URBAN SOCIETY
third edition

Editor

Jeffrey M. Elliot
North Carolina Central University

Jeffrey M. Elliot is Associate Professor of Political Science at North Carolina Central University. He received his Bachelor of Arts degree in 1969 and his Master of Arts in 1970 from the University of Southern California, and his Doctor of Arts from the Claremont Graduate School in 1978. In 1985, he was awarded an honorary Doctor of Humane Letters from Shaw University. He is the author of 44 books and over 500 articles, reviews, and interviews. His work has appeared in more than 250 publications, both in this country and abroad, and has been nominated for several literary awards. Recent book titles include: *Black Voices in American Politics* (Harcourt Brace Jovanovich, 1985), *The Analytical Congressional Directory* (The Borgo Press, 1985), *The Presidential-Congressional Political Dictionary* (ABC-Clio, 1984), and *Tempest in a Teapot: The Falkland Islands War* (The Borgo Press, 1983). In addition to his academic duties, he serves as Distinguished Advisor on Foreign Affairs to Congressman Mervyn M. Dymally (D-Calif.).

Cover illustration by Mike Eagle

Annual Editions
A Library of Information from the Public Press

The Dushkin Publishing Group, Inc.
Sluice Dock, Guilford, Connecticut 06437

The Annual Editions Series

Annual Editions is a series of over thirty-five volumes designed to provide the reader with convenient, low-cost access to a wide range of current, carefully selected articles from some of the most important magazines, newspapers, and journals published today. Annual Editions are updated on a regular basis through a continuous monitoring of over 200 periodical sources. All Annual Editions have a number of features designed to make them particularly useful, including topic guides, annotated tables of contents, unit overviews, and indexes. For the teacher using Annual Editions in the classroom, an Instructor's Resource Guide with test questions is available for each volume.

PUBLISHED

Africa
Aging
American Government
American History, Pre-Civil War
American History, Post-Civil War
Anthropology
Biology
Business
China
Comparative Politics
Computers in Education
Computers in Business
Computers in Society
Criminal Justice
Drugs and Society
Early Childhood Education
Economics
Educating Exceptional Children
Education
Educational Psychology
Environment
Geography

Global Issues
Health
Human Development
Human Sexuality
Latin America
Macroeconomics
Marketing
Marriage and Family
Middle East and the Islamic World
Personal Growth and Behavior
Psychology
Social Problems
Social Psychology
Sociology
Soviet Union and Eastern Europe
State and Local Government
Urban Society
Western Civilization, Pre-Reformation
Western Civilization, Post-Reformation
World Politics

FUTURE VOLUMES

Abnormal Psychology
Death and Dying
Congress
Energy
Ethnic Studies
Foreign Policy
Judiciary
Nutrition
Parenting
Philosophy

Political Science
Presidency
Religion
South Asia
Twentieth Century American History
Western Europe
Women's Studies
World History

Library of Congress Cataloging in Publication Data
Main entry under title: Annual editions: Urban society.
    1. Sociology, Urban—Addresses, essays, lectures—Periodicals.   2. Urban policy—United States—Addresses, essays, lectures—Periodicals.   3. Metropolitan areas—United States—Addresses, essays, lectures—Periodicals.   I. Title: Urban society.
301.34′05   ISBN: 0-87967-618-3   82-646006

Third Edition

Manufactured by The Banta Company, Menasha, Wisconsin 54952

Editors/ Advisory Board

Members of the Advisory Board are instrumental in the final selection of articles for each edition of Annual Editions. Their review of articles for content, level, currency, and appropriateness provides critical direction to the editor and staff. We think you'll find their careful consideration well reflected in this volume.

EDITOR

Jeffrey M. Elliot
North Carolina Central University

ADVISORY BOARD

Chet Ballard
Valdosta State College

David Booth
University of Massachusetts,
Amherst

Pat Edwards
Virginia Polytechnic Institute
and State University

Kurt Finsterbusch
University of Maryland,
College Park

Charles Garrison
East Carolina University

Geoffrey Kapenzie
Babson College

George McKenna
CUNY, City College

Dana Noonan
California State University,
Los Angeles

Fred Parent
Ferris State College

Frederick Peterson
Merrimack College

John Roche
Rhode Island College

Alan Shank
SUNY College, Geneseo

Paul Shott
Plymouth State College

STAFF

Rick Connelly, Publisher
Ian A. Nielsen, Program Manager
Celeste Borg, Editor
Addie Kawula, Acquisitions Editor
Brenda S. Filley, Production Manager
Cheryl Nicholas, Permissions/Photo Coordinator
Charles Vitelli, Designer
Jean Bailey, Graphics Coordinator
Libra A. Cusack, Typesetting Coordinator
Diane Barker, Editorial Assistant

To The Reader

In publishing ANNUAL EDITIONS we recognize the enormous role played by the magazines, newspapers, and journals of the *public press* in providing current, first-rate educational information in a broad spectrum of interest areas. Within the articles, the best scientists, practitioners, researchers, and commentators draw issues into new perspective as accepted theories and viewpoints are called into account by new events, recent discoveries change old facts, and fresh debate breaks out over important controversies.

Many of the articles resulting from this enormous editorial effort are appropriate for students, researchers, and professionals seeking accurate, current material to help bridge the gap between principles and theories and the real world. These articles, however, become more useful for study when those of lasting value are carefully *collected, organized, indexed,* and *reproduced* in a *low-cost format,* which provides easy and permanent access when the material is needed. That is the role played by *Annual Editions.* Under the direction of each volume's *Editor,* who is an expert in the subject area, and with the guidance of an *Advisory Board,* we seek each year to provide in each *ANNUAL EDITION* a current, well-balanced, carefully selected collection of the best of the public press for your study and enjoyment. We think you'll find this volume useful, and we hope you'll take a moment to let us know what you think.

In 1972, Democratic presidential candidate George McGovern beckoned America with these words: "The challenge of our age is whether we shall seize the opportunity to decide what kind of life, what kind of environment, and what kind of opportunities we want for ourselves and for our children." It has been said that survival in today's world is a race between awareness and catastrophe. I believe this to be true. The task of formulating solutions to our present problems—both at home and abroad—is not only extraordinarily complex but extremely urgent. It involves discarding many of our old ideas and fashioning radical new ones. As Rollo May puts it, "the old ideas are dying and the new ones have not yet been born."

This period of crisis, however, has two faces. The ancient Chinese were well aware of this duality, for their character for "crisis" is made up of two characters; one means danger, the other opportunity. America's cities face a plethora of difficult and complex problems: a deteriorating infrastructure, high unemployment, a dwindling tax base, shrinking resources, decaying housing, congestion and noise pollution, inadequate transportation, crime, racial strife, and faltering institutional support systems, among others. These problems defy simple solutions; they are the product of historical forces that have evolved over the past 200 years—forces that have both created and exacerbated the decline of urban America.

Despite these problems, the crisis of America's cities is not unsolvable. Like the early jet pilots who hovered fearfully on their side of the sound barrier, we hover fearfully on this side of transforming our cities into hospitable places in which to live and work. Like these pilots and engineers, we must, with courage and daring, break the barrier, for the consequence of not doing so is continued decline. Clearly, if our cities are to thrive and prosper, we must establish healthful conditions conducive to improved urban life. The attainment of this ideal is dependent upon our ability to create conditions which will allow opportunity and progress to take root and grow. I use the phrase "take root and grow" advisedly, for opportunity and progress resemble a plant, in that they require a balanced environment to develop and mature.

This anthology represents but one step in our search for constructive solutions to the problems of America's cities. The selections reflect a broad approach to the study of urban life. The articles were chosen for their clarity and relevancy in addressing the issues surrounding urbanization, for their usefulness in the teaching/learning process, and for their ability to stimulate interest in students to pursue the study of urban society.

We think *Annual Editions: Urban Society* is one of the most informative, engaging, and current books available, but we would like to know what you think. Please fill out the article rating form on the last page of this book and let us know your opinions. Any anthology can be improved. This one will continue to be, and your comments are important in this process.

Jeffrey M. Elliot

Jeffrey M. Elliot

Editor

Contents

Unit 1

Urbanization

Seven selections review the urbanization process, the development of new patterns of living, and the dynamics of the urban "explosion."

To the Reader	iv
Topic Guide	2
Overview	4

1. How Man Invented Cities, John Pfeiffer, *Horizon,* Autumn 1972.   6

The author maintains that the *city* evolved to reflect the needs of *societies* under pressure. When the city was created, its ultimate form or shape could not have been predicted because it developed in response to the diverse interests and activities of the people.

2. Fear of the City, 1783 to 1983, Alfred Kazin, *American Heritage,* February/March 1983.   12

Kazin examines the age-old threats of the *city*, from a personal and historical perspective. He argues that despite its excesses and aggressiveness, the city possesses an indescribable allure and magic.

3. Symposium: The State of the Nation's Cities, Herbert J. Gans, John D. Kasarda, and Harvey Molotch, *Urban Affairs Quarterly,* December 1982.   18

Three noted urbanologists explore a wide range of contemporary urban problems and possible solutions. These include *urban revitalization*; the role of the *federal*, *state*, and *local governments*; *gentrification* and reinvestment; *urban development*; and the plight of the disadvantaged.

4. The World's Urban Explosion, *The UNESCO Courier,* March 1985.   29

This article is a summary of the proceedings of Metropolis 84, an international symposium held in Paris, France, in October 1984. It focuses on the four main themes of the conference: demography and *town planning*, *economic* and *technological change*, public *transportation*, and culture and environment.

5. The Industrial City: The Environment of the City, Asa Briggs, *Current,* May 1983.   33

Briggs reviews the *city* in history, from a historical and literary point of view. He discusses the social features of the city, variations among cities, the problem of *industrial progress*, and prospects for the future.

6. Building the Empire City, Matthys Levy, *The Sciences,* December 1980.   42

New York City is experiencing a new birth because it attracts "imagineers"—engineers with imagination. Levy examines the realities of the new birth and compares it with old *engineering techniques*.

7. America's Suburbs Still Alive and Doing Fine, *U.S. News & World Report,* March 12, 1984.   46

Caveats and warnings notwithstanding, *suburbia* is fast becoming the center of *economic* and *social life* in America in the 1980s. This report states that despite their problems, suburbs face a far brighter future than the cities they surround.

The concepts in italics are developed in the article. For further expansion please refer to the Topic Guide and the Index.

Unit
2

Varieties of Urban Experiences

Five selections explore the social interactions that, in large measure, direct the urban experience.

Overview   **50**

8. **People of the City,** John Goodman Jr., *American Demographics,* September 1980.   **52**

   Back-to-the-city is a misnomer. Rather, demographics suggest a back-to-selected-*neighborhoods* is the reality of the 1980s. Goodman analyzes the recent demographic data with an eye toward predicting the future of American *cities*.

9. **The New Class,** Patricia Morrisroe, *New York,* May 13, 1985.   **56**

   The author describes the rapid influx of new residents in New York's Upper West Side. Frequently young and rich, single or newly married, they have reshaped an old, mixed *neighborhood* to reflect their own upwardly mobile image and aspirations.

10. **The Dispossessed,** Ellen Hopkins, *New York,* May 13, 1985.   **61**

    Hopkins analyzes the impact of *gentrification* on the *poor* and *elderly* in New York's Upper West Side. She argues that when the needs of *low-rent tenants* clash with those of absentee *landlords* and wealthy property owners, gentrification usually wins out. The article examines the methods employed by these landlords, as well as the strategies utilized by the dispossessed.

11. **For Rent, Cheap, No Heat,** Barbara Koeppel, *The Progressive,* March 1981.   **67**

    A significant number of *urban dwellers* in America are renters. A third of the *renters* in the central urban community can expect to occupy a substandard unit since most enforcement programs ignore the renter and favor the *landlord*.

12. **Home on the Street,** Steven Fustero, *Psychology Today,* February 1984.   **70**

    This article analyzes the problem of *homelessness* and the plight of the more than 2,000,000 persons who inhabit the streets of America's cities. Approximately one-third to one-half of the homeless suffer from mental illness and are doomed to the streets because of "deinstitutionalization."

Unit
3

Urban Problems

Nine selections examine the problems of the decaying urban environment, high rates of unemployment and crime, low tax rates, and high welfare rolls.

Overview   **76**

13. **Crowds and More Crowds—No End to Urban Hassles,** *U.S. News & World Report,* April 5, 1982.   **78**

    Despite the push to the *suburbs, congestion* remains a stark reality in many urban centers. This problem has produced numerous big-city ills, among them: increased traffic, overcrowded buses and subways, serious *housing* shortages, dirty streets, and violent *crime*. These and other problems, reports the article, are expected to grow more severe as society continues to grapple unsuccessfully with the lack of space and its attendant byproducts.

The concepts in italics are developed in the article. For further expansion please refer to the Topic Guide and the Index.

14. **Hunting the Wolf Packs,** Michael Daly, *New York,* June 3, 1985.   80

Daly describes a new breed of robber in New York City—"The Wolf Pack." This band of robbers—often numbering up to 100—haunts subway trains, Times Square, Broadway, and other well-traveled areas. The robbers who prowl the city's wealthier stretches do not conform to past stereotypes. For them, *crime* is a sort of sport.

15. **Black Mayors: Can They Make Their Cities Work?** Thulani Davis, *Mother Jones,* July 1984.   90

Of the eighteen largest cities with populations over 150,000, ten have *black mayors.* In those cities, more than one-half the blacks of voting age are registered. This article analyzes the issue of black empowerment and the special problems faced by black mayors.

16. **The Myths of Mass Transit,** Catherine G. Burke, *USA Today,* July 1982.   97

Mass transit, argues Burke, has outlived its usefulness. She regards it as wasteful, inefficient, inhumane, polluting, and dangerous. Still, most Americans accept the myths of mass transit. In this article, the author explains why.

17. **American Cities and the Future,** David A. Caputo, *Society,* January/February 1985.   101

Caputo examines the shifting nature of federal/state relations and the costs of the *New Federalism.* He pays special attention to the impact of the Reagan proposals on the cities which, he contends, have not been as severe as once feared.

18. **Supercities: The Growing Crisis,** Rashmi Mayur, *The Futurist,* August 1985.   107

Supercities, particularly those in developing countries, face unprecedented problems. These problems are exacerbated by uncontrolled *population growth* in the poor nations. The author calls for the wise use of available resources, equitable resource distribution, and the development of shared new resources.

19. **A Mayor's Dilemma,** Sidney Lens, *The Progressive,* June 1985.   111

The author focuses on the long-running battle between Chicago's *black mayor,* Harold Washington, and the city's entrenched white machine. He describes the Establishment's systematic efforts to sabotage Washington's program, and the various forces opposed to reform. Lens argues that the answer lies in the *political mobilization* of the *poor* and disfranchised Chicagoans.

20. **I Was a Spear Carrier in the War on Poverty,** Jonathan Rowe, *The Washington Monthly,* November 1984.   116

Rowe gives a personal account of his experience in the late 1960s as a *VISTA* volunteer on Manhattan's Lower East Side and the problems associated with combatting urban *poverty.* Although VISTA failed to eliminate poverty, it did encourage people to think creatively about the problems of their neighbors and to avoid simplistic answers to complex problems.

The concepts in italics are developed in the article. For further expansion please refer to the Topic Guide and the Index.

Unit 4

Urban Social Policies

Twelve selections discuss the effects of the social policy process by which an urban center addresses its problems. Often, because of the complexity of these problems, social policies cause unintended consequences or offer inadequate answers.

21. The ACORN Squatters' Campaign, Seth Borgos, *Social Policy,* Summer 1984.   **125**
Borgos describes the attempt by the squatters and their supporters to secure housing for Philadelphia's *poor* in the late 1970s and early 1980s. He examines the campaign's external legitimacy as well as its internal dynamic.

Overview   **134**

22. Running the City for the People, Eve Bach, Nicholas R. Carbone, and Pierre Clavel, *Social Policy,* Winter 1982.   **136**
This case study examines *urban planning* efforts in two well-known progressive cities: Hartford, Connecticut and Berkeley, California. The authors describe the efforts by progressive city administrations to address the needs of the urban *poor*, by challenging the assumptions and demands of elite-oriented planners and proponents of the status quo.

23. Assuring the Economic Health of America's Cities, Henry G. Cisneros, *USA Today,* November 1982.   **145**
Cisneros, the Mayor of San Antonio, Texas, maintains that the future of the cities is inextricably linked to the health of the *economy*. According to Cisneros, the cities must serve as fundamental building blocks for both the national economy and the nation's basic *social ideals*.

24. Urban Strengths/Urban Weaknesses, Donald A. Hicks, *Society,* March/April 1982.   **150**
The article analyzes the new *federal role* regarding America's cities. Hicks contends that the 1930s relationship in which the federal government sought to rescue the nation's poor and powerless may no longer be desirable or possible. He adds that existing bureaucratic problems at the federal, state, and local levels undermine national objectives and limit the ability of subnational groups and *private sector* actors to resolve current problems.

25. Reagan vs. the Neighborhoods, Harry C. Boyte, *Social Policy,* Spring 1982.   **157**
Despite President Reagan's rhetorical commitment to *neighborhood* self-help and rebirth, the administration has dismantled many neighborhood self-help programs. This, insists Reagan's critics, reflects his opposition to redistributive action by the *government*.

26. Small Space Is Beautiful: Design as if People Mattered, William H. Whyte, *Technology Review,* July 1982.   **162**
Urban development, according to the author, should be based on the needs of the people. He maintains that the key to a hospitable environment is to design institutions, facilities, activities, and structures which are conducive to human interaction. People must be able to meet and mingle.

The concepts in italics are developed in the article. For further expansion please refer to the Topic Guide and the Index.

27. **The Case Against Urban Dinosaurs,** William G. Conway,   **173**
Saturday Review, May 14, 1977.
Detroit's massive downtown effort is destined to fail, according to this urban affairs consultant. He argues that *downtowns* are no longer functional and that the new *megastructures* will not change this reality.

28. **Triage as Urban Policy,** Peter Marcuse, Peter Medoff, and   **176**
Andrea Pereira, *Social Policy,* Winter 1982.
The authors examine triage as *urban policy,* focusing on its various forms, the major arguments for and against it, its impact on public policy, and its real and imagined social benefits.

29. **Cities Are Setting Their Sights on International Trade**   **181**
and Investment, Carol Steinbach and and Neal R. Peirce, *National Journal,* April 28, 1984.
The opportunities for increased *international trade* are expanding, according to the article, to the point that almost any city with a local corporate base can enter into mutually profitable relationships. This is nowhere more evident than in Atlanta, where the city is experimenting with several of the most advanced development tools, including trade missions, trade zones, and export trading companies. Many additional cities have followed suit, with equally impressive results.

30. **Achieving Energy Independence by Reviving America's**   **186**
Cities, Neil Goldstein and and Amey Winterer, *USA Today,* November 1982.
Cities can play a pivotal role in America's efforts to achieve *energy independence.* The authors report that the average city dweller expends far less energy than residents of non-urban areas. Unfortunately, existing federal policy often produces the opposite effect by promoting energy-wasting sprawl and *urban decline.* This trend must be reversed if the cities are to continue to serve as the "conservator" of America's resources.

31. **When Public Services Go Private,** Jeremy Main, *Fortune,*   **190**
May 27, 1985.
Increasingly, reports the author, *government* is turning to private contractors to provide basic services, with a savings of twenty percent or more to the taxpayers. In addition, he says, government is looking to private industry to finance, design, build, and administer public facilities. While there are numerous risks associated with *privatization,* public officials are proceeding with marked success.

32. **City-States: Laboratories of the 1980s,** David Morris, *En-*   **194**
vironment, July/August 1983.
America is witnessing the emergence of the *city* as an ecological nation—one that is fast creating clean, biological-based systems. Many cities recognize the importance of self-sufficiency and have taken steps to make optimum use of local resources. Inward-looking, self-reliant cities view themselves as nations and, as such, are better able to design production systems that meet unique local requirements.

The concepts in italics are developed in the article. For further expansion please refer to the Topic Guide and the Index.

Unit 5

Urban Futures

Eight selections examine the implications of a rapidly rising urban population. What effects these changes will have on the entire world population must be taken into consideration and effective planning must be seriously instituted.

33. **Suburban Population Ages, Causing Conflict and Radical Changes,** Joann S. Lublin, *The Wall Street Journal,* November 1, 1984.   207
Lublin analyzes the aging of the *suburbs*, which, she suggests, has served to generate radical changes in the nature and politics of many communities. The problems will continue to worsen, as cities discover they lack the resources necessary to respond to the escalating demands of the *elderly* and aging suburban population.

Overview   210
34. **A City for the Year 2000,** Oscar Niemeyer, *The UNESCO Courier,* March 1985.   212
The author presents a "modest" proposal for the *city of the future*. It should be forward-looking, though respectful of tradition; rooted in human values, not around the machine; and vertical in design, thus fulfilling its primary purpose. In addition, *population density* should be fixed; the city should be free of private automobiles; and sectors should be allocated to health, culture, education, and housing.

35. **Need for New Vision Stirs City Leaders,** Lucia Mouat, *The Christian Science Monitor,* June 1, 1984.   215
The article suggests that the *future* of older *cities* depends upon the emergence of a new class of *civic leaders*—one that is willing to experiment, to expand the city's economic base, to recruit minorities into government, and to redefine existing practices and programs.

36. **Progress Begins Downtown,** Lucia Mouat, *The Christian Science Monitor,* May 29, 1984.   218
Urban restoration depends, to a large extent, on a city's ability to renovate its *downtown* area, in order to make it a hospitable place in which to live and work. According to the article, this will require a determined attack on abandoned warehouses and rundown waterfronts, which represent the raw material that could, if revitalized, entice the return of downtown business and thus benefit needy nearby neighborhoods.

37. **America's Urban "Rust Belt" Cinches Up for the Future,** Lucia Mouat, *The Christian Science Monitor,* May 25, 1983.   222
With imaginative thinking and public support, the once prosperous cities of industrial America can rebuild existing *industry* and expand their *economic base*. This reporter concludes that while *high-tech* offers many concrete benefits, it cannot and will not be the salvation of industrial America. Manufacturing will remain the mainstay of the urban "rust belt."

The concepts in italics are developed in the article. For further expansion please refer to the Topic Guide and the Index.

38. **Suburbs: Revising the American Dream,** Marilyn Gard-   226
    ner, *The Christian Science Monitor,* May 25, 1983.
    Gardner analyzes the problems and prospects of the *suburbs* by
    examining the plight of one such bedroom community—Cupertino,
    California. Despite its lure, the suburbs face serious problems, not
    the least of which is the escalating cost of suburban life.

39. **Politics Is Not the Only Thing That Is Changing**   229
    America's Big Cities, Neal R. Peirce, Robert Guskind, and
    John Gardner, *National Journal,* November 26, 1983.
    America's *cities* are changing significantly. They are plagued by
    racial strife, urban decay, gentrification, dilapidated and scarce
    housing, inadequate transportation, and environmental pollution.
    Their future will depend upon their leaders' ability to better utilize
    existing resources, better control urban growth, and better ad-
    minister existing programs and services.

40. **Dimensions of the Civic Future: Fiscal Restraint and**   233
    Intergovernmental Impacts, S. Kenneth Howard, *National*
    Civic Review, April 1985.
    Although cities can, to a large extent, shape their own futures, they
    are significantly influenced by the *political*, *economic*, and fiscal
    environment of the nation. In the end, argues Howard, their future
    depends upon intergovernmental cooperation. They must active-
    ly work to minimize the negative effects of conflictual politics.

41. **Strategies for the Essential Community: Local Govern-**   235
    ment in the Year 2000, Laurence Rutter, *The Futurist,* June
    1981.
    The author, a political scientist and expert on urban policy, argues
    the need for *local governments* to realistically weigh the resources
    at their disposal and the demands put upon them. Cities will have
    to learn to make do with less, to regulate the demand for services,
    and to buy back their independence from the *federal government*.

Index   242
Article Rating Form   245

Topic Guide

This topic guide suggests how the selections in this book relate to topics of traditional concern to urban society students and professionals. It is very useful in locating articles which relate to each other for reading and research. The guide is arranged alphabetically according to topic. Articles may, of course, treat topics that do not appear in the topic guide. In turn, entries in the topic guide do not necessarily constitute a comprehensive listing of all the contents of each selection.

TOPIC AREA	TREATED AS AN ISSUE IN:	TOPIC AREA	TREATED AS AN ISSUE IN:
Black Mayors	15. Black Mayors 19. A Mayor's Dilemma	**Elderly**	10. The Dispossessed 33. Suburban Population Ages
City (History/Future)	1. How Man Invented Cities 2. Fear of the City 3. Symposium: The State of the Nation's Cities 5. The Industrial City 8. People of the City 18. Supercities 32. City-States 34. A City for the Year 2000 35. Need for New Vision Stirs City Leaders 40. Dimensions of the Civic Future	**Energy Independence** **Engineering Techniques** **Gentrification** **Government: Federal, State, and Local**	30. Achieving Energy Independence 6. Building the Empire City 3. Symposium: The State of the Nation's Cities 10. The Dispossessed 3. Symposium: The State of the Nation's Cities 17. American Cities and the Future 24. Urban Strengths/Urban Weaknesses 25. Reagan vs. the Neighborhood 31. When Public Services Go Private 32. City-States 40. Dimensions of the Civic Future 41. Strategies for the Essential Community
Civic Leaders	35. Need for New Vision Stirs City Leaders		
Congestion	13. Crowds and More Crowds		
Crime	13. Crowds and More Crowds 14. Hunting the Wolf Packs	**Homelessness**	12. Home on the Street
Downtown	27. The Case Against Urban Dinosaurs 36. Progress Begins Downtown	**Housing** **Industrial Development**	13. Crowds and More Crowds 5. The Industrial City 37. America's Urban "Rust Belt"
Economic Issues	4. The World's Urban Explosion 7. America's Suburbs Still Alive and Doing Fine 23. Assuring the Economic Health of America's Cities 31. When Public Services Go Private 37. America's Urban "Rust Belt" 40. Dimensions of the Civic Future	**International Trade** **Landlords**	29. Cities Are Setting Their Sights on International Trade 10. The Dispossessed 11. For Rent, Cheap, No Heat

TOPIC AREA	TREATED AS AN ISSUE IN:	TOPIC AREA	TREATED AS AN ISSUE IN:
Mass Transit	4. The World's Urban Explosion 16. The Myths of Mass Transit	**Society**	1. How Man Invented Cities
Megastructures	27. The Case Against Urban Dinosaurs	**Suburbia**	7. America's Suburbs Still Alive and Doing Fine 13. Crowds and More Crowds 33. Suburban Population Ages 39. Politics Is Not the Only Thing Changing America's Big Cities
Neighborhoods	8. People of the City 9. The New Class 25. Reagan vs. the Neighborhood		
New Federalism	17. American Cities and the Future	**Supercities**	18. Supercities
Political Issues	19. A Mayor's Dilemma 40. Dimensions of the Civic Future	**Technological Change**	4. The World's Urban Explosion 37. America's Urban "Rust Belt"
Poor/Poverty	10. The Dispossessed 19. A Mayor's Dilemma 20. I Was a Spear Carrier in the War on Poverty 21. The ACORN Squatters' Campaign 22. Running the City for the People	**Town Planning**	4. The World's Urban Explosion
		Urban Decline/ Decay	30. Achieving Energy Independence
Population Growth/ Density	18. Supercities 34. A City for the Year 2000	**Urban Development/ Policy**	3. Symposium: The State of the Nation's Cities 22. Running the City for the People 26. Small Space Is Beautiful 28. Triage as Urban Policy
Private Sector/ Privatization	24. Urban Strengths/Urban Weaknesses 31. When Public Services Go Private		
Renters/Tenants	10. The Dispossessed 11. For Rent, Cheap, No Heat	**Urban Dwellers**	11. For Rent, Cheap, No Heat
Social Issues	7. America's Suburbs Still Alive and Doing Fine 23. Assuring the Economic Health of America's Cities	**Urban Restoration/ Revitalization**	3. Symposium: The State of the Nation's Cities 36. Progress Begins Downtown

Urbanization

Historically, the rapid growth of cities was largely a consequence of the developments of agricultural surpluses and factory systems. When farmers produced surpluses, they needed a center for exchange. When factories were developed, the need for a concentrated labor supply and services was apparent. Thus, the city came into existence and became the center of both economic and cultural activity. While scholars agree that cities have existed for many centuries and in most parts of the world, only about three percent of the world's population lived in towns of more than 5,000 inhabitants before 1800. Even today less than thirty percent of the world's population lives in cities larger than 20,000 people. Nevertheless, urbanization has profoundly influenced the course of global development.

Urbanization is a complex and continuous process. It involves the movement of people from rural to urban areas, the creation of new patterns of living, and the communication of these new patterns to both urban and rural populations. In the western world, the emergence of cities as a dominant force in the lives of people has been so rapid, it has been characterized as an "explosion."

Social scientists have been fascinated with the process of urbanization. For the historian, the dynamics of urban growth could illustrate the ways in which entire cultures and nations change over time. For the sociologist, the nature of urbanization became a way of explaining social arrangements and transforming social structures. The psychologist saw urbanization as a force in the ways individuals learned to cope with new threats to survival. Through the process of urbanization, the economist came to recognize cities, and more recently suburbs, as important units for generating wealth and for allocating resources. The political scientists, too, studied urbanization in order to gain a better understanding of the ways in which order and change were maintained in these dynamic units. The change was more gradual for the anthropologist but, nevertheless, urbanization proved to be a rich resource for observing and understanding the nature and importance of subcultural groups within the larger urban culture.

It is clear that urbanization has become a dominant force in the lives of people throughout the world—both those who live in cities and those who remain in rural areas. This examination of urbanization begins with John Pfeiffer's essay on the creation of cities. This is followed by Alfred Kazin's analysis of humankind's longstanding fear of cities. Urban life boasts myriad attractions; it also embodies numerous problems. The following article surveys the state of America's cities. In an attempt to understand the world's urban explosion, an international symposium was convened in Paris, France in 1984. The recommendations of that conference are the subject of the fourth article. Asa Briggs' skillful analysis of the environment of the city from a historical and contemporary perspective follows. Matthys Levy discusses the impact of "imagineers" on the birth of New York City. Finally, the last article surveys the status of America's suburbs, both the ideal and the reality.

Looking Ahead: Challenge Questions

How and why did cities originate? What major functions do they serve?

What historical factors have contributed to humankind's fear of cities? Are these fears well-founded?

What are the main social features of the city? How does the process of urbanization affect social life today?

Has urbanization added to or detracted from the quality of human life? Is suburban life an answer to the problems of urban society?

What are the principal challenges facing the world's great cities? Is it likely that they will meet these challenges?

How can an urban planner shape the content and character of a city? What values and skills should a planner possess?

How Man Invented Cities

John Pfeiffer

The most striking mark of man's genius as a species, as the most adaptable of animals, has been his ability to live in cities. From the perspective of all we know about human evolution, nothing could be more unnatural. For over fifteen million years, from the period when members of the family of man first appeared on earth until relatively recent times, our ancestors were nomadic, small-group, wide-open-spaces creatures. They lived on the move among other moving animals in isolated little bands of a few families, roaming across wildernesses that extended like oceans to the horizon and beyond.

Considering that heritage, the wonder is not that man has trouble getting along in cities but that he can do it at all—that he can learn to live in the same place year round, enclosed in sharp-cornered and brightly-lit rectangular spaces, among noises, most of which are made by machines, within shouting distance of hundreds of other people, most of them strangers. Furthermore, such conditions arose so swiftly, practically overnight on the evolutionary time scale, that he has hardly had a

chance to get used to them. The transition from a world without cities to our present situation took a mere five or six millenniums.

It is precisely because we are so close to our origins that what happened in prehistory bears directly on current problems. In fact, the expectation is that new studies of pre-cities and early cities will contribute as significantly to an understanding of today's urban complexes as studies of infancy and early childhood have to an understanding of adolescence. Cities are signs, symptoms if you will, of an accelerating and intensive phase of human evolution, a process that we are only beginning to investigate scientifically.

The first stages of the process may be traced back some fifteen thousand years to a rather less hectic era. Homo sapiens, that new breed of restless and intelligent primate, had reached a high point in his career as a hunter-gatherer subsisting predominantly on wild plants and animals. He had developed special tools, special tactics and strategies, for dealing with a wide variety of environments, from savannas and semideserts to tundras and tropical rain forests and

mountain regions. Having learned to exploit practically every type of environment, he seemed at last to have found his natural place in the scheme of things—as a hunter living in balance with other species, and with all the world as his hunting ground.

But forces were already at work that would bring an end to this state of equilibrium and ultimately give rise to cities and the state of continuing instability that we are trying to cope with today. New theories, a harder look at the old theories, and an even harder look at our own tendencies to think small have radically changed our ideas about what happened and why.

We used to believe, in effect, that people abandoned hunting and gathering as soon as a reasonable alternative became available to them. It was hardly a safe or reliable way of life. Our ancestors faced sudden death and injury from predators and from prey that fought back, disease from exposure to the elements and from always being on the move, and hunger because the chances were excellent of coming back empty-handed from the hunt. Survival was a full-time struggle. Leisure came only after the invention of agriculture, which brought food surpluses, rising populations, and cities. Such was the accepted picture.

The fact of the matter, supported by studies of living hunter-gatherers as well as by the archaeological record, is that the traditional view is largely melodrama and science fiction. Our preagricultural ancestors were quite healthy, quite safe, and regularly obtained all the food they needed. And they did it with time to burn. As a rule, the job of collecting food, animal and vegetable, required no more than a three-hour day, or a twenty-one-hour week. During that time, collectors brought in enough food for the entire group, which included an appreciable proportion (perhaps 30 per cent or more) of dependents, old persons and children who did little or no work. Leisure is basically a phenomenon of hunting-gathering times, and people have been trying to recover it ever since.

Another assumption ripe for discarding is that civilization first arose in the valleys of the Tigris, Euphrates, and Nile rivers and spread from there to the rest of the world. Accumulating evidence fails to support this notion that civilization is an exclusive product of these regions. To be sure, agriculture and cities may have appeared first in the Near East, but there are powerful arguments for completely independent origins in at least two other widely separated regions, Mesoamerica and Southeast Asia.

In all cases, circumstances forced hunter-gatherers to evolve new ways of surviving. With the decline of the ancient life style, nomadism, problems began piling up. If only people had kept on moving about like sane and respectable primates, life would be a great deal simpler. Instead, they settled down in increasing numbers over wider areas, and society started changing with a vengeance. Although the causes of this settling down remain a mystery, the fact of independent origins calls for an explanation based on worldwide developments.

An important factor, emphasized recently by Lewis Binford of the University of New Mexico, may have been the melting of mile-high glaciers, which was well under way fifteen thousand years ago, and which released enough water to raise the world's oceans 250 to 500 feet, to flood previously exposed coastal plains, and to create shallow bays and estuaries and marshlands. Vast numbers of fish and wild fowl made use of the new environments, and the extra resources permitted people to obtain food without migrating seasonally. In other words, people expended less energy, and life became that much easier, in the beginning anyway.

Yet this sensible and seemingly innocent change was to get mankind into all sorts of difficulties. According to a recent theory, it triggered a chain of events that made cities possible if not inevitable. Apparently, keeping on the move had always served as a natural birth-control mechanism, in part, perhaps, by causing a relatively high incidence of miscarriages. But the population brakes were off as soon as people began settling down.

One clue to what may have happened is provided by contemporary studies of a number of primitive tribes, such as the Bushmen of Africa's Kalahari Desert. Women living in nomadic bands, bands that pick up and move half a dozen or more times a year, have an average of one baby every four years or so, as compared with one baby every two and a half years for Bushman women living in settled communities an increase of five to eight babies per mother during a twenty-year reproductive period.

The archaeological record suggests that in some places at least, a comparable phenomenon accompanied the melting of glaciers during the last ice age. People settled down and multiplied in the Les Eyzies region of southern France, one of the richest and most-studied centers of prehistory. Great limestone cliffs dominate the countryside, and at the foot of the cliffs are natural shelters, caves and rocky overhangs where people built fires, made tools out of flint and bone and ivory, and planned the next day's hunt. On special occasions artists equipped with torches went deep into certain caves like Lascaux and covered the walls with magnificent images of the animals they hunted.

In some places the cliffs and the shelters extend for hundreds of yards; in other places there are good living sites close to one another on the opposite slopes of river valleys. People in the Les Eyzies region were living not in isolated bands but in full-fledged communities, and populations seem to have been on the rise. During the period from seven thousand to twelve thousand years ago, the total number of sites doubled, and an appreciable proportion of them probably represent year-round settlements located in small river valleys. An analysis of excavated animal remains reveals an increasing dietary reliance on migratory birds and fish (chiefly salmon).

People were also settling down at about the same time in the Near East for example, not far from the Mediterranean shoreline of Israel and on the border between the coastal plain and the hills to the east. Ofer Bar-Yosef, of the Institute of Archaeology of Hebrew University in Jerusalem, points out that since they were able to exploit both these areas, they did not have to wander widely in search of food. There were herds of deer and gazelle, wild boar, fish and wild fowl, wild cereals and other plants, and limestone caves and shelters like those in the Les Eyzies region. Somewhat later, however, a new land-use pattern emerged. Coastal villages continued to flourish, but in addition to them, new sites began appearing further inland—and in areas that were drier and less abundant.

Only under special pressure will men abandon a good thing, and in this case it was very likely the pressure of rising populations. The evidence suggests that the best coastal lands were supporting about all the hunter-gatherers they could support; and as living space decreased there was a "budding off," an overflow of surplus population into the second-best back country where game was scarcer. These people depended more and more on plants, particularly on wild cereals, as indicated by the larger numbers of flint sickle blades, mortars and pestles, and storage pits found at their sites (and also by an increased wear and pitting of teeth, presumably caused by chewing more coarse and gritty plant foods).

Another sign of the times was the appearance of stone buildings, often with impressively high and massive walls. The structures served a number of purposes. For one thing, they included storage bins where surplus grain could be kept in reserve for bad times, when there was a shortage of game and wild plants. They also imply danger abroad in the countryside, new kinds of violence, and a mounting need for defenses to protect stored goods from the raids of people who had not settled down.

Above all, the walls convey a feeling of increasing permanence, an increasing commitment to places. Although man was still mainly a hunter-gatherer living on wild species, some of the old options no longer existed for him. In the beginning, settling down may have involved a measure of choice, but now man was no longer quite so free to change locales when the land became less fruitful. Even in those days frontiers were vanishing. Man's problem was to develop new options, new ways of working the land more intensively so that it would provide the food that migration had always provided in more mobile times.

The all-important transition to agriculture came in small steps, establishing itself almost before anyone realized what was going on. Settlers in marginal lands took early measures to get more food out of less abundant environments—roughing up the soil a bit with scraping or digging sticks, sowing wheat and barley seeds, weeding, and generally doing their best to promote growth. To start with at least, it was simply a matter of supplementing regular diets of wild foods with some domesticated species, animals as well as plants, and people probably regarded themselves as hunter-gatherers working hard to maintain their way of life rather than as the revolutionaries they were. They were trying to preserve the old self-sufficiency, but it was a losing effort.

The wilderness way of life became more and more remote, more and more nearly irretrievable. Practically every

advance in the technology of agriculture committed people to an increasing dependence on domesticated species and on the activities of other people living nearby. Kent Flannery of the University of Michigan emphasizes this point in a study of one part of Greater Mesopotamia, prehistoric Iran, during the period between twelve thousand and six thousand years ago. For the hunter-gatherer, an estimated one-third of the country's total land area was good territory, consisting of grassy plains and high mountain valleys where wild species were abundant; the rest of the land was desert and semidesert.

The coming of agriculture meant that people used a smaller proportion of the countryside. Early farming took advantage of naturally distributed water; the best terrain for that, namely terrain with a high water table and marshy areas, amounted to about a tenth of the land area. But only a tenth of that tenth was suitable for the next major development, irrigation. Meanwhile, food yields were soaring spectacularly, and so was the population of Iran, which increased more than fiftyfold; in other words, fifty times the original population was being supported by food produced on one-hundredth of the land.

A detailed picture of the steps involved in this massing of people is coming from studies of one part of southwest Iran, an 880-square-mile region between the Zagros Mountains and the Iraqi border. The Susiana Plain is mostly flat, sandy semidesert, the only notable features being man-made mounds that loom on the horizon like islands, places where people built in successively high levels on the ruins of their ancestors. During the past decade or so, hundreds of mounds have been mapped and dated (mainly through pottery styles) by Robert Adams of the University of Chicago, Jean Perrot of the French Archaeological Mission in Iran, and Henry Wright and Gregory Johnson of the University of Michigan. Their work provides a general idea of when the mounds were occupied, how they varied in size at different periods and how a city may be born.

Imagine a time-lapse motion picture of the early settling of the Susiana Plain, starting about 6500 B.C., each minute of film representing a century. At first the plain is empty, as it has been since the beginning of time. Then the pioneers arrive; half a dozen families move in and build a cluster of mud-brick homes near a river. Soon another cluster appears and another, until, after about five minutes (it is now 6000 B.C.), there are ten settlements, each covering an area of 1 to 3 hectares (1 hectare = 2.47 acres). Five minutes more (5500 B.C.) and we see the start of irrigation, on a small scale, as people dig little ditches to carry water from rivers and tributaries to lands along the banks. Crop yields increase and so do populations, and there are now thirty settlements, all about the same size as the original ten.

This is but a prelude to the main event. Things become really complicated during the next fifteen minutes or so (5500 to 4000 B.C.). Irrigation systems, constructed and maintained by family groups of varying sizes, become more complex. The number of settlements shows a modest increase, from thirty to forty, but a more significant change takes place—the appearance of a hierarchy. Instead of settlements all about the same size, there are now levels of settlements and a kind of ranking: one town (7 hectares), ten large villages (3 to 4 hectares), and twenty-nine smaller villages of less than 3 hectares. During this period large residential and ceremonial structures appear at Susa, a town on the western edge of the Susiana Plain.

Strange happenings can be observed not long after the middle of this period (about 4600 B.C.). For reasons unknown, the number of settlements decreases rapidly. It is not known whether the population of the area decreased simultaneously. Time passes, and the number of settlements increases to about the same level as before, but great changes have occurred. Three cities have appeared with monumental public buildings, elaborate residential architecture, large workshops, major storage and market facilities, and certainly with administrators and bureaucrats. The settlement hierarchy is more complex, and settlements are no longer located to take advantage solely of good agricultural opportunities. Their location is also influenced by the cities and the services and opportunities available there. By the end of our hypothetical time-lapse film, by the early part of the third millennium B.C., the largest settlement of all is the city of Susa, which covers some thirty hectares and will cover up to a square kilometer (100 hectares) of territory before it collapses in historical times.

All Mesopotamia underwent major transformations during this period. Another city was taking shape 150 miles northwest of Susa in the heartland of Sumer. Within a millennium the site of Uruk near the Euphrates River grew from village dimensions to a city enclosing within its defense walls more than thirty thousand people, four hundred hectares, and at the center a temple built on top of a huge brick platform. Archaeological surveys reveal that this period also saw a massive immigration into the region from places and for reasons as yet undetermined, resulting in a tenfold increase in settlements and in the formation of several new cities.

Similar surveys, requiring months and thousands of miles of walking, are completed or under way in many parts of the world. Little more than a millennium after the establishment of Uruk and Susa, cities began making an independent appearance in northern China not far from the conflux of the Wei and Yellow rivers, in an area that also saw the beginnings of agriculture. Still later, and also independently as far as we can tell, intensive settlement and land use developed in the New World.

The valley of Oaxaca in Mexico, where Flannery and his associates are working currently, provides another example of a city in the process of being formed. Around 500 B.C., or perhaps a bit earlier, buildings were erected for the first time on the tops of hills. Some of the hills were small, no more than twenty-five or thirty feet high, and the buildings were correspondingly small; they overlooked a few terraces and a river and probably a hamlet or two. Larger structures appeared on higher hills overlooking many villages. About 400 B.C. the most elaborate set-

tlement began to appear on the highest land, 1,500-foot Monte Albán, with a panoramic view of the valley's three arms; and within two centuries it had developed into an urban center including hundreds of terraces, an irrigation system, a great plaza, ceremonial buildings and residences, and an astronomical observatory.

At about the same time, the New World's largest city, Teotihuacán, was evolving some 225 miles to the northwest in the central highlands of Mexico. Starting as a scattering of villages and hamlets, it covered nearly eight square miles at its height (around A.D. 100 to 200) and probably contained some 125,000 people. Archaeologists are now reconstructing the life and times of this great urban center. William Sanders of Pennsylvania State University is concentrating on an analysis of settlement patterns in the area, while Rene Millon of the University of Rochester and his associates have prepared detailed section-by-section maps of the city as a step toward further extensive excavations. Set in a narrow valley among mountains and with its own man-made mountains, the Pyramid of the Sun and the Pyramid of the Moon, the city flourished on a grand scale. It housed local dignitaries and priests, delegations from other parts of Mesoamerica, and workshop neighborhoods where specialists in the manufacture of textiles, pottery, obsidian blades, and other products lived together in early-style apartments.

The biggest center in what is now the United States probably reached its peak about a millennium after Teotihuacán. But it has not been reconstructed, and archaeologists are just beginning to appreciate the scale of what happened there. Known as Cahokia and located east of the Mississippi near St. Louis, it consists of a cluster of some 125 mounds (including a central mound 100 feet high and covering 15 acres) as well as a line of mounds extending six miles to the west.

So surveys and excavations continue, furnishing the sort of data needed to disprove or prove our theories. Emerging patterns patterns involving the specific locations of different kinds of communities and of buildings and other artifacts within communities

can yield information about the forces that shaped and are still shaping cities and the behavior of people in cities. But one trend stands out above all others: the world was becoming more and more stratified. Every development seemed to favor social distinctions, social classes and elites, and to work against the old hunter-gatherer ways.

Among hunter-gatherers all people are equal. Individuals are recognized as exceptional hunters, healers, or storytellers, and they all have the chance to shine upon appropriate occasions. But it would be unthinkable for one of them, for any one man, to take over as full-time leader. That ethic passed when the nomadic life passed. In fact, a literal explosion of differences accompanied the coming of communities where people lived close together in permanent dwellings and under conditions where moving away was not easy.

The change is reflected clearly in observed changes of settlement patterns. Hierarchies of settlements imply hierarchies of people. Emerging social levels are indicated by the appearance of villages and towns and cities where only villages had existed before, by different levels of complexity culminating in such centers as Susa and Monte Albán and Cahokia. Circumstances practically drove people to establish class societies. In Mesopotamia, for instance, increasingly sophisticated agricultural systems and intensive concentrations of populations brought about enormous and irreversible changes within a short period. People were clamped in a demographic vise, more and more of them living and depending on less and less land—an ideal setting for the rapid rise of status differences.

Large-scale irrigation was a highly effective centralizing force, calling for new duties and new regularities and new levels of discipline. People still depended on the seasons; but in addition, canals had to be dug and maintained, and periodic cleaning was required to prevent the artificial waterways from filling up with silt and assorted litter. Workers had to be brought together, assigned tasks, and fed, which meant schedules and storehouses and rationing stations and mass-produced pottery to serve as food containers. It took time to organize such activities efficiently. There were undoubtedly many false starts, many attempts by local people to work things out among themselves and their neighbors at a community or village level. Many small centers, budding institutions, were undoubtedly formed and many collapsed, and we may yet detect traces of them in future excavations and analyses of settlement patterns.

The ultimate outcome was inevitable. Survival demanded organization on a regional rather than a local basis. It also demanded high-level administrators and managers, and most of them had to be educated people, mainly because of the need to prepare detailed records of supplies and transactions. Record-keeping has a long prehistory, perhaps dating back to certain abstract designs engraved on cave walls and bone twenty-five thousand or more years ago. But in Mesopotamia after 4000 B.C. there was a spurt in the art of inventing and utilizing special marks and symbols.

The trend is shown in the stamp and cylinder seals used by officials to place their "signatures" on clay tags and tablets, man's first documents. At first the designs on the stamp seals were uncomplicated, consisting for the most part of single animals or simple geometric motifs. Later, however, there were bigger stamp seals with more elaborate scenes depicting several objects or people or animals. Finally the cylinder seals appeared, which could be rolled to repeat a complex design. These seals indicate the existence of more and more different signatures and more and more officials and record keepers. Similar trends are evident in potters' marks and other symbols. All these developments precede pictographic writing, which appears around 3200 B.C.

Wherever record keepers and populations were on the rise, in the Near East or Mexico or China, we can be reasonably sure that the need for a police force or the prehistoric equivalent thereof was on the increase, too. Conflict, including everything from fisticuffs to homicide, increases sharply with group size, and people have

known this for a long time. The Bushmen have a strong feeling about avoiding crowds: "We like to get together, but we fear fights." They are most comfortable in bands of about twenty-five persons and when they have to assemble in larger groups which happens for a total of only a few months a year, mainly to conduct initiations, arrange marriages, and be near the few permanent water holes during dry seasons they form separate small groups of about twenty-five, as if they were still living on their own.

Incidentally, twenty-five has been called a "magic number," because it hints at what may be a universal law of group behavior. There have been many counts of hunter-gatherer bands, not only in the Kalahari Desert, but also in such diverse places as the forests of Thailand, the Canadian Northwest, and northern India. Although individual bands may vary from fifteen to seventy-five members, the tendency is to cluster around twenty-five, and in all cases a major reason for keeping groups small is the desire to avoid violence. In other words, the association between large groups and conflict has deep roots and very likely presented law-and-order problems during the early days of cities and pre-cities, as it has ever since.

Along with managers and record keepers and keepers of the peace, there were also specialists in trade. A number of factors besides population growth and intensive land use were involved in the origin of cities, and local and long-distance trade was among the most important. Prehistoric centers in the process of becoming urban were almost always trade centers. They typically occupied favored places, strategic points in developing trade networks, along major waterways and caravan routes or close to supplies of critical raw materials.

Archaeologists are making a renewed attempt to learn more about such developments. Wright's current work in southwest Iran, for example, includes preliminary studies to detect and measure changes in the flow of trade. One site about sixty-five miles from Susa lies close to tar pits, which in prehistoric times served as a source of natural asphalt for fastening stone

blades to handles and waterproofing baskets and roofs. By saving all the waste bits of this important raw material preserved in different excavated levels, Wright was able to estimate fluctuations in its production over a period of time. In one level, for example, he found that the amounts of asphalt produced increased far beyond local requirements; in fact, a quantitative analysis indicates that asphalt exports doubled at this time. The material was probably being traded for such things as high-quality flint obtained from quarries more than one hundred miles away, since counts of material recovered at the site indicate that imports of the flint doubled during the same period.

In other words, the site was taking its place in an expanding trade network, and similar evidence from other sites can be used to indicate the extent and structure of that network. Then the problem will be to find out what other things were happening at the same time, such as significant changes in cylinder-seal designs and in agricultural and religious practices. This is the sort of evidence that may be expected to spell out just how the evolution of trade was related to the evolution of cities.

Another central problem is gaining a fresh understanding of the role of religion. Something connected with enormous concentrations of people, with population pressures and tensions of many kinds that started building up five thousand or more years ago, transformed religion from a matter of simple rituals carried out at village shrines to the great systems of temples and priesthoods invariably associated with early cities. Sacred as well as profane institutions arose to keep society from splitting apart.

Strong divisive tendencies had to be counteracted, and the reason may involve yet another magic number, another intriguing regularity that has been observed in hunter-gatherer societies in different parts of the world. The average size of a tribe, defined as a group of bands all speaking the same dialect, turns out to be about five hundred persons, a figure that depends to some extent on the limits of human memory. A tribe is a community of people who can identify closely with one another and engage in repeated face-to-face encounters and recognitions; and it happens that five hundred may represent about the number of persons a hunter-gatherer can remember well enough to approach on what would amount to a first-name basis in our society. Beyond that number the level of familiarity declines, and there is an increasing tendency to regard individuals as "they" rather than "we," which is when trouble usually starts. (Architects recommend that an elementary school should not exceed five hundred pupils if the principal is to maintain personal contact with all of them, and the headmaster of one prominent prep school recently used this argument to keep his student body at or below the five-hundred mark.)

Religion of the sort that evolved with the first cities may have helped to "beat" the magic number five hundred. Certainly there was an urgent need to establish feelings of solidarity among many thousands of persons rather than a few hundred. Creating allegiances wider than those provided by direct kinship and person-to-person ties became a most important problem, a task for full-time professionals. In this connection Paul Wheatley of the University of Chicago suggests that "specialized priests were among the first persons to be released from the daily round of subsistence labor." Their role was partly to exhort other workers concerned with the building of monuments and temples, workers who probably exerted greater efforts in the belief that they were doing it not for mere men but for the glory of individuals highborn and close to the gods.

The city evolved to meet the needs of societies under pressure. People were being swept up in a process that had been set in motion by their own activities and that they could never have predicted, for the simple reason that they had no insight into what they were doing in the first place. For example, they did not know, and had no way of knowing, that settling down could lead to population explosions.

There is nothing strange about this state of affairs, to be sure. It is the essence of the human condition and involves us just as intensely today. Then as now, people responded by the sheer instinct of survival to forces that they understood vaguely at best—and worked together as well as they could to organize themselves, to preserve order in the face of accelerating change and complexity and the threat of chaos. They could never know that they were creating what we, its beneficiaries and its victims, call civilization.

FEAR of the CITY
1783 to 1983

The city has been a lure for millions, but most of the great American minds have been appalled by its excesses. Here an eminent observer, who knows firsthand the city's threat, surveys the subject.

Alfred Kazin

Alfred Kazin is Distinguished Professor of English at the City University of New York Graduate Center. He is completing An American Procession, *a book about American writers from Emerson to T. S. Eliot.*

EVERY THURSDAY, when I leave my apartment in a vast housing complex on Columbus Avenue to conduct a university seminar on the American city, I reflect on a double life—mine. Most of the people I pass on my way to the subway look as imprisoned by the city as my parents and relatives used to look in the Brooklyn ghetto where I spent my first twenty years. Yet no matter where else I have traveled and taught, I always seem to return to streets and scenes like those on New York's Upper West Side.

Two blocks away on Broadway there is daily carnage. Drunks outside the single-room-occupancy hotel dazedly eye me, a professor laden with books and notes trudging past mounds of broken glass, hills of garbage. Even at eight in the morning a craps game is going on in front of the hydrant that now gives off only a trickle. It has been left open for so many weeks that even the cover has vanished. On the benches lining that poor polluted sliver of green that runs down the center of Broadway, each drunk has his and her bottle in the regulation brown paper bag. A woman on crutches, so battered looking that I can't understand how she stands up, is whooping it up—totally ignored by the cars, trucks, and bicycles impatiently waiting at the red light. None of the proper people absorbed in their schedules has time to give the vagrants more than a glance. Anyway, it's too dangerous. No eye contact is the current rule of the game.

I left all this many times, but the city has never left me. At many universities abroad—there was even one improbable afternoon lecturing in Moscow—I have found myself explaining the American city, tracing its history, reviewing its literature—and with a heavy heart, more and more having to defend it. The American city has a bad reputation now, though there was a time, as the violinist Yehudi Menuhin said during World War II, when one of the great war aims was to get to New York.

There is now general fear of the city. While sharing it, I resent it, for I have never ceased feeling myself to be one of the city's people, even as I have labored in libraries to seize the full background to my life in the city. But when in American history has there not been fear of the city—and especially on the part of those who did not have to live in it?

BEFORE THERE WERE American cities of any significance, the best American minds were either uninterested in cities or were suspicious of them. The Puritans thought of Boston as another Jerusalem, "a city upon a hill," but even their first and deepest impression was of the forest around it. This sense of unlimited space was bewitching until the end of the nineteenth century. In his first inaugural address in 1801, Thomas Jefferson pronounced, as if in a dream, that Americans possessed "a chosen country, with room enough for our descendants to the hundredth and thousandth generation." What was "chosen" was not just an endless frontier but the right people to go with it. This, as a matter of course to a great country squire like Jefferson, surveying the future from his mountaintop at Monticello, meant excluding the mobs he associated with European cities. Jefferson's attitude may have been influenced by the European Philosophes whom Louis XVI blamed for the French Revolution. Jefferson was a Philosophe himself; he would have agreed with a leader of the revolution, Saint-Just, that oppressed people "are a power on the earth." But he did not want to see any oppressed people here at all—they usually

 From *American Heritage*, February/March 1983, pp. 14-23. Reprinted by permission of the author.

lived to become the kind of mob he detested and feared. "The mobs of great cities," he wrote in *Notes on Virginia*, "add just so much to the support of pure government, as sores do to the strength of the human body."

Jefferson knew what the city mob had done to break down ancient Rome as well as feudal France. America was a fresh start, "the world's best hope," and must therefore start without great cities. As a universal savant of sorts, as well as a classicist and scientist, Jefferson knew that Athens and Rome, Florence and Venice, Paris and London, had created the culture that was his proudest possession. And since he was an eighteenth-century skeptic, this cosmopolitan world culture was his religion. But anticipating the damage that "manufactures" could inflict on the individual, he insisted that on an unsettled continent only the proudly self-sustaining American "cultivator" could retain his dignity in the face of the Industrial Revolution.

It is not easy now to appreciate all Jefferson's claims for the rural life, and his ideas were not altogether popular with other great landowners and certainly not with such promoters of industry as Hamilton. Jefferson was a great traveler and world statesman who hardly limited himself to his country estate. Monticello, with its magnificent architecture, its great library, its array of inventions and musical and scientific instruments, more resembled a modern think tank (but imagine one this beautiful!) than the simple American farm he praised as a bastion of virtue.

But "virtue" was just what Jefferson sought for America. Whatever else they did, cities corrupted. The special virtue of rural folk rested on self-reliance, a quality unobtainable in "manufactures and handicraft arts" because these depended "on casualties and caprice of customers. Dependence begets subservience and venality, suffocates the germ of virtue, and prepares fit tools for the designs of ambition."

A few years later Emerson had a more complicated view of his society. The Sage of Concord was no farmer (Thoreau was his handyman) and did not particularly think the farmers in his neighborhood were the seat of all virtue. They were just of the earth, earthy. But believing in nothing so much as solitude, *his* right to solitude, his freedom only when alone to commune with Nature and his own soul ("Alone is wisdom. Alone is happiness."), Emerson found the slightest group to be an obstruction to the perfect life.

There is an unintentionally funny account in Emerson's journal for 1840 of just how irritating he found his fellow idealists. There was a gathering in some hotel—presumably in Boston, but one Emerson likened to New York's Astor House—to discuss the "new Social Plans" for the Brook Farm commune: "And not once could I be inflamed, but sat aloof and thoughtless; my voice faltered and fell. It was not the cave of persecution which is the palace of spiritual power, but only a room in the Astor House hired for the Transcendentalists. . . . To join this body would be to traverse all my long trumpeted theory, and the instinct which spoke from it, that one man is a counterpoise to a city—that a man is stronger than a city, that his solitude is more prevalent and beneficent than the concert of crowds."

Emerson finally agreed to help found Brook Farm but he could not have lived there. Hawthorne tried it for a while and turned his experiences into the wry novel *The Blithedale Romance*. Hawthorne was another Yankee grumpily insisting on his right to be alone but he did not take himself so seriously; he was a novelist and fascinated by the human comedy. A twentieth-century admirer of Emerson, John Jay Chapman, admitted that you can learn more from an Italian opera than from all the works of Emerson; in Italian opera there are always two sexes.

But Emerson is certainly impressive, bringing us back to the now forgotten meaning of "self-reliance" when he trumpets that "one man is a counterpoise to a city—that a man is stronger than a city. . . ." This was primary to many Americans in the nineteenth century and helped produce those great testaments to the individual spirit still found on the walls of American schoolrooms and libraries. Power is in the individual, not in numbers; in "soul," not in matter or material conglomeration. And "soul" is found not in organized religion, which is an obedience to the past, but in the self-sufficient individual whose "reliance" is on his inborn connection, through Nature, with any God it pleases him to find in himself.

CERTAINLY IT WAS easier then to avoid the "crowd." Thoreau, who went back many an evening to his family's boardinghouse for meals when he was at Walden Pond writing a book, said that the road back to Concord was so empty he could see a chicken crossing it half a mile off. Like Thoreau's superiority to sex and—most of the time—to politics, there is something truly awesome in the assurance with which he derogates such social facts as the city of New York: "I don't like the city better, the more I see it, but worse. I am ashamed of my eyes that behold it. It is a thousand times meaner than I could have imagined. . . . The pigs in the street are the most respectable part of the population. When will the world learn that a million men are of no importance compared with *one* man?"

To which Edgar Allan Poe, born in Boston and fated to die in Baltimore, could have replied that Thoreau had nothing to look at but his reflection in Walden Pond. Poe would have agreed with his European disciple Baudelaire on the cultural sacredness of great cities. He would have enjoyed Karl Marx's contempt for "rural idiocy." Poe was a great imagination and our greatest critic; as an inventor of the detective story and a storyteller, he was as dependent on the violence and scandal of New York in the 1840s as a police reporter. "The Mystery of Marie Roget," based on the actual murder of a New York shop assistant named Mary Rogers who was found dead in the Hudson after what is now believed to have been a botched abortion, was the first detective story in which an attempt was made to solve a real crime. Even the more than usual drunkenness that led to his death in Baltimore on Election Day of 1849 was typical of his connection with "low" urban life. He was found in a delirious condition near a saloon that had been used for a voting place. He seems to have been

To prevent immigrants from voting, squads of Know-Nothing party members rampaged through Baltimore on Election Day in 1856. The city had a nationwide reputation for political violence.

captured by a political gang that voted him around the town, after which he collapsed and died.

Yet just as Abraham Lincoln was proud of having a slow, careful countryman's mind, so Poe would have denied that *his* extraordinary mind owed anything to the cities in which he found his material. In the same spirit, John Adams from once rural Quincy, his gifted son John Quincy, and his even more gifted great-grandson Henry, all hated Boston and thought of the financial district on State Street as their antithesis. Herman Melville, born in New York, and forced to spend the last twenty-five years of his life as a customs inspector on the docks, hated New York as a symbol of his merchant father's bankruptcy and of his own worldly failure as an author. In a poem about the Civil War, when the worst insurrection in American history broke out in New York as a protest against the Draft Act, Melville imagined himself standing on the rooftop of his house on East Twenty-sixth Street listening to the roar of the mob and despising it:

. . . Balefully glares red Arson—there—and there.
The Town is taken by its rats—ship-rats

And rats of the wharves. All civil charms
And priestly spells which late held hearts in awe—
Fear-bound, subjected to a better sway
Than sway of self; these like a dream dissolve,
And man rebounds whole aeons back in nature.

BEFORE THE Civil War there was just one exception among the great American writers to the general fear and resentment of the city. Whitman was to be prophetic of the importance of New York as a capital of many races and peoples and of the city as a prime subject in modern American writing. Whitman found himself as man and poet by identifying with New York. None of the gifted writers born and bred in New York—not Melville or Henry James or Edith Wharton—was to make of the city such an expression of personal liberation, such a glowing and extended fable of the possibilities released by democracy. "Old New York," as Edith Wharton called it (a patriciate that Melville could have belonged to among the Rhinelanders and Schuylers if his father had not failed in business), still speaks in Melville's rage against the largely Irish mob burning and looting in 1863. But Whitman, his exact contemporary, did not despair of the city's often lawless democracy when he helped put the first edition of *Leaves of Grass* into type in a shop off Brooklyn's Fulton Street.

Whitman found himself by finding the city to be the great human stage. Unlike earlier and later antagonists of the city, who feared the masses, Whitman saw them as a boundless human fellowship, a wonderful spectacle, *the* great school of ambition. The masses, already visible in New York's population of over a million, were the prime evidence Whitman needed to ground his gospel of American democracy as "comradeship." Formerly a schoolteacher, printer, carpenter, a failure at many occupations who was born into a family of failures and psychic cripples, Whitman felt that the big anonymous city crowd had made it possible for *him* to rise out of it.

One's self I sing, a simple separate person,
Yet utter the word Democratic, the word En-Masse.

Whitman found the model and form of *Leaves of Grass,* the one book he wrote all his life, in the flux and mass of the city—he even compared his book *to* a city. He never reached his countrymen during his lifetime, and the Gilded Age took the foam off his enthusiasm for democracy, but in decline he could still write, "I can hardly tell why, but feel very positively that if anything can justify my revolutionary attempts & utterances, it is such *ensemble*—like a great city to modern civilization & a whole combined clustering paradoxical unity, a man, a woman."

Whitman was that "paradoxical unity, a man, a woman." His powerful and many-sided sexuality gave him friends that only a great city can provide; his constant expectation of love from some stranger in the street, on the ferryboat, even his future reader—"I stop somewhere waiting for you"—made stray intimacies in the city as sweet to him as they were repellent to most Americans.

The trouble with the city, said Henry James, Henry Adams, and Edith Wharton, *is* democracy, the influx of ignorant masses, their lack of manners, their lack of standards. The trouble with the city, said the angry Populist farmers and their free-silver standard-bearer Bryan in 1896, is Wall Street, the "moneyed East," the concentration of capital, the banking system that keeps honest, simple farmers in debt. Before modern Los Angeles, before Dallas, Phoenix, and Houston, it was understood that "the terrible town," as Henry James called New York, could exist only in the crowded East. The West, "wild" or not, was land of heart's ease, nature itself. The East was the marketplace that corrupted Westerners who came East. There was corruption at the ballet box, behind the bank counter, in the "purlieus of vice." The city was ugly by definition because it lacked the elemental harmony of nature. It lacked stability and relentlessly wrecked every monument of the past. It was dirt, slums, gangsters, violence.

Above all it was "dark." The reporter and pioneer photographer Jacob Riis invaded the East Side for his book *How the Other Half Lives* (1890) because he was "bent on letting in the light where it was much needed."

Look at Riis's photograph "Bandit's Roost," 59½ Mulberry Street, taken February 12, 1888. "Bandit's Roost" did not get its name for nothing, and you can still feel threatened as your eye travels down the narrow alley paved with grimy, irregularly paved stone blocks that glisten with wet and dirt. Tough-looking characters in derbies and slouch hats are lining both sides of the alley, staring straight at you; one of them presses a stick at the ground, and his left knee is bent as if he were ready, with that stick, to go into action at a moment's notice. The women at the open windows are staring just as unhelpfully as the derbied young fellow in the right foreground, whose chin looks as aggressive as the long, stiff lines of his derby.

CONSIDER NEW YORK just a century ago: the rooftops above the business district downtown are thick with a confusion of the first telephone lines crossing the existing telegraph wires. The immigrant John Augustus Roebling has built a suspension bridge of unprecedented length over the East River, thanks to the wire rope he has invented. This wire makes for a rooted strength and airy elegance as Roebling ties his ropes across one another in great squares. Brooklyn Bridge will be considered stronger as well as infinitely more beautiful than the other bridges to be built across the East River. But a week after opening day in 1883, the crowd panics as vast numbers cross the bridge, crushing several people to death—and exposing a fear of numbers, of great bridges, of the city itself, that even city dwellers still feel. What they thought of New York in the prairie West and the cotton South may easily be imagined.

But here is Central Park, the first great public park in the New World, finally completed after decades of struggle to reclaim a horrid waste. Unlike the European parks that were once feudal estates, Central Park has been carved, landscaped, gardened, built, and ornamented from scratch and specifically for the people. And this by a Connecticut Yankee, Frederick Law Olmsted, the most far-seeing of democratic visionaries, who saw in the 1850s that New York would soon run out of places in which city dwellers could escape the city. Though he will never cease complaining that the width of his park is confined to the narrow space between Fifth Avenue and what is now Central Park West, he will create a wonderland of walks, "rambles," lakes, gardens, meadows. All this is designed not for sport, political demonstrations, concerts, the imperial Metropolitan Museum, but for the contemplative walker. As early as 1858, before he was chosen superintendent but after having submitted the winning design, "Greensward," in a competition, Olmsted wrote of his park: "The main object and justification is simply to produce a certain influence in the minds of the people and through this to make life in the city healthier and happier. The character of this influence is a poetic one, and it is to be produced by means of scenes, through observation of which the mind may be more or less lifted out of moods and habits in which it is, under the ordinary conditions of life in the city, likely to fall . . ."

Alas, Central Park is not enough to lift some of us out of the "moods and habits" into which we are likely to fall. Even Walt

Museum of the City of New York

"Bandit's Roost" on Mulberry Street by Jacob Riis (1888). Riis later found that five of nine children who lived in one of these houses were dead by the end of the year.

Whitman, who truly loved New York, acidly let it drop in *Democratic Vistas* (1871) that "the United States are destined either to surmount the gorgeous history of feudalism, or else prove the most tremendous failure of time." The "great experiment," as some English sardonically call the democratic Republic, may very well depend on the city into which nearly a million immigrants a year were to pour at the beginning of the next century. Whitman was not prepared to estimate the effect on America of the greatest volunteer migration recorded in history. It was the eclipse of virtue that surprised him at the end of the century. As if he were Jefferson, he wrote: "The great cities reek with respectable as much as nonrespectable robbery and scoundrelism. In fashionable life, flippancy, tepid amours, weak infidelism, small aims, or no aims at all, only to kill time. In business (this all-devouring modern word business), the one sole object is, by any means, pecuniary gain. The magician's serpent in the fable ate up all the other serpents; and money-making is our magician's serpent, remaining today sole master of the field."

ARE CITIES all that important as an index of American health and hope? The French sociologist Raymond Aron thinks that American intellectuals are too much preoccupied with cities. He neglects to say that most Americans now have no other life but the life in those cities. Paris has been the absolute center of France— intellectually, administratively, educationally—for many centuries. America has no center that so fuses government and intellect. Although Americans are more than ever an urban people, many Americans still think of the city as something it is necessary to escape from.

In the nineteenth century slums were the savage places Jacob Riis documented in his photographs, but on the whole the savagery was confined to the slums. The political scientist Andrew Hacker has shown that "there was actually little crime of the kind we know today and in hardly any cases were its victims middle class. The groups that had been violent— most notably the Irish—had by 1900 turned respectable. The next wave of immigrants, largely from Eastern Europe and southern Italy, were more passive to begin with and accepted the conditions they found on their arrival . . . they did not inflict their resentments on the rest of society . . ."

What has finally happened is that fear of the city on the part of those who live in it has caught up with the fear on the part of those who did not have to live in it.

American fear of the city may seem ungrateful, since so much of our social intelligence depends on it. But the tradition of fear persists, and added to it nowadays—since all concern with the city is concern with class—has been fear of the "underclass," of blacks, of the youth gangs that first emerged in the mid-fifties. Vast housing projects have become worse than the slums they replaced and regularly produce situations of extreme peril for the inhabitants themselves. To the hosts of the uprooted and disordered in the city, hypnotized by the images of violence increasingly favored by the media, the city is nothing but a state of war. There is mounting vandalism, blood lust, and indiscriminate aggressiveness.

The mind reels, is soon exhausted, and turns indifferent to the hourly report of still another killing. In Brooklyn's 77th precinct a minister is arrested for keeping a sawed-off shotgun under his pulpit. On Easter Sunday uniformed police officers are assigned to protect churchgoers from muggers and purse snatchers. In parts of Crown Heights and Bedford-Stuyvesant, the *Times* reports that "there, among the boarded-up tenements, the gaudy little stores and the residential neighborhoods of old brownstones and small row houses, 88 people were killed in one year—16 in one three-block area." A hundred thousand people live and work in this precinct, but a local minister intones that "Life has become a mean and frightening struggle." Gunshots are heard all the time.

I was born and brought up alongside that neighborhood; the tenement in which my parents lived for half a century does not exist and nothing has replaced it. The whole block is a mass of rubble; the neighborhood has seen so much arson that the tops of the remaining structures are streaked with black. Alongside them whole buildings are boarded up but have been broken into; they look worse than London did after the blitz.

Democracy has been wonderful to me and for me, and in the teeth of the police state creeping up elsewhere in the world, I welcome every kind of freedom that leaves others free in the city. The endless conflict of races, classes, sexes, is raucous but educational. No other society on earth tolerates so many interest groups, all on the stage at once and all clamoring for attention.

Still, the subway car I take every day to the city university definitely contains a threat. Is it the young black outstretched across the aisle? The misplaced hilarity proceeding from the drinking group beating time to the ya-ya-ya that thumps out of their ghetto blaster? The sweetish marijuana fumes when the train halts too long in this inky tunnel and that make me laugh when I think that once there was no more absolute commandment in the subway than NO SMOKING?

Definitely, there is a threat. Does it proceed from the unhelpful, unsmiling, unseeing strangers around me? The graffiti and aggressive smears of paint on which I have to sit, and which so thickly cover every partition, wall, and window that I cannot make out the stations? Can it be the New York *Post*—"Post-Mortem" as a friend calls it—every edition of which carries the news MOM KILLS SELF AND FIVE KIDS? The battle police of the transit force rushing through one car after another as the motorman in his booth sounds the wailing alarm that signifies trouble?

What a way to live! It is apartness that rules us here, and the apartness makes the threat. Still, there is no other place for me to work and live. Because sitting in the subway, holding the book on which I have to conduct a university seminar this afternoon, I have to laugh again. It is *Uncle Tom's Cabin, or Life Among the Lowly.*

SYMPOSIUM
The State of the Nation's Cities

Herbert J. Gans

Herbert J. Gans is Professor of Sociology at Columbia University. He was trained as both a city planner and a sociologist. He is currently writing on urban and social theory as well as on the news media and American politics. His latest book is an updated and expanded edition of The Urban Villagers *(Free Press, 1982).*

John D. Kasarda

John D. Kasarda is Professor and Chairman of the Department of Sociology at the University of North Carolina—Chapel Hill. His current research focuses on urban economic, demographic, and policy issues.

Harvey Molotch

Harvey Molotch is Professor of Sociology at the University of California—Santa Barbara. He is currently completing a book with John Logan of SUNY—Albany on the political economy of space. He has published articles on neighborhood changes, city growth, and issues in mass media.

Editors' Introduction

We . . . offer a . . . "mini-symposium" of informed opinion from three urbanologists. . . . We asked Herbert Gans, John Kasarda, and Harvey Molotch to respond to a series of questions about current urban problems and public policy prospects for dealing with them.

We selected these three urbanologists, in part, because they represent varying theoretical and political persuasions. Herbert Gans's work in community studies and especially in urban planning represents what may be called a liberal approach to these issues. John Kasarda's work on urban ecology arises from a classical tradition that might now be labeled "neoconservative." And finally, in Harvey Molotch we have the voice of a neo-Marxian political economist. Their responses to the nine questions we have posed, however, represent the enlightened thinking of three scholars, not the political rhetoric of any given dogma. As the reader will see, in spite of theoretical differences, their answers at times surprisingly agree, while at other times they diverge in somewhat unexpected directions.

We also have a diverse geographical representation in our respondents; this was not a consideration in their selection, but rather a happy happenstance. Gans is from the older, frostbelt metropolis of New York City,

Molotoch is from the opposite coast—California, and Kasarda is from the new sunbelt region of North Carolina. Their responses are at times regionally flavored, though none are parochially predetermined. . . .

—*Albert Hunt for the Editors*

(1) What are the fundamental problems confronting urban centers today?

Gans: America's urban centers are so diverse that some are booming while others are declining. Moreover, they are internally so differentiated that boomtowns can suffer from high rates of unemployment while declining cities can brag about growing central business districts. If urban centers have any problem in common, it is the country's fundamental problem: a national economy that has lost its international dominance, has stopped growing, and can therefore no longer supply decent jobs to all who want to work. As a result, existing class, political, racial, and other inequalities worsen, and conflicts over the allocation of resources become more difficult to resolve.

Cities may suffer these consequences earlier and more intensely than other types of settlements, partly because the country's dominant interest groups, particularly corporations and suburbanites, lack incentives to help the cities. Some urban centers face special difficulties because of the widespread closing or exodus of manufacturing firms, or because they are located in economically declining regions. Nonetheless, most problems of most American cities are not distinctively urban, and little is gained for analysis or policymaking by calling the problems urban.

Kasarda: Our urban centers face a host of vexatious problems—the most fundamental of which are rooted in a growing mismatch between their job opportunity structures and resident population skill levels. Modern advances in transportation, communication, and industrial technologies interacting with the changing structure of national and international economic organization have transformed major cities from centers of material goods production to centers of information exchange and higher-order service provision. In the process of urban functional transformation, many blue-collar industries that once constituted the economic backbone of cities and provided ready employment for lesser skilled residents have vanished. These blue-collar industries have been replaced, in part, by knowledge-intensive white-collar industries with requisites for employment entry that entail substantial education or training and, hence, are inappropriate to the expanding numbers of educationally disadvantaged persons residing in our cities.

Aggravating precipitous employment declines in our cities' historic blue-collar industries has been the urban exodus of middle-income residents and the neighborhood business establishments that once served them.

This exodus further weakened secondary labor markets, eroded local tax bases, and increased the spatial isolation of disadvantaged persons in distressed subareas of the city, where prospects for permanent or meaningful employment are negligible.

Rising urban structural unemployment, increased municipal fiscal strains, and the social, economic, and spatial isolation of growing concentrations of urban minorities have contributed to numerous other urban ills, including high crime rates, poor public schools, deteriorating public infrastructures, and the decay of once vibrant commercial and residential subareas of our cities.

Molotch: As long as space, land, and buildings are commodities, pretty much like any others, they can be bought, sold, and otherwise manipulated for private gains. In the United States, this long-standing commoditization of land has been more extreme than in most other societies, and this fact creates special space-related social problems, which fall, in particular, upon those who own no land, those who have little to gain from the intensified uses of land owned by others, or those who are unable to protect the land-based interests that they do have. In modern times, these traditional problems of the landless have been complicated by the erosion of traditional constraints that might have once existed and by the newly created ability of organized entrepreneurs to utilize government to effect large-scale land use changes consistent with their own material interests.

Speaking roughly, but in more concrete terms, this means that ordinary people now confront two different sorts of urban problems, depending upon whether they live in the declining old cities or in the more dynamic (often newer) ones. People's troubles in the old cities stem from unresolved contradictions of former modes of wealth accumulation; those in the new cities are plagued by difficulties associated with more recent dynamics.

Taking the old places first, we find that the social and material residues of nineteenth-century manufacturing remain in place and are still unattended. A *Lumpenklasse* of the unskilled and uncelebrated stagnates as a critical mass, which erodes local fiscal budgets and establishes a sort of hopeless context that inhibits the success of ameliorative interventions. In material terms, a physical plant remains that is increasingly obsolete. The toxic residues (such as water pollutants and chemical wastes) exact severe "neighborhood effects," further inhibiting the attraction of the "glamour capital" that would restore such areas to the forefront of the U.S. economic development.

The new cities, alas, are replicating—in their own way—the irrationalities of past modes of development as investment (both public and private) follows the exigencies of accumulation, with hardly any planning for the needs of appropriate human settlements. Hence, growth in the sunbelt is an attack on a fragile ecosystem that destroys air quality, depletes natural water supplies, and sustains a profligate waste of energy resources. It also lowers people's standard of living by facilitating wild sprees of speculation in housing commodities.

(2) Have cities lost their historic functions for socially and economically upgrading disadvantaged residents?

Gans: It is entirely possible that the good old days never existed and that cities upgraded fewer people than they left in place, downgraded, or let die. In any case, cities have not yet lost their upgrading function, because poor people still come to them to improve their economic condition. In fact, in a period of economic decline, newcomers who are willing to work long hours for very low wages are in particularly great demand, and may therefore be able to upgrade themselves quickly, provided, however, that they do not have to support too many dependents. But this pattern also dates back to the nineteenth century.

Opportunities for upgrading are probably scarcest for the descendents of newcomers, who are sufficiently "Americanized" and "modernized" to expect eight-hour-a-day jobs at decent wages, but cannot get them in economically declining cities.

Kasarda: Yes, to a significant extent they have. Cities served these functions most effectively during an industrial and transportation era that no longer exists. During this era (circa 1880-1915) enormous national industrial expansion occurred, generating millions of low-skill jobs, while prevailing transportation technologies restricted the vast bulk of national employment growth to our urban centers. As a result, our older cities were characterized by entry-level job *surpluses* compared to the entry-level job *deficits* that characterize their employment bases today. These job surpluses attracted the waves of migrants and offered them a foothold in the urban economy. The rapidly expanding employment base accompanying national economic growth, in turn, provided ladders of opportunity and social mobility for the migrants, most of whom were escaping areas of economic distress.

Of course, the access to opportunity and social mobility that our older cities provided disadvantaged migrants were obtained at significant human costs. Prejudice, discrimination, hostility, and often physical violence greeted the new arrivals. They were segregated into overcrowded dwelling units in the least desirable sections of the cities. Their unsanitary living environments contributed to high morbidity and mortality rates, as did hazardous working conditions in the factories. Political corruption and exploitation were common, working hours were long, and there was no such thing as a minimum wage. Using currently fashionable dual labor market theory, virtually all immigrants held "dead-end" jobs.

Yet, to reiterate, there was an abundance of these jobs for which the only requisites were a willingness and physical ability to work. The surplus of low-skill urban jobs and dramatic national economic growth (both of which have now ceased) provided our older cities with their period-specific role in our nation's history as developers of manpower and springboards for social mobility.

Molotch: The word "functions" implies that there was something about "citiness" that provided for greater aggregate mobility than would otherwise have been the case. Cities were the *site* of a great deal of social mobility, but this was part of a larger process in which people in the hinterlands were losing their very ability to sustain life. I don't find much romance in either part of this transformation. I credit urban mobility to the individuals who clawed their way upward and to the larger contingencies that made possible the success of their efforts. The city was not the only site of such mobility; numerous people in the United States made vast fortunes in and off the hinterlands (for example, in agriculture, mining, railroading, real estate speculation).

Regardless of how many people "made it" or didn't make it in the city, the larger point is that this "city mobility" must be viewed as intrinsically a part of a much larger set of events—the development of industrial capitalism. And this process carried with it some very horrible as well as joyful experiences—depending not so much upon *where* you were, but *who* you were and *when* you were.

What is apparently changing today is that mobility and fortune building are to be less evenly spread among U.S. cities and increasingly concentrated in those places that are the centers of technological innovation and elite coordination. Cities are going to be increasingly differentiated in terms of their capacities to serve as the sites of independent wealth generation—and people who are not in such places will have less access to the benefits (some of it by chance) of being in these right places at the right time.

(3) To what extent have federal policies contributed to existing urban problems?

Gans: Most federal policies help and hurt at the same time, but federal urban policies have helped cities, including their poor residents, more than they have hurt them. After all, public housing, "235," "236," and "Section 8," as well as the War on Poverty, CETA, and AFDC, were (or still are) largely urban programs. Their accomplishments may have been meager, but the reappearance of malnutrition and the significant increase in the number of people with incomes below the poverty line since the November 1980 election illustrate that earlier federal urban policies have been beneficial.

Of course, the federal policies that helped drive farmers off the land and made them involuntary urban migrants, and those that facilitated the movement of urban jobs to low-wage areas in America or overseas have hurt many cities and city residents. However, unlike some (but not all) of the beneficial urban policies, these were federal responses to powerful political pressures rather than federally initiated policies.

Likewise, urban renewal hurt the cities, as did the various subsidies that hastened the white exodus to suburbia after World War II, but, again, the federal policymakers were at the mercy of powerful constituencies that gave them little choice. For example, I doubt that politicians who opposed the postwar suburbanization would have been able to get themselves reelected. Besides, if the federal subsidies had not been available, the exodus would have taken place anyway, if on the smaller scale typical of the 1920s. Furthermore, if the exodus could have been prevented, the racial and class segregation that now exists between cities and suburbs would have developed inside the cities. Alternatively, the dark-skinned poor would have been banished to suburban slums, as they are in many foreign urban centers.

Conversely, the currently popular notion that federal policies sapped urban moral fibers and bred dependency patterns that prevented cities and their inhabitants from solving their problems themselves is ideological balderdash to rationalize Republican policies for the rich. The market forces celebrated by the Reagan administration and its intellectual supporters have never worked for people or places that lack the money to operate in the "free" market, and cannot do so now. In the old days, before the federal government developed urban policies and the free market ruled the cities, poor urban residents suffered from joblessness and disease; overcrowded housing turned into slums; low-income areas were wracked by crime; and most other contemporary "urban" problems existed as well. In fact, they were worse, as Edward Banfield demonstrated at length in *The Unheavenly City*.

Kasarda: Conventional wisdom typically targets federal programs such as highway development subsidies, VHA-FHA mortgage insurance, and various tax credits and deductions as the main causes of the deconcentration of people and firms from cities. The fact is, however, that massive demographic and commercial deconcentration commenced well before any of these programs were implemented. Whereas such federal programs no doubt facilitated post-World War II urban deconcentration, their impact has been of secondary importance compared to contemporary technological, market, and social dynamics that underlie the location decisions of people and firms. The overarching strength of these structural dynamics is manifest in a number of Western European nations, where, despite absence of similar federal programs, patterns of deconcentration and urban decline are nearly identical to those occurring in the United States.

Perhaps more harmful to the long-term welfare of our cities and their inhabitants have been well-intentioned federal programs that inadvertently attract and anchor disadvantaged persons in inner-city areas of limited opportunity. Recall that Americans, especially the disadvantaged, historically have been a mobile people, migrating from areas of economic distress to areas of greater opportunity. It appears that government programs may now be interfering with this mobility process. Dependent on public housing and place-oriented income and in-kind transfer programs, the disadvantaged have difficulty following lesser skilled jobs that have dispersed from the cities. Government complacency in racial discrimination and a lack of low-cost housing in many areas of employment growth compound the problem. As a result, a growing urban underclass finds itself increasingly isolated in segregated economic wastelands, where most manage to survive marginally on a combination of government handouts and their own informal (both legal and illegal) economies. Such isolation and dependency of potentially productive persons often breed hopelessness, despair, and alienation from mainstream society, which, in turn, promote family dissolution, drug abuse, and other social ills.

Molotch: I restrict my thinking of "urban problems" to issues having something to do with the social organization of land use in urban environments. In these terms, "federal policies" include such programs as urban renewal, public housing, FHA and VA loan programs, and federal tax policies as they affect land use. And, of course, there is much more—so much more than one would need to carry out a very ambitious cost-benefit analysis to determine how such policies aggregate for each particular segment of the society. We would need an enterprise on the scale of the "Club of Rome" to begin such a task.

My own working hypothesis is that the net consequence of aggregate federal intervention has been to hurt the working classes and the poor—particularly the colored minorities. The cumulative impacts of programs such as urban renewal, federal highway building in urban areas, and so forth are widely known, as are the distributional biases of homeowning incentives (such as property tax and mortgage interest write-offs) given to the white middle classes. I think of these programs, in composite, as being one of the factors that helps keep wealth distribution stable in the United States. Our urban programs are transfer mechanisms (direct and indirect) that offset the gains that the poor and minorities receive from direct welfare expenditures (such as AFDC, Medicare, food stamps, and the like).

(4) What is the most effective policy for economically and demographically revitalizing our major cities?

Gans: Although there are people who believe that "planned shrinkage" or sending the frostbelt's poor to the sunbelt will result in demographic revitalization of the city, the poor are the least mobile—and least wanted—of all urban populations. They can be moved out of the cities by force, which is unthinkable in a democratic society, or by special nonurban economic opportunities, which are difficult to imagine in today's economy. A much more direct, but equally infeasible, demographic policy is income redistribution: to turn the poor into middle-income people, thus enabling most to become middle-class citizens.

As for urban economic revitalization, I have not seen any effective—and politically feasible—policies to achieve it, at least in the foreseeable future. Even policies to restore the national economy to health have not yet been discovered, and most of those currently under discussion would not help declining urban economies anyway. Most likely, however, national economic revitalization will require far-reaching government intervention in the economy and the eventual creation of a distinctively American welfare state, which would blend the virtues of American capitalism and Western European socialism, but without the bureaucratic collectivism and centralization that is foreign to the American tradition. Needless to say, that blend of economic and political democracy has not yet been invented. Even if it can be invented, further economic and political changes are necessary to ameliorate, or compensate for, the powerlessness of the cities, and especially of the urban poor.

Kasarda: Effective policies for economic revitalization will be based on the law of comparative advantage and a fuller understanding of the transforming roles of cities in advanced service economies. Policymakers must strategically appraise the competitive strengths and weaknesses of cities under modern transportation and communication technologies and within a changing national and international economic order. Rather than squandering public dollars in futile attempts to rebuild inexorably declining urban industries, revised policies should help cities adapt to new economic realities and exploit their emerging competitive strengths. These strengths lie primarily in the administrative office, financial, professional, and business service sectors, and in cultural, recreational, and tourist industries. These office and leisure industries offer the greatest potential for central-city economic expansion and job generation in the decades ahead.

To facilitate demographic revitalization, policies are required that will help dissolve bonds that well-meaning prior policies have forged between cities and the dependent poor, that will help structurally unemployed urban residents acquire the skills necessary to participate in their transforming local economies, and that will assist (rather than hinder) the mobility of those who desire to migrate to places where jobs appropriate to their skills are still expanding. A thinner central-city population composed largely of those who actually desire to live in the city (minorities as well as whites) and who have job opportunities nearby would create a far

more vibrant city than results from present policies that unintentionally warehouse millions of disadvantaged persons in our cities, to the benefit of neither.

Planned demographic shrinkage becomes the most humane and socially responsible strategy with the recognition that no government policy that would be either economically or politically feasible can overcome contemporary cost disadvantages of inner-city locations for those blue-collar industries that sustained such large numbers of low-skill residents in previous decades. Revised policies adapted to urban demographic shrinkage should be designed compassionately and should focus on reducing institutional impediments to the mobility of disadvantaged persons who desire to leave the city, rather than on any government program that might force relocation of those who wish to remain. Current policies also should be reviewed to ensure that they are not inadvertently attracting large numbers of disadvantaged migrants to inner-city areas that offer limited opportunities for employment.

Molotch: Some of our major cities are plenty vital—that's one of the main reasons for the problems of the other ones. The vital places have names like Los Angeles, Phoenix, and Dallas; the other group consists of places like Newark, Cleveland, and Detroit. I don't think the latter group is any more "major" than the former. It is, rather, a difference between the newly great and the formerly great.

So, to answer the question in recast form: A way to stimulate growth and development in the formerly great cities is to destimulate growth and development in the newly great ones. I believe that urban growth occurs through the mobilization of organized interests (as opposed to the "natural laws" proffered by the ecologists of old). This means, among other things, that our patterns of growth can be modified by social intervention. We need to investigate systematically, for example, the ways in which federal policies support and enhance the development of the sunbelt regions at the expense of the frostbelt zones. A national development policy could be designed to help reverse the direction of such stimuli. Such a program should not be conceived narrowly as belonging to the "urban" sector of federal decision making (that is, HUD), but as necessarily involving a full mobilization of federal decision making to reverse current distributional trends.

For example, much of the water of the sunbelt regions was delivered through federal funding, subsidy, or enabling legislation. Such taps could be turned off. Similarly, there is no reason that defense and other federal contracts could not be targeted to specific areas as a means of shoring up their faltering economies. A contract to Boeing can mitigate the depression in Seattle, while the same contract to Lockheed will further burden the infrastructure of (relatively) prosperous Los Angeles. Just as significantly, federal support for sunbelt programs of environmental protection, if strong enough, could indeed discourage plant location in such areas, with positive effects on the environments they were designed to assist. The point is that disincentives for development in the sunbelt (including environmental restrictions) act to sustain the economies of the North and East.

Programs of positive incentives, such as those implied by the current administration's "enterprise zones," are, of course, fraught with danger and much potential mischief. Any such incentives to private entrepreneurs run the risk of creating a class of professional beneficiaries—the kind of profiteers who end up collecting major benefits from such programs as home health care, Medicare, and so forth. More specifically, I have the expectation that the subsidies will be picked up by investors making decisions that they would have made anyway—they would just pick up a check along the way (this already goes on in the case of UDAG monies and subsidies resulting from tax increment redevelopment). I also fear subsidies for unproductive investment (another potential danger of such programs), which will only add to the moribund image and reality of the targeted places. Such programs would be extremely inefficient mechanisms of stimulating development in declining places and, in terms of their wealth-distributive effects, would likely be regressive. All of this is to say that they would be consistent with Reagan policies generally.

On the other hand, a case can be made—as the administration has tried to do—that the frostbelt cities should just be left to whither away. This is not a ridiculous option. But I would argue that the distributional effects—both individual and geographic—should receive policy attention. For example, relocation expenses could be paid to those who most need the trip— poor minorities who would benefit from a sort of affirmative action for geographic mobility. This would also help even out the current uneven distribution of misery and local fiscal costs associated with it.

(5) Should policies be implemented to prevent the displacement of disadvantaged residents of urban neighborhoods undergoing gentrification and other forms of reinvestment?

Gans: Most cities badly need gentrification and other forms of reinvestment. Consequently, these should be encouraged, provided, however, that the people to be displaced are rehoused first, in decent dwelling units they can afford, with the costs borne by the beneficiaries of gentrification or by the government. I am, however, more concerned about the far greater displacement generated by housing abandonment and by rent increases that poor people cannot pay.

Kasarda: This is a troublesome question that often juxtaposes people versus place policy and equity versus efficiency issues. Without doubt, urban policies should be sensitive to the problems of those displaced by gentrification and other forms of urban reinvestment.

However, in formulating such policies, government officials must be careful that they do not snuff out the one process that is providing hope that our cities can demographically and economically revitalize.

Indeed, gentrification and other forms of urban reinvestment may offer the best means to help innercity disadvantaged by generating needed fiscal resources, providing employment opportunities, and returning middle-class inputs to neighborhoods and local public schools. More importantly, research conducted at HUD indicates that gentrification and similar forms of reinvestment have actually displaced relatively small numbers of minorities and lower-income groups. The largest cause of their displacement was a *lack* of reinvestment resulting in continuing neighborhood deterioration and eventual forced abandonment. Inhibiting gentrification and urban reinvestment through antidisplacement policies, I fear, would constitute yet another crippling blow to disadvantaged urban residents by policymakers claiming to have the interests of the disadvantaged at heart.

Molotch: The problem of gentrification is part of the larger one of how to provide people with a secure home in which to make their lives. Nowhere is the commoditization of space more consequential than in its capacity to deprive people of a stable place to live. That entire neighborhoods are subject to the same dynamic, as a more or less simultaneous event, is only a more dramatic, more visible form of something that goes on every day, with gentrification or without it.

Such disruptions can occur under many conditions: Ownership of an apartment building can shift into the hands of a more "professional" entrepreneur who envisions a higher rent potential; an existing owner may find it more rewarding to shift occupancy to a different class or cultural group—usually at the expense of the poor, the colored, the aged, and those with children. Government may condemn private land for freeways or culture centers, or to assist entrepreneurs who wish to generate profits through redevelopment. Regardless of the precise mechanism, the results are problematic for those who are often least able to cope with them.

One solution is to provide urban residents with tenure rights. Such policies could take a number of forms:

(a) Rent control, which, according to John Gilderbloom's recent data, has the consequence—under present legal limitations—of smoothing out the rent gradient, rather than effecting any long-run boon to tenants or losses to landlords. Such forms of "moderate" rent control do, however, eliminate the kind of sudden and extreme increases in rents that are most traumatic for tenants.
(b) Evictions could be restricted to conditions of "just cause," which would not include an owner's desire to "upgrade" a building and its tenancy or to replace one sort of use (residential) with another (commercial or industrial).

(c) Compensatory damages could be paid to owners and tenants who lose their homes in lieu of such protections or despite them. Government should be forced to pay not just some approximation of "fair market value" or out-of-pocket "relocation cost"; it should also compensate residents for the trials and tribulations, pain and anguish, that such disruptions tend to create. There is plenty of precedent for such forms of compensation, and they make as much sense in this context as they do in those in which they are now routinely applied. In effect, I am saying that the external costs that developers and governments take out of the lives of poor people should be borne internally by the proposed land use changes themselves.

A benefit of these types of policies, especially the last one, is that they would act as a sort of self-balancing restraint on such processes as gentrification. They would also discourage, because of the increased costs, the use of eminent domain for often trivial and regressive purposes. In other words, we would have a mechanism for preserving types of *communities* through policies that directly safeguard the rights of *individuals*. This channels benefits to people, rather than to areal units, thereby lowering the probability of administrative waste and corruption.

(6) Should urban policies discourage low-density, sprawl-type development in favor of more centralized high-density development?

Gans: I have never seen any persuasive evidence that sprawl has significant bad effects, or high-density development significant virtues. Indeed, I doubt that density itself has much impact on people, except at levels at which it produces overcrowding or isolation. I therefore believe that people should be able to choose the density levels they prefer. Since most Americans who are able to choose have long preferred low-density housing, I favor urban policies that respect their preference, while not ignoring the minority preferring high-rise housing. Still, America is now a suburban country and will remain so, even if gasoline someday costs $5 a gallon or more.

Of course, the poor, having no choice, can be forced to live in high-rise housing, and one could support this solution if the alternative were residence in demonstrably harmful low-density slums or in the streets. However, in most cities land is no longer so expensive as to require tall buildings on economic grounds, at least for the poor. Unfortunately, centralized high-density development, whether built for the poor or for the rich, is also an effective way of isolating one income group from the other.

Kasarda: If one were to accept conventional wisdom that urban sprawl is haphazard, inefficient, and undesirable, then this form of development obviously should be discouraged. This commonly held notion—if ever accurate—is now badly out of date and out of touch. Part of the new urban reality is that modern transportation and communication technologies have transformed the old monocentered industrial metropolis into a far more open and diffuse form of urbanism. For those whose obsolete models still view metropolitan areas as fried eggs (with single uniform cores surrounded by uniform suburban and exurban rings), this new form of urbanism must appear more like scrambled eggs, with very little structure. Yet current research is showing that deconcentrated, multinucleated urban development (negatively referred to as "sprawl") has far more structure than once believed. This structure consists of functionally integrated systems of nodes, networks, and social and economic exchanges sustained via advanced technologies on a time-cost rather than a spatial-distance basis.

Regarding cost effectiveness, it is well documented that many modern industries operate more efficiently in outlying locations than in densely built-up centers, and that costs of living and costs of local government soar in large population concentrations; new evidence is disconfirming the old wisdom that centralized, high-density developments are more energy efficient than dispersed, low-density communities. Apropos of social desirability, residential preference surveys continuously show that the vast majority of Americans *least* desire to live in large, dense population centers. The most preferred location is a low-density peripheral development within commuting distance of a metropolitan central city (that is, the classic "sprawl" development). Given the overwhelming preference of most Americans for low-density living, the growing evidence that large concentrations are more costly, and the greater efficiency and productivity of many industries in decentralized settings, it would be a mistake to rely on which has turned out to be more opinion than fact about "sprawl" to channel people and businesses to centralized, high-density locations that they may neither desire nor find economical.

Molotch: A number of factors have combined to inhibit the sort of sprawl that was practiced in the postwar period, and these changes are increasingly reflected in local zoning and land use policies. The new conditions include increased land costs (in part due to speculation, in part because of simple decrease in buildable land on the urban periphery), higher costs of providing urban infrastructure and services, and the increased price of gasoline needed to fuel long-distance commutes. Nevertheless, sprawl continues (and will increase in its rate when mortgage lending resumes). The best method for controlling such sprawl is to have the full costs that it creates borne internally by the new development. Developers can be forced (as they increasingly are) to offset the marginal costs their projects create by paying for road improvements, park development, or sewer line extensions. Because of its extravagant use of land and its inherently expensive servicing costs, sprawl can be discouraged through such costing procedures.

(7) Is urban decentralization posing a serious threat to our nation's prime farmland and future agricultural productivity?

Gans: There are undoubtedly areas in America where the earth has unique and irreplaceable qualities for particular and highly valued crops, but the remaining 99.99% of the country is so full of vacant farmland that it can feed the entire planet. Consequently, people's homes should have priority over crops. To be sure, the disappearance of exurban truck farming has robbed us of some tasty fruits and vegetables, but I wonder whether these labor-intensive family farms would be economically viable today even if their land had somehow been excluded from residential development.

Kasarda: Our farmland is a precious national resource and should be treated as such. Urban decentralization, however, is not nearly the serious threat to our farmland and future agricultural productivity that preservation advocates would have us believe. Despite highly publicized incidents of farmland conversion to urban development, USDA statistics show that the amount of farmland harvested has substantially increased in all regions of the country during the past 10 years.

The apparent contradiction between urban decentralization and simultaneous increases in farmland harvested can be reconciled when one realizes that all urban development and transportation arteries combined cover less than 3% of our nation's 2.3 billion acres. Conversely, land in farms (the majority of it still inactive) constitutes nearly 50% of our nation's total acreage. Urban development thus poses relatively little competition, in the aggregate, to our cropland base.

Not only has the amount of farmland harvested steadily increased in recent years, but new land brought into service has produced high average yields, contributing to our record harvests. This is because "prime" farmland, when measured in terms of what the land can yield per unit cost, is not a fixed quantity but varies spatially and temporally with the state of agricultural technology. Indeed, with recent advances in food-production technologies, the major expressed concern of farm associations is not a shortage of potential cropland, but growing oversupplies of food commodities, resulting in price returns to farmers so low that most will be forced out of business. Overproduction of basic food crops is the reason our government is continuously trying to expand agricultural export markets while implementing internal price supports, restrictive acreage allotments, and set-aside programs that authorize payments to farmers to keep their land idle when supplies are deemed excessive.

Molotch: For reasons indicated earlier, the rates of sprawl—whether outward from the large cities or from smaller nodes in the hinterland—will probably never be the same. In California, even under conditions of robust economic and population growth, acreage in agriculture has actually increased. That's what the data show for the most important agricultural state in the union. But such "facts" are ambiguous. Some of this California farmland is given over to producing trivia, such as sod (for ornamental lawns), commercial flower crops, and food products that are going to do little to solve the malnutrition problems of the people of the world. Compared to, say, Nebraska, California is less the "breadbasket" of America than it is its avocado dip. I don't know, given these data problems, whether acreage given over to the production of "real food" has been increasing or decreasing, either in California or the nation as a whole. Similarly, there is also the question of what, in fact, constitutes "prime" farmland, as opposed to other sorts. Returning again to the California case, vast amount of its farmland is artificial, in the sense that contrived irrigation is required, along with chemical fertilizer and insecticides. Making this land fertile has thus been accomplished at enormous cost (much of it provided by public subsidy); perhaps the loss of at least some of it to other uses should be welcomed.

Besides the fiscal costs it took to provide this fertility, there is the matter of the larger social and ecological costs. The provision of water in one place requires that it be removed from another place—with resulting damage to habitats at the points of origin. Similarly, the ecology of irrigation itself means that salts are deposited on the lands of destination; these salts can accumulate to eventually destroy *any* productive capacities that such lands might have had (for example, for grazing) if they had not been turned into "gardens" in the first place. Urbanization, of course, doesn't do food production much good either, but it is possible to foster intensive gardening on urban lots; wartime Britain supplied 10% of its food stocks in just that way. The point is thus not "how much" land is used for one purpose or the other but *how* it is used; I am arguing for appropriate technologies in both spheres and the insertion of agricultural productivity into the urban context.

My own composite suspicion (no good data) of what is going on is that urban areas continue to sprawl (albeit at a very reduced rate) into proximate farmland areas, in the process eliminating agricultural lands that are more or less "prime" and that are held by more or less small owners of acreage. In the hinterlands, however, other lands are simultaneously being brought into agricultural production through the expenditure of vast sums of money, in effect providing large public subsidies to big corporations (such as the oil companies) active in agribusiness in places like California. I am suspicious that, especially over the long term, both processes will decrease the capacity of the earth to provide "real food"

1. URBANIZATION

and will detract from its ecological balance, while regressively distributing wealth.

(8) What are the relative roles to be played by local, state, and federal governments in dealing with the nation's urban problems?

Gans: The thousands of local governments and even the 50 state governments are so varied in quality, constituencies, and power that no general answer to this question is possible. Moreover, only the federal government has the funds or the clout to stand up to, or intervene in, the corporate economy. During Democratic administrations, it also has the strongest incentive to help the poor, although that incentive is derived to some extent from Democratically controlled big cities. Even so, too many local and state governments are first and foremost beholden to business constituencies and cannot be relied on to deal with the nation's urban problems.

True, the federal government often has difficulties in delivering services to people (even if not as many as is being claimed today). Still, it is probably best at delivering money. Who is best at delivering services and obtaining the power to get things done in general remains an open question, but the answer cannot be limited to government, and must consider roles also for private firms, voluntary associations, and smaller, informal groups.

My general inclination is to begin with the assumption that most people know best what services and goods they need and want. If incomes were roughly equal, many governmental roles could be taken over by the market (provided it were competitive) and by various kinds of community and block groups. In addition, more economic equality would by itself eliminate many major urban problems. This answer establishes a principle, but begs the question of who will create the egalitarian society.

Kasarda: The U.S. Constitution stipulates that the primary role of formulating public responses to community problems is vested in the states and delegated locally to municipalities and counties. Under our federalist system, states and their constituent local governments are considered to have primary responsibility for influencing economic change within their jurisdictions, as well as for reflecting citizen preferences and meeting local human needs.

During the past two decades, the "Great Society" notion evolved that every urban problem could be defined as a national problem that called for a federal solution. The result was that the federal government progressively became involved in hundreds of narrow, local issues such as urban gardening, snow removal, and the settlement of family disputes. It is increasingly apparent that the federal role in urban affairs has become overextended, inefficient, and, in some instances, counterproductive. A redefinition of roles and responsibilities is needed whereby the federal government will reserve intervention to those urban problems that are both national in scope and that state and local governments cannot themselves adequately address. In so doing, cognizance must be taken of the limited fiscal resources at the disposal of many states and localities so that provision is made to transfer revenue sources along with problem responsibilities back to these states and localities.

Molotch: This is not a particularly important matter compared to the other problems, but, as a general rule of utopian thumb, I (like most) will go on record in favor of local autonomy. The more critical issue is to figure out who will gain substantively if power is at one level and not another. Practical people (me included) evaluate procedural options in terms of the substantive outcomes envisioned. The U.S. system of federalism was created from the beginning, according to Hofstader, as a scheme for balancing interests (both class and regional) rather than as some mechanism developed by management consultants to maximize either efficiency or democratic participation. In terms of certain urban interests, local control can be quite deleterious: Blacks (urban as well as rural) would still be frozen out of the vote in the Deep South were it not for federal intervention in the 1960s. Coastal California would have developed in a less orderly way in recent years had the State Coastal Act (passed through the initiative process) not eliminated certain local options regarding land uses. On the other hand, the legislature of the same state eliminated home rule in regard to siting of liquified natural gas plants, precisely because it was feared that the most likely site for such a plant was in a county that would not permit it. (The precedent of local land use sovereignty was overturned for practical developmental ends.) Similar actions have occurred in other jurisdictions to overcome local resistance to such infrastructural investments as nuclear power plants.

The more general point is that home rule has been a celebrated tradition in the United States primarily because it has been consistent, overall, with the needs of migratory Capital for access to investment sites. As long as localities were eager competitors with one another for development, home rule could be depended upon to deliver the goods. As these circumstances become less prevalent, Capital looks to state and federal levels to somehow reinstitute the same range of siting options. Reagan's "New Federalism" is an effort to provide home rule in regard only to decision making that does not interfere with Capital's maneuverability, while doing nothing to increase meaningful options at the local level, for example, in regard to energy planning, self-sufficient economic development, or housing programs. Instead, by decreasing federal financial and regulatory participation in welfare, the states will be left with local development as their only apparent salvation to offset their increased fiscal burdens. The states will intensify their efforts to attract Capital and to offer disincentives to welfare recipients (lower benefits, more punitively administered). This is one way in which "home rule" becomes a severe liability for the poor, but an asset for Capital.

(9) To what extent does the shifting position of the United States in the world economy account for the plight of our nation's cities?

Gans: Most of the problems of the older cities predate the deterioration of America's position in the world economy, as do the problems of their poor residents. The country's deteriorating economic position has, however, shrunk the resources available for solving these problems. More important, it has engendered widespread feelings of insecurity which have in turn enabled the Reagan administration to shift public funds from solving domestic problems to military expenditures.

The disappearance of American manufacturing and other jobs resulting from the changing international economy is also driving previously working- and lower-middle-class citizens into the ranks of the poor. If they should begin to protest their fate politically, public funds will probably be found to try to solve their problems, perhaps by a latter-day New Deal. If they remain quiescent, however, even a Democratic landslide in the 1984 elections is unlikely to produce drastic change in national economic or urban policies.

Kasarda: Cities are open systems, and their health is inextricably interwoven with the health of our national economy. When the national economy suffers, cities tend to suffer disproportionately. This is why I've argued that the foundation for any national urban policy must be a national development policy conducive to higher rates of overall economic growth. Overall economic growth, in turn, is increasingly tied to our nation's effectiveness in competing on the world economic market. In many traditional industrial sectors, such as the production of electrical components, heavy machinery, textiles, and steel, the competitive position of the United States has been severely weakened by more cost-efficient production elsewhere in the world. Consequently, cities in which employment bases are still dominated by these older industries have been and will remain at a high level of economic distress. Further declines in their total population sizes and employment bases are inevitable.

On the other hand, those cities in which employment bases already are, or are becoming, adapted to newer, internationally oriented service industries will fare much better. In this regard, the U.S. role in the world economy is not declining, but is changing from producing and exporting material goods to producing and exporting information and capital; cities that can exploit their favored positions as international administrative, communication, and financial nodes should experience renewed vitality and net increases in jobs during the 1980s. However, as I've stated above, unless their resident populations are provided with the skills that will equip them for employment in the advanced service industries expanding in these cities, high urban unemployment, poverty, and related social problems will remain intractable.

Molotch: The quality of life in U.S. cities has been cyclical over time, only very roughly correlating (if at all) with the country's international preeminence or overall rate of economic growth. Indeed, some very severe problems for poor people were made possible by the great postwar riches that prosperity brought into the public coffers, resulting in the destructive extravagance of urban renewal, as one example, and the federal highway program, as another. Swedish cities, drawing upon a lower per capita resource base, did a much better job of providing high-amenity, efficient urban settlements than did the United States at the time it was the virtual ruler of the world. The point is that wealth, like rain, can trickle down either as nourishment or as poison; it all depends on the context.

The declining economic power of the United States inhibits its capacity to continue its profligate waste of the world's resources—among other things. Most people are now aware of the changes in urban structure that fuel conservation, for example, must bring. In effect, the U.S. settlement pattern is being forced to converge with that found in the more rationally organized societies.

There is another major sort of change afoot that has less to do with the decline in U.S. "standing" and more to do with the reorganization of Capital across the world. This reorganization involves the "internationalization" of Capital as corporations increasingly transcend their national boundaries—not just in terms of markets and production sites (the multinational phenomenon), but in terms of the fabrication of a given product and the very constitution of the corporation itself. Recent trends include the tendency for firms of different countries to share in the financing, design, and manufacture of a single product, with different components made at sites within the various countries. Exchanges of stock are sometimes part of such deals, making ownership as international as the commodity produced. These changes have some potential implications for U.S. urban areas:

(a) The fact that a product, say a jet passenger plane, will consist of engines made in Britain by a British firm, electronic controls produced in Japan by a Japanese firm, tires made in Italy, and so on, means that the plane is "made" nowhere, but is instead "sourced" in many places. This means that cities will not occupy a place in a division of labor that can be identified with a particular product or type of product (for example, Detroit as the "motor city"), but will instead play a more simple role in an increasingly complex international system of production. In other words, many U.S. cities will function as "modules" in an international productive apparatus. This implies a "deskilling" of cities, analogous to the deskilling that is said to have occurred in the workplace. The apparatus of coordination shifts to fewer control centers—some of which will remain in the United States (such as in New York and Los Angeles) and some of which will be abroad (such as in London and Tokyo).

(b) An implication of these developments is that the "module city" will be dependent upon an increasingly international system of Capital. The potential for "runaway" shops will be vastly increased when what is running away is not an industry (such as car production), but merely the production of a component. As much as the runaway shop has seemed a threat to U.S. cities, it is a much more formidable problem within a place such as Taiwan, where there are virtually no constraints whatever to Capital migration because the simple nature of the production system makes its replication in another place a constant option. Only by keeping conditions optimal—from the standpoint of Capital—can such countries sustain foreign investment. U.S. cities are also going to need to sustain each investment—virtually all investment becoming, in some sense, "foreign," U.S. cities may have to pay the going price in terms of wages and environmental standards.

(c) Related to these events, it will be increasingly difficult, as a practical matter, to exact concessions from Capital—in the form of higher paychecks or increases in welfare benefits. Besides the problem of the runaway shop, there is the problem of the changing identity of the corporations that do business within U.S. boundaries. When there are no longer "American" corporations, but international hybrids, who are we going to tax? How can erecting tariffs against "foreign-made" products even make sense in such a context? Which cartels are we going to break up, if none of them are "ours"? Perhaps some system of international controls can be developed, although, given the precedents on the books, that seems extremely unlikely.

In summary, it will be increasingly difficult for working classes to exact a trickle as Capital ceases to be a fixed target. Traditional interurban competitions for Capital will be augmented by an increasingly international sort of competition, with U.S. places reduced to the level of almost ordinary competitors. We seem to be headed for a merger of social units at the top of the international wealth structure, with a consequent merger (at least of conditions) at the bottom as well. That is, if these speculations have any plausibility, there is a tendency for a leveling out of urban roles across nations (although variegation within them), with resulting homogenization of the social classes across world regions. Such a future outcome is at least consistent with certain tendencies discernible at the moment and not altogether inconsistent with much prior theorizing by others.

The world's urban explosion

By the year 2000, for the first time in history, more people will be living in towns and cities than in rural areas. Most urban dwellers (over 1.5 thousand million persons) will be living in conurbations of over one million inhabitants. Demographic pressure on cities bursting at their seams is illustrated in this photo of a Tokyo crowd. In 1980 the 28.7 million inhabitants of the Tokyo Metropolitan Region represented one quarter of Japan's entire population.

The problems and the future of the great metropolitan areas of the world were discussed by 800 participants at an international symposium, *Metropolis 84,* organized by the Regional Council of the Ile-de-France and held in Paris from 10 to 12 October 1984. The report on the proceedings of the symposium, on which this article is based, has been published in *Les Cahiers de la I.A.U.R.I.F. (Institut d'Aménagement et d'Urbanisme de la Région d'Ile de France), Paris (N° 74).* It covers the four main themes of the symposium: demography and town planning, economic and technological change, transport, and culture and environment.

FROM 1900 to 1975, the number of cities with a million inhabitants increased tenfold and that of cities with over five million inhabitants multiplied by twenty. During the same period, the total population of the twenty-five largest cities more than quadrupled and will be multiplied eight to ten times by the year 2000. Their average size will pass from two to sixteen million inhabitants and they will include about six per cent of the world's population and twelve per cent of its urban population. In the year 2000 more than half of the twenty-five cities with more than ten million inhabitants and nearly half the cities with over four million inhabitants will be located in Asia.

The universalization of urbanism is a new fact. Before the year 2000, for the first time in the history of humanity, the world will have more town dwellers than country dwellers. If conurbations with over one million inhabitants are included, metropolitan areas will assemble sixty per cent of the urban population, or over 1,500 million individuals.

This change will be accompanied by a swing in the relative importance of metropolitan areas. Those in the industrialized countries are stagnating and regressing (London, for example, has lost

Long a problem in countries that first used the automobile on a large scale, urban traffic congestion is now a growing cause for concern in many Third World cities as well. Monumental traffic jams occur regularly in such cities as Lagos, Bangkok and São Paulo (above). Handicapped by insufficient infrastructures to meet current needs, cities in the developing world are today facing massive and ever-mounting demands for public transport by low-income users.

Reproduced from the *Unesco Courier*, March 1985, pp. 24-29, by permission.

1. URBANIZATION

In the next 30-40 years the largest increase in urban growth will take place in developing regions. All the problems inherent in rapid urbanization will be compounded by the crushing poverty, disease, and social pressure of these least developed areas.

By the year 2025 Mexico City will be the largest metropolitan area in the world. It is estimated that in excess of 30 million people will live in the greater Mexico City area. This scene is typical of the random and spontaneous urban development that is going on today.

two million people in forty years) and those in the Third World are rapidly expanding. In 1975 there were 262 million people in the metropolitan areas of the developed countries as against 244 million in those of the Third World. In the year 2000 Third World metropolitan areas will have 914 million people, more than double the 444 million forecast for the industrialized countries.

This demographic and urban evolution is taking place in the context of an economic crisis and the imbalance in population distribution will be accompanied by an increasing gap in the distribution of wealth. All this will occur in a world brought closer together by improved transport facilities, the multiplication of commercial exchanges and the increasing openness of boundaries and cultures to the spread of information.

The increase in the mobility of mankind is inescapable—from one country to another, from one continent to another, under the attraction of the real or imagined opportunities offered by metropolitan areas beyond the barriers of the frontiers of today. California's powerful magnetic appeal to the people of Latin America is perhaps premonitory.

In the metropolitan areas of developed countries with low growth or falling populations, the problem today is one of reviving activity, preserving and highlighting the cultural heritage, preventing the depreciation of certain districts before they are transformed into ghettos, and making the best possible use of existing infrastructures.

The metropolitan areas of the developing countries, on the other hand, are seeking to control their demographic growth, to organize urban extensions, to make good their lack of facilities and services and to make productive use of the available labour force.

Those responsible for the metropolitan areas in developing countries are faced with problems of alarmingly rapid growth. The urban conurbations in these countries have average growth rates of between five per cent and seven per cent per annum which means that they double every fifteen years. Each year additions to their populations can be counted in hundreds of thousands (350,000 in Cairo, 300,000 in Bangkok, 750,000 in Mexico City) and the areas of agricultural land lost in thousands of hectares, often in the richest agricultural areas in the country.

The evidence is that this rapid growth is going to continue for several years. The rural population today is still very considerable. Its birth rate is greater than that in the cities and generates demographic growth far superior to that which agriculture can absorb (1.5 per cent per annum according to the experts). While, for cultural reasons, the birth rate is lower in the cities, the mortality rate there is lower still. As a result the normal growth of the urban population is more rapid than that of the rural population, as witness the examples of Mexico, India and China.

Faced with this problem a number of countries and metropolitan areas are doing their best to control metropolitan growth in a variety of ways: demographic policies and national encouragement to decrease the birth rate—China provides the most striking example, promotion of agricultural activities and development of related activities in small rural towns, development of medium-sized towns, etc. Nevertheless, it is generally agreed that metropolitan growth will remain, for several decades, at a level close to that being experienced today. Those responsible for metropolitan areas in the Third World will therefore have to make provision for the reception of these huge inflows of new inhabitants.

A variety of often complementary solutions have been adopted: the creation of development zones, new districts, new towns; the extension of infrastructural networks, prefabricated or do-it-yourself housing, etc. However, the speed at which such operations can be undertaken does not match the rapidity of population growth. In addition there is the problem of the poverty of the newcomers which is intensified by the current crisis. It is everywhere evident that economic development and therefore employment are not progressing fast enough to meet their needs. The difficulties of employment and poverty in the metropolitan areas of the Third World are reflected in the anxiety of the worker whose budget is whittled away by accommodation costs and the anguish of those who know that their accommodation is only temporary.

Employment is the number one challenge. Yet at the same time it offers a way towards a solution to all the problems described above, whether in the metropolitan areas or elsewhere.

In addition there is the high cost of urbanization in the large conurbations. In developing countries, national resources are limited. It is not easy to define an urban policy that allows satisfactory development of metropolitan areas without signing away the economic and social development of the country as a whole.

Throughout this century, the metropolitan areas of the developed countries have witnessed periods of rapid growth which those in charge have usually tried to halt by various methods. The situation today is very different and although some conurbations (such as Los Angeles, Moscow and Madrid) are still expanding, others appear to have stable (Ile-de-France; the Randstad—the urban circle in the Netherlands comprising Rotterdam, The Hague, Leiden, Haarlem, Amsterdam, Hilversum, and Utrecht) or decreasing (London, New York, Brussels) population figures. The desired limitation has been achieved, yet there remains a certain dissatisfaction.

This stems from the fact that, even when the populations of the conurbations are no longer increasing or are even decreasing, the space occupied continues to grow up to the

Metropolitan areas in developing countries are confronted with demographic increases on a scale never before known. Below, modern housing in Abidjan, capital of Ivory Coast. The city's population, estimated at 2 million in 1982, is doubling every 7 years.

Photo Georg Gerster © Rapho, Paris

very limit of what is acceptable in the economic context of today, particularly with respect to networks and facilities.

At the same time, due to the effect of the economic crisis, qualitative problems are multiplying: socio-professional changes connected with developments taking place in industry, increasing impoverishment of large sectors of the metropolitan population and the development of social problems, delinquency, drug addiction, and criminality. The increase in the number of the impoverished is a sign of the poor health of society as a whole. In the towns these vulnerable population groups are concentrated in particular areas, emphasizing the social stratification.

Experience acquired over the last fifty years, however, has made possible the elaboration of a generally accepted "urban technique" which is being put into practice in most countries in various forms. Its main elements are:

Polycentrism. It has become clear that the organization of an urban area must be based on a hierarchical system of centres each dispensing services to the inhabitants. The Ile-de-France, Los Angeles, Randstad and London provide good examples of this;

The notion of discontinuity. Green belts can halt the blanket urbanization that is now everywhere rejected. Varied examples are provided by Montreal, Los Angeles, Moscow, Brussels, Copenhagen, the Ile-de-France and Randstad;

Urban renewal. This appears to be an essential factor in improved integration of inhabitants;

The optimization of town planning operations. The scale of these operations has been considerably reduced, allowing forms of intervention to become more subtle and therefore better adapted, more human and better integrated into the urban framework;

Energy conservation. After the crisis of the 1970s concern for energy conservation modified town planning perspectives. Too much dispersion is costly in energy. Linear development, overspill areas and the grouping of services have become the guiding themes of present-day town planning.

Experience has exposed the great complexity of metropolitan phenomena. The large metropolis is neither a static organism nor an isolated fortress. It is involved in multiple exchanges with the surrounding regions. Even when it is experiencing a net loss of inhabitants it continues to receive newcomers in their tens, hundreds or thousands. Intensive and permanent exchanges take place in its midst: while population is diminishing in some parts of a conurbation—often the city centre—in other parts it is increasing. This is why urban extension and the replanning of city centres are often problems which must be tackled simultaneously.

Are common solutions appropriate given the diversity of the situations? The demographic, social, economic and cultural differences between the continents are obvious. Moreover, each concrete situation is the product of a particular geographical and historical setting and therefore unique.

Everywhere the metropolitan area is emerging as the most suitable level for reflection and action. Even though the outlines of the metropolitan area remain unclear and changing, and it has to work in collaboration with local, regional, federal and national communities, the urban region must clearly be considered as a whole.

The technical, cultural and financial feasibility of different urban policies is a key factor. Experience throughout the world shows that what makes the difference between success and failure is not the town planning or aesthetic aspects of the projects, that is to say their intrinsic qualities, but their appropriateness to the local technical, administrative and financial context. Immense progress remains to be made in this area and is all the more necessary in view of the economic crisis and the weak financial situation of the Third World urban populations.

This is why the participation of citizens in town planning choices is being widely advocated. The fast pace of growth, the cultural diversity, the size of the populations in question, the complexity of the procedures, are all obstacles to be overcome in order to ensure a genuine citizen participation—and the best chance of success for future projects.

The Industrial City: The Environment of the City

Asa Briggs

Mr. Briggs is Provost of Worcester College, Oxford, and Chancellor of the Open University.

No reflection on the human odyssey, however sketchy or cursory, could leave out the city—the city as place of survival, often precarious, highly vulnerable survival; the city as centre of civilisation, or rather of richly varied civilisations in time and space; and, not least, the city as metaphor, with the metaphor itself twisting and turning through the centuries into old and new shapes.

The etymological fact that with the Western tradition the words "*city*" and "*civilisation*" have a common root, along with "*citizenship*" and "*civility*", points to the second of these aspects of the city as an influence in history—to something far more than survival, to the temple and the theatre rather than to walls or shelters, to the creativity of the individual and of the society, and to the enrichment of human culture. So also does the haunting preoccupation through the centuries with the "Ideal City", the city of dreams to which restless and striving men should aspire; and at this point, of course, fact turns into metaphor, the metaphor not only of the New Jerusalem but of Babylon.

Yet the first aspect of the city—as place of survival or destruction—also has its scaffolding of imagery: Venice under the sea, T. S. Eliot's tumbling of the towers. When Lewis Mumford, a leading 20th-century surveyor of cities, wrote his second massive book on the city, *The City in History*, 23 years after the first (*The Culture of Cities*, 1938)—with a World War and the Atomic Bomb in between—it was to the theme of the city as insecure citadel that he returned when pondering characteristically on the relationship between first and last things.

"Urban life spans the historic space between the earliest burial ground for dawn man and the final cemetery, the Necropolis, in which one civilisation after another has met its end."

Science fiction takes over in the 20th century where history ends, often attempting a complete rewriting of history in the process. The city can become nightmare rather than dream as "civilised" relations crack. Yet the technology of the citadel can be strengthened. In one of his short stories, "Caves of Steel", Isaac Asimov envisaged 800 cities on earth with an average population of 10 millions.

"Each city became a semi-autonomous unit economically all but self-sufficient. It could roof itself, gird itself about, burrow itself under. It became a steel cave, a tremendous self-contained cave of steel and concrete."

In other science fiction the city returns as symbol after disaster . . . in what Arthur C. Clarke has called appropriately "the Aeneas theme." As the hero in John Christopher's *The Death of Grass* goes out toward a new settlement, he says to the heroine. "There's a lot to do. A city to be built."

THE CITY IN HISTORY

The building adaption and transformation of cities has been a major human achievement, providing us in the 20th century with a whole "prospect of cities", even the newest of them already historically layered. Paradoxically, destruction has often uncovered civilisation:

"The Industrial City: The Environment of the City," Asa Briggs, *Encounter*, December 1982, pp. 25-35. Reprinted by permission.

thus, the bombing of London in World War II revealed Roman London for the first time. If the 20th century has changed skylines, the 19th century created a whole new city-network underground, a network of pipes and sewers, a technological triumph even greater than that of the Romans. We are constantly reviewing our assessments of the achievements of previous ages, not only contrasting present with past but finding in historic cities "similes and analogies for the contemporary architect and urban designer." Napoleon III thought of himself as a new Augustus. Nor is it only autocrats who turn back to the past. As a contemporary American architect said in 1980:

> "When this new wave of architects comes out of the schools, with a sense of caring about context, it seems to me that cities are going to have the concern that you see in a place like Florence . . . some sense of continuity even with changing styles."

It is because both city builders and city dwellers can compare one actual city with another actual city and not simply with the Ideal City, however envisaged, that time scales are as significant as the use of spacing in judging the appearance of cities. There were more 19th-century references to Florence as a particular "place of concern" than there have been 20th-century references. In Britain's industrial Birmingham, for example, "adventurous orators" in the 1860s would "dwell on the glories of Florence and of the other cities of Italy in the Middle Ages and express the hope that Birmingham too might become the home of noble literature and art. . . ." There was, indeed, a double framework of historical reference in the 19th century, with some city reformers and commentators looking back to the city states of the Middle Ages and the Renaissance and some looking further back still to the city in the ancient world, the Greek *polis* and the Roman *civitas*. In each case, there was a strong sense not only of continuity—and of community—but of civic pride. At a time when the actual cities of a new industrial society were generally thought of as problem places, this pride was conspicuous. It was in the United States, not in Britain, that F. C. Howe could write (in 1903) that through the city "a new society has been created. Life in all its relations has been altered. A new civilisation has been born, a civilisation whose identity with the past is one of historic continuity." It was in Communist Poland that historic Warsaw was reconstructed after 1945.

City pride most usually meant not pride in the city but in particular cities; each one was recognised as having an individual identity. Philadelphia was different from Boston or Baltimore or Cincinnati or Chicago; Manchester was different from Liverpool or Birmingham; Warsaw from Cracow; Budapest from Vienna. In Britain, the historian Edward Freeman complained bitterly that some of his contemporaries could not understand how "the tracing out of the features and history" of particular cities could be "as truly a scientific business to one man

as the study of the surrounding *flora* and *fauna* is to another." In the attempt to make history "scientific", analysis and imagery could become somewhat confused, as they were when ancient organic metaphors of the city were given new life. Yet the more emphasis is placed on particular cities and the differences between them, the closer we can draw to lost experience. The best 19th-century observers recognised (as clearly as Jane Jacobs has done in recent years) that "city processes in real life are too complex to be routine, too particularised for application as abstractions. They are always made up of the interaction of particulars, and there is no substitute for knowing the particulars. . . ." This is as true of Vienna or Paris or London as it is of New York.

Yet though cities as environments have to be treated separately before we can start to generalise about urban structures and styles—and some, like Venice or Kyoto, are visually unique—the city has never been, in fact, self-contained in history as in Asimov's short story, least of all Venice. The city has come into existence and developed—sometimes declined—through interdependence both with the rural hinterland and within a wider system of cities, linked through trade. The marketplace has mattered at least as much as temple or cathedral, fortress and walls. There have, of course, been capital cities which have been above all else centres of power and display, but for every capital city, rival of other capital cities, there have been many which above all else have been centres of commerce. As we classify cities or rank them in hierarchies, we can never leave economics out, whether we are concerned with buildings or with ways of life. Indeed, the most fascinating feature of the study of cities is that it must take account of so many subjects which are too often considered separately—along with economics, demography, geography, ecology, history, sociology, political science, anthropology, architecture, archaeology, to name only some of the most obvious.

DISCOVERING THE "REAL" CITY

No self-contained discipline can cope with the city or with cities. Nor, moreover, are all the disciplines taken together quite enough. Ignoring for a time the Ideal City—for this we have to turn to the philosophers—the real city has to be explored before it can be explained. Freeman's historian contemporary J. R. Green was once described by Lord Bryce as exploring a strange town and "darting hither and thither through the streets like a dog trying to find a scent." On the other side of the Atlantic, Robert Ezra Park, pioneer of the Chicago School of Urban Sociology, the first academic school of its kind in the world, was fully aware of the need to find scents even in a city which was not (on the surface at least) "strange." In inviting his students to explore Chicago, he always stressed that

> "the city is not . . . merely a physical mechanism and an artificial construction. It is involved in the vital

processes of the people who compose it: it is a product of nature and particularly of 'human nature.' "

There was a similar awareness in Park's British predecessor, the sociologist Charles Booth, whose vast survey of London (then the world's largest city) during the last years of the Victorian Age entailed as much exploration as that associated with the names of Livingstone and Stanley in Africa.

"It is in the town and not in the country [Booth wrote] that *terra incognita* needs to be written on our social maps. In the country the machinery of human life is plainly to be seen and easily recognised . . . The equipoise on which existing order rests, whether satisfactory or not, is palpable and evident. It is far otherwise with cities, where as to these questions we live in darkness."

In some respects, we still live in darkness almost 100 years after Booth—despite the boom of the last quarter-century in urban studies, specialised and interdisciplinary—although we are perhaps clearer now than Freeman, Park or Booth were about the influences of the explorer's own attitudes and experience on the selection of facts about the city which he chooses to collect and the images which he seeks to present. The same city means quite different things to different people, even to residents of the city, and in considering impressions we have to distinguish between those of residents and visitors, of privileged and deprived, of reformers and boosters, to note only a few of the relevant categories. If the boom in urban studies has increased our understanding of the city, it is mainly through a sharper realisation of the different elements involved in our diverse perceptions, visual and social, of the city. In other words, we have to add psychology to the list of associated disciplines necessary for understanding. As one of the most stimulating recent British writers on the city, Peter Smith, has put it, "Experiencing environment is a creative act. It depends as much upon the subject interpreting the visual array as upon the disposition of objects in space."

LITERARY MINDS AND THE CITY

During the 19th century, the collection of facts about the city was one of the most active preoccupations of a new generation of statisticians, some involved in boosting cities, some in problem-solving within the city—and no account of 19th-century positivism would be complete without taking stock of it. During the late 20th century, however, we have focused our attention more on the range of human experience within the city, and the perceived pluses and minuses associated with it. Of course, we have left to experts—who were not there in the early 19th century—the practical tasks of dealing with the city's pressing problems: surveyors, engineers, traffic analysts, housing managers, leisure controllers, social workers, and above all, planners. There is a gulf between the two kinds of approach, and in recent years the "expertise" of each of the expert groups has been subjected to increasing scrutiny. Meanwhile, city tensions multiply as the volume of writing about the city at every level, not least journalistic, increases. The 19th century talked of "the age of the cities". We talk of "the crisis."

Some observers (like Melvin Webber) have been claiming for more than a decade that we are moving into "the post-city age." As Patrick Geddes, Mumford's mentor, put it succinctly in 1905, "A City is more than a place in space, it is a drama in time." Before I dwell on our current preoccupations, which turn as much on survival as on civilisation, it is necessary to acknowledge that in perspective there has seldom been any consensus about the role of the city in human affairs. There has usually been a debate, often crude, occasionally sophisticated, with some crossing of sides. The Christian Bible begins in a garden and ends in a city; and both before and after the Christian Bible, garden and wilderness have been pitted against town, city, and conurbation. At times, classical literature has swayed later generations at least as much as the Bible, both in its portrayal of the urban and of the pastoral. Of course, we quickly move into metaphor here, as we do in Albert Camus's 20th-century *Cahiers*, where he writes that "as a remedy to life in society, I would suggest the big city. Nowadays, it is the only desert within our means."

The modern debate preceded the industrial revolution and was not a by-product of the rise of the industrial city, which was described in one magazine of the late 1830s as "a system of life constructed according to entirely new principles." Go back to the 1770s, the decade of American independence, and you have on the one side William Cowper's unforgettable lines *"God made the country, and Man made the town"*, and on the other Dr. Samuel Johnson's almost equally famous rebuke to Boswell: "No sir, when a man is tired of London, he is tired of life; for there is in London all that life can afford."

In newly independent America, too, the city had its detractors and its defenders. One of the best known passages in Jefferson's *Notes on the State of Virginia* (1784–85) is that in which he asserts that

"the mobs of great cities add just so much to the support of pure government as sores do to the strength of the human body. It is the manners and spirit of a people which preserve a republic in vigor. A degeneracy in these is a cancer which soon eats to the heart of its laws and constitution."

The conception of the city as cancer—the organic metaphor gone wrong—was never to disappear thereafter. Indeed, for this reason, biology and physiology should doubtless be added to the list of associated disciplines which have been applied to the study of cities . . . and not merely through imagery, as in Jefferson's case, but through theory, like the theory that city growth depended ultimately on the fusion of healthy tissue from the countryside, on different and older demographic patterns.

1. URBANIZATION

The late 18th-century debate, which found a place for noise and nuisance as much as for numbers, often looked backwards. Yet it had many new ingredients. Thus, at the very time that there was talk of "cancers", the new word "*civilisation*"—and it is difficult to think that it *was* a new word—was coming into use. Related though it was historically to the word "city", "civilisation" did not come into use until the late 18th century. Johnson might sing the praises of London and question the delights of the countryside; yet as late as 1772 when Boswell discovered him preparing the fourth edition of his folio *Dictionary,* he learned that Johnson would not admit "civilisation" as a word, but only "civility."

In a decade of dramatic change, which also saw the introduction of the new word "technology" and of Watt's steam engine, not to speak of the drafting of the American Declaration of Independence and the publication of Adam Smith's *Wealth of Nations,* both "civilisation" and "the city" were already controversial subjects. Indeed, the decade ended in London with urban riot and the open expression of what many Londoners thought of as barbarity in the heart of a great city. Boswell, in talking about the words "civilised" and "civilisation", did not add that there was already an alternative vocabulary, itself to become controversial, pivoted on the words "cultivated" and "culture"—words derived not from the city but from the countryside.

Some cultivated people then and later were sceptical about or hostile toward "civilisation", as were romantic writers like Rousseau and Wordsworth, the former comparing cities with prisons, the latter pointing to the association of the city both with crime—the adjective he used was "dissolute"—and with meaningless bustle, "the same perpetual whirl of trivial objects, melted and reduced to one identity." "Civilisation itself is but a mixed good", Coleridge was to write, "if not far more a corrupting influence, the hectic of disease, not the bloom of health."

Ambiguous responses to the idea of "civilisation" were equally apparent two decades later, when John Stuart Mill in his brilliant essay on Coleridge, frequently discussed more than a hundred years later, attempted to draw up a balance sheet measuring "how far mankind has gained by civilisation." Mill was less interested in centuries-old contrasts between the urban and the pastoral, or in romantic evocations of nature as against culture of the rough against the polished, than in a qualified utilitarian assessment of social and cultural change.

On the credit side, Mill recorded "the multiplication of physical comforts; the advancement and diffusion of knowledge; the decay of superstition; the facilities of mutual intercourse; the softening of manners, the decline of war and personal conflict; the progressive limitation of the strong over the weak [and] the great works accomplished throughout the globe by the co-operation of multitudes." Not all these manifestations of "civilisation" explicitly or obviously derived from the city context, although there was a tendency then and later—not least within the Chicago School of Urban Sociology—to relate all social indicators, socially favourable or unfavourable, to the influence of the city and of urban life styles. Certainly when Mill, following Coleridge, identified the items on the debit side, he had the city very much in mind. They include "the creation of artificial wants" . . . "monotony" . . . "narrow mechanical understanding" . . . "inequality and hopeless poverty"—even though "monotony", at least, and "inequality and hopeless poverty" had often been and were still being associated as much with the countryside as with the city. Then, as now, it was possible to argue about whether or not the city as such was a causal factor, rather than the society as a whole, and how to weight the different items in the balance sheet. What is curious to note, however, is that there was no specific reference in Mill's balance sheet to the rise of a new kind of city, the industrial city, the advent of which to some extent turned the terms of the argument and in the shadows of which we have lived ever since.

For although there had been cities since the beginnings of recorded history—and earlier—it was only at the time when Mill was writing that it was possible to speak of "the age of great cities."

In 1800, there were only 22 cities in Europe with a population of more than 100,000 (and none in America). By 1850, these numbers had increased to 45 and 8; there were also 4 cities in the world with a population of over a million. By 1900, there were 160 cities in the world with a population of more than 100,000 and 19 with a population of over a million. Significantly, there were as many as 23 with a population over 500,000, including new products of the century—often described as "prodigies"—like Chicago in the USA and Melbourne in Australia. The population of London, "the world city", had risen to over 4 million people. Patrick Geddes called it an octopus or polypus, "a vast irregular growth without previous parallel in the world of life—perhaps likest to the spreading of a great coral reef."

In one turbulent decade, the 1880s, the number of cities of between 40,000 and 70,000 in the United States increased from 21 to 35 and the number of still bigger cities from 23 to 39, so that one young American scholar could proclaim in the last year of the century that "the tendency towards concentration or agglomeration is all but universal in the Western world."

Industrial cities constituted only one group of cities in this huge urban expansion, and even the most renowned of them, like Manchester, which was a Mecca for visitors during the 1840s, often became service centres as much as manufacturing concentrations, serving the needs of an adjacent industrial region. It became fashionable, indeed, to classify cities like flora and fauna as well as to deal with them individually or to trace the general processes or urbanisation. Yet it was the industrial city which shocked contemporaries into an awareness of the social implications of urbanisation. Manchester, where facts were worshipped, became a symbol. In Manchester, wrote the most famous of all 19th-century travellers, Alexis de Tocqueville,

"humanity attains its most complete development and its most brutish; here civilisation works its miracles, and civilised man is turned back almost into a savage."

SOCIAL FEATURES OF THE CITY

There were four features of the industrial city which received particular attention from critics: deterioration of the environment; social segregation; impersonal human relations; and materialism.

The first was obvious enough to the nose as well as to the eye, and it did not need prophets like Ruskin or novelists like Dickens to identify it. It was a business visitor from Rotherham in Yorkshire's West Riding, itself no Athens, who remarked of Manchester as early as 1808,

"the town is abominably filthy, the Steam Engine is pestiferous, the Dyehouses noisome and offensive, and the water of the river as black as ink or the Stygian lake."

Yet Ruskin, interested as he was in the cities of Switzerland and of Italy, was moved by the experience of the industrial city to probe the relationship between the visual and the social as well as to indict a whole society and culture, and Dickens in his symbolic picture of Coketown—Chapter V of *Hard Times,* where the picture drawn is called "the Keynote"—has caught the sense of something more than appearances.

Like Tocqueville, Dickens places the savage—very much not the noble savage—in the middle of the city. "It was a town of red brick which would have been red if the smoke and ashes had allowed it; but, as matters stood, it was a town of unnatural red and black, like the face of a painted savage." For Dickens, deterioration of the environment and impersonal human relations were two sides of the same question—they are often separated in the 20th-century—and both were related to materialism and monotony:

"It was a town of machinery and tall chimneys, out of which interminable serpents of smoke trailed themselves for ever and ever, and never got uncoiled. It had a black canal in it, and a river that ran purple with ill-smelling dye, and vast piles of buildings full of windows where there was a trembling and rattling all day long, and where the pistons of the steam engine worked monotonously up and down, like the head of an elephant in a state of melancholy madness."

This was highly personal imagery, reminding us that Dickens should always be treated as painter rather than photographer; but what satire could do, statistics could do also, even though *Hard Times* was a satire on statistics. The facts of segregation were obvious enough in the industrial city, and they were made the most of by another of the early critics of Manchester, Friedrich Engels. In the pre-industrial city there were social gradations and propinquities. In Manchester, according to Engels—and he was not alone in his analysis—there were hostile classes and socially segregated districts.

"He who visits Manchester simply on business or pleasure need never see the slums, mainly because the working-class districts and the middle-class districts are quite distinct. This division is due partly to policy and partly to instinctive and tacit agreement between the two social groups."

The word *slum* was another new word, recorded for the first time by the *Oxford Dictionary* in 1825. Characteristically, it had no ancient roots and emerged from slang. Yet everywhere during the 19th century the industrial city became identified with slums as well as with factories.

The processes of segregation are fascinating to trace, whether or not we are dealing, as in 19th-century Britain, with segregation by income or, as in the later 19th century in the United States, with income and ethnic grouping. Indeed, in the Manchester of Engels, Irish segregation was a particular feature which he dealt with at length, and it was from the vantage point of Melbourne in Australia, a land of rural myth and city fact, that a writer observed in 1886 that

"the rich live with the rich and the poor live with the poor. The palace and the hovel, except in the imagination of the socialistic romancer, seldom adjut."

VARIATIONS AMONG CITIES

The Chicago school, operating in a city which was as much the shock city of its time as Manchester had been half a century earlier, interested itself not only in segregation but in all aspects of urban morphology, in the processes as much as in the structures. "Natural areas", Robert Park was to write, "are the habitats of natural groups. Every typical urban area is likely to contain a characteristic selection of the population of the community as a whole. In great cities the divergence in manner, in standards of living and in general outlook on life in different areas is often astonishing." Park went on to talk of a "sorting-out process" and, as memorably as Engels, of "little worlds" in the city "which touch but do not interpenetrate." Indeed, in a city where there was far more change of land use than in Manchester, he went on to claim that it was only because "social relations are so frequently and so inevitably correlated with spatial relations", and because "physical distances so frequently are or seem to be, the indexes of social distances, that statistics have any significance whatever for sociology."

Many 20th-century urban sociologists—and geographers—have tried to place Park (and for that matter

Engels) in social perspective, explaining why they felt as they did. If we wish to see the industrial city itself in perspective, we must not restrict our attention to the four features of it which received most attention from critics or with the generalisations that Lewis Mumford drew out of their and his own criticisms in his description of what he called (in 1938) the "insensate" industrial city.

It is not true that the new cities of the industrial revolution were really "man-heaps, machine warrens, not agents of human association for the promotion of a better life", as Mumford argued both in 1938 and in 1961. Nor is it true that "there were no effective centers in this urban massing: no institutions capable of uniting its members into an active city life; no political organization capable of unifying its common activities." Can 19th-century English history, let alone French or German history, be written in terms of the judgment that "in every quarter, the older principles of aristocratic education and rural culture were replaced by a single-minded devotion to industrial power and pecuniary success, sometimes disguised as democracy"?

Finally, it is not true that industrial cities were "all the same, variants of Dickens' Coketown, alias Smokeover, alias Mechanicsville, alias Manchester, Leeds, Birmingham, Merseberg, Essen, Elberfield, Lille, Roubaix, Newark, Pittsburgh or Youngstown." When night falls it did not fall—and does not fall—on the same urban environment in all these places.

Industrial cities were as varied even in their appearance as pre-industrial cities. They had different social structures as well as different appearances. They drew on different heritages from the past, when they had a pre-industrial past, and they did not always invent the same history or duplicate the same monuments when they sought to create a heritage for posterity. Many of their buildings, monumental and functional, are worth preserving, and since in some societies they represent the whole of the past, the recent effort to preserve them or to adapt them to new purposes has intensified. They generated more voluntary effort in their own great age of expansion than had ever been generated in cities before, and through the focusing of attention on their problems, which were never minimised by contemporaries, they directed attention for the first time in human history to the full possibilities of social control. They were capable of enunciating civic gospels which combined concern, commitment and vigour, and their cultural as well as their social life attracts the interest of historians and today can both command respect and evoke nostalgic regret. Perhaps one of the most misleading of Mumford's judgments was that in the industrial city "sonorous oratory served the double function of stimulant and anaesthetic; exciting the populace and making it oblivious to its actual environment."

THE PROBLEM OF INDUSTRIAL PROGRESS

If I had to generalise in one sentence, I would not be euphoric. I would still fall back on the view I presented in *Victorian Cities,* in which I described the growth of industrial cities in Britain as "a characteristic Victorian achievement, impressive in scale but limited in vision, creating new opportunities but also providing massive problems." I would also want to note the strange coexistence of pride and fear in all the contemporary writing about the industrial city, and the continued preoccupation with the creation of an Ideal City, not least the idea of a "garden city", marrying town and countryside.

If the pride has until recently been somewhat neglected, the fear continues to dominate historical narrative of the period. One British observer during the early 1840s—and he was an optimist about industrial progress—described it for us thus:

> "As a stranger passes through the masses of human beings which have been accumulated round the mills [in the industrial north], he cannot contemplate these crowded hives without feelings of anxiety and apprehension amounting almost to dismay. The population is hourly increasing in breadth and strength. It is an aggregate of masses, our conceptions of which clothe themselves in terms which express something portentous and fearful."

The fear could be so great that, as in this case, the observer turned to the upheavals of nature for metaphor, comparing the rise of the masses to "the slow rising and gradual swelling of an ocean", as striking a metaphor as the comparable 20th-century "winds of change."

Yet the mysterious *terra incognita* (as Charles Booth called it) was not, of course, *terra incognita* to the people who actually lived there. Nor, *pace* Engels, did most of the people who lived there think of themselves as *"masses."* The term was originally applied from outside, a new variant in the industrial city of the older term *"mob"*, associated with the pre-industrial city. There were wise city dwellers, who appreciated the dangers of thinking in these terms even at the time. For the most part they were doctors, clergymen and leaders of voluntary movements, who were prepared—indeed, expected—to cross urban frontiers into the *terra incognita.* One of them, a Leeds Nonconformist minister, warned his congregation in the 1840s against using the term "masses" too easily.

> "Our judgments are distorted by the phrase. We unconsciously glide into a prejudice. We have gained a total without thinking of the parts. It is a heap, but it has strangely become indivisible."

Not all 20th-century social criticism is so perceptive. We are bound to assess the industrial city, indeed, in the light of our own urban experience in the 20th century as well as in the light of preindustrial urban experience. It may well be that our cities look more alike than theirs did, that it is we not they who have tampered with the sense of place, that we are more fearful than they were of what we do not experience ourselves within the life of the city, that we are less active in our voluntarism and more disillusioned about the expertise. Mumford has criticised the 20th-century city as sharply as he criticised the 19th-century industrial city, dwelling mainly on what he calls "the increasing pathology of the whole mode of life in the metropolis." The mess is the message.

It is fair to note that Mumford's is not the only view, and that the city generates as much argument now as it did in the 1840s or the 1890s, with first Los Angeles and then Sao Paulo standing out as the shock cities of recent history where all the problems and all the excitments seem to converge. Los Angeles, at least— and it has now passed into a new phase of its history— has always had its passionate defenders as Manchester had, although it was in neutral Palo Alto, not in Los Angeles, that a conference was held not long ago to compare as "shock cities" Manchester and Sao Paulo. The English architectural critic Reyner Banham's fascinating *Los Angeles, the Architecture of Four Ecologies* (published ten years ago and concerned with far more than architecture) explains why the 20th-century city continues to defy consensus. The mobility of Los Angeles can attract or disturb, the visual appearances stimulate or repel, even the weather (apart from smog) seems right or wrong. "Los Angeles has not weather", remarked a journalist in 1969, and added, "Los Angeles has beautiful sunsets—if man-made."

NINETEENTH CENTURY PRECEDENTS

For the precedents of comments of this kind we have to turn back not to the 19th-century industrial city but to the 19th-century capital city, particularly London, Paris and (though it was not the administrative national capital) New York. It was of London, endowed with what Henry James called "general vibration", that Virginia Woolf wrote in her diary in 1918, "They say it's been raining heavily, but such is the civilization of life in London that I really don't know." Twenty years earlier the poet Richard Le Gallienne had proclaimed,

London, London, our delight,
Great flower that opens but at night,
Great city of the midnight sun,
Whose day begins when day is done

The 19th-century metropolis inspired more poetry than the industrial city, particularly in Baudelaire. Balzac saw Paris as a stage, the greatest stage in France for human ambition to express itself; Zola saw it as a challenge, where individuals and groups were caught in its grip. Baudelaire, however, saw Paris as a place of perpetual change, of fleeting moments and quickened consciousness, beyond good and evil, and he communicated his vision not only to his often disturbed contemporaries

but to future generations of writers. Thereafter, the old formal distinctions between urban and pastoral acquired new dimensions, as they were to do in the 20th-century writings of James Joyce, who (as Harry Levin once pointed out) lived in as many cities as the author of *The Odyssey,* each more polyglot and more metropolitan than the last. Yet his unique vision of the city rested not only on his own experience, but on a rich texture of historical and literary association. We move with him from *Dubliners* not only to Paris but to *Ulysses.* Feelings of attraction, and of recoil, toward the great metropolitan city, of total absorption and complete disengagement, are all expressed in his work, which is not only of immense imaginative power but of the most subtle complexity—as complex, indeed, as the early and mid-20th-century city itself.

The pictorial artist, too, has expressed something of this complex-city in the 20th century, so that every serious student of cities must visit art galleries as well as archives or newspaper offices. Even in the 18th century—in the age of Johnson and Cowper—the poet George Crabbe was advising his readers that

Cities and towns, the various haunts of men,
Require the pencil, they defy the pen. . . .

Yet it is only in the 20th century that Western artists, beginning with the Italian futurists, turned enthusiastically to cityscapes. The German Expressionists followed, and in New York John Marin anticipated much verbal and visual comment on Manhattan with his paintings of major monuments like the Woolworth Building or Brooklyn Bridge—shaken by a brittle light and seeming to fuse with the sky. They are as much a product of their time as Dutch views of the city in the 17th and 18th centuries, many of them reaching at the city through green fields and across canals. There is an apocalyptic element in some 20th-century paintings— and photographs—of cities, for the camera too has come into history in the 19th and 20th centuries, through films as well as photographs. An appreciation of this apocalyptic element—and it should be added that the camera has brought in a new sense of city beauty also—brings us round by a full circle to what Mumford had to say about megalopolis as necropolis.

REFLECTIONS ON MODERN URBANIZATION

I conclude with four reflections on the contemporary scene (reflections on, not prescriptions for). None of them is original, and none of them focuses either on defence or disaster.

First, however rapid rates of urbanisation were in the 19th century, they have been dwarfed by 20th-century rates. *Second,* much urban growth in the last half of this century has been in so-called Third World countries. This brings in different approaches to problems and opportunities, some outside our tradition. *Third,* the

1. URBANIZATION

position in the West, coexisting at a different stage of development, continues to raise profound questions about the nature of "civilisation"—though we seldom now choose to call it such—as well as about survival. *Fourth,* for various reasons we have a more shaky sense than we used to have of place and what it means, and we find it increasingly difficult to isolate the urban factor either in our analysis or in our policy-making.

The reflections must be brief. On the first—more rapid urbanisation rates than in earlier centuries—reflection starts in places like Hong Kong (if there is any place quite like Hong Kong) where skyscrapers grow together like trees in a forest and where new towns as big as Manchester was in 1900 can be built within a decade. In 1950 there were 75 cities in the world with populations of more than a million; in 1960, 141; in 1975, 191. The figure for 1985, it has been projected, will be 273. Moreover, as a result of the technological changes of the 20th century, particularly those associated with power and transportation, there are in many countries huge metropolitan areas, scarcely broken by anything which can be called rural, which may contain 25 million people or more. These are so different in scale and in organisation even from 19th-century cities, which were, as we have seen, already breaking with tradition, that (as Patrick Geddes foresaw in the first decade of this century) they seem to constitute a new species.

Second, such cities and bigger concentrations have emerged not only in the so-called "advanced" countries but outside. The proportion of people in "developing countries" increased from 16.5% in 1950 to 28.3% in 1975. For South Korea, the comparable figures were 18.4% and 50.9%. *Asia Urbanizing* is the evocative title of a recent collection of essays, yet in Africa, too, and above all in Latin America, urbanisation has moved faster than it ever moved in Europe in the 19th Century. The shock effect has certainly been great, at least to visitors. As Richard Meier put it in *India's Urban Future,* "the restrictions placed by poverty upon urban design always come as a shock to Western visitors", and it is interesting to compare Levi-Struss with Tocqueville. Noting—and, as we have seen, it is only one side of the picture—that we are accustomed to associate our highest values, both material and spiritual with urban life", he found in India

> "the urban phenomenon reduced to its ultimate expression . . . filth, chaos, promiscuity, congestion; ruins, huts, mud, dirt . . . all the things against which we expect urban life to give us organized protection, all the things we hate and guard against at such great cost."

This, too, is one side of the picture, for a very different reason. It relates Indian experience entirely to our own views of the city in history to the tradition that stretches back to Greece and Rome. The Asian or African city continues to provoke clashing reactions within and between societies and cultures, not least between generations. Thus, in a study of Korean urbanisation, a particularly striking phenomenon, the authors insist that it would be much more accurate to refer to Asia's "teeming countryside" than to its "teeming cities", and that while all countries that urbanise rapidly have urban problems—of dislocation, adjustment and serving— urbanisation itself is "a normal and desirable concomitant of economic growth."

> "Korean urbanization [they conclude] has been a great success story during the third quarter of the 20th century. The basic reason is that the national government has focused its efforts on the promotion of economic growth instead of on control of urban growth and structure."

However different the traditions, the same remark might have been made in 19th-century Europe or America. On the other side, we have Jose Arthur Rios's comment on the Rio de Janeiro of the late 1960s, which recalls comments on London in the 17th and 18th centuries before the rise of modern industry:

> "Rio is the product of a vast maladjustment. Its growth is unparalleled by any other city in the nation. The tendency has been to enslave the whole country to this abnormal growth, like a tumor which drains all the energies of the body. Its high life is fed upon by the misery and backwardness of the rural population."

My third reflection is renewed, if not inspired, by almost every magazine and Sunday colour supplement. Mumford's contemporary pathology also seems to dominate newspaper headlines when they deal with crisis in urban finance (common to many parts of the world) or with riot (ethnic or social, or both). Biology seems to reinforce history. Thus, from a different angle from that of Mumford—though with equal concern—René Dubois has complained that "life in the modern city"—by which he meant the so-called advanced city of the West—"has become a symbol of the fact that man can become adapted to starless skies, treeless avenues, shapeless buildings, tasteless bread, joyless celebrations."

Such generalisation always invites *riposte.* The inner cities remain problem areas, particularly in Britain, but there have been immense changes in these inner areas—too few in Britain—not all for the worse, since the 1950s. The number of groups of people concerned not with being adapted, but with themselves adapting the urban environment, has greatly increased. There are more trees in the avenues and more people walking on them, more buildings with shape, and not all celebrations are joyless. There is more scepticism about accepted policies and more willingness to look for new answers. The awareness of the visual has been sharpened, although there is still a serious deficiency in visual education.

Fourth, and last, we have a more shaky sense than we used to have of place and what it means, and we find it increasingly difficult to isolate the urban factor in our analysis and in our policy making. There has always been a tendency to attribute causal influences to the city which would be better attributed to the society and the culture, not to speak of the economy. Melvin Webber, who has hailed "spatial dispersion" in a new post-city age, argues that

> neither crime-in-the streets, poverty, unemployment, broken families, race riots, drug addiction, mental illness, juvenile delinquency, nor any of the commonly noted 'social pathologies, marking the contemporary city can find its cause or its cure there. We cannot hope to invent local treatments for conditions whose origins are not local in character, nor can we expect territorially defined governments to deal effectively with problems whose causes are unrelated to territory or geography."

It is a salutary remark, yet merely a first point in an argument. If the city cannot deal with all these problems, neither, by itself, can the nation state. There are too many interdependencies. Cities have always been part of a network, even when nation states have been at war. Moreover, we cannot afford to leave out the local from our reckoning. Even with spatial dispersion, it is useful to have senses of belonging which extend beyond the private or the national. Indeed, we have to work out new relationships between the local (through our involvement in a particular place) and the global (through our involvement, whether we like it or not, in our whole planet). A touch of pride in where we are as well as where we came from is not out of place. At the end of our odyssey, however, we might not all agree with Euripides that "the first requisite to happiness is that a man be born in a famous city."

Building the Empire City

Matthys Levy

Matthys Levy is a partner at Weidlinger Associates, Distinguished Professor at the Pratt Institute, and Adjunct Professor in architecture at Columbia University. He is the author, with Mario Salvadori, of STRUCTURAL DESIGN IN ARCHITECTURE *(Prentice-Hall, Inc., 1980), and he is the structural engineer for the New York Convention Center.*

Living in the middle of Manhattan, surrounded by towering walls of masonry and glass, it is often difficult to remember that New York City has 578 miles of waterfront, a distance equal to that from Portland, Maine to Norfolk, Virginia. It is this connection to the sea which spurred the fantastic growth of the metropolis in the last 150 years, transforming it from a city of one-quarter million inhabitants crowded into the lower tip of Manhattan to a colossus of eight million people. This growth brought with it unique problems in every branch of engineering. The challenge of invention and creativity attracted the greatest engineers of the past: John Roebling (designer of the Brooklyn Bridge), Gunvald Aus (engineer of the Woolworth Building), H.G. Balcom (engineer of the Empire State Building) and many others.

Growth of a city is dependent on the strength of its infrastructure, that network of roads and power and water distribution which permits development of individual parcels of land. The first problems encountered by the civil engineers of the 19th century dealt with water supply and led to the construction of the Croton aquaduct — designed by Sir James Renwick in 1842 — and the development of the Catskill system 75 years later, which now brings 250 million gallons of water a day to the city through an ingenious siphon under the Hudson River. Over the years, more than 6,000 miles of water mains were buried under city streets. Today, one of the major problems facing the city is the aging of this infrastructure. In Manhattan, over 120 miles of water mains were installed prior to 1870 and recently there have been more and more breaks in these lines — they need to be replaced. The original cost of these facilities was financed by a growing metropolis. Now, the cost of replacement cannot be met by the current income of a stable or slightly shrinking population. It is therefore necessary to seek federal financing. This same problem exists with all aging elements of the infrastructure: roads, bridges, sewer systems, solid waste disposal. A further pressure on the system comes from changing social attitudes. Sewers originally dumped their effluent into the rivers and the ocean around the city. This is no longer permissible, and extensive treatment facilities have had to be built — with help from federal moneys.

The city, an island seeking interconnections and links to the continent, required the construction of 65 bridges and 12 tunnels over and under the various bodies of water around it. The Brooklyn Bridge, built by Roebling in 1883, paved the way for unification of the outer boroughs into the city and the incorporation of the city in 1898. The George Washington Bridge, designed by O.H. Ammann in 1930, opened the gate to the suburban development of northern New Jersey, which took place after the Second World War.

The rectangular grid which defined the pattern of growth in the city above the lower Manhattan enclave was established in 1811 and was based on a seemingly endless multiple of 25-foot by 100-foot lots progressing along the north-south axis of the island. From this, plans for tenements and so-called brownstones were developed to house the rapidly multiplying population. Wood houses on individual lots gave way to row houses. The flat roof characteristic of New York row houses was based on the development of asphalt and cheap metal roofing techniques. Two great fires, in 1835 and 1845, destroyed almost 1,000 houses in lower Manhattan, and in 1848 the first wave of German immigrants spurred a demand for new housing construction. These two events eventually led to the regulation of building for public safety and the establishment of minimum standards for room size, ventilation and sanitation. It was not until 1916, however, that the first zoning law was established and it was 1923 when the Setback Law was instituted to control the height and configuration of new buildings by defining maximum building size in relation to lot size and by defining building setback from streets varying with building height. This much-needed legislation came rather late: We can see the evidence of its tardiness in the canyons of the Wall Street area, where skyscrapers were superimposed on a street grid laid out for three-story buildings. Nevertheless, as Pier Luigi Nervi, the innovative Italian engineer, remarked after touring downtown New York, "Don't talk to me about Paris or London. Even the horrors are beautiful in this city."

Steel Skeletons

More than any other metropolis, New York is known as the city of skyscrapers. Fundamental to their development was the introduction of the elevator, which first began moving passengers vertically in the six-story Fifth Avenue Hotel in 1859. With the development of the electric motor in 1889, building heights jumped to 10 stories,

 From *The Sciences*, December 1980. ©1980 by The New York Academy of Sciences.

limited only by the weight of their masonry structure. The year 1888, remembered in local lore as the year of the "Great Blizzard," saw the first steel skeleton rise on lower Broadway.

Steel, with a strength 30 times that of masonry, permitted the development of high-rise structures because much less floor space had to be given over to vertical supports. Masonry walls (which for a 16-story building had to be five feet thick) gave way to widely spaced columns less than a foot square. The development of the steel skeleton, which made the skyscraper a reality, necessitated innovations in foundation construction. The high loads concentrated in the columns of the skyscrapers required foundations resting on rock. A pneumatic caisson perfected by Daniel Moran solved the problem of sinking foundations down to rock in lower Manhattan—and permitted columns to sit on footings down as much as 80 feet below street level, well below the ground water table.

The skyscraper, which was born in Chicago, blossomed and reached maturity in New York. The 486-foot City Investing Company Building erected in the early 1900s was the start of an intense development in lower Manhattan which saw the rise of the 760-foot neo-gothic Woolworth Building in 1913. Three factors contributed to the heavy concentration of building in that part of the city: the rising value of land, the availability of technology, and the lack of regulations to restrict building density. The opening of the Erie Canal in 1825, which made New York the origin of westward trade during an expansionist era, and the availability of the best deepwater port on the East Coast, helped make the city the financial capital of the United States. This generated the office building boom of the last quarter of the 19th century and supported the construction of so many skyscrapers in the first quarter of the 20th.

After the Setback Law froze further development downtown, and developers began seeking cheaper land, the center of gravity of skyscrapers shifted uptown with the construction of the Chrysler Building in 1930 and the "Queen of Skyscrapers," the Empire State Building, which opened in 1931. With a height of 1,472 feet to the top of its TV antenna, the Empire State Building was the symbol of New York for more than 40 years.

Insulated Eyebrows
Explosive growth in the decades straddling the beginning of this century made that an exciting era for engineers, and by comparison, the post-World War II period might seem slow and restrained. Nevertheless, construction still faces new challenges, which lead, in most cases, to refinements in the basic work laid down in the golden decades of the recent past. The Eiffels, Roeblings and Ammanns of that time have been replaced by innovative engineers like Fazlur Khan, whose "tube concept" (which will be described later) was used by the designers of the World Trade Center towers.

Le Corbusier wrote, "A considerable part of New York is nothing more than a provisional city, a city which will be replaced by another city." Before zoning regulations defined the maximum area of building that could be placed on a particular lot, only market conditions and the desires of the owner (who was often the prime tenant) dictated the size and configuration of a structure. Today, rising land values and changing market conditions make buildings erected only 50 years ago uneconomical today even though the buildings themselves may be in sound physical condition. Because land and space are so valuable, there is often more profit in demolition and reconstruction than in renovation. This market pressure, coupled with the normal aging process, results in a city in a continuous state of change.

In 1974 the 612-foot Singer Building, one of the early skyscrapers (it was built in 1905) was demolished to make room for a new building, One Liberty Plaza. This unique new project grew out of a research effort sponsored by the U.S. Steel Corporation to explore new approaches to the construction of high-rise office buildings. Architectural and structural studies were prepared for it well in advance of its erection. The structural studies explored ways in which the facade of a rectangular building could be used to resist wind forces by transforming the rectangle into a tube. This approach, which had been pioneered by Fazlur Khan in the John Hancock Building in Chicago, reduces to a minimum the substantial amount of additional steel required for wind resistance, and is expressed in the Hancock Building by the cross-bracing on its facades. The scheme chosen for One Liberty Plaza uses spandrel girders (horizontal external beams) six feet deep, rigidly connected to columns and forming a multistory tubular frame. (Though this was the innovation eventually chosen, the rejected prior designs constitute a real catalog of solutions to the problem of wind resistance.)

A second novelty in the One Liberty Plaza project was the use of an exposed steel structure. Steel loses its strength at a temperature of 600°C and the problem of fireproofing steel structures has conventionally been solved by covering the steel with a blanket of insulating material. But in this building a so-called "flame shield" was developed and adopted: Rather than insulating the vertical webs of the spandrel girders, they were shielded from direct contact with the flames of a fire by insulated "eyebrows"—wide horizontal flanges on the beams. (This concept has since been picked up and used in many other structures.)

Finally, in another preliminary study for One Liberty Plaza, the floor construction of office buildings was carefully examined and it was found that by spanning with deep trusses (a truss is a triangular assemblage of bars forming a rigid frame) rather than with beams from the core of the building to its facade, and by threading the mechanical distribution systems through the trusses' bars, one could obtain an integrated structural-mechanical system, more efficient and economical than the traditional separate systems. Although this concept was not used at One Liberty Plaza, it found application in the

World Trade Center towers, for which Leslie Robertson was the engineer.

The Waffle Slab

New York contains almost every conceivable type of structure. Within the five boroughs one finds structures built of steel, concrete and wood, resting on foundations varying from solid Manhattan schist to the organic silts under the John F. Kennedy airport. Under these varied conditions the choice of the structure for a particular project is often narrowed down by economic considerations. Until the early 1960s, office buildings in New York were always built of steel. In fact, concrete apartment buildings using the now-familiar flat plate construction system (solid slab floors supported on columns) had moved north from Washington, D.C., only a few years earlier. It is hard to believe that the flat plate did not originate in New York, where thousands of apartment buildings have been erected by this system, but the fact is that, like the "Chicago" skyscraper, the "New York" flat plate was only *perfected* in this city (so much so that New York engineers like Robert Rosenwasser became known as masters of this structural system).

In 1963, the 40-story Columbia Broadcasting System building (Eero Saarinen, architect) demonstrated the economic feasibility of the use of concrete for office buildings. Architecturally, the CBS building, like the Lever House a decade earlier, became an inspiration to a generation of designers. In planning the building a steel design was prepared just to satisfy those practitioners who mistrusted the intuition of the engineer of the concrete design, Paul Weidlinger; the concrete structure could be seen to be economical in comparison. The floor structure of the building used a concrete "waffle slab" (a flat slab stiffened by a grid of beams) with no interior columns between the facade and the inner core. This concept, which permits complete flexibility in the layout of office space, has been widely used all over the world in concrete skyscrapers designed since that time.

The Relics of the Generations

New Yorkers are constantly looking up at the changes taking place in their well-known skyline. With building sites so scarce and expensive, with economic pressures to build up, and to replace low- with high-density buildings, so intense, it is not surprising that New York is becoming more and more a vertical city. Recently, however, a new awareness of our heritage has arisen and also a new pressure to improve the quality of life by improving the physical environment. New York, as one of the oldest cities on this continent, has a stock of historic buildings which needs to be preserved. The wrecking ball can no longer be accepted as the *only* means of renewal; we must consider historic preservation and energy conservation. Preservation and restoration are both a new planning policy and a new economic necessity. The landmark Grand Central Station case, in which preservationists survived the assault of developers wanting to "crown" the station with a 50-story building, served to focus the issue and made everybody conscious that the valuable past can and must be kept in the fabric of the metropolis. More recently, the historic Villard Houses have been saved and integrated into a design for a new hotel. In lower Manhattan, Fraunces Tavern (named after Samuel Fraunces, who opened a tavern there in 1792) has been spared from destruction and integrated into an historic block of buildings scheduled for renovation. This trend presents a totally new challenge to engineers involved both in the reconstruction of these historic buildings and in the erection of new buildings on adjacent sites.

For example, a new project for a 30-story building happens to be located directly across the street from the Fraunces Tavern block. The site for the new tower is typical of many in lower Manhattan. It is underlain by the relics of the generations of buildings that preceded it and has been the site of an archeological dig to uncover relics from the Dutch era. The site is adjacent to Broad Street (which was an old inlet) and has an underground stream crossing it diagonally. The rock which is to serve as the foundation of the new tower is about 40 feet below street level, while the ground water is only 15 feet below street level. All these elements complicate construction, obviously, but are not overwhelming. However, the presence within the zone around the projected building of a group of old houses on unknown foundations and in delicate structural condition introduces a significant challenge to design engineers. In this kind of situation they must first survey the existing buildings, and assess the possibility of damage due to vibrations from the new construction and to fluctuations in the water level resulting from the new excavation. The engineers must then establish monitoring procedures to control all the factors which are identified as potentially damaging, and moreover, carry out this investigative process not in the comfortable safety of their offices but in the public arena of community boards, preservation groups and special interest factions. Thus the challenge becomes both technical and political, and involves the art of compromise as well as the science of building.

Jane Jacobs, in the early 1960s, battled against Robert Moses' imperious attitude toward urban renewal, and helped change the role of the engineer. She had just written *The Death and Life of Great American Cities* in which she disputed the predicted demise of cities by detractors such as Le Corbusier and identified the elements of hope—the neighborhoods, the people, the lights. The bulldozer approach was no longer acceptable; selective demolition, coupled with intense renovation of structurally sound housing, became the accepted practice. Neighborhoods which had fallen into decay were suddenly "discovered" and bloomed again. A new intensity and vigor appeared in the streets, and a new pride and sense of place grew in the city. The "environmental engineer" played a major role in this episode of New York's evolution.

Since the mid-Seventies, when energy concerns came into focus as a result of blackouts and fuel shortages, the renewal process has taken a new turn. Conservation of non-renewable resources means that both new and renovated buildings must be designed to meet more stringent standards of energy efficiency. Just as the auto industry is witnessing the disappearance of the "gas guzzler," the construction industry has awakened to the fact that fuel savings of 30 percent are economically within reach purely by changes in architectural design and construction.

Obvious solutions, supported by hard economic facts, have surfaced in the form of shorter and shorter payback periods of invested capital. Better insulated walls and roofs, double and triple glazing, solar hot water, thermostatic valves on radiators have made their appearance in residential applications; heat recovery cycles, lower levels of illumination, and other more sophisticated technical solutions have appeared in commercial applications. The changing attitude is clearly visible in both new and renovated buildings. The new office building at 85 Broad Street has small windows instead of the sheer glass facade of the sixties; it has an inviting arcade at ground level instead of an inhospitable wall; and it has an archaeological remnant of old New York in a tree-lined garden instead of a bronze plaque.

Imagineers

The proposed new convention center, to be built over the old Pennsylvania Railroad yards on West 34th Street, is probably the most ambitious single project to be built in New York in many decades. The center, with almost two million square feet on a five-city-block site, presents a superb opportunity to its architects and engineers. The site for the center is mostly on landfill, extending out to the Hudson River from the original shoreline of Manhattan, and is traversed by two of the tubes of the Lincoln Tunnel. Foundations for the new structure vary from shallow spread-footings of concrete to deep piles and caissons of concrete-filled steel cylinders. A system of deep girders bridges over the Lincoln Tunnel from caisson to caisson drilled into rock and located so as to impose negligible loads on the tunnel. The superstructure is as varied as the foundations and includes concrete, steel and precast concrete. The structure of the exhibition floor is closer to that of a bridge than to that of a building since it must sustain the weight of trucks and heavy industrial exhibits in a vast exhibition hall.

The roof, possibly the most spectacular element of the center, is a space structure of interconnected steel tubes spanning a square grid of columns spaced 90 feet apart in both directions. The grid itself consists of diamond-shaped trusses assembled from the same tubular elements. A crystalline entrance hall is formed by a stepped pile of cubes rising dramatically to a sort of summit 150 feet above the floor. These cubes are glazed and structured with the same tubular space structure used in the exhibition hall. When completed, the space structure will be the largest ever built.

In keeping with the desire to make the center an active public building, a block-long skylit gallery, lined with shops, acts as a public boulevard linking the entrance hall with restaurants overlooking the Hudson River.

Planning of the center began over ten years ago. Just before the threat of bankruptcy forced the city to stop all new construction, a center was being planned on a platform over the Hudson River on a different site. At the same time, a hotel in Times Square was in the planning stage. Both projects were to serve as a focus for the intense redevelopment of two declining areas of the city and both two declining areas of the city and both projects were revived when the fiscal health of the city improved. The convention center is well on its way to becoming a reality. The hotel project, a 2,000-room high-rise conceived by John Portman, is still in question. This hotel would be a daring structure with a 400-foot-high skylit atrium surrounded by rings of hotel rooms. Laid out in a U shape, the plan calls for the closure of the U to be made up of five-story stacks of hotel rooms spanning the 112-foot atrium and arranged in a series of giant steps. A free-standing concrete elevator core with glass-enclosed outside elevators terminates in a multi-level rooftop revolving restaurant. The overall effect is nothing short of spectacular and has more of a show business than a utilitarian character. Translating this concept into steel and concrete requires a level of imagination and innovation above average. For example, the stacks of rooms which span the atrium are designed as multi-level "Vierendeel frames" made of rigidly connected horizontal beams and vertical columns. Precast concrete decks cantilever beyond the frames to create the corridor overlooking the atrium. This solution to the support problem looks quite different from the conventional approach—floors supported by trusses; it has a more dramatic visual impact with its rooms seemingly suspended in space. Walt Disney coined the word "imagineers" for those engineers capable of translating concepts of the city of tomorrow into reality. Perhaps New York needs more imagineers to create the metropolis of tomorrow.

The city attracts engineers from all over the world because it offers a variety of opportunities and challenges that cannot be matched elsewhere. Its projects range from the highest towers to the deepest tunnels, from the longest bridges to the smallest houses; from the most complex of water supply systems to the simplest street "furniture." Although New York is no longer growing demographically, it is entering a phase of rebirth and reconstruction—recreating the atmosphere that made the city a hundred years ago a magnet for the brightest engineering and architectural achievements in the world.

America's Suburbs Still Alive and Doing Fine

Once viewed as boring bedroom communities and cultural wastelands, suburbia has evolved into a vibrant center for jobs, shopping, arts and entertainment.

For all that has been said and written in the last decade about the so-called comeback of the cities, one simple fact remains: Suburbia overwhelmingly dominates the course of economic and social life in the America of the 1980s.

Gleaming malls, sprawling office parks and high-tech manufacturing centers have ended the need for millions of suburbanites to go downtown for shopping or jobs.

New housing developments and hopes for safer and better schools keep most families firmly entrenched in the suburbs, leaving city life largely to singles, childless couples and the poor, who can't afford to move out.

Outlying communities, once viewed as boring bedroom areas and cultural wastelands, have sprouted countless restaurants—many as good as those found in even the most cosmopolitan cities. Also joining the exodus to suburbia: Art centers, music halls and professional sports.

Says sociologist John Kasarda of the University of North Carolina: "The city has moved to the suburbs, which now have all the services and amenities people could ever want. To a great extent, they have made cities superfluous."

Yet suburbia isn't utopia. Some aging, "inner ring" suburbs suffer the same deterioration found in the cruelest of big-city slums. Newer, fast-growing suburbs are often choked with traffic and beset with soaring housing prices and zoning battles. Preoccupied with their own problems, few care about the fate of the central cities that spawned them.

Magnets for Growth

While singles and childless couples trickle back to stylish big-city neighborhoods, a far greater number of individuals and families are pouring into the suburbs from cities, small towns and rural areas.

From 1950 to 1980, the population of suburbia nearly tripled, from 35.2 million to 101.5 million—about 45 percent of the nation's total population. During the same period, central cities grew only modestly, from about 50 million to 68 million, or 30 percent of total U.S. population. Many Northern cities lost hundreds of thousands of people.

Examples of enormous suburban growth are everywhere. In California, Orange County—a huge suburban area south of Los Angeles—has become a center for high-technology industries, particularly aerospace and computers. The county has gained so many jobs in the last decade that it has been responsible for one quarter of California's migration. Planners expect Orange to have a total of 1.25 million jobs by 1990, nearly 40 percent more than the present total.

The situation is similar in Northern California suburbs. Pleasanton, a former hop-growing community of 36,000 southeast of San Francisco, has 898 acres of land under development in six major office parks that will create 25,000 jobs. The high cost of office space in San Francisco also is leading companies into larger suburbs such as Concord, which is now enjoying an office boom, including a six-block, 150-million-dollar Bank of America facility.

"The stereotype of a suburban city, a little hamlet dominated by single-family homes and dependent on the urban core for jobs and culture, needs rethinking," says planner Susan Hootkins of the Association of Bay Area Governments.

"No one's suburb today." In Colorado, the population of Aurora, a suburb just east of Denver, has zoomed from 75,000 in 1970 to about 200,000 today. In the process, the community is creating a whole new downtown, called City Center, with shopping, offices and residences. Several new hotels have opened recently, and a new 5 percent lodger's tax will help finance a 12-million-dollar convention center to open in 1988. Says Mayor Dennis Champine: "Aurora is no one's suburb today."

Chicago, which lost 123,000 private-sector jobs in the 1972-to-1981 period, is watching new growth move to its suburbs—adding 286,700 jobs during the same period. Among the big gainers: Northwest communities such as Schaumburg, Elk Grove Village and Arlington Heights.

In Washington, D.C., a recent report by the Council of Governments showed that suburbia accounted for 57,000 of the 82,000 jobs created in the 1976-to-1980 period. Leading the way was the Tysons Corner area of Northern Virginia, with its burgeoning office and shopping complexes. The lifeblood of New York City's business base also continues to flow outward. The number of *Fortune* 500 firms headquartered in New York has dropped from 136 in the late 1960s to about 65 today. Many have moved to suburban areas such as Greenwich and Stamford, Conn.; White Plains, N.Y., and Bergen County, N.J.

Even in some sun-belt cities, such as Atlanta, suburbs rival the downtown areas. Northern suburbs, making up what is known as the "Golden Crescent," accounted for about 70 percent of metropolitan Atlanta's growth in the 1970s. Says real-estate consultant Harry Saxton of the Redi-Data Corporation: "The mentality used to be downtown, but over the past five to seven years, particularly with the advent of the suburban office park, that's no longer the case."

What these examples show is that suburbia has become a fertile economic center in its own right. Increasingly, people not only live but also work in the suburbs. The Census Bureau's most recent national study of commuting showed that 25 percent of all workers lived and worked in the suburbs in 1980, while only 18 percent lived and worked in central cities. "Jobs have decentralized faster than people have," notes Brian Berry, dean of the Graduate School of Urban and Public Affairs at Carnegie-Mellon University.

Goodbye to Boredom

Establishing new centers of culture and entertainment often can be more difficult than creating jobs, but here, too, suburbs are catching up fast.

In nearly every big city, the popular centers for summer music and drama festivals are located mainly in the outskirts—Ravinia, north of Chicago; Wolf Trap, in a Virginia suburb of Washington, and Pine Knob, in north suburban Detroit. Other areas have built new theater, music and arts complexes. Dinner theaters, which spare patrons the hassles of downtown parking, are cropping up everywhere.

Concord, Calif., has its 8,000-seat Concord Pavilion, where offerings run the gamut from the New York Philharmonic to the Boston Pops and Linda Ronstadt. In surging Orange County, a 59-million-dollar performing-arts center being built in Costa Mesa is the latest in a series of new repertory theaters and art museums.

In Stamford, the 1,600-seat Hartman Theatre hosts two repertory companies and an opera company, and plans are under way for a new 7-million-dollar arts center to be built around the theater. Thriving artist colonies have sprung up in Suffolk County on Long Island and along the waterfront in Hudson County, N.J. Also in New Jersey, the Whole Theater Company has converted a former bank in Montclair into a 200-seat theater that draws 36,000 people in a typical season.

The Arvada Center for the Arts and Humanities near Denver boasts a 500-seat theater and a 2,000-seat amphitheater, plus art galleries and studios, and is home to four resident performing-arts companies. "The arts center is symbolic of a statement by the city that it's interested in more than just basic services, that it's interested in a unique quality of life," says center director Frank Jacobson.

Restaurants also are thriving in what was once a culinary Siberia. In *Chicago Magazine's* latest readers' poll of restaurants, four of the top 10 were suburban, including Wheeling's Le Français, which draws customers from all over the country. "The restaurants are moving to where the money is—the North Shore," says geographer Irving Cutler.

One of metropolitan Denver's most distinctive dining experiences is Café Kandahar in Littleton, a southern suburb. The owners spent more than 1 million dollars to convert a former jail into a combination restaurant/ski museum. "We feel that Littleton is probably at the core of what will be some of the biggest development and activity in greater Denver," says co-owner Steve Knowlton.

More popular spots. Downtown Detroit attracts little night life any more, but diners from all over the area flock to restaurants and lounges in suburban Southfield, such as the Bijou, the Golden Mushroom and Excalibur. Perhaps the top-rated restaurant in the Indianapolis area, the Glass Chimney, lies north of that city's sprawling borders, and Washingtonians often must call two weeks in advance for reservations at L'Auberge Chez François in suburban Great Falls, Va.

As for professional sports, team after team has moved to a suburban location. To cite just a few: The Los Angeles Rams football team actually plays in Anaheim, and the Detroit Lions play in Pontiac. The New York Giants have their home in the Meadowlands, a 435-million-dollar sports complex in East Rutherford, N.J., and will be joined there in the fall by the Jets, the area's other National Football League team.

The Rosemont Horizon, a convention center and arena opened in 1980 in the northwest suburb of Rosemont, is now the site of many big-time college basketball games, as well as concerts, wrestling matches and other spectacles once held in Chicago arenas.

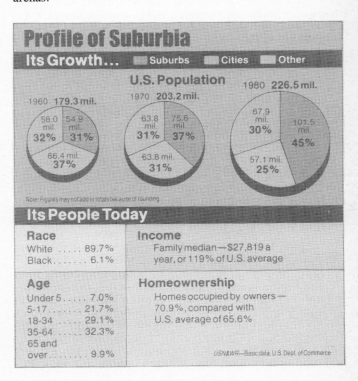

Side Effects of Prosperity

The maturing of suburbia hasn't come without a wide range of problems, not the least of which is traffic. In many areas, highways fronting shopping malls and office parks are every bit as clogged as busy city thoroughfares.

The Portman development, a massive office park under way along Georgia Highway 400 in Fulton County north of Atlanta, is expected to add 25,000 autos a day to an already crowded road. "Either we try to develop new ways of moving people around, control growth or we have to live with congestion," says Dan Antobelli of the Federal Highway Administration in Atlanta.

Companies in San Francisco's suburbs use staggered work hours to relieve congestion near office parks and encourage car and van pooling, often giving preferred parking spaces to such groups. South of Los Angeles, Fluor Corporation provides subsidized van service to more than 600 employes of the construction firm's Irvine office.

Equally worrisome to many fast-expanding suburbs is the skyrocketing cost of housing. In Orange County, where the average price of a home is about $145,000, "many workers are forced to live 50, 60 or even 70 miles away in Riverside County," says planner Richard Bailey. Some prospective employers are choosing to locate elsewhere.

Across the country in New York City's suburbs, companies are confronted with the same problem. The American Can Company, which moved its headquarters from New York City to Greenwich, Conn., 13 years ago, now is looking for another site, largely because of the lack of affordable housing in the immediate area. Some employes, says Chairman William Woodside, put up with a 90-minute drive from Danbury, Conn., where housing is cheaper. Another firm, Mutual of New York, has promised to subsidize mortgage rates and pay rental supplements to employes, when the firm moves a major part of its operation to Westchester County this year.

Although some suburbs are beginning to allow more zoning for condominiums and luxury-apartment projects, most outlying communities still oppose construction of low and moderate-income apartments. Not even major court cases, such as the landmark Mount Laurel II decision in which the New Jersey Supreme Court ordered suburbs to provide such shelter, have made much of a dent in suburban attitudes. "On one level, there's a racial component to this opposition," says Hugh Wilson, director of the Institute for Suburban Studies at Adelphi University on Long Island, N.Y. "But often, you find affluent suburban blacks joining with whites of the same class in opposing apartments."

Moreover, federal budget cuts have virtually wiped out funds for new subsidized housing. With the growing apartment shortage, owners of single-family homes, particularly in older suburbs such as Levittown, N.Y., and Evanston, Ill., are renting out sections of their homes, sometimes in violation of local ordinances.

Debate Over Growth

Whether it's housing shortages, traffic snarls or sprawling commercial development, many suburbanites don't like what is happening to what they once considered ideal environments. Spreading office construction near their development in Georgia's Fulton County prompted owners of 24 homes in the Aruba Circle neighborhood to put their houses and land up for sale for commercial development. Says one resident: "People will get many times what they paid for their homes, but if we could have this place like it was five years ago, I'd pay $15,000 to stay."

In other places, officials and residents grapple over the pace of growth. Residents of burgeoning Lakewood, Colo., voted down three major projects that had been approved by the city council. In Southampton, Long Island, the city council has approved 5-acre zoning for the remaining 26,000 acres of undeveloped land in that community as a hedge against advancing suburbia. At least one county supervisor in booming Fairfax County, Va.—Audrey Moore—speaks out often against that area's rapid growth. "When I came here, I thought, 'What a beautiful place and what lovely land and what a better life than in New York,'" she recalls. "Then, as I watched the development, I thought we weren't planning to take care of it very well."

Still, for every official leery of growth, there is another who welcomes it. Fulton County recently spent $100,000 to promote the southern end of its boundaries to developers. "I hesitate to say 'limit development' because why would I want to limit a trend that has kept our economy growing?" asks Michael Lomax, chairman of the county commission.

The Many Faces of Suburbia

The varying attitudes toward growth are just one example of the great differences found in American suburbs. "Suburbs are not a monolith but rather a kaleidoscope," says geographer Peter Muller of the University of Miami at Coral Gables. "You can pick the exact suburb to match your income and lifestyle."

Typical is suburban Chicago. In the old but exclusive North Shore suburb of Kenilworth, homes are valued at more than $200,000, and the commercial district is mostly stylish boutiques. Evanston, the first suburb north of the city, has an established downtown and a mix of neighborhoods that range from the very fine in the north to seedy sections in the south that have been marred by gang activity. South of Chicago lies the poor and mostly black suburb of Robbins, where the median home value is less than $25,000. Still others like Berwyn and Cicero cater to white, working-class families, while Glenview and Oak Brook are home to middle-class white-collar workers. Then there are the booming new commercial centers, such as Schaumburg.

Varied as they may be, most suburbs are faring well—but not all. A 1982 study by the Rand Corporation found that 1 in 5 of the 408 largest incorporated suburbs was troubled by factors such as poverty, high unemployment, deteriorating housing stock and crime. Among the worst cases were aging, close-in communities such as the Philadelphia suburb of Chester and Highland Park near Detroit.

In some sun-belt cities, developments thrown up in haste in the 1950s already have become eyesores. Less than 3 miles from Disneyland in Garden City, Calif., 4,500 residents pay $400 to $500 a month for dilapidated apartments in the Buena Clinton development built only 23 years ago. On an average night, Buena Clinton's streets are jammed by poor Hispanic children at play and prostitutes on patrol, with drug dealers and junkies shooting up in abandoned buildings.

Some long-established suburbs such as Mount Lebanon near Pittsburgh are still attractive but are faced with the task of closing schools left vacant by declining enrollments and establishing new services for aging residents. Others, such as the Detroit suburbs of Westland, Taylor and Garden City, have suffered right along with their residents—many of them laid-off auto workers. There, property values have plummeted, cars have been repossessed and municipal and school budgets have been slashed.

The crime factor. Fast-growing suburbs face still another problem: Crime. In Colorado, Aurora recorded 18,340 crimes in 1978. By 1981, the number had grown to 24,630.

The police department has 322 commissioned officers, up from 198 in 1978. Says Police Chief B. K. Blake: "When I started here 21 years ago, homicide was unique and armed robbery was something even the chief responded to. But in the last three or four years, we've had one homicide a month and an armed robbery every two days."

Yet to be addressed in many suburbs is the issue of racial integration. "Nobody has welcomed minorities," states William B. Shore, senior vice president of the Regional Planning Association in the New York City area.

Although the number of blacks living in the suburbs increased from 4.2 million in 1970 to 6 million in 1980, they constitute just 6.1 percent of suburbanites. Moreover, says Wilson of Adelphi University, blacks tend to live for the most part in traditionally black suburbs.

Many studies show that real-estate agents continue to "steer" black families to primarily black neighborhoods of suburbs and that landlords still find excuses for not renting to minorities. Incidents of violence against blacks who move into white neighborhoods are not uncommon. In October, the home and car of a black family who moved into the Atlanta suburb of Mabelton were hit with shotgun blasts.

Other minorities, such as the Vietnamese, have an easier time of it. Yet even they tend to congregate in close-knit neighborhoods. One section of Arlington County, Va., across the Potomac from Washington, is known as Little Saigon. The number of non-English-speaking people living in Arlington rose from 1.6 percent of the population in 1970 to 8.2 percent in 1980, posing new challenges for schools and emergency personnel.

Suburbs vs. Cities

Despite their problems, most suburbs face a far rosier future than the cities they surround. Already richer—average family income is $27,819, compared with $21,650 in central cities—suburbs are expected to get even wealthier. Meanwhile, cities will increasingly become home to what urban experts call the underclass—the poor, the elderly, the unskilled. "The trend is clearly a growing disparity between cities and their suburbs in economic and social conditions," says economist Richard Nathan of Princeton University.

President Jimmy Carter's plan to rebuild cities by pouring in more dollars and changing federal policies encouraging flight to suburbia is all but forgotten in an era of budget cuts. Rather than having the federal government target aid programs, the Reagan philosophy of New Federalism is designed to give local governments more authority to spend the dollars that come from Washington.

As suburbs become more self-sufficient and politically powerful, says urbanologist Pierre de Vise of Chicago's Roosevelt University, they are becoming even more reluctant to aid struggling cities. "The distrust between city and suburbs is getting much worse," he observes.

Proposals for giving cities a part of the tax windfall of mushrooming suburbs, such as the tax-base-sharing system in effect in the Minneapolis–St. Paul area, are going nowhere, says finance expert Thomas Muller of the Urban Institute in Washington, D.C. He adds that "you can forget" schemes for consolidating city and county governments. "The suburbs figure they have little to gain," explains Muller. Such city-county consolidations exist in only a handful of areas, such as Indianapolis, Nashville and Jacksonville, Fla., and none has been established recently.

City-suburb cooperation is limited primarily to issues designed to solve areawide pollution and transportation problems such as the new plans for rail systems voted in the Dallas and Los Angeles areas.

The temptation is for cities to fight back by taxing suburbanites who work in the city or use city services. The nation's capital has a steep 8 percent sales tax on meals. New York City, Philadelphia and Detroit all have payroll taxes aimed at suburbanites. Yet these steps can be counterproductive. "If you push these taxes too high, you will encourage workers and companies to move out of the city," says Muller.

Nor does suburbia, with its growing political power, hesitate to fight back. The New York suburban counties of Nassau and Suffolk have as many representatives in the State Legislature and the House of Representatives as do Manhattan and the Bronx. Those suburban legislators have resisted increases in New York City's commuter tax and were able to vote millions of dollars in state funds for commuter railroads while New York's subways deteriorated.

While cities languish, experts see suburbia becoming even stronger, taking ever bigger bites of rural America, as people and businesses flee congestion and high costs. Says urban planner Peter Gordon of the University of Southern California: "Only if you watch movies that fantasize about the future will you see cityscapes with huge buildings concentrated downtown. That's not the future of American cities. It's the past."

By LAWRENCE D. MALONEY with the magazine's domestic bureaus

Varieties of Urban Experiences

Social scientists who study the urban community agree that there exists in our society a wide variety of life-styles and life experiences. This has been observed in every unit from neighborhoods to entire cities. Ethnic and religious communities exist in which the traditional values and behaviors are mixed with the new patterns of urban life. Slums, and all that is implied by the term, present still another set of life experiences. Suburbs, once conceived of as the refuge of the wealthy and upwardly mobile, have become as diverse as the central city. There are poor suburban communities, ethnic suburbs, and suburbs that are nearly or totally occupied by black Americans. In summary, there are nearly as many possible experiences as there are groups to provide those experiences.

One characteristic of urbanization is that the rate of change is increased. The swiftness with which change takes place allows entire communites to alter their populations within a single decade. For example, many suburbs immediately surrounding the central city are dominated by a particular ethnic group through the invasion-succession process only to be replaced by another group a few years later.

How individuals respond to urbanization is also a concern of the social scientist. Some people enjoy the pace and dynamics of crowded cities; others respond much more negatively to the city and grow to hate it. Some find happiness in the city; for others it becomes a tragic, alienating experience. Some ethnic groups find despair in the changes while others adjust rapidly and even become agents for change.

Another task for the social scientist is describing, comparing, and analyzing the similarities and differences between the many urban contexts. The goal of this section is to explore the dynamic social interactions that have an impact upon and, in large measure, direct the urban experience. John Goodman, Jr.'s demographic analysis of the city examines urban movement in the 1980s. Patricia Morrisroe describes the impact of a new, upwardly mobile population upon New York's Upper West Side. Ellen Hopkins analyzes the impact of gentrification upon the poor and elderly in New York's Upper West Side. Barbara Koeppel discusses the problems and prospects faced by renters in America's large cities and the inevitable clashes between tenants and landlords. Finally, Steven Fustero describes the problem of homelessness faced by the more than 2,000,000 people who inhabit America's streets.

Looking Ahead: Challenge Questions

What factors, if any, make urban life different from rural life? Does urban life alter behavior? If so, how?

Is the process of gentrification inevitable? If so, what will become of the dispossessed?

To what extent has deinstitutionalization contributed to the problem of homelessness? Do private and voluntary organizations possess the resources and will necessary to solve the problem?

What explains the present attraction of neighborhoods in transition? Is the new urban dweller an asset or a liability to these old, mixed neighborhoods?

People of the City

John Goodman, Jr.

John Goodman, Jr., is a member of the research staff of The Urban Institute in Washington, D.C. Views expressed are those of the author and should not be attributed to The Urban Institute.

Although more people are moving out of cities today than are moving in, popular accounts of a back-to-the-city movement have some truth to them. As was the case during the 1960s, the 1970s saw revitalization of some inner-city neighborhoods in many of the nation's largest cities. Even though the extent of this revitalization is not yet documented, the manner in which it has occurred is a noteworthy break from the past.

Federal urban renewal programs in the 1950s and 1960s often demolished the housing of the poor and built new housing for the not-so-poor. In contrast, much of the housing activity during the 1970s, whether through government programs or the private market, involved renovation of existing structures. Nationwide, expenditures for additions and alterations to existing residences doubled in only four years during the mid-1970s.

A shift in how properties change hands has also accompanied these renovations — at least in the neighborhoods affected by the back-to-the-city trend. Historically, housing has filtered down to lower-income households as it is vacated voluntarily by higher-income households moving on to better housing. Everyone gained. But now, in some areas, older housing which previously filtered down to lower income households, has begun to percolate back up to higher-income households. Unlike filtering, such percolation leads to displacement — forced moves by lower-income households, often to less desirable or more expensive dwellings.

Because it is such a distinct break from the past, and because frequently blacks are displaced by whites, it does not take many of these moves to arouse public interest. The changes are all the more visible because, both for economic and psychological reasons akin to blockbusting, but in reverse, they tend to concentrate on one neighborhood at a time.

Back-to-Neighborhoods

As measured by either numbers of people or their socioeconomic status, however, there is little evidence of a nationwide back-to-the-city movement. For every person who moved into a central city during the 1970s, nearly two left. The average population of the central cities of the nation's metropolitan areas declined by 4.6 percent between 1970 and 1977. In fact, a slight increase occurred in the rate at which people are leaving cities, and a slight decrease in the rate at which they move into them.

All age groups contributed to this net movement out of cities. The poverty rate in cities increased slightly between 1969 and 1976, while the poverty rate in suburbs declined. Despite substantial gains in black suburbanization during the 1970s, the gap between the percentage of blacks in the cities and the percentage of blacks in the suburbs is still great.

National statistics mask differences among cities. Such cities as Boston, Cleveland, Phoenix, and Newark did not fare identically over the 1970s. Tracking the demographic details of a back-to-the-city movement has been difficult because migration statistics for individual cities and their neighborhoods are spotty. Yet the available evidence provides little support for a broad, back-to-the-city trend. For example, Washington, D.C. — often considered as typifying the movement — actually experienced a population decline of 13 percent between 1970 and 1979, and the median income of district households did not rise in relationship to the household income of surrounding areas. The slight increase over the past several years in the percentage of the Washington, D.C., population that is white is a turnabout from past trends, but it should not be confused with changes in population size, mobility patterns, or average economic status.

The fact remains that some of the nation's cities did experience dramatic demographic change during the 1970s. The explanation is that the change has been largely internal to the cities and has taken place at the neighborhood level. Back-to-the-city is the demographic misnomer of the decade. Back-to-selected-neighborhoods would be a much more accurate label.

Why the Confusion?

Urban resurgence, like urban decline, has three dimensions: economic development — growth in industry and retail trade, with the accompanying change in the number and type of private-sector jobs; housing improvement — new construction and housing rehabilitation; and population change — change in the number and composition of city residents. Changes among the three di-

In recent years urban centers have been experiencing increased population movements. However, this back-to-the-city trend is really more of a back-to-selected-neighborhoods migration. The urban resurgence must not be confused with changes in the size and composition of city population.

mensions are correlated, but perhaps not as highly as is often assumed. A 10 percent increase in occupied downtown office space does not necessarily imply a like increase in city population, nor does a 10 percent increase in retail trade volume. New housing construction and increased housing rehabilitation do not necessarily imply more people.

To give an example, a back-to-the-city article in the *Saturday Review* in 1978 singled out six cities — Atlanta, Birmingham, Cincinnati, Detroit, Hartford, Minneapolis — as examples of a "monumental renaissance." As Paul Porter noted recently in commenting on this article, each of these cities actually declined in population by at least 7 percent from 1970 to 1976. However significant the gentrification movement in particular neighborhoods, it must not be confused with changes in the size and composition of city populations.

Coverage by the popular media

also has contributed to misperceptions about a back-to-the-city movement. One could speculate that there has been a newspaper or magazine article for every case of a white, middle-class, childless couple moving from the suburbs to an inner-city neighborhood and renovating an older house. Such attention is understandable: A back-to-the-city article has the attraction of a man-bites-dog story. In an era of urban decline, any offsetting change is noteworthy — and especially when it arises through private actions. Anecdotal observation is sufficient to reveal that change is taking place, but we do not yet know all the details. In fact, it is still an open question whether the tempo of revitalization even increased from the 1960s to the 1970s.

Inside Gentrification

First among the demographic forces instrumental in urban neighborhood change is the continuing growth in

the number of households, a more important factor than population increase or decline in determining housing demand. Sustained growth in the number of households has put additional pressure on the existing housing stock. Due to the decline in average household size, the number of households in central cities increased by 8 percent during the first seven years of the 1970s, even though central cities declined nearly 5 percent in population over the same period.

Recent changes in household composition have also favored city populations. Non-family households accounted for most of the growth in the number of households in the country during the first seven years of the 1970s. Individuals in households of this type historically have had below-average rates of movement out of cities and above average rates of movement into cities. The 1970s also witnessed a large increase in the number of two-earner households, which many people believe favor central residential locations.

In light of these important demographic shifts, it may seem surprising that city-wide population trends have not changed even more than they have. Offsetting the changes in number and composition of households, however, is the fact that growth was most rapid among households headed by persons between the ages of 25 and 34 — the age group with the highest rate of net migration out of cities. Statistics on the growing number of young adults in cities are sometimes cited as evidence of a back-to-the-city movement. But the truth is that the number of young adults outside of cities is growing even more rapidly. Both inside and outside cities the increase in the numbers of young adults is due less to migration than to the aging in place of the baby-boom generation.

Moreover, most age groups increased their rate of migration out of cities and decreased their rate of migration into cities between the periods 1970–1973 and 1975–1978: The number who moved out between 1975 and 1978 was 6 percent higher, and the number who moved in 8 percent lower, than if the age-specific rates of 1970–1973 had been maintained.

Finally, two-earner households may not favor the central city as much as is believed, based on where such households have chosen to live in the past. In 1970, 42 percent of women living in suburbs were labor-force participants, almost matching the 44 percent rate for women living in cities. For married women living with their husbands, the rate in the suburbs was 39 percent, and 41 percent in cities. At the very least, the notion that homemakers live in the suburbs and women working outside the home live in the city is an exaggeration.

The housing economics of the 1970s offer further explanation of neighborhood revitalization. The large baby-boom group has reached the age when a high percentage purchase first homes just when it has become more difficult for first-time buyers to purchase a new home, as measured by an increase in the percentage of income that must be allocated to housing expenses. At the same time, it has also become more financially attractive to own rather than rent, because of tax savings and the investment value of homes. Older houses in the city have provided an alternative for many young buyers who have found themselves priced out of the new home market.

Changing residential preferences and improved attitudes toward city living are sometimes cited as causes of a return to the city. This argument is difficult to accept, however, especially when much of the evidence comes only from surveys of people who have chosen to move into neighborhoods that are being revitalized. National polls show no such increasing preference for city living. A recent Harris poll of attitudes toward cities clearly indicated that most Americans across the nation think that cities offered the best cultural activities, jobs, and health care, but the worst housing, public schools, and crime. They may be pleasant to visit, but not to live in. It is perhaps not so much a change in where people want to live that is responsible for the neighborhood revitalization of the 1970s, as the fact that their choices have been limited by economic and demographic pressures.

Prospects for the 1980s

What can the experience of the 1970s tell us about the likely urban population trends of the 1980s? The total number of households will probably continue to increase by at least 1 percent a year through 1990, putting continuing pressure on the existing housing stock.

Other demographic changes during the 1980s may partially offset this growth. Rates of movement out of cities may increase further during the 1980s, because people who can afford a home usually want to own one. Nationwide, the percentage of households owning their housing increased during the 1970s, with the increase most pronounced in the 25 to 34 age group. Continuing a long-term trend, home-ownership opportunities recently have been increasing fastest in the suburbs. Between 1970 and 1977, suburbs had 80 percent of the total metropolitan growth of owner-occupied housing, compared to only 69 percent of the metropolitan rental growth. In the mid-1970s, a desire for home ownership most clearly distinguished movers to the suburbs from those to the city, according to a study of 27 metropolitan areas. The aging of the baby-boom generation into the age groups with higher home-ownership rates, therefore, could increase migration rates out of the cities.

Other plausible, but uncertain, demographic trends of the 1980s may shift population out of the cities. Married women are remaining childless to an older age than before. If these couples become parents during the 1980s — as most will, if current indications hold true — the suburbs may become more attractive to them. Depending on the rate at which new mothers temporarily withdraw from the labor force, the composition of two-earner households may shift during the 1980s. Young childless couples may want to live near the city offices where they work, but mothers re-entering the labor force may be more likely to seek work near their suburban homes.

The Importance of Energy

Economic forces will be more important than background demographic conditions in determining whether people move out of, or into, central cities during the 1980s. Real income growth provides the freedom for families and individuals to buy or rent the type of housing they want, where they want it. A stagnant economy would restrict this freedom. Tax laws affecting housing are perhaps the most effective tool at the federal government's disposal for influencing the type of housing people occupy and, indirectly, where they live. At the local level, zoning laws, building codes, and growth controls all determine the price of newer, primarily suburban housing and thus influence the attractiveness of older, primarily city housing. Condominium conversion laws will affect the availability of owner-occupant housing in the cities.

In the private sector, business and industry choices of whether to locate in cities or suburbs will affect residential location choices, just as such choices are often affected by population trends. Any acceleration in the shift of industry out of the Northeast and North Central regions will make it more difficult for the cities in those regions to compete successfully with their suburbs for people remaining.

Of all the uncertain factors that will shape urban population change during the 1980s, energy looms as the most important. With its effect on transportation, industry, and building technology, the availability and price of energy will help determine whether the 1980s become a decade of movement toward what recent congressional hearings termed the "compact city."

THE NEW CLASS

They're young and rich, single
or starting families, and they're making
over an old, mixed neighborhood
in their own upwardly mobile image.

PATRICIA MORRISROE

IT'S A SATURDAY NIGHT AT 96TH and Broadway. Inside the new Caramba!!!, everybody's drinking frozen margaritas and talking real estate, while outside on the traffic strip, a derelict swigs Wild Turkey and shouts obscenities. By 11 P.M., he's sound asleep on the bench, but the crowd at Caramba!!! is still going strong.

"These are the most lethal margaritas in Manhattan," says a man in a blue pin-striped suit by Polo. He staggers out of the restaurant and into David's Cookies next door. "Get the double-chunk choco-late chip," says his girlfriend, who is win-dow-shopping at Pildes Optical.

At the newsstand across the street, a middle-aged woman buys the Sunday *Times* and looks at the dozens of young professionals spilling out of Caramba!!! "Yuppies," she shouts. "Go home!"

But they are home. Ads in the the *Times* tout the Upper West Side as "Yup-pie Country," and Amsterdam is being called "Cinderella Avenue." According to a study of the years 1970 through 1980 by New York's Department of City Plan-ning, 7,500 people between the ages of 25 and 44 flooded the area between West 70th and 86th Streets. That age-group now makes up 47 percent of the popula-tion there. At the same time, the number of singles went up by 31 percent, while the number of families dropped 24 per-cent. "You want to know who's moving into the West Side?" says a woman who owns an antiques store on Amsterdam Avenue. "It's the young, the rich, and the restless."

SOME OLDER WEST SIDERS blame the newcomers for the skyrocketing rents and the up-rooting of local merchants. They deplore the cuteness of Columbus Avenue and the hordes of tourists who congest the sidewalks. They worry that the neighborhood's solid middle-class values will be replaced by the yuppie ver-sion of the West Side Dream: a pre-war apartment with a Food Emporium around the corner.

They can't relate to the 30-year-old on Central Park West who takes her hus-band's shirts to the East Side because she can't find a "quality" laundry in the neighborhood. Or to the tenants at the Sofia on West 61st Street, 50 percent of whom bought their apartments after seeing a model of the bathroom. ("They're big and very Deco," says Rich-ard Zinn, the building's director of sales.)

The Columbia, a condominium on West 96th Street, has been called the "Yuppie Housing Project" by locals who can't believe anyone would *pay* to live on Broadway. "Didn't anyone tell these peo-ple it's a *commercial* street?" says an el-derly man who is buying Rice Krispies at the Red Apple on the corner. "If I had the money for a condo, I'd move to Florida."

One third of the Columbia's units were bought by lawyers; the average income

From *New York*, May 13, 1985, pp. 34-39. Copyright © 1985 by News Group Publications, Inc. Reprinted with permission of *New York*.

SUE LEIBMAN

"Columbus is getting to be like a middle-class Rodeo Drive. The restaurants are so self-consciously trendy. I don't want brunch. I want breakfast."

per apartment is $100,000. "It's a nice first home for couples on their way up," says developer Arthur Zeckendorf, who worked with his father, William, to build the Columbia. Once they've made it, they can move to the Park Belvedere, a condominium on West 79th Street also built by the Zeckendorfs. Sold for an average of $400 per square foot, it has attracted a better-off buyer. "I looked at the Columbia," says a 27-year-old Wall Street bond trader, "but the neighborhood was just too borderline for me." So he bought an apartment in one of the Belvedere's towers and persuaded a friend to buy one, too. "It's a great deal," he says of his $400,000 one-bedroom.

Many West Side co-ops are besieged by Wall Street financiers who use their bonuses to make down payments. "The last five apartments in my building went to investment bankers," says a woman who owns a co-op on West End Avenue. "I want to protect my property, so it's good to have people with money move in. But I worry about the population in the next ten years. Are you going to need an MBA to get into Zabar's?"

Of course, not everybody apartment hunting on the West Side is young and on the make. Advertising wizard Jerry Della Femina and his wife, TV reporter Judy Licht, are looking for a co-op on Riverside Drive. "The West Side is the most exciting part of New York City," says Della Femina. "But the prices are ridiculous. Recently, a real-estate agent asked us how much we wanted to spend, and when we said, 'about a million,' she turned up her nose. 'Well, obviously you can't afford Central Park West,' she said. 'Have you considered Park Avenue?'"

Yet for all the money being poured into the neighborhood, some of the new West Siders have a decidedly old-fashioned point of view. For every yuppie who dreams about moving from Broadway to Central Park West there are others who chose the West Side because it seemed unpretentious. "I always hated everything the East Side represented," says 33-year-old Joe Powers in between feeding mashed carrots to his five-month-old son, Mark. "The West Side always seemed to have less airs about it. To me, it's Zabar's and Fairway. Not Rúelles and Pasta & Cheese."

Powers, a loan officer at a major New York bank, bought a two-bedroom condominium at the Columbia with his wife, Polly, a product manager for General Foods. Though the move from their apartment on West End Avenue and 89th Street was in some ways a move up, the new neighborhood is a little daunting. "Before the Columbia was built, the area was pretty much off-limits," says Polly. "Mostly, I remember bodegas and numbers parlors. A lot of them are still here, and while that doesn't bother me, I sometimes get nervous taking the baby for a walk. There's still a lot of drug dealing on the side streets."

Two years ago, the Powerses bought their apartment for $150,000. Today, they could probably sell it for $200,000. "But where would we go?" Polly asks. "I've already moved from West 73rd to 89th, and now to 96th Street. This is about as far north as I could handle. A lot of our friends are heading to Queens and New Jersey, but I'm not ready for the suburbs. I love the city.

"People ask me, 'What do you do for entertainment on West 96th Street?' and I say, 'Who has time for entertainment?' When I come home from work, I see everybody heading into the four elevators looking exhausted. At about 7 P.M., you can practically hear 300 bodies collapsing on their living-room sofas. Everybody's lives are so hectic that it just isn't part of the culture to socialize."

Polly looks out the window. "There he is again," she says, pointing to a man who is sitting in his underwear. "We've got an SRO across the street, and that man is always looking into our apartment." She pulls down the blinds. "It's so annoying," she says.

"It's the West Side," says Joe.

Ten blocks uptown, 31-year-old Richard Conway is setting up his VCR to tape Jacqueline Bisset in *Anna Karenina*. A vice-president at a Wall Street investment firm, Conway recently bought a twelfth-floor five-room co-op at 106th Street and Riverside Drive. In the past fifteen years, Conway has moved from Greenwich to Harvard to Third Avenue to Yale to Chelsea, and now to Duke Ellington Boulevard.

"This is not a yuppie neighborhood," says Conway, uncorking a bottle of white wine. "That's what I like about it. In my building, we have a wonderful mix of people. The head of the co-op board is a musical director, and we've got artists and writers and movie producers."

When Conway decided to buy a co-op, he wanted to look only north of West 96th Street. "I think a lot of the glamour is gone from the East Side," he says. "Besides, I considered it boring and staid, too much like Greenwich. I like living in a neighborhood that's ethnically diverse. Broadway has a lot of bodegas and mom-and-pop stores. To me, that's nice."

From his living room, Conway has a spectacular view of the Hudson. From the opposite end of the apartment, in the dining room, he can see a cityscape of charming turn-of-the-century brownstones. "I wonder how long they'll last," he says. "It's ironic, but everything I like about the neighborhood will probably disappear. And unfortunately, the reason is that people like me are moving into it."

"The West Side has always been on the brink of becoming fashionable," says Dr. Elliott Sclar, who teaches urban planning at Columbia University. "It

THE REINERS

"Everyone wants to come to the Upper West Side. There's nothing more exciting than living in a neighborhood in transition."

RICHARD CONWAY

"Everything I like about the neighborhood will probably disappear. And unfortunately, the reason is that people like me are moving into it."

had more land than the East Side, and it was bordered by two parks. But it never really made it for the rich. Instead, it captured the essence of middle-class life in all its various stages."

The Upper West Side really didn't start to develop until the Ninth Avenue elevated line was extended from 42nd Street to 104th Street in 1879. Row houses were built along the side streets for middle-income people, while the working-class lived in the tenements along Columbus and Amsterdam Avenues. By the turn of the century, large apartment houses like the Ansonia were going up.

At the end of World War II, however, the West Side declined as suburbia flourished. The people who had lived in the row houses fled to Westchester and Long Island and were replaced by a wave of Puerto Rican immigrants. "Those who stayed on," says Sclar, "had a real urban mentality. A lot of them were musicians, writers, and people who were left of center. To an outsider, the West Side looked like it was falling apart, but some of the middle class stuck with it."

With the West Side urban-renewal program in the mid-sixties, $1 billion of public money went into low- and middle-income housing projects (and such developments as Lincoln Center). That helped to rejuvenate the area between 87th and 97th Streets, and the decaying row houses soon became desirable. "A few years earlier, nobody had wanted them," says real-estate broker Austin K. Haldenstein. "I remember the day when eleven were put up for sale, and they sold only one. And they were only asking between $22,000 and $37,000."

Realtors like Haldenstein began persuading young couples to go west. "It was a real pioneering effort," he says. "We got a lot of people in their twenties and thirties to fix up the brownstones. Many of them had a liberal bent, and they believed in living in an ethnically mixed neighborhood."

By the mid-seventies, many of the brownstones had been renovated and were selling for as much as $300,000. Now, says Haldenstein, they can easily bring $1 million. In 1978, the co-op market began to boom. "Right from the start," says a broker at the Corcoran

Group, "we got a different type of client on the West Side. A lot of them were the kids of the sixties who didn't want to live on the East Side because it was too 'Establishment.' Besides, the West Side co-op boards were considered more socially liberal and were much looser with their financial requirements."

Barry Nathanson and Liliane Mager lived on East 84th Street before buying a co-op on Central Park West two years ago. "I was a hippie with hair down my back," says Barry, 36, who publishes a trade magazine. "After college, I traveled around the world for six years. Finally, I said, 'Hey, you're a Jewish kid from Great Neck. Go home already.'

"So this," Barry says, giving a tour of his two-bedroom co-op, "is home." The apartment, which the couple bought for $162,000, is decorated in shades of beige, with a modern canvas sofa and lacquered Italian furniture. "We got everything wholesale," says Barry. "At first, I was scared to death to get a co-op. But now, just telling cabdrivers I live on Central Park West is an ego trip. Anyway, the same apartment upstairs just went for $300,000, so we've doubled our money."

Liliane, who recently left her job as a teacher to take care of their four-month-old daughter, isn't quite as enthusiastic. "I feel very isolated here," she says. "I miss the services on the East Side. If I want to go to a good deli, I have to walk eight blocks to Zabar's." She tries to give the baby a bath in between preparing hors d'oeuvre for guests. "You know what else I don't like? People just don't dress up here. On the East Side, you had to look great to take out the garbage. But here, I feel uncomfortable wearing my fur coat, and after all it's only *raccoon*."

Barry holds the baby while Liliane tests

the bathwater. "The West Side is the best place to have kids," Barry says. "Every Saturday and Sunday, we go down Columbus with the baby, and it's like stroller avenue. All the other young couples are out there with their babies, and you feel you're a part of all the trends. You're right in the middle of where it's happening."

"That's the problem," says 28-year-old Sue Leibman, who works for a film-production company. "It's like, yeah, I'm young, single, and live on the Upper West Side. Next I'll be appearing on the Phil Donahue show."

Leibman, who lived in Los Angeles for a year and a half, recently moved into a one-bedroom co-op on Central Park West. "I spent months looking for a rental," she says. "Agents would show me $1,000 studios with a 'balcony,' which would turn out to be a fire escape overlooking the garbage pails." Finally, she persuaded her parents to help her "invest" in a piece of Central Park West real estate.

With some hand-me-down furniture and a little help from an interior-designer friend, Leibman has created a good-looking, comfortable apartment. "This is Paul Mazursky's couch," she says, "and that chair and table come from a movie set." She shrugs. "It's just sort of thrown together."

Leibman is not so nonchalant about what she calls the Columbus Avenue nouveau-chic parade. "It's getting to be like a middle-class Rodeo Drive," she says. "It's so faddish and plastic. And you can't even get a good Italian dinner anywhere in the neighborhood. Where are the decent restaurants? The ones on Columbus are so self-consciously trendy. I don't want brunch. I want breakfast. I

THE HANDLERS

"These pre-war buildings need new blood. The old people resist everything. They can't switch their rental mentalities into a co-op mode."

JAY ZAMANSKY

"The displacement is unfortunate, but where are we supposed to live? Whether people realize it or not, we're real assets to this community."

want my eggs plain, without hollandaise and a Bloody Mary."

DESPITE ALL THE CUTE CUI-sine, the six Charivaris, and the expensive co-ops, West Siders tend to ignore fashion: The neighborhood uniform is jeans, sneakers, and a sweatshirt.

"The West Side is for people who don't want the jacket-and-tie life," says Ira Fogel, who lives with his wife, Stephanie, in a modern, two-bedroom co-op in the West Seventies. "The minute I get home from work, I put on my jeans. It's an attitude. Go to any of the restaurants and you can pick out the outsiders a mile away. They're the ones wearing the trendy stuff. Not us."

Three years ago, the Fogels gave up a house in Los Angeles to move back to New York. The house had a pool and overlooked Benedict Canyon and the San Fernando Valley. "After that, we didn't want a tiny box with views of an air shaft," Ira says. The couple looked for a year before finding the right apartment. "On the East Side, we could never have afforded to live so close to the park," Stephanie says. "Since our apartment is relatively small, the concept of outdoor space was important to us. That's why I love the sidewalk cafés on Columbus. It's like St. Germaine de Pres in Paris. It's so much fun looking at everybody else."

The West Side's increasingly rich street culture is part of the reason Emily Greenspan, a free-lance writer, moved from East 93rd Street to a co-op in the West Seventies. "The East Side is a very indoor place," says Greenspan, who shares the apartment with her husband, Howard Kelting. "At 8 P.M., the blinds come down and the shutters close. If you're out on the street, you feel very isolated and alone."

Kelting, who works in the arbitrage department of PaineWebber, agrees. "I think West Siders tend to see their leisure time as having more dimension to it," he says. "Walk into Harper's or Uzi's on the East Side and people are still in their business suits, and they're talking stocks and bonds. Here, people leave it

behind. Besides, it's relaxing just to walk on the streets. With everybody around, it feels safe."

That wasn't always so. In the late fifties, the tabloids were calling 84th Street between Columbus and Amsterdam the most dangerous block in the city. WNBC News executive producer Bret Marcus, who grew up on Central Park West and moved to West 74th Street not long ago, recalls that people used to think he lived in a combat zone. "Whenever I gave friends my address," he says, "their parents looked at me like, 'Do you sleep with a gun under your pillow?'"

TWO PRECINCTS COVER THE Upper West Side—the 20th, from 59th to 86th Street, and the 24th, from 86th Street to Cathedral Parkway. Last year, there were 8,635 reported felonies in the 20th Precinct, down from 8,937 in 1983. In the 24th Precinct, there were 7,264 felonies, compared with 7,253 the previous year.

For lawyer Jay Zamansky, fear of crime isn't a problem, although his dates aren't always that secure. "There was one woman a couple of weeks ago who arrived at my door, pale and trembling," he says. "She kept repeating, 'How can you live in a place like this?' Needless to say, we didn't go out again."

Zamansky, who grew up in Philadelphia, now makes his home in a renovated SRO next door to the Salvation Army senior citizen's home on West 95th Street. "I really wanted a place where I could establish roots," he says. Constructed around the turn of the century, the building has 30 apartments, most of which are inhabited by young professionals. "We're a real unique building" he explains. "In the summer, we have barbecues, and when our first co-op baby was born, everybody was thrilled."

Zamansky bought his apartment, a duplex with a roof garden, for a little over $100,000. "I'm real proud of it," he says. "It's the consummate bachelor pad." The ceiling is painted black, with lots of track lighting. "I met an interior designer at the Vertical Club," he explains, "and she helped me with the overall concept."

But Zamansky says he doesn't want to be the kind of person who does nothing but "work, eat at restaurants, and go to a health club. I really want to be a part of this neighborhood," he says. "I attend community-board meetings, and I registered voters in front of Zabar's. I even went into the Salvation Army's old people's home and registered senior citizens. They were just so glad to see a young face that I don't think they cared how they voted. By the way, I'm a Republican. I think it's important to put that in the article.

"I'm also very pro-development," he adds. "It makes me angry when people criticize a lot of the changes. The displacement is unfortunate, but where are we supposed to live? We have rights. We pay taxes. Whether people realize it or not, we're real assets to this community."

Twenty-nine-year-old Paula Handler, who lives with her husband in a three-bedroom apartment in the Eldorado on Central Park West between 90th and 91st Streets agrees. "These big pre-war buildings need young blood," she says. "The old people can't maintain their apartments. They resist everything, from redoing the lobby to putting in new windows. The problem is they can't switch their rental mentalities into a co-op mode."

The Handlers moved from the East Side to the Eldorado a year ago. "Frankly, I didn't know anything about Central Park West," says Paula. "I mean, I knew the Dakota, but the Eldorado? What? All I knew was that I wanted space, and I wanted old. Old is chic."

"Originally, I said no to the West Side," says Scott, a quiet man who is involved in commercial real estate.

"That's right, he did," Paula says. "He didn't like it because it was dirty and nobody we knew lived there. But I fell in love with this apartment. It was a total wreck, but it was me. We gave them an offer the minute we saw it. We even offered more than they asked because we wanted it so much."

The Handlers put in two new bathrooms and a new kitchen, and redid the plumbing and wiring. Today, the apartment, which faces the park, is completely renovated. "See what I mean about new blood?" Paula says. "It doesn't take money. It just takes creativity."

Six floors above the Handlers, Linda and Mark Reiner also had to redo their apartment completely. "It was considered the worst disaster in the building," Linda says. "The walls, which were painted magenta, royal blue, and orange, were falling down. But we really wanted to live here. We recognized how the West Side was growing, and we wanted to be a part of that."

Two years ago, they moved from a house in Hewlett Harbor, where Mark Reiner had a medical practice. "It was a risk giving up everything," he says, "but Hewlett Harbor was very sterile and uniform."

"That's why we didn't want the East Side," adds Linda, who until recently was a practicing psychologist. "Now I sell real estate," she says. "I became addicted to it while we were looking for this apartment." The au pair brings their two-year-old son into the living room to say good night. "You wouldn't believe the children's playground in the park," Linda says. "You can barely get a place for your kid in the sandbox."

"Everybody wants to come here," says Mark. "There's nothing more exciting than living in a neighborhood in transition. It's sad, because a lot of people who live here can't afford to shop in the stores. But they're being pushed out of Manhattan, not just the West Side."

"The West Side makes you feel the difference between the haves and the have-nots," says Linda, who is dressed in a silk Chanel shirt, black pants, and pumps. "Right in our building, there's a real schism between the pre-conversion and post-conversion people. A new breed is taking over, and there's a lot of hostility. People are separated by age and economic class. The senior citizens got insider prices so low that there's a lot of resentment on all sides. At a recent meeting, one elderly person shouted, 'Well, I'm not rich like you.' But what can you do?"

"Basically, we're very optimistic," Mark says. "We feel good about the changes. The neighborhood is going to continue to improve."

Linda nods. "Definitely," she says. "For the West Side, there's no turning back."

THE DISPOSSESSED

Many are old and poor, many others are middle class, and though tenants have protections, gentrification usually wins.

ELLEN HOPKINS

JOE MAURI LIVES IN A ROOM THAT IS JUST long enough for his single bed; a man with long arms could almost span the width. There is no kitchen, no bathroom; he shares a toilet off the hall with two other tenants. In his fifties and out of work, Mauri wants nothing more than the chance to live the rest of his life as he has the last twelve years—in this room. Mauri, though, will not be able to realize this modest dream, because his room is not in a Bowery flophouse but in a lovely brownstone on West 70th Street, right in the heart of Upper West Side gentrification. His landlady, Denise Sobel, is trying to evict him because she wants to use the space as a sewing room.

Mauri's situation is emblematic of what's happening on the Upper West Side today—the squeeze that gentrification is putting on some longtime residents. People who live in the brownstones they buy can take over any portion of the building for their own needs. And personal-use evictions, say lawyers, are on the rise, even with rent-stabilized tenants. Landlords like Denise Sobel do not fit any ghoulish cliché: They are simply people with some money who want a perfect home—and their tenants are standing in the way of that dream.

Absentee landlords are no less eager to clear out low-rent tenants. But with either sort of landlord, the days of arson and goon squads are pretty much over. Even cutbacks on services such as heat

and hot water don't seem to happen as often as they used to. Tenants are better at fighting back, and they can count on the support of the West Side's elected officials and tenant-advocacy groups. As a result, the tactics have become much more subtle, much more *civilized.*

There are all kinds of ways to get people out of their homes, many of them perfectly legal. The Appellate Term Court ruled last December that there is no limit on the amount of space an individual landlord can take for "personal use." Denise Sobel, who is married and has a child, already uses the bottom half of her brownstone. Mauri's room is on the top floor and faces north. "You're telling me that every time she wants to sew a seam she's gonna run up all those stairs to sew in bad light?" he asks.

Mauri found out about the court decision in the New York *Post*—the story was called APPEALS COURT SEWS UP EVICTION. "A smart little headline wrapping up my life," he says. Mauri has since given away his books, among the few possessions he had. "I won't have no need of them where I'm going," he says. "I put them on the street and cried like a baby." Mauri expects he, too, will soon be on the street. He could never find a room at a comparable rent—$98 a month.

Personal-use evictions aren't being attempted just on people in SRO rooms. Brian Black, an institutional consultant,

lived for five years in a one-bedroom apartment with elegant wood trim—he had stripped and refinished the wood himself. Black left three weeks ago because his landlords, Floyd and Sarah Brezavar, wanted separate bedrooms for their two daughters and a more convenient space for their au pair girl. The au pair has been living on the fourth floor of the West 95th Street townhouse; the Brezavars live on the bottom two floors. "They want my living room for a child's room; my bedroom will be for the au pair," says Black. "Tenants can't protect themselves." Actress and writer Cathy Arden, the other tenant on Black's floor, will probably go next, when her lease expires in June; her apartment will become the other daughter's bedroom.

SOME LANDLORDS WHO DON'T want to go through the eviction process find subtle ways to harass tenants. Whenever one elderly woman left her apartment, she would return to find that her furniture had been moved a bit. Nothing was stolen or destroyed—just a seating arrangement altered, a chair pulled out that had been against a wall. One day, she came back and found that someone had put price tags on her tables and chairs. She agreed to leave her eight-

BRIAN BLACK

"My landlords want my living room for a child's room; my bedroom will be for the au pair. Tenants can't protect themselves from a personal-use eviction."

room rent-controlled apartment for a few thousand dollars.

Perhaps the most straightforward way to get rid of a tenant is to raise the rent. Administrative agencies have allowed landlords to replace a boiler and then pass along the cost to tenants in the form of major capital improvement charges (MCI's). For anyone on a fixed income, MCI's can be the same as an eviction notice.

When rents are raised substantially, people on fixed incomes have two choices—leaving or doubling up. Many West Siders, elderly ones in particular, are sharing overcrowded apartments because they can't bear to leave the area.

Until recently, Ines Miranda, 75, a former biology professor at the University of Havana, lived with ten other people in a six-bedroom apartment in the West Nineties. She paid $218 a month for a room just big enough for her bed, chair, and TV. There was no living room (it was the seventh bedroom), and all eleven people shared the same cooking area. Because of this, Miranda often ate only reheated soup. "I don't like to get in anybody's way," she says. "Besides, they were not much clean. They leave food in the pots, there were many roaches. I *hate* roaches." On days that the kitchen was extremely dirty, Miranda just drank tea.

Even though she could not do much cooking or bring her friends over—"We were many people; friends is not good for the house"—Miranda had almost no complaints. "Sometimes they noisy," she shrugs. "What could I do?" She leans forward and confides with a sweet smile: "Sometimes I turned the TV loud when I do not want to hear the shouting. I do not like to hear the things they say."

Last week, Miranda left the West Side. After years of waiting, she was lucky enough to get into subsidized housing.

Even elderly people with money are having a hard time staying in the neighborhood. The rents at the Lincoln Square Home for Adults on West 74th Street are far from cheap—its tenant leader, Rose Gale, pays $960 a month for a rather small bedroom, a private bath, and meals (there are no kitchens; all meals are served in a communal dining room). She and her fellow tenants, whose average

age is 75, have spent the last year and a half fighting eviction. In November 1983, their building was contracted to be sold; as part of the agreement, the owners promised to deliver it empty. Most of the tenants panicked and left within days of the announcement.

Today, the tenants are hopeful that things can be worked out. The new landlord, after being barraged by community activists, local politicians, and the tenants, agreed to let the remaining residents stay (41 of the original 200 are left). Even if these people *were* evicted, they would not end up on the street. In fact, because they are old people with money, other metropolitan-area homes would be delighted to have them. The problem is they don't *want* to live in the boroughs.

Rose Gale is in her seventies. She has a subscription to the Chamber Music Society of Lincoln Center, goes to the ballet, and sees the latest movies (she was enchanted by *A Sunday in the Country*). She came to Lincoln Square because living in Brooklyn depressed her.

THE OPTIONS FOR ELDERLY people who want to stay on the West Side are slim. Lincoln Square is the only home of its kind in Manhattan. And if a person is old and has little money, the options dwindle even further. The recently built Goddard-Riverside home provides about 170 subsidized apartments for the elderly and handicapped; tenants cannot have an income of over $11,400. The accommodations are splendid—large, sunny one-bedrooms with modern kitchens and baths. Half of the apartments look across the street at a newly built brick building that is Goddard's virtual twin, and where apartments are selling for upwards of $185,000.

Mae Hickey has lived in Goddard since it opened almost two years ago. An Irish immigrant who prefers to keep her age a secret (her hair is still jet black), Hickey spent her working life in New York as a waitress. She used to live on West 74th Street, but her landlord evicted her because he wanted to ren-

ovate the building. Hickey looked at city-owned housing in the East Twenties, but she was repelled by what she saw. "I decided the park is preferable to this," she says, slapping her hand against her knee. So she gave away all her possessions. "I had a big, beautiful, 23-inch color television, remote-control. . . . It was the *grrrrreatest.* Ooooh, good Lord! How could I take that to the park?"

At the eleventh hour, Hickey was accepted into Goddard. She is gradually accumulating new furniture, and the apartment is adorned by the few small items she did save—including her treasured memorial plate of John F. Kennedy. "Ooooh, good Lord, I loved that man!" she says. "I saw him once when he came to New York—I've had my crowning glory. That's why I could never leave Manhattan, you know." She waves her hand at the stack of daily papers she gets. "I love politics. I read it all. I couldn't go to the Bronx. I'd rather live in the park. And Staten Island is the pits. They're all a bunch of Reagan-lovers out there."

Hickey is one of the fortunate few. There is hardly any available subsidized housing for older people on the Upper West Side (or anywhere else in Manhattan). The waiting list at Goddard has over 3,500 names. For most, the only solution is to hope for a bit of space in an apartment shared by strangers.

Sharing apartments isn't just for the elderly. A large number of apartments meant for one family are being shared by several generations, simply because there is no place else to go. There is no official count on the number of families waiting for public housing on the Upper West Side; some eligible people have been waiting as long as twenty years to get into a subsidized apartment.

Lower-income people aren't the only ones being priced out. Unless new legislation is drawn up in Albany this month, a lot of middle-class housing will soon lose its rent-stabilized status. During the seventies, landlords were encouraged to upgrade their buildings by using J51 tax abatements—but those tax benefits last only twelve years. Once they stop, owners of buildings with fewer than six units are freed from rent stabilization and can raise rents to the "fair market" rate when a lease is up.

Jerry and Pat Ouderkirk, members of the J51 Tenants Coalition, are typical of the sort of people who will be driven out of the Upper West Side if J51 abatements are not extended. They are a middle-class couple with two little boys. He is in the securities business; she stays at home to take care of the children. They have lived for twelve years in a charming, if slightly cramped two-bedroom apartment on West 70th Street; their rent is $599. When their lease runs out in July,

JOHN PATERAS

the landlord will raise the rent to $2,500.

"We could certainly dip into our savings for a while," says Jerry, "but that's not the point. I suppose some people might look at us and say, 'So what? They're not going to end up on the street.' But we certainly can't stay here very long at that rent."

"We don't want to live in the suburbs—we're city people," says Pat. "This building is almost all families. You're just furthering the flight of the middle class by doing this."

RAISING RENTS TO "FAIR market" has been responsible for one of the greatest disruptions on the Upper West Side—the squeezing out of small businesses. There has been no

"**I**s not right for me tomorrow to tell the customer to give me $10 for a haircut that was $5, just to pay the rent. They go somewhere else."

commercial rent control since 1963; landlords are free to charge whatever rent they choose, and it is not unusual now to see rent increases of several hundred percent.

People like John Pateras, owner of the Lido Barber Shop on 87th Street off Broadway, cannot absorb much of a rent increase at all. Pateras, 59, is a Greek immigrant, and until seven years ago, he worked as a barber in someone else's shop. He took all his savings and bought

the Lido. It's an old-fashioned barbershop with three antique red leather chairs, fluorescent lighting, and a red-and-white striped pole.

Pateras has been warned by his landlord that the building will probably be demolished soon after Pateras's lease runs out in November. If the building is not torn down, Pateras expects a large increase in rent. He is paying $615, a low rent for the area, but even so, he just gets by.

The BROADWAY BLUES

ON WEST 89TH STREET, AROUND THE CORNER FROM BROADway, is a small faded sign: LYNN OLIVER STUDIOS. The sign is faded because it's 35 years old. Years ago, before the studio had air-conditioning, the sounds of Benny Goodman's and Woody Herman's bands used to float through the second-floor windows on warm summer nights, lingering over the honking cars of Broadway. Today, the warren of yellowed practice and recording rooms still lies at the top of a narrow flight of stairs. Stacks of now brittle music—"Stranger in Paradise," "Love for Sale," "My Melancholy Baby"—transcribed in Lynn Oliver's spidery hand are piled underneath, on top of, and in between drums, speakers, pianos, trombones, vibraphones, and music stands. Even the walls are crowded: Every inch is plastered with snapshots of the people who used to play here—Maynard Ferguson, Stan Getz, Gerry Mulligan.

Lynn Oliver and his wife, Anne, have spent the last few weeks packing it all away. The building was sold in February, and they were told to leave by April 30.

Lynn, 63, is a voluble, heavyset man with gravel in his voice and large white hands that he uses to great dramatic effect; he's been in the music business for 38 years, first as a drummer, then as a bandleader. He opened the studio, which provides rooms for practicing, recording, and teaching, with Anne, an Ann Miller look-alike softened with a dash of motherliness.

Anne isn't a musician. "They're very temperamental, honey," she confides. "One in the family is enough. It's a good thing I'm so calm." Anne is responsible for the business end of things; Lynn teaches the workshops and leads his own seventeen-member band. It isn't an easy life—they haven't had a vacation in over four years and the music business is sporadic at best—but they have enjoyed it.

Since the beginning of February, when the Olivers were told they had less than two months to vacate, they have spent almost

every waking hour looking for a new studio. They have called brokers, combed the classifieds, even taken out an ad in the *Times*. Only one place was even vaguely suitable, and that fell through.

"The places I've seen are either exorbitant rents or total sleaze," says Lynn. "Many places are talking $20, $50, $100 a square foot—and the foot you're getting is diseased. It's *cancerous*." Leaving the city is not an option—both the studio and Lynn's own band depend on a central location to survive. "If I wasn't in this business, I would have gotten out of this city long ago. Musicians have the least amount of work outside of hoboes, bag ladies, and bums."

Lynn makes his way through the obstacle course of a rehearsal room, jabbing his index finger against snapshots for emphasis: "I've got walls full of dead people that used to rehearse here. Here's Gene Krupa. Dead. Duke Ellington. Dead. Hazel Scott, Paul Gonsalves, Wes Montgomery—dead, dead, dead. People who think it doesn't hurt to leave, I say, '*Take my place.*'"

Anne slips into the room wearing a black T-shirt with yellow letters that spell out LYNN OLIVER STUDIOS. She hands her husband a cup of coffee and stands by the door listening quietly.

Lynn leans heavily on the battered concert piano: "I've thought about putting up the white flag and saying, 'I surrender.' But it's hard to walk away. I don't get passionate driving a truck, but I can get sensuous playing a piece of music. What am I supposed to do, plug up my ears?

"Let's say I leave it all. I'm in the wilderness chopping some wood, you understand, and then all of a sudden, I hear Artie Shaw playing the clarinet." Lynn holds up his large hands for a pause and then drops them, shaking his head. "Jeez, I'd have to stop right there, put down that ax, and say, 'Oh, boy! How the hell did I get *here*?'" —E.H.

If Pateras's rent were to go up, he is not sure there would be any point in continuing. "Is not right for me tomorrow to tell the customer give me $10 for a haircut that was $5, just to pay the rent," he says. "They go somewhere else. And if the customer not stay with me, I do bankruptcy, that's it." And then, Pateras will probably go back to being a barber in someone else's shop.

Barbershops, cleaners, shoe-repair places—all West Siders know that these are disappearing. There's also a sea change with small businesses that isn't quite so obvious as the LOST OUR LEASE signs. Alan Rubin, owner of the two RCI discount-appliance stores on Broadway, says, "Because all the leases now are short ones, the merchant can no longer plan for growth in his business."

It isn't just the marginal businesses that are going under, either, says Rubin. "Good strong businesses are folding. These places can absorb a certain amount of rent increase, but they can't go from $2,000 to $10,000. And if an RCI that's been around 50 years disappears from your neighborhood, some chain comes in. If it's at all uneconomical, they'll pull out. Whereas a business that only has one, two stores, they'll stay during the tough times. In the '77 blackout, our 98th Street store was looted and damaged. I could have collected my insurance, got out, and done quite well. But I stayed."

Some stores may be able to stay, but they won't be the same. Golden's Stationery, on Broadway between 94th and 95th Streets, has two years left on its lease. It is in a prime location for demolition—the block consists of two-story buildings, all the leases on the site will expire in 1987, and no attempt has been made to rebuild the store on the corner of 94th Street, which was destroyed by fire a year ago.

Paul Kaplan, one of Golden's owners, has tried to discuss renewing his lease, but he says his landlord won't talk about it. Kaplan assumes he will lose his store. But even if the block is not torn down and he is offered a new lease, he is discouraged about what that will mean for his business. Golden's is a vast dingy space, crammed to the last inch with a staggering amount of merchandise—the quintessential stationery store.

"If my rent were to go up substantially, which I assume it would if we aren't torn down, it's not as though I could just start charging higher prices," says Kaplan. "I can't charge $2.99 for a Scotch tape that everyone else is charging $2.49 for. What it does mean is that I'll only carry the expensive lines.

"We've built a reputation on the fact that we've got a wide variety—we carry 35 kinds of markers, 30 brands of greeting cards. I won't be able to afford that anymore. I won't carry 100 kinds of tumblers. I'll stop carrying that 36-column book someone wants once a year. Pretty soon you end up with a boutique."

Kaplan looks at his scuffed linoleum floor: "I planned that this would be a nice retirement for me. It's a family business, I've put in 30 years, I'm 59 years old. It's all worth zero now, zero."

There's another group of commercial tenants having trouble on the West Side, a group most people haven't lost much sleep over—dentists. Central Park West is lined with lavish dental offices; it's difficult to muster much sympathy for people who are clearly doing so well. But the future may be bleak for them, too, because the cost of moving is especially high for dentists.

Dr. Ronald Topal, chairman of the West Side Dentists Association, estimates that it would cost a minimum of $100,000 today to set up a dental office, with its specialized plumbing and electrical requirements. Vacuum-suction hoses have to be installed, along with high-pressure air hoses, gas lines for Bunsen burners, and plumbing for the darkroom. None of these fixtures can be moved; they are all sunk cost. "Someone opens a practice, puts an enormous amount of money on the table, and a few years later his rent has been raised so much he has to move," says Topal.

He knows of five established local dentists who were recently forced to abandon their offices. Topal believes that the day of the solo practitioner is drawing to an end on the Upper West Side. Smile Centers—those glossy clinics with several dentists rotating patients—will be where most West Siders go for a filling someday. And Topal is disturbed about this, both for the patients' sake—"If there's no ongoing relationship, a patient's needs may be ignored"—and for that of his colleagues. "This is a profession of very prideful individuals. It's difficult for men like this to feel that they're in a department-store setting."

ONE OF THE THINGS THAT seem most unfair about Upper West Side gentrification is that the people who paved the way for it, the musicians and artists who made it chic, are now among the ones being forced out by higher prices. Linda, a bass player, lives in her tiny studio on Broadway near 107th Street for two reasons: It's cheap ($236 a month), and it's convenient. Originally, her building was filled with musicians; Linda is one of the few left. Her landlady has tried twice within recent months to evict her. In January, Linda's rent check bounced. She called her landlady to ask her to redeposit it. Instead, her landlady sent a notice telling Linda she was being evicted for nonpayment.

"This is the second time she's done this to me," says Linda. "The last was when I paid my rent five days late. What she's forcing me to do is drop everything—which is hard when you're a musician—and hire a lawyer, which I can't afford." Most of Linda's musician friends now live in Washington Heights. "In a few years, we're going to have to live outside the city altogether," she says. "Musicians will live in these dumps, and all of a sudden, it's cool and groovy and your neighborhood's a Perrier highway."

The situation is just as bad for artists. Artists' studios are generally in commercial spaces with no rent control. Ken Juon, a 39-year-old sculptor, has had his studio on West 88th Street for ten years. It's a large area— 1,400 square feet—and he has always shared it. But now that his work has got bigger—he is making large, flat wall pieces with black tile—he needs more space. "Realistically, I can't make any more pieces until I get a commission or sell the ones I already have," Juon says. He and the two other artists he shares the studio with are paying $1,425 a month. That will go up $100 a month until it reaches $1,750, at which point Juon's lease will be up. He cannot afford a

HELEN

"My life was not meant to be walking back and forth on streets. I was always on my way, going somewhere, doing something."

higher rent and assumes he will then have to begin commuting.

Living in Manhattan is so important to artists and musicians that they will sometimes put up with bizarre living conditions. A few years ago, an organization known as Artists Assistance Services rented out inexpensive apartments in Bretton Hall, on Broadway and 86th Street, to people in the arts. But there was a little clause attached: The tenant had to share his living room with a "cultural activity."

Abby Cahn shared her apartment with a karate class. She soon found out that she wasn't even *sharing* the living room— the karate teacher wouldn't allow her to put any furniture in it ("It was his dojo; he decorated it like a Buddhist temple," she says), and if classes were going on, Cahn was not supposed to enter the apartment. Classes generally went from 5 to 10 P.M. five nights a week. Other tenants suffered with rock-band rehearsals that went on all night long. Some tenants left. Others put up with the conditions simply because they couldn't afford to leave.

CREATIVITY HAS BECOME THE key to removing tenants, but when all else fails, sometimes good old-fashioned harassment will do the trick. Anne Pollack, a 26-year-old flutist, lives in a West 84th Street building that is an obvious candidate for demolition. Three vacant lots lie on one side; on the other is a school yard. Pollack's building has a precarious look, standing by itself in the midst of all that open space; the fire escapes are separating from the building, and the west wall is crumbling away.

Pollack and her fellow tenants claim they have been suffering for the last three years from classic harassment—no heat, no hot water, and rotting stairs, windows, and floors. By the fall of 1982, tenants say, 250 complaints on the building had been filed with the city, and a rent strike had started. In 1983, Judge Ralph Sparks agreed to let the tenant association use the money that had accumulated from the rent strike to make repairs on the building.

Nine months later, the court asked for an accounting. It decided the tenant association had overspent by $7,000 and had to replace the money. "We were never given any spending ceiling before," says Pollack. It was then, in the spring of 1984, that the judge appointed a 7A administrator.

In buildings where the landlord is not providing services, the court may appoint a 7A, who collects the rents—the landlord no longer has access to them—and uses the money to make repairs. Since the 7A took over in Pollack's building a year ago, almost no repairs have been made. And from October through March, the building had heat and hot water for approximately 30 days.

Pollack works only part-time now. "You can't work a full-time job and still fight this kind of nonsense effectively," she says. "It's amazing how much it consumes your life—calling lawyers, making complaints, going to court, keeping records. And they know it takes time. As long as you're keeping anyone in court, you're keeping them busy and broke." Judge Sparks has urged the tenants to leave if the landlord makes them an offer. Pollack isn't interested. "Where the hell can I afford to move to?" she asks.

MONEY UNDER THE TABLE is still an accepted way to remove tenants. But there's always the person who isn't easily bought. Sarah (not her real name) is a single mother with two sons, aged thirteen and six. She's 32, has lived on public assistance, and until two months ago had a three-bedroom rent-controlled apartment in the West Eighties—the rent was $109 a month. She was the last tenant left in a building emptied for renovation. "They started out offering me $5,000 and then went up," says Sarah. "But whatever they gave me, in the long run I lose, 'cause where could I ever find something like this?"

In September, the only other tenant had moved out. Walls were knocked down around Sarah's apartment; large portions of her ceiling caved in, one time knocking her younger son unconscious; the staircase was removed, leaving them virtual prisoners; and four days before Christmas, a fire broke out in the building. The children had to be hospitalized for smoke inhalation; their kittens died in the fire. "Almost everything we had was destroyed," Sarah says. "The Christmas tree was melted and all the presents too—most of the things we had was plastic."

Shortly afterward, Sarah was visited by an investigator from Special Services for Children. An anonymous report that she was abusing her children had been made. The report was soon found to be false. (Oddly enough, another woman with two children on the same block, whose landlord was also trying to evict her, was reported to be abusing her children around the same time. That report was also unfounded.) By then, Sarah's resolve was beginning to crumble: "Another fire could wipe us out. And even if we could stay, they'd be accusing me of being a prostitute or a drug addict. They'd get me in the end."

In March, Sarah finally agreed to leave for an undisclosed sum of money. "When I came here twelve years ago, it seemed like such a wonderful place to be," she says. "A library nearby and a church across the street. It's been nice having that watching over me." She worried that Medicaid would find out about her settlement, because all benefits would be cut off—her younger son is a hemophiliac, and his treatments then cost about $3,000 a month, which would quickly eat up Sarah's entire windfall. She has not calculated how long the money will last, given the higher rent she must expect to pay.

"The judge kept on saying to me, 'You're crazy; just pretend you won the lottery. This is more money than you'll ever see.' But I didn't want to win no lottery. I just wanted to stay where I was and have a little peace of mind."

IN THE LAST TEN YEARS, OVER 85 percent of the single-room-occupancy stock has been destroyed or converted into luxury housing. SRO's have a bad reputation, sometimes deserved, because of the drug addicts and former mental patients who have lived in them. But there is another side to SRO's—they are the last viable means of housing for low-income people on the Upper West Side. And today, there are almost none of these rooms available. Mayor Koch has proposed a moratorium on SRO conversion, but the damage has been done. There are so few SRO's left in the area that a group of people are living in an abandoned one on West 85th Street, once known as the Sunset.

In 1982, the Sunset was emptied by landlord Tony Postiglione, who later went to jail for coercion. He then sold the building to Alan Sackman, a landlord who has been accused of illegal eviction.

In January 1984, David Jacobs, a 33-year-old from California, found his way to the Sunset. According to Jacobs, it had been left wide open, and several people were living there. Jacobs had been about to take up residence on the street when he stumbled onto the Sunset. There was no heat, water, or electricity, but it was better than the street. The new residents got rid of the garbage that had collected in the halls. They designated a few areas as communal living space, installed propane heaters, and put plastic on the windows. Water was brought in jugs from a nearby fire hydrant. More people began to move in. By the time Sackman filed for a squatter's eviction, over twenty people were living in the Sunset.

It is the residents' belief that the landlord gave his tacit approval to their moving in because, they claim, he left the building open. While their position is legally questionable, there is no question about what their fate will be if their case is lost. Many came off the street or from Central Park—a few had been living in the band shell. If they are forced to leave, they will return to the places they came from. They will be sorry to go.

Last summer, they helped create a community garden in the abandoned lot behind the Sunset. "The dayroom overlooked the garden," says Jacobs. "It was a real pleasure to sit and look at the flowers, smoke a cigarette, have a glass of wine, and talk about life."

A month ago, the garden was uprooted by a bulldozer; visitors are no longer invited to the "dayroom"—or anywhere else in the building. Experience has made its occupants wary. A man claiming to be a *Village Voice* reporter came in to interview them at that time. He later turned up at the trial, testifying for the landlord.

"I've tried to live my life according to the teachings of the Founding Fathers," says Jacobs. "Why should this management have the right to throw *us* out onto the streets?"

ONE OF THE HARDEST QUEStions posed by gentrification is, Where do all the squeezed-out people go? A few small businesses have managed to relocate to less desirable places within the same area. Louis Jon used to be a street-level beauty parlor on West 72nd Street right off Columbus. The location was prime, and so was the rent—$1,850 per month. Then Louis Cavagnuolo, its owner, was told his new lease would have a demolition clause—meaning that if the building was sold (a distinct possibility these days), his lease would be worthless. The only alternative seemed to be leaving the West Side altogether, but Cavagnuolo was lucky enough to find a second-floor space. The rent is no bargain—$3,300—and he's lost much of his walk-in clientele, but he feels fortunate because the lease is for ten years with no demolition clause.

But for the most part, businesses do not relocate. Valerie Hill, who owned Powers Fish Market on Columbus near 86th Street, lost her store over a year ago. When Hill bought the business seven years ago, "I didn't know one fish from another," she says with a giggle. "Salmon I knew because it was red. But I learned fish fast. The hard way." Hill, 52, then was working as a nurse. For a short while, she kept up both jobs and would go straight from the hospital to the market at three in the morning to buy fish.

Her rent started at $650 and gradually rose to $1,000. Her last lease was up in October 1982. Instead of sending a renewal lease, her landlady sent an eviction notice. In order to get a new lease, Hill agreed to pay $2,500 and sell no prepared foods such as chowders (which had become the most profitable part of Hill's business). "I got to the point where I couldn't pay my bills," says Hill. "And she told me she was going to raise my rent even more the next October."

So Hill closed the store. She was out of work for seven months. She couldn't go back to nursing without first taking a refresher course and going through hospital orientation. When it was time to enroll, however, the nursing strike was on. Today, she is a nurse again, though she still thinks occasionally about owning a store. "I'm a glutton for punishment," she laughs. "But not right away. I'm $40,000 in debt, and at the rate I'm going, it's going to take me twenty years to pay it all back! I miss my store, though—it was *prestige* for me. I'd do it again. But never in New York. I couldn't even consider it."

VALERIE HILL AT LEAST had something to fall back on when her store was shut down. There are sometimes no alternatives when a person's home is lost. When lower-income housing is eliminated (SRO units in particular), one of the results is homeless people: About a third of all shelter residents once lived in SRO's. The homeless on the West Side are not imported.

Helen, who lives outside Euclid Hall, an SRO on Broadway and 86th Street, is a West Sider. For the last fifteen years, Helen had her own room in the hotel, a room for which she paid $120 a month. A 75-year-old former chambermaid, she emigrated from Romania half a century ago and is all alone—she has no friends, and her husband is dead.

About a year ago, Helen became ill.

She stopped paying her rent—she says her money ran out. She ignored the letters management sent her; her glasses were lost and legalities fluster her. On March 5, she was evicted for nonpayment. "They barged in my room and said, 'Out, out, out!'" says Helen. "They took big black plastic bags, and they throw all my stuff in. They was the bosses in my room. These men, they shouldn't touch a woman's things."

She adds wistfully, "I wasn't going to try to take anything." Helen was legally evicted; she had not paid her rent for over a year. Like many elderly people, she becomes upset when confronted with unpleasant monetary realities. Now that she is a recognizable hardship case, she's been approached by workers from Project Reachout who have tried to persuade her to come to a shelter. She is unwilling to leave with these strangers.

"We don't know each other," she explains. "I don't want to take no more chances. I live here fifteen years, I think I know them, and look what happen to me.

"My life was never meant to be walking back and forth on the streets," she says sadly. "I was always on my way, going somewhere, doing something. I was *ambitious*. Why this West Side destroy my life altogether?"

Many middle-class people have also begun to recognize the negative side of gentrification. Several years ago, Sally Goodgold, then chairman of Community Board 7, asked a block association if it would like its street, which was rather grungy, to be made into a model block. "They fought it tooth and nail," says Goodgold. "'Once you repair the street, plant trees, paint the buildings, developers will discover what a terrific block this is,' they said. 'And we will never benefit.'"

But not everyone has figured this out. Many SRO residents are delighted with the cleaned-up streets, pretty boutiques, and lower crime rate. "This area used to be a dump. I love living here now," says one young woman whose landlord is trying to evict her.

Even Joe Mauri, who is losing his home precisely because it is where it is, has kept his affection for the area. "[Denise Sobel] kept on saying in court how much she liked this neighborhood," he says. "Well, I like it, too. I like the parks, I like to go for a jog, read a newspaper under the trees. Mrs. Sobel's a mother. Why couldn't she have had some compassion? Most of my life's over. Couldn't she have let me stay in the area I care about, couldn't she have waited until I got old and died?"

For rent, cheap, no heat

A third of all renters live in substandard housing in Detroit, Baltimore, Chicago....

Barbara Koeppel

Barbara Koeppel is a contributing editor of The Progressive.

In the heart of East Baltimore's black ghetto, the brick on the six-room rowhouse is crumbling, the steps sag, and the wooden trim is rotten. But the stark signs of decay are no warning for the scene inside.

On the top floor, two rooms lie buried knee-deep in the rubble of a roof that collapsed six months earlier. The ground floor is dank and without heat. Two small rooms on the middle floor are the only usable space for the fifty-three-year-old tenant, her unemployed brother, and her eighty-six-year-old grandfather, who stares vacantly from his wheelchair. But these rooms are hardly livable; in winter, wind sweeps through the loose windows, and the only heat drifts from the open oven. "It's so cold downstairs that some water in a glass froze," the woman says.

"I cried to [the landlady] on the phone, 'Will you please make it warm for us and also move the debris from the roof?' But she only laughed and said the litter would keep in the heat."

"The housing inspector came and said, 'Why don't you move?' But where can we go? Rents are too high and we've been waiting for public housing for six years.

"I've given up," she says softly. "I don't cry any more."

Across the country, in Los Angeles, tenants in a downtown building owned by neurosurgeon Milton Avol filed suits against their landlord four times. They live without heat or hot water. Avol was found guilty and fined $250.

In subsequent trials, the fine was increased to $500, and most recently, he was ordered to do public service for the city. Repairs, as well as service, have yet to materialize.

Besides heating and plumbing problems, a quick tour of inner-city housing reveals similar problems everywhere—walls with holes large enough to put a body through, collapsing walls and floors, exposed wiring, and a nightmare of rats and roaches.

Baltimore's case is instructive. Touted nationally as a city responsive to its poor, Baltimore has a Department of Housing and Community Development (HCD) that is armed with standards, teams of inspectors, repair crews, a computerized system for recording complaints, and two state's attorneys who do nothing but handle court cases involving code violations. The city also has a Housing Court that hears an average of 1,000 cases a year and a Rent Court, which, though originally established as a tool for landlords, is now also used by tenants to establish escrow accounts and sue negligent owners.

Still, officials admit 31 per cent of Baltimore's rental housing is substandard, and much of that is downright dangerous. Baltimore is far from unique: In Chicago, city officials put the figure at 33 per cent; in Detroit, 32 per cent, and in Washington and Los Angeles, 25 per cent.

Why?

"The whole enforcement system is stacked from the start—against renters," says former Legal Aid lawyer Jean Hitchcock. Landlords, speculators, banks, city officials, laws, and tenants interact in such a way as to ensure that wherever the poor rent, slum housing is there.

From the landlords, there are the standard complaints: "We make repairs quickly and well, but irresponsible tenants destroy our properties"; or, "There is almost no profit in low-cost housing." To these, new gripes have been added: Rising property taxes and inflation have cut so deeply into the already meager profits, they say, that the whole effort is hardly worth the hassle.

While some of these grievances are valid, most ring false. To begin with, tenants are hardly responsible for the severe structural problems that plague the aging housing stock. Second, taxes in badly-blighted areas have generally remained constant for the last few years. Most important, mortgage payments—which account for about 50 per cent of the landlords' overhead costs—are set at the time the owner buys the building and are totally untouched by inflation.

Of course, landlords are in business to earn profits, and from that point of view they do have a justifiable complaint about their tenants. "Many families in this city cannot afford more than $150 a month rent," says one Baltimore landlord. (The monthly welfare payment for a family of four now stands at $326.) "How can I turn even a modest profit and provide a decent house, at today's prices, for that?" Faced with a need to turn a profit, landlords in low-income neighborhoods automatically choose to skimp on maintenance. Normal upkeep—let alone costly repairs on deteriorating structures—therefore becomes a rarity for the least well-off tenants.

One option for landlords is to let the building become uninhabitable, evict the tenants, board up the windows, pay taxes, and sell when rising property values make the price right.

But it is the awareness that their tenants have no alternative that offers landlords the greatest incentive to skimp. As slum properties disappear—as they are either torn down entirely, renovated for higher-income occupants, or abandoned—the poor have fewer and fewer units to rent.

San Francisco's record is typical: Over the last fifteen years, 5,000 new units of Federally subsidized housing were constructed. But 30,000 units were torn down where new ones were built.

Though the Federal Government defines any vacancy rate of less than 5 per cent as an emergency, rates in many American cities are far worse: 2 per cent in Baltimore, less than 1 per cent in San Francisco and Newark, and 2.6 per cent in Washington. In Los Angeles, where the rate plummets to .5 per cent in Hispanic and .4 per cent in black ghettos, more and more of the poor are living in autos and paying between $20 and $30 a month for bathroom or kitchen privileges in nearby apartments.

The waiting list for Federally subsidized private units (Section 8 housing) or public housing is long and growing. In Baltimore, 34,000 families were listed at last count, with an average wait of five to ten years, while in Chicago, 53,000 families are waiting. In Los Angeles, the list is shorter—only 18,055 families. But Los Angeles closes the list from time to time, refusing to accept new applications.

Landlords and tenants are well aware of the impasse. "Thus a bargain is struck," says Brendan Walsh, founder of Baltimore's city-wide Coalition Against Displacement. "Tenants don't complain about horrendous conditions and landlords agree not to raise rents dramatically or to evict them. But the people live in misery."

Finally, landlords risk violating the housing code and laws because the chance of being caught and penalized—to any real degree—is slim.

Conditions are grim, yet tenants rarely complain. First, there is the overriding fear of reprisals. For centuries, landlords have enjoyed the right to evict at will, and they continue to do so today. Where tenants' groups have campaigned for "just cause eviction" laws (laws that protect renters from retaliatory evictions after they've complained about conditions or taken landlords to court), the bills are usually defeated by real estate interests. In the very few locales where such laws exist, protection is limited only to a certain period—say, six months after complaints. Then, tenants are on their own.

"Even with the law, a landlord can always get rid of you," says Katherine Lewis, a former state's attorney with Baltimore's HCD. "He can say your children are too noisy, you play music too loudly, or you are late in your rent. Thus it's too great a risk to complain."

Above all, there is hopelessness. "Poor people just don't think anything will change, since they've been living in desperate conditions for so long," says Lucille Gorham, head of Baltimore Citizens for Fair Housing, an inner-city advocate group. The pattern is well known. "They talk to the landlord, and nothing happens. They call HCD, an inspector comes, and nothing happens. Even when HCD takes the case to court, nothing happens.

"From the first day they complain, it can be a year or longer until repairs are made, or never," says Gorham. "By this time, if the condition was unbearable, the tenants have moved. The new place is just as bad—but the next time repairs are needed, the people don't bother calling."

On paper, the cities' housing code enforcement systems look sound. Using a variety of sticks and carrots, Baltimore's HCD, for example, claims to woo landlords into voluntary compliance in 95 per cent of the cases—a tactic born of necessity since the Housing Court can only handle 1,000 cases a year.

Critics, however, charge the "compliance" is questionable and the time involved indefensible. Says one housing inspector, "Most repairs are of the Band-aid variety, and within a short while, we're called back for the same condition." Also, though cities may require that violations be corrected within days or weeks, cases still drag on for months and years because property owners manipulate the system.

"The landlords' goal," says Lewis, "is to put off repairs for as long as possible, because these obviously cut into profits." Landlords ignore violation notices, refuse to accept court summonses, fail to show for trials or ask for postponements, start repairs and leave the work incomplete, or threaten to evict tenants and abandon the properties altogether. Each delay means housing notices that must be reissued, meetings and trials that must be rescheduled. Further, if a summons contains a misspelled name, a wrong middle initial, or an incorrect company title, the landlord may legally refuse to accept it, and the whole process must begin afresh.

"Ironically, enforcement becomes progressively more difficult as you descend the ladder of housing quality," says David Harvey, an urban expert at Johns Hopkins University. "The result—housing code enforcement is least effective where it is most needed and most effective where it is least needed."

A *Baltimore Sun* investigation revealed the depth of the problem in that city. Of 816 random cases of outstanding code violations, "25 per cent were more than ten months old and dozens of others were two, three, and four years old."

The city's HCD is drowning under an impossible caseload. There are between 50,000 and 70,000 substandard housing units in Baltimore, most of which are rental, yet there are just sixty inspectors who must regularly inspect all multi-family dwellings, check an average of 42,000 complaints a year, and follow the cases all the way to court. Because of staff cutbacks, multi-family buildings, formerly inspected once a year, are now checked every twenty-four months, and then only common spaces such as hallways and a sample unit are examined. Moreover, single-family homes, which constitute the bulk of Baltimore's dilapidated inner-city housing, are never inspected on the inside, except in response to complaints.

In Chicago, there are 160 inspectors. But there are 208,000 substandard rental units, and in the last few years there have been numerous indictments of housing inspectors for taking bribes from landlords.

Even when inspectors turn up violations, enforcing the code is not easy. Landlords use various forms of ownership (for tax breaks and other purposes) that don't require individual names on deeds. Thus, just determining who should be served with a violation notice or court summons can require lengthy investigation. And out-of-state or out-of-country absentee owners stymie the process even further.

"Whom do you serve," asks John Huppert, head of Baltimore's inspection division, "when the owner of 100 dilapidated houses is a Panamanian corporation, managed by a German national living in Venezuela?"

Critics say the cities could, in fact, do better, even with their flawed enforcement systems. Ralph Moore, a staff member of St. Ambrose Housing, a Baltimore counseling and rehabilitation center, insists Baltimore's HCD won't push too hard or cite all the violations it could because the owners might abandon their properties. And this is the last thing city officials want, since empty buildings spell lost taxes.

In part, city laws themselves are responsible for the decay, as they blatantly favor owners over renters of property. Again Baltimore provides a typical example: "The way the law reads, the burden is on tenants to ensure their housing is maintained properly," says Hitchcock. "It's they who must call the landlords, they who must complain to HCD or Legal Aid, and they who must prove beyond a shadow of a doubt that conditions are truly bad. Everyone is responsible, except the landlord."

Moreover, the law does not require landlords to know that violations exist on new properties they buy. Thus, when a case against a landlord is in progress, even if major violations are cited, the whole process must begin again from scratch if he or she sells the building to someone else. Aware of this, landlords often transfer properties to other corporations they or their relatives own under different names.

While Baltimore tenants do have the right to withhold rent in escrow accounts until repairs are made and even to sue landlords for the months they endure unhealthy or hazardous conditions, most of the poor are unaware of these procedures. When a tenant *does* choose to use the rent escrow law, he or she must first send a letter to the landlord by certified mail, stating what the conditions are. Even this minor detail shows how lopsided the rules are, Hitchcock observes: "When landlords send eviction or rent-increase notices, they can use regular mail."

When property owners take court action, the process is simple and swift. "The landlord files for back rent and there is a hearing in Baltimore's Rent Court within fifteen to thirty days," she notes. "But it takes at least four to six months from the time a tenant files a complaint for a case to reach Housing Court—even if the condition is really dangerous. And with postponement, a case might not be heard for over a year."

The drawbacks with Housing Court, where Baltimore's HCD sends all but a handful of its cases, are glaring. The biggest obstacle is that code violations are criminal offenses; thus, the only possible penalties are fines or jail sentences. The court cannot order owners to make repairs. Likewise, in Los Angeles, guilty landlords can be jailed, but "it never happens," says Barbara Blanco, a Legal Aid staff attorney. "The judges don't believe renting out bad housing is a serious crime and won't put landlords in jail."

As for the fines, the small amounts are hardly deterrents to large landlords. In Los Angeles, even when a landlord is found guilty of serious violations, the total fine is no more than $250. The judges simply impose "summary probation" and tell offend-ers not to violate the code again. Since the city rarely follows through to see if repairs are made, nothing changes.

In the late 1940s, Senator Robert ("Mr. Republican") Taft, then leader of the conservative wing of his party, sponsored a public housing bill. It was needed, he claimed, since there was no way private enterprise could provide housing for the poor and turn a profit. Taft was wrong. Landlords do provide it and profits *are* made. But decent, safe, and sanitary housing it is not. Nor will it ever be if the present system of housing remains unchanged.

The system is stacked against America's urban poor; the pieces are so interlocked that piecemeal changes just will not do. "You would need an army of inspectors to check all the substandard properties, and that will never happen," says Moore about proposals to beef up code enforcement as a solution to the problem.

There is in fact no way that America's inner-city housing blight can be alleviated without a massive redistribution of income in society. If this should take place in the form of cash, then a whole battery of legislation and regulation must follow to keep it from being sucked back out by landlords as extra profits. Rent control laws, coupled with housing maintenance provisions, code enforcement, and the like, can then make sense. And if landlords disinvest, there must be back-up ways of converting rental housing into cooperative forms of ownership.

Otherwise, the government must pick up the tab through more public housing (boosting the current dismal 3 per cent to something closer to the British figure of 25 per cent) and subsidized rentals.

Until such change comes, slum housing will continue to scar the landscape and the lives of its occupants.

Home on the Street

*It's winter and homelessness is a hot issue again, but solutions
to the problem are as hard to find as a warm place to sleep.*

STEVEN FUSTERO

Steven Fustero is on the staff of Psychology Today.

You are awakened by the flutter of pigeons circling the statue of General McPherson and by the distant droning of an early-morning train. A cold drizzle is falling, and the steam grate on which you slept is hard against your back. Rolling to your side, you carefully eye the plastic bags and milk cartons at your feet to make sure none of your possessions were stolen during the night.

As the morning mist rises, you see a line of nine-to-fivers stepping off a city bus, some of them heading your way. As they pass, you notice their tucked newspapers and leather valises, both symbols of a world to which you no longer belong. Exposed, you feel indignantly naked, your bedroom forever trespassed by strangers. Quietly, you gather your belongings, and foresake this place of rest to begin another long day as one of the nation's more than 2,000,000 homeless persons.

Runaway children, immigrants, bag ladies, displaced families, a growing number of unemployed, alcoholics and drug abusers and the mentally ill— these are the homeless persons who live on the mean streets of our cities. Every winter, their plight is dramatized by the media, and every winter, groups investigate the causes of and possible solutions to this age-old problem.

THE PRESENCE OF NUMEROUS MENTALLY ILL PERSONS ON THE SKID ROWS OF THE UNITED STATES IS FURTHER TESTIMONY TO THE FAILURE OF THE PRIVATE AND COMMUNITY MENTAL-HEALTH SYSTEMS.

Approximately one-third to one-half of the homeless are believed to be mentally ill and on the streets primarily because of a process known as deinstitutionalization, which was initiated more than 20 years ago, when thousands of patients began to be released from state mental hospitals. At the time, the idea was a noble one. Deinstitutionalization was supposed to bring new hope, freedom and a second chance to those living behind the walls of overcrowded mental institutions. Instead of being cut off from the real world, they would be placed in the care of community mental-health centers, where they could continue their treatment in more humane social settings.

The deinstitutionalization movement was spurred on by advances in the development of psychotropic drugs (tranquilizers) that could be used to treat the more serious cases of mental illness and by landmark legal decisions. In 1971, deinstitutionalization changed from policy to law as a result of the *Wyatt v. Stickney* suit in Alabama, which guaranteed the right to treatment in the least restrictive set-ting. Other cases expanded the rights of patients to community care. The result was hasty release of patients into the care of unprepared community facilities and the development of a policy of more restrictive admissions requirements. Almost anything was seen as being more benevolent than putting people in state hospitals. And to an extent, this is still the feeling.

The restrictive admission policies and continuing funding and personnel cutbacks at state hospitals make it unlikely that many of the deinstitutionalized will be reinstitutionalized. In addition, because of these restrictive admission policies, there is a fast-growing population of young, chronically mentally ill persons who have never been admitted to an institution and are living on the streets.

The results of the massive depopulation of the state mental hospitals are only now being realized. In 1955, there were more than 550,000 patients in state institutions. Today the figure is roughly 125,000, a reduction of 75 percent. Where did these people go? Many found places for themselves in the community, but many others ended up homeless. In Illinois, for instance, more than 30,000 patients have been deinstitutionalized within the past 20 years. Many were released into the care of underfunded and understaffed community facilities that could not provide the extensive care and follow-up treatment they needed. An abyss of bureaucratic red tape, holes in the treatment system and ineffective case management left many of the mentally ill with little or no continuity of care.

Judi Berry, a senior planning specialist at the New York State Department of Social Services, offers an example of how the system can fail to meet adequately the needs of the deinstitutionalized. One of the more common types of street person likely to be found begging on the upper West Side of New York, she says, can be described as an alcoholic schizophrenic male. Early in his life, he was diagnosed as schizophrenic and sent to a state hospital, where he spent anywhere between two and 10 years before being discharged. Upon release, he was given a subway token to the welfare office, a disability check, if he was lucky and a bed in a public shelter. Eventually he dropped out of the system—perhaps he didn't even make it to his first psychiatric appointment—and began drinking on the street with other outcasts in similar predicaments. Soon he developed drinking patterns so close to those of an alcoholic that when he gets picked up off the street and taken to the emergency room of a hospital, the intern can't tell whether he is an alcoholic or a schizophrenic. A human pinball game follows, with this person being bounced back and forth between the psychiatrist and the alcoholic wards, getting no coordinated service from either. He ends up on city corners, begging.

The presence of numerous mentally ill persons on the skid rows of the United States is further testimony to the failure of the private and community mental-health systems to treat deinstitutionalized patients successfully, says Rodger Farr, head of Adult Psychiatric Services in Los Angeles. Many of these patients end up on skid row, Farr explains, because of a practice known as "bus therapy." Farr has documented cases of public institutions releasing patients and giving

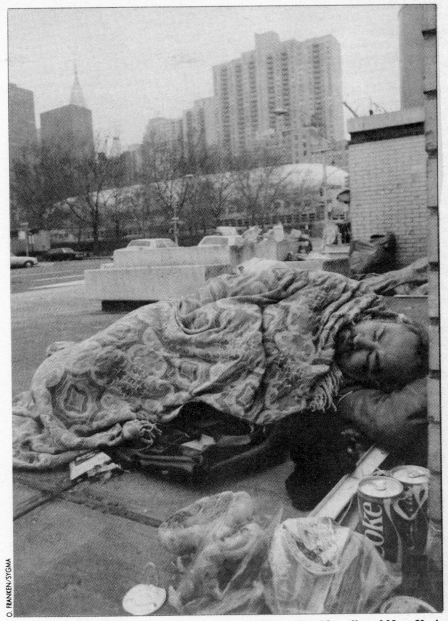

An estimated 36,000 persons make their homes on the sidewalks of New York.

them bus fare to another city as their only form of therapy. Los Angeles, with its mild climate and a social atmosphere that tolerates their presence, is a natural magnet for many of these patients. Once they get off the bus—in the worst part of town—they lack the resources and abilities necessary to locate the existing care facilities. They end up as denizens of skid row. "These people," Farr says, "have changed the homeless population of L.A.'s skid row over the past 15 years from the alcoholic derelict population we used to see to a repository of chronically and seriously mentally ill people. Because of its allure, California is becoming a

dumping ground for what is a national problem."

The population of skid row may have changed in the past 15 years, but that is a result of deinstitutionalization and economic conditions, not because alcoholism is no longer a cause of homelessness. It is estimated that alcoholics and drug abusers represent up to 40 percent of the homeless population. Because of addictions, they cannot get or keep jobs, they cannot afford adequate housing and they usually can't get organized enough to take advantage of the services that are available.

In addition to suffering the problems associated with alcohol, drug abuse and mental illness, many of the homeless suffer from a wide range of physical disabilities. A recent study by Philadelphia psychiatrist A. Anthony Arce and his colleagues found that 22 percent of those who sought refuge in the city's emergency shelters had evidence of physical illness. Their ailments ranged from frostbite to heart problems to drug withdrawal. And as if life on the street weren't hopeless enough, there is also the ever-present danger of personal violence. In Los Angeles, Farr says, "the chances of spending a four-hour period on Fifth Street, or The Nickel, without being stabbed or beaten or robbed are almost nil."

A few months ago, the president of the Philadelphia Committee for the Homeless, Robert E. Jones, cited additional causes of homelessness in an article in the *Journal of Hospital and Community Psychiatry* (Vol. 34, No. 9). He blamed deinstitutionalization as the major cause, but he also mentioned, as significant contributors, economic recession, high unemployment rates and cutbacks in federal programs. In addition to blaming cutbacks in aid to individuals, he cited the cutbacks in programs for medical care, aging studies, alcoholism and drug abuse, families and children and employment training. He also cited urban renewal for severely cutting into the number of available low-cost housing units and for increasing the number of evictions.

For years, the downtowns and inner cities of our large metropolitan areas have been the havens of the homeless. It was in these places that they found church missions, shelters, SRO's (single-room occupancy hotels) and some sense of community support. However, urban development is changing this picture. In Chicago, 5,000 low-cost rooms have been lost since 1970. In Phoenix, 27 residence hotels in the inner city have been torn down in the past 10 years. In downtown Washington, D.C., housing and services used by the homeless were lost when a new convention center and hotels were built.

The buying up and remodeling of inner-city houses and changing them from inexpensive rooming houses into single-family dwellings and expensive condos is also contributing to

*S*OLUTIONS PROBABLY WILL BE AS DIVERSE AS THE CAUSES, WITH THE PRIVATE AND PUBLIC SECTORS AS WELL AS THE LEGAL SYSTEM PLAYING IMPORTANT ROLES.

homelessness. New York, for instance, has lost thousands of such units in the past decade.

Increased unemployment has also contributed to the homeless problems in recent years. In New York, for instance, the unemployment rate among young black males is running between 40 and 50 percent. The job situation is similar and equally serious in most major cities in the Northeast.

Many of the unemployed, frustrated with the lack of job opportunities where they live, migrate from the Northeast, making the homeless problem worse for Sun-Belt cities. According to anthropologist Louisa Stark of the St. Vincent De Paul Shelter for the Homeless, in Phoenix, Arizona, 60 percent of those using the shelter have been homeless for six months or less. These include many Mexican nationals who fled a ruined economy and Native Americans who left their reservations, where unemployment approaches 50 percent.

The employment picture is bleak for the mentally ill. E. Fuller Torrey, a clinical and research psychiatrist, says in his book *Surviving Schizophrenia* that vocational rehabilitation efforts in the United States have, for the most part, excluded the mentally handicapped. The major focus of programs of the Labor and Health and Human Services departments, he says, has been the poorly educated members of society, especially minority groups. Consequently, there is no program especially designed for those schizophrenics who are able to return to the work force on at least a part-time basis. This is not the case, however, in other parts of the world. Sweden and

England have both job opportunities and housing units for the mentally ill. This includes sheltered workshops for long-term, partial employment of psychiatric patients. In the Soviet Union, employment of schizophrenics in sheltered workshops is "the rule and not the exception," Torrey says, "and such workshops work closely with psychiatric hospitals."

"Homelessness probably has been a way of life for a certain segment of the human population since before Old Testament times," says William Mayer, administrator of the Alcohol, Drug Abuse and Mental Health Administration (ADAMHA). One of the reasons that homelessness continues to be a problem is that our society has tolerated it. In a round-table discussion sponsored by ADAMHA last spring, professionals who work with the homeless cited this tolerance as an important reason that homelessness has never been resolved or effectively dealt with. And when tolerance is lacking, some localities simply try to hide or get rid of the problem.

Phoenix has been especially inventive in its dealings with the homeless. In 1982, the city decided to rid itself of the homeless population because it felt these people were scaring away tourists and potentially lucrative business prospects. So, Phoenix began a dispersal policy. The thinking went that if the city had no facilities, no social-service agencies and no private voluntary organizations, then the homeless would all leave—take the next bus to L.A. or Salt Lake City. Consequently, a lot of anti-transient, or "anti-bum," legislation was passed. For example, anyone found scavenging through a full dumpster looking for recyclable cans or food could be accused of stealing city property.

The city also managed, through zoning, to shut down most of the food programs and shelters for the homeless. Between January and June 1982, the city condemned two missions that were providing shelter and two food programs. In August of that year, the Salvation Army shut down its shelter and food program because of mounting pressure from the city. (It reopened this winter.)

You're standing in line, waiting for a lunchtime meal at Martha's Table, a soup kitchen for the needy in Wash-

Homeless "snow birds" flock to cities like Miami to escape the cold winters of the Northeast and Midwest.

ington, D.C. The line is long, extending two blocks past the storefront carry-outs and liquor stores. Your feet are aching from walking all day—the public bathrooms and soup kitchens are few and far between. Waiting with you are the city's poor, some sitting because they are tired, others pressing together in an attempt to shield each other from the rain and sleet with broken umbrellas, rags and tattered coats. You don't feel safe on this street, where drug trafficking and violence are not uncommon.

Inside, it's warm and the chicken soup is surprisingly tasty. Across from you is an elderly man who has been drinking and has problems spooning his soup. At the table to your left, an angry young woman is shouting obscenities to no one in particular. Most of the people, though, are quiet. With the soup eaten, you're pressed to go out again, where the temperature is falling fast. Bundled up, you hit the sidewalks.

Solutions to the problem of homelessness are likely to be as diverse as the causes, and in the next few years, all of us are going to become actively involved, whether we want to or not. The kind of involvement could vary anywhere from casting a vote for a specific housing initiative to fighting for or against the opening of a soup kitchen near where we live or work. For example, for years the D.C. government has been burdened with the homeless residents of surrounding counties. It is only recently that the states of Maryland and Virginia have acknowledged that they have a homeless problem. And only recently have local advocacy groups pressured those states into accountability.

Because of the efforts of these groups, county facilities for the needy are now being opened—but not without opposition. In Bethesda, Maryland, argument still rages among the local merchants and the county government, the Salvation Army and an advocacy group called Threshold AMI over a soup kitchen and a shelter for homeless men. Liz Farrell, a clinical social worker employed by Threshold AMI,

says this type of hoopla is nothing new. "Part of the problem with opening this kind of kitchen," she says, "is community acceptance. There is still the old problem of what is called the criminal element—thinking all of the homeless are criminals. Most of the people coming to eat here," she stresses, "will be families and local residents."

The merchants of Bethesda have expressed several concerns in their series of meetings with the county. Foremost on their list is the fear that the kitchen, along with its group of indigent men, will disrupt business during the day and create a safety problem at night. They are also worried that the kitchen might attract undesirables or "a bunch of drifting criminals," as one of the merchants put it. Similar fears were expressed when a soup kitchen was opened in affluent Westport, Connecticut. But Ted Hoskins, a minister of the church that helps run that kitchen, says that since the kitchen opened last year, crime in the neighborhood has gone down more than 20 percent.

In Fairfax, Virginia, proposals for

shelters or special housing for any disadvantaged group have spawned protests of all sorts from neighboring residents. Many cry that the homeless would bring property values down. Others say that they would cause an increase in crime.

Despite the negative images associated with the homeless problem, their cause is by no means hopeless. There are several aggressive groups acting and focusing on this issue. One of the most prominent is the Coalition for the Homeless, whose legal advocate Robert M. Hayes successfully sued New York City on behalf of the homeless. The suit forced city officials to provide emergency shelters for the needy and to provide dining areas, lockers, toilets and showers.

Mitch Snyder, of the Community for Creative Non-Violence (CCNV), based in Washington, D.C., is familiar with this type of litigation. His group has a suit in the Supreme Court that is set to be decided upon early this year. Two years ago, to protest President Reagan's domestic program cuts, members of CCNV, along with many of the District's homeless, set up tents in Lafayette Park, where their large number became a visible, but silent, protest in front of the White House. The group, after being ordered out of the park, claimed violation of its First Amendment rights and sued, saying protest by sleeping is permitted and protected by the Constitution. The case is to be argued this month or next.

CCNV is also trying to place an initiative on the November ballot of this year's D.C. elections. The question this initiative raises is whether shelter should be a legally guaranteed right. If it does make the November ballot, and wins, then all of the District's homeless will be required by law to have shelter. Snyder hopes this type of initiative will set a precedent for other cities, so that no citizen will ever be without shelter.

On a federal level, Rep. Stewart B. McKinney, R-Conn., has introduced legislation aimed at correcting the defects of deinstitutionalization. The McKinney bill, offered as an amendment to the Public Health Services Act, would replace the requirement for "least restrictive setting" in the standard care for a mental patient to one of "optimum therapeutic setting." The

PRIVATE AND VOLUNTARY ORGANIZATIONS HAVE BEEN SUCCESSFUL IN MOVING SOME OF THE HOMELESS OFF THE STREETS.

bill is specific in stating that a hospital or other form of institution may be optimum for some patients, while community living is most desirable for others. The bill also puts responsibility on the states for insuring that the chronically mentally ill receive appropriate care, tying that responsibility to eligibility for federal block-grant funds.

The needs of the homeless are many and varied, but they can be met in effective ways. The participants of last year's ADAMHA round-table discussions and the Coalition for the Homeless of New York agree that this could be done with an aggressive outreach program that moves the homeless off the streets into emergency facilities, from there to transitional shelter and finally into permanent housing.

Outreach involves meeting the homeless on their own ground and making initial contacts that allow for the time and care necessary to develop trusting relationships. These first meetings should offer easy access to basic needs and should be used to increase gradually the willingness of the homeless person to take advantage of food services, drop-in facilities and emergency shelter. The Midtown Outreach Project in New York City is actively involved in finding street people who frequently avoid treatment and administering on-the-spot medical and psychiatric therapy. Along with finding those who avoid the available treatment facilities, the Midtown project locates people who show signs of mental illness and those who cannot fend for themselves without intervention by psychiatric professionals. Marsha Martin, director of the project, says that they also provide information on the nearest shelters and psychiatric centers, and that they will

sometimes even take people to their appointments at clinics.

In 1981, social researchers Ellen Baxter and Kim Hopper published *Private Lives/Public Spaces*, about homeless people. The authors described the Pine Street Inn of Boston, the city's oldest and largest emergency shelter for men and women, as a model three-tier shelter program. The inn offers security, meals, counseling and nursing services to more than 500 men and women a day.

A program based on the three-tier model has been proposed recently in Phoenix by the Consortium for the Homeless, a coalition of more than 30 public and private groups.

Each tier is designed to provide a step toward complete independence and stabilization of the homeless person. Under Tier I, armories, church basements and school buildings could serve as short-term (up to 72 hours) emergency shelters where the basic needs of homeless people could be met until they are ready to move to Tier II.

Tier II is transitional shelter, where more demands are made on residents and more services provided. The goals of Tier II are independence and normalization of lifestyle. Services would include job training, the securing of entitlements (such as welfare or disability payments) and providing links with clinical services.

Unlike Tier II, which would allow people to stay up to six months, Tier III is long-term. The residences would have low-cost housing, food services and other services built in as part of the structure of everyday life.

For example, Rodger Farr's Los Angeles Skid Row Project has been successful in taking advantage of existing private community and volunteer agencies in the area and piggybacking mental-health treatment programs onto them. The Salvation Army, like other agencies in the skid row area, Farr explains, welcomes the involvement of mental health professionals to their program. "Our most valuable service as a mental health department to these nonprofit groups," he says, "is to act as consultants, educators and expediters to the various mental-health problems of their clients." The Salvation Army has an adult rehabilitation center in Los Angeles with 180 beds. They are self-supported by their satellite Salvation Army thrift stores.

The residents sleep, eat and work in a four-story building donated by a local private industry. The repair and rebuilding of various items that have been donated to the Salvation Army constitute the bulk of the rehabilitation services. This includes such things as electrical and television repair and wood refinishing. Farr believes that the combined efforts of the public and private sectors of our society are needed to alleviate this reservoir of human suffering.

The not-for-profit sponsorship and operation of such residences, like the St. Francis Friends of the Poor Residence in New York, exemplify the humanity of this approach. Similar programs in other cities have shown that private and voluntary organizations can be successful in moving some of the homeless off the streets, sometimes permanently.

Increased federal funding, however, will be necessary to further such efforts. With regard to deinstitutionalization, for instance, Charles Kiesler of Carnegie-Mellon University and his colleagues recommend in the *American Psychologist* (Vol. 38, No. 12) that federal funds be used to improve existing methods of collecting data on mental-health services. Too often, they say, there are conflicting conclusions drawn by different groups, making the quantifying of any data nearly impossible. The report also suggests that the government be more supportive in the funding of basic behavioral and biomedical research in the area of mental health, and that it assist in the development of guidelines for a minimally acceptable level of mental-health care as a national policy.

There is little doubt that the problem of homelessness will continue to exist and will be dramatized again next winter as more people freeze to death on the streets. If the problem is ever to be solved, if people are to stop living and dying on the streets, there will have to be a reduction in the public's willingness to tolerate the situation and a concerted, coordinated ef-

PSYCHOLOGY AND THE HOMELESS

The homeless, the "street people," are an acute embarrassment to us ordinary middle-class or blue-collar types. I am still uneasy as I remember how I felt about the street person, seemingly an alcoholic schizophrenic in his 30s, who was sleeping in the entryway of our upper East Side walk-up in Manhattan last winter—until the other tenants insisted on a new lock on the outside door. It is disturbing to have to step over such a stinking person, and it is more disturbing to feel utterly baffled about how to help. Back home in Santa Cruz, I see many more street people, who are attracted by a mostly benign climate and by a civic culture that is very tolerant, for the time being, but is strained almost to the breaking point by the desire of the conservative business community to roust the unwelcome visitors out of town. The situation is getting humanly intolerable.

Here is an emerging focus of public concern where psychology obviously has no ready answers, but where psychologists have a special responsibility all the same. Psychologists participated in the movement of deinstitutionalization—cleaning out the back wards of the big state "insane asylums" in favor of "community treatment"—which is one source of the present problem. (There are clearly others.) After taking part as officers of the Joint Commission on Mental Illness and Health, which laid the basis for the deinstitutionalization that followed, Nick Hobbs and I drafted the position paper on *The Community and the Community Mental Health Center*, in which we placed special emphasis on the importance of "continuity of concern" for people in trouble and on "reaching those most in need of help." In retrospect, "community treatment" of the deinstitutionalized never dealt adequately with the problems that were shoved off on it. Since the excellent report of President Carter's Commission on Mental Health came to nought in the general retrenchment of human services under President Reagan, unwanted incompetents have been nobody's problem—until by sheer numbers and intrusive visibility they are making themselves everybody's problem.

By M. Brewster Smith, a psychologist at the University of California at Santa Cruz.

fort, involving the courts, lawmakers and public and private organizations.

It's night, the northern winds are snapping hard at your fingers and toes. It's the first day of a cold wave, the kind that killed your buddy, Freddy, last year. The papers are warning pet owners to bring their animals inside. As you turn the corner of L and 15th, you are met by a screaming siren. Looking up into the windows that icily reflect *swinging yellow and green streetlights, you see the red blur of a speeding ambulance. The streets are slick and suddenly vacant. Your feet are aching. Frightened, you pick up the pace. The warm grids are far away and probably crowded, but you're sure there's a spot for you somewhere. And so you walk your endless walk, occasionally wandering into dark corners, always moving, forever homeless.*

Urban Problems

Nearly every edition of the daily paper or evening news broadcast contains some reference to a crisis in one urban community or another. It has become a topic with which most Americans are quite familiar. More often than not, the reference is to some form of social disorganization. One important characteristic of the urban community, however, is a very high degree of organization. It would be impossible for so many people to live in such a small geographical area, demanding services such as food, housing, and work without some sort of organized effort to meet those needs. Nevertheless, there is a strain on the society that attempts to meet these needs which is often reflected in the large number of problems that beset the urban community.

Suburbanization began as a movement of people from the central city to the outlying regions. However, the movement was not limited to people; commerce and industry also began to move. What started as a "bedroom community," where people went to spend the night after working in the central city, became a "full day community," where people worked, shopped, entertained, and slept. In short, the entire day was spent in the context of suburbia. Combine this fact with the growing obsolescence of the central city—where the factories and retail establishments as well as the housing are often old and in despair—and it becomes clear that the economic strength of the central city was diminished. Physical decay, high unemployment, crime, low tax rates, and burgeoning welfare rolls are the problems most often mentioned with regard to the central city, but the suburban communities have developed problems of their own. High land costs, poor transportation, and increased demands for services are just a few of the problems that the suburban communities share with the central cities.

In those nations with a strong central government, the allocation of resources can be, and often are, made in such a way as to attack the problems of both suburban and central city communities equally. In our society, however, such a strong central government does not exist. Instead, each city tends to operate independently of the other cities. Rivalries develop when cities compete with each other for the resources to solve problems. These rivalries are intensified by problems of powerlessness, poverty, favoritism, discrimination, and economic change.

Because cities tend to provide more in the way of work opportunities, education, and cultural enrichment, most urban dwellers consider themselves fortunate. While they recognize the personal alienation as well as the other problems associated with urban life, they view these inconveniences as the price to be paid for the increased opportunities presented by living in cities.

This section explores a wide variety of urban problems. It begins with an insightful article on the problem of big-city congestion and its attendant byproducts, one of which is crime. The next article explores the emergence of a new breed of criminal—the Wolf Pack—which has become a major problem in Manhattan's affluent communities. This is followed by an essay on black mayors, which explores the unique problems faced by black leaders. Catherine G. Burke's article on the myths surrounding mass transit follows. The next article analyzes the nature and impact of President Reagan's New Federalism and what it has meant and will mean to America's cities. Rashmi Mayur chronicles the major problems confronting the supercities in the Third World. The fierce battle between Mayor Harold Washington's administration and Chicago's white Establishment, and the impact of that struggle on the mayor's reform program is discussed by Sidney Lens. Jonathan Rowe presents an autobiographical piece on his experiences in VISTA. An account of a successful squatters' campaign in Philadelphia concludes this section.

Looking Ahead: Challenge Questions

How does urban growth create urban problems? Are these problems compounded by the present decentralized approach to urban problem solving?

What factors have caused big-city congestion? What are the main byproducts of overcrowding?

How do the new, big-city robbers differ from those of the past? What, if anything, can the public do to protect itself against groups such as the Wolf Packs?

Will black empowerment foster an improvement in urban life? Do black mayors face problems that do not confront their white counterparts?

Is mass transit a valid response to the problems of public

transporation? What are the main alternatives to mass transit?

What impact has President Reagan's New Federalism had on the cities? Is the American federal system resilient enough to meet the challenges of urban life?

Why are conservatives wary of such federal programs as VISTA? Do they have reason to be concerned?

Is squatting an appropriate response to the housing shortages in many American cities? Why, or why not?

What factors have contributed to the urban crisis of the Third World? What can be done, if anything, to combat these problems?

Crowds and More Crowds —No End to Urban Hassles

Formula for frustration: City and suburban residents jousting daily to win more elbowroom for commuting, living space and recreation.

The nation's cities aren't the teeming centers of population they were 50 years ago, but congestion still remains an unpleasant fact of life for millions of urban dwellers.

Even with the push to the suburbs, three quarters of the U.S. population—about 173 million people—live on just 16 percent of the country's land. In many places, the result is traffic that moves at a snail's pace, packed buses and subways, housing shortages, filthy streets and crime.

For some people, the advantages of the city, such as proximity to work and cultural attractions, outweigh the drawbacks, but many find the strain of urban life overwhelming. Samuel Leff, a New York anthropologist who has studied urban overcrowding, says that "stress builds up and leads to a lot of diseases," including high blood pressure. Older people, the very ones who are least able to escape, are particularly susceptible to these strains.

No. 1: New York City. By most accounts—and by statistical standards—the nation's king of congestion is New York City, which has an average density of 23,453 people per square mile.

In the borough of Manhattan, crosstown auto traffic creeps along at 5.2 miles an hour, even slower than the 6 miles an hour registered three years ago. Traffic moves so slowly that ambulances take twice as long to respond to an emergency as in any other city in the nation, according to officials.

For those New Yorkers who prefer public transportation to automobiles, the news is no better. Subways are twice as late and twice as likely to break down as they were in 1980.

James DeFilippis, an ABC Radio engineer in Manhattan, says he tries to "ignore the congestion, but there are times I suddenly feel closed in—on a crowded subway or in a line in a store. When tension really builds up, I go skiing, visit my parents in New Jersey or just generally get out of town."

The hassles of city life are evident in Chicago, too, where escalating transit fares are sending more people to their cars. Highways built to handle 1,500 vehicles per lane per hour are now forced to accommodate 2,000 vehicles during the morning and evening rush hours. Even traffic moving against the tide gets jammed up as thousands leave the city each morning for jobs in the suburbs.

In San Francisco, Betty and John Dearborn thought that moving into the city from the suburbs would ease the commuting grind that left them frazzled and frustrated at the end of each day. But, says Betty, "it takes us just as long to travel 3 miles as it did to travel 30. The bus seems to run on its own schedule. It's always standing room only, and if I have to work past dark, I don't feel safe waiting out on the street."

Already harrowing traffic problems in Philadelphia could get even worse when the Schuylkill Expressway—referred to facetiously by residents as the "Sure Kill Expressway"—undergoes repairs. The diversion of auto traffic, along with the possible shutdown of the city's commuter rail line because of a financial shortfall, worries officials. David Girard-diCarlo, chairman of the Southeastern Pennsylvania Transportation Authority, finds the prospect of this double blow "too nightmarish to contemplate."

A shortage of parking spaces, both downtown and in residential areas, is adding to the strains in other cities. Frederic Caponiti, public-parking administrator for the District of Columbia government, says that in some neighborhoods "residents coming home at 11 or 12 o'clock at night usually have to park six or eight blocks from their homes. And more two and three-car families make the problem worse."

In downtown Miami, about 40,000 vehicles vie daily for approximately 32,000 parking spaces, producing frantic searches for metered spaces, which are cheaper than garage parking. "You don't think people are actually arriving at work early because of a devotion to their jobs, do you?" quips Maria Barros, a Dade County official.

Miami's parking problem is expected to get worse as new office construction reduces the number of spaces by 2,000. Complains Reginald Walters, Dade County director of planning: "It's almost to the point of being a horror story." Officials hope a planned rapid-rail-transit system will eventually relieve some of the pressure.

Supermarkets, too. Big-city congestion is not limited to transportation snarls. In Jersey City, the checkout line at a 24-hour supermarket on Route 440 sometimes stretches all the way from the cash registers to the back of the store.

Jersey City parks also are filled to overflowing. Lincoln Park often has five softball games occurring simultaneously. Says Stephanie Pidhorecki, secretary for a drug company: "There are balls flying all over the place."

In New York City, too, lines and crowds for leisure activities are a way of life. Lawyer Ted Schachter says he has devised a system to reduce the wait at the movies: "You go to the early show, say at 5 o'clock, or the very late one at 11 p.m., especially on a Sunday night. No one goes to them." Schachter adds that living in New York has to be viewed "as a challenge."

On summer weekends in Chicago, lakeside beaches are often jammed to the point of being uncomfortable, and bicycle paths are more like downtown sidewalks because of all the pedestrian traffic.

Ugly byproducts. Some experts see overcrowding as contributing to other urban problems, such as crime and littering. Philadelphia Councilman Lucien Blackwell says congestion "breeds rapes, muggings and dope."

New York police officers last year issued some 500,000 summonses in connection with the symptoms of overcrowding: Uncovered garbage cans, loud music in public, sidewalk obstructions, loitering and disorderly conduct.

In Baltimore and Washington, attacking litter and dirty streets remains an uphill battle. Richard Smith, director of an antilitter program in the nation's capital, complains that many people "use shopping bags as litter containers, which get torn open by dogs or cats or fall apart when it rains."

Denise Jacobs of Detroit observes that her garbage is supposed to be picked up every week, but ends up being collected, on average, only once in three weeks.

Still another sign of congestion: Housing shortages. The apartment-vacancy rate is about 2 percent in New York City. Baltimore and Washington face a similar crunch, as does San Francisco, where one-bedroom apartments in good neighborhoods often rent for more than $600 a month.

Larry Weston, an official of the Metropolitan Washington Planning and Housing Association, says that "with fewer units, people have to crowd into the ones there are, which leads to a whole other set of sanitary, safety and social problems."

The problem is particularly acute for low-income families. Aisha Bediako, a cook with four children, squeezed her family into a two-bedroom apartment for four years. Her two sons shared one bedroom, and she shared the other with her younger daughter. Her older daughter slept on a living-room sofa. Bediako recently found a three-bedroom apartment—after two years of searching.

In Philadelphia, Councilman Blackwell says, "There are no empty houses anywhere. The few we have are unfit for habitation."

Office-space squeeze. Businesses looking for office space face a comparable squeeze in many cities. In San Francisco, the Planning and Urban Research Association says that 97 percent of the 4 million square feet of new office space scheduled for completion this year has already been leased.

A 1981 study of the Baltimore office market found that of 4 million square feet of space in the central business district, less than 20,000 was available for direct lease.

In New York, the international-real-estate consulting firm of Jones Lang Wooten predicts that there will be virtually no available office space in lower Manhattan in the next two years.

These and other problems are expected to get worse before they get better. Fewer federal dollars will be available for urban revitalization, and most cities are in a poor position to expand and refurbish public facilities on their own.

George Sternlieb, director of the Center for Urban Policy Research at Rutgers University, says that compared with suburbs "cities look like dinosaurs—slow to adapt and slow to change."

Still, for all of the stresses, many residents believe that the excitement and diversity of urban living compensate for at least some of the hassles. Stan Heuisler, a Baltimore magazine editor, says that the city "doesn't really feel crowded. Actually, I think it's quite spacious."

A Detroit woman adds: "The cost of living is lower than in the suburbs, and I'm close to everything. I have a butcher, a baker and a grocery store all within walking distance of where I live. And my two children attend the elementary school right across the street from our house."

But even the most avid urbanite finds it necessary to escape now and then. Glenn Shreffler, a Philadelphia machine operator, heads to the country for hunting. He observes: "The way to deal with congestion is not to think about it. There's nothing you can do about it, anyway, except go bananas."

America's 30 Most Densely Packed Cities . . .

Among cities with 1980 population of 100,000 or more—

	Area (sq. mi.)	People Per Square Mile
1. New York	302	23,453
2. Jersey City	13	16,934
3. Paterson, N.J.	8	16,623
4. San Francisco	46	14,633
5. Newark	24	13,662
6. Chicago	228	13,174
7. Philadelphia	136	12,413
8. Boston	47	11,928
9. Yonkers, N.Y.	18	10,675
10. Washington, D.C.	63	10,170
11. Miami	34	10,115
12. Baltimore	80	9,798
13. Berkeley, Calif.	11	9,480
14. Elizabeth, N.J.	12	9,077
15. Detroit	136	8,874
16. Bridgeport, Conn.	16	8,745
17. Buffalo	42	8,561
18. Providence	19	8,297
19. Hartford	18	7,662
20. Pittsburgh	55	7,652
21. Hialeah, Fla.	19	7,487
22. Santa Ana, Calif.	27	7,435
23. St. Louis	61	7,379
24. Cleveland	79	7,264
25. Long Beach, Calif.	50	7,256
26. Syracuse	24	7,147
27. Rochester, N.Y.	34	7,068
28. Garden Grove, Calif.	17	7,049
29. Alexandria, Va.	15	6,881
30. Minneapolis	55	6,732

. . . And the 30 Least Congested

	Area (sq. mi.)	People Per Square Mile
1. Anchorage	1,732	100
2. Chesapeake, Va.	340	336
3. Oklahoma City	604	668
4. Jacksonville, Fla.	760	712
5. Lexington-Fayette, Ky.	285	717
6. Columbus, Ga.	217	779
7. Nashville-Davidson	479	950
8. Virginia Beach	256	1,025
9. Huntsville, Ala.	114	1,256
10. Waco, Tex.	74	1,367
11. Chattanooga	124	1,370
12. Independence, Mo.	81	1,387
13. Montgomery, Ala.	128	1,389
14. Kansas City, Mo.	316	1,417
15. Bakersfield, Calif.	74	1,435
16. Kansas City, Kans.	107	1,500
17. Fort Worth	240	1,604
18. Beaumont, Tex.	73	1,618
19. Mobile	123	1,630
20. Irving, Tex.	67	1,634
21. Fremont, Calif.	78	1,683
22. Davenport, Iowa	59	1,736
23. El Paso	239	1,778
24. Amarillo	80	1,863
25. Jackson, Miss.	106	1,910
26. Lubbock	91	1,920
27. Tulsa	186	1,945
28. Indianapolis	352	1,991
29. Little Rock	79	1,996
30. Arlington, Tex.	79	2,024

USN&WR—Basic Data: U.S. Dept. of Commerce

HUNTING THE
WOLF PACKS

A new breed of robber is stalking the city. Hunting in packs, these bold, agile young men account for half the street crime in midtown. Now savvy decoy cops are fighting back.

O N THE FIRST FRIDAY IN APRIL, EIGHTEEN-YEAR-old Mark Ross of Brooklyn heard a familiar voice call up to his second-floor bedroom window. Mark peered down and saw a friend named Alan waving nine 100-dollar bills. Alan said he had "taxed" a man of $946 on 39th Street in Manhattan. Mark said he would have to reconsider a recent vow to give up crime.

"Alan say, 'Yo, Mark, these is hundreds,'" Mark remembers. "I say, 'I got to get some money, too.'"

Over the next week, Mark spent most of his time at home. He had dropped out of Lane High School two years before, and he now spoke of getting a general-education diploma. He was hoping to get a job as a security guard. In the meantime, his widowed mother gave him what little she could spare to tide him over.

"He always saying, 'I got to have this, I got to have that,'" his mother says. "I say, 'What you got to have is patience.'"

Around noon on the second Friday in April, Mark was awakened by seventeen-year-old Kelly Thompson. He and sixteen-year-old Alex Williams had also learned of Alan's $946 score. They invited Mark to join them that evening on a jaunt to Manhattan. There, they would "get paid," or commit a robbery. Alex would "fiend," or choke, somebody. Mark could help Kelly take whatever the "head," the victim, had. Then they could all "go get fresh," buy new clothes.

"Alex said, 'Yo, Ross, word up, I'm going to fiend a head,'" Mark remembers.

That afternoon, Mark lounged in bed. He flicked on the radio and the television. His girlfriend stopped by for a few hours, and she offered to return in the evening. He said he would be in Manhattan. He did not tell her or his mother what he planned to be doing.

"I don't like telling my mother I be robbing," Mark says. "She be wondering, 'Where you get this money from?' I be telling her, 'I found it.' Last time I got locked up, she got kind of brokenhearted."

As evening approached, Mark got up. He is always careful to eat before heading out, and he cooked a hamburger supper. He then donned blue pants, a blue hooded sweatshirt, and a $52 red "starter" jacket with "Alabama" stitched across the chest. He also grabbed a plaid shirt. During his apprenticeship as a robber, he had learned to pull a "throwaway" over his jacket just before a robbery and discard it as he fled.

"You just pick up the basic things," Mark says. "Crime is crime."

At 8:30 P.M., Mark headed out with Kelly and Alex. Kelly also had a plaid throwaway. Alex had a blue nylon Windbreaker his mother had given him. On the way to the subway, they picked up a teenager named Sha-Kim to serve as a lookout. He was still a juvenile under the law, and he therefore had little to fear.

"Under sixteen, the judge just look at you and send you home," Mark says. "If I had to do it again, I'd probably would have robbed, but after sixteen, I would have left it alone."

In the Grant Avenue station, they all hopped the turnstiles and boarded an A train. The three older boys remember feeling edgy. Mark reminded them of the importance of a positive attitude. Mark says, "People think they ain't going to get paid, nine out of ten times, they get knocked"—arrested.

During the ride into Manhattan, the teenagers talked about Alan's $946 score. If they, too, could "catch a stack," Alex

THE BEARDED MAN STAGGERED AND APPEARED TO BE DRUNK. "I SAID, 'YO, THAT'S *THE VIC*,'" ALEX RECALLS.

planned to buy a Guess? denim-and-leather suit. Kelly hoped to get a suede outfit and sky-blue Puma sneakers. Mark had a yen for a blue leather coat and matching suede shoes.

"Every time you go to rob, you do get that nervous feeling," Mark says. "You say, 'No,' but the money makes you say, 'Yeah.'"

AN HOUR LATER, THEY ARRIVED AT WEST 42ND Street and Eighth Avenue. They strolled along "the Deuce" and ran into a thief known as Bugout. They declined an invitation to go with him to 125th Street and "get busy," rob people. They paused to flirt with two girls and then drifted east. They grew quiet as they searched for a "poppy love," a middle-aged or elderly gentleman likely to have cash.

"That's all you do is go hunting, go hunting for a vic," Mark says.

Over the next three hours, they ranged as far east as York Avenue and as far north as the Seventies. Mark had studied this hunting ground, and he says, "You know between the buildings they have those little fences you can still climb over. You go down the alley and into the next block." They passed several groups of white teenagers.

"White kids wear faded jeans, old sneakers, stuff they had *last year*, and they be having money," Mark says.

On one of the avenues, they spotted a lone poppy love. They trailed him downtown, hoping he would turn onto a side street. Alex reminded the others of Bernhard Goetz and instructed them to search the man for a weapon as well as cash. Alex says, "We got these Bernie G. dudes around. I kept telling them, 'Since I'm doing the fiending, make sure you give him a pat down, because we be running with our backs to him.'"

When the man entered a deli, Mark pulled up the hood of his sweatshirt and followed. Mark bought a bag of pretzels and studied the man's pocket for the outline of folded bills. While there were no "pocket prints," the man was clearly well heeled.

"If he'd gone on the right block, I'd have been for it," Mark says.

After six blocks, the man was still on the avenue. The teenagers lost interest and cut across 42nd Street to Times Square. They stopped at Godfather's Pizza on Broadway and bought three slices. This left them with combined assets of 25 cents. Kelly remembers feeling that there was little chance they would go home with anything more than that, much less a score like Alan's $946.

"I felt like we were giving up," Kelly says.

Back out on Broadway, they ambled uptown. They paused for traffic at West 47th Street and bobbed their heads to rap music blasting from a portable cassette player. The player belonged to a man who stood just around the corner, beside a darkened Florsheim shoe store. The man sported a red St. John's jacket. On his head he wore a black do-rag and a red baseball cap turned sideways.

"It looked like an ordinary dude," Mark says.

As they crossed the street, Alex spotted a bearded man wearing a double-breasted blazer and a striped tie. Alex alerted the others, and they watched the man head from a subway stairway to a darkened alcove on West 47th Street. They noted that the man staggered slightly.

"Friday night, just got paid, just coming out of the bar, he looked like the type," Alex remembers. "I said, 'Yo, that look like a drunk head.'"

In an instant, they had on their throwaways. Sha-Kim leaned against a trash bin on the corner and began looking out for "jakes," police. Alex approached the alcove alone to "size" the prey. He was to check for pocket prints and jewelry. He was also to look for signs of drunkenness, fear, or weakness.

"Nobody going to just rush up on you and rob you," Alex says. "They going to watch you, see what moves you make, see how big your pockets, see if you be that easy to rob."

The bearded man was leaning against the far wall of the alcove, coughing. Alex spoke in a soft voice. He remembers, "I said, 'Mister, are you all right? Do you need a tissue?' He said he was all right, he just had a few too many beers." Alex pretended to urinate and then rejoined the others.

"I said, 'Yo, that's *the vic*,'" Alex says.

Kelly went with Alex to see for himself. Kelly pretended to urinate while Alex again asked the bearded man if he was all right. Mark stayed on the corner across from Sha-Kim. He remembers having a vague, inexplicable sense that something was wrong.

"It felt funny," Mark says. "I was kind of leery."

A uniformed cop came up Broadway, and Sha-Kim waved his hands. Alex and Kelly scurried back to the corner. They watched the bearded man step onto the sidewalk and then lean back into the shadows. Mark expressed his misgivings. Alex and Kelly said that the target was wearing gold chains.

"They were saying, 'He got on *much* jewelry,'" Mark remembers.

A young woman with red hair brushed by Sha-Kim and headed down the block past the alcove. On the opposite corner, the man in the black do-rag was still rocking out with his cassette player. Kelly and Alex suggested that the man was watching them too closely.

"I said, 'He ain't no jake,'" Mark says. "I thought he was one of those niggers that was going to rob. I thought he was trying to get money, too."

The man with the black do-rag almost certainly knew what was going on, and that put Mark on a kind of stage. Mark remembers feeling that he did not want to "front," or back down, before an audience. He decided to go ahead despite his lingering doubts.

"What did it was the home boy blazing with the box," Mark says.

Eight feet from the alcove, Mark crouched as if to tie his shoe. He kept an eye on Sha-Kim's lookout post as Kelly slipped behind the target. Alex stepped up to throw the "yoke," or choke hold. His feet inched back and forth as he summoned his nerve. He insists that he did not speak. The bearded man says that Alex uttered a few final words and that the soft voice was tight with urgency.

"He said, 'Yo, man, what you got?'" the man says. "Then he said, 'Give it up.'"

Suddenly, the bearded man whirled and knocked Alex over with his forearm. The man pinned Alex facedown and pressed

A ROBBER WHO MAKES A BIG SCORE BECOMES WHAT ALEX CALLS A "PROJECT CELEBRITY."

a gun barrel against the back of his head. The silver flash of a badge joined the glitter of the gold chains.

"Police," said Officer Jeff Aiello.

Kelly burst from the alcove and bolted toward Eighth Avenue. As he cut across the street, a young woman with red hair stepped from behind a charter bus. In her right hand, she held a revolver.

"Police," said Officer Elizabeth Sheridan.

Mark turned toward Broadway. He saw Sha-Kim disappear uptown, and he decided to head down to the Deuce and the sanctuary of the subway. As he neared the corner, he saw the man with the black do-rag extend his right arm.

"Police," said Officer Billy Carter. "Freeze."

After he had obeyed the order, Mark realized that Carter's hand was empty. Carter had not wanted to panic some passing cop with the sight of a "home boy" waving a revolver, and he was imitating a gun the way a child would. Mark had been stopped by an index finger.

"Everything was happening *too* fast," Mark says.

Two other officers had been hiding in the Gaiety Delicatessen, and they helped lead Mark and Kelly over to the alcove. The two teenagers lay with Alex on the dank pavement and listened to the cops of the new Transit Police Decoy Squad congratulate one another.

"Still want me to give it up?" Aiello asked.

"No, sir," Alex said.

THE NEW BREED

THERE IS A NEW BREED OF ROBBER IN THE CITY. Wolf packs of young men rampage after a Diana Ross concert. Bands of robbers up to 100 strong "bum rush" volunteers at a March of Dimes walkathon. Early one morning, a hunting party hits a subway train and rips through one car after another. One afternoon, a small band mauls a pair of actors on their way to prepare for the opening of an Off Broadway show. One evening, a mob of 35 strikes a single elderly man in Times Square. The man finds himself in a new urban nightmare where there are no faces, only a blur of snatching hands and punching fists and kicking feet.

"They see a poppy love going by and they rush up on him and you can't see him no more," Mark Ross says. "They go in pockets, and everybody be gone. And the man, he don't know what hit him. He just standing there, saying, 'What? What?'"

Over half the street crime in Manhattan is now committed by jobless young men who journey in from Brooklyn and the Bronx to prowl the city's wealthier stretches. The new robber is not the lone, tattered junkie of the past. He is a fit young man who shuns narcotics and who stalks his victims with all the skill and deliberation of a woodsman hunting wild game. For him, crime is a kind of sport that has been franchised to the poor.

"Criminals aren't bad people, you know," Alex says.

Those who rob on a professional level take an athlete's care in looking sharp and staying fit. Mark does 150 push-ups at a time, and he says, "I hit hard for my size." He tells of a dedicated thug known as Drac who does not drink or smoke.

"You know how fast Drac run?" Mark says.

Often, the robbers leave their neighborhoods in "posses," or

groups. Mark says, "I just get a whole lot of people from my way and say, 'Let's go to the city and get paid.'" The drill calls for them to decide before they set out who will incapacitate the victim. Some use fists or a weapon. Many prefer to fiend. The secret here is stealth.

"Anybody can fiend a head," Mark says. "It's not how fast you is. It's how you sneak up. Once you got them, it's over."

After a small band hits, the robbers are supposed to divide the money evenly. Sometimes a pocket man "gets fast," or secretly withholds a little for himself. Mark says, "You be robbing with your friends, and you see a whole envelope of money, you might take one bill. There's no honor among thieves."

When the posse grows to more than four or five, the individual thief keeps whatever he can snare. These bigger groups often assemble in Times Square, and Mark has seen his colleague Drac recruit gangs there up to 35 strong. Mark says, "Everybody know each other. You see somebody, and you say, 'What's up? You all getting busy on dollars? Let's take it up Broadway.'"

As the weather turns warm and the citizens stroll without coats, the robbers declare "diamond season." Wolf packs rampage through the theater crowds, snatching at exposed necks. Mark says, "Get whatever comes along. See diamonds, get it. See money, get it. See jewelry, get it."

A robber who returns home with a big score becomes what Alex calls "a project celebrity." Almost all the money usually goes toward getting fresh. Many robbers seem to live for the moment they first step out wearing a Guess? suit or flashing a pair of monogrammed gold teeth.

"When you get extra, extra, out-of-the-ordinary fresh, people be watching you," Mark says.

"You feel like above the rest, and you get girls," Kelly says.

"You might not have a penny in your pockets, but the clothes be nice," Alex says.

To snare these project celebrities, Transit Police Chief James Meehan this March assembled 24 "subway stars." These specially trained officers usually work in teams of four and set out a decoy posing as an executive or a student or some other often victimized type. The disguises of the backup cops range from a rabbi to a pizza man to a home boy to a blind man with a Braille edition of *Better Homes & Gardens*.

In the first two weeks of operation, the Decoy Squad made 39 arrests. These included a nine-year-old pickpocket, a dwarf stickup man, and a robber who worked with an attack dog. When they grabbed Mark Ross and his friends, the cops knew they had a good act. Mark still seemed to be in shock when he spoke to the other prisoners at Manhattan Central Booking.

"Oh, man, of all the people I could have robbed," Mark said.

PLAYING THE VIC

THE FIRST DAY OF APRIL MARKED MONDAY OF Holy Week, April Fools' Day, and the Decoy Squad's first tour in the field. In a back room at the unit's Brooklyn headquarters, Sergeant Jack Maple set out 72 pieces of fake gold jewelry, twelve watches, nine cameras, six radio-cassette players, fifteen wallets, ten handbags, six briefcases, and three pairs of sunglasses. Police Officer Carol Sciannameo picked three chains and a fake Rolex watch. Police Officer Elizabeth Sheridan took several chains, a fake Seiko watch, a wallet, and a handbag.

"How about a camera?" Lieutenant Richard Gollinge said.

By 2 P.M., the rest of the cops had reported. With a black do-rag, Officer Julie Eubanks was very much a man of the streets. Officer Richie Doran came in a black leather jacket and a brown cap that his mother wears while working at a Sizzler Steak House. Handcuffs dangled from his belt loops. Officer Ronnie Pellechia wore jeans and a blue hooded sweatshirt and looked remarkably like a plainclothes cop.

"I didn't know what everybody else would be wearing," Pellechia said.

After roll call, the cops deployed in groups of three and four. Pellechia, Eubanks, Doran, and Sheridan strolled to the LL line. Sheridan had never carried a purse before, and she clutched her black leather bag as if it were a football. Maple came up and slipped the strap over her shoulder.

"It's done like this," Maple said.

When the train rolled in, the four cops stopped talking and became strangers. Sheridan was the decoy, and she sat by a door with her "gold" and an open pocketbook. The others scattered through the car and kept a furtive watch. At East New York, they followed Sheridan off the train and toward the A line. The only person who accosted her was a middle-aged woman.

"Excuse me, but your bag is open," the woman said.

"Oh, uh, thanks," Sheridan said.

The group trolled back and forth between East New York and Hoyt Street. Sheridan displayed her jewelry and read Nevil Shute's *On the Beach* and struggled not to laugh when she glanced at Doran. A teenager wearing Cazal glasses studied Sheridan and turned to a friend.

"The bitch might not have but $100," the teenager said.

In the late afternoon, the group headed into Manhattan to "play" the rush hour. They got off the A train at West 42nd Street, and Eubanks assumed the lead. Sheridan trailed him toward Times Square and past one shady-looking character after another. The two remaining cops drifted behind as backups.

At the Times Square station, Eubanks took Sheridan by a change booth. She paused to buy a token, and a teenager in a gray leather jacket bumped her from the front. She felt a slight, fishing-line sort of tug on the shoulder strap of her bag. She glanced to the right and saw a teenager in a brown leather jacket remove her wallet. The two teenagers then ambled toward the stairs.

"Julie," Sheridan said.

A street person shouted, "Hey, blood," to warn the teenagers as Eubanks came up behind them. Eubanks is a hefty six foot four, and he swept the teenagers up in his arms before they could react. As he pushed them against a wall, the one in the brown leather jacket dropped the wallet.

"What's the matter?" the teenager said.

A T 4:50 P.M., DORAN AND PELLECHIA LED THE Decoy Squad's first two catches into the police room at the West 42nd Street subway station. The teenager in the gray jacket identified himself as Ernest Smith, sixteen, of Bedford-Stuyvesant. He had $3.05 in his pants pocket. The teenager in the brown jacket said he was He-Allah Broadhead, also sixteen, of Coney Island. He had no money.

"I'll be seventeen soon," He-Allah said.

"When was the last time you were arrested?" Maple asked.

"Never."

"*Never?*"

"I was in family court."

"For what?"

"Running wild."

"What else did they call it?"

"Robbery."

"What else?"

"Burglary. Assault."

"How about a chain snatch?"

"Yeah, once. But I didn't do it."

In a back room, Sheridan gave a good performance as a shaken complainant and identified He-Allah as the one who had lifted her wallet. He-Allah said, "Come on, Miss. What did I do to deserve this kind of treatment?" Doran searched He-Allah's leather jacket and found a Macy's price tag. The jacket had been marked down from $235 to $100.

"Since you stole this on sale, it's only a misdemeanor," Maple said. "At the regular price, it'd be a felony."

"I bought that jacket hot, but it's my jacket," He-Allah said.

When Doran went off to call Macy's, He-Allah said that the jacket actually belonged to his sister. He insisted that he did not know Ernest and that he had just come off a train from Brooklyn when he was arrested. Eubanks asked why he had stepped into the token line.

"I got on line because I'm mentally disturbed and I got no other place to go," He-Allah said.

A few minutes later, the results of a computer check on He-Allah came in. Maple read aloud each of the ten arrests, including two for robbery. He-Allah sat silently on a wood bench and gazed at the list. Then he took a deep breath.

"I didn't do nothing," He-Allah said. "I didn't put my hand in no bag. I gave up my life of crime."

Maple put his arm around He-Allah.

"I don't think you're a bad guy," Maple said.

"I'm not," He-Allah said. "I'm nice."

Maple smiled.

"I want you to look me straight in the eye and say 'I didn't do nothing' ten times," Maple said.

He-Allah smiled.

"See," Maple said. "You're laughing already."

"I'll pay whatever penalty," He-Allah said. "Do what you want with me."

With a shrug, He-Allah rose to pose for a mug shot. He turned his tweed cap backward, cocked his chin, and puffed out his chest. The cops remarked on his muscles, and He-Allah said that he hoped to box in the 1988 Olympics. Pellechia predicted that he was more likely to become a "maytag," a servant to other prisoners in jail.

"I hit too hard to be a maytag," He-Allah said. "I'm going to be top dog."

"What grade are you in?" Maple asked.

"Ninth."

"Who's your homeroom teacher?"

"Homeroom teacher?"

"I thought you said you were in the ninth grade."

"I am, but I been out of school for years."

When Ernest was questioned, he also insisted that he and He-Allah did not know each other. The cops said they had determined that the address he had given them was a burned-out building and that he actually lived in the same housing project as He-Allah. Ernest's only visible reaction was to flick his cigarette.

"I just want to go home," Ernest said.

As Ernest rejoined He-Allah in the lockup, Doran turned on his cassette player. The teenagers started dancing. Their handcuffs jiggling, they told Doran that they were accomplished rap singers and that they often performed together.

"I never did a crime, I never took a dime," He-Allah chanted.

SERGEANT MAPLE WARNED THE SQUAD OF DECOY COPS NOT TO MAKE THE BAIT TOO "SWEET."

The following day, the teams reported a series of near-hits. Maple suggested that the cops might be looking around too much. He told them to watch their body language and to make sure the bait was not too "sweet." He reminded them that criminals seem to have some instinctive sense that grows more acute in that final instant.

"There's something the victim does or doesn't do that sets them off," Maple said. "You have to *be* a victim. You have to believe the role you play. If you believe it, everybody's going to believe it."

As the squad began the third tour, Sheridan embellished her student look by carrying a literary text and a philosophy book. She said, "I had a couple of Supreme Court books, but I figured I better not bring those." Officer Vertel Martin went as a tourist with a camera and a purse. Officer Wayne Richardson was a denim-clad punk, complete with blaring box and a Lipton-tea "joint" behind his ear. Officer Jerry Lyons's outfit featured a tie, a tweed jacket, wire-rimmed glasses, and a yarmulke.

"If we lock anybody up, I'll go over and ask if they need a good lawyer," Lyons said.

With Richardson and Lyons as backup, Martin hopped the A train to Times Square. As Martin emerged from a stairway, a youngster in a gray leather hat saw that the flap of her purse was open. The youngster bounced on the toes of his sneakers and flapped his arms. He called in a school-yard voice to a crew of older boys.

"Look at the lady," the youngster said.

A teenager in a gray sweatshirt slipped in front of Martin to slow her down. The youngster scurried up from behind and reached out with his right hand. There was the slap of shoes on concrete as Richardson and Lyons hurried to close in.

The bobbing purse was moving too fast for a good "dip," and the youngster peeled away. The backup cops slowed to a stroll and watched the youngster pull the teenager in the gray sweatshirt aside by the sleeve. The cops again heard the school-yard voice as the youngster cocked his head back and scolded a boy who was two feet taller and maybe four years older than himself.

"You don't know *how* to block," the youngster said.

The youngster then ran ahead to a soda stand and asked a crowd of kids if one of them was interested in hitting a purse. A boy in a Yankee jacket said he was "down." While the youngster performed a truly professional block, the boy in the Yankee jacket pulled a wallet from Martin's bag.

A moment later, the two lay handcuffed on the sidewalk. The youngster's gray leather cap ended up three feet from his head, and he said, "My hat, my hat," until one of the cops picked it up. The teenager in the gray sweatshirt ran up to watch, and he was also arrested. They were all loaded into a squad car.

"Sir, am I going to jail?" the boy in the Yankee jacket asked.

"No," Richardson said. "We're joking."

At the Columbus Circle station house, the boy in the Yankee jacket identified himself as Dinell Stanberry, seventeen, of the Bronx. Dinell waived his right to remain silent and said, "Soon as I lifted [the wallet] up, somebody shoved me to the floor." When Dinell agreed to make a written statement, Lyons asked him to note that an officer had informed him of his rights.

"How do you spell 'officer'?" Dinell asked.

After Dinell signed the confession, Martin asked him if pocketbooks were his specialty. Dinell said that he considered himself a good pickpocket, adding, "I'm always saying, 'I'll show you how to jostle.'" Martin suggested that his present predicament

indicated that he was not exactly a virtuoso.

"If you wouldn't have caught me, then this wouldn't have happened," Dinell said.

As Dinell was led into the lockup, he eyed the box that was part of Richardson's disguise. Dinell said, "That my friend radio. He told me to hold it." Dinell then turned his attention to a prisoner with a shaved head, tattoos, earrings, and a black leather jacket.

"I be here long, you'll be bleedin'," Dinell said.

The teenager in the gray sweatshirt was Wade Jolly, sixteen, of the Bronx. He initially insisted that he had been shopping for a new jacket when he was arrested. Richardson asked how much money he had. Wade said, "I was just pricing. Window-shopping." Richardson said the cops had heard Wade being dressed down. Wade lowered his eyes.

"All right," Wade said. "I was blocking. But when they took it, I wasn't even there."

"Listen," Richardson said, "I want you to write a story for me."

"When Wade completed a written statement, Richardson complimented him on his prose style. Wade said that he was getting 80s at Taft High and that he wanted to be either a fireman or an engineer when he got older. Richardson said Wade could make a phone call. Wade dialed his aunt's number.

"Hi, it's . . .," Wade said.

Wade put down the receiver. "She said she's asleep," Wade said.

"Ask her to wake up," Richardson said.

Wade redialed and spoke in a small, polite voice. "Would you wake up for a minute, please?" Wade asked.

Wade turned to Richardson.

"She hung up," Wade said.

The youngster who had first spotted the purse was named Eddie. He sat hand-cuffed to a wood bench in the juvenile room. He donned mirrored sunglasses and tilted the brim of his gray leather cap to just the right angle. His mouth stretched into a yawn as he faced the woman he had tried to rob.

"You got identification, young man?" Martin asked.

"No," Eddie said.

"How old are you?"

"Twelve."

No emotion showed on Eddie's face until Richardson came in with sausage pizza. Richardson held out half a slice, and Eddie said, "Pay for it?" Richardson shook his head. Eddie chewed and waited for his uncle to claim him. When his uncle arrived, he rapped Eddie's head with his knuckles.

"You're not supposed to be here," the uncle said.

"They said I was pickpocketing a lady," Eddie said.

The uncle strode out of the station house. Eddie paused at the door.

"Thanks for the pizza," Eddie said. "I really appreciate it."

THE DWARF AND LITTLE C

On Holy Thursday, none of the groups were hit. On Good Friday, Sheridan and Doran teamed up with Lyons, and they were all heartened to find West 34th Street swarming with thieves. A man in a vest began stalking Sheridan at the top of a Sixth Avenue stairway. As she paused and pretended to watch a sidewalk magician squeeze a quarter into a Heineken bottle, the man delicately removed the wallet from her purse. Lyons was carrying a New York *Times,* and he held the paper out to the man.

"MANHATTAN MAKE IT AND BROOKLYN TAKE IT," EXPLAINED FIFTEEN-YEAR-OLD DERRIAH.

I DO SO DECLARE THAT I WAS UP SET ABOUT HAVING TO GO TO A REABELATION HOME ON THURSDAY SO I HAD SOME MONEY AND I WENT DOWN-TOWN TO BY SO... I got HIGH CN THE TRAIN

AT THIS TIME I WOULD LIKE TO CLEAR THE RECORD ABOUT THE ROBBERIES IN STATEN ISLAND.
① JERSEY AND RICHMOND - WHITE MAN - 7/83 - 1,120 dollars. PRINCE, BASH
② WESTERVELT AND RICHMOND - WHITE LADY - 7/83 - 200 dollars
③ YORK AND RICHMOND - WHITE MAN - 7/83 - 363.35 dollars.
④ YORK AND RICHMOND - ... TE MAN - 7/83 - 2 00 dollars + 2 PACKS of cig

He told ME TO take her walet or He was going to beat ME up

"I confess": *Statements from suspects caught by the Decoy Squad.*

"Could you hold this for me, please?" Lyons said.

By reflex, the man reached for the paper. He had a confused look on his face until Lyons and Doran grabbed him. His expression was one of pure fury as he was led in handcuffs down to the subway. When Lyons picked up an emergency phone to summon a radio car, the man tried to depress the disconnect lever with his chin.

"That's not really necessary," the man said.

At the Columbus Circle station house, the man was charged with grand larceny. He identified himself as Anthony Freeman, eighteen, of Brooklyn. In his wallet, he had a pack of pay stubs showing that he earned $150 a week at the Billanti Jewelry Casting Company. He also had a summons for jumping a turnstile and an invitation to a birthday party that night at the Night Owl in Brooklyn. He had no money.

During questioning, Anthony said that he had the day off from work because it was Good Friday. He insisted he had only been window-shopping on 34th Street. Maple produced a copy of Anthony's adult criminal history and noted arrests for burglary and robbery with a gun. Maple asked about his youth record, and Anthony said it was clean.

"I ain't no hoodlum in the street," Anthony said. "I can't afford to go to jail. I got too much going for me. Too many people love me."

After Doran solemnly announced that the victim was the mayor's niece, Anthony consented to make a statement. In a neat script, he wrote, "In this case it was a matter of cowensadence. I am a very nice person and will never hurt anybody. Not even there feelings. . . . It was just something that happened I don't know what came over me. I just in a bad perciou-

sian [position] right now but I am not a hood. I am a honest decent American mostly a loiner [loner]. And a family guy I don't hang out a lot. Thank you. I'm sorry."

With three hours of the tour left, Sheridan's group bought a white vinyl wallet at a Woolworth's and returned to West 34th Street. By the stairway where Anthony Freeman had just been snared, Sheridan was jostled by a dwarf and a young man in a Yankee jacket. A child in a red Izod jacket went up on his toes and slipped a tiny hand into her purse. The tiny hand came away with the white vinyl wallet, and the child took off. Lyons chased him into the subway and past a newsstand.

"Police," Lyons said.

The child froze and let the wallet fall from under his jacket. Lyons took him in handcuffs to join his two cohorts. The dwarf seemed distressed. The young man in the Yankee jacket was crying. The child grinned and began chewing a huge wad of gum he had tucked in his cheek.

"How old are you?" Lyons asked.

"Nine," the child said.

At the station house, the tearful young man in the Yankee jacket was identified as Derrick Hodges, sixteen, of Brooklyn. He said that he had seen "Shorty" hit Sheridan's bag. Lyons asked if he meant the dwarf or the nine-year-old.

"I call them both Shorty, because they both shorter than me," Hodges said.

"What were you doing on 34th Street?" Lyons asked.

"Nothing to do in Brooklyn."

"How much money do you have?"

"I was window-shopping."

After he made a written statement, Hodges called his

mother. He said, "Mom, I'm going to court tomorrow. They're going to charge me with jostling. You know little Shorty? He went in a lady's pocketbook. They're trying to hold me for the same thing. Yo, I got to hang up. I'll call you tomorrow. Bye."

The nine-year-old sat handcuffed to the bench in the juvenile room. He swung his legs, passed around an economy-size pack of Juicy Fruit gum, and watched Sheridan fill out his arrest form. He identified himself as C-Allah, known on "Trey-Four" Street as Little C.

"How tall are you?" Sheridan asked.

"Four foot five," C-Allah said.

"How much do you weigh?"

"Seventy pounds."

"What grade are you in?"

"Sixth. I mean fourth."

C-Allah extended his fingers and slipped his hand out of the handcuffs.

"Hey, look at this," he said.

Under questioning, C-Allah said that a husky adult had forced him to "throw the dip." Sheridan asked him to make a written statement. In a child's large, deliberate letters, he wrote, "He told me to take her walet or he was going to beat me up. He's stout got big lips an big eyes. Brown Lees. Blue and White New Balance. Blue IZOD shirt."

The dwarf was named Robert, and he was fourteen. A computer check showed that he had recently been arrested for armed robbery. Maple asked him if he had used a gun. Robert pointed to the biggest of five juveniles who had just been arrested for attempting to rob Sciannameo.

"No, he had   Robert said.

The big juvenile was named Derriah. He said that he had a prior arrest for attempted murder. He also announced that he was the father of two children.

"How old are they?" Richardson asked.

"Three and two," Derriah answered.

"How old are you?"

"Fifteen."

At a nearby desk, Sheridan was on the telephone to Derriah's mother. Sheridan hung up and said, "She says his being arrested is a blessing. She doesn't want him, and she doesn't like him." Derriah said, "If my mother slap me, I hit her back." The rest of Derriah's posse laughed. A fourteen-year-old named Thomas said, "Me too. Someday, I'm going to have to snuff her."

When the juveniles asked for water, the cops filled Styrofoam cups. The juveniles asked for more, and each made fingernail marks in the Styrofoam so he would not end up drinking from somebody else's cup. Thomas ran his tongue over his gold incisors. In keeping with the latest fashion, three of the juveniles had a pair of eighteen-karat teeth bearing their initials. C-Allah said he was going to outdo them all.

"I'm going to get my whole name straight across," C-Allah said.

When Officer Joe Quirke walked into the room, both C-Allah and Robert offered him a stick of gum. Quirke asked if they all had clothes for Easter, and Robert said, "Sneakers and everything. . . . I always got fresh clothes. They say, 'Where did you get that?' I say, 'I get it my own way.' If we be out for Easter, I be looking fly." Quirke further inquired if they had any goals.

"Yeah, I got that," Robert said. "Jewelry."

"Not *gold*," Quirke said. "*Goals*."

"I just want to be rich," Robert said.

Derriah expressed the same ambition and repeated a saying now current among his home borough's robbers.

"Manhattan make it and Brooklyn take it," Derriah said.

A woman appeared and identified herself with a welfare card as C-Allah's aunt. Sheridan handed her a family-court appearance ticket and explained the circumstances of the arrest. The aunt nodded and gave C-Allah a long look. He chewed on his Juicy Fruit and met her weary gaze with bright, unblinking eyes.

"Get rid of that gum," the aunt said.

The five juveniles who were not claimed by their families included Robert, Thomas, and Derriah. Maple faced them in different directions and ran handcuffs through belt loops and created a sort of huge pretzel. He then led them out to the street and held open the back door of an unmarked car.

"All right, guys, hop in," Maple said.

With grunts and curses and finally giggles, the juveniles somehow squeezed into the rear seat. Thomas said, "Yo, put on Kiss-F.M. 98." Music mixed with the calls on the police radio as the car cut through Central Park and across the Upper East Side.

When the car entered the South Bronx, voices from the back directed Maple to a white-brick complex. This was the Spofford Detention Center, known on the street as Great Adventure. Derriah reminded Maple that new prisoners should be delivered at the side entrance.

"I hope my cousin don't sleep in my bed while I'm gone," Derriah said.

The juveniles spilled out of the car and fell silent as they entered the yard. The only sound was the hum of the high-intensity lights that glinted off the razor wire. A guard in the reception area asked them for their dates of birth and if they were injured. He then directed them to go into a cubicle and strip. One of them apparently had not been able to afford a pair of shoes that fit.

"You won't believe this," the guard said. "Six pairs of socks on each leg."

The guard pulled on clear plastic gloves and conducted a thorough search. Name-brand sneakers and leather jackets and designer jeans were replaced by laceless discount-store sneakers and worn blue bathrobes. A heavyset woman called the juveniles over to give their particulars, and Robert had to hike up the hem of his robe so he would not trip. Derriah approached with a bowed head.

"Welcome home," the woman said.

THE NIGHT SHIFT

DURING THE SECOND WEEK OF OPERATIONS, Maple's team went after the predators who prowl at night. These robbers are more likely to hit men, and male officers became the decoys. They were hit three times in the first two nights. Those arrested included Carlos Miranda, nineteen, of the Bronx. He had last been apprehended in February, for robbery and assault with a gun.

"I was up set about having to go to reabelation home on Thursday so I had some money and I went downtown to buy some dust," Carlos's statement read. "I got high on the train and I was bugging out. . . . I rip the chain from his neck because I was having a flashback. I am sorry for what I did."

The next night, Officer Jeff Aiello's group was back on the I.R.T. Pellechia was the decoy, and he sat in the last car with Officer Billy Carter. Aiello and Sciannameo kept watch from the next car. They all noticed a young man in red nylon pants who sat on Pellechia's right.

"As soon as I saw him, I said, 'He's going to go for it,'" Pellechia recalls.

As the train rolled downtown from West 135th Street, a second young man came into the car. Pellechia closed his eyes and pretended to nod off. He could hear the one in nylon pants and the new arrival start talking in excited voices.

Across from Pellechia, Carter laughed and smoked a Lipton-tea joint. Pellechia smelled the smoke and took it for real marijuana. He heard the nylon pants swish toward him. Two pairs of hands felt his pockets. Fingers jiggled his wrist.

"I felt them grab my hand, and I said, 'This is it,'" Pellechia

WHILE OFFICER RICHARDSON PRETENDED TO SLEEP, A DOBERMAN SNIFFED AT HIS FACE.

remembers. "I felt my heart going. I was saying, 'It's going to go down. It's going to go down.' Then it didn't happen."

At Times Square, Pellechia heard a nightstick rattling on a belt and knew that a uniformed cop had boarded the train. Carter pretended to ask the cop for directions and muttered for him to leave the car. The rattle of the nightstick stopped, and the swish of nylon began again.

On the way downtown, the young man in the nylon pants waved his fists at Pellechia and mimed a beating. He grabbed a strap and raised his foot. Carter heard him say, "This guy moves, we're going to stomp him to death." Pellechia heard only an unintelligible voice and the rumble of the train. As his ears strained to make out the words, his eyelids began to flutter.

"Then I concentrated on keeping my eyes closed," Pellechia remembers.

When the train pulled into Wall Street, Pellechia felt a tug at his neck and a gust of wind. Carter grabbed the young man in nylon pants as he tried to flee with Pellechia's chain. Pellechia opened his eyes and reached for the second man.

THE FOLLOWING EVENING, RICHARDSON'S TEAM rode the A train out to Queens. Richardson wore a blue overcoat, a white suit, a gold tie, a black yarmulke, and a droopy expression that summoned the word "nerd." A chain dangled from his neck, and a fake gold Rolex shone on his right wrist. He was feigning sleep when a man got on with a youngster and a Doberman. Richardson felt the dog's black, wet nose sniff his face.

"I was thinking, 'I wish I was back in Kansas,'" Richardson recalls.

The dog's snout pulled away. Richardson felt the man slide next to him and pull off the watch. Eubanks and Martin rose and said, "Police." Pellechia hurried in from the next car. He found the man already leaning against a door with handcuffs on his wrists and Martin's revolver at the back of his head.

"Everybody makes mistakes," the man said.

The cops left the Doberman with the youngster and took the man off at the next stop. Richardson sat on a bench and posed as a complainant named Mr. Vicstein. He said that the Rolex was worth $3,100, and the prisoner spit out a half-smoked cigarette.

"I'm going to get you, Jewboy," the prisoner said.

"I'm ascared," Richardson said.

"Go back to Jewland," the prisoner said.

At the Rockaway station house, the prisoner identified himself as Edwin Cordova, 24, of Queens. He signed a paper confirming that he had exactly 25 cents on his person. He said he had planned to fence the watch and buy a hero sandwich.

"I figured I'd eat something if I got away, and if I didn't, they'd feed me anyway," Edwin said.

"Do you *want* to go to jail?" Pellechia asked.

"I need a vacation. In jail, they feed me, they give me clothes. I can wear jewelry. I can beat up who I want."

"Are you sorry you took the watch?"

"He shouldn't have been asleep.... You got a Doberman pinscher sniffing in your face and you don't wake up, there's something wrong with you."

As Edwin was escorted to Queens Central Booking, he spied Richardson. Edwin said, "You're one dead Jew." The cops not-

ed Edwin's various threats in the report. This was read by Assistant District Attorney Abraham Berkowitz, who immediately went for a more serious charge.

"I said, 'What we have here is a grand larceny,'" Martin remembers. "He said, 'No, this looks like a robbery to me.'"

THE ROUNDUP

AT 11:30 P.M. ON FRIDAY, THE TEAM ASSEMBLED for the last tour of the week. Carter appeared in a black do-rag, a red St. John's jacket, imitation Cazal glasses, and a red baseball cap turned sideways. Maple asked if he was also wearing a bulletproof vest.

"Under no circumstances take out your gun tonight," Maple half-joked.

To complete his getup, Carter brought along a box. The team rode into Manhattan in a van, and Carter played Mendelssohn's Symphony No. 8 for Strings. As the van hit Times Square, he switched to a tape of "Roxanne." The night was clear and warm, and the sidewalks were teeming.

"I expect big things tonight," Carter said.

At Broadway and 47th Street, Aiello performed a drunk act around a stairway. Sheridan watched from a nearby pay phone. Doran and Lyons mingled with the pedestrians. Carter posted himself by a Florsheim shoe store on the opposite corner. He set the box at top volume.

Four teenagers came up Broadway with the slow, fluid stride of robbers on the prowl. They stopped at the corner and bobbed their heads to Carter's music. Then they saw Aiello wander into a dark alcove. In a flash, they had throwaways over their jackets.

A tall teenager crossed the street and leaned against a trash bin a foot away from the pay phone. Sheridan spoke into the dead receiver and watched a teenager in a nylon Windbreaker approach Aiello. The one in the Windbreaker went back to the corner and returned to the alcove with a teenager in a green plaid shirt.

The tall one by the trash can spotted a uniformed cop meandering up Broadway, and he raised his hands over his head. The two in the alcove scurried back to the corner. Sheridan hung up and strolled down West 47th Street. Aiello covered his mouth with a handkerchief as she passed.

"Are they still there?" Aiello asked.

"Yeah," Sheridan said.

Near the end of the block, Sheridan boarded a parked charter bus filled with middle-aged ladies. Sheridan showed her badge, and the ladies said they had just come from Chippendales, a club that features male strippers. They chatted and giggled while Sheridan silently peered up the street.

The tall teenager stayed by the trash bin as a lookout while the other youths crept up on Aiello. There was a flash of movement, and the lookout vanished around the corner. One of the three by the alcove was grabbed by Aiello. A second was stopped when Carter held out his finger. The third started running directly at Sheridan.

The ladies on the bus pressed their faces to the windows as Sheridan raced into the street and drew her revolver. She led the teenager back to the alcove in handcuffs. As the three pris-

"I GOT TO GET INTO COMPUTERS," SAID MARK ON HIS WAY DOWN TO CENTRAL BOOKING.

oners lay on the pavement, Aiello shone a flashlight in their faces and asked how old they were.

"Sixteen," Alex Williams said.

"Seventeen," Kelly Thompson said.

"Eighteen," Mark Ross said.

At the West 42nd Street police room, the throwaways were vouchered as evidence. The teenagers were searched and placed in a cell with a foul-smelling transvestite who had just robbed Richardson. Alex held out the single quarter that the teenagers had among them.

"Could I get some potato chips, please?" Alex asked.

After Mark waived his Miranda rights, he admitted to a single previous robbery. He said, "A man said me and eight others tried to rob him. It was only four males and three girls." He insisted that he had since given up crime.

"I don't be robbing," Mark said.

"What are you, a nut?" Maple said. "What's this?"

"I stopped."

"Until tonight?"

"Until tonight. I got no money."

"Are you sorry?"

"I'm sorry I'm here."

Maple put his arm around Mark and asked him in a tender voice to write a statement. Mark agreed and wrote in small, neat letters that he and his friends had come from Brooklyn to "rob some heads." Maple patted him on the back.

"You have nice handwriting," Maple said.

Without looking up, Mark continued. He wrote: "We walk around th area without see no one to rob. We came back to 42nd and Broadway and start walking down to the 50's. We stop at 47th and Broadway. Were we seen the officer in question. . . . I know in my heart it was wrong that's why I back out but it was too late. They had already start to rob him and the officers arrested me to. . . . I brought my plaint [plaid] shirt so if we rob so body I could throw it a way and have my Alambama jacket."

As Mark labored on, Kelly and Alex consented to make statements. They were handcuffed to chairs, and the room resembled a class with armed proctors as the three teenagers hunched over sheets of white paper. Mark confessed to ten felonies. Kelly listed four serious crimes.

"They weren't really robberies," Kelly said. "Just some guys I was with grab a guy and punch them and take their money."

At the bottom of the paper, Kelly wrote, "I'm heartly sorry for all the robberies I did or attempted to do. I do so declare that everything I wrote here is true. And I hope god can forgive me and help me to turn over a brand new leaf."

When Maple reviewed the statements, he saw that one of Mark's first robberies had netted him just under $300. Mark now said, "It was too easy. After that, I was hooked." Mark's smallest score had been $2 and two packs of Newport cigarettes. His biggest haul had been $363.35. He had spent this in a single day on Calvin Klein pants and three pairs of shoes and a gray pin-striped Bill Blass suit.

"Money really don't last too long," Mark said.

There was no mention in Mark's confession of a mugging Kelly said they had done at the Euclid Avenue station. Maple said to Mark, "Why would [Kelly] lie?" Mark said, "Because everybody lie." Mark finally made an addendum.

"Excute [except] when I yoq a man at Euclid Avenue," Mark wrote.

At Maple's request, Mark gave a demonstration of how to yoke or fiend. He stepped up from behind and placed his left forearm across Maple's throat. His left hand clasped his right bicep, and his right hand pressed against the back of Maple's head.

"It got something to do with air to your brain," Mark said. "Heads try to scream, and they go 'echhh.' Once you let out that breath, it's over. You go right to sleep."

Maple then asked Mark how much time he thought he should get for attempting to rob Aiello.

"To be fair?" Mark said. "Eight months."

Back in the lockup, Kelly worked his upper lip over a 24-karat-gold front tooth engraved with the letter K. He asked Mark if they would really go to prison. Mark later said, "I don't know why, but Kel's scared of jail. He calls himself a robber, and he's scared of jail."

SHORTLY AFTER SUNRISE, THE TEENAGERS WERE loaded into the back of the van. They talked about Guess? suits, and Mark said, "Would you believe they be selling a vest for $85? The pants with leather is $54 and change, plus tax." Mark paused as the cops stopped for a daylight look at the alcove on West 47th Street.

"I got to get into computers," Mark said.

As the van continued downtown, the teenagers stared out at the bright April morning. The air coming through the windows was warm, and the few pedestrians strolled without coats.

"You know diamond season is coming," Alex said.

Doran turned and gazed at the three prisoners. "You don't look like criminals," Doran said.

"Not supposed to," Mark said.

At Central Booking, Mark stepped onto a pair of footprints that had been spray-painted on the concrete floor. He stared into the Polaroid camera without expression. As he entered one of the cells, he nodded to a pair of young men who were crouched in the corner.

"What's up?" Mark said.

When Kelly and Alex joined him, they smoked cigarettes and spoke in "swain talk." This is a sort of pig Latin where "iz" is added to the first sound of a word. Mark said that he could not believe that a home boy with a "bizox" turned out to be a cop. He said he would have escaped if he had got off the "bizlock."

"Yeah?" Aiello said. "Well, you almost met a Smiz & Wesson."

"Can I ask how much you had?" Mark said.

"Eleven dollars."

"It would have been a shame to fiend you out for $11."

The teenagers spent that night in a cellblock at the 1st Precinct. In the morning, they were transferred to a holding pen at Manhattan Criminal Court and fed bologna-and-cheese sandwiches. The judge released Kelly and Alex on their own recognizance. Mark was already on probation for robbery. and he was remanded. He was bused to Rikers Island for the fourth time in two years.

"The first time I went, I was kind of scared," Mark remembers. "When I was on the bus, I still really couldn't believe it. When I got there, I said, 'I'm really locked up. This is it. It's over.' But, by the third time, I knew what was up."

The following Friday, the teenagers reappeared in court. They entered pleas of not guilty and were freed pending further proceedings. In front of the court building, they encountered the familiar figure of Officer Billy Carter in his red St. John's jacket.

"He say he be there because some other people try to steal the police jewelry," Mark later said.

As they headed home to Brooklyn, Mark heard about the latest exploits of their friend Alan. The boy who had made his name by scoring $946 on West 39th Street had grabbed $5,400 on West 49th Street while Mark was in jail. Alan now planned to buy a motorcycle.

That evening, the teenagers went to the Grant Avenue subway station. Mark decided to catch an outbound train to his girlfriend's home in Rockaway. Kelly and Alex headed into Manhattan with Sha-Kim, the fifteen-year-old who had been their lookout.

A week almost to the minute after the arrest, Maple found Kelly and Alex standing with a posse on West 42nd Street. Kelly said he liked Maple's new pink sneakers. Maple asked him about their lookout.

"Haven't seen him," Kelly said.

"Just trying to stay out of trouble," Alex said. "Word up."

As Maple went with Sheridan for a bite to eat, they spotted the robber who had hit her bag that first day of decoy work. Maple informed He-Allah Broadhead that he was likely to do heavy time.

"So what? What that mean?" He-Allah said.

When Maple and Sheridan returned to the Deuce, they saw that everybody in the posse but Kelly had moved on.

"They were going to get some money," Kelly said.

"Robbing people?" Maple asked.

"Yeah," Kelly said.

Early in the morning, Mark went to the Winfield Security Corporation hoping to get $5-an-hour fill-in work during the impending doormen's strike. The strike was called off at the last minute, and Mark returned home to the Cypress Hills projects. He went back to bed and woke in the early afternoon to the smell of frying chicken.

"You cook, Ma?" Mark asked.

In a gray T-shirt and red Jockey shorts, Mark padded into the kitchen. He returned to the bedroom with a plate of chicken and mashed potatoes and a bowl of salad. He flicked his television to a Mets game and the radio to Kiss-F.M., and he ate sitting on his bed. He left no meat on the bones.

As he smoked a Newport cigarette, Mark gazed out the window. The people out enjoying the fine spring day included Drac, the gold-fanged neighbor who marshals huge posses in Manhattan. Mark watched Drac for a while and finally rose to wash and dress.

His mother was in the living room watching television. She looked up as Mark came down the hall to the bathroom, and she spoke of his graduation from P.S. 306. She remembered that none of the other children had seemed interested in the math and spelling awards Mark had won.

"All they were saying was, 'What kind of shoes you got?' " the mother now said.

At that moment, Mark appeared wearing the gray pin-striped Bill Blass suit he had bought after his biggest score. The mother noted his gray-and-black shoelaces and said, "Even the strings have to match." Then the mother turned back to a *Ben Casey* rerun. And, without a penny in the pockets of his $150 outfit, Mark Ross headed out into the city.

"I'll be back, Ma," Mark said.

BLACK MAYORS

CAN THEY MAKE THE CITIES WORK?

Thulani Davis

When I visited the Detroit Institute of Arts, everyone I met told me not to miss the 1933 murals by Diego Rivera, the institute's most prized art work, and, like the gorgeously designed building and the city itself, a creation of the Fords and their auto empire. The frescoes, which are breathtaking, show Detroit as it may have once seemed to those living there, or a Detroit that *might* have been—a new kind of landscape created by the industry of man.

Rivera's complex universe surrounds you with a pale, gentle industry: clean, safe, flowing naturally from the raw resources of the earth to machines that glide through the sky. And humankind, the creator, is shown in the ideal, our races lying languidly across the firmament and then moving side by side in labor, connected by umbilical conveyor belts. In the final fresco a completed car rolls off the line, just as one rolled off earlier this year with Democratic presidential candidate Walter Mondale at the wheel, reminding voters that he helped save Chrysler from its own logical end.

Detroit and its industry began to list after the oil embargo of 1973 and, during the depression that followed, began to sink. Already saddled with the label

of "murder capital" and suffering population losses that came to most big cities in the wake of the insurrections of the '60s, Detroit has over the years come to resemble less the vision of Diego Rivera than that of his wife, painter Frida Kahlo. Kahlo's Detroit (not collected by the Institute of Arts) is a landscape where smokestacks spell out the name F-O-R-D, and emit heavy, threatening clouds. Appliances grow like mutants into the ground, electrical cords trace off paths toward odd destinations in work Kahlo did at the same time as Rivera's. She saw what was meant by the long lines of people in search of jobs, the lines of men who'd gone to war, and would go again; Detroit is almost bare, except for the specter of an auto plant. Rivera's work is a shrine to progress, Kahlo's a *retablo* for the costs.

The Detroit inherited by its first black mayor has the Rivera mythology as part of its history, and the Kahlo vision as part of its present. The racial harmony shown by Rivera was never achieved on the assembly line; the city's black community, hounded by white supremacist bands in the '30s, spawned the Black Muslim movement. But the wasteland Kahlo saw never took full shape, in part because the black community began in the '60s and '70s to exercise its political force. Coleman A. Young, now in his tenth year as mayor,

represents that power and the will of a city to survive.

"I had hardly been sworn in before it became evident that we were going to be seriously impacted by the Arab oil embargo," he told me, as we talked in his spotless, sunny office overlooking the riverfront. "Because starting in 1974 the wheel came off the buggy, literally —in Detroit, off the automobile—and we've been in a ten-year depression. It's had its ups and downs, but you would have to describe the ten-year period as one of severe economic crisis. And I think this economic crisis has overshadowed—has been a warp and woof of everything that's happened."

For Young's inauguration, Diana Ross and other Motown stars, who brought the "motor city" its only glamour after the glory days of the auto magnates, returned to the town abandoned by one of the biggest black businesses in the United States. The now deserted Motown building stands overlooking a bit of highway, and is emblazoned with a cryptic sign suggesting, "this was it." Indeed, for many, the home of Stevie Wonder, The Four Tops, The Supremes, Marvin Gaye, Mary Wells, the Marvelettes, and Martha (Reeves) and the Vandellas, could only be the black community where they started. The sign is a grim reminder of the million-in-one chance to escape the depression that was to hit Detroit in the '70s.

From *Mother Jones,* July 1984, pp. 30-41, 51. Reprinted with permission from *Mother Jones* magazine, ©1984 the Foundation for National Progress.

As Young took office, like other black mayors (most recently Chicago's Harold Washington), he faced a declining city credit rating. Detroit's Standard & Poor's rating is today a BB, or speculative grade—meaning that city bonds are considered high-risk and cost more to buy. Newark's is only slightly better at BBB. Chicago's was dropped from an A- to a BBB + ; analysts attribute the drop to the belief that Mayor Harold Washington could not control his city council. (Atlanta, a different story that I'll get to later, has a very strong AA.) I asked Coleman Young if he thought most black mayors coming into office would face this problem.

"Only in the sense that black mayors have been elected and blacks have come into a majority, or a substantial plurality, in cities," he said. "And I think we ought to note that it's only in those cities where blacks are a majority or a near majority that it's possible to elect a black mayor." Thomas Cavanagh of the Joint Center for Political Studies says a black population of 40 percent is the threshold for a black victory. Detroit's was approaching 50 percent when Young was elected (63 percent of the population is now black). That increased percentage of blacks resulted from the exodus of whites— "white flight"—that other big cities were experiencing; it also resulted from the influx of blacks who, Young said, were coming in, by and large, looking for jobs and not in a position to become tax-paying citizens immediately. Both causes of the population shift hurt the city's economic stability.

As the first generation of black mayors struggled to stop the slide in the early '70s, "many people were asking if black mayors were the undertakers or the saviors of the cities," Young said. "It was a legitimate question." He let a laugh roll out as he remembered those years. Now four of the six biggest U.S. cities have black mayors, and of the 18 biggest cities with black populations of more than 150,000, ten have black mayors (see page 34). "It is *still* a legitimate question," he said, "but many precipitously predicted the demise of our cities."

The economy was not yet the major issue in Detroit when Coleman Young became Detroit's first black mayor, after a polarizing race that had basically one issue: the Detroit police depart-

ment. A former state senator, labor leader, and a man known for standing up to the House Committee on Un-American Activities in the 1950s, Young was pitted against then-Chief of Police "Black Jack" John Nichols. Once an army officer, Nichols headed a police entrapment squad known by its ironic acronym, STRESS (Stop the Robberies Enjoy Safe Streets). "There had been any number of killings of young black people at the hands of STRESS and a few police officers had been killed," Young recalled. In 1973, STRESS was responsible for the deaths of 16 blacks. Although blacks made up 50 percent of the population, less than 18 percent of the total police force and only 8 percent of officers were black.

Under Young, the city's police department became a model of how a black mayor can build a black and white force. Despite layoffs forced by the depression, blacks now make up 32 percent of the force. They account for 30 percent of the lieutenants and 23 percent of the sergeants. Young began hiring blacks at a rate of 75-80 percent in the police and fire departments in 1974, a practice considered revolutionary at the time. But promotion rules remained a problem. Young instituted a plan for promoting equal numbers of blacks and whites in the police department, and the court battle over the plan went to the Supreme Court, where it was upheld. (I sat in Coleman Young's office the day the now-eviscerated federal Commission on Civil Rights declared itself against quotas in a case arising out of Young's efforts to implement the new promotion scheme. "An off-the-wall opinion," he said. "It's diabolic that they should choose a woman and a member of a minority to wield the ax.")

One of Young's first executive orders when he took office was the abolishment of STRESS. Complaints of police brutality declined from 2,323 in 1975 to 825 in 1982. Young oversaw the appointment of a civilian review board and named Detroit's first black police chief, William Hart. People I spoke to there repeatedly commented that the general perception is that relations with the police have improved.

Solving the city's economic problems was a tougher proposition. Detroit's unemployment rate is still 17 percent, or nearly twice the national average. Young puts black unemployment at about 35 percent and black teen-age

unemployment at 60 to 70 percent. These facts suggest why Young has taken several risks as mayor. Twice he has instituted, for example, a curfew for young people. And he has supported the construction of a Cadillac plant in one of the city's remnant ethnic neighborhoods, Poletown. The homes in Poletown had to be razed, eliminating another of the once numerous neighborhoods built by Detroit's various immigrant groups. According to the mayor, the residents received settlements at three to four times the value of their property, but there was a struggle to keep the plant out. Young won.

And Young has won over his business community during the past decade, after many of those who abandoned the city for Troy and Pontiac fought to keep growth outside of town. In a move familiar to Northeast mayors, particularly black mayors, as the suburbs swelled, the suburbanites began to fight for larger shares of state revenues— shares that took a bite out of urban money. Suburban real-estate developers built a stadium for the Detroit Lions that would draw patronage away from the city. Battles have been waged from New Jersey to Mississippi over school funding and redistricting as regional planning came to popularity in the early '70s. It has all had the effect of potentially undermining the political strengths of urban black mayors.

But Young has used the power given him by the city's 1974 "strong mayor" charter to get projects built in downtown. Along the riverfront, huge centers bump into one another: the Joe Louis Arena; the odd-shaped community college with its cylindrical structures and elevated tunnel; the convention center housing this year's car show; the Oz-like Ren Cen, or Renaissance Center. In the works is an upper-income housing development to be called Riverfront West, which is to have its own marina and security abutments to keep out burglars. (While the old "murder capital" label was always something of a misnomer, Detroit is still a town where security is a priority; there is a high incidence of gun ownership, and the papers are loaded with stories of valiant citizens beating off would-be robbers at the door. If you live there you learn to put your dry cleaning through a plexiglass window rather than across an open counter.)

3. URBAN PROBLEMS

Former Councilman Kenneth Cockrel, who was (until 1981, when he decided not to run again) the lone Marxist on the city council and frequently the only dissenting vote, and a critic of Young on issues such as tax abatements for business, has assessed Young's development progress:

"I have differed with the mayor on the terms of trade . . . the conditions on which the economic development takes place. There are a number of tools available to the mayor that are employed on terms I thought a tad bit disadvantageous to the general population, relative to the downtown area. But having said that, let me say that I don't think anyone can deny Coleman's ability to form a coalition with leaders of the economic elite and harness their concerted energy and marshall it behind his economic development projects."

Coleman Young's reign has not been any romance out of the Jackie Robin-son mythology. A black mayor is no freer than a black ballplayer to just go in and get along because he plays a good game, or has a good right arm. In Young's view he has been hounded throughout his career as mayor by a hostile press. He speaks at length on the subject whenever he gets the chance. Detroit's two remaining dailies, the *Detroit Free Press* and *The Detroit News*, have given heavy coverage to the two federal investigations that have dogged his past three years. There has been "a drumfire of constant pressure," Young told me. In one case, Young's tax records were subpoenaed in an attempt to link him to a black-owned firm, Magnum Oil, that was advanced $1 million at low interest by the city to buy bus fuel that was in turn sold back to the city. The city maintained that the company could not get traditional financing. Three people, including two former city officials, were indicted on state charges. The case was dismissed in state district court for lack of "credible evidence."

Federal investigators tapped the mayor's home phone in a case involving Vista Disposal, Inc., and a contract to haul sludge from the city's water treatment plant. Charles Beckham, former director of the Water and Sewerage Department, was indicted for bribery and conspiracy along with Darralyn Bowers, Vista's owner and a friend of the mayor, and four others. There was an unsuccessful attempt by federal prosecutors to have Young made an unindicted coconspirator.

Young charges that such investigations are commonly aimed at black elected officials (although, he notes, some white officials are also coming in for similar investigations). In fact, Detroit Congressmen John Conyers, Jr., and George W. Crockett, Jr., have called for hearings into the possible singling out of black officials for investigation. Young cites a pattern dating back

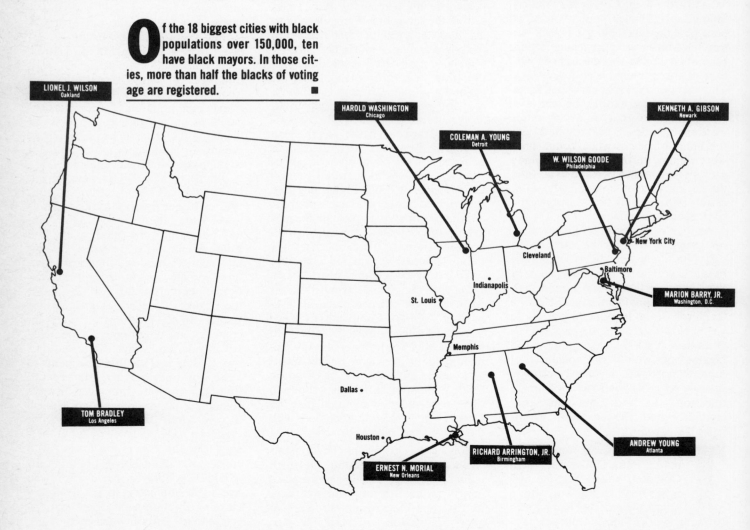

Of the 18 biggest cities with black populations over 150,000, ten have black mayors. In those cities, more than half the blacks of voting age are registered. ■

LIONEL J. WILSON
Oakland

HAROLD WASHINGTON
Chicago

COLEMAN A. YOUNG
Detroit

W. WILSON GOODE
Philadelphia

KENNETH A. GIBSON
Newark

New York City

Cleveland

Baltimore

Indianapolis

MARION BARRY, JR.
Washington, D.C.

St. Louis

Memphis

TOM BRADLEY
Los Angeles

Dallas

Houston

ERNEST N. MORIAL
New Orleans

RICHARD ARRINGTON, JR.
Birmingham

ANDREW YOUNG
Atlanta

to former Congressmen Adam Clayton Powell, Jr. and Charles Diggs; California Congressman Ronald V. Dellums; Eddie Carthans, former mayor of Choula, Mississippi; and others.

Coleman Young has fought the battles all first black mayors must fight. He had to dispel white fears of black leadership. He had to break the stronghold of the all-white past in the police and fire departments and other municipal employment groups. He had to work against the flight of the white working and middle class and for the incoming, unemployed blacks. He still faces high unemployment, an uphill battle for a better credit rating for the city, and construction of a desperately needed rapid transit system to help people get to work. When $600 million was allocated for rapid transit under the Ford administration, a legislative battle, waged by the "white flight" interests in the suburbs, stalled any use of the funds. (Detroit is one of the few major cities without a rapid transit system.) Like Chicago's Harold Washington, Coleman Young has had to deal with a contentious press and bide through investigations close to home like Newark's Kenneth Gibson. Yet he has become a known quantity to builders and investors, and he enjoys better relations with corporate executives than might have been imagined ten years ago. He has built a loyal machine and usually gets the city council to see things his way. Like Washington, D.C.'s Marion Barry and Atlanta's Andrew Young, both second-generation black mayors, Coleman Young is now positioned to refine the broad strokes of change.

In *Black Political Power in America*, Chuck Stone called 1967 "the year of the black mayor." It was the year that black men ran for mayor in six major cities and got elected in two: Cleveland, Ohio (Carl B. Stokes), and Gary, Indiana (Richard G. Hatcher). And it was the year, Stone noted, that a president from Texas felt pressured, as a step toward home rule, to appoint a black man as mayor of the nation's capital, whose blacks made up 55 percent of the population (they now account for 71 percent). Roger Wilkins, a senior fellow at the Institute for Policy Studies, Washington, D.C., told me that story, which illustrates differences between black urban power then and now:

"What Johnson was going to do was appoint a guy named Theodore Roose-velt McKeldin [a white], who had been governor of Maryland and mayor of Baltimore, as the mayor," said Wilkins. "And he was going to appoint me deputy mayor. Then, after a year or 18 months, McKeldin was going to resign and I would be mayor. And I said no, I would not do that. And they asked why, and I said, 'First of all, I'm too young,' I was 34 maybe. And secondly, I said, 'This is supposed to be a step toward home rule, and it is ridiculous to appoint two outsiders.' I said, 'Yes, I live here, but I am not of Washington—I came here to work in the federal government, and I'm a transient, I don't intend to stay here . . . and the black people of Washington don't regard me as one of their own and they should not. They should have one of their own.'

"He [Johnson] had it all set up. He was going to do it without any say-so from me. And I finally told Ramsey [Clark], just before the thing was going to be announced, if he appoints me, I'm going to say, 'Thank you, but no, thank you.' So they called it off at the last minute. They then got Walter [Washington], who a lot of people in town wanted in the first place. And they dropped the McKeldin idea."

Walter Washington was appointed mayor commissioner in 1967 and elected in the District of Columbia's first mayoral election in 1974. His greatest task was to get whites, particularly on Capitol Hill, to accept the fact of his existence, without punishing the district and bolting on the idea of home rule. This he did. He was labeled an Uncle Tom by some who objected to the mayor-as-diplomat idea in the first place, and by others who regarded his style as too low-key and conciliatory to whites. In his first elected term, criticism focused more on his administration.

"A lot of people think that Walter Washington was ineffectual," said Wilkins. "They think he was just a fellow who went around glad-handing . . . and there were a lot of people who felt that the city administration was not handled very well when Walter was there. But, even if that's true, and I don't know it to be true, Walter performed a great service. This is a Southern town, and you don't just have a bunch of Southerners and quasi-Southerners living in this town. You've got a bunch of them on Capitol Hill with their fingers on the purse strings. And the first black mayor in this town had to reassure lots and lots of people, because there were lots of people in this town who had visions of the blacks taking over, and Walter did that superbly. . . . He made Marion Barry possible."

Now in his second term as Washington's mayor, Marion Barry, Jr.—like his predecessor—has wrestled with the legal and financial problems that are unique to this stateless city, still in an uneasy relationship with the federal government it houses. But Barry, considered one of the more progressive black mayors, has managed to increase social spending, particularly for the poor, the schools, and the elderly.

"It's unusual for mayors to be doing that in tough times," he told me. "But my own view is that even when you have tough times you have to look after three categories of people: those in the dawn of life, like children and their education—it's critical, particularly in the black community. The poor, the mentally retarded—AFDC, public housing—those persons have to be supported; and I'm increasing monies for the elderly, the pillars of our community. I don't think you need to cut back on social services and education just because these are tough times; that's when you need these services the most."

A former civil rights organizer, Barry belongs to a second generation of black mayors who can go beyond reassuring the powerful: these mayors can cast themselves as friends to the newly empowered who live in public housing, are unemployed in numbers larger than usually admitted, and worry about both crime and police brutality. But black mayors now in office can also claim as their issues good management and reform of city government. Ivanhoe Donaldson, the investment banker who ran Barry's campaign, cites appointment of Elijah Rogers as D.C.'s city administrator as one of Barry's most important changes when he took office. "One of the criticisms of Walter Washington was that he probably did not take an active enough role in professionalizing city management, and Marion decided that one of the things the city needed was a professional manager."

Reform was a clear issue in Chicago when Harold Washington came into power in 1983. While Chicago had the earmarks of a city ready for a black mayor—a population that was about 40 percent black, black ward leaders and congressmen, and an increasingly active Latino population—it also had a powerful machine that turned around Mayor Jane Byrne. Blacks and Latinos in Chicago (of the Latino vote, 76 percent went to Washington) were voting for a change of politics as well as a change of color in Chicago. In that city, blacks had had enough black machine leadership to know that patronage and racism work in similar ways against those who need jobs and services.

Good management has been central to the agenda of Tom Bradley in Los Angeles. In Philadelphia, W. Wilson Goode won in 1983 by stressing that he would trim government, push public projects like a convention center, improve the port, work for international trade, and create a comprehensive economic plan for the city. A bureaucrat who had worked his way up through the system and Democratic party channels, Goode won 54 percent of the vote—including 27 percent of the white vote (he got 95 percent of the black vote).

Roger Wilkins remembers that in the beginning, Dick Hatcher and Carl Stokes, the first Northern black mayors, "were freaks. And everybody went and looked at them and examined them head to toe, and made them national celebrities. There are some people who think that Carl [Stokes] would have been a much more successful mayor if he hadn't been pushed up into the clouds from the beginning. Now here comes Wilson Goode becoming mayor 16 years after that. And he's the first black mayor of Philadelphia, but he is not a national freak. After the first pictures are taken, and he's been inaugurated, everybody goes away and leaves him alone." Wilson Goode may be able to concentrate on managing his city. He may enjoy some of the latitude of the second black mayor in Atlanta.

Two things strike me on a return to Atlanta. Construction is everywhere, and this is shocking, in a way that perhaps only a Northeasterner can appreciate. I'm just unaccustomed to seeing large tracts of overturned earth where subways, stores, housing, and hotels are going up.

This first shock comes only after an encounter with the remarkable Atlanta airport. The William B. Hartsfield Atlanta International Airport, now the world's second busiest airport (behind Chicago's O'Hare), is former Mayor Maynard Jackson's baby. With a projected revenue of $84 million in 1984,

the airport has turned out to be the boon Jackson had hoped for. But that fact in no way prepares visitors for this metropolis on what used to be a dirt race track owned by a Coca-Cola president. The floor space is about the size of 54 football fields over which are spread 30,000 employees, 1,200 coin-operated phones, 470 public toilets, 38 elevators, two jail cells, a post office, a chapel, four fire stations, and a quarter-mile jogging track for the firefighters.

The second striking thing about Atlanta, once you get past all the construction and into offices and homes, is that everybody loves Andy, that is, the mayor, Andrew Young. While the first black mayor, Maynard Jackson, cut an imposing shadow in Atlanta as a well-respected (and often well-disliked), intimidating politician, Andy Young, quieter but nationally—even internationally—famous, is respected in a different way. The papers carp about his frequent absences for trips abroad, but most people seem to feel his business diplomacy is good for Atlanta.

Atlanta is a city that has had to grow sophisticated as it grew prosperous. It has risen from its *Gone With the Wind* embers, times when you could buy a Lester Maddox souvenir anywhere downtown, to embrace its history as the home of the Reverend Martin Luther King, Jr., and a successful civil rights movement, and to become a major city with an ever-taller skyline. A tour from Martin Luther King, Jr. Drive in the southwest across town to the MLK Center for Nonviolent Social Change in the southeast leads the visitor past the traditionally black colleges of the Atlanta University Graduate School, Morehouse, Spelman, Clark, Morris Brown, the Interdenominational Theological Center. There is the athletic field of Booker T. Washington High School, for years the largest all-black high school in the South. And then Paschal's hotel and restaurant, where a conference of grassroots organizers is breaking up and a woman comes into the lunchroom to tell everybody having fried chicken that her sister called from New York to tell her the latest on Jesse Jackson.

Across on the southeast side, on "sweet" Auburn Avenue, there is the pristine new headquarters of Atlanta Life Insurance Company (founded in 1905 by the son of an ex-slave), the Ebenezer Baptist Church, King's tomb

at the MLK Center for Nonviolent Social Change, the MLK Community Center, and King's birthplace. Across from the birthplace, the street is lined with tiny wooden houses, probably built 75 years ago—unhappy reminders that not all of Atlanta prospers and lives in homes fit for the souvenir book of black Atlanta. The houses are eyed for restoration by Mrs. King and the MLK Center, I'm told. The residents, not too happy with being pressured to come up with money to fix their houses, must wonder at the irony of it.

In the downtown area, an addition to the World Congress Convention Center is under construction not far from the Omni complex, a huge structure that houses a concert and sports facility and offices for downtown businesses. Department stores in shopping malls are expanding, and so is the mass transit system, MARTA (jokingly referred to by some as Moving Afro-Americans Rapidly Through Atlanta). About 430 of the *Forbes* 500 companies have offices in Atlanta; $800 million in building permits were issued in Andy Young's first year in office, and more than a billion dollars since his election.

Atlanta has a high Standard & Poor's credit rating, a budget balanced by law and good prospects. The operating budget for 1984 was $195 million, with projected revenues of more than $200 million. A healthy supply of businesses and homeowners provides a strong tax base, although the unemployment rate is about average. (Black unemployment in Atlanta still runs double the national general average.) Mayor Young told me, "Our problem is not unemployment. It's underemployment." The convention industry has taken up some of the unemployed, but placed them in low-paying jobs.

Of Atlanta's population 67 percent is black. After two terms of Maynard Jackson and more than two years of Andy Young, not only the power base is black, but the power structure is as well. The majority of the 19-member city council are black, along with Young's commissioner of public safety, George Napper, City Attorney Marva Brooks, Fulton County Commission Chair Michael Lomax, Commissioner of Administrative Services Clara Axam, and a host of others.

The civil rights movement schooled much of the generation now in power in Atlanta, including the mayor, State Senator Julian Bond, and Councilman

John Lewis. Still another generation is making its mark in local elections. Reginald Eaves, Fulton County commissioner, who ran against Young and won about 16 percent of the vote, mostly among the black and poor, is part of that generation. So is Marvin Arrington, president of the council and a frequent Young critic. Michael Lomax, a Maynard Jackson protege and his director of cultural affairs, is another who will continue to move up in local politics. Atlanta is a city likely to have strong, well-groomed black leadership for some time to come. Interest in its politics is high; the blacks who were rebellious students in the '60s have indeed "joined the system." On a southwest street in early morning, you can see David Reeves, a member of the governor's staff, jogging by with a sign that simply reads, "Register to Vote." Four or five miles, every day.

I am reminded by that simple sign of how Andy Young used the printed word—bumperstickers and a handsome poster of the city—and radio instead of television in his campaign, because to Young race was still an issue. Reeves, who worked on Young's campaign, said Young felt the television image would not help, even after two terms of Jackson. And perhaps he was right. On a visit to Chicago I saw a local station airing a string of uninterrupted TV ads from the mayoral campaign. Washington's face was used by his opponents in a grievous series of threatening accusations. But then, Andrew Young, former United Nations ambassador, is known the world over, and in Atlanta that carries a lot of weight. Reporters I spoke with who cover city hall accounted for his success with the council and critics by way of his image. They described Young as a man who has the image of being bigger than the job.

Ivanhoe Donaldson, campaign strategist for a number of important black political campaigns, told me, "Andy offers the international community to Atlanta. He's a mayor who can pick up the phone and call anybody in the world. He takes trade delegations abroad, he helps out the minority community, he helps the business community, and gets them into partnerships. . . . He inherited a good tradition from Maynard (Jackson). Maynard deserves his due, too, because he did a hell of a job."

Young's biggest flap to date seems to have been his introduction of a sales tax. This is expected to bring a $40 million windfall to city revenues. The use to which the windfall might be put struck up a few doubting editorials. The money will go to capital improvement projects, both for government and business. "I think we've never done that kind of thing before," Young said. "We're proposing a city hall annex, a new municipal courts building and a new public safety complex, and about $15 million into the revitalization of Underground Atlanta" (an area once restored, now decaying, at the site of the old Atlanta train station, shown in *Gone with the Wind*).

As you enter the city room of *The Atlanta Journal and Constitution* you face yellowing 19th century editions of the papers. An August 16, 1914, paper carries a story headlined "Negro Uses Hatchet against 9 White Persons." Stepping beyond the old headlines you enter the quarters of an integrated workforce of the New South, as it was once called. I visited one of the editorial board meetings, where upcoming editorials were being discussed. The writers there were not from the South, with the exception of the one black board member present; the talk centered largely on the pressures from Washington, D.C., to roll back progress made in the South in civil rights areas.

Speaking later with reporters, I found that Andy Young was catching political heat for his refusal to endorse either Jackson or Mondale. This had done some political damage, they claimed, despite the fact that Mondale's people had taken an understanding attitude toward Young's silence. (After I spoke with him, Young went on record saying Jackson is too inexperienced for the office.) When we talked, Young cited other mayors who are not supporting Jackson and took a cavalier approach to trouble it might cause him at home. Asked if he would concede that Jackson's candidacy might get more blacks into the electoral process, Young said, "I hope so, but there's nothing yet to test that. I don't think people vote emotionally. I think they vote because they're organized."

Many of Young's own young, well-heeled crowd put together a hefty-donation brunch for Jackson's arrival. But some of Atlanta's old-time grassroots movers and shakers were at the Butler Street Y for lunch one afternoon, at the weekly meeting of an old institution called the Hungry Club Forum. Fulton County Commission Chairman Michael Lomax was speaking, trying to drum up much needed support for a new county jail. Selling black folks on a jail is not an easy task, but Lomax had at his disposal the desperate necessity imposed by a court order to provide better inmate housing or release close to 700 inmates. Over chicken, gravy, rice, and greens, black senior citizens and young people alike asked their questions, interrupted by reporters querying as hard as they could. But Lomax was not going to be roasted at the Hungry Club—he is, after all, part of the next generation, inheritors of their own powerful legacy. They would think about his bond issue (it subsequently passed). And the following week they would hear Atlanta's black political pollster, Harry Ross, on his analysis of the Democratic presidential primaries. Black empowerment in Atlanta, any Wednesday at noon.

The power behind Jesse Jackson's candidacy for president is the urban black voting power that has emerged since the 1965 Voting Rights Act. While 4.4 million blacks voted in 1966, 8.2 million did so in 1980, and more than a million have been registered since 1980. Detroit has 76 percent of eligible blacks registered; Chicago, 77 percent; New Orleans, 68.5 percent. These voters vote Democratic at a rate of 90 percent. In seven states where Reagan won slim victories in 1980, they could make a difference in 1984, and the Democrats know it.

But not all black political leaders—and few of the big-city mayors—have supported Jackson. Walter Mondale has been endorsed by Coleman Young, Birmingham Mayor Richard Arrington, Jr., Georgia State Senator Julian Bond, Philadelphia Mayor Wilson Goode, and Los Angeles Mayor Tom Bradley.

As Coleman Young sees it, blacks have to look at their situation beyond the profile of a single candidate, a single broker, such as the Reverend Jesse Jackson. It was only days after Jesse Jackson's campaign troops had rolled through to woo a crowd of several thousand and then sit down to soul food with hometown legend Aretha Franklin. But Young, who remembers that Mondale helped bail out Chrysler, did not mince words on Jackson's candidacy: "This is a very serious contest for president. As far as I'm concerned the most serious issue facing the American people is the absolute imperative of ushering Reagan out of the White House. And any phenomenon within the electoral process must be measured as to whether it adds to or detracts from that goal."

Coleman Young called Jackson's run an "ego-trip." "At best, he is bargaining . . . to play our chips at the political convention. And we don't need any single person to bargain for us. He is a self-appointed bargainer at that." At worst, Young said, those disenchanted by Jackson's failure to capture the nomination may desert the political process. "I know Jesse and I respect his abilities, [but he has] no platform, no background. I think it's irresponsible. The only person I can see who'll profit from it at this point is Reagan. Reagan holds a disastrous threat. I don't know what will happen to this country with four more years of him." Young's voice rose in indignation, "Can you imagine what will happen to the Supreme Court?"

But Jackson has gained the support of Mayors Barry of D.C. and Hatcher of Gary; Tuskegee Mayor Johnny Ford; Congressmen John Conyers (D-Michigan) and Ron Dellums (D-California); State Representatives Maxine Waters (D-California) and Albert Vann (D-New York). Asked about black officials who did not support Jackson's candidacy, Barry—whose city gave Jackson a primary victory—said: "Most people in their guts would like to support Jesse. Some of the black elected officials made these private understandings with these white elected officials. We just don't think that's the way you do business. You have a *public* agenda for *people*; some of us don't want anything out of the federal government but money to run our cities."

Jesse Jackson's supporters see his candidacy as a way to bring life back to the Democratic party and to give blacks a stronger voice in the party. "We need to strengthen electoral politics as it relates to blacks and Jesse offers a new course," says Barry. "Complacency has set in, in the Democratic party. We lost to President Reagan, not because Reagan was better organized, or better. We lost because Democrats stayed at home. And some of those who came out voted for Reagan. They just weren't excited about the Democratic

agenda. I think Jesse's getting us back on the Democratic agenda."

Black empowerment in the '80s is not simply a continuation of the assumption of urban power begun in the '60s. As long as the black numbers are there, one can assume blacks will come to office, but what is going on now is more significant than that.

A black mayor is no longer simply black, simply a liberal Democrat; black empowerment has meant the election of blacks from across a wide spectrum of political views. This means, in a race involving several blacks, that the community elects an agenda, as well as an identity. Oakland's conservative first black mayor, Lionel J. Wilson, is now being challenged by a more progressive black, Wilson Riles, Jr., who claims Wilson has ignored poor blacks.

Andy Young, on the other hand, sits clearly in the middle. A conservative economic planner who introduced a regressive sales tax in Atlanta, he was once excoriated for radical political views on international politics. Marion Barry and Melvin H. King, unsuccessful candidate for mayor in Boston, come from the most progressive end of the spectrum. Barry and others behind the closed doors of D.C. politics came out of the most revolutionary wing of the civil rights movement. They have made black empowerment a reality in the South where the greatest growth in the black electorate is now taking place, and in cities where black power just needed to be registered and organized.

Some say blacks are only following in the steps of various immigrant groups— like the Irish and Italians who rose to power in successive decades in U.S. cities. But the rise to power of blacks and Latinos is accompanied by an understanding of the dynamics that permitted the Irish, for instance, to become simply American and prevents black and brown people from doing the same. This possibility of addressing long-term ills alone creates some of the excitement so evident in these elections and just after.

The races run by Mel King, Marion Barry, and Harold Washington not only drew black and Latino electorates into enthusiastic participation in electoral politics; they also showed that *genuine* coalition-building is taking place among the cities' disenfranchised. Last year when King ran for mayor against Ray-

mond L. Flynn, a progressive, in Boston, a city with a 30 percent black and Latino population, 90 percent of Boston's blacks and 70 percent of its Latinos voted for King and his rainbow coalition. The race, which ended with Flynn's victory in a run-off, presented a situation, not unlike that in Chicago, where coalition politics proved effective, and the historical racial tensions in the city played a major role. However, in Boston, where the black candidate did not win, the campaign itself became a victory because it did not degenerate into a war between "them" and "us."

"Probably at that moment in history," says Ivanhoe Donaldson, "it was more important to the city of Boston to feel that two individuals, irrespective of background, class, intellect, and ethnic standing, could make a run at it in peaceful coexistence. Mel made it to the run-off—that was indeed important and fantastic and a tremendous effort on his part, and Boston is to be given credit; it didn't allow the stuff to break down into garbage."

The energy and grace of the King campaign can be compared to the exhilaration in New York, when Jesse Jackson passed through, or still evident in Chicago, when I visited in April. A lawyer there told me how many people excited by the Washington race had worked in the race for his old congressional seat (won by Charles Hayes, Washington's choice). A long-time Chicago resident and an administrator in the welfare office in the hard-hit northwest side said to me, "I'm just glad to know a black man is down there in city hall, and a smart black man at that."

"Black mayors unleash a lot of black creativity which white mayors were overlooking," says Roger Wilkins. When a black mayor is elected, "all of a sudden it gives white people who have any eyes and sense a pause. They say, 'My God, just because we have a black majority in this town does not mean the town is bad. Something real and alive is occurring and there's hope and possibilities.' And the greatest example of that is Detroit. My judgment is that Coleman Young is one of the great politicians of our time. You go to Detroit and people will *tell* you that they feel good about their city. A white mayor could not have done that."

Thulani Davis, a senior editor at The Village Voice, *lives in New York City.*

The Myths of Mass Transit

"Whether we consider buses or trains, urban public transit systems offer inferior service, both in quantity and quality."

San Francisco cable car.

Catherine G. Burke
Associate Professor, School of Public Administration, University of Southern California, Los Angeles

MASS transit is an idea whose time has passed. It is costly, ineffective, inhumane, wasteful of energy, can not serve our real needs for transportation, and helps to increase congestion and air pollution. If all this sounds shocking and absolutely wrong to you, be assured you are not alone. One of the most widely believed myths in our society is that the problems cited above are created by the automobile and can be solved by mass transit.

Letting go of cherished beliefs is one of life's most difficult undertakings. There are some things we simply "know" are true, and we refuse to be confused by mere facts. Such cherished beliefs are myths—stories whose origins are forgotten, but which ostensibly relate to historical events which are usually of such character to explain some practice, belief, institution, or natural phenomenon.

These myths are so widely believed that they are assumed to be common knowledge and are rarely questioned. Even when contrary facts are presented, they are quickly forgotten and the myths prevail. Part of this has to do with a natural human characteristic not to abandon a theory, even when it has problems, at least until a better theory appears. Another part of the reason, however, may have to do with potential beneficiaries should the myths prevail and the public invest large amounts of money in mass transit systems.

Before examining the myths in detail, some definitions of terms may help. For many people, the term mass transit can refer to any type of public transportation. The idea of mass transit, however, implies the movement of large numbers of people (masses) at the same time along fixed routes. Today, it is best confined to rail rapid transit, whether subways, elevated trains, or ground-level trains which are separated from other types of traffic. Such systems serve internal transportation needs of an urban region and usually include commuter services as well as intra-city services.

Public transportation, on the other hand, can include not only mass transit (rail systems), but also buses (large and small), taxis, moving sidewalks, people movers, elevators, personal rapid transit, and other means of transporting people and goods. Their common characteristic is that they are available to the public at large, rather than involving private ownership and usage provided by the automobile or bicycles.

Thus, it is perfectly possible to believe in the necessity for public transportation while at the same time opposing mass transit or other particular forms of public transit because of service quality, cost, or other problems. As with all public projects, it is not enough to argue that something is good or it is bad; what is needed is an examination of the purposes to be served by a particular project, the most effective means to achieve those purposes, and the costs and benefits to be achieved.

Although over-all costs and benefits are important, it is also important to disaggregate the costs and benefits to find out specifically who benefits and how much, who pays and how much. Public policies which are promoted without such examination are unlikely to have longterm success or public acceptance. They will be based on myths, not on fact, and their ultimate failure will make it even more difficult to institute innovative policies which show much greater promise for success.

Myth 1: We once had adequate public transit systems in our cities and these were destroyed through a conspiracy of large corporations—National City Lines, General Motors, Firestone Tire and Rubber, Standard Oil, and others.

This myth is one of the most pernicious, because it assumes things were better in the past and, if we could only return to what we had, things would be good again. It is also one of the most persistent myths, since there is considerable evidence to support it. Part of the evidence comes from fond memories of the Big Red Cars in Los Angeles or the streetcars which provided good service in many cities in the early part of the 20th century.

There is also a Supreme Court case—*United States v. National City Lines et al,* 341 U.S. 916 (1951)—which indicates that National City Lines was incorporated in 1936 to purchase transit systems in cities where streetcars were no longer practicable and convert them to motorbus operations. To raise capital to make such purchases, a plan was devised to procure funds from manufacturers whose products would be used by the operating companies. This was the basis of the conspiracy wherein National City Lines and the other defendants were convicted of monopolizing the markets.

For those who would like to build new rail systems today, it is attractive to assert we once had good rail systems which were destroyed for narrow profit motives. The evidence, however, does not support the conspiracy theory. Rail transit systems began having serious financial difficulties during and just after World War I. Rail systems which had been built to support real estate ventures could no longer be maintained, since the land was long since developed and the profits realized. Real estate development began to take place between the rail lines, making the rail service inadequate for many people. Beginning in 1912, people turned to the convenience of the auto and—despite hard times, wars, and energy crises—the trend has not

changed. By 1919, one-third of the rail operating companies were bankrupt.

The death of street railways

The first competitors to the rail systems were the jitneys—private autos which offered fast and flexible service for a nickel. Many people financed their first car by traveling along streetcar lines picking up waiting passengers for a quicker and more convenient trip. Some jitney operations apparently attracted up to 50% of the peak-hour electric rail ridership. The situation of the urban transit industry became so serious that Pres. Wilson appointed a Federal Electric Railway Commission after World War I to investigate it. The solutions offered by the industry were to restore corporate credit by reestablishing their monopoly, to ban the competition (jitneys), and to raise fares.

The transit industry got what it wanted, but it was not enough to save the street railways. The trend toward autos accelerated. Within transit operations, the trend toward buses began in the 1920's, as some jitney operations were taken over by the street railways and placed on schedules using buses rather than rail lines. Buses offered a number of advantages as track construction and maintenance were eliminated: one mechanical failure did not shut down an entire line and buses could be rerouted if demand shifted or if a street were blocked due to construction or some other emergency.

The critical factor leading to the conversion of street railways to buses and to the further decline of the industry may have been the Public Utility Holding Company Act of 1935. In 1931, over 50% of the street railways and over 80% of the total revenue passengers rode bus or streetcar lines controlled by the power holding companies. The original street railways had been drawn by horses, and the new electric companies bought out the street railways in order to convert them to electricity and develop a market for their generating capacity.

Even during the Depression, most of these holding companies could make a reasonable profit through their electric, gas, lighting, and other ventures. In 1935, however, the Utility Holding Company act was passed, which required these firms to divest themselves of their urban transit operations. During the legislative hearings on the act, the power trusts did not mention the subject of transit, and one can assume they were anxious to get rid of these unprofitable operations without incurring the wrath of local communities, which might jeopardize their more lucrative franchises.

It was at this point that National City Lines and the other "conspirators" entered and played a significant role in

offsetting the contraction of capital for transit modernization caused by the 1935 act. Clearly, they also had a profit motive, and the chance to write off ancient, obsolete equipment still carrying high book values was an important attraction for outside capital.

Later, in the 1950's, when the National City Lines case led to another major loss of capital backing from suppliers, this, coupled with the loss of patronage, made it unprofitable for large holding companies to remain in the transit business. Public ownership became essential to keep the transit systems operating. Thus, it seems clear that economics, not conspiracy, destroyed the street railways. The abandonment of streetcars probably prevented the financial collapse of the industry.

Almost overnight an industry with high fixed costs of maintenance of way, generation of power, and, in some cases, engineering and construction of rolling stock, found itself buying standardized products from a limited group of manufacturers, as well as relieved of the problem of maintenance of right of way. The motor bus brought other significant savings. In many cities, two-man streetcars were replaced with one-man buses. . . . [The companies] were able to close down unneeded depots, sell excess real estate. . . .[1]

Myth 2: Rail rapid transit can promote high-density growth and high land values in the concentrated central city districts.

The idea is that rail systems can counteract the multi-centered urban areas such as Los Angeles and Houston and move us toward more concentrated patterns such as New York or San Francisco. Urban density is assumed to be good and urban sprawl bad. Even if one prefers density (and it is quite clear that many do not), it is not certain that rail systems can cause more dense development. In Toronto, there are indications that the development that took place along the Yonge Street subway would have occurred anyway due to the city's high rate of growth in the 1950's. The rearrangement of development that took place was accomplished as much with zoning as with transit development.

Whereas some claim the billion-dollar construction boom along Market Street in San Francisco was caused by BART, others believe the growth in San Francisco was due to its service-type economy and would have taken place with or without BART. In Houston, Dallas, and Denver, which rely solely on automobiles and buses, even greater expansion in high-rise central office building has occurred.

Urban sprawl may also be a product of rail transit development, since these

[1]L.M. Schneider, *Marketing Urban Mass Transit* (Boston: Harvard University Press, 1965).

systems best serve those who work in the central city and live in distant suburbs. These are usually the more affluent members of society who reach the train by auto. Rail systems make long-distance commuting tolerable and the land boom that has taken place around San Francisco (especially Contra Costa County) offers some evidence of this pattern.

In situations of little growth, or even decline, as in many of our large central cities, it seems likely that growth in some areas will reduce demand in other areas. Whether these increases and declines offset each other is uncertain from existing information. Aggregate estimates of costs and benefits frequently fail to reveal that values are being transferred, rather than created.

Even where growth is assumed, a major rail network may not have major impact on development. Washington Metro officials estimate that the number of jobs in downtown Washington, D.C., will increase from 500,000 in 1974 to 750,000 in 1990. At the same time, jobs in Washington suburbs are expected to grow from 500,000 to 1,500,000, despite the building of the $8,000,000,000 fixed-rail system.

One reason for this is the low diversion rate from automobiles to trains. BART reduced the number of cars on most heavily used lines by five per cent. In Chicago, the Dan Ryan expressway train line carries less than 20,000 people per day in rush hours, while the adjoining freeways carry 160,000. Experience is consistent that diversion from automobiles is equal to about one year's increase in vehicle counts. Much of the diversion to rails comes from people who rode in buses or carpools before or from those who could not travel before (latent demand). This puts considerable strain on bus systems, since the trains frequently compete for their most profitable lines.

Myth 3: Rail rapid transit systems can reduce home-to-work rush hour congestion. The low diversion rates cited above indicate why rail systems can not have major effects upon rush hour congestion. New rail systems may even increase central city congestion.

If a high-rise office building is erected in the central city in order to house economic activity that might otherwise have been located in a diffuse pattern, only some 15% of the employees can ordinarily be expected to use the rail facility to reach it. The other 85% use the streets, either in buses, in automobiles, or on foot.[2]

Myth 4: Rail rapid transit systems can help alleviate air pollution problems. To the extent a concentrated pattern of

development does occur, it may act to concentrate pollutants from automobiles, making air pollution worse. Vehicles moving at low speeds and stopping frequently produce four times the pollutants than are emitted by vehicles moving freely on an expressway.

Even if there were no increase in congestion, rail rapid transit can have only negligible effects on over-all pollution. This is partly due to the low diversion of people from their autos and also due to the controls on automobiles which attack the problem directly by reducing their polluting qualities.

Myth 5: Rail rapid transit systems can reduce our energy requirements, especially petroleum energy.

Based on the operating energy required per passenger-mile, rail systems appear to be real savers of energy. Such appearances vanish, however, once trains must be run at less than full capacity. Under typical operating conditions, full capacity is met for, at most, 20 hours per week during rush hours. At other times, trains must still run, and new rapid rail systems such as BART in San Francisco or the Washington Metro are actually energy wasters, rather than savers.

The principal reasons for this waste are the widespread use of low-occupancy private automobiles to gain access to the system, the attraction of people from more energy-efficient forms of public transportation, and the high use of energy to build the system and to operate stations—46% of the energy which will be consumed by BART over the next 50 years was consumed before the first train was run. Most recent studies suggest the best opportunity for energy savings is to improve the energy efficiency of the automobile. According to a 1977 study prepared for the Senate Committee on Environment and Public Works, "Rail rapid transit offers little aid to the nation's effort to save fuel."

Why rail rapid transit does not work

Myth 6: Mass transit can provide good service for a large (or significant) portion of the population, especialy the transit-dependent such as the poor, elderly, young, physically handicapped, and others without easy access to the automobile.

The main reason rail rapid transit systems can not work well for these people is the same reason it can not work well for anyone else. Our cities are now multi-centered urban regions with housing, commerce, and industry scattered over large areas. Both residence and employment are becoming increasingly dispersed, modifying the demand patterns for urban transportation. The causes of these patterns are multiple and varied. It is too sim-

ple to say they have been caused by the automobile, though the auto clearly has permitted such development which began long before the auto came on the scene.

As people became more affluent, they had more choices in housing, and the early street railways allowed urban expansion in roughly star-shaped corridors. Later, the development of electric motors made land-extensive horizontal factories in outlying areas more economic than the vertically organized steam-powered factories in the central core. Telephones removed the need for hand-delivered messages between offices and also allowed people to communicate with those who lived in more distant neighborhoods. Trucks freed manufacturers from the need to be near a central rail system, and these factors plus the lower cost of land and taxes in outlying areas made greater dispersal of industry attractive.

Government housing policies regarding zoning, taxation, and financing of home purchases also encouraged the move to the suburbs. With the expansion of both housing and industry, many jobs, especially industrial jobs, are now found outside the central city. In perhaps the extreme case, Los Angeles, only 6.6% of all jobs are found in what passes there for a central business district. Even a concentrated city such as New York has lost over 600,000 jobs since 1969, many of them to outlying suburban areas.

Since rail systems tend to best serve those in the suburbs who wish to travel to the central city, poor people who live in the central city and need to get out of the city to industrial jobs find the train systems offer little or nothing. Other needs for mobility (roughly 75% of all urban trips) can not be easily met by train systems—the needs to go to market, to visit friends, to reach a doctor, or to get to a recreation area. Granted the auto-dominant system we now have offers little for the transit-dependent, the mass transit systems proposed for our cities will do little to alleviate their problems.

Myth 7: Mass transit systems will save travel time.

It is assumed that cutting travel time will attract riders to mass transit systems. Therefore, stations are placed at least a mile apart, and frequently more than a mile apart. Thus, there are few points of access to and egress from the system. The 71-mile BART system has only 34 stations. the larger Chicago system has 150, and Boston has 70. While this may reduce the time on the train, total trip time becomes longer as it takes more time to get access to the system and more time to get from the system to one's final destination. It is total trip time, however, which is most important to the consumer. Waiting time and other out-of-vehicle activity are very onerous to potential customers.

---

[2]G.W. Hilton, *Federal Transit Subsidies: The Urban Mass Transportation Assistance Program* (Washington, D.C.: The American Enterprise Institute, 1974), p. 101.

Myth 8: Mass transit systems will result in lower costs for transportation in cities.

The costs to build urban rail systems is extremely high. The most recent construction for the Washington Metro is running roughly $100,000,000 per mile. Nonetheless, despite high capital costs, proponents of rail systems claim operating costs are much lower than for, say, bus systems, The evidence for this is quite the contrary, with the all-bus Southern California Rapid Transit District showing much lower costs than other big city systems which have rail transit as part of their operations. In San Francisco, costs of the BART system exceed not only those of buses, but also those of subcompact and even standard autos.

With all these difficulties, it is not surprising that rail transit systems are viewed with little favor by their users. Around the world, rail systems are declining in ridership as more affluent people seek more convenient alternatives. Rail systems also decline because of their inflexibility. As cities develop and change, the rail systems can not be moved to accommodate the change. The growth of low-density rings around metropolitan areas discussed earlier is part of this problem. Another factor is the growth and development of new attractions. A considerable portion of the decline in use of the New York subway system can be attributed to its lack of service to attractions that have been built in the 50 years since its completion. A new sports complex, airport, or other major traffic generator is unlikely to be served by existing rail lines.

Despite all these problems, rail systems have enjoyed considerable support in major cities and in the Federal government (prior to the Reagan Administration). Much of the support comes from downtown business interests, which want increased property values, and the consultants and contractors who will design and build the system. Big-city mayors (who get much of their support from downtown business interests) also support these systems. A number of observers attribute this to a kind of boosterism—a city isn't really a city unless it has a rail transit system.

Some people seem to have an emotional attachment to trains—a predisposition to rail transit because of a childhood fascination. "They don't have to have a reason for wanting it, they just want it." For local politicians, there is also a desire for a visible accomplishment—something that can be pointed to with pride during the next election.

Environmentalists have been important supporters of train systems. Many of them have fought the road gang for years and they "know" rail systems are the answer. They genuinely believe these systems will reduce energy consumption, air pollution, and congestion, as well as help the transit-dependent and improve the over-all quality of urban life.

A significant segment of the public apparently agrees with them, at least on the issue of air pollution. A poll taken in Los Angeles prior to a 1974 vote on a rail transit proposal indicated an overwhelming proportion of voters felt it would reduce smog. This was not enough to gain a favorable vote on the proposal, however, perhaps because another poll in the same area indicated 86.8% of the respondents believed Los Angeles needed a new transit system, but only 4.7% said they definitely would ride it.

Finally, there are the rapid transit districts. Their support has come primarily from the downtown business groups and the consultants and contractors who build rail systems. The transit districts appear to respond to this support by offering rail solutions time and again. Until recently, such systems offered the promise of Federal money, and such money would give more power to the transit districts, more jobs, and more income for the technostructure of the agency.

Alternative approaches

First, it must be recognized we have an auto-dominant system, not because people are perverse, but because this system offers more people greater mobility and access to the goods of our society than any transportation system in history. It is the very success of this system which has created difficulties for society as a whole and for those who can not or do not wish to use it.

Whether we consider buses or trains, urban public transit systems offer inferior service, both in quantity and quality. Riding on these systems is usually slow and often a dehumanizing experience. Crowding and crime both take their toll. Given this situation, our best strategy is to alleviate and ameliorate the problems of the auto-dominant system while, at the same time, we attempt to create new transit systems which can better meet our needs.

To reduce petroleum consumption, we do not add one per cent of the people to public transit, we reduce the size of the automobile and increase its fuel efficiency—something which the high cost of petroleum is already bringing about. Automotive air pollution can be attacked through better engine design and by changing to non-polluting fuels. Public policies to encourage the use of methanol (which can be made from any organic matter, including garbage) could help reduce petroleum usage and contribute to pollution control.

Auto safety can be improved through the use of roll cages and fuel tank bladders such as those which protect race drivers. Their additional weight could be offset by using lighter materials elesewhere.

Congestion can be reduced through improved traffic controls, as well as such social devices as flex-time. We can also make better use of existing systems by encouraging paratransit—carpools, vanpools, jitneys, subscription buses, and shared taxis.

Often overlooked as public transit, taxis can provide important service, especially if we support the move to computerized dispatch, as has been done in a number of European cities. For a cost of roughly $5,000,000, we could develop a central computerized dispatch system for a city like Los Angeles which would greatly improve the productivity and profitability of all taxi companies as well as enable them to provide superior service. For those who can not afford taxis, it would be far less costly to subsidize taxi rides and it would provide far better service than mass rail systems.

Such short-term solutions could meet immediate transportation needs and also help attack the ancillary problems associated with our present transportation system. In the long run, we must develop new technologies which will fit the multi-centered and dispersed shape of our cities. Elsewhere, I have argued that Personal Rapid Transit (a small automatic electric vehicle system) shows the most promise for meeting our individual and societal needs for a cost-effective, energy-efficient, non-polluting, and aesthetically attractive transportation system.[3] It is my belief that work on such a system should begin now; in the meantime, we should make every effort to meet today's transportation needs with systems which are low in capital cost and which promise a high return in both service and costs. We should avoid systems with high capital costs which lack flexibility and are vulnerable to changes in values, the physical dimensions of cities, working hours and patterns, and human failures such as strikes, criminal violence, and civil disturbance.

Mass rail rapid transit offers the highest costs and the least flexibility. It is truly an idea whose time has passed. If the Reagan Administration sticks to its intention to cut off funds for rail rapid transit, it will be doing all of us a favor. By saving money which would otherwise have been wasted on expensive and ineffective rail systems, we can begin to work to improve our auto-dominant system. We can also begin to explore and develop new technologies which will improve upon the present system and offer us better service, greater opportunities, and a better quality of life.

---

[3]C.G. Burke, *Innovation and Public Policy: The Case of Personal Rapid Transit* (Lexington, Mass.: D.C. Heath, 1979).

American Cities and the Future

David A. Caputo

David A. Caputo is professor and head of the Department of Political Science at Purdue University. His research interests are in public policy, urban politics, and intergovernmental relations. He has published many articles and books, including, coauthored with Richard L. Cole, Urban Politics and Decentralization. *His current projects include evaluations of President Reagan's urban policies.*

Urban leaders in the United States have experienced a substantial shift in their relationship with the federal government in the past twenty years. Although it is tempting to label recent policy proposals by the Reagan administration as far-reaching and even "revolutionary," another possible and logical explanation is that what has occurred in the past three years is only an acceleration of trends and policies begun in the early 1970s. There is ample evidence to support this position. I deal with the descriptive aspects of contemporary federalism, its impact on American cities, and the general implications from these developments for American society as it enters the mid and late 1980s.

Considerable effort could be spent attempting to label contemporary federalism, but it should be clear that no single label adequately covers the nuances of American federalism today. While terms such as "permissive federalism" or "picketfence federalism" are often used, they do not convey the complexities and subtleties involved. American federalism, as always, is in a state of flux. To maintain that any particular description is characteristic for any sustained period is to invite empirical contradiction. Yet American federalism has been changing in regard to the cities for more than a decade. Changes during this time have led to greater administrative decentralization, and changes in the past few years have also resulted in a decrease in federal financial responsibility.

Twenty years ago, President Lyndon Johnson's Great Society resulted in accelerated domestic spending and a near tripling in the number of federal grant-in-aid programs from 1960 to 1968. These included such well-known programs as the War on Poverty and lesser-known programs dealing with mass transit and highways. These programs led to more than a doubling of federal expenditures between 1960 ($10.2 billion) and 1968 ($22.5 billion), an increase that was partially responsible for heightened concern over United States military involvement in Southeast Asia.

Many political, economic, and social forces accounted for these increases and the adoption of new programs, but in 1968 the scope and magnitude of the federal government were far different from what they were when John F. Kennedy took office just eight years earlier. It was a different intergovernmental system, and city-federal relationships had changed. For instance, the Economic Opportunity legislation of 1964 created Community Action Agencies (CAAs), local antipoverty organizations some of which were often independent of local political control. While numerous types of CAAs developed, one type was independent from local political control, but received direct grants from the federal government. This frequently caused political controversy.

The CAAs often had jobs to offer through their various training programs, as well as other rewards usually the province of local public officials only. The emphasis for the 1963–68 period was on increased or new federal funding and more direct contact between the federal government and local governments and organizations, which often led to more federal and local bureaucrats monitoring programs, enforcing requirements, and monitoring local compliance. "Red tape" multiplied and programs often inched toward completion.

Enter Richard M. Nixon. The president and his staff, confronted by a war in Southeast Asia and an increasingly complicated and expensive set of domestic programs, moved quickly to control spending, to reorganize a variety of domestic programs, and to simplify the entire bureaucratic process associated with the Great Society. There was a consistent effort to reduce the power of the bureaucrat and to add to the power of the locally elected official. In his 1971 state of the union message, Nixon argued, "The time has now come in America to reverse the flow of power and resources from the states and communities to Washington, and start power and resources flowing back . . . to the states and communities and, more important, to the people all across America." This theme, in one way or another, not only characterized Nixon's domestic policy but became an important part of the next three presidents' domestic policy as well.

What occurred during this period was a substantial reduction in the administrative hierarchy and apparatus that had developed during the Great Society days. There was an increase in the federal funds provided by Washington to local jurisdictions, but Nixon did eliminate, reduce, or change a variety of Great Society programs. The Office of Economic Opportunity was dismantled and the most popular programs (Headstart, Upward Bound, etc.) were transferred to other departments.

In addition to this type of change, Nixon introduced two programs that were to have a profound impact on the cities. The first was general revenue sharing (GRS), which was enacted in the form of the State and Local Fiscal Assistance Act of 1972. The legislation provided federal revenues to more than 38,000 general-purpose units of government for five years. The governments did not have to apply for the funds but only meet minimal reporting and expenditure requirements. Even more important, the program allocated its funds on a formula basis that eliminated the congressional role once the formula was agreed to. Large administrative staffs at the federal, state, or local governmental levels were not needed. GRS quickly became popular, not just because of the money involved but because it provided consider-

---

Many local political leaders are not pleased with the Reagan policies.

---

able flexibility and autonomy to locally elected officials who determined, with few federal restrictions, how the funds were to be spent.

The second innovation was special revenue sharing; the Law Enforcement Assistance Act and the Housing and Community Development Block Grant program typify such initiatives, which stressed state and local administrative flexibility while combining several federal grant-in-aid programs into one program. The result was greater federal funding and a decrease in local administrative costs.

The Nixon administration was indeed partially successful in meeting its stated goals of returning power and resources to local governments. Both federal funding levels and the amount of local autonomy and control over the various programs increased. In some respects, local governments and cities became even more dependent on federal funding than during the 1960s. The percentage of local governmental revenues from the federal government grew from 5.1 percent to 12.9 percent from 1970 to 1975; for municipalities, from 7.1 percent to 19.3 percent. While cities may have had greater autonomy in the use of the funds, they also became more vulnerable to federal budget cuts.

After Nixon resigned his presidential office in August 1974, little was done to change the basic drift of domestic policy by either the Ford or the Carter administrations. General revenue sharing was renewed in 1976 and 1980. While it is not surprising that Gerald Ford, given his political inclination and the brevity of his time in the White House, would not embark on new domestic policy initiatives, it is somewhat surprising that Jimmy Carter did not.

It was not until 1978 that Carter introduced his domestic policy labeled "The New Partnership." It was a mixture of things, but its key emphasis was on "targeting" federal funds, especially community development and urban development funds, to the more impoverished areas of the cities. It was an attempt to reestablish national priorities, but in a very limited way. What was unexpected about the Carter policies was the absence of any new policy initiatives or a request for increased expenditures. Carter argued for a continuation of past practices, with more emphasis on federal control over how and where local jurisdictions spent their federal funds. Even the guidelines and regulations in this area were rather mild. In many cases, to prove targeting of funds to low-income areas, local officials simply had to certify the funds were going to such areas or would directly benefit them. This did not require extensive federal bureaucratic involvment and had only a modest impact on the use of federal funds.

As with the Nixon and Ford presidencies, Carter's behavior was consistent with his own perception of American federalism. His policies reflected a strong distrust of centralized power, and he was especially disdainful of the Washington "establishment." His political experience in Georgia had convinced him of the need to be wary of Washington and its tendency to legislate broad national programs.

Given all this, it should not be surprising that major new federal programs were not proposed. It is interesting that during the Carter years, the federal government's financial importance to subnational governments reached its peak: In 1978, $51.8 billion was available to them. If we look at local government and municipal revenues from federal intergovernmental aid programs between 1960 and 1981, there are increases in revenues for each five-year period, beginning with 1960 to 1965, and a very substantial increase from 1970 to 1975. The percentage of revenues received between 1975 and 1980 increased but less so than during the previous five-year period. In 1981, although the total aid increased, the percentage of local revenues it represented declined. President Ronald Reagan took office in 1981, after federal involvement in state/local affairs had already slowed. The actions of the Nixon administration (1969–74) curtailed many of the federal government's administrative and bureaucratic centralization efforts, and the Carter presidency resulted in a leveling off of federal expenditures. The Reagan proposals and policies are best understood within this context.

We lack perspective on the Reagan administration's domestic policy achievements, but its policy recommendations have been based on a well-stated and consistent set of beliefs about the role of the federal government in providing programs and funding for state and local government. Reagan summarized this approach in a statement about federalism after ten months in office:

> We have seen the federal government take too much taxes from the people, too much authority from the states, and too much liberty with the Constitution. My administration is committed heart and soul to returning authority, responsibility, and flexibility to state and local governments.

It was a sweeping indictment of the intergovernmental grant system, but was it appropriate in 1981, given the apparent high-water mark of federal spending in the late 1970s and the less than vigorous federal action in other intergovernmental areas by the late 1970s? This statement is representative of a basic desire to change not only the amount and type of federal aid going to the states and cities but the basic nature of American intergovernmental relations and American federalism. What are the key elements of the strategy to achieve these goals?

In January 1982, the Reagan administration introduced "The President's Federalism Initiative," which had two main components. The first dealt with a "swap": the federal government would take over responsibility for Medicaid, while the states would take over food stamps and the Aid to Families with Dependent Children program. The second component was a "turnback" proposal: the federal government would return to the states over forty federal education, transportation, community development, and social service programs, which would be financed by a trust fund of $28 billion for three years, and then the federal support would be phased out by 1991.

There were a variety of arguments and justifications for the proposal, including claims that (1) it would lead to a "far clearer delineation of federal and state responsibilities," (2) the states were now both economically and politically better equipped to deal with the problems facing them, (3) it would release federally elected officials to deal with the major issues of our time, (4) it would increase state authority and responsibility, (5) it would reduce federal lobbying, and (6) it would increase the likelihood that elected officials would be in a better position to make policy.

While we could argue with each of these assertions, they do have a common theme and they are consistent with the earlier-stated philosophy that the federal government is too big and too unresponsive. A correlate is that state governments have abdicated many of their constitutional obligations and have been willing to let the federal government do what they should be doing. The result is the belief that the intergovernmental system wastes tremendous amounts of money due to inefficiency and ineffectiveness, and, perhaps worst of all, is unresponsive to the citizenry.

To offset this lack of interaction between elected officials and the public, the Reagan administration committed itself "to removing obstacles to local initiative and experiment, to allowing governments close to their communities to make the vital decisions affecting their citizens and to freezing resources which have been drawn to Washington so that individual communities are free to use their own resources for their own locally determined goals." The president's report on national urban policy went on to offer assistance in disseminating information and to encourage "privatization" whenever and wherever possible.

The most comprehensive description of "privatization" may be offered by E.S. Savas in *Privatizing the Public Sector:*

> Local shedding, together with greater reliance on nongovernmental arrangements and the introduction of competition through voucher systems and by contracting, are policies that have enormous potential for restricting and reversing the growth of government, improving the delivery of public services, and enhancing the lot of citizens.

The thesis is simple and direct. Government not only does too much but does a great deal badly, and often discourages local initiative and citizen responsibility. Privatization would lead to increased local participation and would result in more realistic expectations about what government can do.

The Reagan administration has accelerated a trend begun in the Nixon administration and continued through the Carter years. Administrative decentralization has been a consistently pursued goal, and the events of the past ten years indicate it has been met to some extent. There are fewer grant-in-aid programs and local autonomy has been increased while federal control has been decreased. The rate of spending increases have been slowed, and the purposes for which federal dollars can be spent have been broadened. This means that while a city may receive the same or even more federal funds than in the 1970s, the funds are likely to be used much differently than in the past. If the budgetary reductions that are being discussed take place, the cities will suffer a net loss in federal aid.

While it is difficult to draw major conclusions now about the sustained impact of the Reagan policies on the cities, a variety of research efforts have explored their political impact. One of the first and most comprehensive efforts was Palmer and Sawhill's *The Reagan Experiment*. This collection of essays considered the various policies of the first eighteen months of the Reagan administration. The editors conclude "it is clear that the changes introduced thus far make the distribution of income less equal and require some sacrifices by low-income families while granting large tax cuts to high-income families." As low-income families need more services, cities will be unable to provide them due to the loss of federal revenues and inability to raise local revenues.

Empirical research has focused on the impact of the Reagan proposals and actual policies on American cities. Richard L. Cole and Delbert Taebel have "surveyed urban officials of Texas and other states in an attempt to assess the attitudes and anticipated responses of urban officials to the President's proposals." Terry Clark, in the *Newsletter of the Committee for Community Research*, has coordinated an effort to investigate local decision making in a time of budgetary retrenchment.

The purposes for which federal dollars can be spent have been broadened.

Richard Nathan has coordinated a team of investigators observing local decision making in a variety of settings across the country; the material is being published in both project form and as individual work by the project's field observers. The Nathan research, patterned after his earlier general revenue sharing and community block grant research, is concerned with how communities have dealt with changing budgetary and fiscal situations. The findings are largely consistent with those reached by the other researchers previously mentioned, and provide a useful perspective on not only the impacts but the nature of American federalism today.

In 1981 and 1982, a relatively short mail questionnaire was sent to the chief executive and finance officers in cities with a population over 25,000 in Illinois, Indiana, Michigan, and Wisconsin. The aggregate response rates for each year were 52 percent and 51 percent, respectively. The response rates were consistent for each state except Indiana: 61 percent and 30 percent. One hundred thirty-one respondents, 33 percent of the total respondents, answered both questionnaires. The respondents were similar to the nonrespondents in terms of city size, state, and position held. The 131 respondents answering both questionnaires are used in the analysis.

Among the questions asked the city officials were their expectations about reductions in city services (asked in 1981), whether reductions had taken place (asked in 1982), and whether future reductions were likely (asked in 1982). Except for Illinois, at least 70 percent of the

local officials in each state anticipated service reductions because of the policies of the Reagan administration. In Illinois, slightly over half the respondents (52 percent) indicated service reductions were anticipated. By 1982, in all four states, actual service reductions were less than anticipated; 21 percent of the Wisconsin, 22 percent of the Illinois, 46 percent of the Michigan, and 70 percent of the Indiana respondents indicated service reductions occurred in 1982. Despite this experience, the respondents indicated future service reductions were expected to be higher than the initial ones they had experienced.

When city size is used to explain service reductions, another interesting pattern develops: The larger the city, the more immediate service cutbacks have been and the more they are anticipated in the future. In cities with a population over 100,000, the Reagan policies are seen as having caused nearly universal service reductions. For cities with a population between 50,000 and 100,000, the policies have led to service reductions in less than half. About 25 percent of cities under 50,000 had actual service cutbacks. This pattern holds when future service cutbacks were considered, with the exception that more respondents from smaller cities anticipated a considerable increase.

The data support several conclusions. First, more than 20 percent of the respondents in each of the four states reported actual service reductions because of the Reagan budget cuts. Second, city officials were initially wrong in their estimation of the anticipated impact on service reductions; respondents tended to be poor predictors of service reductions and usually overestimated the size of the reductions. Third, city size is associated with the likelihood of service reductions: The larger the city, the more likely service reduction has occurred and will occur. Fourth, city officials are again predicting service reductions despite the fact that their initial anticipation of service cuts was too high. If they are correct, the budget cuts will have even a greater impact on their cities and city services in the future than the cuts did initially.

For the three questions dealing with the impact of the Reagan proposals on local tax increases, a high percentage of only the Wisconsin respondents anticipated local tax increases; the respondents in the other three states did not anticipate local tax increases. When the respondents indicated what actually had happened in 1982, only Indiana had a higher percentage indicating more local tax increases had occurred than anticipated. In the other three states, actual tax increases were less than anticipated, especially in Wisconsin. When asked about the possibility of future increases, respondents from Indiana were the most likely to indicate future increases while a lower percentage of respondents in the other three states indicated future local tax increases were less likely than in 1981. Based on the data, it appears that for most respondents the Reagan proposals have not meant as great an increase in local taxes as expected, but a sizable number of respondents expect a future increase.

City size had a slight impact on anticipated tax increases in 1981, for the range was from 50 percent for cities between 100,000 and 250,000 to 41 percent for respondents in cities between 50,000 and 100,000. The respondents in cities between 100,000 and 250,000 were more likely to indicate an actual tax increase than smaller cities. On the other hand, the smaller cities were more likely to indicate anticipated increases. Size did not have the impact on tax increases that it did on reductions in city services or that state location did.

The Reagan policies have had a substantial impact in these cities and the policies have led to substantial reductions in city services and increases in local taxes in many cases. Despite this, the dominant conclusion is that the Reagan policies have not led to the drastic reductions in services and increases in local taxes many city officials feared. What the impact of the policies will be over a longer period of time is more difficult to assess and other research is needed to answer the questions of which services were eliminated and which citizens were affected by the cutbacks. Despite these caveats, it remains important to stress that the short-term impact of the Reagan proposals has not been widespread service reductions or tax increases.

In three of the four states, more respondents were satisfied with the New Federalism than dissatisfied; Indiana respondents were equally divided in their evaluation. Despite this, a majority of only the Wisconsin respondents were satisfied with the program; majorities of the respondents in the other three states were either dissatisfied or uncertain in their evaluation of the program. When the respondents are categorized by city size a clear pattern emerges: The smaller the city, the higher the percentage of respondents favoring the Reagan program;

> The Reagan proposals have had a major impact on the cities, but the impact has not been as drastic as originally expected and feared.

---

however, even in the smallest cities, less than half of the respondents were satisfied with it. When respondent party identification is introduced, the division becomes even sharper: 12 percent of the Democratic respondents and 77 percent of the Republican respondents favor it. Independents were nearly equally divided, but 27 percent of them were uncertain.

When the Reagan policies are compared with the Carter domestic policies, the former lost some support between 1981 and 1982; in neither year did a majority of the respondents favor Reagan's policies over Carter's. In 1982, the smaller the city, the more likely the satisfaction with Reagan's policies. In no case did the level of preference increase from 1981 to 1982. Also, there is sharp division when party identification is introduced. The Independents are almost evenly divided, and the Republican and Democrat respondents overwhelmingly select the policies of the president of their party.

When the Nixon domestic policies are compared, the responses are more varied. The respondents were more favorable toward Nixon's policies than Reagan's. The respondents did not change their opinion to a considerable extent between 1981 and 1982 (about 40 percent favoring Reagan's proposals), with the respondents in three states (Indiana the exception) indicating a slight increase in preference for the Reagan policies. The smaller the city, the more favorable the comparison, but even in the most favorable case, only 42 percent of the respondents favored the Reagan policies to Nixon's in 1981 and 47 percent in 1982. In 1982, 38 percent of the respondents who were Democrats favored Reagan's policies over Nixon's.

Reagan's domestic policies are not popular with the local leaders who responded to the questionnaire. In addition, the policies are not seen as favorable alternatives to those of Carter and Nixon. Respondents rank the domestic policies of both Carter and Nixon over Reagan's and, more importantly, in most cases fewer than half are satisfied with the Reagan policies.

While it is difficult for the social scientist to identify the precise moment broad social changes take place, it is possible to identify the forces set in motion by the changes. Such is the case with recent intergovernmental relations in the United States. The critical watershed was the 1970s; the social programs and increased federal involvement of the 1960s reached their peak and then were reduced. While few of the participants realized it, the debates of the 1970s centered on how best to limit or reduce the activities of the federal government, not on how to expand the scope of federal involvement. The Reagan administration has accelerated the reductions in federal financial support for the cities. The important questions remaining are whether the pendulum will once again begin to swing in the opposite direction or whether it will swing even farther in the present direction.

The Reagan proposals have had a major impact on the cities, but the impact has not been as drastic as originally expected and feared. The larger the city, the more pronounced the impact on both service reductions and tax increases. The cities and their political leaders will have to reorganize the provision of basic services and the range of such services.

The Reagan program is having a profound impact on the intergovernmental system. As the data indicate, many local political leaders are not pleased with the policies, but the policies are achieving their goals: Federal involvement, both programmatic and financial, is declining. Some city governments are now being faced with major budgetary crises as the amount of federal funding decreases. Cities that have the needed tax base and the political will to raise taxes are more likely to avoid short-term problems, but in the long term all cities will be forced to reexamine the range of services they offer and how they are financed.

While it is tempting to predict widespread collapse and difficult times for the cities, it is important to point out that the Reagan program, in its initial stages, has been implemented during a time of nearly unprecedented economic problems. High unemployment rates and low economic growth make it more difficult for cities to cope with their situation. As in the past, the American federal system has shown remarkable resiliency. There is little reason to doubt that this will not continue. Certainly Reagan's domestic policies during his second term will have an impact on the nature of American federalism and on the American city. □

READINGS SUGGESTED BY THE AUTHOR:

Cole, Richard L. and Taebel, Delbert A. *Attitudes of Texas Urban Officials to New Federalism: The First Year*. Arlington, Tex.: Institute of Urban Studies, 1983.

Nathan, Richard P. *The Plot That Failed*. New York: John Wiley, 1975.

Nathan, Richard P. et al. "Initial Effects of Fiscal Year 1982 Reductions in Federal Domestic Spending." In John W. Ellwood, ed. *Reductions in U.S. Domestic Spending: How They Affect State and Local Governments*. New Brunswick, N.J.: Transaction Books, 1982.

Palmer, John V. and Sawhill, Isabel V. *The Reagan Experiment*. Washington, D.C.: Urban Institute, 1982.

Savas, E.S. *Privatizing the Public Sector*. Chatham, N.J.: Chatham House, 1982.

Supercities

The Growing Crisis

Supercities—congested, polluted, and unmanageable urban centers containing millions of residents—already exist in a number of Third World nations. We must act now to control such unmanaged urban growth, says author Rashmi Mayur.

Rashmi Mayur

Rashmi Mayur, an urban systems scientist and environmental planner, is president of the Global Futures Network. His address is 38F Maker Tower, Cuffe Parade, Bombay 400 005, India.

The human population of most developing countries is increasing at a threatening pace. If rapid population growth in poor nations is not controlled soon, there will be mass starvation, widespread misery, and breakdown of the local and even global social fabric.

Earth's population stands at 4.8 billion. Eighty-two million were added during 1984. This means that over 1.5 million children are born each week. In India, for example, there are 40,000 new mouths to feed *each day*. By the dawn of the twenty-first century, forecasts call for there to be 6.2 billion people on earth. If current trends continue, the earth's population will reach 8.2 billion by 2025 and is projected to stabilize at an incredible 10.5 billion sometime during the twenty-first century.

The tragedy of this population growth is that 90% of it will take place in poor, underdeveloped, and overcrowded countries in Africa, Asia, and South America. This has horrendous implications for the future of these civilizations.

Today, 41% of the world's people live in cities and towns.

Within the next 15 years, 52% of the earth's population will reside in urban centers. Some cities are becoming so gargantuan that, for most of the people living in them, life has become a nightmare.

Large Cities of Today And Tomorrow

Ninety percent of the earth's population will likely be urbanized by the end of the next century. Much of this urbanization will take place in "supercities" in Third World countries.

Today, Mexico City, with a current population of 17 million, epitomizes the supercity. Mexico City is an anthill of people, activities, cars, industries, and offices. It is already a city characterized by breakdown—of air quality, of traffic control, of crime. Slums are mushrooming everywhere. Worst of all, many of its residents are losing hope that they will ever have civilized lives.

Bombay, Lagos, Sao Paulo, and Jakarta are rapidly heading in the same direction. Their ecologies are being destroyed, and existence there, as in Mexico City, is becoming a diseased existence.

The United Nations has estimated that eight large cities of the Third World will have a combined population of 170 million by the year 2000. These cities are Mexico City (28 million by the year 2000), Sao Paulo (26 million), Shanghai (23 million), Calcutta (20 million), Beijing (20 million), Rio de Janeiro (19 million), Bombay (17 million), and Jakarta (17 million).

More than 50% of urban growth in the southern hemisphere is due to migration—the poor leaving their centuries-old homelands in search of survival. More than 20 million people migrate to cities each year in less-developed countries. And, while large cities of the Third World are exploding, small towns are dying or declining.

While urban populations are growing at almost twice the rate of national growth, large cities are growing at a rate three to four times as high. Streams of people are moving into overcrowded cities in order to escape wretched conditions in the countryside, although the situation in many of these cities seems even more horrendous.

At the same time that urban population centers grow uncontrolledly, the infrastructures necessary to meet the demand for water, housing, sewerage, roads, transportation, education, and medical facilities continue to decline and erode. There are simply not enough resources to meet the multiplying demands.

Bombay, like Mexico City, is a classic example. Bombay's population, which was 3 million in 1950, is already 9 million and is expected to reach 17 million within the next 20 years. It is one of the fastest growing metropolises in the world (4.2% growth annually), almost equalling some of the front-ranking cities like Mexico City (5%), Cairo, Jakarta, Sao Paulo, and Nairobi.

Reprinted from *The Futurist* August 1985, pp. 27-30. Published by the World Future Society, 4916 St. Elmo Avenue, Washington, D.C. 20014.

"Some cities are becoming so gargantuan that, for most of the people living in them, life has become a nightmare."

Urban planners cannot cope with the growth.

During the last three decades, Bombay, like some other cities, has experienced ruthless expansion. The verdant beauty of the city has been destroyed. Bombay today is a vast expanse of shanty towns with heaps of garbage, no greenery, a thick pall of smog hanging over the city, and millions of residents trying to eke out their survival.

As in other such cities, Bombay exists in a state verging on anarchy and chaos. There is simply no room. Demography and resources are in imbalance. Fifty-two percent of the people are refugees, with 500,000 living on sidewalks. If trends continue, at least 75% of Bombay's population will live in squalid conditions, with the resultant breakdown of services and amenities, deterioration of living conditions, and decline of the qual-

ity of environment, not to mention social, political, and institutional collapse. Such is the prognosis and forecast for many large cities in the Third World.

An Alternative Scenario

Although further urbanization is probably inevitable, the present deterioration of human conditions is not necessary. There are cities such as Zurich, Montreal, Edinburgh, Vienna, Leningrad, and Beijing that show the way by providing promising alternatives for a sustainable, desirable, and enjoyable human habitat.

There is still hope and reason for

Downtown district in Seoul, Korea.
CARL PURCELL/AID

"Populations cannot be allowed to grow uncontrolledly. Yet, in spite of rapid population growth, most countries have made no serious attempts to grapple with this desperate problem."

CARL PURCELL/AID

Rural family listens to family planning representative near New Delhi. In spite of rapid population growth, only 25% of the 130 million couples in the reproductive age group in India have received any information about family planning or birth control.

optimism. Large cities in the less-developed regions can be controlled and saved from disaster. The task is uphill but not impossible. The answer is in people and not necessarily in technology.

Populations cannot be allowed to grow uncontrolledly. Yet, in spite of rapid population growth, most countries have made no serious attempts to grapple with this desperate problem. In India, for example, only 25% of the 130 million couples in the reproductive age group have been reached with information about family planning and birth control. Clearly, education rather than new technology is needed. In order to reach manageable proportions, India's population growth must be brought down to 1.5% within five years and to less than 1% by the end of the century. Equivalent levels should be reached in other developing nations.

Planning and Managing Urban Development

Next, the growth of Third World cities must be stopped or at least drastically slowed. Then, further development of such cities must be carefully planned. The first step would be to create a metropolitan administration that would supersede all the existing authorities and function independently from the national government. This metropolitan administration should have an elected executive, as well as a cabinet consisting of the functional heads of departments such as housing, transportation, health, police, etc.

The metropolitan region would then be subdivided into various manageable local bodies so that authority can be delegated as close to the people as possible. The boundaries of the communities embraced by the metropolis should not be de-

cided on historical or political grounds but on economic, social welfare, and other urban considerations.

A metropolitan development plan should be prepared, based on resources and requirements. There should be a short-range as well as a long-range plan. The metropolitan administration would coordinate, supervise, and implement the plan. Its first concern should be to "decongest" the center city and develop the total metropolitan area.

The metropolitan development plan should be part of a wider regional development plan prepared by the national government. If the regional development plan brings growth and benefits to the entire region, it could halt the mass migration of people to metropolitan areas. The metropolitan administration could establish priorities for development and allocate resources accordingly. Such priorities would not only be based on urgent needs but also be related to other development efforts.

For example, cities should be demotorized through the use of efficient public transportation systems and bicycles. Low-energy and low-pollution transportation systems should be planned. Heavy investment should be made to modernize and develop electronic communications systems, ushering in an age of information for developing cities and regions. Massive programs should be designed for recycling waste and recovering materials, particularly those that are non-renewable. Urban planners should move toward the use of renewable energy sources such as biogas and solar power. And modern management techniques should be applied for administration and decision-making efficiency.

Proper Use of Resources

Third World cities cannot afford to squander scarce and dwindling resources through a policy of laissez-faire. The present waste of resources by a minority of citizens has converted many Third World cities into systems of exploitation, speculation, and selfish aggrandizement and, consequently, has degraded the masses.

Three urgent tasks face urban planners:

● Available resources must be judiciously and selectively used, and efforts must be made to develop new indigenous resources.

● The benefits of resources must be distributed equitably.

● A fair system of sharing and contributing resources must be assured.

It is also imperative that an urban data bank be set up to ensure that policies and planning are based on facts and not on ad hoc whims and fancies, as is the practice today.

Cities throughout the world must be revitalized. Only then can the great opportunities and potentials of mankind be realized. Balanced planning, systematic developments, and global unity are needed. Cities are opportunities for the future. Our task of designing the future must begin today.

A Mayor's Dilemma

In Chicago, the system fights City Hall

SIDNEY LENS

Sidney Lens, a long-time resident of Chicago, is The Progressive's Senior Editor.

Chicago's small revolution is in mid-term limbo.

It was two years ago that Harold Washington became mayor by slaying Goliath, the city's entrenched political machine. Washington, a black member of Congress, defeated two powerhouses—incumbent Mayor Jane Byrne and State's Attorney Richard M. Daley—in the Democratic primary and then overcame white backlash to prevail against the Republican candidate, Bernard Epton.

His victory was an upset, and Washington was praised nationally and internationally. He appeared on the covers of *Newsweek*, *The New York Times Magazine*, and many other publications; he gave radio and television interviews by the dozen.

Washington's win brought spiritual renewal to the black, liberal, and progressive forces that had joined hands to put him in office. They had been waiting decades to settle scores with the machine. "It's our turn now," said hundreds of thousands of Chicagoans. Washington received 97 per cent of the black vote, strong support from liberals, and solid backing from radicals.

"This is the first time in my life that I've ever voted for a capitalist candidate," said a feminist who, in the 1960s, had been a leader of Students for a Democratic Society. Washington, a lawyer, had staked out progressive positions throughout his career.

To be sure, his record was not unblemished. Years before the 1983 campaign, he had served forty days in jail for failing to file income tax returns—the actual taxes were paid, but the forms were not filled out—and for not rendering service to six clients from whom he had accepted $265 in fees. Still, these seemed trivial and ancient offenses, and they were overshadowed by the man's talent and charm. He was a determined reformer: charismatic, witty, and surprisingly well-read. You could find him discussing Plato after midnight with the doorman at his apartment house.

Washington's opposition to the arms race was a matter of genuine conviction, not the flim-flam his Congressional colleagues manufactured for public consumption. He often spoke at antinuclear rallies, strongly supported labor, and championed affirmative action. He was committed to scrapping the patronage system that sustained the Chicago machine and retarded the city's development. He held out the hope of stemming the disintegration of the Second City (which had slipped to third, behind Los Angeles). And he promised to turn Chicago into a habitable place for its injured and oppressed.

Now, at the mid-point of Washington's four-year term, the great expectations are tempered by reality. What was hailed as a victory for social reform has settled into a day-to-day government operation, with progressive touches here and there, but also with bickering, disaffection, ineptitude, and traces of timidity and cronyism.

"Harold just doesn't know how to govern," says a nationally known figure who served on his transition team. "He doesn't know how to assign work or keep in touch with his administration. He has permitted a large incursion of the black bourgeoisie, and I can't stomach that any more than I can stomach the white bourgeoisie."

Alderman Martin Oberman, dean of the liberals and a Washington supporter in the City Council, gives the mayor credit for ending the patronage system, curtailing corruption in city contracting, introducing a local Freedom of Information program, and spurring other advances. "But insofar as a cohesive, workable strategy on how to govern the city, he has done a poor job," says Oberman. "He has no plan for economic development, for creating the kind of atmosphere—good schools, good housing, reduced crime levels—that would attract new business and new jobs."

"He had a great opportunity, but he didn't use it," Oberman adds. "He attacked people he didn't have to attack and made a bad situation worse."

There are 286 black mayors in American cities today, many of them radical leaders of yesteryear—Coleman Young of Detroit, for example, and Andrew Young of Atlanta. They have excited hopes of a new day in their cities, and they have broken with the ways of past administrations. But the system, the powers that be, have a way of containing such people.

Harold Washington has discovered this in Chicago.

When Washington assumed office, his supporters in the fifty-member City Council were five votes short of constituting a majority.

All sixteen black aldermen, including those who had been part of the late Mayor Richard J. Daley's machine, lined up behind the new mayor because it would have been political suicide to do otherwise. Four liberals, including Oberman, joined with Washington as a matter of course, and one other alderman went along because of a dispute with the machine.

Many observers thought Washington could have picked up the five additional votes he needed by appealing to wavering aldermen or by making minor deals. "If he had agreed to appoint a good white police chief, instead of a good black one, he would have had his majority," asserts one political analyst. But he didn't. Instead, the old machine, headed by Alderman Edward (Fast Eddie) Vrdolyak, closed ranks and formed a bloc of twenty-nine. Goliath was not dead after all.

The "Council 29," as the mayor's opponents came to be called, were determined to hold on to as many prerogatives as possible until the 1987 election, when they will try to regain City Hall. They settled in for a protracted battle with Washington that is known as Council Wars.

Vrdolyak and his chief lieutenant, Edward Burke, chairman of the powerful fi-

nance committee, have obstructed and undermined some of the mayor's key programs. Under the Council 29's assault, the city scrapped a $300 million project to rehabilitate Navy Pier as an entertainment and business center. A $1.25 billion O'Hare Airport redevelopment program was delayed while the Council 29 tried to muscle from Washington the right to approve medium- and large-scale contracts. The budget has annually been held hostage to power grabs by Vrdolyak's cronies. (For instance, they promise agreement on the budget in exchange for authority to pass on promotions in the police department.) Relatively small projects, such as the reopening of an abandoned factory to build buses, have died in Burke's finance committee.

For months and now years, the Council 29 have withheld approval of seventy-two major mayoral appointments, making it impossible for Washington to put his stamp on important units of government. A conservative foe of Washington, Ed Kelly, retains control of the Park District because the Council 29 will not review four appointees to that body who would oust Kelly. Though sixteen minor appointments were recently approved, the mayor has not been able to seat his nominees on the Board of Education, the Library Board, and other agencies.

"Our tradition has always been weak executive, strong legislature," says Alderman Roman Pucinski, one of the leaders of the Council 29 and a possible mayoral candidate in 1987.

Of course, that was not true during Richard J. Daley's long reign. But in those days, a subservient Council was rewarded with opportunities for personal enrichment. Aldermen could sell insurance to businesses that worked for the city, or provide legal work at inflated rates, or buy into a host of land and development deals.

In 1974, U.S. Attorney James R. Thompson, now Governor of Illinois, boasted that he had seventy-five "Daley notches" on his belt; he had convicted dozens of politicians close to Daley, including former Governor Otto Kerner and former Cook County Clerk Edward J. Barrett, plus fifty employees of the highly political Chicago police force.

During the Daley era, each alderman and ward comitteeman was allowed to place a few hundred friends, relatives, and neighbors on city and county payrolls, thereby assuring the machine of an army of doorbell ringers in the next election.

This has substantially changed under Washington, but the mayor's achievements have been obscured by Council Wars. Patronage jobs are gone, except for the few allotted by autonomous subgovernments still under machine control, such as the Park District and the Sanitation District. Financial wheeling and dealing is less frequent because of new open-government standards and because an affirmative action program sets aside 25 to 30 per cent of all municipal business for blacks, Hispanics, and women.

The Council Wars are an attempt to reverse this state of affairs—to regain lost clout through political blackmail.

Unfortunately, the Washington administration has been bedeviled by its own impulses of opportunism, cronyism, and bureaucracy. In the absence of major economic and social breakthroughs, these stand out.

Chicago has a new management that has never tasted power before—or not this much power—and some of the players tend to abuse it. The Mayor's reformist image is often challenged by the headlines:

¶ Five of Washington's aides, including Corporation Counsel James Montgomery, make a trip to Europe to study "people-movers" for the O'Hare Airport renovation project. It is a small matter, involving only a few thousand dollars, but the administration cannot explain why its chief lawyer had to study an engineering problem abroad.

¶ A black lawyer from Atlanta pays $100 for a $1 million interest in a multimillion-dollar newsstand concession at O'Hare.

¶ Two lawyers close to the mayor are

appointed as co-counsel on some municipal bond work. The press says they will each make $200,000 a year on the deal (though one of the two tells me the contract will net her only $47,000 in the first year). Such work had long been monopolized by white lawyers, so it seems reasonable to cut blacks in on the action. But the transaction raises questions about favoritism.

¶ A black politician who had never been in the court reporting business is given a court reporting contract covering the whole city.

¶ Some "minority" companies turn out to be white companies that have a few blacks or women in key posts as window dressing.

¶ The cousin of a black alderman is awarded a $2.5 million no-bid contract with American Airlines after seven black aldermen meet with the company.

And so on. If there is any consolation, it is that the improprieties are still incidental, sporadic exceptions. They have not become institutionalized, as they were during past administrations. In Chicago, it is progress when corruption stops being the order of the day.

But what about the promise of a new and better Chicago? What has Harold Washington done for the Windy City?

'We're boxed into a system,' says Mayor Washington; 'we're barely a pimple on an elephant's rear end'

"Practically nothing" so far, says Don Rose, Chicago's leading political analyst and a Washington supporter. In Rose's shorthand, "practically nothing" is not zero, but little of major substance. He and other left-of-center theorists—such as former Alderman Dick Simpson—point to a sizable folio of Washington achievements, but taken together, these amount to no big deal.

Washington has certainly made city government more responsive to the citizenry. The Office of Professional Standards, which hears complaints against the police department, has been moved out of police headquarters—where it inevitably ruled in favor of the police—to a neutral location. The police commander of each

district now sets aside (or is supposed to set aside) two to three hours a week for chats with area residents.

Pregnant women and those with small children are being provided with coupons for cereals, baby foods, and dairy products. Washington added 1,200 beds for the homeless. He raised mortgage money for 8,000 housing units in twenty-two months. The previous administration funded 2,964 units in four years.

The mayor unsealed government files that had been hidden from the public for ages; he struck a blow against inertia and indifference by terminating the patronage system; he began rectifying old injustices by increasing public and private opportunities for minorities and women. And even his adversaries admit that Washington's cabinet appointments have been excellent—good technicians who know how to solve problems.

By recognizing unions for 40,000 city workers, Washington reversed the paternalistic policy of Mayor Daley, who eschewed written agreements and conferred raises at whim (except for skilled craft workers). Washington has also placed an emphasis on economic development in the neighborhoods; such progressive community leaders as Gail Cincotta and Slim Coleman have participated in the planning.

No one can gainsay these improvements or the enthusiasm with which Washington's assistants implement them. But if you compare them to the city's needs, they still add up to practically nothing.

Don Rose does not put the whole blame on Mayor Washington. "There are reasons," he says, and chief among them is the machine, whose rule left Chicago lagging decades behind other cities.

"The City that Works" really never did. It worked only for the elites—for big business, the banks, the real estate firms, the labor hierarchy, a small number of leading blacks. The majority of Chicago's residents were left to fester. According to a Northwestern University professor who studies poverty, half of the city's seventy-six neighborhoods were permanently poor because they had no base for economic sustenance. Between 1950 and 1970, half a million whites fled to the suburbs, while the black population almost tripled.

According to the official figures, 857,000 Chicagoans live below the poverty level; others say the number is as high as 1.2 million. The city's permanent depression hits minority youth hardest, leaving them prey to drugs, crime, and other afflictions of impoverishment.

Though white flight has been stemmed in the last few years, the city's tax base remains gravely weakened, constraining what Washington can do. The population of Chicago shrank from 3.6 million in 1950 to less than 3 million in 1980. Since 1969, 2,258 factories—more than one fourth of the total—have closed shop or moved else-

where. Last year, 103 small plants opened, but they do not begin to make up for the shutdown of Wisconsin Steel (3,000 jobs), the contraction of U.S. Steel (9,000 jobs), or the overall disappearance of 248,000 jobs since 1972.

Washington's challenge is not to provide episodic patch-up but to institute systemic change. And like it or not, it is impossible to solve deep social and economic problems within the confines of a single city.

A mayor—Washington or any other—depends on Federal and state funds. What's more, even the most visionary program can be derailed by the captains of industry, banking, and real estate (along with their allies in the media). Washington understands the bind better than most politicians.

"We're boxed into a system," he recently told me. "Simply by local initiative we can't resolve all city problems. We're limited in what we can do—we're barely a pimple on an elephant's rear end."

Taxes were raised in Chicago, as Washington had promised during the 1983 campaign, but the revenue is not enough to put thousands back to work, to rebuild scores of substandard housing units, or to feed the poor. If Washington tried to launch a more expansive program—one that involved higher taxes on business—a dozen business leaders would compel him to retreat. They can lower credit ratings, cut off financing, close down factories, choke off new commercial development, and persuade state and Federal officials to put the squeeze on the recalcitrant mayor.

The chief executive of a small steel town in the Middle West once gave me a short lecture on the subject: "If I announce a major plan that the steel mill opposes, I suddenly face a threat they will move operations elsewhere, or reduce operations, leaving our economy here in tatters. The governor calls me to say he intends to cut state aid to my city, and I hear rumbles from Washington, D.C., about possible similar action. I have little choice but to yield."

Chicago is a much bigger place, but equally vulnerable to pressure from the Establishment. Fully 15 per cent of the city's funds come from the Federal Government. President Reagan's proposed 1986 budget cuts would cost the city $307 million in a single year and $1 billion over three years. There would be major reductions in community development, job training, and housing.

In human terms, says Mayor Washington, the Reagan Administration's budget would reduce city health services by more than half, cause the layoff of 1,900 health and sanitation workers, push transit fares from 90 cents to $1.35 a ride, eliminate 12,000 summer jobs for low-income youth, and cause many other setbacks.

A Fresh Start in Boston, Too

Tonight, Boston made history," declared Raymond Flynn, the city's newly elected mayor, at his victory party in 1983. "We've proven that the hopes that unite us are greater than the fears that separate us."

In his first year as mayor, Flynn has managed to infuse the chronically divided city with a sense of optimism and renewal. He is committed to bridging Boston's racial fissures, strengthening the besieged neighborhoods, and assuring tenant rights. Flynn brought openness and a progressive program to an office that, during the sixteen-year tenure of former Mayor Kevin White, trafficked in back-room political deals and kowtowed to real estate and business interests.

"The difference between the way we were treated by the White administration and the relationship we have with the Flynn administration is just night and day," observes Grant Young, vice president of the Massachusetts Tenants Organization. "When we used to go into the White administration with problems, they would say 'fine,' and we'd never hear from them again—it was like talking to a brick wall."

Flynn, forty-five, was born and raised in the conservative Irish working-class area of South Boston. His early stands as a state legislator reflected the values of his constituency: He was an outspoken critic of school busing and the Equal Rights Amendment. Since then, however, his politics have evolved.

"Flynn has a genuine concern and a real empathy for poor people and for working people," says Peter Dreier, the mayor's housing adviser. "His basic goal is to make government a way to help residents who are vulnerable."

But there is growing concern that the Flynn administration may not be capable of delivering on its compassion or of solving the city's fiscal woes. Questions about managerial competence have dogged the mayor and his aides since they took office. And some in the coalition that helped elect Flynn are starting to wonder if his liberal pronouncements and policies contain more style than substance.

"Flynn has succeeded in projecting a certain image, a progressive image," says Adam Parker, Boston regional director of Massachusetts Fair Share, the citizens' group. "Now he has to live up to that image, and already there are some complaints that he isn't. The challenge he faces is to both run the city well and run it in a progressive manner."

One of the toughest tests will be guiding Boston out of its financial straits. The squeeze that began when the state capped property taxes in 1982 has worsened under the budget-slashing policies of Ronald Reagan.

To boost revenues, Flynn has asked the legislature for authority to tax Boston's visitors and nonresident consumers, using hotel, entertainment, and parking levies. The idea is unpopular in the suburbs, and it will not be an easy task to persuade capitol politicians that Boston deserves special consideration as the "jewel" of Massachusetts.

In meeting the city's needs, Flynn has had to pick through a minefield of competing interests.

He promised a bigger piece of the pie to neighborhoods and low-income residents, but he must also accommodate the business and real estate community that is cashing in on the largest development boom in Boston's history. The mayor continued his predecessor's program of "linkage," in which commercial developers pay into a special housing fund. Flynn also wrested jobs for city residents from various large downtown development projects.

But Flynn still faces the most significant and complicated development initiative, "Dudley station," where property buyers are casting greedy eyes on the poor area of Roxbury. An unrestrained market there could displace thousands of low-income and minority residents.

"Things are not perfect now," says Young of the Tenants Organization. "There are some outstanding issues we are waiting for Flynn to deal with, and there have been disappointments."

Rent control was one such letdown. Flynn could not pass a strong protection ordinance through the Boston City Council last fall. Real estate and development firms bitterly opposed the housing package, and the mayor did not mount an aggressive lobbying effort in behalf of rent control and restrictions on condominium conversions. Eventually, a much weaker compromise was introduced by a supporter of the development interests, and Flynn supported it.

"They did a crummy job of handling it," says Jack Hall, an aide to Boston City Councilor David Scondras, who is an outspoken liberal. "They completely dropped the ball."

As for Boston's historically thorny racial problems, Flynn gets high marks from the city's minority leadership for evincing a desire to improve relations. Tensions between the races appear to have lessened, and much of the improvement is credited to Flynn, who seems to be transcending his South Boston roots. (The mayor occasionally plays basketball with youngsters in black neighborhoods.)

But here again, Flynn's allies ask whether the image matches the reality of the situation. A report filed last summer by the Massachusetts Commission Against Discrimination showed that only 33 per cent of 303 new employees in the Flynn administration were minorities, and the vast majority of those were hired for jobs paying less than $20,000 a year. Flynn is also criticized for not involving Roxbury's black community in the preliminary planning for Dudley station.

Nonetheless, "Flynn has made great strides in race relations and in making the public perceive that things are better," says Jack Robinson, president of the Boston chapter of the National Association for the Advancement of Colored People. "That is a great achievement."

To succeed in his second year, Flynn will have to change more than just perceptions.

—MINDY BLODGETT

(Mindy Blodgett is a reporter for The Tab, a Boston-area weekly.)

Faced with this situation, Washington has had to choose between a strategy of class conflict—a head-on clash with the First National Bank, Standard Oil, Sears, the Arthur Rubloff real estate firm, the *Chicago Tribune*, the Council 29, and the White House—and a strategy that mutes class conflict in favor of modest reform. He has taken the latter route, perhaps in the hope that his power will be firmly consolidated after the 1987 election.

Dave Canter, who advises the Mayor on electoral issues, expects Washington to win in 1987, although backing from white liberals will soften and the percentage of black supporters will decrease (while the total black vote increases). More important, Canter anticipates that the number of pro-Washington aldermen will grow to at least twenty-eight because of court orders revising the boundaries of certain wards.

So Washington is not rocking the boat, and the Establishment is coming to the conclusion that Chicago must have a black mayor—preferably a moderate one—or face chaos. The city's black community is asserting itself; other segments of the population are dormant or in retreat.

In its mid-term appraisal of Washington, the *Tribune* called on the private sector to "muster the courage to help him."

Washington meets every month with leaders of the business community. He offers assistance and enlists their support in efforts to "improve city government." The mayor is believed to oppose having the World's Fair in Chicago in 1992, but he pays lip service to the idea to avoid offending the moneyed forces that support it.

On the labor front, he has taken an uncharacteristic "neutral" stand and, in at least one instance, sided actively with management. In January 1984, he urged city bus drivers to accept a proposal from the Chicago Transit Authority that would defer payment of $26 million into their pension fund—a sore point with the union's rank and file.

Washington failed to head off two strikes by 27,000 school teachers and related employees, and he refused to castigate Board of Education Chairman George Munoz (a Washington appointee), who was trying to break the strikes. The mayor's efforts in behalf of unemployed steelworkers have been lame; a participant in the meetings aimed at preventing a shutdown of U.S. Steel's South Works says Washington's representative "tries hard not to offend management for fear he will lose business support in the next election."

Timidity was also displayed in the strike at the Danly Machine Corporation. It took sixteen weeks, according to a strike leader, for the Washington administration to order Chicago police officers to stop moonlighting as scabs at the suburban plant.

The mayor showed more initiative in the case of Playskool, which announced its intention to leave town despite a city investment in the toy factory. Under a compromise, Playskool will spend almost $500,000 to place laid-off employees elsewhere.

Washington's staff is not organized for a big breakthrough, and its ineptitude sometimes descends to surprising depths: Phone calls are not returned, letters go unanswered, the mayor misses meetings. Moreover, many of Washington's senior aides are more pragmatic than progressive, most notably Chief of Staff Bill Ware.

The mayor's personality and politics may incline him toward radicalism, but the business interests, the Federal Government, and the machine block his path. To transcend the policy of moderation, he would have to mobilize poor and disfranchised Chicagoans for mass activity and join hundreds of other mayors to challenge the American Establishment.

He may yet do so, but halfway through his first term, Washington has not.

At VISTA we were less interested in priming the pump than in fixing the boiler

I Was a Spear Carrier in the War on Poverty

Jonathan Rowe

Jonathan Rowe is an editor of The Washington Monthly.

When I tell people that in the late sixties I was a VISTA Volunteer on Manhattan's Lower East Side, I sometimes sense in them a certain reverential awe, as though I were a veteran of the good war. This I greatly enjoy. But the impression is not entirely accurate.

Though a member of the generation that came of age during the sixties, I was never really of it. The turmoil I experienced during my college years was largely personal, and unlikely as it now sounds, both the civil rights movement and the Vietnam war were like a commotion in a room down the hall. The closest I came in those college years to a political act was joining the Young Republicans.

This was mainly to help a friend who needed votes for an opposition slate, but it was not out of character either. One of my first enduring political memories was the time my grandfather pulled me aside at a family gathering to dispense a bit of advice. He had suffered through a dozen ulcerous years of Roosevelt and he was not about to let his grandson go down that ideological drain. "Jonny," he admonished me, apropos of nothing, "I want you to remember one thing. YOU CAN'T PRIME THE PUMP." My formative political reading consisted of such fare as Barry Goldwater's *Conscience of a Conservative*,

Herbert W. Philbrick's *I Led Three Lives*, and Harry and Bonaro Overstreet's *What We Must Know About Communism*. Were he still around when I finished high school, my grandfather would have been proud of my long senior paper on John Maynard Keynes, in which I concluded that a government that manipulated the economy was a menace to our freedom.

College didn't really alter any of these beliefs. But somehow in my mind, conservatism had always been connected to the idea of service; if the government wasn't supposed to do very much, then wasn't it all the more important that individuals pick up the slack? I didn't see how you could fob off humanity's well-being onto automatic cosmic processes, the way communists do with their historical dialectic and capitalists do with their invisible hand. This was the Boy Scout Manual view of individual good deeds rather than a yen for what was called, at the time, "social change."

During the summer after my junior year, I worked on a house painting and tutoring project in the black Boston ghetto of Roxbury. At the end of my senior year, the "future" suddenly looming before me like a cantankerous creditor, and the draft beginning to loom up as well, I found a VISTA application outside my college dining hall. Actually, it was the Peace Corps that had captured my imagination. But the Peace Corps application was long and complicated, and they seemed to want skills like animal husbandry that were not my strong suit. The VISTA application was much simpler. I felt some trepidation, nevertheless, submitting my meager creden-

From *The Washington Monthly*, November 1984, pp. 38-47. Reprinted by permission of The Washington Monthly, 1711 Connecticut Avenue, N.W., Washington, D.C., 20009.

tials before those high people in Washington. A few days later they called, person to person, and asked if I could start training in June.

These events, and those that followed, have been on my mind during the last four years. President Reagan might have been expected to embrace VISTA's volunteer spirit: the way it tries to help communities help themselves, the patriotism that is implicit in taking time out to help your country. He might have seen what a bargain the government and the country get when they tap the enthusiasm of young (and old and middle-aged) people for, at present, $7,800 a year, all costs included. But Reagan first tried to eliminate the program, and when Congress wouldn't let him, his underlings set out to run it into the ground. Key positions have gone unfilled for months, even years. There has been absolutely no national recruiting of the kind that made it possible for me to pick up an application outside my college dining hall. They even removed VISTA from the stationery of Action, the agency of which VISTA is a part.

For people like Thomas Pauken, Reagan's Action director, VISTA is a symbol: social "activism," the antiwar protests, Hayden and Fonda, the works. Indeed, VISTA did arise as part of Lyndon Johnson's War on Poverty. It *has* tended to attract volunteers of other than Reaganite persuasion, largely because they seem less interested than Reaganites in making money. VISTA volunteers *have* found that to improve the lot of people low on the ladder, they sometimes have had to do what the realtors, gun-owners, and cigarette companies do, which is to try to bring some pressure to bear upon elected officials.

More specifically, the Reaganites have objected to the way Sam Brown, who was Carter's Action head, dispensed large VISTA grants to groups with nationwide organizing agendas, like Associated Community Organizations for Reform Now (ACORN). Fair enough. But they have inflated this objection into a caricature of the entire program that bears virtually zero relationship to what I experienced as a VISTA volunteer. The funny part is that I think Ronald Reagan himself would approve of at least part of what I saw and learned. As for the other part, I wish he had been there to see it with me. Pauken too.

Sobering up the white boys

When I set off for Springfield, Massachusetts a few days after graduation for VISTA "training," I felt a little like a Marine recruit headed for Camp Lejeune. It did not turn out quite that way.

I lived with a blind woman—a real live member of the community—who kept getting the mineral oil and the cooking oil confused, and I was assigned to a local storefront action group of the kind that were proliferating at the time. The director of this group, a large

"I stayed with a blind woman in Springfield, Massachusetts."

man of obvious Mau-Mauing potential, told two other volunteers and me to go register new voters in a housing project that was set off like a dump on the outskirts of town. That was it.

Looking back, I think the primary purpose of this assignment may have been to give the white boys something to do, and perhaps sober them up a bit. Not appreciating such subtleties at the time, I undertook the task with earnest zeal, trooping up and down the stinking stairwells, knocking on doors, trying to cajole people into coming with us to city hall a week or so hence. Innocence is a greatly undervalued asset, and we actually spent an entire day at the end of this canvass ferrying new voters back and forth. The people at the store front seemed no less surprised than those at city hall.

All the while, there were uplifting lectures on poverty by officials from Washington, visits to black churches, and excursions to such places as a migrant labor camp, where we were all duly appalled. What I really needed was advice on walking a ghetto street at 1 a.m. and on attaching a lock to a tenement doorframe that has been reduced to sawdust by holes drilled upon holes (not to mention a little Spanish). The VISTA training program, unfortunately, seemed to have been designed by sociologists, not police patrolmen and locksmiths.

There was no sergeant presiding over this training. Instead, there was a gregarious local social worker we called "Auntie Harriet," who fed and cheer-led us, and generally represented the acme of Jewish motherhood. Aside from a pregnancy in the ranks, the cause of most concern was the volunteers who complained they were given neither sufficient supervision nor "meaningful" work to do. I ignored most of this and went about registering voters, a response which caused the program psychiatrist to puff thoughtfully on his pipe at the required interview at the end of the training. ("You just, ah, withdrew, is that correct . . .?") Again, a locksmith would have been more helpful.

From there, I was assigned to something called the Mobilization for Youth, on Manhattan's Lower East Side. The gangs, the drugs, the crime— I had no idea how I was going to fight poverty in a place like that. It was pretty scary.

'There is nothing you can do'

The Lower East Side was the port of entry for the wave of immigrants, especially Eastern European Jews, that flooded the city in the late 19th century. It is a place of legend, captured in the movie, *Hester Street,* and the classic American novel, *Call It Sleep.* Entertainers like George Jessel and Eddie Cantor grew up here; Jacob Riis discovered how the other half lives;. institutions like the Henry Street Settlement, the Educational Alliance, and the garment workers union defined a whole era of American idealism. Garment district tycoons with homes in Scarsdale or on Long Island started as pushcart peddlers on these same streets.

As these original occupants—many of them at least—moved out, and new immigrants from the Caribbean and the South moved in, the neighborhood began to unravel. In the old days nobody locked his door, even though the Lower East Side was the most crowded area in the world, and neighbors visited from one tenement floor to the next. Now there were still enclaves of stability. But the ubiquitous metal grates across windows and storefronts gave the dark streets the feeling of a city under seige.

That summer, 1967, was like the autumn ripeness before the final decline. Owing largely to the controlled rents—apartments could be had for $37.50 a month—the Lower East Side had become Haight-Ashbury East, the Atlantic capital of the Flower Children. Emaciated acid freaks and Hare Krishna chanters peopled the street corners. The processional organ strains of Procol Harem and the Doors somehow blended with the Latin music blaring from the record stores, the black nationalists, store front evangelists and Hasidim. There were front stoop domino games on milk crates, polkas at the Ukrainian social clubs, and bocci at the corner of East Houston and First Street. And always, those window grates and the specter of crime. It was at first terrifying, but then rapturous. My first night there, I went to Katz's delicatessen and sat next to a man who said he was Art Gar-

funkel's uncle. I could barely imagine what wonders must lie ahead.

Life was not so rapturous, of course, for those who were there because they had no choice. It was for these—the Puerto Ricans and blacks, primarily—that the Mobilization for Youth was founded in 1962. MFY's main focus was job training, including the creation of enterprises, such as a gas station and a luncheonette, to employ the people so trained. But MFY also engaged in direct action against what its organizers saw as the perpetrators of distress in the neighborhood. They organized rent strikes, picketed construction sites over union hiring practices, took on public school principals, and in general made a ruckus not seen on the Lower East Side since the garment workers took on the bosses earlier in the century.

None of this direct action endeared MFY to its targets. At the same time, factions at city hall thought that the millions MFY was receiving from the federal government should be channeled instead through themselves. In 1964 the *Daily News* accused the organization of being a "Red honeycomb," prompting an orgy of investigation that was referred to within MFY simply as "the trouble." MFY survived, but the place was never the same. It was the prototype, I heard repeatedly, for the federal War on Poverty. But by the time I arrived at 255 East Houston Street, an old catering establishment that had been converted into an MFY center, the organization was approaching middle age.

"Which one of you is from Harvard?" Rita was asking. "Is there someone here from Harvard?" Rita was a sturdy Latin woman, bronze and handsome, who had just emerged from a classroom in PS 82 at the corner of Madison and Grand Streets. I had just reported here with another VISTA volunteer to work with the Neighborhood Youth Corps, a summer job program for teenagers that MFY had contracted to run. As the object of Rita's question, I was embarrassed and a little confused. Why did she have to bring up Harvard?

She ushered me into the old classroom, where ochre computer cards were stacked up on hinge-top desks. Tito, a gangly Puerto Rican youth with one arm, sat at one of the desks, flipping doggedly through a stack. Elsewhere in the room sat one or two others, similarly engaged.

These punch cards, I learned, had spawned a crisis in the Youth Corps program. The crew leaders at the service agencies that served as job sites had filled them out incorrectly, and as a result the entire payroll process had gagged. Checks for the Lower East Side were being sent to Bedford-Stuyvesant and Brownsville, kids had not been paid for weeks, and there had been sit-ins and threats of violence. Harvard was going to help straighten things out.

This was not exactly the sort of work the VISTA posters and forward-looking logo had suggested. But since New York was overwhelming and I had no idea how else to wage war on poverty there, the punch cards were at least a way to keep busy and feel like I was contributing.

I worked under Ron, a canny young black from Harlem who had the gift of ironic detachment from the confusion around him. We sat in the classroom, correcting card upon card, while "Whiter Shades of Pale" came from Tito's radio on the window sill. There was no shortage of administrators, who seemed to issue forth from the inner sanctums of PS 82 like clowns from the Volkswagen in the old circus trick. What they all did, I never quite grasped. I began to supect that the Neighborhood Youth Corps was intended to provide summer employment not just for ghetto youth but for high school guidance counselors from Brooklyn as well. There was also, of course, a generous provision for MFY's administrative expenses.

As best I can recall, neither these administrators nor I got out into the field a great deal to actually see the program. What I did see gave me cause for concern. On the positive side, Youth Corps workers were reading to elderly folks with failing eyesight and doing other things along that line. But there were also "recreational aides" or "community support workers," who might hang around a playground and perhaps push some kids on the swings. I was less inclined than others of my generation to question authority, but I did feel impelled to call attention to this.

At the end of one typically sweltering afternoon, I approached Irv (not his real name), one of the top administrators, as he was departing, leather portfolio under arm. Irv was a somber man whose hang-dog expression suggested he had processed a few thousand too many forms in the New York City schools. "Errr," I began, "don't you think we should get out to the job sites more and make sure the kids are doing something useful?"

"Believe me," Irv intoned, with just a trace of irritation, "there is nothing you can do."

Disemburdening the camel

VISTA pay was $205 per month, which had to cover rent, food, everything. This amount was not as little as it may seem. My $49.50 per month rent included utilities, and you could get imperfect eggs and cheese at the Essex Street Market at seconds prices. Ninety-five cents would buy a weighty veal cutlet platter at the Ukrainian restaurants on Tompkins Square Park, or a plate of lo mein in Chinatown. For considerably less you could get a knoblewurst at Katz's. I thought I was living pretty well.

A greater problem than money was crime. There was an absurd incongruity between my rickety doorframe and the hostile world that this

> The common belief is that legal service offices are hotbeds of 'activism.' In reality, Rutgers Street was more of a divorce and welfare mill.

barrier was supposed to protect me against. My window opened out to a fire escape that seemed ominously accessible from the ground. For weeks I lay awake at night concocting medievalish devices for foiling intruders—spikes in the window sill and the like.

In the end, the obvious solution was not to fortify the camel but to disemburden it. I rid myself of everything I might worry about losing and lived in one-and-a-half rooms with only clothes, pots, and plates from a second-hand store on the Bowery, and the old radio on which I listened to Lyndon Johnson announce that he would not seek another term. Poverty is always more pleasant when it is voluntary, but the effect of lightening the load in this fashion was unexpectedly liberating. Since I had little to fear losing, New York became, in a sense, mine. In terms of friendship and experience, it was by far the richest year of my life.

Process server for the people

When the summer was over, I was assigned to one of the MFY legal services offices, the shining stars in the MFY galaxy at the time. The office was the first floor of a tenement at 26 Rutgers Street, at the far bottom of the Lower East Side, near the stanchions of the Brooklyn Bridge. The neighborhood was a living archeological dig. Around one corner, on East Broadway, sober young Hasidim in black robes and *payess* (ear curls) lined up at shul. At the other end of the street, across from the public housing projects, blacks and Puerto Ricans lined up for their late afternoon pharmaceutical trade. To the east, on East Broadway, were the Garden Cafeteria, thick with the aromas of pea soup and challeh, Noah Zark's kosher pizza, and bodegas. To the west the Chinese were spilling over from Chinatown.

The legal services office reflected this polyglot brew. The head attorney was a former youth worker named Bernie. Under him were a Puerto Rican, a black, and a WASP. There were two social workers: Ping, whose conciliatory style might have driven the confrontation types to distraction, and Nadia, who was indifferent to her beauty, both cherubic and world-wise.

The common belief is that such offices were

> Conservatives are wary of VISTA because they see it as a haven for liberals who want to make trouble for society. But I don't see how you could fix the boiler on Henry Street without making trouble for *somebody*.

hot-beds of legal "activism." In reality, Rutgers Street was more a divorce and welfare mill. Ninety-five percent of the cases, it seemed, had to do with the tenuous ordering of unordered lives. I, for the most part, was a messenger. This wasn't exactly on the VISTA posters, either. But I could watch trials from the back of courtrooms and traipse around New York, with which I was infatuated. (This often included, not incidentally, traipsing through Chinatown at lunchtime, on the way to the city courts.) Being a messenger often meant being a "process server." When you start a lawsuit in New York, someone has to deliver a copy of the complaint to the person being sued. This can be interesting work.

I remember one case in which a black woman was divorcing her husband for atrocities I cannot now recall. For some reason the husband, who ran a fish and chips joint not listed in the Michelin guide, had to be served that evening. It was a blustery December night, the streets were desolate, and the scene inside the fish joint was like an Edward Hopper painting racially transposed. Men in Goodwill overcoats and tattered army jackets leaned lank and tired under a fluorescent light, cupping cigarettes in their fingers, waiting for nothing in particular. In the rear, an ox of a man was hacking away at a fish with an enormous cleaver. He was the one I had to inform that his wife was suing for divorce.

I stood across the street, looking through the cracked plate glass, watching the cleaver go up and down, whacking through the fish. I studied the faces for a hint of benevolence. I shivered, and waited; perhaps there would be a fire, or a power outage, or perhaps a rabbi would drop in for a chat. Finally, no such reprieve in sight, I resigned myself to my fate. I am not brave but dutiful to the core. Holding the blue-covered complaint in front of me like a soldier bearing the cross into the crusades, I entered and walked across the room. The cleaver stopped. Everything

stopped. I can still feel those eyes bearing down on me. "This is for you," I forced from my mouth.

He took it, without visible emotion. Then, in a voice that seemed to rumble up from the gravel pits, that sounded like Sonny Terry hung over, "Wha's dis shit?"

Then there was the pianist, a nervous little Jewish man whose wife hated his piano playing so much that she would shut the piano lid on his fingers. He wanted a divorce. But it was a Jiggs and Maggie situation, and he was so terrified of her that he refused to point her out to me in person. This made it difficult for me to serve the complaint. Bernie devised a plan. The pianist and I would secrete ourselves in a broom closet in the senior citizen's center where Mrs. Pianist spent her afternoons. We would peer through a crack in the door. When Mrs. Pianist passed by, he would give the signal, and I would burst forth and present the notice of the divorce.

I have since suspected that Bernie was having fun with my dutifulness, but I regarded this as a solemn assignment and carried it out accordingly. The only hitch was that at first sight of his wife, Mr. Pianist lost his composure and made a break for the stairs, leaving me standing in the broom closet, its door wide open, for all to see.

With Nadia I often made social work calls, investigating family squabbles and welfare problems and occasionally taking an alcoholic husband to Bellevue or Long Island to dry out. The apartments tended to be similar. A television set along with wall hangings of John F. Kennedy and Martin Luther King or the pope formed the family shrine. There was vinyl-covered living room furniture and a formica dinette set. Purist that I am, the television sets surprised me. I questioned whether welfare should provide for such things and took a dim view of those who, I thought, wanted to raise the detritus of the consumer culture to a matter of right.

For this reason I was somewhat skeptical of the major lawsuit in our office of the kind that so annoys the Reagan types. We were trying to establish, to some degree, that welfare recipients should have a telephone as a matter of right. When Jefferson and the others drew up the Bill of Rights in Philadelphia, was telephone service in Lower Manhattan really what they had in mind? I didn't think so. Still, this was my team.

One of the hazards of such lawsuits is that plaintiffs have a way of disappearing. This possibility is especially distressing for legal services attorneys, to whom such suits represent a blow not only for social justice but for career advancement as well. Thus there was some anxiety on Rutgers Street when the plaintiff in the telephone case didn't appear to sign some required papers. I was dispatched to find her.

On the Lower East Side the neighborhood becomes generally worse as you go from Second

Avenue on the west towards Avenue D and the river on the east. Our plaintiff, whom I will call Mrs. Martinez, lived on Avenue C, in a tenement indistinguishable from hundreds of others except that it was shabbier. The mailboxes were gouged and pried almost to the point of uselessness, and the entryway was a littered invitation to junkies and whoever else would take refuge in the building's dark recesses.

I knocked at the apartment. Again. And again. Finally there was a barely audible "Quien es [Who's there]?"

"El abagado [the attorney]," I replied—the magic password. She opened the door a crack and then let me in. With her were a sister, or neighbor, and a little boy who seemed to be ill. Mrs. Martinez had not left the apartment for two or three days. The reason, I was told, was the Columbia riots.

The story on the street was that so many policemen had been summoned to deal with the students rioting uptown that patrols on the Lower East Side had diminished. Junkies and muggers were having a field day, and people like Mrs. Martinez were so terrified that they locked their doors for the duration. Lacking a telephone, she was not able to call a doctor, a lawyer, anyone, when her child became ill.

It is still hard for me to swallow the idea of a "right" to a telephone. But it's almost as hard for me to argue that people like Mrs. Martinez don't need one—perhaps not as a right, but as something the rest of us ought, by public policy, to provide. To the lawyers it may be a distinction without a difference. But to me it seems important that we put a little more emphasis on responsibilities and a little less on rights.

One strike against VISTA in the Reaganesque mind is that its volunteers have, on occasion, interfered with the benevolent workings of the private sector. I helped cause such interference. The private sector was in the person of an individual I will call Shepstein.

Shepstein owned two tenement buildings on Henry Street, about two blocks from the office. When one of the tenants came timidly to our office one afternoon, the building had been without heat and hot water for, I believe, more than a week. This was the dead of winter, with temperatures in single digits. Mothers were huddling with their children in front of open ovens at night to keep from freezing, while elderly ladies were burning charcoal in trash barrels. For at least two days there was no running water at all.

In the world of New York landlord-tenant relations, which resemble relations on the Iran-Iraq border, a primary weapon of battle is something called a "7A." Under a 7A tenants can withhold their rents from the landlord and pay them to a trustee, who will use the money to make needed repairs. To start a 7A the tenants must sign a petition. This is where I came in.

When I tell of my VISTA days, the "tenant organizing" is the part I take greatest pleasure in recounting, sounding as it does like service on the front lines. Actually, I pretty much just held the clipboard. At the first apartment I knocked at that cold February evening I was greeted by Mrs. Tomasita Rivera. Tomasita was somewhere in that foggy territory between 22 and 45 that Puerto Rican women enter when they have not much money and a brood of kids. She had a cap on a front tooth and moved with a kind of tomboy swagger. The bloom may have been off the rose, but her puckish humor and spunk were still there. Tomasita Rivera was a tenant organizer's dream.

Despite her imperfect English, Tomasita understood immediately what was afoot and seized hold of it like a Common Cause chapter head undertaking a good-government drive. For the next several days she and I made our evening troop through the tenements, she doing the talking with her rat-a-tat-tat Spanish, I standing there trying to nod in the right places. Despite the dire conditions, getting the signatures was not always easy. It is a rule of life in such places to minimize contacts with authority, since just about everyone has a skeleton in his or her closet, such as an undisclosed source of income that stands to be exposed. Besides, people on the financial edge just don't like to make trouble. Still, we got the signatures, calling in Ping to translate for the Chinese.

Before we could get Shepstein, however, we had to serve him with the complaint, and before we could do that, we had to find him. This was not a simple matter either, since Shepstein's only listed address was a maildrop, and repeated calls and letters went unanswered. I even tracked down elderly couples who were listed as second mortgagees on his deeds; sitting in a living room on the Grand Concourse in the Bronx, I listened to one such couple lament how Shepstein had welshed on his debt to them. This was reinforcing but it didn't get me any closer to Shepstein.

Finally Bernie decided that if the maildrop was all Shepstein had listed, then the maildrop was what we would serve. It was on 42nd Street, not far from the New York Public Library. The narrow staircase looked forbidding—what ghouls and goons might Shepstein have lurking up there? As it turned out, he had neither ghouls nor goons but rather a lone woman manning a switchboard as though it were a battleship's controls. She was square-shouldered and brawny, her black hair lacquered fast, lipstick blazing, and breasts boosted atop an expanding girth, contoured by her cashmere sweater. She was fearsome, and at the sight of the legal complaint in its telltale blue binding, she exploded.

"You get that *out* of here," she shrieked. "There's no Shepstein here. You have no business...you get that *thing* out of here." As

"We celebrated the occasion with a picket line in which tenants carried placards announcing their views of Shepstein and the city administration."

she was barricaded behind the switchboard, there was no way I could touch her physically with the complaint—the legal requirement of service—and I wasn't sure whether throwing it was sufficient. The only alternative was retreat. Shepstein knew his business. Minutes before I had had visions of him handcuffed before a judge, begging for mercy. Now he was off free.

This was my first failure as a process-server. I wandered down 42nd Street towards Grand Central Station, wondering what to do next. I recalled hearing somewhere that the police had to help you serve process if you asked them. It sounded unlikely, but having no better plan, I set off to find the police.

I came upon a couple of burly policemen, picking their teeth as they emerged from a luncheonette on Madison Avenue. My request seemed to puzzle them, but to my amazement, they agreed to help. As I followed them up the staircase, their shoulders just about touching the walls, I felt I now knew how Charlie Conerly, the New York Giants quarterback, felt when he dropped back into the pocket behind Jack Stroud and Roosevelt Brown. Mrs. Commando, however, was not impressed. "What did you bring *them* for?" she shrieked, with no less belligerence than before. "This is an *office*. You get them *out* of here." She was up and waving her arms, but the complaint was served. Shepstein was begging for mercy before the judge again.

Only, not quite yet. The American judicial system was not formulated with people like the Henry Street tenants in mind. To start the 7A, these tenants needed to appear in court at 10 a.m. one morning in early March—no problem for Shepstein's lawyer, but quite a production for two buildings full of tenants, some of whom were elderly and infirm. We stood in the back of the courtroom for what seemed like hours as we waited for the clerk to get to our case. When he finally did, we learned that Shepstein had somehow managed to get a postponement. Hardship, no doubt.

Finally, we obtained the court order. It was with a sense of exultation that I made the rounds with Mrs. Rivera to help collect the rents—a bit perhaps like the Sandinistas felt when they took over the Nicaraguan treasury. But the money in slum housing is not in rents; it is in such things as depreciation, which were of use to the landlord but of absolutely no use to ourselves. And let's be honest: not everyone pays his rent on time, and under rent control, not that much cash was coming in to begin with. My recollection is that after we had paid the bills we didn't have a great deal left over for repairs. At least this was so for the months I was there. The revolution is exhilarating. Running the state afterwards is something else.

While this 7A was working its way slowly through the esophagus of the courts, the people at Henry Street were still without heat and hot water. This was the administration of Mayor John Lindsay, and while the streets on the Lower East Side were not paved with gold, there *was* an emergency heating program, under which the city would send a truck to fill an empty oil tank and even fix the boiler. It sounded too good to be true.

It was. Every time we called, it was another story. First they said they would send an inspector. Then they said they had to contact the landlord (an inspired regulation, that). Then they said they could not do anything because the tenants weren't paying their rents to the city. Then they started sending over employees who said they couldn't do the work because they were boiler men and not plumbers; or were plumbers and not boiler men. It was totally beyond me how a city could set up a program to help desperate tenants, and then erect impediments like these.

I drafted a letter of protest to Mayor Lindsay, reciting all these difficulties and others I haven't mentioned. We translated it into Spanish and Chinese so that everyone in the two buildings could sign and sent copies to *The New York Times*. In my naiveté, I thought this was the blockbuster move that would really shake up city hall. By some miracle, the letters seemed to work. Just a few days later, a city truck appeared, accompanied by a police escort and a bigshot in a brown leather trenchcoat, whose solicitous manner suggested that someone had chewed him out. We celebrated the occasion with a picket line in which tenants carried placards declaring, again in three languages, their views of Shepstein and the city administration. "No toilets," one proclaimed. "We'll all get typhoid."

By the end of the day, the heat was on. Over the past 13 years I have been engaged in various kinds of "public interest" work here in Washington. But I can think of nothing I've done in that period that helped concrete individuals the way we did when we got the boiler fixed on Henry Street.

By the late sixties, having been tamed by the investigators, MFY also was falling out of favor with the quasi-political leaders of the Lower East Side. Poverty money represented, simply, jobs and power; and leaders of local organizations were wondering why the uptown types —such was now the perception—who ran MFY were getting so much of both. Staff salaries at MFY were quite competitive, and the term "poverty pimp" was appearing in the raucous "letters" columns of *The Village Voice*.

Nevertheless, MFY had retained the contract to run the Youth Corps program for another summer, and in the spring I was transferred back to this program.

It was during the registration for this Youth Corps program that I first began to think in a serious way about what has come to be called "waste, fraud, and abuse." A long line of teenagers extended down the staircase at 255 East Houston, and I was one of the people conducting the registration on the second floor. The regulations said that only those below the "poverty level" were eligible; this meant, as best I can recall, $4,500 a year for a family of four, or $21.63 per person per week. More than that, you were too well off.

"Family income" can be a pretty nebulous concept in places like the Lower East Side. Does the niece sleeping on the couch for a few months count as "family"? What about the money your mother gets—in cash—for working in the laundromat on weekends? The way such questions were resolved was simply to ask the kids. Most offered sums safely beneath the ceiling; word does get around. A few, however, blurted out some higher figure—$4,900 perhaps or even $6,200—causing me to wince. These were invariably the nicest kids, the ones you saw dressed in white on Sundays with bibles under their arms, who showed you a deference that you didn't deserve. Still, the regulations were the regulations, weren't they? When you told them you were sorry, these kids actually thanked you, and departed as politely as they had come.

An MFY supervisor, whom I will call Enrique, came by on a routine check. Proud of my diligence, I showed Enrique my stack of rejects. He, however, was not pleased, especially about those that were near the borderline. "We do *not* want to turn those kids away," he said, in a way

that made me remember, with shame, that I was after all only a guest in someone else's house. Enrique seated himself at my registration station and showed me how it was done. "How much do your parents make?" he asked the next person in line.

"Uh, $4,800," this teenager replied tentatively, as though wary of thin ice.

"But are you completely sure? Or is that just an estimate?"

"Uh. Uh-huh."

"Your father may have missed a week or two of work because he was sick...?" And so on until, if possible, the individual was down to the requisite level. It was a little like the drill a tax preparer runs you through. Enrique then turned the station back to me, and I proceeded to follow his example.

Whenever I hear Reagan recite his litany of antipoverty "abuse," I think of that Youth Corps registration, and wonder what exactly he has in mind. I wonder too whether *he* would sit there and tell a 13-year-old that he can't have a job because he may be living on a little more than $21.63 a week.

A different poverty

A year, two years, after I left the Lower East Side, my old apartment at 131 Pitt Street had become a psychedelic crash pad. A few years after that, the building had been gutted by fire. A few years after that, 131 Pitt Street was a pile of rubble. The surrounding streets that had been so alive had become a grim combat zone. In the eerie mid-day quiet, drug dealers were doing business from abandoned buildings, passing their envelopes through holes in the concrete blocks with which the city had tried to seal these buildings off. Hot dog vendors would set up their carts nearby, so brisk and open was the trade. Some blocks east of Avenue B had been virtually demolished; the neighborhood wasn't even there. 255 East Houston Street had become a branch of the New York City Department of Social Services.

"There is no demonstrable record" that VISTA had "any effect on poverty in this country." So declared James H. Burnley IV, Reagan's first VISTA chief and a Republican district chairman in North Carolina prior to his appointment. To be sure, VISTA volunteers like myself didn't make much of a dent in poverty on the Lower East Side. If there is less poverty there now, it's mainly because there are fewer dwellings in which it can reside. And as the real estate operators now move in, buying and selling the remaining buildings at enormous markups, raising rents to the $700-a-month level and even higher, making life miserable for existing low-rent tenants to force them out, there will be still fewer dwellings for those at the bottom. It is widely suspected that when Mayor Koch finally routed the pushers from parts of the Lower East Side a number of months ago, it was not entirely for the benefit of the welfare mothers there.

Still, I like to think that my year in VISTA was not totally without value. At the very least, I developed an immunity to the cliched views of poverty and how to reduce it that issue forth from people like Reagan and his counterparts on the political left. Many volunteers, especially in smaller communities and rural areas, have made a significant impact. But the primary value of a program like VISTA may be in addressing a kind of poverty that the Reaganites are inclined to overlook—the kind which causes comfortable Americans to live oblivious to the need that exists in our own country and the world. If there were not so much of this kind of poverty, there wouldn't be as much of the other kind either.

Indeed, a substantial portion of VISTA volunteers have gone on to lives of public service. A government program, of course, is hardly the only way to promote a culture of service. But the government affects our mores and culture for better or worse; abolishing VISTA, as the Reagan administration wants to do, wouldn't change that. When you consider the other things the federal government fosters and promotes—from synfuels to tobacco—at much greater expense, then VISTA stacks up fairly well by comparison.

In theory, I am inclined to agree with the Reaganites that people shouldn't expect the government to fund "social change." In practice, however, I don't see how you could get the boiler working on Henry Street without making trouble for *somebody*. Should we simply have handed out charcoal and blankets to the freezing tenants? But even if such realities are unacceptable to the Reaganites, what about the VISTA volunteers who have helped start local enterprises such as crafts co-ops for low income producers in West Virginia and South Dakota? Isn't such entreprenuership worth supporting?

VISTA hasn't eliminated poverty. But if that were the standard, capitalism would be judged a failure as well. In Washington's clamor of self-interest, we need ways like VISTA to encourage people to think about the problems of their neighbors.

The ACORN Squatters' Campaign

Seth Borgos

SETH BORGOS, formerly research director at ACORN, is currently finishing a pictorial history of the American protest movement, This Mighty Dream, *forthcoming from Routledge & Kegan Paul. This article is excerpted from a chapter in* Critical Perspectives on Housing, *edited by Chester Hartman, Ann Meyerson, and Rachel Bratt.*

By official estimates, there are more than 20,000 abandoned houses in Philadelphia, concentrated mostly in North Philadelphia, flanking Broad Street for hundreds of blocks from City Hall to the city line.

The characteristic housing of North Philadelphia is the single-family brick row house: narrow, unadorned, and unpretentious. For decades following their construction in the 19th century, these houses provided a stable and affordable environment to the lower middle-class and working-class families of the city. In the years following World War II, this environment was violated. Houses were purchased by speculators and subsequently abandoned; houses were foreclosed and left vacant; houses were demolished leaving gaps in formerly solid blocks. Paradoxically, as the number of vacant houses increased so did the number of low- and moderate-income Philadelphians who lacked safe and affordable housing.

On a bright cold Saturday in March, 1982, 200 people gathered on the street in front of Calvary Church at 29th and Lehigh in North Philadelphia. After a round of speeches decrying the abandonment and neglect of their neighborhoods, the demonstrators marched a few blocks down Lehigh, chanting "2-4-6-8,

we want houses, we can't wait!" and "We're fired up, can't take no more!", then swept down a narrow side street with TV cameras, plainclothes police, and curious onlookers in their wake. Passing houses draped with makeshift banners proclaiming "Welcome,

---

During a period characterized by political reaction and social quiescence, ACORN mobilized hundreds of militant squatters, backed by thousands of organized supporters.

ACORN squatters," the crowd halted in front of a boarded-up house in the center of the block. A young Black woman mounted the steps and addressed the crowd:

> I decided to squat because I couldn't stand to live in public housing anymore. We are in Richard Allen project and you know what that's like—the rats and the crime and the stink and all....I need a house for my children! This is our moment. We are going to fix up this house and make it a place to live.

The crowd applauded. Two men with crowbars climbed the steps and pried the sheet-metal off the doorway. The young woman raised her arm in a gesture of victory and the crowd cheered. She turned and entered the house, followed by cameras and the curious. It was noted that the house was in good condition,

considering the neglect it had suffered; the young woman was pleased. Some neighbors brought brooms and plastic trashbags to remove the debris. The police remained outside, observing the scene and relaying perfunctory reports on their walkie-talkies.

Through the afternoon, the march snaked its way across the neighborhood, stopping every few blocks to tear the boards off an abandoned house. The ritual was re-enacted at each site. Later there was an impromptu barbecue in a vacant lot. The crowd slowly diminished as cars departed for parallel actions in South and Southwest Philadelphia. By the end of the day, squatters had seized 30 more houses in the city.

A TIME-HALLOWED PRACTICE

To squat is to occupy property without permission of its owner. It is the time-hallowed response of the landless to the contradiction between their own impoverishment and a surfeit of unutilized property.

In the 19th century, squatting was a common way of life in the United States. Though widely sanctioned on the frontier, its extension to settled and urbanizing areas was more problematic. When gold was discovered near Sacramento in 1849, the boom attracted land speculators who acquired lots cheaply and rented them for thousands of dollars a month. Prospectors couldn't or wouldn't pay those prices, so they settled where they pleased and formed a Settlers Association to represent their interests. The landowners responded in 1850 by getting a law passed that allowed evictions without the customary legal protections. In August of that year, a squatter was evicted from his land and thrown in jail. Members of the Settlers

Association immediately united to defend him, and a shoot-out ensued.[1]

A similar mode of squatting flourishes today in developing cities around the world, from San Juan, Puerto Rico, to Capetown, South Africa. In cities such as these, swollen by migration from rural areas, housing for the poor is crowded, unsafe, or simply unavailable. The poor solve the problem by squatting on vacant land at the margins of the city. In some instances, squatters have succeeded in creating full-fledged communities, with streets, utilities, schools, and permanent houses. In other cases their settlements have been bulldozed by the authorities.[2]

Squatting inevitably conveys a political message—a critical one—even when squatters are not conscious of it. The symbolic authority of the act has not gone unnoticed by political movements seeking an effective protest tactic.

An example from our own history is the Bonus Expeditionary Force of 1932. Three hundred unemployed World War I veterans began a journey to Washington to demand an advance payment of veterans' bonuses promised by Congress. The idea caught on, and some 20,000 veterans descended on the capital, where they squatted in vacant buildings and on federal land. The squatters were an embarrassment to President Hoover, who asked Congress to pay the way home of any veteran who wanted to leave. Few took advantage of the offer. Finally, Hoover called in the army. Six tanks and 700 troops rousted the squatters. However, the protest could not be considered a failure; Hoover lost the election that year, and Roosevelt's New Deal provided some relief to the unemployed.[3]

Later in that decade, a group called the Southern Tenant Farmers Union organized a protest by 1,700 sharecropper families who had been evicted from their farms. These families camped out beside a major highway in southeast Missouri. After confrontations with the police, they eventually won cash relief and resettlement in Farm Security Administration housing.[4]

In the past 15 years, squatters movements have bloomed in the major cities of Western Europe. The character of these movements is explicitly political. Although some of the predominantly young squatters are motivated by personal housing needs, and a few disclaim political intent, the fundamental thrust

of the action is a collective protest against the policies that have created severe housing shortages in these affluent cities, and against the development-oriented values that undergird these policies. The new European squatters have not yet succeeded in stemming the tide of development. But they have fought the authorities to a standstill in their own enclaves, and have established *de facto* "squatters rights" on many occasions.[5]

A "HIGHLY RISKY VENTURE"

This capsule survey suggests that governments may respond to squatting with repression or concession. Another common response is to "tame" squatting by licensing it within a restricted context. In the United States this has gone under the name of "homesteading."

The first national homesteading legislation was approved by Congress in 1862. It provided free grants of federal land to applicants who would improve the land for agriculture and reside there for five years.

The Homestead Act was the product of a 20-year debate over the disposition of public land on the frontier. Supporters of homesteading contended that it would encourage owner-occupancy of land and accelerate settlement; they also saw homesteading as an "escape valve for the urban poor and a way of avoiding downward pressure on wages." Opponents of homesteading argued that:

> . . . giving away land would lower property values of remaining land and create an injustice to those who had paid for the property. They also argued that it would entice the unprepared and unwary into a highly risky venture. Finally, they argued that homesteading was an indiscriminate form of charity that helped those perfectly able to support themselves instead of those who legitimately needed public aid.[6]

The initial homesteading proposals reflected the radical views of their sponsors: grants were to be limited to the poor, and the sale of government land was to be curtailed. But many legislators felt that the urban poor would be unable to meet the expenses of moving to the frontier and improving the land. As finally enacted, the Homestead Act of

1862 contained no eligibility restrictions on income or assets. And the federal government continued to sell prime land to speculators and award large tracts to railroad companies.

On its own terms the Homestead Act was a success. Hundreds of thousands of individuals received land grants, and many succeeded as farmers. The main beneficiaries of the program were families of moderate means who could afford the cost of travel, supplies, and equipment. The program declined, however, as the frontier moved west to agriculturally marginal land, and it was finally closed down in the 1930s.

A generation later the concept of an "urban frontier" came into vogue, and with it came a new field for homesteading. Urban homesteading was a response to two distinct problems. One was the flight of private investment from inner-city neighborhoods, which led to a rapid increase in housing abandonment. In the early 1970s, Wilmington, Baltimore, and Philadelphia established experimental programs that sold abandoned houses for a nominal fee to homesteaders who agreed to rehabilitate them. The other problem was a growing inventory of vacant federally-owned houses, generated mainly by foreclosures of FHA-insured mortgages.[7] In 1970, the FHA owned 21,000 single-family properties; by 1974 it owned 78,000.[8] Congress responded by authorizing a federal homesteading program in Section 810 of the Housing and Community Development Act of 1974.

The Congressional floor debate on this measure contained striking parallels to the 19th century homesteading controversy. Proponents claimed that homesteading of vacant federally-owned properties would reduce the blighting influence of these structures and alleviate the shortage of housing for low- and moderate-income families. Others questioned whether lower-income families could afford the costs of rehabilitation, and suggested that more affluent families would be the ultimate beneficiaries. "Middle-income and upper-income people are coming into Baltimore and paying $1 for these houses, and making mansions out of them," noted Representative William Barrett of Pennsylvania. Concerns were also expressed about the indeterminate costs of the program and its unproven methods. Interestingly, the debate did not break along conventional party or ideological lines. The leading proponents of the legislation were two Representatives from Maryland: Marjorie Holt, a conservative suburban Republican, and Parren Mitchell, a Black Democrat. Among the more vocal skeptics were Barrett, a Philadelphia Democrat, and Republican Gerry Brown of Michigan.[9]

The act which emerged from Congress in 1974 was, like the Homestead Act of 1862, a compromise of sorts. On the critical matter of homesteader selection, the legislation required that "special consideration" be given to the applicants' need for housing and to the applicants' capacity to make the required improvements. The inevitable tension between the "housing need" criterion, which favored lower-income applicants, and the "capacity to repair" criterion, which favored higher-income applicants, was left unresolved. Although the houses were to be provided by the federal government, management of the program was entrusted to localities, which were given wide discretion over homesteader selection and other aspects of program administration. The language of the act suggested that Section 810 was conceived as a "demonstration" of homesteading's viability in carefully targeted neighborhoods.

As the program was implemented in the years following its enactment, the issue of homesteader selection was conclusively resolved in favor of middle-income applicants. HUD initially provided local homesteading agencies with a special allocation of "Section 312" low-interest rehabilitation loans, designed to encourage low- and moderate-income participation, although not limited to that purpose. But appropriations for Section 312 were steadily reduced after 1978 and no alternative mechanism was created.[10] Instead, HUD advised localities to use their Community Development Block Grants as a source of rehabilitation assistance. Some did so, but competition for CDBG funds was so intense that relatively little assistance was generated in this fashion.

Local officials concluded that providing homesteads to a tiny cadre of young, upwardly-mobile families was a more prudent course than an ambitious low-income effort, and HUD did nothing to discourage this view. The program remained small, turning over less than 1,000 houses annually, and middle-class families received the lion's

> **Squatting was to be the tactical vehicle for a protest against the failure of the nation to provide decent and affordable housing to low- and moderate-income families, homesteading its programmatic vehicle.**

share of the houses in most cities. In 1979, the latest year for which data are available, the mean household income for homesteaders was about $17,000, only slightly below the national average of $17,700.[11]

Needless to say, the federal homesteading program—whatever its experimental merits—was having little impact on the twin problems of abandonment and low-income housing need, both of which were reaching crisis proportions in distressed cities such as Philadelphia. In 1977 there were 40,000 abandoned buildings in Philadelphia, many of them HUD-owned; North Philadelphia alone had 5,000 HUD homes. The situation impelled a bold and charismatic neighborhood leader named Milton Street to organize a grassroots "Walk-In Urban Homesteading Program"—less euphemistically, a squatters movement.

Street's organization put 200 squatters into HUD-owned single-family houses. The action produced a heated response from public officials. HUD Secretary Patricia Harris described the squatters as "no better than shoplifters" and the president of the Philadelphia City Council warned of the "beginning of anarchy." But the public generally supported the squatters and the press was sympathetic as well. A Philadelphia *Daily News* editorial (August 8, 1977) proclaimed that Street "is putting people who need homes into houses that have stood vacant far too long.... Rather than doing battle with Street, the Rizzo Administration and HUD should get behind the man and help him."[12]

Though loathe to "get behind" a man who had thoroughly embarrassed them, federal and city officials quietly capitulated. Half of the squatters eventually received title to their houses at nominal cost, 50 purchased their homes,

and another 25 remained under rental agreements with HUD.

"NEED A HOUSE? CALL ACORN"

When the Association of Community Organizations for Reform Now, or ACORN, opened an office in Philadelphia in 1977, it was an established grassroots community organization with affiliates in ten states. Its membership ranged from welfare recipients to middle-class professionals, but the heart of its constituency in Philadelphia, as elsewhere, was the working poor. The typical ACORN member, tenant or homeowner, was firmly attached to a neighborhood and committed to its improvement. And the most visible and pervasive blight in ACORN's Philadelphia neighborhoods was housing abandonment.

By 1979, two years after the initial squatting wave, the character of Philadelphia's abandonment problem had significantly altered. Embarrassed by its status as the nation's largest slumlord, HUD was rapidly liquidating its inventory through demolition, sale, and transfer of properties to localities. During the same period the City of Philadelphia was gaining title to thousands of vacant houses, mainly as a result of foreclosure for nonpayment of taxes. Neighborhood activists began to shift their attention to the city-owned housing stock and to the City's "Gift Property" program, the local homesteading effort.

On paper, Gift Property was a conventional urban homesteading program, providing houses for $13 to families who agreed to rehabilitate them. Deeper scrutiny revealed systematic mismanagement and corruption. In defiance of textbook distinctions between legislative and executive functions, the program was administered by the office of City Councilman Harry P. Jannotti, a Democratic-machine stalwart. In four years Jannotti had conveyed a few hundred homes, many of them to real estate interests and political cronies. One speculator had obtained 30 Gift Property houses, which he was renting out in violation of program rules. In the meantime, 5,000 applicants languished on the waiting list and the stock of city-owned houses seemed to be mounting, although the records were so poor that no one could say with certainty how many houses the City owned.

On March 7, 1979, 75 members of

ACORN and the allied Kensington Joint Action Committee (KJAC) descended on Jannotti's office carrying scraps of paper with the addresses of 300 vacant properties. They demanded that Jannotti match these properties to applicants within two weeks, and that he release the waiting list of applicants along with a listing of all the houses that had been conveyed under the program.[13]

When the two-week deadline was up, the group returned to find Jannotti's office locked and under armed guard. After ACORN threatened to sue for the files, the City agreed to release them. A week later the records mysteriously disappeared in a "burglary." The campaign then shifted its focus to the City Council, where independent Councilman Lucien Blackwell introduced a bill to remove control of the program from Jannotti. With the machine faction in command of the Council, Blackwell's bill was consigned to limbo.

By this point, ACORN's leadership had reached certain conclusions. It was agreed that reform of the Gift Property program should remain an organizational priority despite the level of resistance from the City; the issue was so critical, and the conduct of the program so indefensible, that some kind of victory seemed assured if ACORN and KJAC could maintain the pressure. Second, there was a consensus that a new and more militant tactic was needed. Squatting was the obvious choice. Finally, it was clear that ACORN's active membership could supply relatively few prospective squatters. The most likely squatters were the applicants on the Gift Property waiting list and other families like them. Mobilizing this young, transient constituency and integrating it with the existing neighborhood base became the primary challenge of the ACORN homesteading campaign.

Since Jannotti refused to release the waiting list, this constituency had to be located in other ways. The most effective mechanism was a flyer that proclaimed, "Need a House? Call ACORN." The flyer cautioned that ACORN didn't have houses to give away, but that, by organizing, the Gift Property program could be made to work. It drew thousands of phone calls to the ACORN office and hundreds of people to meetings in North, South, and Southwest Philadelphia. Some of those who responded had been on the Gift Property list for years, others had never

heard of the program. They were united by a deep dissatisfaction with their existing housing situation. Typically, they were sharing a cramped residence with relatives or living in one of Philadelphia's notoriously decrepit and unsafe public housing projects.

Prospective squatters were informed that squatting was illegal, physically taxing, and risky. There was no guarantee that any squatter would obtain title to a house. At the same time, they were told that squatting was morally justifiable in this instance, that it might be the only way to force the City into action, and that ACORN would put its full organizational weight behind the squatting effort.

Scores of people decided to take the risk. Prior to squatting, they were asked to take certain functional steps that were also designed to reinforce their understanding and commitment. First, squatters were asked to identify five vacant houses in which they were interested. They then proceeded to check the deeds and property tax records for these houses.[14] Next, they were required to sign a "squatters contract," which obligated them to participate in meetings, rallies, and other activities generated by the campaign to reform Gift Property; this was to be a collective struggle, not just a battle for one's own house. Finally, squatters were instructed to obtain the signatures of 75 percent of their prospective neighbors on a petition endorsing the squatting action, and to obtain concrete assistance from these neighbors wherever feasible.

The squatting action itself developed certain regular features. There was always a rally to demonstrate neighborhood support for the squatter. Ministers and sympathetic elected officials were invited to participate in order to lend legitimacy to the tactic; two ministers removed the boards from the first ACORN squatter's house. The press was generally invited as well. After the boards were removed, neighbors and supporters remained through the afternoon helping to clean the house and serving as guards against eviction.

The first ACORN squatters moved in on July 27, 1979, impelling the City Council to resurrect Lucien Blackwell's reform bill. A public hearing on the bill degenerated into a shouting match and 100 ACORN and KJAC members walked out when the bill was tabled. But they had succeeded in making Gift Property a

major political issue and a liability for the machine faction on the Council. Adding to the machine's woes was a string of indictments stemming from the federal "Abscam" investigation; Jannotti was among those indicted. In the fall elections the machine's grip on the Council was loosened, and a new mayor, William Green, was elected with a clear mandate to reform the City's housing programs. Control of the Gift Property program was subsequently transferred from Jannotti to the Office of Housing and Community Development, whose director was a mayoral appointee. The squatters had won their first victory.

THE PHILADELPHIA MODEL

With Jannotti out of the picture, the squatters upped the ante. They demanded the deeds to the houses they were occupying and immediate reforms in the Gift Property program, including an orderly application process, free access to information, tighter restrictions on eligibility, and a tenfold expansion in the number of houses being turned over.

Green and his appointees did not readily accede to these demands. The pattern was one of alternating confrontation and negotiation. In response to a wave of squatting, the City would offer some programmatic reforms, a commitment to transfer some deeds, and *de facto* legal amnesty for all existing squatters, in exchange for an agreement from ACORN and KJAC that no new squatting actions would be organized. ACORN and KJAC would accept the deal, subject to revocation if the City's performance was unsatisfactory. For a short while peace would reign, but the City inevitably failed to fulfill all of its commitments, and the squatting cycle would begin anew.

Yet each cycle moved the program forward, and out of this conflict-ridden process emerged a new concept of urban homesteading—the Philadelphia model. The essence of the Philadelphia model was to conceive homesteading primarily as a housing program rather than as a property rehabilitation program, and as a large-scale effort rather than as a showcase demonstration. The requirements of this model were as follows.

Restriction of eligibility to low- and moderate-income families. Local homesteading programs have tended to favor middle-income applicants, partly for political reasons, and partly on the assumption that middle-income families have more cash and more skills to apply to home rehabilitation and improvement. But if homesteading is conceived primarily as a housing program, an eligibility standard based on need seems appropriate. Furthermore, the assumption that lower-income families cannot perform rehabilitation without massive assistance is questionable. The Philadelphia squatters insisted that the City's rehabilitation cost estimates were inflated, and they cited examples of low-income squatters who were rehabilitating their houses on a "self-help" basis with the assistance of their neighbors and relatives. Their position was bolstered by an Office of Housing and Community Development study which concluded that there was no significant relationship between the income of Gift Property applicants and their success rate as homesteaders.[15] Philadelphia ultimately restricted eligibility to households whose income was 80 percent or less of the median for the Philadelphia SMSA.

Sufficient time to bring homesteads up to code. Self-help rehabilitation by homesteaders "generally took longer to complete but produced work that was equal in quality to that performed by professional contractors," according to a report by HUD's Office of Policy Development and Research.[16] Yet many local homesteading programs require participants to eliminate all code violations within six months to a year. By contrast, the Philadelphia model calls for a more extended two-step process: one year to eliminate "all major housing code defects posing a substantial danger to life and safety," after which the homesteader receives the deed to the property and two additional years to complete the renovation.

Financial assistance for rehabilitation. Despite the importance of the self-help component in low-income homesteading, structural repairs and renovation of major systems (wiring, plumbing, and heating) must often be performed by contractors. Few lower-income families can afford these expenses without some form of financial assistance.

The most common form of government assistance is a low-interest loan. Because homesteaders do not have to make mortgage or rental payments, they are able to carry sizable rehab loans if the interest loans are sufficiently low. For example, a $10,000 loan at 3 per-

cent, payable over ten years, requires a monthly payment of $96.56, well within the budget of most low-income households.

Of course, a 3 percent loan requires a substantial public subsidy. Philadelphia ACORN advocated a "leveraged" subsidy mechanism, under which Community Development Block Grant funds would be used to lower the interest rates on loans financed by tax-exempt housing revenue bonds. By depositing the full amount of the subsidy in an interest-bearing account at the initiation of the loan, the City could generate $10,000 loans at 3 percent for $2,000-$2,500 per loan, depending on the prevailing market interest rates. A sliding scale would permit the City to vary the bor-

---

Squatters cast their demands in terms of individual initiative, mutual assistance, and the superiority of homeownership.

---

rower's interest rate, and hence the required subsidy, according to the income level of the applicant.[17]

Philadelphia eventually established a program, known as Action Loans, precisely along these lines, but it did not allocate sufficient funds to make low-interest loans available to all homesteaders who need them. The program's credit guidelines also excluded some low-income homesteaders. In short, the City assimilated the technical components of the model, without implementing the underlying entitlement principle.

Production quotas. The model calls for a monthly quota appropriate to the City's size, administrative capacity, and level of abandonment. The value of a quota as an accountability mechanism is obvious. It also reinforces the concept of homesteading as a program designed to have real impact on the problems of abandonment and housing distress, in contrast to the well-intentioned irrelevance of many homesteading demonstrations.

The Philadelphia squatters demanded that the City convey 200 houses a month. City officials resisted the quotas,

but expanded the program from an average of five to ten houses a month to over 50. And the demand for more houses raised the question of why many abandoned properties were not available for homesteading purposes.

Aggressive solicitation of houses. In Philadelphia, as in many other cities around the country, the largest proportion of vacant properties are neither city-owned nor federally-owned but privately-owned and tax delinquent. Many of these houses have been abandoned for years. Eventually they will be foreclosed for nonpayment of property taxes, and will be auctioned off at an event known as "tax sale" or "sheriff's sale." Those which remain unsold at sheriff's sale fall into public ownership, where they are potentially available for homesteading. But the process takes so long—five years or more is not unusual—that the houses may have fallen apart in the meantime. Thus, proponents of large-scale homesteading efforts have an interest in accelerating the tax foreclosure process or developing alternatives to it.

Before the squatters entered the picture, Philadelphia had developed one alternative: a "donor/taker" provision that allowed delinquent taxpayers to donate their houses to the homesteading pool and deduct the assessed value from back taxes owed. (This was the "gift" provision to which the program's name referred.) Under pressure from the squatters, the City began to use Community Development Block Grant funds to purchase low-value houses from their owners and bid on houses at sheriff's sale to prevent them from being acquired by speculators. City officials implemented a technical change that accelerated the acquisition of full title to tax-foreclosed properties by six to nine months. They also experimented with the use of "spot condemnation" powers derived from urban renewal legislation to obtain properties designated by homesteaders.

All of these measures helped to expand the pool of homestead properties, but their impact was relatively minor. A more radical solution was proposed by Councilman John Street, Milton's brother, and ultimately adopted by the Council. Street's ordinance permits the City to declare an abandoned house a public nuisance and contract with a Gift Property applicant to occupy the house immediately and commence improvements. If the City subsequently obtains title to the house, the homesteader may claim it; if the original owner manages to redeem the property, he must reimburse the City for contracted improvements and the City in turn reimburses the homesteader. By shortcircuiting the cycle of abandonment and foreclosure, the Street ordinance aims not only to expand the homesteading pool, but to reduce the unit cost of rehabilitation, since houses which are "caught" earlier in the cycle are likely to require less extensive renovation.[18]

THE ROAD TO TENT CITY

By the end of 1981, the City Council and the Office of Housing and Community Development had implemented many elements of the Philadelphia model. City officials continued to denounce squatting, but none of the ACORN and KJAC squatters had been evicted, and some had received the deeds to their houses.

The news spread to ACORN affiliates in other cities, which began to scrutinize their local homesteading programs. The situation in some cities bordered on the scandalous. Detroit, with the largest inventory of HUD-owned houses in the country, had a tiny program limited to two neighborhoods; 12 houses had been conveyed in a two-year period. Detroit's general policy was to demolish vacant houses and "landbank" the property. In St. Louis, another city with a massive abandonment problem, the homesteading agency was refusing to turn over 32 houses that had been claimed from the federal government for homesteading purposes. The St. Louis Land Reutilization Authority, an autonomous state-chartered agency, owned 1,000 vacant houses, many of which had been languishing in its inventory for years.

HUD frequently cited the homesteading programs of Dallas, Texas, and Columbus, Ohio, as models. Both cities had turned over more than 300 houses to homesteaders, with few subsequent failures. But ACORN groups in Dallas and Columbus discovered that this "success" had been achieved by conveying most of the houses to middle-class families. Neither city had established an adequate rehabilitation assistance program. These cities had a low rate of failure because they took few risks.

Local ACORN organizations responded to these findings with conventional protest tactics and squatting.

Squatters and leaders from Philadelphia visited other cities to explain how it was done. By April, 1982, there were more than 200 ACORN squatters in 13 cities; the largest numbers were in distressed cities such as Detroit, Pittsburgh, and St. Louis, but there were also squatters in Houston, Dallas, Tulsa, and Phoenix.

City and federal authorities cracked down hard in some locations. Squatters were arrested in Pittsburgh and St. Louis; a HUD Area Office manager led a midnight raid on a squatter's house in Dallas; the St. Louis Land Reutilization Authority filed a $500,000 civil suit against ACORN and the leaders of its squatting group. With rare exceptions, mayors denounced the squatters and refused to negotiate with them. But the response was more positive in some quarters: the Detroit City Council passed a resolution asking for the establishment of a large-scale urban homesteading program and clemency for the squatters; favorable columns and editorials appeared in the metropolitan newspapers of Ft. Worth, Atlanta, and St. Louis; the St. Louis tax collector agreed to accelerate the tax foreclosure process on abandoned houses suitable for homesteading; Mayor Andrew Young of Atlanta agreed to negotiate; homesteading ordinances based on the Philadelphia model were filed in Pittsburgh, St. Louis, and Detroit.

As squatting erupted around the country, the goals of the campaign became more diverse. The Tulsa squatting effort was part of a longstanding protest against redevelopment and displacement on the city's North Side. An ACORN group fighting public housing vacancies in Jacksonville, Florida, squatted briefly in a housing project to dramatize the issue. In cities such as Houston and Phoenix, which have relatively few abandoned houses, the squatters' primary goal was not to create large-scale urban homesteading programs, but to challenge the complacent assumption that the poor are adequately housed in these "Sunbelt" communities.

During the same period—winter and spring of 1982—the campaign began to develop a national focus. In cities such as Detroit and Dallas, unlike Philadelphia, a large portion of the vacant housing stock was federally-owned, giving HUD a more direct involvement in the issue. Furthermore, ACORN's national leadership was beginning to appreciate the symbolic power of squatting and its

potential for broader impact. The leadership began to conceive of the campaign not only as a fight for local homesteading reforms, but as a protest against the failure of the nation to provide decent and affordable housing to low- and moderate-income families. Squatting was to be the tactical vehicle for this protest, homesteading its programmatic vehicle.

As ACORN members became more familiar with the federal role in homesteading policy, they concluded that HUD was the source of many problems they were encountering at the local level. HUD officials insisted that localities were free to design their own programs, but although this was technically correct in many instances, it was obvious that the cities took their cues from Washington. For example, the squatters were often infuriated when cities refused to expand homesteading programs beyond a few target neighborhoods. City officials inevitably attributed this policy to HUD. The truth was a bit more complicated: HUD's regulations did not flatly prohibit a more expansive approach to homesteading, but the tone of the regulation was hostile to this approach, and in practice HUD strongly discouraged it. The agency also seemed unconcerned about the middle-class character of the program, the shortage of funds for homestead rehabilitation, and the disparity between the enormous scope of the abandonment problem and the miniscule homesteading effort.[19]

On June 5, 1982, ACORN members in seven cities squatted in HUD-owned houses despite threats of eviction and arrest from HUD officials. Two days later, more than 300 persons sat in at HUD offices in 12 cities. Both actions were intended to underline the federal responsibility for effective homesteading programs and for addressing the housing problems of low- and moderate-income Americans. In doing so, they set the stage for the culminating event of the "national strategy"—a squatters' Tent City in Washington, D.C.

Tent City was established on the Ellipse, a few hundred yards from the back porch of the White House, and housed more than 200 squatters from ten cities. The squatters used a press conference, a rally, a Congressional hearing, and a march on the HUD building to press their case for reform of the federal homesteading program. They demanded that homesteading efforts be targeted to low- and moderate-income families, that more vacant houses be made available for homesteading, and that more funds be allocated for low-interest rehabilitation loans.

The action produced an unsatisfactory response from HUD; although HUD Secretary Samuel Pierce later met with a delegation of ACORN leaders, he demonstrated scant knowledge of the issues and conceded nothing. However, the squatters received a friendly reception on Capitol Hill. At a hearing conducted by the House Subcommittee on Housing and Community Development, Representative St. Germain of Rhode Island told the squatters, "I don't consider you criminals.... You are doing the community a favor." The sentiment was echoed by Democratic and Republican members of the subcommittee, and Congressman William Coyne of Pennsylvania promised to introduce legislation which would implement ACORN's demands.[20]

The Congressional hearing and other Tent City activities were reported in the squatters' hometown newspapers and received some national media coverage as well. "Squatting for Homeless Gains Support" was the headline in the Tulsa *Tribune*; "ACORN Finally Gets HUD's Ear" proclaimed the Columbus *Citizen-Journal*. By publicizing and legitimizing the squatters' cause, the D.C. action helped to sustain the momentum of local homesteading campaigns, which have since borne fruit. Bridgeport, Connecticut, and Des Moines, Iowa, have established homesteading programs on the Philadelphia model. New funds for homestead acquisition and rehabilitation assistance have been appropriated in Phoenix ($200,000), Columbus ($800,000), and Brooklyn ($1 million). Mayor Coleman Young of Detroit, previously an implacable opponent of the squatters, has announced a program to give away 500 properties, and the Detroit City Council has approved a bill —modeled on John Street's nuisance abatement ordinance—which would permit homesteading in privately-owned, tax-delinquent houses.

In March, 1983, Congressman Coyne introduced legislation to reshape the federal homesteading program along the lines advocated by ACORN. The legislation was opposed by HUD but supported by a bipartisan consensus on the Housing and Community Development subcommittee. It has since passed the House of Representatives and awaits action by the Senate.[21]

RADICAL PRINCIPLES, FRIENDLY TERRAIN

Five years ago, single-family urban homesteading programs were, at best, irrelevant to the needs of poor people and, at worst, a means for their displacement. The notion that these programs could serve a mass, low-income constituency had scant credibility and had never been seriously tested. Today, this notion has not only acquired a concrete, programmatic form—the Philadelphia

> The desperation of the squatters mocked the assumption that Americans are well-housed.

model—but is influencing local and national policies. This achievement can be credited almost entirely to the action of the squatters.

It would be gratifying to conclude that the squatters had succeeded in their broader objective of forcing government to take increased responsibility for low-income housing. But although the squatters undoubtedly drew attention to housing issues and disturbed the complacency of public officials, they were swimming against a powerful current. The Reagan Administration budgets have cut federal housing programs more deeply than any other major area.[22] This reflects not only the Administration's antipathy to these programs, but the weakness of the political constituency for housing. With or without Reagan, the immediate prospects for a renewed national commitment to low-income housing appear dim.

For many observers, therefore, the most remarkable aspect of the squatters' campaign is that it succeeded at all. During a period characterized by political reaction and social quiescence, ACORN mobilized hundreds of militant squatters, backed by thousands of organized supporters, and won significant policy reforms in the face of deep resistance from public officials. What made this possible?

Viewed nakedly as a tactic, squatting

was enormously effective. Its visual drama and clarity drew TV cameras and newspaper photographers. Its programmatic clarity—filling empty houses with families who need shelter—lent it both power and legitimacy. To many among the public, the press, the ministry, and even some housing officials, the moral logic of the action outweighed its patent illegality.

The combination of intense militancy and public legitimacy reflects the manner in which the campaign's tactics and programmatic demands embodied radical principles in a politically compelling context. The squatters insisted that they had a right to decent housing, and that this right took precedence over the rights of property. In the abstract, such principles do not command the support of a majority of Americans; national housing policy is certainly not founded on them. Yet in the particular form posed by the squatters, these principles were almost unassailable.

At a time when Americans were increasingly hostile to anything perceived as a "giveaway" program, the squatters proclaimed that they were not looking for a handout, but an opportunity. They cast their demands in terms of individual initiative, mutual assistance, and the superiority of homeownership—all culturally sanctioned values in the United States. Their position was bolstered by the visible failure of the for-profit "private sector" to maintain housing in their neighborhoods. And homesteading had fiscal appeal as well; even with the provision of generous rehabilitation loans, it appeared to be a relatively inexpensive means of producing low-income housing, and it promised to restore abandoned property to the tax rolls.

Just as important as the campaign's external legitimacy was its internal dynamic. In the classic mode of community organizing, the squatters' campaign appealed to a fundamental need in a direct and immediate way. "Need a house? Call ACORN"—the flyer was sometimes criticized for its audacity, but it was the audacity of that appeal which drew hundreds of previously unorganized individuals to ACORN offices, just as the simplicity of the campaign's central premise—"the houses are ours!"—propelled them to action. As we have seen, ACORN eventually developed a fairly sophisticated critique of urban homesteading policy and a detailed program for reform. But these emerged from the campaign, rather than vice versa. The squatters understood the policy issues and "owned" the policy demands because the issues and demands took their ultimate shape from the collective experience of protest.

Another factor in the campaign's success was ACORN's capacity to forge links between the squatters and its traditional neighborhood-based constituency. The neighborhood base provided squatters with material and psychological support, as well as public legitimacy. (Many TV news accounts included interviews with squatters' neighbors, who inevitably said they preferred to have a squatter next door than an abandoned haven for rats and junkies.) And ACORN's experienced neighborhood leaders contributed political and organizational sophistication, which tempered the youthful militance of the squatters without smothering it.

ENTITLEMENT OBSTACLES

One reason that the cause of low-income housing has suffered defeats in recent years is the absence of a grassroots constituency to generate, monitor, and defend programs. Some low-income housing programs are too complex or diffuse to attract grassroots support; others, like public housing, are unwelcome in many communities and are viewed ambivalently even by their beneficiaries. Homesteading, on the other hand, is blessed with two large, enthusiastic constituencies: families who need houses, and residents of neighborhoods with serious abandonment problems. If the identification and mobilization of such "natural" constituencies is not a precondition for policy reform, it is certainly a major asset.

But this analysis of the squatters' campaign raises as many questions as it answers. Even if all the abandoned houses in the United States suitable for homesteading were turned over to poor people, how much impact would it have on the nation's low-income housing problem? Aren't the economics of low-income homeownership so daunting that it represents a dubious basis for policy, and a cruel and dangerous myth for the poor? Doesn't the appeal to values such as self-reliance and fiscal efficiency play into the hands of those who wish to absolve the government of responsibility for housing? If the objective is fun-

damental reform of housing policies, why not develop proposals and campaigns which confront the central issues of equity, entitlement, and resources in a comprehensive fashion rather than nibbling at their edges? In short, could one characterize the squatters' campaign as tactically instructive, but peripheral to the main lines of strategy for housing reform?

The most superficial response is that the campaign encompassed a much broader range of issues than the management and design of homesteading programs. In the course of their efforts to obtain houses, the squatters had an impact on federal property disposition policies, the tax foreclosure process, housing speculation, redevelopment plans, and code enforcement. They disseminated new approaches to home rehabilitation financing, which benefited existing homeowners as often as homesteaders. John Street's "nuisance abatement" ordinance, a product of the campaign, was a radical innovation in local housing policy.

And squatting embodied much more than the policy demands of the squatters; it was a blatant challenge to the assumptions and values upon which U.S. housing policy is founded. The desperation of the squatters mocked the assumption that Americans are well housed; their eagerness to tear down the boards asserted the primacy of housing needs over property rights; their uncompromising demand for the deeds lent substance to the nascent principle of entitlement. Of course, they cast this challenge on friendly terrain: the social terrain of their home neighborhoods, the ideological terrain of the American dream. But that is precisely what is instructive about their experience.

At present, comprehensive policy reforms such as the establishment of a national housing entitlement are improbable under any scenario; the costs are too high, the political constituency for reform too weak, the bias against government action too well entrenched. The only way to advance fundamental reform is through the accretion of small but principled victories, which undermine the hegemony of dominant values and assumptions and enhance the credibility of alternatives. When these victories involve ordinary people in the criticism and formulation of policy, they build an informed popular constituency for change. Hence, the key to the

strategy is identifying friendly terrain—campaigns that can mobilize large numbers of people on their home grounds, and win a broad base of public legitimacy.

Where is the terrain? Our own view is that it is most likely to be found in two areas. One is the effort to lend rental housing some of the characteristics of equity: security of tenure, predictability of costs, control over quality. The other is the effort to make equity affordable to the lowest income groups, whether in the form of conventional homeownership, homesteading, or new forms of equity such as cooperatives and mutual housing associations.

Is the expansion of low-income homeownership a realistic policy goal? It is not within the scope of this article to consider the question. Here we would simply note that, despite the political and historical legitimacy of that goal, politicians and policy makers are currently showing little interest or support for the development of new mechanisms by which the poor can obtain equity in their housing. Indeed, the experience of the squatters suggests that there is resistance to the goal where one would least expect it—among the traditional supporters of low-income housing.

One of the supreme ironies of the squatters' campaign is that the support it received from political moderates and conservatives was frequently offset by the opposition it generated from liberal mayors, housing officials, and their allies. This opposition was attributable in part to crude political considerations: squatting was a rebuke to those in power at City Hall, regardless of their political complexion. But there was also a strong odor of paternalism in the resistance of some officials to the idea that poor people could renovate and maintain their own homes. It was exemplified by a liberal member of the St. Louis Board of Aldermen, previously one of ACORN's strongest supporters on that body, who refused to support a homesteading ordinance unless massive financial assistance was guaranteed to homesteaders. Since the funds for such massive assistance were not likely to be forthcoming in hard-pressed St. Louis, it was in effect a stand against homesteading. Mixed in with a low estimation of the capacities of poor people was an attitude that homeownership was an expensive luxury, along with a deep reluctance to take programmatic risks of any kind—a fear of being associated with "another failed program."

The squatters would have none of this. They insisted that they could make their houses livable; financial assistance would make the process faster and smoother, but they wanted the deeds regardless. Of course there were risks, but the risks were acceptable, because even a problematic house was better than what they could reasonably expect otherwise—a perspective that few public officials could comprehend. The squatters felt that homeownership, far from being a luxury, was the only way to escape the domination of others. They drew strength from the same values that legitimated their militant actions to the wider public. As ACORN leader Grover Wright informed a Congressional panel, the squatters "are here because they have an insatiable desire to become a part, an integral part, of this great American life."[23] Such "myths" are the engines of change.

NOTES

[1]Josiah Royce, "The Squatter Riot of '50 in Sacramento," *Overland Monthly* (September, 1885).

[2]Marc Howard Ross, *The Political Integration of Urban Squatters* (Evanston: Northwestern University Press, 1973); Richard E. Stren, *Urban Inequality and Housing Policy in Tanzania: The Problem of Squatting* (Berkeley: Institute of International Studies, University of California, c1975); "Assault by Cape Town Police Ends Squatters Dogged Stand," *The Washington Post*, (May 20, 1983).

[3]Harris Gaylord Warren, *Herbert Hoover and the Great Depression* (New York: Norton, 1967).

[4]Donald Grubbs, *Cry from the Cotton: The STFU and the New Deal* (Chapel Hill: University of North Carolina Press, 1971); H. L. Mitchell, *Mean Things Happening in This Land* (Montclair, N.J.: Allenheld, Osmun, 1979).

[5]Kevin Kearns, "Urban Squatting: Social Activism in the Housing Sector," *Social Policy* (September/October 1980); Richard P. Greenfield, "The 'Krakers' Strike Again," *The Nation* (January 3-10, 1981).

[6]This quotation and the account of the 1862 Homestead Act are drawn from *The Urban Homesteading Catalogue, Volume 3*, Office of Policy Development and Research, U.S. Department of Housing and Urban Development, 1977, pp. 1-29.

[7]Brian Boyer, *Cities Destroyed for Cash: The FHA Scandal at HUD* (Chicago: Follett, 1973).

[8]Statistics on the HUD-owned houses are available from HUD's Office of Single-Family Housing, Preservation, and Sales Division.

[9]*The Urban Homesteading Catalogue, Volume 3*, op. cit.

[10]The Reagan Administration attempted to close down Section 312, but succeeded only in cutting off new appropriations. The program is currently funded entirely by loan repayments.

[11]*Evaluation of the Urban Homesteading Demonstration Program: Final Report, Volume I: Summary Assessment*, Office of Policy Development and Research, U.S. Department of Housing and Urban Development, 1983.

[12]The account of Milton Street's campaign is drawn from Chester Hartman, Dennis Keating, Richard LeGates, *Displacement: How to Fight It* (Berkeley: National Housing Law Project, 1982), pp. 68-71.

[13]The best account of the early stages (1979-1980) of Philadelphia ACORN's squatting campaign is Madeleine Adamson, "Need a House? Call ACORN," *The Organizer* (Summer 1981).

[14]Potential squatters were asked to check deeds and property tax records because squatting was encouraged only in city-owned houses and in seriously tax-delinquent houses owned by persons outside the neighborhood—in short, houses where the squatter had a reasonable chance of obtaining the deed, and where squatting was unlikely to create conflict within the neighborhood.

[15]The study, conducted by the Planning and Policy Research Department, was unfortunately never published. Copies may be available from Paul Levy, 235 Queen St., Philadelphia, PA 19147.

[16]Howard J. Sumka, "Urban Homesteading," paper prepared for the Homeownership Task Force, The President's Commission on Housing (January 11, 1982).

[17]A good sourcebook on such leveraged mechanisms is *Designing Rehab Programs*, Office of Policy Development and Research, U.S. Department of Housing and Urban Development, 1980.

[18]The ordinance was introduced as Bill 1202 on April 1, 1982. The program, known as "1202A, Emergency Nuisance Abatement," is administered by Philadelphia's Office of Housing and Community Development.

[19]Regulations for the Section 810 program are in 24 CFR Part 590; the ambiguous language on neighborhood targeting is in 590.7(a).

[20]"Hearing before the Subcommittee on Housing and Community Development, of the Committee on Banking, Finance, and Urban Affairs, House of Representatives, 97th Congress," June 24, 1982.

[21]The bill was introduced as H.R. 2150 on March 16, 1983, and later incorporated in the Omnibus Housing Bill, H.R. 1.

[22]The best source of information on the federal housing budget is the National Low-Income Housing Coalition, 323 8th St. N.E., Washington, D.C. 20002.

[23]"Hearing Before the Subcommittee on Housing and Community Development," op. cit., pg. 42.

Urban Social Policies

When an urban problem is recognized and clarified, solutions are often, but not always, proposed. These solutions generally take the form of social policies designed to deal with the critical issues surrounding the problem. Since urban problems are often quite complex, the policies that are designed to solve them are also likely to be equally complicated and to generate considerable debate and conflict.

In recent years, social scientists have been involved in both policy proposals and in the ensuing debates which follow. The result usually takes the form of some proposal such as the recent one to create enterprise zones in the decaying sections of urban communities. This policy calls for clearing lands of old housing and creating new space for economic enterprise to build. Attached to this policy are certain tax benefits designed to encourage the new economic enterprise. The student of the urban condition can readily see that this proposal might generate considerable debate and conflict. Nevertheless, rational and ongoing examination of the urban condition will require that social scientists continue to examine the issues, explain the variables that operate in the urban community, and present possible alternatives.

Social policies are usually directed at specific ends, but the unintended consequences of a given policy sometimes have unusual effects. Some policies have been proposed and action has been initiated without adequate resources to accomplish the goals. Other policies, while successfully ending one problem, have created or uncovered another set of problems. Unfortunately, we do not possess the skills to predict accurately all the outcomes of a specific social policy. The articles in this section illustrate the processes involved in effecting social change. The section begins with an article on the efforts of two progressive communities—Hartford, Connecticut and Berkeley, California—to assist the urban disadvantaged. In the next section, San Antonio Mayor Henry G. Cisneros argues that the future of the cities is closely linked to the economic health of America's economy. Donald A. Hicks follows with an analysis of the strengths and weaknesses of the present federal-state relationship and offers several possible suggestions for the future. Harry C. Boyte reviews President Reagan's neighborhood self-help program and its impact on community preservation. William H. Whyte then argues that cities should be designed as if people mattered, and suggests that urban design should strive to make cities "friendlier." In the following piece, William G. Conway contends that Detroit's downtown area is dysfunctional, and that the present approach is doomed to failure. Two articles examine two new approaches to urban policy—triage and privatization. Also included is a discussion of the efforts of several cities to engage in international trade and investment. Neil Goldstein and Amey Winterer explore the relationship between America's cities and energy independence. David Morris analyzes the city as an ecological nation. Finally, Joann S. Lublin chronicles the difficult problems associated with the aging of the suburbs.

Looking Ahead: Challenge Questions

Can government solve the problems of the cities? Why, or why not?

To what extent, if any, have federal policies contributed to existing urban problems? What is the ideal relationship between the federal, state, and local governments in addressing urban ills?

What social, political, and economic forces typically influence the development of urban policy? Do these forces contribute to enlightened public policy?

Are America's cities administered in the interests of the people or the ruling elite? Has citizen participation changed the fabric of urban life?

Does America have a national urban policy? If not, why?

What can and should be done to assure the economic health of America's cities? What is the economic future of the nation's cities?

What principles should govern the design of cities? Is small necessarily better?

Is triage a viable approach to the problems of urban America? What are its primary strengths and weaknesses?

Why are many cities turning to private contractors to perform government services? What does this portend for the future?

What is the relationship between energy conservation and the future of cities? Why do cities promote more energy-efficient life-styles than non-urban areas?

Why are many cities, such as Atlanta, determined to seek foreign trade and investment? Is this policy likely to prove successful?

How are self-reliant cities different from other cities? What obstacles prevent greater self-sufficiency?

What factors have produced the aging of suburbia? How has this altered the character and politics of many communities?

What are the major costs, both tangible and intangible, of unplanned growth? What will this mean to the future of America's big cities?

Running the City for the People

Eve Bach, Nicholas R. Carbone, and Pierre Clavel

EVE BACH is special assistant to the City Manager, Berkeley, Calif. NICHOLAS R. CARBONE is at the Hartford Policy Center. Pierre CLAVEL is professor of city and regional planning, Cornell University. This article is adapted from "Progressive Planning: A Report from Berkeley and Hartford," Working Papers in Planning 51, Cornell University.

Urban renewal, the federal highway program, Model Cities, community action, and later programs developed in the last decade came into existence under an umbrella of planning, and they each demanded, and provided support for, planning staffs. But even as these programs have been eclipsed by fiscal restraint, a new kind of planning has emerged in several cities. In the face of fiscal cutbacks, these cities pioneered redistributive policies while other cities cut back services ever more severely.* Berkeley, Calif., and Hartford, Conn., are striking examples of planning and implementation under progressive majorities. Their planning, more than most, expressly focused on the interests of relatively disadvantaged groups, on challenging

*For example, Cleveland elected populist Mayor Dennis Kucinich and for two years experienced a number of progressive administrative initiatives—many of them based on earlier advocacy in the City Planning Department. Madison, Wisc., Burlington, Vt., and Santa Monica, Calif., are other cases in point.

the agendas of elite-oriented planning, and on institutional innovation carefully adapted to local circumstances.

HARTFORD AND BERKELEY

Progressive planning developed in different ways in each place. In Hartford, there had been competent and vigorous staff work since at least the mid-1960s, but the major growth in planning came after 1969 as a new coalition of neighborhood activists and liberals gained seats in the city council. By the early 1970s this group had gained effective political leadership of the city and began making key administrative appointments. From the beginning, they were conscious of their neighborhood constituency and the desperate economic and fiscal obstacles to survival as a community. Hartford was a major insurance, banking, and government center, but its population was primarily poor white ethnics, Blacks, and Puerto Ricans who provided 43 percent of Connecticut's welfare caseload. A Brookings Institution study found the economic disparity between the city and its suburbs to be the third worst in the nation. In these circumstances the council majority led by Nicholas Carbone vowed a policy of advocacy on behalf of the have-nots, and argued the legitimacy of using all the resources of local government in pursuit of that policy. They were to develop and implement this policy through the decade, until their defeat at the polls in 1979.

In Berkeley, the progressives for many years had minority representation in the city council, prior to moving into a leadership role in 1979. This began with the election of Ron Dellums—now Berkeley's U.S. Congressman—in 1967. The progressives used their minority position to advocate the use of public capital for cooperative housing, economic development, and community-based energy and social-service programs. They designed these programs in the 1970s as city resources were expanding, and capital accumulation could take place at the margin of growth. In April 1979 the citizens of Berkeley elected five progressive city officials: the Mayor—Gus Newport; three council members—Florence MacDonald, Veronika Fukson, and John Denton; and the City Auditor—Anna Rabkin. The three council members plus the Mayor comprised a near majority in the nine-person council because they had the frequent support of a then-unaffiliated member, Carol Davis. In 1979 this group set about implementing some of the programs that had been part of progressive platforms for over a decade. This period of progressive influence lasted two years. The 1981 election was swept by more conservative candidates who have regained control of the city council.

Intense planning over a long period of time marked both the Hartford and Berkeley groups. This planning was marked by a commitment to redistribu-

From *Social Policy*, Winter 1982, pp. 15-23. Copyright 1982 by Social Policy Corp.

tion, which distinguished the Hartford and Berkeley progressive leadership from the "liberal" ideals that prevailed in a great many other cities with equally impoverished constituencies. The Hartford and Berkeley leadership aimed to serve the poor quite openly and publicly. The result was that they did quite a lot of open, synthetic, public, and progressive planning.

In Hartford, starting from a general position of advocacy for the have-nots, the city council moved through a series of analyses to detail its strategy. There had been a Plan of Action prepared by a "Committee of 100," and a two-year Model Cities planning process that involved a lot of neighborhood interaction. The studies impressed the council with both the extent of the economic depression facing city residents and the extent to which these economic problems were a distributional issue between city and suburbs.

Hartford had lost over 10,000 manufacturing jobs. Of the existing work force of 134,000 people at the beginning of the 1970s, only 34,000 were city residents. Of the 98,000 jobs in eight surrounding towns, only 18,000 were held by city residents. Hartford had the highest percentage of the unemployment, over 50 percent of the work force in some neighborhoods. The city's population was marginal in terms of income. It was a population that needed subsidy for housing, for health, for recreation. They had inadequate income; any they might have went to pay for basic essentials: food, clothing, and shelter. An analysis by the Council on Municipal Performance clarified these inadequacies for the city council. Comparing 1970 population census figures to the Bureau of Labor Statistics' deprivation level showed that the incomes of 61 percent of the population of 158,000 were substandard by an average of $1,528 per year. There was no way the city could find the tax revenues to make up that difference.

From this analysis, the council developed two major strategies. One was to reduce the cost of living within the city through a series of innovative public-service systems such as energy conservation and a community food system. The second strategy was to increase incomes. The key to this end was a land use and transportation strategy that included litigation to block suburban industrial development and highways and mass transportation policies that would encourage suburban development at the expense of the city, as well as a set of positive development plans.

These latter plans evolved along with council action, and were elaborated piece by piece as they were needed. There was no one published document that could be pointed to as the "Hartford Plan." But public statements were frequent, and in early 1976 the council formally adopted a series of policy papers, which, with succeeding documents, boiled down the underlying themes into three:

1. To increase jobs and income for unemployed and underemployed Hartford residents.
2. To improve the fiscal health of the city of Hartford.
3. To revitalize Hartford's neighborhoods.

These ideas, with their implicit and explicit redistributive implications, were dramatized by the Hartford leadership. Most spectacular was a suit, brought by the city against HUD and six suburban towns, to stop the distribution of Community Development Block Grants because those towns had not filed adequate low-income-housing plans. The suit was successful in that it provided a context for negotiation between city and suburbs on other issues, and allowed the council to make public its case for Hartford's redistributive claims: on welfare, federal highway funds, suburban affirmative action, and others, in addition to housing.

In Berkeley, progressive forces operated from a minority position from 1967 until their council victories of 1979. During that period, Berkeley Citizen's Action (BCA) and similar coalitions that preceded it produced a succession of separate programs operating from outside the central control points of city government. BCA was able to pressure a reluctant council to support some of its programs, such as the Savo Island Housing Cooperative. In addition, the city made rapid affirmative-action gains during this period due to a significant degree to the aggressive demands of the progressive minority on the council.

During the decade of minority participation in city government, BCA also successfully used the initiative process to change city policies and practices. BCA placed before the voters initiatives that established a civilian police review commission, controls over housing demolition, inclusionary requirements for low- and moderate-income housing in new housing developments, strengthened citizen participation on city boards and commissions, and rent control.

Public statements of overall strategy emerged from this experience in opposition—most notably a book, *The Cities' Wealth*, by E. Bach, et al., published in 1976—which combined discussion of tactics with substantive policy and programs. The authors included tactics that they saw as

> examples of structural, or nonreformist, reform, extending the actual or potential realm of people's power. We have tried to avoid techniques for conventional political shifts, where one group with similar goals nudges out another for position at the top, but the structure remains intact.

They interpreted the goals of the progressive coalitions as

> efforts to improve the economic position of the city's many renters and small homeowners . . . support for free social services to the underserved poor, the transient, the young, the disabled and elderly . . . for affirmative-action programs for ethnic minorities and women, and other programs to rectify past injustices . . . [and] concern with a long list of environmental problems, from industrial pollution to waste recycling.

They saw cities as offering a vehicle to effect these goals. At the time, their main emphasis was on the city as a source of capital: they had the power to tax, own property, annex territory, borrow capital, and own and operate productive enterprises, in addition to being subject, at least formally, to popular control. This combination of redistributive goals, the drive toward institutionalizing popular control, and the notion of using the city as a vehicle for capital formation characterized the list of proposals that followed. These included rent control; a scheme for neighborhood land-use control; cooperative housing; public ownership and control of electric power, telephones,

> **A general principle behind much of the Hartford innovation was that of substituting local organization for expensive bureaucratic and professional agencies.**

and cable TV; proposals for generating cooperative and municipal businesses; a city-operated bank; redistributive tax and fee measures; and the development of increased community participation in and control of various kinds of social services.

In summary, both the Hartford and Berkeley groups articulated public plans and principles that set their agendas and guided their actions. Both rejected the idea that private-sector forces were the main engine of economic welfare and instead opted for public ownership, enterprise, regulation, and services in major ways. They differed in that the Hartford group began with political leadership, while the Berkeley coalition spent a decade in opposition positions. In both cases, policy was to develop out of actions, but they were different kinds of action. In Berkeley, policies evolved from outside of government, from minority-based actions. In Hartford, policies evolved in the course of substantial control of government over a long period of time. Moreover, the background was different in each case: Berkeley was less pressed by economic decline, though it shared the problems of fiscal stress in government, particularly when BCA came into power at the end of the 1970s.

HARTFORD: FROM INVESTMENT TO SERVICE STRATEGIES

In each place, the combination of redistributive policies and plans and the opportunities and challenges of involvement in city administration resulted in an extraordinary record of innovation. Some of the new institutions and practices, particularly those implemented early in the 1970s, were the results of exploitation of federal funding resources, in addition to private investment projects carried over from previous years. But the essence of the innovation was the use of public policy to redirect private priorities. In Hartford, this occurred through public pressure on the tax structure, through a public land development policy, and through the development of new and reorganized public services.

The City as Tax Reformer

In 1978, a state-mandated property-tax reassessment was confronting Hartford with two kinds of effects: a shift of tax burden from neighborhoods that had been experiencing deterioration to those where some reinvestment had been occurring, and an overall shift from business to residential properties. There was the basis for fragmentation of interests and conflict. White ethnic community leaders, representing the areas whose assessments would go up, called for the city council to throw out the revaluation. Black political leaders and civil-rights activists would not stand for any talk of a delay in implementing the new scheme—which would have reduced assessments in their neighborhoods. Municipal unions were mainly concerned about the prospects of revaluation shifting the tax burden from business and commercial property to homeowners—fueling a taxpayers' revolt, they feared, that could lead to massive budget cuts and layoffs. Business leaders argued that their property was overassessed, and wanted an immediate revaluation to lower their property assessments.

In this climate, the council leadership set out to reach the fairest possible solution to the revaluation dilemma. They caused legislation to be introduced in the state legislature covering several resolutions of the problem without committing the city to any one, simply to buy time. They then began meeting with the groups concerned. They pointed out to the Black leaders that, even if the reassessment achieved a redistribution of burden to the relatively better-off residential neighborhoods, their taxes would still go up if the shift from business assessments went through. They talked to the white ethnic groups about the deleterious effects on Black neighborhoods if they continued to bear their present disproportionate burden, and got them to agree to the principle of equity among homeowners regardless of neighborhood. The city council then filed a new bill in the legislature, which fixed the total tax bill that would be paid by homeowners after revaluation at 14.6 percent, the same proportion contributed by residential property before revaluation.

At this point, the Hartford leadership had gotten preliminary agreement on a solution to revaluation that would satisfy the different neighborhoods and, potentially, the public-sector unions. But they faced heavy opposition in the legislature. They then encouraged the formation of the Citizens Lobby to apply pressure to the state legislature. Municipal unions then rallied around the bill, and many city employees, over 3,000 of them residing in the suburbs, began to work in their neighborhoods urging neighbors to contact their state representatives and senators in support of the bill.

The key to passage, however, would be business support. At one meeting with representatives of the Greater Hartford Chamber of Commerce, city leaders' arguments were to no avail: the chamber's executive committee voted to oppose any effort to defer shifting the tax burden from business to residential property. Carbone then sent a telegram to each member of the chamber executive committee, repeating the urgency of the situation and asking for face-to-face meetings among business leaders, community people, and local elected officials. Citizens Lobby members made similar requests of the chief executive officers of the city's largest corporations. As a result, some corporate leaders changed their positions, agreeing to remain neutral in the upcoming legislative battle.

Despite this, some business leaders remained adamantly opposed. Community leaders began demonstrating against the business community, demanding that no more public money be used for downtown improvements. They picketed tax-delinquent corporations and large companies that were appealing their property-tax assessments. And some groups argued that the city should spend no more tax dollars to rebuild the Hartford Civic Center Coliseum, which had been destroyed when its roof collapsed earlier that winter. At city hall, the leadership began to take a tougher line, looking for bargaining points that could help leverage business support (or neutrality) for property-tax relief. Their top legislative priority was the revaluation bill, which became known as the "differential" bill because it set different rates of assessment for residential and business properties.

At this time, with the business community still generally opposed to the bill, the city council was pressed to approve funds for the Civic Center Coliseum. Hartford's corporate community had a heavy investment in a professional hockey team, the Whalers, which was part of the merger plans between the two major hockey leagues. Without a firm commitment on the new coliseum, the Whalers would be out of the expanded National Hockey League. The franchise—and millions of local corporate dollars—would be lost.

When the request to allocate funds for the new coliseum reached the council floor, Carbone stated he had been too busy working on the revaluation issue to study the resolution concerning the coliseum. He said he needed more time to review the request for funds. Several other council members made similar remarks, and the proposal was tabled. They had made their point. The strongest opponents of the differential bill agreed not to lobby against it, and other business leaders let it be known that they favored the differential as a temporary solution. If a sunset provision were written into the bill, they would support it.

The short-term struggle was won. For a while, at least, a $6 million tax shift to homeowners was avoided. In addition, the coalition-building around reassessment—and subsequent lobbying—generated other legislation beneficial to the city, and created new organizational capacity within the city and linked the city to sympathetic supporters in the suburbs.

The City as Investor and Regulator

At the beginning of the 1970s, Hartford was already a partner in various investment schemes, including urban-renewal projects. The city's role in these projects had so far been relatively limited. It had put up the local share of project subsidies, provided some public works and administrative support, and had left development—and profits—to private developers. But the analyses of the city's welfare population that the council had initiated earlier suggested that a new approach was needed, where the primary objective of city policy should be to supplement local incomes. Consequently every investment possibility was to be evaluated according to the extent it contributed toward this objective, and the city was to use what means it had to direct and regulate investment in this direction. The city's strategy to improve income was accomplished in part by means of the courts and by taking advantage of administrative rules, particularly the federal affirmative-action hiring rules, that had not previously been vigorously followed. In a sense this was a negative strategy, meant to redirect private-sector development that was moving toward the suburbs from the city, and which favored the relatively well-educated white labor force over Hartford's Black, Hispanic, poor, and untrained one. The other side of the strategy was a more positive one: to use vacant land and buildings in the central city as a resource for employing city people. The council decided that the city should become the retail, entertainment, cultural, and food service center for the region, a development that would create a great many entry level and part-time jobs that educationally deprived inner-city residents could get to supplement family incomes.

The first and major project implementing this strategy was the Hartford Civic Center, a $90 million complex in which the city put up $30 million, the private sector the balance. The Civic Center included a hotel and 360,000 square feet of retail space on air rights. The city owned the land but leased the air rights to the hotel, office, and retail space, retaining a part of the equity and a percentage of any profits through the air rights leases. The city had the state legislature enact laws to facilitate these arrangements. It created a Civic Center Authority, which allowed them to set up a body independent from the city yet able to employ people as city employees: the Authority would thus be under the policies of the city government but outside the bureaucracy and the civil-service system so that it could be run as a business. Because of the employees being considered city employees, the council could still impose a residency requirement. The council then negotiated with the school system that all the part-time jobs for young people had to go through the Hartford school system through the work-study program, an important link. Thus they took young people from welfare homes (75 percent of the persons in the Hartford school system came from AFDC homes) and linked them into the Civic Center with part-time jobs—if they were in school.

Aetna Life and Casualty, which built the retail part of the Civic Center, was required to have as part of its affirmative-action plan the condition that they would (1) have minority businesses in the center and (2) would help capitalize small businesses. To fulfill this, Aetna put up $8 million for furniture, fixtures, and capitalization for small businesses. They took small businesses that were successful, that had a good product: for example, a grinder shop from Franklin Avenue was brought in that sold grinders (a submarine-type sandwich) and Italian foods as part of the Civic Center's marketplace—a small restaurant with a fast turnover that seated about 25 people. They took a Black man who ran a marginal liquor store but who was doing a good job and put him in the Civic Center right next to the hotel, where he upgraded his store. A Black baker who worked in a hotel as the pastry chef opened the John Williams Bake Shop. Hartford did this sort of thing in several buildings in which the city had an interest. They developed a policy of taking equity holdings in buildings and land and leasing them back to private developers with stipulations, essentially making the city a partner in commercial and housing ventures. They asked the legislature for changes in the law to make it possible to do this: for any development over $10 million they proposed to negotiate the taxes for up to seven years in return for one percent of gross rentals. If the city was to give tax deferrals for risky ventures, it wanted to participate in the profits later. They then formulated the City and Town Development Act, which went through the legislature in 1975, providing that the city could fix taxes for up to 20 years, own real estate, and lease it to businesses. The city could build factories, and it could use industrial-revenue bonds for a sinking bond for up to two years, resulting in somewhat cheaper rates to build factories, or housing. Thus the city was in the real-estate business. With that the city took ownership of an old abandoned Korvettes department store and leased it to American Airlines. This brought 1,000 jobs into the city, with the American Airlines office plus—as a condition of the lease—the use of the first two floors for small businesses.

The city also began to restructure administrative budgets and service delivery systems. It gave greater attention to education functions, adding 400 positions to the Board of Education payrolls, while subtracting 200 from the police and fire departments, 200 from public works. It initiated new school dental, lunch, and breakfast programs—an indirect income subsidy—while replacing teachers with paraprofessionals with local-residency requirements. It redirected $1.5 million of Community Development Block Grant funds, traditionally used for capital investments, toward the school system.

Nonservice Options

A general principle behind much of the Hartford innovation was that of substituting local organization for expensive bureaucratic and professional agencies. The city council began to encourage citizen participation, not just in policy decisions but in performance—in the actual delivery of services to residents.

They began with the police department, instituting neighborhood police teams that were assigned to specific districts, in a return to the old "cop on the beat" theory that it was helpful for police officers and residents to know and respect one another. Every two weeks, neighborhood representatives met with police team leaders to talk about problem areas. One police lieutenant told Carbone that he initially resisted neighborhood demands to crack down on street prostitution. Five and a half years behind a desk downtown had taught him that prostitution is a victimless crime that should be ignored by the police. Residents who lived with the problem saw it differently. And he found that as the amount of street prostitution declined, so did the number of muggings, assaults, and other violent crimes. Burglaries and drug traffic also declined. That kind of experience began to generate feelings of mutual respect and

cooperation between police officers and residents.

In some neighborhoods, residents became even more directly involved in crime prevention efforts. Street observer programs put citizen foot-patrol teams in direct radio contact with police officers in the area. Other neighborhood groups went door-to-door, with police officers, to help people engrave their valuables with identification numbers and offer suggestions on how to improve the security of their houses and apartments.

One of the neighborhood policy advisory committees sponsored a cultural awareness night, which brought together police officers and their families and people who lived in the neighborhood. More than 300 people attended this social event, which included ethnic music and a dinner of soul food and Puerto Rican dishes. Previously, police officers and residents of that neighborhood had viewed each other with hostility. The team police concept was beginning to change this attitude. They now began to see each other as allies with common goals.

Similar efforts were made to bring local residents into the provision of recreation services. Over 40 percent of the city's part-time recreation leaders had been suburban residents, but Hartford created a neighborhood incentive program that allowed residents to plan and operate their own activities. If someone in a neighborhood wanted to teach a class in oil painting, for example, he or she would submit a proposal to a neighborhood planning group. If it appeared that the person was qualified and there would be sufficient interest to warrant a class in oil painting, the resident would be paid to teach the class. This system involved far more people and offered a greater variety of recreational activities than the former, more traditional program. Classes developed in cross-country skiing, squash, acting, weaving, the guitar, vegetarian cooking, and hundreds of other areas.

Citizen Participation

By the middle of the 1970s, it was apparent that public and private investment, and consequent employment, would not by itself solve Hartford's personal income problems. Nor was it possible to raise the flow of public

funds into the city. Federal categorical programs like urban renewal and Model Cities were cut back; what had been an $18 million yearly subsidy was cut to $10.8 million in 1970, then $6 million under the Community Development Block Grant formulae. The limited fiscal resources that had greeted the city council in 1969 got even tighter, and an economic development study in 1979 counted a net decrease of 196 person-years since 1972 despite large increases in federal operating subsidies. The problem was how to manage decline, not growth. The property-tax base could not be raised, there was inflation pressure on taxpayers and landlords, so that the population was generally getting poorer. In 1974 the city canceled its capital expenditures for police cruisers to cover welfare costs, and the council increasingly directed its efforts at turning programs toward the objective of supplementing local family incomes. The city wrote its housing assistance plan under Section 8 of the Housing Act so that all subsidies would go to existing rental units rather than the construction of new housing—a move dictated by the pressure on family incomes and threats of landlord abandonments.

Neighborhood Cost-Reduction Programs

Toward the latter part of the 1970s, Hartford planners adopted a strategy to reduce the cost of basic necessities, focusing on Hartford neighborhoods. They realized that even the most optimistic forecasts of local job creation through infusion of outside capital would not suffice to provide jobs for every resident. They felt if they could help reduce the costs of such basic necessities as food, energy, transportation, and health care, more purchasing power would be available for other local activities. There would be additional resources available for purchase of private market housing and for patronage of neighborhood retail and service enterprises.

The city got farthest in food and energy cost-reduction programs. The Hartford food system included a downtown food market, a community cannery, community gardens, youth gardens, neighborhood buying clubs, solar greenhouses, roof-top container gardening, and a city-wide composting program. All elements were planned to complement one another. The system was justified as developing traits of self-reliance and cooperative consumption in residents and as generating a job environment for training that could later be applied to private-sector employment.

The energy program was initiated as a result of steep increases in fuel oil prices, which led to abandonment of many rental units by owners during the winter of 1978. This not only produced heating crises for many residents, it produced secondary effects of neighborhood economic deterioration and loss of housing units. In response, Hartford planners made surveys to determine the factors that made specific structures subject to abandonment because of energy costs or likely to generate complaints of heating failure. They used a computer-based information system to determine what structures in the city were at risk in these respects, and used the information to target outreach workers. They created a Coordinated Energy Response Center with a central "heat line" to permit quick responses to heating complaints. They coordinated the distribution of weatherization kits, claiming that these materials could save up to 20 percent of each tenant's fuel consumption. They established a rent receivership program as a last resort to maintain minimum heat levels and to reduce the likelihood of housing abandonment. The combined effect of targeted code enforcement and rent receivership programs was reported for the winter of 1979-80. Officials stated that the landlords of 217 housing units corrected heat violations and that 51 units were placed into rent receivership, requiring the city to pay the cost of correcting violations.

BERKELEY: INNOVATION IN THE FACE OF CUTBACKS

When Berkeley Citizens Action moved into a position of influence in 1979, it, like the progressive leadership in Hartford, was faced with serious budget problems. The newly elected leadership, which had earlier seen the city as a source of capital formation—a vehicle that could carry cooperative housing, economic development, tax reform, community-based energy, and social-services programs—had moved into the driver's seat just as the needle on the gas gauge moved toward empty. BCA had gained experience promot-

ing and forcing the implementation of some of its proposals. This was important, but nothing could have completely prepared newly elected officials for what they encountered in April 1979.

Battle of the Budget

The new council faced a proposed budget that had been developed by the City Manager who was appointed by the previous, more conservative council. It called for massive service cuts because, under Proposition 13, city-generated revenues were lagging seriously behind the expense of maintaining them at existing levels.

The budget that then-City Manager Michael Lawson proposed would close down two fire houses, eliminate programs in the police department that the community had fought to include (the Unit on Crimes Against Women, the Juvenile Bureau, the foot patrol, for example), cut deeply into the library budget for the second year in a row, and completely eliminate allocations to community-based social-service providers (the various community clinics and the women's shelter, for example).

The first response of the new council was to appoint a 27-member Citizens Budget Review Committee. At the request of the committee, the date for passing the 1979–80 city budget was delayed until mid-July.

After six weeks of study and deliberation, the Budget Committee submitted its proposals for changes in Lawson's budget, which were generally adopted by the city council. The fire stations would remain open, but vacant deputy chief and lieutenant positions were eliminated. The positions in the police department that provided direct services—such as school-crossing guards, foot patrol, the rape detail, and all positions on the street—were restored, with comparable dollar cuts made within the department by eliminating administrative and rank officer positions. (Lawson's budget called for the elimination of 46.5 positions in the police department, all at the point of service, while the Budget Committee called for elimination of 19 higher-paid positions, none providing direct services.)

The Budget Committee was also able to recommend restoration of funds for the library and for community services by developing additional

revenues for the city. The committee recommended several significant methods:

1. A property transfer tax that was already on the books was to be implemented. Passed by the previous council, it was not as progressively structured as those called for by BCA over the years, but it included important features that targeted speculative sales and exempted long-time owner occupants.

2. Services provided by the city to developers and businesses that had been partially or wholly supported by property taxes were shifted to total fee support. Building permits, for example, which had traditionally been subsidized by the city's General Fund, were to be totally supported by fees. The committee proposed to revise the fee schedule, which had previously been highly regressive (as much as 2 percent of project costs for small projects and less than .002 percent for very large ones) to a flat rate (about 1.4 percent of project costs). In addition the committee recommended charging a fee for fire inspections of businesses and industries for which no fee had ever been charged.

3. Activities supported by special funds were charged for their use of city services. The most important example was the City Marina Fund, which had generated healthy surpluses over the years that could only be spent in the marina area. This had led to expenditures for luxurious facilities in the yacht basin. State regulations did not allow these funds to be utilized elsewhere in the city but did allow the city to be reimbursed for fire, police, accounting, and other administrative services it provided. This reimbursement had not been previously required.

4. Additional revenue was also generated from automobile disincentives. Parking meters in an upper-income commercial area, increased meter rates, and long-overdue increases in parking violations fines were all put forward by the Budget Committee.

After its first heroic six weeks, the Budget Committee continued to meet. Members of the committee, as well as those from the city's 30 other citizen boards, were invited to participate in the budget discussions between the City Manager and city departments. In its second year, the Budget Committee took the initiative in present-

When Berkeley Citizens Action moved into a position of influence in 1979, it moved into the driver's seat just as the needle on the gas gauge moved toward empty.

ing a new tax to the voters of Berkeley for their approval. Under Proposition 13, California localities are prohibited from raising the ad valorum property-tax rate at all and can only institute other new taxes with the approval of two-thirds of the voters. Working with another citizen body, the Board of Library Trustees, the Budget Committee designed a new tax based on the floor area of buildings to support the city libraries. A sample survey indicated that this method was feasible to implement and generally progressive. The progressivity was reinforced by writing in a split rate. The tax, which requires residential property owners to pay 2.3 cents per square foot and commercial and industrial property owners to pay 3.5 cents per square foot, was approved by almost 70 percent of the voters in June 1980. While the main emphasis of the tax is its support of library services, all other services in the city receive support indirectly, since dollars from the General Fund that would otherwise support the library have been liberated.

Rent Stabilization and Eviction Control

From the very earliest years of its history, the progressive coalition in Berkeley had worked to regulate the rental housing market. The history includes an interesting mixture of successes and failures. Berkeley's first rent-control ordinance was put on the ballot through the initiative process in 1972, and passed with 51 percent approval. It was subsequently overturned in court as unconstitutional. Opponents had successfully argued that it was unfair to legislate rent control by plebiscite, since there were more tenants than landlords among the voters. A second attempt to gain rent regulation through the polls in 1977 failed to gain majority support.

Then, in the aftermath of Proposition 13, Berkeley—along with numerous other California cities—voted in a mild form of regulation in 1978 by requiring property owners to return a portion of their Proposition 13 property-tax savings to their renters. It prevented rent increases for months, and the issue of whether the controls on rent increases would be extended and institutionalized on a permanent basis was pivotal in the 1979 city elections. BCA candidates favored rent control; the other group opposed it.

When BCA gained its four seats, there was an immediate commitment from the nonaffiliated swing voter on the council to support rent regulation.

The next major task that BCA council members undertook after passage of the first budget was the development of an ordinance that would stabilize rents and protect tenants from unfair evictions. By late fall, a far-reaching ordinance had gained council approval. However, the City Charter required a second reading after several weeks.

While the ordinance was awaiting its second reading, property owners, realtors, and others opposed to rent control were on the streets collecting signatures to have the ordinance nullified. Berkeley was reminded, for the third time in less than 20 years, of a powerful feature in the City Charter, whereby a small number of voters (10 percent of those voting for Mayor in the last election) can petition against an ordinance passed by the city council. When presented with the signatures, the council can either repeal the ordinance or place it on the ballot at the next regularly scheduled election. If the council chooses to take the issue to the voters, the ordinance does not go into effect until after it has gained their approval.

Previously this provision of the charter had been used in the early 1960s to overturn the council-approved fair-housing ordinance. During the 1970s, the city's progressive forces turned to this charter requirement to overturn the council's decision refusing to study the feasibility of municipalizing the privately owned electric-distribution system. (The study indicated it would indeed be feasible; given the actual rate of inflation since the study was performed, it turns out the study underestimated the feasibility. Acquisi-

tion of the system was, however, twice rejected by Berkeley voters.)

When rent-control opponents turned to petitions with the requisite number of signatures (collected from some people who believed they were signing in favor of rent control), the BCA council members had to develop a strategy that would extend the soon-to-expire rent regulations in effect until a permanent ordinance could be passed in the June 1980 election. It was very important that there be no gap in the protection that renters were receiving.

The BCA council members were successful in providing the unbroken coverage. The voters approved Berkeley's Rent Stabilization and Good Cause Eviction Ordinance at the polls. The council appointed members of the Rent Stabilization Board and set up a staff to implement what is necessarily a complex regulatory mechanism. Tremendous effort still has to be devoted to legal defense of the ordinance. The courts have not yet become comfortable with a law that shifts the balance between owners and renters. After a year, opposition to the ordinance is still strong.

Cooperative Housing

Another major BCA commitment over the years had been to the development of cooperatively owned housing for low- and moderate-income people. Just as the new council members took office, the city's first project opened (Florence MacDonald, one of the new council members, was among the first residents). A second co-op housing project was in the planning stages. Many members of the community active in housing issues believed that the outcome of the 1979 election would determine whether or not this second project would see the light of day.

Like developments elsewhere, the construction and financing costs of this new project were skyrocketing. Between a committed city council and creative developers who pulled in every outside available federal and state direct and indirect subsidy, the project moved toward realization. The magnitude of the costs emphasized, however, that delivering low- and moderate-income housing requires a strong commitment, which will be tested repeatedly.

Redevelopment

One of the issues that separated political factions in Berkeley for many years was the city's Redevelopment Project. Originally planned for an industrial park, the redevelopment area was the site of intense, sometimes violent, conflict, as BCA fought to preserve existing housing and target the vacant subsidized land for housing rather than industrial and commercial uses. Over the years, BCA had won battles that delayed industrial development, but only after the 1979 election could BCA change the plan to build housing.

It seemed that it would be a simple matter, until the council learned that once again Proposition 13 was blocking them. In the fine print of the redevelopment bonds was language requiring the Redevelopment Agency to collect one-third more in taxes than it had to pay out in debt service in order to amend the Redevelopment Plan. By cutting tax revenues below this level, Berkeley would have to contact bondholders and receive their approval before amending the plan. Just after the election, the Redevelopment Agency staff developed a method of defeasance to meet the legal requirements. As the legal clouds lift, the city will now need to find the millions of dollars of investment capital required to build low- and moderate-income housing.

Energy Programs
Energy issues in Berkeley presented themselves very differently in 1980 than they did in 1970. For many years, the thrust of the BCA program was to have the city buy out the electric system. Rates that Berkeley residents were paying reflected the costs of expanding the system in the suburbs. Relieving ratepayers in Berkeley of this expense and other savings inherent in a publicly owned system necessitated some form of public ownership. In recent years, the Pacific Gas and Electric Company's rate schedule was shifted by the California Public Utilities Commission from the declining block structure to lifeline rates favoring small users over large ones. As a result, Berkeley ratepayers, who have been successful at conservation, generally have benefited.

Meanwhile, new city programs were developed to foster conservation, especially for lower-income people. Instruction in no-cost and low-cost improvements in housing was provided by the city. Young people were

trained to weatherize houses and provide services for elderly residents. In addition, the Energy Commission, another citizen board, studied ways the city might save on its heating and fuel bills

Eliminating Waste
Given the tight financial situation in Berkeley and the commitment of the city council to solve basic but expensive problems, the city administration explored ways of improving the organization's productivity, reducing wasteful expenditures, and reorganizing to improve efficiency. While Berkeley's city council was hardly unique in its commitment to these objectives, there was an urgency about their realization that is directly related to its other progressive goals.

A more conservative city government has options that the BCA council members rejected, such as cutting costs by contracting out services to firms paying nonunion wages or eliminating programs that serve the poorest (often nonvoting) people. BCA is a coalition—to a very large degree comprised of people who have been passed over by BCA's more conservative opposition. The coalition depended on meeting each group's needs—fully meeting them was no longer possible, but each one had weight.

In the 1979–81 period, BCA council members scraped together resources to meet the broader community needs in part by skimming a little off the top (the split rate in the library tax and the changes in the fee structure are examples). The council members also learned that there are significant obstacles that prevented significant redistribution—in Proposition 13, in the City Charter, in the fine balance of electoral politics. In this context, efficiency and elimination of waste took on an urgency that would otherwise be surprising in progressive circles.

Berkeley's campaign against waste was directed by Wise Allen, the City Manager appointed by the city council in February 1980. He immediately targeted an array of nonproductive but increasingly expensive costs—workmen's compensation payments, for example. He initiated an occupational health and safety program. In California cities, attention to these costs was not unusual. What may distinguish the Berkeley approach, however, is Al-

len's belief that the problems had to be solved by the people working for the city. Solutions designed by the people who face the problems can be carried out in a way that the ideas of an outside consultant—no matter how creative—are unlikely to be.

Public Services Committees
The Labor-Management-Citizen Public Services Committee Project is a collaborative effort involving the city of Berkeley, unions representing city employees (SEIU Locals 535 and 390, IBEW Local 1245, and the Berkeley Firefighters Association), and members of citizen commissions and citizen organizations. The thrust of the program is to focus the attention of the three parties on the overriding problem they share—that is, how to maintain and improve the delivery of municipal services in an environment of fiscal scarcity.

The Public Services Committees provide a cooperative, nonadversarial forum for identifying service delivery and work organization problems and solutions to those problems. The Project supplements but does not supersede the collective-bargaining agreement between the city and the unions. A unique feature of the Project's approach is to involve citizens, the consumers of city services, in the collaborative labor-management work review process.

The locus of the Project's work is in discrete work units in different city departments, where three-sided Public Services Committees are being established to identify and rectify problems in work organization and service delivery. A three-sided city-wide coordinating committee makes broad policy for the Project and monitors and supports the functioning of the work-site committees. The Project was suggested by the Citizens' Budget Review Commission in November 1979. Since that time, dozens of well-attended informational and exploratory meetings have cleared the way for the enthusiastic commitment of all three parties to the Project.

CITIZEN ACTION IN AND OUT OF OFFICE
Clearly, progressive ideas infused both cities' administrations. In Hartford and Berkeley, progressive movements depended on local organizing

Liberal governments have always been theoretically in favor of "citizen participation," but Berkeley and Hartford actively encouraged it, tapping a source of energy, creativity, and support.

efforts. Hartford's Citizens Lobby had city hall support, as did Berkeley's Citizen Budget Committee, but these were only the most dramatic, peak-level examples of what was a much more widespread phenomenon. Liberal governments have always been theoretically in favor of "citizen participation," but Berkeley and Hartford actively encouraged it, tapping a source of energy, creativity, and support. Thus, planning took on an importance and role it had not had previously. In Hartford, technical planning analyses quantified and reinforced the premises of the general advocacy policy, and then suggested specific programs that the council could pursue. In Berkeley, plans were elaborated in opposition that were only partially carried out later, but they

nevertheless served to punctuate a generally progressive agenda.

Now out of power, the Hartford and Berkeley progressives face the question of what legacy they leave. On the one hand, there is the painful knowledge that progressive municipal politics is an uphill struggle against great odds. The most immediate difficulties in both places came from the fiscal pressures on city budgets. Proposition 13 in California and the generally increasing gap between needs and revenue sources in Hartford resulted in very severe restrictions in local autonomy. This has meant that progressives have to work very hard just to keep the service levels of yesterday. The possibilities for significant change are severely diminished. Hartford's experience clearly demonstrates the political liability of redistribution at the margin of shrinkage. Berkeley's begins to show the liability that progressives face when their fancy technical footwork does not keep up with an accelerating crisis in public finance.

With electoral defeat, there was also an awareness of the fragile nature of most progressive innovations. Most participants in the Hartford administration dispersed after 1979, and many innovative practices were reversed. In Berkeley, the BCA retained a minority position on the council, and it is not yet clear what reverses will occur. But in both places electoral defeat raised

the question of how to institutionalize the changes that seemed to work. The Hartford and Berkeley progressives have had some permanent accomplishments—a civic center in one case, housing cooperatives in the other. The long-term lease arrangements in Hartford cannot be altered, and the experience of the Citizens Budget Review Committee in Berkeley might be remembered for a while. But the enemies made by these arrangements were probably better organized than their friends were. And the general structure of municipal practice in affirmative action, regulation, and public enterprise can be dismantled rather easily—and was in Hartford. These innovations requiring a continuing commitment are easier to replace with more traditional modes of government than it is to initiate them in the first place.

Nevertheless, what had been achieved made more sense for the people who had been served—the majority—than the "moderate" or even reactionary themes adopted by their successors. Future elections might show this. Moreover, other cities, facing similar economic issues, have tried to move in similar directions. Even as BCA went down to defeat in Berkeley, a rent-control coalition swept to victory in Santa Monica. There and in other places, progressive administration will continue to be tested and experience will accumulate.

Assuring the Economic Health of AMERICA'S CITIES

"The health of the cities requires as a precondition a prosperous national economy."

Henry G. Cisneros

Mr. Cisneros is the Mayor of San Antonio, Tex.

America's cities are the windows through which the world looks at American society. It is true that, at various moments, each of us in our own way, for our own reasons, would define things that we are proud of about America—the level of our culture, the advancement of our science, the fairness of our democracy—by citing examples from technology or art or music, from architecture, or from business accomplishments. However, the fact remains that the most comprehensive and the likeliest measure of American society is found at a glance in the American cities.

The cities are the focal point of American life today because they are the integrating mechanism for all the essential dynamics of our modern society, the point of convergence for those dynamics—the quest for justice and the dialogue by which we find opportunities for people. People who seek a place on the American ladder of opportunity come to the cities from other countries. New art forms are presented at the galleries and the museums of the great cities. New communication technologies are developed in the cities, such as the paperless office and cable television innovations. There is experimentation and research in the great centers of learning and, when the cure for cancer is found, it is likely to be found in one of the medical centers of a great American city. New forms of architecture are proposed. The search for a better quality of life and for ways in which people can live together goes on in the neighborhood movement sweeping virtually all of America's large cities.

That role of the city as an integrating mechanism for such essential dynamics is particularly true with respect to the economic life of the nation. Cities are key entities in the economic life of America. They are economic factors in several important ways. First, because when you look at the origins and the histories of the city, they are generally the result of economic decisions and common sense. Secondly, because the daily mechanics of the functioning of cities and their change and development are economic in nature. Thirdly, because the role they will play in the future of American society involves the national economic future.

Cities are created and they grow, or they stagnate, based on economic decisions which take into account the sweep of economic history and economic trends that confront the nation. We tend to forget that reality. We see cities in many other ways— as the places where we live, as the places where people congregate, as social centers— in so many different ways that we often forget that the origins of cities generally stem from economic decisions and economic common sense. Cities grow or stagnate depending on realities that relate to the adequacy of infrastructure, the adequacy of transportation, or the maturation and change in the makeup of the national economy as is occurring at the present.

Cities are also economic entities in the daily dynamics of their change and functioning. Consider briefly the all-too-familiar ways in which economic phenomena buffet and batter cities today. In times of cyclical turndown in the national economy, it is the cities that are hurt the worst—their economies the hardest hit, their tax bases reduced most, their social services expenditure requirements the hardest pressed. When demand is weak, production is usually curtailed first or stopped altogether at the oldest plants, which tend to be located in the central cities. As a result, at the peak of the 1975 recession, when national unemployment peaked at 8.5%, the rate in the cities was 9.6% and in the central city poverty areas it was more than 15%. Even worse disparities exist in the recession we are experiencing today.

The other side of the economic roller coaster, inflation, also batters the cities with particular severity. The costs of goods and services purchased by city government tend to rise faster than consumer prices. From 1972 to 1977, for example, when the consumer price index rose by about 48.6%, the costs of purchases by state and local governments rose by well over 50%. However, the real losses to cities from the inflationary spiral can be seen only by comparing the inflation in required expenditures—the package of goods that the city has to buy—with the slower rise in revenues available to meet those expenditures. The fact is that city revenues do not keep pace with the escalating costs because,

. . . although sales and income taxes rise automatically with inflation, the property tax, which is the mainstay of local finance, must be readjusted through conscious reassessments. Such reassessments generally occur only at specific intervals and are politically difficult to accomplish during periods of high inflation. The result is that cities lose purchasing power faster than the rest of society. Atlanta, for example, in a recent two-year period lost 16.6% of the value of its revenue by experiencing an effective property tax rate decline of 14%.[1]

Reprinted from *USA TODAY* November 1982, pp. 43-47. Copyright 1982 by Society for the Advancement of Education.

4. URBAN SOCIAL POLICIES

Still another effect of national economic problems for cities is the range of issues that comes under the heading of structural change in the U.S. economy. Structural changes, such as the decline of specific industry sectors, have created patterns of regional advantage and disadvantage, population shifts, and industrial migration. The story of population and job loss in central cities is all too familiar. Today's news carries the story that 137,000 General Motors workers are now "on furlough." The implications are clear for Detroit, Akron, Toledo, South Bend, and all of those other cities where GM plants are located or where the factories exist that make automobile tires, windshields, ball bearings, and engine parts. The conclusion is clear—cities are daily buffeted by economic realities to a degree that the economic assault is the dominant fact of life for city governments.

A National Urban Policy

In examining the economic future of the cities of America, there is an immediate temptation to point to the need for a national urban policy. As we review national urban problems, the natural response for one searching for solutions is to look for national solutions. A person such as myself, a mayor of a growing Southwestern city, observing the current economic circumstances in the nation and in the cities, tries to draw conclusions about a national urban policy, but that is a very difficult thing to do, because the differences across the cities and the regions of this country are great. Yet, I do think it is possible to make two points about the relationship between the cities and the nation, perhaps as a basis for national policy.

The first is obvious and is often stated— the health of the cities requires as a precondition a prosperous national economy. The second point is less well-understood, but I believe it needs to be developed as part of our basic understanding of the workings of our society—to attain a prosperous national economy, one that is able to deal with ideals of American society, requires the general health of a balanced system of cities. I see the role of the cities not as incidental beneficiaries or unintended victims of economic trends, but, instead, as fundamental building blocks for the national economy and building blocks for the social ideals of American society. It is a two-sided coin.

Let us examine the two sides of that coin separately. First, the health of the cities requires as a precondition a prosperous national economy. I have already stated some of the elements of my case:
• When national unemployment is up, it is higher in the cities by as much as five per cent.

• When inflation is high, it affects the package of city expenditures worse.
• When inflation is up, it outstrips the revenue-producing power of such basic taxes as the property tax.
• When interest rates are high, cities must pay more for public debt, the need for which can not be postponed because replacement or expansion of such critical public requirements as sewer systems or water services can not long be delayed.
• When recession induces plant closings, they occur first in the cities and often it is the city plants which remain closed even after cyclical recoveries.
• When the national savings rate declines and capital business reinvestment in modernization is unavailable, it is the productivity of older city-based plants which suffers by comparison with newer facilities.

Although these facts tend to be true for cities all across the nation, some people would argue that the health of every city in fact does not depend upon national prosperity; that it is possible to have some—in fact, many—city economies remain strong even in a severe national recession by virtue of prosperous regional or local conditions. As evidence, one could cite the fact that Oklahoma City today, to pick but one example of a dynamic Sunbelt city, had an unemployment rate of only three per cent through much of 1981 and that about 15% more new jobs were created in the oil business, agriculture, retailing, and real estate. Nearly similar statistics could be cited for Phoenix, Denver, Tampa, Jacksonville, Tulsa, Houston, Dallas, San Diego, San Jose, San Antonio, Austin, or Tucson. There is frankly a great temptation to cite such successes as an indication of what is possible and write off the problems of the Northeastern and North Central cities. That temptation has found expression in the implicit thrust of a national commission's recommendation that citizens from depressed areas should "vote with their feet" and pursue opportunities elsewhere. Such feelings are reinforced by Sunbelt convictions that, in previous periods of our national history, the regions that are today's losers—the depressed cities—were heavy-handed oppressors of the rest of the nation. There is a sense that this is a period of reckoning for the eastern bankers, the railroad barons, the steel producers, and the so-called Eastern Establishment politicians who held such a stranglehold on the machinery of production, the raw materials, and the capital so badly needed to fully develop the South, the West, and the Southwest in earlier periods of our history. If calling these feelings "revenge" is too strong, then there is at least a sense that much of the North's problems are of its own making, the products of profligate spending of big-city political organizations, of out-of-control labor unions, or of overpromising

that assumes dimensions of a political-economic ethic.

Such feelings are most certainly out there and they run deeply through the currents of the public consciousness in the Southwest and throughout the South. Thus, they become an element of making those public policies that are to deal with vastly different conditions and trends across the regions and the cities of our country. Whether those convictions have basis in fact or not is not nearly so important as that they are the shared convictions of many citizens west of the Mississippi; therefore, in the modern political arena, they find expression more and more in public policy.

Yet, despite the fact that there are those temptations to split the nation along lines that divide growing regions from mature regions, the fact remains that we are a nation. First and foremost, we are one nation! One has to question whether escalating the competition for advantage between regions is the best way to behave as a nation. We have to ask whether it is possible under those circumstances to hold together any semblance of a national consensus on how to deal with the poor, the old, the unskilled, and those for whom social justice is still a dream. I read in national policy statements today a clear preference for policies which would encourage unbridled competition between regions. Implicit in those policies is the hope that somehow, as the migration out of declining areas reaches a sufficient momentum, the market mechanism will right some of the wrongs; there will be corrections to costs, wages, and governmental organization in the Northeast. However, there are critical questions we have to ask ourselves: "What is the human price that will be paid as those who are the least mobile in our society suffer from that kind of competition?" "Is such an intense interregional competition the best way to meet the challenges of an international environment in which we have to behave more as a nation than ever before?"

That begins to address the other side of the coin, so let us forget sentimentality or ideals or the subjective value of national cohesiveness and talk instead just of economic benefits. The other side of that coin is this: to attain a prosperous national economy which is able to sustain an open society requires the health of a balanced system of cities across the country. Consider these facts:
• When structural unemployment in the central cities rises from inattention, each increase of one per cent in the national unemployment rate adds $25,000,000,000 to the national deficit in a combination of decreased tax payments and increased benefits entitlements.
• When cities are unable to meet the cost of building roads, bridges, ports, or sewer systems, there are bottlenecks and ineffi-

ciencies that affect the national economic prosperity.

• When central city schools are no longer able to train youngsters and prepare them for technological jobs, the nation pays a price in manpower shortages and gaps in the technical skills base needed for re-industrialization.

• When racial strife becomes one of the dominant features of urban life, the nation sustains a high crime rate and must live with alienation and division.

• When the cities are characterized by deterioration and when the urban landscape is a picture of decline and despair, then I believe there occurs a psychological change of mood such that national optimism is replaced by national pessimism.

All of this suggests that policies which promote or reward regional abandonment are damaging, both to the cities and to the larger national economy. It suggests that a national policy whose essential thrust is to "let them vote with their feet," leaving behind pockets of despair for the least mobile citizens of the society, is flawed both for the cities and for the national economy. It suggests that, because of the nature of American society today, to make national economic policy is to make national urban policy; and the best national urban policy is one that integrates the problems of the cities into national economic policymaking. These two great interests of national policy need to be considered.

What does it mean to think of them concurrently? What should we expect of a national economic policy that relates to urban areas? What is the overarching framework for a Federal economic role in the cities? What are the principles or basic elements of such an approach? I would like to suggest three elements.

The Need for Cooperation

The first element would be to create a sense of integration of the concerns of the cities into national economic thinking. This is a delicate area because it deals with a kind of cooperation that we have not had in our nation, but it parallels the spirit that the national government, the cities, and business need to foster in order to create the framework that best enables business to prosper and create jobs in the long run, drawing lightly as it does from the Japanese concern for "long-run vision." Actually, that term is a nickname for one of the most important divisions of the Japanese Ministry of International Trade and Industry. We need to think not in terms of subsidy, control, guidance, or supervision of business, but in terms of creating the conditions for business that are necessary to realize long-term visions and infuse in that process some sense of the high stakes for the survival of the cities. In the Japanese case, an organization which serves as a clearing-

house for several ministries, the Economic Planning Agency, avoids attempting to manage the economy, but it does ". . . provide targets reflecting long-term trends and specifying what would be necessary for balanced national development. It is, in effect, a point of communication, coordinating estimates of future growth made by governmental branches and by the business community. It helps draw attention to various needs and helps shape the thinking about what is required for a certain level of growth."[2]

The Ministry of International Trade and Industry itself shows initiatives beyond what has been considered acceptable in our economy. Ministry of International Trade and Industry officials try to

. . . push the pace of modernization ahead of market forces by setting high standards for modernization of plants and equipment and by promoting means to shore up companies that lack the capital to meet those standards. They point out areas where resources need to be concentrated in order to keep Japan competitive internationally in the future. MITI officials consider it their responsibility to assist companies and declining industries to merge or go out of business while encouraging new ones to move into the localities and employ the personnel who were laid off.[3]

A key aspect to this entire process in Japan is that its success cannot in general be attributed to statutory powers or authorities, which would be resisted. "Overwhelmingly, the success of the Ministry is derived not from rules or regulations but from its efforts at administrative guidance and from the voluntary cooperation of the business community."[4]

It is a cooperation which derives from a spirit that conveys a genuine interest in the welfare of the companies, from a high degree of competence and professionalism, and from constant formal and informal discussions within industrial sectors. This spirit of cooperation applied to our case, to our economy, would seek "to create an understanding that a partnership of business and government is a necessary condition for achieving individual and social objectives," prominent among them the need to rebuild the central cities.[5] Cooperation has been tried before:

Every U.S. administration since that of Calvin Coolidge has established tribunals composed of government, business, and occasionally labor with responsibility for the economic development of particular industries. Herbert Hoover, as Secretary of Commerce, sought industry-wide associations to rationalize production

and increase productivity. Similar notions underlay Franklin Roosevelt's National Recovery Administration and the various business-government boards responsible for production during World War II. More recently, the Carter Administration set up tripartite boards to develop policy for the steel, auto and coal industries.[6]

However, those efforts have been hampered by bureaucratic disorganization, characterized by fragmentation which prevents promoting the idea of a "big picture" approach to the revitalization and reinvestment efforts, and by a philosophical resistance to understand and cooperate on the supply and production side of the economy at the level of regions and geographic areas. In addition, the traditional adversary relationship between government and business is so engrained that it prevents meaningful cooperation, and many of the people who have the greatest stake in the policies—for example, representatives of cities—have not been included. They could help assure that cooperative government-business efforts stay on track toward success instead of being torn apart by defenders of the *status quo*.

There is one effort which is interesting as a demonstration of how close cooperation genuinely committed to building a prosperous industrial sector can succeed and prevent a great deal of human misery. In 1977, the American shoe industry was being driven out of business by imports. Employement had been cut down from 230,000 to 165,000 jobs in less than a decade. Production had dropped from 640,000,000 pairs of shoes to 400,000,000, while imports had doubled from 175,000,000 to 370,000,000. In the face of demands for import barriers and tariffs, the Carter Administration, in an effort spearheaded by Under Secretary of Commerce Sidney Harman, embarked on an effort to overcome the gaps in information and the competition between the Departments of Labor and Commerce in providing assistance to the nation's shoe producers. In contrast to mounting efforts to shore up the shoe industry in Europe, officials in the U.S. had neglected the creation of early warning forecasting systems for anticipating structural adjustment problems.

The program, coordinated by Harman with the Department of Labor, was more than just an effort to speed up standard adjustment assistance to a dying industry. It innovated assistance for the industry's self-help by improving the quality and volume of private technical expertise provided to companies. Domestic retailers and manufacturers were brought together to identify market trends and style changes. An export promotion program was developed. The Office of Science and Technology was directed to work on new technologies, the first government-industry program to develop a new generation of technology in a nondefense field. By pointing out this kind of direction, the program showed results within six months. Half of the 150 companies eligible for help applied for it. Imports were dropping as a result of marketing agreements that staved off the need for strict import quotas. Employment and production began rising. Some companies began to report record sales and earnings and, by 1978, Commerce Department statistics showed that America's shoe exports had increased by 28%.

That is not to say that the shoe industry does not remain a troubled one nor is it to say that the program that Harman instituted continues. With his departure, enthusiasm and interest in the program diminished. However, the pilot program did bring some results: the revitalization of essentially sound firms and the conversion to other manufacturing fields or firms that would never have been competitive in the industry. The pilot program helped bolster the strong and facilitated conversion of the weak. Harman considers the approach a contrast to the policies that we are normally more ready to employ, but which have often failed, such as imposing quotas on imports. Such reactions do not solve the inherent problems of the industry involved.

While the Harman experiment with U.S. shoe firms is novel by U.S. standards, it is one that is approached more regularly by our allies and competitors. For example, Germany, under Economics Minister Carl Schiller, designed a four-fold framework to guide the government's assistance to private firms in ailing industries. Those guidelines stated that the entire sector, not just some firms, must be in difficulty; that the actual restructuring program chosen be the decision of the private firms; that the government's role be only to trigger self-help efforts to restore the sector's competitiveness; and that the aids be both temporary and result in competitiveness and efficiency.

In practice, the German program has involved targeted depreciation allowances, has encouraged industrial innovation, and has set up voluntary agreements among firms in a sector to provide breathing space for testing new production methods.

In summary, I believe that a first principle of national urban policy must be to begin to institutionalize the forms of cooperation which I believe are going to be more necessary in the economy of the future.

A second principle, and perhaps a specific outcome of the cooperation which I have just described, is investment in public infrastructure. Many of the investments necessary to the continued health of the U.S. economy—ports, bridges, and disposal sites—are public goods; they need to be provided by government. Yet, ". . . investment in infrastructure by government has

been declining, from $38,600,000,000 in 1965 to less than $31,000,000,000 in 1977, a drop of 21% measured in constant 1972 dollars. As a percentage of GNP, infrastructure investment declined from 4.1% in 1965 to 2.3% in 1977, a drop of 44%."[7]

Now, to make the picture even bleaker, Pres. Reagan's New Federalism proposals would turn over to state and city governments complete financing responsibility for such essential economic development infrastructure as roads and highways, airports, sewer systems, and disposal facilities. Keep in mind that these responsibilities will be turned over to the same levels of government which will shoulder even more human services burdens and education costs. I would suggest that, in "sorting out" which programs the Administration is going to send back as the responsibility of the states, it set up a test for what should not be included. A key test for what ought to remain funded from Federal resources would result from an identification of those infrastructural programs that are required for dealing with the problems of the national economy as it affects the cities in both a short-term cyclical sense and, in the longer-term sense, that involves structural blockages caused by declining infrastructure. That would be the public investment element of a true supply-side strategy to revitalize U.S. industry and help the cities at the same time, and it ought to be considered as a principle in reviewing the New Federalism proposals which would send programs back, without economic rationale, to state and local governments.

The third principle which I would suggest be part of national urban policy would be recognition that, if indeed we are to load responsibilities on local government, then we must give local government more capacity and resources. It is a characteristic of our intergovernmental development that all over this country there are dying cities at the center of metropolitan areas that are, in fact, essentially healthy. The truth of the matter is that there are no devices in our present system for relatively healthy metropolitan areas to participate in solving the problems of the central cities. While there exist no means for mandating such participation, it is advisable to begin to think of ways to provide incentives for regional solutions. We should look at umbrella levels of financing and of providing services that make sense on a regional basis. It may be useful to consider, for example, a system of Federal tax credits to citizens in metropolitan areas which have taken the initiative to finance central-city problems on a metropolitan-wide basis, such as the Dayton Housing Plan or the public works and water works services more commonly delivered on a metropolitan basis. Citizens under such metropolitan systems would then be paying taxes or service fees to an umbrella

metropolitan organization, but would receive credit on their Federal income taxes for having set up such metropolitan services that would help unburden the central cities.

Developing An Economic Strategy

I have described three principles which I hope will be discussed as elements of national urban policy as it merges with the considerations of national economic policy. Fundamentally, however, the economic future of the cities is going to rest with the cities themselves. Those cities that know what they want and where they are going are the ones that are going to be more successful. Even in the declining regions of the nation, those cities which have set goals, devised strategies for how to achieve those goals, and generated the organizational discipline to make the machinery of city government work for economic objectives will be better off. An example is Baltimore and the clear sense of direction that Mayor William Schaffer has provided. Recognizing that such direction can be effective, I would like to highlight five themes which I think will be important to any city administration that is trying to develop an economic strategy.

First, cities must understand their essential economic origins and must understand the role that the shifts in the American economy portend for them. Against that backdrop, city leaders must think hard in order to understand what it is they really want to accomplish. In our case in San Antonio, the driving goal is to raise the incomes of a large percentage of the population living below the national median. Our short-term strategy to achieve that goal involves the development of a high-technology sector that is first labor-intensive, but that builds the base for developing jobs. Those jobs will have long career ladders and higher skills requirements and provide channels for this generation, and certainly the next, to climb out of poverty and underemployed circumstances. Dallas, on the other hand, has different goals, as befits a city at a very different stage of life and with a much higher income level. The Dallas strategy is not raising incomes *per se,* but preparing the city for national leadership in the 21st century. As a result, its leaders are making infrastructural decisions today that will build the communications complex which will assure Dallas' role as the communication capital of the Southwest. Houston leaders understand that, to remain a growth city for the long run, they must deal with serious traffic congestion, and so they have embarked upon a $16,000,000,000 program integrating mass transit, highways, and double-decked expressways. The long and short of it is that a city has to make explicit what it is trying to accomplish in an economic sense and then must express in clear terms how it intends to go about it.

Secondly, cities have to organize themselves for economic development. That means creating a municipal organization that has entrepreneurial qualities. We believe we have created such an entrepreneurial team in San Antonio. In fact, we have gone beyond that to create an economic agenda which allows us to filter policy discussions in seemingly unrelated areas through the screen of its significance for the economic future of our community.

The third theme which I believe cities will have to master is an understanding of what it means to create a climate in which the private sector can produce jobs. We in San Antonio have developed what we refer to as our "two-fisted" approach to job creation. The first "fist" is understanding, in practical common sense terms, what it actually takes to create jobs. That kind of recognition is expressed in the most recent issue of the City Club of New York's newsletter, *The Gadfly,* in which Ed Logue of the South Bronx development effort is quoted as saying: "The fundamental need in the South Bronx is to create jobs." The second fist of our strategy is to make sure that the jobs occur in ways and in locations such that the poorest of the society can benefit.

The fourth theme to which I believe cities will have to be attentive involves the "building blocks" of the national economy of the future. That means stressing education for high-technology, technical-vocational programs, and engineering curricula offered in the central cities, motivating central-city youth to gravitate toward technological jobs. This is critically important. I say this because I believe that the divisions in our society have the potential to be deeper and more serious than even the present racial division, as national technological development separates those who are technologically illiterate from those who are technologically competent. That is not a line which can be crossed via affirmative action programs; it is a line that can be crossed only by investing in the educational system and early technological training for youngsters in the central cities.

The fifth and final point I would make is that I believe a component of local policies must be a tangible optimism that fuels our relentless effort to invest in the future. The surest way to perpetuate the cycle of decline in depressed regions and to create the conditions of eventual decline in the regions that are presently growing would be to slow down or hold back the process of investment in infrastructure.

Notes

1. Robert O. Reischauer, "The Economy, the Federal Budget, and the Prospects for the Cities," in Roy Bahl, ed., *The Fiscal Outlook for Cities* (Syracuse, N.Y.: Syracuse University Press, 1978), p. 95.
2. *Ibid.,* p. 70.
3. *Ibid.,* p. 71.
4. *Ibid.,* p. 73.
5. Ronald E. Muller, *Revitalizing America: Politics for Prosperity* (New York: Simon and Schuster, 1980), p. 222.
6. Robert B. Reich, "Why the U.S. Needs an Industrial Policy," *Harvard Business Review,* January-February, 1982, p. 81.
7. *Ibid.,* p. 78.

Urban Strengths/Urban Weaknesses

Donald A. Hicks

Donald A. Hicks is associate professor in the Political Econony Program at the University of Texas at Dallas. This article is taken from Urban America in the Eighties: Perspectives and Prospects, *prepared by the Panel on Policies and Prospects for Metropolitan and Nonmetropolitan America (one of nine Panels of the President's Commission for a National Agenda for the Eighties), for which Hicks was Senior Professional Staff.* Urban America in the Eighties *was recently published by Transaction Books.*

Until 50 years ago, the proper federal role vis-à-vis the nation's cities was easily summarized. Because the Constitution had not explicitly specified otherwise, the responsibility for cities devolved to state governments. With the onslaught of the Depression, the federal government began for the first time to consider cities as national, rather than merely state, assets. Accordingly, New Deal recovery policies included federal assistance for both distressed people and beleaguered local governments. The rationale behind this action was, according to R.B. Miller, that "the American economy was dependent upon the health of the many urban industrial economies within it and that it was in the best interests of the federal government to aid those [local] economies." This national economic calamity henceforth legitimized the appropriateness of a general federal urban policy presence, even though a commitment to continuing federal involvement in the functioning of local economies was never intended.

In the past twenty years, the time-honored logic of a federal commitment to assisting people in cities has been extended to assisting the cities as well. Welfare and income maintenance programs have been supplemented by programs that emphasize physical redevelopment, local economic development, and direct fiscal aid to local governments. The transition from the War on Poverty and Great Society era of the 1960s to the New Federalism of the 1970s did much to legitimize an increasing federal emphasis on places in the country. This emergent spatial sensitivity in public policy had become particularly apparent during the Carter administration, as illustrated by the dominant thrusts of the national urban policy and executive orders devoted to urban impact analysis, federal facility siting, and targeted procurement. The New Deal emphasis on helping distressed people in cities directly has evolved into an emphasis on helping distressed places (local business and government) directly for the purpose of helping people indirectly. Today most federal funds directed to urban problems go to "place" recipients rather than distressed people. In the late 1970s, a spatial sensitivity appears to have overtaken in large part a social sensitivity developed during the previous decade. Politically, this shift is justified by the assertion that aiding places with problems is easier than aiding people with problems. Economically, this shift is justified by the assertion that direct aid to local economies multiplies its impact so that benefits reverberate throughout the economy in ways that direct aid to people does not.

The 1980s may well require a new perspective on aiding distressed people in urban America. To import the 1930s rationale for a federal urban policy role across the decades may not be wise. Although the economy in the 1930s was indeed dependent on the health of local urban industrial economies in ways not fully appreciated, and it undoubtedly was in the best interest of the federal government to aid those local economies, circumstances have conspired to weaken that rationale.

Unlike a half-century ago, contemporary urban economies are no longer confined within the political jurisdictions of cities. Modern urban economies have an expanded scope that integrates central city, suburban, and nonmetropolitan economies. The deconcentration trends accompanying the arrival of a postindustrial era highlight the fact that the nation's economic vitality no longer arises from or is tied to specific types of places. It increasingly derives its strength from all kinds of places, both local political jurisdictions and beyond. Today it may be in the best interest of the nation to commit itself to the promotion of locationally neutral economic and social policies rather than spatially sensitive urban policies that either explicitly or inadvertently seek to preserve cities in their historical roles. A federal policy presence that allows places to transform and assists them in adjusting to difficult circumstances can justify shifting greater explicit emphasis to helping directly those people who are suffering from the transformation process.

Our cities are truly national assets. Hence, the federal policy presence should recognize that the health of a city, or any other settlement, is determined not by population

Published by permission of Transaction, Inc. from *SOCIETY*, March/April 1982, pp. 10-16, copyright © 1982 by Transaction, Inc.

or employment levels, but by its ability to perform vital functions for the larger society. As national assets, cities and their residents are the resources and responsibilities of us all during their adjustment to the postindustrial era. With this perspective in mind, a redefined federal policy role in urban America for the coming decade is presented.

Urban Policy Reconsidered

The economic health of our nation's communities ultimately depends on the health of our nation's economy. Federal efforts to revitalize urban areas through a national urban policy concerned principally with the health of specific places will inevitably conflict with efforts to revitalize the larger economy. Federal efforts to nurture economic growth through increased productivity, expanded markets, job creation, and controlled inflation will require that settlements, their residents, and local governments adjust to changing economic realities. Accordingly, the purpose and orientation of a "national urban policy" should be reconsidered. There are no "national urban problems," only an endless variety of local ones. Consequently, a centrally administered national urban policy that legitimizes activities inconsistent with the revitalization of the larger national economy may be ill advised.

Priority should not be assigned to the implementation of a spatially sensitive policy effort designed to retard or reverse the emergence of new economic patterns and relationships within and among the nation's settlements. The federal government should assign greater priority to meeting the needs of the residents of the nation's communities rather than to reconciling or resolving the array of constituent intrametropolitan and interregional conflicts. The federal government should exercise its policy presence carefully so as not to exacerbate unnecessarily the circumstances facing certain localities and regions that cause them to lose population and economic vitality. Where federal policies and programs are used to assist the transformation of local communities to achieve health and vitality at new population levels and with restructured economic bases, such national policies should endeavor to ameliorate the undesirable impacts of these transitions on people, primarily, and on places, secondarily.

Although no national urban problems exist, myriad problems do exist within all localities and regions of the nation. Our nation's settlements, and the households, firms, and local governments within them, exhibit a bewildering diversity of conditions that reflect the confluence of long-term demographic, economic, and governance trends and that link them to emerging patterns of metropolitan and regional change. The forces underlying these transformations are relatively persistent and immutable. However, the local and regional problems left in their wake are not uniform in cause; therefore, the urban policies proposed as remedies cannot be expected to be uniform in consequence.

It is unlikely that the federal government can act wisely on behalf of the nation as a whole if economically healthy metropolitan areas are not appreciated because their vitality is discounted or obscured by a preoccupation with transforming core areas of central cities. Neither will the nation benefit if the newly prospering regions that historically have been economically depressed are defined as inimical to historically prosperous regions that are now experiencing relative economic decline. A national urban policy cannot be enunciated and implemented when the very national focus it should assume and the national well-being it should foster are sacrificed to a concern for the diverse fates and fortunes among cities, among metropolitan areas, among states, and among regions.

Certainly, there is merit in anticipating the locational consequences of federal government actions, but many federal policies aimed at promoting the efficiency and productivity of the nation have unavoidable negative consequences for certain localities and regions. Knowing that spatial tilts are embedded in federal policies provides no necessary justification for weeding them out. They often may be entirely justified. Indeed, anti-industry biases in federal policies may be more pernicious than anti-urban biases, given that the health of all places is directly or indirectly dependent on the strength of the larger economy. These tradeoffs should be clearly recognized, and choices should be made consistent with the functioning of the national system of settlements and the national economy, which benefits the entire country at the risk of abiding a series of smaller scale, and often painful, subnational adjustments. A national urban policy designed to place the swirl of local and regional concerns ahead of an overall concern for the nation is both inappropriate and ill advised.

Federal urban policy can be used to channel and target the enormous, if seldom adequate, resources of the federal government and to guide or influence the flows of private sector resources. Nonetheless, despite the importance of the government resources, and the far greater weight of the private resources that at times may be influenced, problems do not yield to massive infusions of resources alone. Rather, a great proportion of urban ills stems from inevitable competition for advantage among groups within localities and between regions. The litany of urban problems is a reflection of this underlying competition in a pluralistic urban society. The very competition that dictates our urban strengths may determine the nature of our urban ills, although not the character of the solutions to those ills. An explicit national urban policy can do little more than make that irony more salient.

The limits to what a federal urban policy effort can achieve are defined by several factors. First, recognition should be made of the near immutability of the technological, economic, social, and demographic trends that herald the emergence of a postindustrial society and that are responsible for the transformation of our nation's settlements and life within them. These major formative trends are likely to continue not only through the coming decade, but also well into the next century. Major deflection or reversal of these broad-gauge trends is not likely to result from purposive government action. Clearly, on the basis of these trends, a federal policy of active anticipation, accommodation, and adjustment makes more sense than efforts to retard or reverse them. The efforts to revitalize those communities whose fortunes are adversely affected principally by the inadvertent consequences of past public policies are entirely justified, but these instances are judged to be rare. It is far more judicious to recognize that the major circumstances that characterize our nation's settlements have not been and will not be significantly dependent on what the federal government does or does not do.

Federal Role Redefined

What should constitute a reasonable federal urban policy role in the light of domestic trends that are transforming this nation and transnational trends that are drawing us into closer community with the world? Policy responses to such complex and changing circumstances are inevitably difficult to conceive and develop. Not only do limits to what can be accomplished with policies and programs exist, but also in many substantive areas, the local readjustments may not require vigorous federal intervention. Accordingly, a proper federal presence in urban affairs should reflect a blend of actions to be avoided as well as actions to be taken. That powerful forces are creating multiple forms of distress in local communities and regions, and that they are not likely to be deflected or defused by public policy, do not inherently justify more or less federal urban policy. Rather, this situation serves as an argument for a different concept of what the federal urban policy role should be.

The federal government can best assure the well-being of the nation's people and the vitality of the communities in which they live by striving to create and maintain a vibrant national economy characterized by an attractive investment climate that is conducive to high rates of economic productivity and growth and defined by low rates of inflation, unemployment, and dependency. Where disadvantage and inequality are selective and cumulative, federal efforts should be expended to ameliorate these consequences in ways that are consistent with developmental trends within the society and the economy as a whole.

The federal government, in partnership with the business community and state and local governments, should carefully consider developing a policy perspective on industry in order to maintain a dynamic national economy and secure a strong role in the transforming international economy. The industrial bases of our nation's economic strength must be allowed to transform, and localities and regions should be assisted in anticipating and adjusting to national and international trends. A positive industry policy should include national economic planning, a coherent science policy, and invigorated research and de-velopment efforts to nurture and enhance our existing comparative advantages within and between industrial sectors vis-à-vis other nations. Such efforts should acknowledge that much can be learned from certain individual firms that may be in the most challenged industrial sectors but are able to compete successfully in international and domestic markets. Increased productivity and employment growth, together with diminished inflation, will do more to benefit people in this nation, regardless of where they may live, than efforts to resist the local and regional impacts of a changing international economic order.

People-oriented national social policies that aim to aid people directly wherever they may live should be accorded priority over place-oriented national urban policies that attempt to aid people indirectly by aiding places directly. If the ultimate goal of federal policies and programs is to aid people in their adjustment to or migration from transforming local circumstances, the most direct and effective ways to do that should be chosen. A national social policy should be based on key cornerstones, including a guaranteed job program for those who can work and a guaranteed cash assistance plan for both the "working poor" and those who cannot work. Federal job creation, subsidies to private employers, and manpower training and retraining programs can significantly reduce minority, youth, and displaced worker unemployment. Where public employment programs are used, they should be considered a temporary supplement for and provide a transition into private-sector employment. A federal guaranteed-income plan, implemented through either a negative income tax or a direct cash transfer program, would effectively and properly shift the welfare burden to the federal government, which can

---

> The nation's cities are national assets that will continue to perform vital, although changing, functions for the United States.

---

administer it more efficiently and with a greater capacity for responding to equity considerations than subnational governments.

Where the problems faced by people exist in such concentrations that the impacts of people-oriented social policies and programs are negated, or where communities bear the brunt of special circumstances (such as massive foreign immigration), federal funds should be carefully targeted to local governments and to the private sector to assist them in meeting collective needs. Nonetheless, the federal government should develop the will and capability to assist local governments in identifying both places that are unlikely to realize any significant improvement through targeted urban aid and appropriate strategies to disinvest public resources and to channel public and private resources to locations that retain the capacity to absorb and benefit from federal assistance.

These major social policy initiatives and realignments should largely substitute for, rather than add to, existing federal policies. Prime candidates among the federal urban (and rural) development assistance program efforts that should be scrutinized for eventual reduction or elimination are in the place-oriented policy domains, including economic development, community development and public facilities investment, housing, transportation, and development planning. Instrumentalities such as community development block grants, urban development action grants, general and countercyclical revenue sharing, CETA grants, and water and sewer construction grants can be useful tools for an adjustment process. However, their use can be justified only during localities' major transitions in size and function. In addition, such mechanisms should be tilted toward the goal of assisting localities to adjust to changing circumstances and should be used to supplement marginally, but not substitute for, efforts that aid people directly. Because guidelines for establishing timeframes for ending interim transitional efforts in view of a more spatially neutral federal presence will be exceedingly difficult to adopt, efforts should begin now.

It is important to realize that identifying tradeoffs among policies and programs with explicit urban foci is not sufficient. Tradeoffs among nominally nonurban federal policies and programs also should be considered, because they often have major, if inadvertent, urban impacts. Among the explicitly nonurban policies and programs that should be scrutinized for major restructuring or elimination are the panoply of in-kind benefits for the poor (such as legal aid services and Medicaid), the growing inventory of subsidies that indiscriminately aid the nonpoor as well as the poor (for example, veterans' benefits), protectionist measures for industry (trade barriers for manufacturers and price supports for farmers), and minimum wage legislation.

Although the original goals of each policy and program may be laudable in isolation, once set into place alongside all others, their aggregate result has been policy incoherence, inconsistency, internal contradictions, and inertia. Solutions regarded as permanent or sacrosanct tend to outlive and become poorly articulated with the characteristics of the problems that they were intended to address. The thrust of this extended proposal is that the problems of people and the places where they live can be handled in better ways than by continuing to tinker with hundreds of different programs that assist individuals, households, neighborhoods, businesses, and subnational governments. Although a "people-place" distinction may often be more apparent than real, the aim should be a reorientation of emphasis, which involves

avoiding the temptation to use place-oriented assistance to prop up localities rather than allowing them to transform. People are best assisted directly, and policies that best insulate people from or compensate them for painful transitional consequences should be emphasized.

Federal urban policy efforts should not necessarily be used to discourage the deconcentration and dispersal of industry and households from central urban locations. Interregional and intrametropolitan shifts of households and industry are essential to the efficient functioning of the national economic system on a scale that supersedes local and regional economies. Each emerging deconcentration trend is nothing more than an aggregate of

---

The health of a city is determined by its ability to perform vital functions for the larger society.

---

countless choices by and actions of individuals, families, and firms influenced by social, cultural, and economic considerations; our public policy tools are least useful when attempting to alter in a predictable way what the individual household or firm will do. Yet an inability to alter these developments should be appreciated apart from the fact that their net impact is probably positive and beneficial. The ongoing deconcentration processes that leave very undesirable local consequences in their wake justify a federal policy role that principally attends to these consequences, rather than flails against the change processes that generate them.

The relocation of population and economic vitality to nonmetropolitan and previously rural areas also should not be discouraged. The current revitalization of traditionally rural areas should neither obscure the fact that much of the traditional basis for urban-rural distinctions no longer exists, nor veil the fact that much of formerly rural America remains unaffected by expanding and diversified economic bases. Although the poor of this nation are largely city-bound, the incidence of poverty in rural areas still exceeds that in urban areas.

The energy and environmental implications of the continuing trends toward relatively low-density development in new growth areas and the thinning out of existing high-density areas do not unequivocally justify the need for a national effort to encourage reconcentration in historically central locations. The emergence of decentralized social and economic systems, which encompass increasing scope and territory and dictate that new, more specialized functions be performed by cities, should generally be encouraged. Although energy and environmental considerations will and should assert themselves in important policy debates in the coming decade and beyond, as yet little compelling and unambiguous empirical evidence exists to justify explicit public policy designed to alter the way in which our nation's communities grow and contract. Conservation of existing energy and environmental resources is not necessarily inconsistent with, and may even be enhanced by, the shift to lower density development, small-scale reconcentration in new growth areas, and the thinning out of

---

The very competition that dictates our urban strengths may determine the nature of our urban ills.

---

large-scale, centrally located concentrations of people and activities. Nonetheless, the federal government should not abdicate its responsibility to assist localities and states in anticipating and countering the negative consequences that low-density development may have in some locations, including those instances where prime agricultural land is invaded indiscriminately by urban uses.

Federal policies should not be revamped, without careful consideration given to their primary functions and net effects, simply because unintended or inadvertent "anti-urban" consequences are discovered. Bending federal policies that do not have an explicit urban focus to serve locational or spatial outcomes may be undesirable. Although countless federal policies initiate a barrage of unintended anti-urban effects, these policy thrusts most often have simply reinforced larger demographic and economic trends or marginally increased the pace at which they have unfolded.

In the end, the federal government does not have that much control over what happens to localities and regions. There is little justification for using explicit urban policies to do more than assist people primarily and places secondarily to anticipate and adjust to the emergence of a continually transforming national economy and society. Federal policies, including investment tax credits and environmental regulations, have important narrow sectoral goals that may be unwisely sacrificed if they are manipulated to secure specific urban outcomes.

In close partnership with the private sector, the federal government should develop strategies to assist localities in adjusting to economic-base transformation and population change. In a federal policy lexicon, "development policy" should be expanded to imply policy-guided local contraction and not simply local revitalization and expansion. Policy-guided contraction and disinvestment can help to ease the impact of decline on individuals and local institutions and to position communities for re-

gaining their health at new lower levels of population and industrial activity.

The federal government should acknowledge that the problems of population and economic growth can be as troublesome and painful as those of shrinkage. Shifts in population and economic activity, which current policy instrumentalities probably cannot reverse, pose specific adjustment problems for metropolitan and nonmetropolitan communities in all regions. Both growth and decline present opportunities to local governments to become better articulated with their populations and economic bases through carefully planned expansion or contraction. The federal government should assist communities during their transition and adjustment to new levels of population and economic activity.

Federal policies aimed at achieving beneficial urban outcomes should be consistent with efforts to ensure a strong national economy and to implement national programs in health, welfare, housing, transportation, energy, environmental protection, and local governmental assistance that are consistent with dominant trends. These policy domains should not use allocational strategies for federal efforts that attempt to counter larger social and economic transformations or to maintain specific local or regional advantages that are slowly being eroded in the course of metropolitan and regional development. Nonetheless, the federal government should be fully sensitive to the fact that even though certain large-scale transformations bode well for the nation, they do imply serious transitional distress for some localities.

Accordingly, the federal government should continue to assist localities in providing basic services to local residents. Meeting the collective needs of citizens wherever they live will continue to require close federal-local cooperation. The federal government should refrain wherever possible from assigning new responsibilities to localities unless they also provide the resources that localities need to meet those obligations. This intergovernmental relationship recognizes both the well-developed capacity of the federal tax system to collect and disperse revenues efficiently and the developing capacity of localities to provide the necessary services in the most efficient manner. Although much place-oriented federal assistance to localities is ill advised to the extent that it is expended to reverse the largely inevitable shrinkage of larger and older communities, some short-term federal transitional assistance to localities is justified to assist them in meeting the expanding range of their responsibilities. As localities experience difficulty in funding basic services or in meeting the financial obligations incurred through federal orders and mandates, the principle of federal adjustment assistance to localities should be inviolate.

Improved access to jobs involves helping people relocate to take advantage of economic opportunities in other places, as well as retraining them to take advantage of economic opportunity in their own communities. Enhancing the mobility of Americans to enable them to relocate to areas where economic opportunity exists should receive greater attention. Accordingly, a people-to-jobs strategy should be crafted with priority over, but in concert with, the jobs-to-people strategy that serves as a major theme in current federal urban policy. Greater emphasis on developing a policy of assisted migration would help underemployed and displaced workers who wish to migrate to locations of long-term economic growth. This option is especially necessary for residents of severely distressed, older industrial cities facing relatively permanent contraction of their economic and population bases.

States should be encouraged and aided in their efforts to assist local governments, as well as their individual and corporate residents, to adjust to changing social and economic circumstances. The nation's cities are national assets that will continue to perform vital, although changing, functions for the United States. Although transforming socially and economically, cities remain the legal creations of the states. In past decades, many subnational governments have improved substantially their capacities to implement economic, community, and manpower development policies. Intergovernmental relationships in the coming decade should preserve the spirit of the federal-local government ties without undermining the emergence of state governments as key urban policy partners.

Localities should be encouraged to reexamine their municipal service packages and their funding and deliv-

---

In the end, the federal government does not have that much control over what happens to localities and regions.

---

ery arrangements. Much local fiscal distress can be traced to an inability to adjust public service infrastructures to changing population size and composition. Municipal service arrangements should either expand in growing communities or contract in shrinking communities in ways that give localities the flexibility to adjust to future changes. Growing localities should be encouraged to consider carefully the breadth of functions and depth of responsibilities that they wish to assume, thereby avoiding a ritualistic imitation of those local governments that assumed their responsibilities in an earlier historical era. Greater reliance on private sector delivery of public services and the transfer of fiscal/ad-

ministrative responsibility for selected functions to other levels of government should be carefully considered.

Partners and Partnerships

The patterns of relationships between localities, counties, states, and the federal government have grown increasingly complex. Responsibilities for funding and administration have become hopelessly intergovernmentalized. The unfortunate and inescapable consequence of our broader, bigger, and deeper federal aid system is intergovernmental overload. This report endorses the general recommendations made by the Advisory Commission on Intergovernmental Relations aimed at the decongestion of the federal system.

The federal role in urban policy should allow for the sorting out of roles and responsibilities among levels of government and between the public and private sectors. Once those reassignments are made, policy and program activity should seek to abide by and to maintain those assignments. In addition to seeking to reintroduce distinctions between federal and subnational responsibilities, efforts should proceed to decide under what conditions and to what extent state and local budgets should become dependent on federal revenues.

Any policies targeted at the nation's communities should engage the federal government as a policy partner with other levels of government and with the private sector to assist people (primarily), places, business, and political jurisdictions (secondarily) to cope with changing circumstances. The resulting policy division of labor should continue to emphasize the decentralization of federal power and the assignment to each partner of the tasks that it can best undertake.

The federal level of government is relatively efficient at enunciating broad policy goals and raising revenues for distribution to subnational levels of government which, in turn, can best define specific program features. Over time many subnational governments have expanded their capacities to initiate and to implement localized community and economic development efforts without complex federal controls. Local general purpose governments should continue to be the principal policy implementers at the local level, and policy instruments that encourage local initiative consistent with national purpose should be emphasized. Despite problems associated with granting wider discretion to local governments, on balance, accepting local judgments is wiser than implementing federal policies that are relatively unable to be articulated with local circumstances.

The federal government should retain responsibility for ensuring that local initiatives, while reflecting local circumstances, are consistent with national goals—particularly in the area of civil rights. The nation needs to develop ways of accomplishing this valid purpose without requiring duplication of the federal government's organizational complexity at the local level. The public sector should endeavor to enhance and encourage private

4. URBAN SOCIAL POLICIES

sector vitality and, where necessary, to alleviate its undesirable consequences without hampering that vitality.

Although place-oriented federal urban and rural development policies and programs eventually should be reduced in significance in favor or more people-oriented national economic and social policies, during the transition between emphases, the former should become more coordinated and coherent, with greater emphasis on policy consistency than on level of program funding. While housing, transportation, and urban economic, community, and manpower development programs marshal relatively meager resources in efforts to ameliorate the impacts of unfolding demographic and economic trends, their potency can be enhanced through better organization and consolidation. General fiscal and monetary policies, transfer payments to individuals, and development assistance to the public and private sectors have their collective impact diluted by indefinite lines of responsibility, divergent delivery systems, and program procedures (including idiosyncratic funding cycles, planning requirements, and eligibility criteria) that often differ and even conflict. Consequently, the efforts of subnational governments and the decisions of private sector actors are unnecessarily hampered by gaps, overlaps, and shifting goals at the federal level.

Reagan vs. the Neighborhoods

Harry C. Boyte

HARRY C. BOYTE, author of The Backyard Revolution: Understanding the New Citizen Movement *(Temple University Press), is director of the Citizen Heritage Center.*

Along the commercial strip that forms the arterial hub of Williamsburg, the old Italian neighborhood in Brooklyn, a remarkable transformation has taken place in recent years. Graffiti and chipped paint are gone. Instead, the steam-cleaned brick facades and painted cornices on the storefronts complement new brick sidewalks and street lamps in the style of gas fixtures from the neighborhood's distant past. A sign in a large vacant lot announces the shopping mall soon to be constructed. In front of each store, painted styrofoam sculptures add whimsy to the serious business of attracting customers. A boy on a bicycle hangs over the door of Albert's Bargain Store. An old-fashioned wishing well adorns the entrance to Special Occasions. Customers shopping in the Grand Bazaar walk underneath a smiling teddy bear. For those dining at the barbecue place, a large pig out front gives an anticipatory welcome.

The changes are a part of the revitalization plan for Williamsburg that has been developed by St. Nicholas Neighborhood Preservation and Housing Rehabilitation Corporation, a community organization to which all neighborhood residents belong. In concert with the merchants group that St. Nick's helped set up, the organization has combined such physical improvements with an aggressive public-relations campaign, with postcards, calendars, advertisements, and other devices to lure back customers to the Grand Metro Shopping District, as the area is now labeled. It has all succeeded far beyond expectations.

Most of the funds for the community efforts came from the local area. A city grant for the commercial district's improvement, which required local mer-

chants to add a dollar to every two provided publicly, precipitated a rush of private capital. For every dollar the city put in, local merchants themselves ended up spending eight. Federal funds also played an important role. St. Nick's obtained a grant from the National Endowment for the Arts to help with the sculptures. Seed funding for the planned shopping mall came through a neighborhood self-help program at the Department of Housing and Urban Development, begun during the Carter Administration.

One might imagine that such entrepreneurial zeal and local initiative would find an even warmer reception from the appointees of President Reagan. The entire endeavor, after all, would seem to embody precisely that American spirit that candidate Reagan pledged at every opportunity to renew. Thus St. Nick's encounters with the government after January 20, 1981, contain no small irony. "We couldn't even get our phone calls answered," recounts Gary Hattem, St. Nick's executive director, describing the organization's efforts to work out details of the self-help grant already secured. "It was like we were Godzilla. Everyone in the bureaucracy ran."

St. Nicholas Corporation's experience is not unique. Across the country, neighborhood-based projects—many of which took the rhetorical commitments of candidate Reagan to neighborhood self-help at face value—have often met with brusque indifference from the new office-holders in Washington. Indeed, the attitudes of the Administration toward the community self-help movement that has emerged in recent years furnish a fascinating counterpoint to the eloquent presidential challenge for a rebirth of old American cooperative and voluntary traditions.

REAWAKENING COMMUNITY TRADITION

On no subject has Ronald Reagan been more articulate, or more insistent. The Republican party platform of 1980, taking the lead from the top, pledged a

government "committed to nurturing the spirit of self-help and cooperation through which so many neighborhoods have revitalized themselves." In every speech on the campaign trail, Governor Reagan declared his allegiance to the "five simple words": family, neighborhood, work, peace, and freedom. Since taking office, the President has justified proposals ranging from budget-cutting to the New Federalism partly through invocation of the need for increased local control and a revitalization of voluntary community initiatives.

These themes strike a responsive chord. They recall old American values and practices of the sort described by the French observer, Alexis de Tocqueville, 150 years ago. According to Tocqueville, "Americans of all ages, all conditions, and all dispositions constantly form associations." Barn raisings, quilting bees, voluntary fire departments, and farm organizations in rural areas had such urban counterparts as immigrant mutual-aid societies, religious reform associations, and trade groups.

Moreover, public responsiveness represents much more than nostalgia for the world of our grandparents, filtered through *Little House on the Prairie* and *The Waltons*. In fact, through the supposedly self-absorbed seventies, traditional levels of voluntary activity remained constant—and very high. According to a recent Gallup poll conducted for Independent Sector, the Washington-based coalition of voluntary agencies and foundations, 31 percent of Americans regularly engage in voluntary activity to help others, such as men's service clubs and church aid societies, roughly the same figure as a decade ago.

Moreover, by the late seventies a new generation of community-based voluntary organizations had spread on a large scale. The number of incorporated nonprofit organizations, for instance (the great bulk of which are community-based), increased from 500,000 in 1975 to nearly 900,000 in 1980. In New York City alone, several thousand block associations appeared from 1975 to 1978, working on projects that ranged from crime control to health care and urban gardening. Literally thousands of larger neighborhood advocacy and development groups like St. Nick's developed as well in poor, minority, white ethnic, working- and middle-class areas alike. Their names often recall the civic traditions from which they have grown: Queens Citizen Organization in New York; Communities Organized for Public Service in San Antonio; Citizens Action Coalition in Indiana; Citizens Action League in California. The National Commission of Neighborhoods in its 1979 report listed 8,000 such groups.

Fusing grass roots, participatory language, and values reminiscent of the sixties with a down-to-earth practicality and connection with established businesses and religious and other community institutions, these efforts have, with some success, tackled problems like job creation, housing rehabilitation, and crime control that have confounded traditional liberal, big-government approaches. "I keep hearing that everything's dead and that there's no big cause since civil rights and the Vietnam War," argues Gale Cincotta, chair of the National People's Action neighborhood coalition. "But that's a myth. There's a neighborhood movement that started in the sixties. It's not as dramatic with everybody out in the streets, but it's steadily gaining strength in every city and state."

Neighborhood groups have commonly begun as battles against unresponsive bureaucracy or large economic interests. But the hallmark of the thousands of organizations that have developed in American communities in recent years has not primarily been criticism. Their main thrust as they have evolved has been, rather, positive, a revival of the old American traditions of community involvement and self-help once embodied in such practices as barn raising and quilting bees. In the Bronx and on Manhattan's Lower East Side, in the barrios of East Los Angeles and ethnic neighborhoods of Chicago, across the country in communities once considered "garbage dumps" by city administrators—redlined by banks for years, and starved of traditional social services—stirrings of a new spirit, what Ron Shiffman of the Pratt Institute calls "the same pioneer-

ing spirit that built so many communities across the country," have become visible.

Community development corporations, neighborhood advocacy groups, preservation efforts, neighborhood-based social services and self-help projects, tenant associations, cooperatives, small-business associations, and other groupings have all been a part of this reawakened community tradition. And as they have grown and matured, challenging old government policies, they have demanded not an *end* to government programs but their transformation into efforts that aid communities in their own endeavors. From the perspective of neighborhoods, as Gale Cincotta explains, "there are a lot of things government can do even if they are not dramatic." The Neighborhood Commission concluded that the key to an effective federal policy on cities and communities must be to "work in, for, and through the neighborhoods for the people who live there."

Government working "in, for, and through the neighborhoods" has meant in some cases providing through legislation new tools that citizens can use in organizing against unresponsive private power. Thus, for instance, after many years of effort the National People's Action finally won a major victory in their campaign against redlining when Congress passed the Home Mortgage Disclosure Act, requiring lending institutions to open their books for public inspection of where they were making loans. Armed with the data of where loans were actually going, community groups across the country have been able to pressure local lenders far more effectively. In another case, by 1979 tenant coalitions in some 20 states had forced legislatures to create laws on issues like leases, terms of rental agreements, reasonableness of landlord rules, and security deposits. With such laws on the books, tenant organizations then found they had many more tools with which to organize against unfair and arbitrary practices.

Furthermore, community groups have also sought to win changes in government programs to sustain and support community initiatives and self-help efforts. Energy programs that provide funds for communities to develop conservation plans on their own, to weatherize houses, and to increase

use of alternative, renewable energy sources like solar, wind, and biomass are far more effective, from a neighborhood point of view, than vast

In the Bronx and on Manhattan's Lower East Side, in the barrios of East Los Angeles and ethnic neighborhoods of Chicago, across the country in communities once considered "garbage dumps" by city administrators—redlined by banks for years, and starved of traditional social services—stirrings of a new spirit have become visible.

government subsidies for synthetic energy. Job training through community institutions, staffing neighborhood betterment projects, tailoring programs to local needs and opportunities, produce far more permanent and useful jobs than huge tax "incentive" plans to large industry.

By the late 1970s, the neighborhood movement, bringing together an array of community-based institutions, had begun to have a noticeable effect. Government programs such as CETA and VISTA had been considerably redesigned so that most positions were filled by local residents who were recruited through community institutions and associated with community efforts. Crime prevention programs had been changed, partially, so that more funds went directly to neighborhood groups. Housing programs through the Department of Housing and Urban Development furnished funds to community associations for rehabilitation. Stronger and more sophisticated community organizations were able to win major grants through programs like the Economic Development Administration for community economic revitalization.

Finally, under the Carter Administration, communities had won some notable new programs providing technical assistance and resources for neighborhood initiatives. For instance, the new Office of Neighborhoods, Voluntary Associations, and Consumer Protection—headed by longtime neighborhood activist and organizer Msgr. Geno Baroni—initiated the Neighborhood Self-Help Development program, which provided grants and other forms of aid to community organizations for economic development, housing, and other kinds of self-help. Under the Livable Cities Act, local and state governments were to receive funds to expand community-based cultural programs in low- and moderate-income neighborhoods. Through the Youth Demonstration Project, Baroni's office administered funds from the Department of Labor for housing and commercial development efforts in which young people were employed.

Such diverse programs for community self-help varied in their effectiveness and usefulness, of course. But, on balance, they furnished critical and increasing resources for voluntary grassroots organizations, strengthening the capacity of communities to do things for themselves.

A vein of neoconservative social theory has pointed to the success of the new community self-help efforts as a part of its criticism of liberalism. For instance, Robert Woodson of the American Enterprise Institute in his work on youth crime has shown how classic approaches to juvenile delinquency rely almost exclusively on professional welfare systems and the courts. Yet the high rates of recidivism and the ravaging effects of youth crime and violence on inner-city communities continue, impervious to such programs.

Woodson maintains that professionalized and bureaucratic approaches fail because they treat young offenders as isolated individuals, victimized by the pathologies in their environment, and entirely neglect the positive resources —the strengths—available in families and communities that must be a part of any solution. "It is time to move in a different direction," Woodson argues, "toward a realization that some of the answers to mental health, crime, and other social enigmas already exist within the neighborhoods themselves and within their indigenous institutions, both formal and informal."

Substantiating his argument, Woodson found that programs that were successfully addressing issues of gang violence and youth delinquency build on community institutions like the family. One striking example that he studied for several years is the House of Umoja, a group home for boys on the West Side of Philadelphia that has been in existence since 1968. Umoja has had a dramatic effect on gang killings throughout the entire area. On a tour of Philadelphia in the fall of 1981, President Reagan cited the home as a model of voluntary community initiative.

THE HOUSE OF UMOJA

The House of Umoja grew out of a magazine, *Umoja,* edited by two advocates of Black power, Sister Falaka Fattah and her husband, David. Umoja, the Swahili word for unity, perfectly expressed the philosophy of the two. They were convinced that the Black community had to pull together, cease its internal violence, and develop new resources for itself on its own terms.

The issue of gang violence in the Black community suddenly came home to the two editors when they discovered one of their sons had joined a local gang. Convinced that the other gang members, like her son, could be reached through a revival of the patterns of the African extended family, Sister Fattah invited all 15 members to live in their house.

The structure was based on the extended African family system, which Sister Fattah had once researched in her work as a journalist. Older boys served as "big brothers" for the younger ones, and when possible got jobs to help the "family" income. All obeyed firm rules and met regularly to evaluate members' behavior. For several years, Umoja barely scraped by, living partly on donations from local church and civic groups when funds ran out. By 1972, however, it had established a reputation sufficient to overcome the initial skepticism of police and welfare bureaucracies. The state furnished a welfare grant to turn it into a group home for delinquent boys. Falaka and David Fattah then turned their attention to the broader problems of gang violence and youth unemployment on the West Side.

Sister Fattah initiated a series of gang conferences to see if peace could be achieved—with amazing results. Gang-related deaths, 43 in 1973, had dropped to one by 1977. Umoja began to acquire properties on their block and rehabilitate buildings. Through an anticrime and security program, they trained dozens of local youth in crime prevention, working with local businesses and community residents to guard against burglaries. Through an economic development program, they began to develop what was called "Boystown Businesses" to train the unemployed teen-agers for jobs and to produce revenue for their other efforts.

Since its inception, the House of Umoja has seen itself in unorthodox ways, as a tribute to the kids with whom it works. "When we show our plans to different people, they think it is just brick and mortar; we try to explain that the building of the boys' town is a monument to the brothers' word," explained Sister Fattah to a conference on youth violence at the American Enterprise Institute in 1980. It has defined success in a way that is different from the conception of the courts or the welfare system. "They're measuring by recidivism rates. We think that a person is a success if he is able to function in society whether he has a job or not, if he respects himself."

With some trepidation that its voluntary spirit would be jeopardized, Umoja began to seek funds as its operations expanded. There were problems. "When you start paying people for what they had done because they felt that they wanted to, it doesn't always work well," Sister Fattah observed. But funds from the LEAA, from CETA, and from the Economic Development Administration allowed major expansion in their programs, furnishing jobs for youth and ex-offenders who desperately needed them. Moreover, Umoja saw the money as a kind of seed capital, not permanent support. "We wanted the money to get off the ground," explained Rhonda Bigelow, Umoja's director for the Boystown project. "We needed start-up funds. After that, leave us alone."

Umoja's skepticism about federal funds was common among community groups in the seventies. Yet, as such organizations evolved, turning attention toward positive problem-solving efforts, Umoja's experience was also common. Neighborhood organizations sought new resources for seed capital and technical assistance that would help build the foundations for future independent community initiative. Joseph McNeely, an official in the Department of Housing and Urban Development during the Carter years, calls this a shift toward an "investment approach toward federal resources." In McNeely's terms, community groups in the sixties tended to demand that government programs be re-funded each year for an indefinite period. By the late seventies, neighborhood organizations wanted help in becoming

Job training through community institutions, staffing neighborhood betterment projects, tailoring programs to local needs and opportunities, produce far more permanent and useful jobs than huge tax "incentive" plans to large industry.

self-sufficient, and looked for programs that would produce a return on each investment for the neighborhood itself.

By the late seventies, neighborhood groups had a direct impact on an array of other programs. Established crime prevention efforts like the LEAA had begun to make available the sort of funds that helped Umoja's anticrime effort get off the ground. The decentralization of job programs like CETA enabled Umoja, along with hundreds of other community groups, to provide job training, fix up neighborhood structures, and undertake a variety of other community projects. St. Nicho-

Banana Kelly Community Improvement Association, New York City

las Corporation, for instance, began with one of the first allocations of CETA jobs to a community in 1975. From the perspective of neighborhood leaders, enclaves in the bureaucracy began to appear that gave them a hearing. "The self-help office in HUD was a spiritual home for a lot of community groups," recounted executive director Hattem about the St. Nick's experience. "For the first time there was recognition on the national level that what we were doing was legitimate. It added credibility to our cause. It was someplace to touch base with every once and a while."

DISMANTLING NEIGHBORHOOD PROGRAMS

Taking the rhetoric of Ronald Reagan simply, one might have anticipated an expansion of such programs under the new Administration. But when the first Reagan budget was announced, many communities had an abrupt awakening. In the name of the return of power to local communities and a paring away of federal bureaucracy to enable the "flowering" of community and voluntary initiatives, the Reagan Administration has eliminated and severely curtailed those very programs that communities have been able to use in their self-help efforts. The impression is inescapable that the present Administration, behind all the rhetoric, has subordinated all other values to the raw economic forces of the marketplace. When the President declared that those whose communities and lives suffered as a result of his economic policy should simply move, the irony became stark. How can you pull yourself up if your bootstraps are sliced away? How can there be neighborhoods, and a spirit of neighborliness, without neighbors?

As the Administration's urban plan has unfolded, communities have discovered increasingly the contradictions between rhetoric and reality. Again and again, Ronald Reagan has pledged to create "a government that can do the people's work without dominating their lives" and to "return power to the people." One major aspect of his program has been the consolidation of 57 categorical federal programs into nine block grants run by state governments. Yet poor, minority, and even moderate-income communities, with scarce resources and historically little access to state government, can only

hope to secure a hearing at local and state levels through the new generation of grass-roots self-help and advocacy organizations, which the Administration has sought to undermine in every way possible.

To evaluate the cuts and their impact, the Catholic Bishops' own self-help funding program for community groups, the Campaign for Human Development, conducted a survey of the organizations with which they worked. Eighty-five percent of their respondents used some sort of federal program. More than half used specific programs like CETA and VISTA. All eight programs that the Catholic Bishops' group judged most useful to community self-help efforts were targeted for elimination. At the moment that President Reagan was praising the House of Umoja, federal cutbacks of $100,000 in promised funds were jeopardizing its economic development program. Associate director of the Catholic Bishops' program, Kathy Desmond, who conducted the survey, concludes wryly, "When you demythologize the rhetoric and look at the specific things the Administration has cut, you find that they've specifically targeted all those programs that we think of as essential components of self-help."

In some cases, cutbacks have brought clear, if unintended, benefits. For instance, through changes in the VISTA program in recent years that have resulted in primarily local recruitment, community groups regularly began to use such volunteers to fill staff positions. At times, such aid was a vital resource; other times, volunteers undertook work that community leaders would have otherwise undertaken. "We've certainly seen instances of community members taking on more responsibility and organizational involvement over the past year," notes Desmond.

But such results seem incidental to the intent of the Administration's policies. Desmond believes that the basic motivation for cuts in VISTA, along with other programs, is aversion to community organization itself: "The Reagan people didn't want the government to fund groups that were going to stir things up, anything that was organizing or advocacy." Such a suspicion is widespread among neighborhood networks, fed by new policy guidelines barring VISTA volunteers

from any community project engaged in "organizing." The agency's list of supposedly left-wing organizations from which VISTA volunteers have been taken includes studiously nonpartisan, apolitical community betterment programs like the Massachusetts Association of Older Americans, which is engaged in services and housing repair, and the Whitmore Neighborhood Corporation in Kansas City, a working-class neighborhood preservation effort whose president, Mary Rose, calls herself a "middle-of-the-road conservative."

In a climate of general budget-cutting, it is possible to read too much into the dismantling of neighborhood self-help programs. Some would argue that the Neighborhood Self-Help Development program has been eliminated simply because it is relatively new, and has a slender base of support.

More generally, cuts reflect ideological assumptions of the Administration. As Joseph McNeely sees it, "They believe that each neighborhood should be entirely on its own." Such a laissez faire attitude finds ample counterpart in other Administration approaches. Most basically, it eschews the legitimacy of any redistributive action by the government. "To the Reagan Administration, any idea that smacks of redistribution is completely out," observes McNeely. In the neoconservative faith as interpreted by the current occupant of the White House, the main concern is not that government replace community-based problem-solving efforts, but whether government should involve itself with community problems at all, through any mechanism other than the economic marketplace.

Meanwhile, the ethnic and working-class groups intrigued by the Reagan campaign and rhetorical vision begin to show signs of disillusionment. John Kromkowski, president of the National Center for Urban Ethnic Affairs, voiced early on the sentiment that has been steadily growing: "Although neighborhood self-help and rebirth was a major plank in the Reagan campaign, in the Reagan White House the concerns of neighborhoods and ethnics no longer warrant a Special Assistant to the President; and in a 'streamlined' HUD, the Office of Neighborhoods and Voluntary Associations is extinct. The only special interest not being heard from is 'the people.'"

Small Space Is Beautiful:
Design as if People Mattered

The successful design of small urban spaces
ultimately depends on watching
the "experts"—people—using them.

William H. Whyte

William H. Whyte is director of the Street Life Project in New York City. This article is based on research conducted by that group since 1971 and is excerpted from his book *The Social Life of Small Urban Spaces* (the Conservation Foundation, Washington, D.C., 1980). Among his other books are *The Organization Man, Open Space Action, Cluster Development,* and *The Last Landscape.*

The editors acknowledge the *NOVA* program "City Spaces, Human Places" (originally broadcast on PBS November 29, 1981), which served as inspiration for this article.

In 1970, I formed a small research group, the Street Life Project, and began looking at city spaces—to learn why some work for people, and some do not, and what the practical lessons might be. At that time, direct observation had long been used for the study of people in far-off lands. It had not been used to any great extent in the American city. There was much concern over urban crowding, but most of the research on the issue was done somewhere other than where it supposedly occurred. The most notable studies were of crowded animals, or of students and members of institutions responding to experimental situations—often valuable research, to be sure, but somewhat vicarious.

The Street Life Project began its study by looking at New York City parks and playgrounds and such informal recreation areas as city blocks. One of the first things that struck us was the *lack* of crowding in many of these areas. A few were jammed, but more were nearer empty than full, often in neighborhoods that ranked very high in density of people. Sheer space, obviously, was not itself attracting children. Many streets were.

It is often assumed that children play in the street because they lack playground space. But many children play in the streets because they like to. One of the best play areas we came across was a block on 101st Street in East Harlem. It had its problems, but it worked. The street itself was the play area. Adjoining stoops and fire escapes provided prime viewing across the street and were highly functional for mothers and older people. There were other factors at work, too, and, had we been more prescient, we could have saved ourselves a lot of time spent later looking at plazas. Though we did not know it then, this block had within it all the basic elements of a successful urban place.

As our studies took us nearer the center of New York, the imbalance in use of space was even more apparent. Most crowding could be traced to a series of choke points—particularly subway stations. In total, these spaces constitute only a fraction of downtown, but the number of people using them is so high and their experience so abysmal that it colors our perception of the city out of all proportion. The fact that there may be lots of empty space somewhere else little mitigates the discomfort.

This phenomenon affects researchers, too. We see what we expect to see, and have been so conditioned to see crowded spaces in center city that it is often difficult to see empty ones. But when we looked, there they were.

Furthermore, the amount of space was increasing. Since 1961, New York City has given incentive bonuses to builders who provide plazas. For each square foot of plaza, builders can add 10 square feet of commercial floor space over and above the amount normally permitted by zoning. So they have—without exception. Every new office building we studied provided a plaza or comparable space: by 1972, some 20 acres of the world's most expensive open space.

We discovered that some plazas, especially at lunchtime, attracted a lot of people. One, the plaza of the Seagram Building, helped give the city the idea for the plaza bonus. Built in 1958, this austerely elegant area was not planned as a people's plaza, but that

The most attractive fountains,
the most striking designs, cannot induce people to come and sit if there is no place to sit.

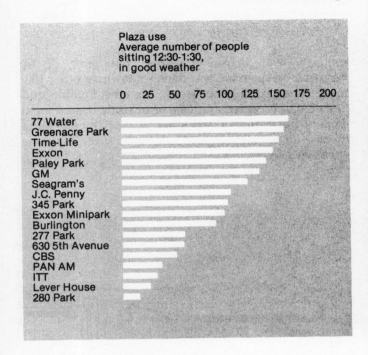

Plaza use
Average number of people
sitting 12:30-1:30,
in good weather

0 25 50 75 100 125 150 175 200

77 Water
Greenacre Park
Time-Life
Exxon
Paley Park
GM
Seagram's
J.C. Penny
345 Park
Exxon Minipark
Burlington
277 Park
630 5th Avenue
CBS
PAN AM
ITT
Lever House
280 Park

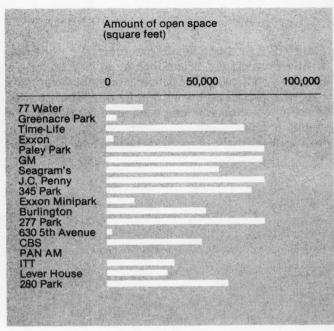

Amount of open space
(square feet)

0   50,000   100,000

77 Water
Greenacre Park
Time-Life
Exxon
Paley Park
GM
Seagram's
J.C. Penny
345 Park
Exxon Minipark
Burlington
277 Park
630 5th Avenue
CBS
PAN AM
ITT
Lever House
280 Park

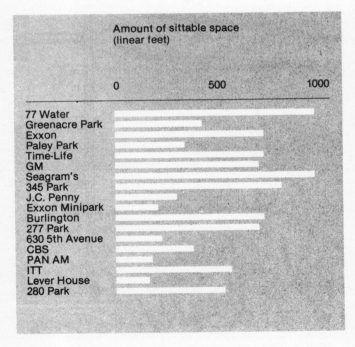

Amount of sittable space
(linear feet)

0   500   1000

77 Water
Greenacre Park
Exxon
Paley Park
Time-Life
GM
Seagram's
345 Park
J.C. Penny
Exxon Minipark
Burlington
277 Park
630 5th Avenue
CBS
PAN AM
ITT
Lever House
280 Park

is what it became. On a good day, there would be a hundred and fifty people sitting, sunbathing, picnicking, and shmoozing—idly gossiping, talking "nothing talk." People also liked 77 Water Street, known as "swingers" plaza because of the young crowd that populated it.

But on most plazas, we didn't see many people. The plazas weren't used for much except walking across. In the middle of lunch hour on a beautiful, sunny day, the number of people sitting on plazas averaged four per 1,000 square feet of space—an extraordinarily low figure for so dense a center. The tightest-knit CBD (central business district) anywhere contained a surprising amount of open space that was relatively empty and unused.

If places such as Seagram's and 77 Water Street could work so well, why not the others? We began studying a cross-section of spaces—in all, 16 plazas, 3 small parks, and a number of odds and ends. We mounted time-lapse cameras and recorded daily patterns. We talked to people to find where they came from, where they worked, how frequently they used the place, and what they thought of it. But mostly we watched people to see what they did.

There were a lot of false starts and dead ends, and the research was nowhere as tidy and sequential as in the telling. The findings would also have been staggeringly obvious had we thought of them in the first place. But we didn't. Often, what seemed plainly evident turned out to be incorrect. We arrived at our findings by a succession of busted hypotheses.

Patterns of the People

The best-used plazas are sociable places, with a higher

"A dimension architects seem to have forgotten is the human backside. Rarely will you find a ledge that is sittable on both sides. Most ledges are inherently sittable, but with a little ingenuity and additional expense they can be made unsittable."

proportion of couples than you find in less-used places, more people meeting people or exchanging goodbyes. A high proportion of people in groups is an index of selectivity. When people go to a place in twos or threes or rendezvous there, it is most often because they have decided to. Nor are these sociable places less congenial to the individual—they attract more individuals than less-used spaces. If you are alone, a lively place can be the best place to be.

What attracts people most, it would appear, is other people. But many urban spaces are being designed as though the opposite were true. People often do talk along such lines; this is why their responses to questionnaires can be so misleading. How many people would say they like to sit in the middle of a crowd? Instead, they speak of getting away from it all, and use terms such as "escape," "oasis," and "retreat." What people do, however, reveals another priority.

This was first brought home to us in a study of street conversations. When people stop to have a conversation, we wondered, how far away do they move from the main pedestrian flow? People didn't move out of it. They stayed in or moved *into* it, and the great bulk of the conversations were smack in the center of the flow. The same gravitation characterized "traveling conversations"—the kind in which two people move about, alternating the roles of "straight man" and principal talker. Although there is a lot of

apparent motion, if you plot the orbits, they turn out to be quite restricted.

People also sit in the mainstream. At the Seagram plaza, the main pedestrian paths are on diagonals from the building entrance to the corners of the steps. These are natural junction and transfer points and the site of lots of activity. They are also a favored place for sitting and picnicking. Sometimes there will be so many people that pedestrians have to step carefully to negotiate the steps. The pedestrians rarely complain. While some will detour around the blockage, most will thread their way through it.

Standing patterns are similar. When people stop to talk on a plaza, they usually do so in the middle of the traffic stream. They also show an inclination to station themselves near objects such as a flagpole or a statue. They like well-defined places such as steps or the border of a pool. What they rarely choose is the middle of a large space.

Whatever they may mean, people's movements are one of the great spectacles of a plaza. You do not see this in architectural photographs, which typically are empty of life and taken from a perspective few people share. It is a quite misleading one. At eye level the scene comes alive with movement and color—people walking quickly, walking slowly, skipping up steps, weaving in and out on crossing patterns, accelerating and retarding to match the moves of others. There is a beauty that is beguiling to watch, and one senses that the players are quite aware of it themselves. You see this, too, in the way they arrange themselves on steps and ledges—they often do so with grace. With its brown-gray monochrome, Seagram's is the best of settings—especially in the rain, when an umbrella or two adds color in the right places, like Corot's red dots.

How peculiar are such patterns to New York? We assumed that behavior in other cities would probably differ little, and subsequent comparisons proved our assumption correct. The important variable is city size—the strongest similarities are found among the world's largest cities. People tend to behave more like their counterparts in other world cities than like fellow nationals in smaller cities. Big-city people walk faster, for one thing, and they self-congest. After we had completed our New York study, we made a brief comparison study of Tokyo and found that the proclivity to stop and talk in the middle of department-store doorways, busy corners, and the like is just as strong as in New York.

For all the cultural differences, sitting patterns in various parks and plazas around the world are much the same, too. Similarly, shmoozing patterns in Milan's Galleria are remarkably like those in New York's garment center. The modest conclusion: given the basic element of a center city—such as high pedestrian volumes and the concentration and mixture of activities—people in one place tend to act much like people in another.

The Bottom Line

In their use of plazas, New Yorkers were very consistent. Day in, day out, many of them would sit at certain plazas, few at others. On the face of it, there should not have been this variance—most of the plazas we were studying were fairly comparable. With few exceptions, they were on major avenues and usually occupied a block front. They were close to bus stops and subway stations and had strong pedestrian flows on the sidewalks beside them. Yet when we rated plazas according to the number of people sitting on them at peak time, there was a very wide range—from 160 people at 77 Water Street to 17 at 280 Park Avenue (*see the upper-left chart on page 163*).

How come? The first factor we studied was the sun. We thought it might well be the critical one, and our initial time-lapse studies seemed to bear this out. Subsequent studies did not. As I will note later, they showed that the sun was important but did not explain the difference in the popularity of plazas. Nor did aesthetics. The elegance and purity of a building's design seems to have little relationship to the use of the spaces around it. The designer sees the whole building—the clean verticals, the horizontals, the way Mies van der Rohe turned his corners, and so on. People sitting on the plaza may be quite unaware of such matters. They are more apt to be looking in another direction: not up at other buildings, but at what is going on at eye level.

Another factor we considered was shape. Urban designers believed this was extremely important and hoped our findings might support tight criteria for proportion and placement. Our data did not support such criteria, but neither did they prove shape unimportant or designers' instincts misguided. As with the sun, however, they did prove that other factors are more critical.

If not shape, could the *amount* of space be the key factor? Some conservationists were sure this would be it. In their view, people seek open spaces as a relief from the overcrowding they are normally subjected to, and it would follow that places affording the great-

Rules for Regulators

Ledges ought to be "sittable." But how should this be defined? If we wanted sittable ledges in the New York City zoning amendments, we thought we would have to indicate how high and deep ledges should be and then back up the specifications with facts.

The zoning proceedings during 1974 were unexpectedly adversarial. The attack came on the grounds that the zoning was *too specific*. And it came not from builders, but from members of a local planning board. Rather than spell out the requirements in specific detail, the board argued, the zoning should deal with broad directives—for example, "make the place sittable"—and leave details to be settled on a case-by-case basis.

This argument is persuasive, especially for laypeople, and, at the inevitable moment in zoning meetings when someone gets up and says, "Let's cut through all this crap and get down to basics," everyone applauds. Be done with bureaucratic nitpicking and legal gobbledygook.

But ambiguity is a worse problem. Most incentive zoning ordinances are very, very specific as to what developers get. The trouble is that they are mushy as to what they are to give, and mushier yet as to what will happen if later they don't. Vague stipulations, as many cities have learned, are unenforceable. What you do not prescribe quite explicitly you do not get.

This lack of guidelines does not give buildings and architects more freedom; it reinforces convention. That is why so few good plazas were built under the 1961 zoning resolution. There was no law preventing builders from providing better plazas, but there weren't any guidelines either. And most builders do not do anything far out of the ordinary. A few had sought special permits for amenities not countenanced by existing regulations. But this time-consuming route makes the builder and architect run a gauntlet of city agencies, with innovation as likely to be punished as rewarded.—*W.H.W.* □

est feeling of light and space would draw the most. Once again, we found no clear relationship. As can be seen from the upper-right chart on page 163, sheer space does not draw people. In some circumstances, it can have the opposite effect.

What about the amount of *sittable* space? Here we begin to get close. As the lower chart on page 163 shows, the most popular plazas tend to have a lot more sitting space than the less well used ones, but the relationship is rough. For one reason, the amount of sitting space does not include any qualitative factors: a foot of concrete ledge counts for as much as a foot of comfortable bench space. We considered weighing the data on a point basis—so may points for a foot of bench with backrest, with armrests, and so on. This would have produced a nicer conformance on the chart. We gave up the idea, however, as too manipulative. Once you start working backward this way, there's no end to it.

There was no necessity. No matter how many variables we checked, one point kept coming through:

People tend to sit most where there are places to sit.

This may not strike you as an intellectual bombshell, and, now that I look back on our study, I wonder why it was not more apparent from the beginning. Sitting space, to be sure, is only one of many variables, and without a control situation one cannot be sure of cause and effect. But sitting space is most certainly prerequisite. The most attractive fountains, the most striking designs, cannot induce people to come and sit if there is no place to sit.

Design with Human Nature

Ideally, sitting should be physically comfortable—benches with backrests, well-contoured chairs. However, it's most important that it be *socially* comfortable. This means a choice: to sit up front, in back, to the side, in the sun, in the shade, in groups, off alone.

Choice should be built into the basic design. Even though benches and chairs can be added, the best course is to maximize the "sittability" of inherent features. This means making ledges that are sittable or making other flat surfaces do double duty as table-tops or seats. There are almost always such opportunities. Because the elevation changes somewhat on most building sites, there are bound to be several levels of flat space—it is no more trouble to make them sittable than not to. It takes real work to create a lousy place. Ledges have to be made high and bulky, railings put in, surfaces canted. Money can be saved by not doing such things, and the open space is more likely to be amenable.

A dimension architects seem to have forgotten is the human backside. Rarely will you find a ledge or

bench deep enough to be sittable on both sides; some aren't deep enough to be sittable on one. Most frustrating are the ledges just deep enough to tempt people to sit on both sides, but too shallow to let them do so comfortably.

Thus to another of our startling findings: ledges and spaces two backsides deep seat more people comfortably than those that are not as deep. For a few additional inches of depth, then, builders can double the amount of sitting space. This does not mean that double the number of people will use the space, but that is not the point. The benefit of the extra space is social comfort—more room for groups and individuals to sort themselves out, more choices and more perception of choices.

Steps work for the same reason. The range of space provides an infinity of possible groupings, and the excellent sightlines make virtually all the seats great for watching the theater of the street. And corners are functional. You will notice that people often bunch at the far end of steps, especially when an abutting ledge provides a right angle. These areas are good for face-to-face sitting. People in groups gravitate to them.

One might, as a result, expect a conflict, for corners are also the places where pedestrian traffic is heaviest. But for all the bustle, or because of it, the sitters seem to feel comfortable. And the walkers don't seem to mind.

We find similar patterns at other places. Other things being equal, you can calculate that where pedestrian flows bisect a sittable place, that is where people will most likely sit. And it is not so perverse of them—it is by choice. If there is some congestion, it is an amiable one and a testimonial to the place. Circulation and sitting, in sum, are not antithetical but complementary. The easier the flow between street and plaza, the more likely people are to move between the two—and to tarry and sit.

This is true of the handicapped, too. If circulation and amenities are planned with them in mind, the place is apt to function more easily for everyone. Drinking fountains low enough for wheelchair users are low enough for children. Pedestrian paths that are made easier for the handicapped by ramps, handrails, and steps of gentle pitch are easier for all. The idea is to make all of a place usable for everyone.

Planned Enlightenment

The most satisfying film I've ever seen is our first time-lapse record of the sun passing across the Seagram plaza. In late morning, the plaza was in shadow. Then, shortly before noon, a narrow wedge of sunlight began moving across the plaza and, as it did, so did the sitters. Where there was sun, they sat; where there was none, they didn't. It was a perfectly splendid correlation, and I cherished it. Like urban designers, I believed a southern exposure to be of critical importance. Here was abundant proof.

Then something went wrong. The correlations vanished—not only at Seagram's but at other places we were studying. The sun still moved; the people didn't. At length the obvious dawned on us: May had been followed by June. While midday temperatures hadn't risen a great deal, the extra warmth was enough to make the sun no longer the critical factor.

It was about this time that much of Paley Park's sunlight began to be cut off by an office building going up across the street. From its scaffolding we focused time-lapse cameras on the park and recorded the effect of the new building. It was surprisingly little. Although the sunlight was curtailed, people used Paley as much as they had before. Perhaps they would have used it more had the sun remained; without studying an identical place as a control, one can never be sure. The more important point is that, unfortunate as the loss may have been, the park was able to sustain it.

Access to the sun should be protected, of course, but places that have little or no sun because of a northern exposure or intervening buildings are not a lost cause. With adroit design, sun can be "bor-

rowed." The same new buildings that cast shadows also reflect considerable light. Along with mirror walls, glass, and stainless steel, architects have been laying on travertine marble with a heavy hand, and light has been bouncing into many places that didn't receive it before. In eight years of filming, I have found that several streets have become photographically a half-stop faster. A number of open spaces that otherwise would be dark much of the time are bathed in reflected light, sometimes on the second or third bounce. Grace plaza, for example, gets no direct sun at all but benefits most of the afternoon from light reflected by the southern exposure of the building to the north. Give travertine its due. It bounces light admirably, especially in the late afternoon, when it can give a benign glow to the streetscape.

So far, such effects are wholly inadvertent. Sun studies made for big new buildings tend to be defensive, so that planning boards can be shown the building won't cast an awful lot more shadow than is cast already by other buildings. Few studies try to determine the light a new building will cast, what benefits might result, to whom, and when. Yet benefits of great potential value can be planned and negotiated in advance.

Open Seating

A wonderful invention is the movable chair. Having a back, it is comfortable; more so if it has an armrest as well. But the big asset is movability. Chairs enlarge choice: to move into the sun or out of it; to make room for groups or move away from them. The possibility of choice is as important as the exercise of it. If you know you can move if you want to, you feel more comfortable staying put. That is why, perhaps, people so often move a chair a few inches this way and that before sitting on it, with the chair ending up about where it was in the first place. The moves are functional, however. They are a declaration of autonomy, to oneself, and rather satisfying.

Small moves say things to other people. If a newcomer chooses a chair next to a couple or a larger group, he may make some intricate moves. Again, he may not take the chair very far, but he conveys a message. Sorry about the

closeness, but there's no room elsewhere, and I am going to respect your privacy, as you will mine. A reciprocal move by one of the others may follow. Watching these exercises in civility is itself one of the pleasures of a good place.

Fixed individual seats are not good. They are a design conceit. Brightly painted and artfully grouped, they can make fine decorative elements: metal loveseats, revolving stools, squares of stone, sitting stumps. But they are set pieces. Social distance is a subtle measure, ever changing, and the distances of fixed seats do not change, which is why they are rarely quite right for anybody. Loveseats may be all right for lovers, but they're too close for acquaintances, and much too close for strangers. Loners tend to take them over, placing their feet squarely on the other seat lest someone else sit on it.

Fixed seats are awkward in open spaces because there's so much space around them. In theaters, strangers sit next to

one another without qualm; closeness is a necessity, and convention makes it quite tolerable. On plazas, the closeness is gratuitous. With so much space around, fixed-seat groupings have a manipulative cuteness to them. The designer is saying, now you sit right here and you sit there. People balk. In some instances, they wrench the seats from their moorings. Where there is a choice between fixed seats and other kinds of sitting, it is the other that people choose.

To encourage the use of movable chairs, we recommended that in the New York zoning amendment they be credited as 30 inches of sitting space, though most are only about 19 inches wide. The Building Department objected. It objected to the idea of movable chairs at all. The department had the responsibility of seeing that builders lived up to requirements. Suppose the chairs were stolen or broken and the builder didn't replace them? Whether the department would ever check

up in any event was a moot point, but the fewer such amenities to monitor, the easier the monitoring would be.

Happily, there was a successful record at Paley and Greenacre parks to point to, and it was persuasive. The chairs stayed in the amendment. They have become a standard amenity at new places, and the maintenance experience has been excellent. Managements have also been putting in chairs to liven up existing spaces, and even without incentives they have been adding more chairs. The most generous provider is the Metropolitan Museum of Art. Alongside its front steps, it puts out up to 200 movable chairs and it leaves them out, 24 hours a day, seven days a week. The Met figured that it might be less expensive to trust people and to buy replacements periodically rather than have guards gather the chairs in every night. That is the way it has worked out. There is little vandalism.—*W.H.W.* □

4. URBAN SOCIAL POLICIES

Wind and the Willows

What people seek are suntraps. And the absence of wind and drafts are as critical as sun. In this respect, small parks, especially those enclosed on three sides, function well. Physically and psychologically, they feel comfortable, and this is one of the reasons why their relative carrying capacity is so high. New York's Greenacre Park has infrared heaters, but they are used only in extremely cold weather. With sun and protection from wind, the park is quite habitable even on nippy days.

Spaces around new buildings are quite another matter. In winter, many are cold and drafty, and even in moderate weather few people tarry in such places. The errors are of omission. Wind-tunnel tests on models of new buildings are now customary, but they are not made with people much in mind. The tests for the World Trade Center largely determined stresses on the towers and the type of structural steel required. What the towers themselves might generate in the way of wind, and the effects on people below, apparently were not of much concern.

These effects, however, are quite measurable. It is now well established that very tall, free-standing towers can generate tremendous drafts down their sides. This fact has in no way inhibited the construction of such towers, with the predictable result that some spaces are frequently uninhabitable. At one bank plaza in Seattle, the gusts are sometimes so fierce that safety lines must be strung across the plaza to give people something to hang on to. Chicago has the windiest places, not because of the local wind (which isn't really so very much stronger than in other cities), but because the drafts down the sides of the giant John Hancock and Sears towers are macro in force—often so strong as to prevent people from using the plazas, even if they had reason to.

James Marston Fitch, who has done more than any other architect to badger the profession to consider environmental effects, points out that the problem is conceptual, not technical. "Adverse effects are simply ignored," he says, and outdoor spaces are designed as if for some ideal climate, ever sunny and pleasantly warm. Thus [the spaces] fail in their central pretension—that of eliminating gross differences between architectural and urbanistic spaces, of extending in time the areas in which urban life could freely flow back and forth between the two."

Technically, as Fitch points out, we can greatly lengthen the effective season of outdoor spaces. By asking the right questions about sun and wind, by experimentation, we can find better ways to hoard the sun, double its light, obscure it, or cut down breezes in winter and induce them in summer (*See "Rediscovering Energy-Conscious Architecture," August/ September 1980, page 68*). We can learn lessons from

"Unless the plaza is on the way to the subway, why go down into it? Once there, you feel rather as if you were at the bottom of a well."

the semiopen niches and crannies that people often seek. Most new urban spaces are either all outdoors or all indoors; more could be done to encourge in-betweens. With the use of glass canopies or small pavilions, semioutdoor spaces could be created that would be usable in all but the worst weather. They would be particularly appropriate in rainy cities such as Seattle and Portland.

There are all sorts of good reasons for trees, but for climatic reasons alone we should press for many more of them, big ones too, along the sidewalks and open spaces of the city.

Trees ought to be related much more closely to sitting spaces than they usually are. Of the spaces we have studied, by far the best liked are those affording a good look at the passing scene and the pleasure of being comfortably under a tree while doing so. This provides a satisfying enclosure; people feel cuddled, protected—very much as they do under the awning of a street cafe. As always, they'll be cooler, too.

Unfortunately, guy wires and planting beds often serve to rule out any sitting, and even if they don't, the fussiness of design details works to the same effect. Everything is so wired and fenced you can neither get to the tree nor sit on what surrounds it. Where large planters are used, they are generally too high and their rims too narrow for comfort.

Developers should be encouraged to combine trees and sitting spaces. They should also encourage planting trees in groves. As Paley Park has demonstrated, if trees are planted closely together, the overlapping foliage provides a combination of shade and sunlight that is very pleasing. Arbors can do the same.

Water is another fine element, and designers are

doing rather well with it. New plazas and parks provide water in all sorts of forms: waterfalls, waterwalls, rapids, sluiceways, tranquil pools, water tunnels, meandering brooks, fountains of all kinds. In only one major respect is something lacking: access.

One of the best things about water is the look and feel of it. I have always thought that the water at Seagram's looked unusually liquid, and I think it's because you know you can splash your hand in it if you are of a mind to. But in many places water is only for looking at. Let a foot touch it and a guard will be there in an instant: Not allowed. Chemicals in the water. Danger of contamination. If you let people start touching water, you are told, the next thing you know they'll start swimming in it.

It's not right to put water before people and keep them away from it. But this is what has been happening across the country. Pools and fountains are installed, then immediately posted with signs admonishing people not to touch. Equally egregious is the excessive zeal with which many pools are continually emptied, refilled, vacuumed, and cleaned, as though their primary function was their maintenance.

Another great thing about water is the sound of it. When people explain why they find Paley Park so quiet and restful, they always mention the waterwall. In fact, the waterwall is quite loud: the noise level is about 75 decibels close by, measurably higher than the level out on the street. Furthermore, taken by itself the sound is not especially pleasant. I have played tapes to people and asked them what they thought it was. Usually they grimace and say a subway train, trucks on a freeway, or something just as bad. In the park, however, the sound is perceived as quite pleasant. It is white sound and masks the intermittent honks and bangs that are the most annoying aspects of street noise. It also masks conversations. Even though there are many others nearby, you can talk quite loudly to a companion—sometimes you almost have to—and enjoy a feeling of privacy. On the occasions when the waterwall is turned off, a spell is broken, and the place seems nowhere as congenial. Or as quiet.

Eat, Drink and Be Merry

If you want to seed a place with activity, put out food. In New York, at every plaza or set of steps with a lively social life, you will almost invariably find food vendors at the corner and a knot of people around them—eating, shmoozing, or just standing.

Vendors have a good nose for spaces that work. They have to. They are constantly testing the market, and if business picks up in one spot, there will soon be a cluster of vendors there. By default, the vendors have become the caterers of the city's outdoor life. They flourish because they're servicing a demand not being met by the regular commercial establishment. Plazas are particularly parasitic in this respect. Hardly a one has been constructed that did not involve the demolition of luncheonettes and restaurants. Vendors thus fill a void, and this can become quite clear when they are shooed away. A lot of the life of the space goes with them.

New York City is less puritanical than some other places. Many cities have ordinances that not only prevent purveying food outdoors but eating there as well. If you ask officials about this, they tell you of the dreadful things that would happen were the restrictions lifted—of unhealthful food, terrible litter problems, and so on. Partly because of these restrictions, most of the plaza and building complexes constructed during the past ten years have no provision of any kind for outdoor eating. The few that do have had to do some pioneering. The First National Bank of Chicago, for example, found that even to provide such a minimal facility as a popcorn cart they had to get special dispensation from the city.

The most basic facility is a snackbar. Paley and Greenacre parks both have pass-through counters featuring good food at reasonable prices and making a moderate profit. Plenty of tables are provided, and people are welcome to bring their own food—wine, too, if they wish. From the street it sometimes looks like a great big party, and if the line of people for the snackbar gets long passersby will join. Food, to repeat, draws people, and they draw more people.

Where Street and Plaza Meet

Now we come to the key space for a plaza. It is not on the plaza; it is the street. The other amenities we have been discussing are indeed important: sitting space, sun, trees, water, food. But they can be added. The relationship to the street is integral, and it is far and away the critical design factor.

A good plaza starts at the street corner. If it's a busy corner, it has a brisk social life of its own. The activity on the corner is a great show and one of the best ways to make the most of it is simply not to wall it off. A front-row position is prime space, and if it is sittable, it draws the most people.

The area where the street and plaza or open space meet is the key to success or failure. Ideally, the transition should be such that it's hard to tell where one ends and the other begins. Paley Park is the best example. The sidewalk in front is an integral part of the park, and an arborlike foliage of trees extends over the sidewalk. There are urns of flowers at the curb and, on either side of the steps, curved sitting ledges. In this foyer you can usually find somebody waiting for someone else—it is a convenient rendezvous point—and people sitting on the ledges, and, in the middle of the entrance, several people in conversations.

Before the New York Telephone Co. installed chairs, tables, and a buffet in its plaza at 42nd Street and the Avenue of the Americas, it was frequented mostly by "undesirables." It soon became a success for employees and passersby alike, and most of the undesirables went somewhere else.

Passersby are users of Paley, too. About half will turn and look in. Of these, about half will smile. I haven't calculated a smile index, but this vicarious, secondary enjoyment is extremely important—the sight of the park, the knowledge that it is there, becomes part of the image we have of a much wider area. (If one had to make a cost-benefit study, I think it would show that secondary use provides as much, if not more, benefit than primary use. If one could put a monetary value on a minute of visual enjoyment and multiply that by those many instances day after day, year after year, one would obtain a rather stupendous sum even after applying a high discount rate.)

The park stimulates impulse use. Many people will do a double take as they pass by, pause, move a few steps, and then, with a slight acceleration, go on up the steps. Watch these flows and you will appreciate how very important steps can be. The steps at Paley are so low and easy that one is almost pulled to them. They add a nice ambiguity to your movement. You can stand and watch, move up a foot, another, and then, without having made a conscious decision, find yourself in the park. The steps at Greenacre Park and Seagram's plaza are similarly low and inviting.

A slight elevation, then, can be beckoning. Go a foot or so higher, however, and usage will fall off sharply. There is no set cutoff level—it is as much

psychological as physical—but it does seem bound up with how much of a choice the steps require. One plaza that people could be expected to use, but don't, is only a foot or so higher than two comparable ones nearby. It seems much higher. The steps are constricted in width, sharply defined by railings, and their pitch is brisk. No ambiguity here, no dawdling, no drifting up.

Sightlines are important. If people do not see a space, they will not use it. In the center of Kansas City is a park just high enough above eye level that most passersby do not realize it is there. As a result, it is lost. Similarly lost is a small, sunny plaza in Seattle. It would be excellent and likely quite popular for sitting—if people could see it from the street, which they cannot.

Unless there is a compelling reason, an open space shouldn't be sunk any more than it should be raised. With two or three notable exceptions, sunken plazas are dead spaces. You find few people in them; if there are stores, there are apt to be dummy window displays to mask the vacancies. Unless the plaza is on the way to the subway, why go down into it? Once there, you feel rather as if you were at the bottom of a well. People look at you. You don't look at them.

We have gone over the principle factors that make a place work. But there is one more factor. I call it

Boston's Quincy Market, in contrast to a megastructure, is open, inclusive, safe, and part of a real city.

Dinosaurs of Urban Design

The ultimate development in the flight from the street is the urban fortress. In the form of "megastructures," more and more of these things are being put up—huge, multipurpose complexes combining offices, hotels, and shops, such as Detroit's Renaissance Center and Atlanta's Omni International. Their distinguishing characteristic is self-containment. While they are supposed to be the salvation of downtown, they are often some distance from the center of downtown, and in any event tend to be quite independent of their surroundings, which are usually parking lots. The megastructures are wholly internalized environments with their own life-support systems. Their enclosing walls are blank, windowless, and to the street they turn an almost solid face of concrete or brick.

A car is the favored means of entry. At Houston Center you can drive in from the freeway to the center's parking garage, walk through a skyway to one tower, thence to another, work the day through, and then head back to the garage and the freeway without ever once having set foot in Houston at all.

There wouldn't be much reason to. Down at the street level of Houston Center there are no store windows. There are no stores. There are not many people. The sole retail activity is a drive-in bank, and the only acknowledgment of pedestrians consists of flashing lights and signs telling them they'd better damn well watch out for cars.

The resemblance to fortresses is not accidental; it is the philosophical base. "Yes, they do look a little forbidding," says one proponent, "but they really have to. The fact is, the only way we can lure middle-class shoppers back to downtown is to promise them security." So, in spirit as well as form, the interstate shopping mall is transplanted to downtown and security raised to the *n*th degree. The complexes abound with guards and elaborate electronic surveillance systems. Any kind of suspicious activity is quickly spotted and attended to (including, as I have found, the taking of photographs). Ports of entry from the city outside are few in number and their design is manifestly defensive. Where Renaissance Center faces Detroit, large concrete walls flank the entrance. The message is clear: afraid of Detroit? Come in and be safe.

The complexes bid to become larger. Increasingly, the megastructures are being combined with convention and sports facilities, which, like megastructures, tend to be located at the edge of downtown or beyond. And these can be mated with other megastructures, via skybridges and concourses, to form an almost completely closed circuit. As a result, some American cities now have two cities—regular city and visitor city.

Conventioneers sometimes complain of a lack of variety. A logical next step will be the creation within the complexes of facsimiles of streets. There is one at Disneyland, and it is very popular; there are several at the White Flint Mall outside Washington, D.C. With similar showmanship, indoor theme parks could be set up to give an experience of the city without the dangers of it. In addition to such physical features as sidewalks and gaslights, barber poles, and cigarstore Indians, streetlike activities could be programmed, with costumed players acting as street people.

A better approach would be to tie in with real streets in the first place. There are some solid attractions in megastructures—excellent hotels and restaurants, good shops, waterfalls, elevators in glass pods, and public spaces of a drama and luxury not seen since the movie palaces of the twenties. Must isolation be a condition of their attraction? The megastructure thesis is somewhat self-proving. If people go in, it is argued, they must be seeking escape from the city and its insecurities.

But are they? Do people go into Peachtree Plaza Center because there are spikes on its front ledge on Peachtree Street? They went in when there weren't spikes. Do people go into Renaissance Center because of the concrete barriers? Or despite them? The evidence suggests that they go in because there are attractions to enjoy. These attractions do not require separation from the city to be enjoyed and are more enjoyable when not separated. Boston's Faneuil Hall Marketplace is witness to this. It's a bit hokey, shrewdly so, but it's part of a real city and has a splendid sense of place.

This is what megastructures so lack. One feels somewhat disembodied in these places. Is it night or day? Spring or winter? And where are you? You cannot see out of the place. You do not know what city you are in, or if you are in a city at all. The complex could be at an airport or a new town. It could be in the East or the West. The piped music gives no clue. It is the same as it is everywhere. You could be in a foreign country or on a space satellite. You are in a universal controlled environment.

And it is going to date very badly. Forms of transportation and their attendant cultures have historically produced their most elaborate manifestations just after they have started to become obsolete. So it may be with megastructures and the freeway era that bred them. They are the last convulsive embodiment of a time passing and a wretched model for the future of the city.—*W.H.W.* □

"triangulation." By this I mean that process by which some external stimulus provides a linkage between people and prompts strangers to talk to one another.

The stimulus can be a physical object or sight. At the small park at the Promenade in Brooklyn Heights is a spectacular view of the towers of lower Manhattan across the East River. It is a great conversation opener and strangers normally remark to each other on it. When you come upon such a scene, it would be rude not to.

Sculpture can have strong social effects. Before-and-after studies of the Chase Manhattan plaza showed that the installation of Dubuffet's "Four Trees" has had a beneficent impact on pedestrian activity. People are drawn to the sculpture, and through it; they talk about it. At the Federal Plaza in Chicago, Alexander Calder's huge stabile has had similar effects.

Musicians and entertainers draw people together. Rockefeller Plaza and the First National Bank of Chicago regularly schedule touring school bands, rock groups, and the like. And the real show is usually the audience. Many people will be looking as much at one another as at what's on stage.

It is not the excellence of the act that is important. It is the fact that it is there that bonds people, and sometimes a really bad act will work even better than a good one. Street entertainers, for example, can run the gamut from very, very bad to sublime, but the virtue of street acts is their unexpectedness. When people form a crowd around an entertainer—it happens very quickly, in 40 to 50 seconds—they look much like children who have come upon a treat; some will be smiling in simple delight. These moments are true recreation, though they are rarely thought of as

such, certainly not by the retailers who try so hard to outlaw them. But there is something of great value here, and it should be fostered.

Why not invite entertainers onto a plaza instead of banning them? One corporation is considering a plan to welcome the best of the street entertainers to its new building. They would be given the equivalent of several good collections for doing their act.

Most of the elements that induce the triangulation effect are worthwhile in their own right. Simply on aesthetic grounds, Dubuffet's "Four Trees" much improves the scale and sense of place in the Chase Manhattan plaza. But the social effects are important. By observing them, we can find how they can be anticipated and planned.

I am not, by the way, arguing for places of maximum gregariousness or social directors for plazas. Anomie would be preferable. What I'm suggesting, simply, is that we make places friendlier. We know how—in both the design and management of spaces, there are many ways to make it much easier for people to mingle and meet. Some of the most felicitous spaces have been provided inadvertently. Think what might happen if someone planned them.

It is wonderfully encouraging that places people like best of all, that they find least crowded and most restful, are small spaces marked by a high density of people and very efficient use of space.

I end, then, in praise of small spaces. The multiplier effect is tremendous. It is not just the number of people using them but the larger number who pass by and enjoy them vicariously, or the even larger number who feel better about the city center for knowledge of them. For a city, such places are priceless. Yet they are built on a set of basics that are right in front of our noses. If we will look.

IDS Building, Minneapolis, Minnesota

Gerald Brimacombe/Black Star

The Case Against Urban Dinosaurs

William G. Conway

William G. Conway, an urban affairs consultant, was formerly associated with Atlanta's architect-developer John C. Portman.

A S CONTEMPORARY wisdom would have it, the future of the American city depends on megastructures—those huge but slickly sophisticated commercial real estate projects that have been springing up in American cities for the past decade. Tax-starved mayors, along with the owners of dwindling downtown business establishments, persist in their claim that these giant renewal efforts are all that keep their cities from irreversible decay.

The truth is, however, that the megastructure guarantees neither the investment of its owners nor the future of the city. Far from lending strength to downtown areas, these complexes create little more than a suburban island in mid-city. The hope had been that the architectural behemoths would be the most promising of the creations thus far produced by the boom-bust cycle of real estate speculation. But it is the cycle itself, together with the size and complexity of the projects, that spells financial trouble for megastructure owners. Plagued by cost overruns, the overbuilding that accompanies speculative fever, and onerous finance charges, more and more owners are turning over control of their projects to the out-of-town financial institutions that made them possible in the first place. The size of the structures keeps financial institutions committed to the projects after owner troubles ensue.

Trailing in the wake of financial concerns has been the unforeseen dilemma these edifices impose on their host community: building them stimulates inflation—and thereby further agitates the deterioration of the central city, which further divides the poor from the middle and upper classes.

But what of the much touted benefits of the megastructures? They were intended as more than profit-making ventures for their investors: they were supposed to revive the central city. Generally, they draw people to the city no more successfully than they attract revenue.

It is understandable why mayors and businessmen would cling to anything that promised to stop the decentralization of downtown. The dwindling of population, retail trade, and jobs erodes the tax base. Those citizens left behind make bigger and bigger demands on the public treasury.

Billions have been spent in the United States to stem this flow from city to suburb. But despite the full-page ads and megastructural magnificence—or perhaps because of them—the exodus continues. Minneapolis, for example, after two decades of hard-selling of the city—including the IDS building—has lost more than a fifth of its population. In Atlanta and Los Angeles, both of which boast a great many of the mammoth complexes, researchers discovered that downtown patrons are usually "captive" central-city employees and transients.

Why? Because the megastructure enshrouds the creator's visions of a controlled environment. It respects neither the texture nor the geography of its surroundings. From the street, which the megastructure normally blind-sides with the exception of a grand entrance or two, the unrelieved boredom of whatever material is in vogue reveals the designer's hostility to the cities he professes to save.

Removed from the heights of their angular abstractions, we on the ground can bear witness to a few of the things the megastructures and their apostles have done to our cities. As Paul Goldberger, architecture critic for *The New York Times*, wrote recently about Renaissance Center (Detroit's answer to its severe case of the urban blues): "The . . . towers are set on a multi-story base, which turns a massive wall to the rest of the city. . . . It wants to stand alone, and fails to do the crucial thing that all good urban buildings do—relate carefully to what is around them."

Renaissance Center has so far cost $330 million, more or less. It is removed from and creates a barrier to most pedestrian movement, except for those inside, who enjoy the mazelike and private-cop-supervised rigors of what Goldberger calls the "conceptually . . . suburban development." Visitors to these projects are never in the city. They, and these projects, could be anywhere.

Meanwhile, in reaction to the street crime and sales erosion that these projects were supposed to end, department stores and jewelers are abandoning downtown—in Detroit, Baltimore, and elsewhere—for the suburbs, where cash registers tend to be open more often than they are closed.

Peter Wolf, in *The Future of the City*, writes that if the big-base megastructure trend continues, the existing city will be "closed out," and "the already perilous decline in the amenity offered by public spaces within the city" will be accelerated. The street, as the traditional organizer of urban life and design, will be replaced by enclaves.

ATLANTA exemplifies the curse of megastructuralism. The five huge architectural jewels in the South's queen city are transforming her crown into fool's gold. This reverse alchemy is laying waste the downtown areas *between* the megastructures. In so doing, it obeys the laws of economics now ignored by the projects' sponsors and by the city officials who clamor for more megastructures without first knowing the effects of those already constructed.

In 1960, Atlanta's "first class" office space was spread among 40-odd buildings, and much of this prime office space was centered near the heart of the business district, Five Points. Land values decreased rapidly as the distance from this intersection increased. Property ownership was fragmented; downtown lost the lead in office space and retail sales to the suburbs. Enter the megastructure.

It all begins with the land; and megastructures require acres in zones where property is measured in square feet. With one exception, the land acquired for Atlanta's renewal projects is on the fringe of the business district, between the peak of the land-value "pyramid" and its base. The focus of the center has thus been blurred. Other major acquisitions, for projects that may be abandoned, have also been made. The result is a previously unknown concentration of property ownership—at some distance from the traditional center—and the creation of several new and absurdly inflated "value pyramids."

Property in the vicinity of the $250 million Peachtree

Allen Green/Visual Departures

View from the ashes—" 'It fails to do the crucial thing . . . relate to what is around it.' "

Center that traded for less than $10 per square foot in 1960 cannot be purchased for less than $50 per square foot this year. The pattern is repeated around the other acquisitions. If inflation this severe were experienced by the economy as a whole, it would be crippling. In downtown Atlanta, it has been most destructive to the small firms that hoped to incubate their calculations of prosperity in the warmth of large, accessible markets and cheap space. The cheap space is gone, and so are many of the small firms.

Big employers are also beginning to feel the pinch. The distributing firm of Beck and Gregg, one of downtown Atlanta's larger employers, has quietly declared its intention to leave for more efficient quarters. St. Joseph's Hospital has put its property on the market for $75 per square foot and is building new facilities 15 miles from downtown. Either to be closer to a better-trained labor force or to reduce costs, the South's largest bank, The Citizens and Southern National Bank, along with many insurance companies and airlines, has removed some computer operations and many office functions with high clerical requirements.

If only because of the real estate taxes they pay, the sponsors of megastructures acquire certain enduring political influence. The economic weight and the burden-sharing of the new real estate pyramids are not calculated in the environmental impact statements that breeze through city hall on the wings of political ambition. But in forgoing such concerns, the sponsors of these projects have permanently altered the social and economic ecology of downtown.

At the behest of megastructure owners, city officials plead with state and federal governments to build new highways and to install new anti-crime lights for the owners and their tenants—who, more often than not, no longer live in town and are even afraid to go there unless they can park within the walls of the megastructure. The well-lighted streets empty when they go home. Nevertheless, requests for rapid transit, people-movers, and other capital-consuming projects follow. The city, of course, tries to meet many of these demands.

spending to its limits. Meanwhile, the needs of the under-served are relegated to lower and lower priorities.

"Every bank and insurance company with money wanted to get a piece of the developer's action in Atlanta," said a bank officer whose department placed over $100 million in real estate loans there during the Sixties. "We were under unbelievable pressure to get the money out, despite the fact that we had an inexperienced staff and only passing familiarity with the markets." A colleague, pondering his moribund portfolio of megastructure investments, commented that "lenders were too quick to elevate architects and developers from the status of manufacturers of space to visionaries."

The visionaries have secured more than one billion dollars from the lenders in the past 15 years. While that sum was being invested in downtown Atlanta, employment there remained almost steady—in the range of 80,000 jobs. And while "upward" shifts in the composition of employment occurred, the changes have not been sufficient to justify the hot-market monuments to hope.

Atlanta and many other cities now have a surplus of office space that can be expected to last five to seven years. The average size of new office buildings has trebled. Seven projects account for over half of Atlanta's downtown office space. After three years of leasing efforts, the megastructures' shopping arcades are little more than half full. Tenants are complaining. As for hotels, Donald Ratajczak, Atlanta's leading economic forecaster, has said that the city built three (averaging 1,000 rooms apiece) when it needed only one.

The dismal economic performance of these projects has put the lenders squarely in a role they do not relish. Lenders are now actively involved in the financial administration of four of Atlanta's five megastructures.

Economies of scale are an important tenet of the developers' faith. Build one more big one, believers say; revitalization is around the corner. But if Atlanta builds another, its promised land of urban salvation may be populated solely by the megastructuralists and their bankers, waving to each other through see-through floors, elevated from the parking lots and abandoned blocks that await the next vote of confidence in downtown.

A block north of Peachtree Center is a group of buildings once leased by firms that designed stores, did printing, fixed teeth, sold books, served cheap food, repaired cars. These firms have been replaced by one of the few tenant types that will not be admitted to the megastructures—porn shops. The new tenants will pay whatever rent is asked. They are now the object of outbursts of civic virtue and midnight raids.

The property near Omni International is not as expensive as the stuff up on Peachtree Street. It is much emptier, though. Marietta Street, connecting the Omni with Coca-Cola's world headquarters, wends its way through a series of largely unoccupied industrial structures that for years housed several key employers of those Atlantans who lived near the center of the city. These buildings now provide shelter for itinerant winos while they polish off shared pints of scuppernong before heading out to huddle in the next building down the block. The land the winos stand on sells for $20 per square foot, compared with $5 per square foot for the industrial property in a suburban zone that has increased its employment 630 percent in the past 15 years.

Two other concentrations of small businesses, close to or at the center of downtown, were removed primarily for aesthetic considerations. Most of these firms provided a variety of goods and services to bus riders who, because of the route structure, transferred nearby. But in the past three years, the buildings containing many more than 200 of these establishments have been torn down by the wrecker's ball.

On one site, a sterile park now gives photogenic prominence to the bank from which flowed the funds that purchased the parkland. The other site, presently a fenced-in pit, is comically straddled by a five-and-dime, the only retail tenant on the block that has a listing in Standard and Poor's. Gone is the bebop and diddy-wah from the record stores, the fragrance of the peanut stand, the harsh colors of the Day-Glo socks hung amid the sundries of no name. When the city's mass transit system is completed, this land will be the site of yet another plaza on which some developer will be granted "air rights" to build yet another rebuttal to the "Towering Inferno."

The customers that frequented the now vanished establishments were the people who, in the words of Central Atlanta Progress, an establishment-backed planning group, caused "racial imbalance on the streets," from which the megastructures were supposed to be a refuge. The stores themselves once offered goods and services not found on North Michigan Avenue or Fifth Avenue or Rodeo Drive, elite streets that the megastructures attempt to emulate in their self-contained, monocultural ambience.

Atlanta, which in the premegastructure era billed itself as "the city too busy to hate," is now hyperbolically "the city without limits." Perhaps there is still time for that city, and for the other cities that have fallen under the spell of the megastructure shamans, to demonstrate that it is not "too big to care" about the essential destructiveness of these lumbering urban dinosaurs.

Triage as Urban Policy

Peter Marcuse, Peter Medoff, and Andrea Pereira

PETER MARCUSE is professor of urban planning at Columbia University. PETER MEDOFF is a student in, and ANDREA PEREIRA has recently completed, the graduate program of urban planning, Columbia University. Work on this article was done in part for The Working Group for Community Development Reform, National Citizens' Monitoring Project.

If the city is to survive with a smaller population, the population must be encouraged to concentrate itself in the sections that remain alive. . . . The natural flow out of the areas that have lost general attraction must be encouraged. . . . The role of the city planner is to observe and use [the trend of abandonment] so that public investment will be hoarded for those areas where it will sustain life.

Federal housing subsidies can be used to encourage movement away from deteriorating areas. The stretches of empty blocks may then be knocked down, services can be stopped, subway stations closed, and the land left to lie fallow until a change in economic and demographic assumptions makes the land useful once again.—Roger Starr, *The New York Times*, Nov. 15, 1976

I [have] argued for a land management strategy that would guide central-city depopulation toward the complete clearing out of population from the weaker subdivisions and the clustering of
the remaining households in the stronger communities. . . . Sizable savings in the cost of producing and delivering public services are most likely to be achieved only if whole service areas can be emptied out, so that the service can be completely withdrawn.—Wilbur R. Thompson, in testimony before the Subcommittee on the City of the Committee on Banking, Finance, and Urban Affairs, U.S. House of Representatives, 96th Congress, Second session, Sept. 16–17, 1980

There are advantages in clearing first at the edge of the areas we intend to save and moving from there on inward. . . . The worst decay most often is in the center of the area to be eventually cleared. . . . We [might] choose to clear land first very near to the most marginal areas we are trying to save and then work back toward the center (worst) of the blight. We could use this land as an open-space buffer zone.—Wilbur Thompson, ''Land Management Strategies
for Central City Depopulation,'' in *How Cities Can Grow Old Gracefully*, Subcommittee on the City, Committee on Banking, Finance, and Urban Affairs, U.S. House of Representatives, 95th Congress, First session, Dec. 1977

Triage is a term that came into general use during the Vietnamese War to describe the policy adopted to establish priorities in treating wounded soldiers.[1] As they were brought into the medical treatment area, they were classified into one of three groups: those whose injuries were slight or for whom no medical emergency existed, those hurt so badly that no available medical treatment would be of real use, and the remainder. It was the third category, the remainder, that was given priority, on the theory that the first group would get better even without emergency medical treatment, and the second group would not be served by such treatment in any event.

Triage is quite at variance with the more conventional approach of first treating those whose condition is the most critical, helping those most who are most in need. It was nevertheless argued that its use was justified in

From *Social Policy*, Winter 1982, pp. 33–37. Copyright 1982 by Social Policy Corp.

situations where the supply of medical services was grossly overwhelmed by the number of those needing treatment, whatever medical ethics might say on the matter.

Triage has also come to be used to describe a certain policy dealing with neighborhoods in recent times. The concept underlying it was first explicitly enunciated (although its implementation may well have preceded its enunciation) in a famous article by Roger Starr in *The New York Times Magazine* in 1976. Starr, who had just left his position as administrator of the Housing Development Administration, New York City's superagency dealing with issues of housing and community development, argued that cities like New York were declining in population, employment, and resources; that such decline was inevitable, resulting from forces far beyond the power of the city to control; and that the most rational response to that decline was a policy of "planned shrinkage." Rather than attempting to maintain public facilities and services throughout the city, at levels that could no longer be justified, in view of the city's decline, he suggested that the city rationally and consciously select those areas that it would make most sense to abandon. It should then concentrate its resources in other areas. The city would be able to strengthen those areas that it could make greater efforts to save by being able to transfer resources to them from the areas it was writing off. Two advantages would thus result. For the city, the net efficiency of its operation would be increased because of the cost-effectiveness of concentrating services in viable areas and the savings achieved in the written-off areas; for the neighborhoods, although those being written off would decline more rapidly than they might otherwise, only the rate of decline, not its fact, would change, while other neighborhoods would be saved that otherwise might have been lost.

Because of its resemblance to the policy for treating patients in conditions of wartime, Starr's policy was soon described by commentators as one of triage.

Starr's arguments have a certain superficial plausibility about them. Given limited resources, the cost-effectiveness of this policy may well

be enhanced by its concentrated application in certain neigborhoods, it might seem. If other neighborhoods are inevitably going to decline, given macroeconomic and demographic circumstances beyond the control of public policy, then it could be argued that the continued expenditure of funds to preserve those neighborhoods at their old levels is only an attempt to hold back the tide. Better to accept and plan for the inevitable than to squander resources fighting it to no avail. There should be a net public savings from

The allocation of benefits useful only to areas of growth does not have to entail the writing off of an area of stability or decline, but it may have a similar effect.

the strategy, it can be said; part of that savings could then be allocated to alleviating the hardships caused to those in the abandoned neighborhoods and assisting in relocating, retraining, or supporting in other ways their last remaining residents. They, as well as the citizens and taxpayers of the community at large, will benefit in the long run. To help those in the South Bronx hold out just a few years or even months longer in the face of decay and blight all around them is doing neither them nor anyone else a service, the argument runs.

THE FORMS OF TRIAGE
As used in the present context, triage means the exclusion of a particular geographic area from service by governmental programs, despite its need for them, on the grounds that the very intensity of those needs make that service in the area inefficient. Such an area is thus "written off" for purposes of those programs.

This is the narrow definition of triage. A broader definition might also include (1) public actions favoring certain areas as well as those disfavoring them and (2) public inaction as well as action. The allocation of benefits use-

ful only to areas of growth, for instance, does not have to entail the writing off of an area of stability or decline, but it may have a similar effect. The failure to adopt any program to deal with certain issues, by the same token, may result in the writing off of certain areas. The failure to deal with arson for profit, for instance, or to provide for programs addressed to specific problems of new groups of immigrants may have as much effect in contributing to the decline of a geographic area as any policy formally adopted, even though it constitutes nonfeasance rather than misfeasance.

There are four possible forms of triage.

Triage I. At the most innocent end is Triage I, which means the distribution of public services or facilities in accordance with nongeographic, nonlocational standards, but which has the unintentional consequence of eliminating a specific geographical area from the investment or funding program. The distribution of library facilities in accordance with existing reader demand, for instance—as was shown in a recent Los Angeles review—has the clear impact of favoring higher-income areas and may result in so little investment in certain low-income neighborhoods that (partly as a result of the vicious circle of inadequate supply turning off demand, partly as a result of orthodox "cost-effectiveness" analysis) library facilities may be entirely removed from that neighborhood.

Triage II. Triage II is the use of locational standards for the distribution of public goods or services, but without the delineation of specific geographic areas to be favored or avoided. Under Triage II, for instance, the rule might be formulated that rehabilitation grants will only be given in a block where there are less than 10 percent abandoned, demolished, or sealed-up buildings. The same results might be produced by providing that rehabilitation funds only be granted where after rehabilitation the economic viability of the unit on the private market will sustain its proper maintenance and occupancy, or where a program is conditional on private participation, which in turn uses locational criteria. Such policies have the effect of eliminating from the program consideration of specific geographic areas where abandonment is widespread, but without at the outset outlining the areas to be avoided.

Triage III. In Triage III, either blocks or census tracts may be designated from the beginning to which, because of the high concentration of abandoned buildings or for other economic or physical reasons, rehabilitation grants will not be given, or other census tracts or areas may be designated that would have priority claim on rehabilitation funds.

Triage IV. Triage IV, finally, is the designation of specific geographic areas for the distribution of public goods and services. Certain areas may be given a high priority for all services across the board, as in Neighborhood Strategy Areas, for instance, but others would be effectively redlined. Whether Triage IV is done only indirectly, by putting all resources in favored areas and leaving none for triaged areas, or whether it is done as a matter of an explicit policy of planned shrinkage does not seem particularly relevant.

The crucial issue throughout is not one of motivation or intent, but of the clear, known, and foreseeable result of the policy.

Only in Triage I could the argument be made that the consequence was "accidental." In each of the others, it is a specified and explicit policy that areas be treated differentially, that geographic distinctions be made. In Triage II, the distinctions arise from program formulations rather than from the designation of geographic areas, as in Triage III and IV. The difference between Triage III and Triage IV is only in the comprehensiveness of the approach; Triage III may be applied only to one or two programs, while Triage IV establishes policy more totally for a whole variety of investment or funding decisions.

Distinctions among the forms of triage are set forth specifically to make it clear that all of the types of public action as noted above can be appropriately classified as triage, regardless of the particular intent of the parties involved or the explicitness of the geographical criteria used.

THE CASE AGAINST TRIAGE

There are six major arguments against the policy of triage.

- Many of the problems of neigh-borhoods are by no means inevitable but, in fact, come from prior public policies that can be altered and reversed.

- The policy of triage itself is in part responsible for creating the precise conditions that seem to create the need for it—the loss of jobs and people from neighborhoods in the inner city.

- It is by no means clear, even accepting the inevitability of some decline in employment and population in a city, that a policy of writing off specific neighborhoods and concentrating resources in others is a more

> **The policy of triage itself is in part responsible for creating the precise conditions that seem to create the need for it—the loss of jobs and people from neighborhoods in the inner city.**

effective use of resources than alternate methods of establishing priorities and distributing resources.

- Triage destroys communities just at a time when the values of community preservation are being recognized as central to national urban policy.

- There are adverse distributional effects in a policy of triage. It is invariably the poor who will suffer—overwhelmingly minority group members, women, the elderly, and youth; the rich, the business community, the well-to-do, and officialdom will not. While a policy of triage may be cost-effective for some, it may be devastating for others, generally those least able to deal with its consequences. That hardly seems a distribution of costs and benefits that public policy should seek out.

- Finally, resources are not limited in the sense of the Vietnamese medical situation; it is well within the resources of the United States of America to treat successfully the problems of its neighborhoods.

The decline of city neighborhoods is not inevitable. The argument that the changes in the character and location of economic activity are not the inevitable result of the play of free-market forces, but also the result of deliberate and massive public policy, has been spelled out in detail elsewhere.[2] Tax laws, rewarding the writing off of existing plant and equipment and providing accelerated depreciation and investment credits for new construction and equipment; local government bonanzas for businesses moving into a community, leaving minimum wages low and permitting state action such as right-to-work laws that foster significant wage differentials among different parts of the country; public stimulation of high-technology, capital-intensive industries and products rather than labor-intensive, community-based enterprises; inducements offered to business by state and local governments to relocate facilities within their borders—all these have greatly encouraged the movement of capital and economic activity out of certain areas and into others. The fact that the cost of such moves is borne publicly, while the benefits are reaped privately, worsens the complicity of public policy in the adverse consequences of shifting locations of economic activity. Instead of dealing with the symptoms and consequences of these shifts in business activity, their causes can be directly addressed. This can be done at least in large part by simply reversing existing public policies. The patient is only terminally ill because of the treatment; a different treatment might effect a miraculous change.

The policy of triage itself accentuates the very conditions it is designed to cure. Even assuming, for the sake of argument, that a city's economic base is declining, that capital, employment, and consequently the population are leaving because of forces beyond the city's control, the policy of triage is likely to accentuate these evils rather than cure them. Neighborhood conditions are themselves frequently a reason to move, even where continued occupancy is otherwise preferred. Given the abandonment of half the structures on a block because their residents have moved elsewhere, those wishing to remain will find themselves quickly motivated to move out as well. The process has been well documented.

Once a city policy of triage is adopted, once a given area, still partially occupied, is abandoned by the city, its residents will have no alternative but to move. Given the decision to move, it will more likely be out of the city than within. The same holds true for business firms. Once the infrastructure, the access to a labor market, the transportation facilities, the public security, the environmental quality of a neighborhood, are written off by the city, firms will move that might otherwise have preferred to stay. Nor is there any reason to believe that their movement will be to another location within the city. Once a move is decided on, a new and more attractive site out of town—often even out of the region—will generally be found.

The triage of entire neighborhoods is less economical than a planned reduction in density more broadly distributed throughout the city. Again, assuming for the sake of argument, that loss of population and economic activity will take place, there are advantages as well as disadvantages that can be obtained by a community from the process. Most older cities have areas of extraordinarily high density. They have buildings constructed for uses that are outdated, technologically and socially obsolete. They have a need for more open space, for recreation facilities, for more light and air. They have overcrowded transit facilities, congested sidewalks and streets, noise and pollution resulting from heavy use. They lack playgrounds, trees, benches, attractive green spaces for outside activities.

A policy of planned reduction in density might, in fact, make a great deal of sense in many older cities. It would involve looking at the quality of individual structures, their age, their suitability for their current uses. It would involve looking at the quantity and quality of community facilities available and calculating the densities most appropriate for optimum use of those facilities. It would involve looking at existing fixed-route transit facilities and planning the best use of their layout. It may then involve a policy of very strict code enforcement in areas where reductions in density are desirable, labeling obsolete arrangements as nonconforming, and condemning other structures where alternative public uses are desirable.

Planning thus becomes planning for reduction in size and planning for reduced densities and improved quality of life, rather than planning for the amputation and death of entire neighborhoods.

New York City figures suggest the problem. A majority of all apartments in the city are in either "Old Law Tenements" or "New Law Tenements." Old Law Tenements are those built before 1901, generally to much lower building standards—with much greater lot coverage, less light and air, et cetera—than exist in those buildings built after the new Tenement House Act became effective in 1901. A total of 135,000 units were removed from the housing inventory between 1975 and 1978: 33,000 of these, from the available figures,[3] were Old Law Tenements, but 75,000 were New Law Tenements. This is not the market removing the oldest and worst of the housing stock as the overall quality of housing improves; rather, this is a process, whether deliberate triage or not, that removes more newer units than old from current use and leaves behind a vacancy rate of 2.9 percent, the present figure in the city, well below what a balanced market would show. Even the increased vacancies and loosened market for housing that could be the silver lining in the cloud of population loss does not take place in New York today. Surely these results cannot be defended as part of a desirable public policy.

What an alternative approach would look like is, in fact, not so hard to imagine; by something less than coincidence, New York City has a classic example right at hand. The very first public housing in the country, sponsored by the Public Housing Administration in the early years of the New Deal, was in New York. First Houses, on the Lower East Side, was in fact not new construction but the rehabilitation of Old Law Tenements. One of the ingredients that made it a universally acknowledged success was that every third building on the block was demolished to make light and air for the remaining two, and back portions of buildings were taken down to create pedestrian ways and play spaces for residents. In a city with a declining population and an older housing stock, such an approach makes superb common sense. As selected units are taken

off the market and demolished, the remaining units are improved, the neighborhood changes for the better, and the community is preserved and strengthened. These results are just the opposite of those produced by a policy of triage.

Triage destroys communities. The loss of the spirit of a community that accompanies a policy of planned shrinkage is one of its serious drawbacks. It is the relationship to the community in which one lives, after all, that creates a great deal of the satisfaction one obtains from one's residential environment. Neighbors one has known a long time, stores offering known goods, patterns, networks of support, habits, traditions of a community, all mean a great deal to people—and their disruption and destruction can take away much of the attraction of life in a city. The strength of the opposition to policies of neglect and abandonment shown by residents and community groups in the South Bronx attests to the strength of the spirit of community even in such a devastated area.[4] Yet triage deliberately sets out precisely to destroy such communities. In a period in which the forces of community, neighborliness, and belonging are increasingly looked to as a bulwark against anomie, delinquency, vandalism, hopelessness, and where the preservation of existing communities in other areas of the city are major objectives of public policy, the deliberate destruction of these very values in areas of triage seems a dubious policy.

Beyond this, of course, the destruction of communities accelerates the very losses of population and housing that are supposed to have produced the need for their destruction to begin with; the circle is tight and vicious indeed.

The damage done by triage hurts those most who can afford it least. The areas of the wealthy are not likely to be subject to triage: central business districts are not likely to be neglected; luxury apartments are not likely to be abandoned; solid single-family homeowners will protect their own neighborhoods and schools—often to the exclusion of others. Those excluded from both the residential and economic benefits of this society are precisely the ones who will be most negatively affected by triage. Those are inevitably Blacks, Hispanics, recent immigrants, women and households headed by women, teen-agers who are out of work, the elderly. It is their schools that will be abandoned, their streets that will be neglected, their sidewalks filled with broken glass, their transportation cut off, their employment moved away, their buildings neglected, their safety ignored. The vague promises to make up to them elsewhere for the losses occasioned by their geographical location are lip service indeed. If economic and/or demographic decline dictate that some in a community must bear unusual if temporary costs, surely public policy should seek to distribute those costs more equitably than by a policy of triage of the poorest neighborhoods.

Resources for the preservation of neighborhoods are not inadequate. This is perhaps the most important and simplest point, although the one most often lost sight of. It is, at the very least, startling to assume that the national resources of the United States are inadequate to cope with the problems of our most depressed neighborhoods. In absolute wealth, this country is the richest nation on earth; in Gross National Product per capita, it is in the top five; its technology is unrivaled, its government stable, its commitment to democratic values longstanding and widely heralded. To give but one example, in a comparison between the United States, the United Kingdom, and West Germany in the extent of public support for new housing construction, the United States

shows up as a very poor third over the years.

The concept that this nation is materially unable to deal with the problems of the South Bronx because of some inherent limitation on its national resources would, one might think, be accepted only with the greatest reluctance, intellectual as well as moral. It certainly should not be made the starting point of public policy.

Dispute about the pros and cons of triage is by no means academic. It is a policy that, in the form of Triage I or II, has been with us for some time; Triage III and IV are more newly arrived, the advent of the latest "urban fiscal crisis" ushering in their wholesale use. The closing of schools, the elimination of transportation services, cessation of upkeep of parks, elimination of building inspections, denial of rehabilitation funds, have all been accelerated in areas where blight is "too severe." The National Citizens' Monitoring Project of the Working Group for Community Development Reform[5] of the Center for Community Change has documented the way in which community development block grant funds have been used to effectuate triage, despite the (weak) federal regulations against certain forms of it. Now, with the further weakening of federal guidelines for a variety of programs, and the increased discretion given municipalities and states, the threat of triage is dramatically increased.

In this context, community groups, all faced with reduced funding, may easily find themselves fighting among themselves for the crumbs that remain,

and it will be harder to keep a focus on the big picture. Yet that is where the focus must be, if triage is not to be allowed to be part of a divide-and-conquer strategy. Community groups must fight to have adopted local guidelines at least as strong as those that have existed (or have been advocated) at the federal level. They must join together in insisting that severity of need and human benefits, including the protection of communities, be the priority for the allocation of funds, not some abstract economic cost-benefit measure that ignores distributional effects entirely.

NOTES

[1]The word "triage" is an old one, dating back to at least 1727, and comes from the same root as the word "try." Its original meaning was simply "to sort, to select." In the nineteenth century, "triaged coffee" came to mean coffee that has been rejected in the normal sorting-out process when the beans were inspected, and was sold at a cut price. The application to setting priorities for medical treatment apparently dates back to the French army during the First World War, but the connotation of writing off "hopeless" cases only came into vogue with the Vietnam War.

[2]Peter Marcuse, "Public Crisis for Private Profits: On the Usefulness of the Urban Fiscal Crisis," *Working Paper* 20, Division of Urban Planning, Columbia University, 1981.

[3]Peter Marcuse, *Rental Housing in the City of New York: Supply and Condition, 1975–1978,* New York Department of Housing Preservation and Development, Rent Control Division, January 1979.

[4]See the excellent catalogue of the exhibition on the South Bronx prepared at the Bronx Museum, *Devastation/Resurrection: The South Bronx,* 1979.

[5]The project may be reached at 1000 Wisconsin Avenue, N.W., Washington, D.C. 20007. Paul Bloyd is project director.

Cities Are Setting Their Sights On International Trade and Investment

More cities are following Atlanta's lead and trying the newest local economic development tools: trade missions, trade zones and export trading companies.

CAROL STEINBACH
AND NEAL R. PEIRCE

March was a busy month for Mayor Andrew Young and a profitable one for Atlanta. On the 12th, Young entertained a delegation of Korean business leaders who had added Atlanta to their itinerary after a plea from Young to South Korean President Chun Doo Hwan during a Far East trip this year.

March 15-16 found Young at a trade conference in Sousse, Tunisia. The result: two contracts to buy $200 million worth of goods from Atlanta firms.

On March 24, Young hosted French President Francois Mitterrand to discuss, among other things, establishing a direct Atlanta-Paris air route. Accompanying Mitterrand was a representative of the largest architectural firm in France, which wants to establish a U.S. office, possibly in Atlanta.

With Young as the catalyst, Atlanta is at the forefront of the newest municipal trend—development of local foreign trade policies. Other mayors who are plagued by budget deficits, work force cutbacks, deteriorating infrastructure and overwhelming capital spending needs are becoming internationalists, too. They see foreign trade and investment as a way to increase jobs without luring away domestic companies from other U.S. cities.

"International trade represents jobs and tax revenues," said Alan Beals, executive director of the National League of Cities, which is spearheading an effort to help cities expand trade programs. Catharine H. Findiesen, an international trade

consultant with Coopers & Lybrand, put it more bluntly: "The survival of many urban economies through the 1980s may hinge on the success of their export development efforts."

Atlanta captures the limelight, in part because its mayor, who was ambassador to the United Nations during the Carter Administration, is still known as "the ambassador."

"Young has the ability, because of his world reknown, to draw attention to Atlanta," said Carol Martel, director of the international department of the Atlanta Chamber of Commerce. "He is the most significant internationalist we've ever had in the mayor's office."

During the past 10 years, direct foreign investment in Atlanta totaled $2.2 billion. An estimated 36,000 Atlantans work for 720 foreign-owned Georgia firms, compared with only 200 foreign-owned firms eight years ago.

The trade programs in Atlanta and other cities have two main goals: attracting foreign manufacturing firms and increasing foreign sales of locally produced goods and services. And a few cities are promoting themselves as "must stops" for foreign tourists.

Municipal competition for foreign business involves several strategies. The most popular include organizing overseas investment and trade missions, establishing foreign trade zones and one-stop export assistance shops and promoting tourism. Many cities are also teaming up with

the private sector to promote trade, and a few are trying to set up export trading companies, which were authorized by Congress in 1982.

Several cities have set up international development offices. San Antonio's two-year-old office operates on a $900,000, city-funded annual budget. In Los Angeles and San Diego, the job is done by independent, nonprofit corporations. In other cities, the international program is part of the city economic development office. And increasingly, cities are learning how to tap state and federal trade and export programs for funds.

The city efforts get rave reviews from federal officials who see expanded local trade as a way to help reduce the national trade deficit. Federal support takes the form of scattered increases in trade promotion grants and promises to improve coordination of the hodgepodge of federal trade and export programs.

But the cities' attempts to develop cozier relationships with foreign businesses have also drawn criticism. Large domestic industries that are seeking protection from foreign imports are nervous about stronger ties between cities and foreign businesses. And some state officials contend that foreign investment efforts are properly their function. Cities that are too dependent on foreign trade could find their economies weakened by world forces beyond their control. Finally, some critics contend that local officials should devote their scarce resources and ener-

Battle Creek, Mich., is relying heavily on foreign trade and investment to rebuild a recession-shattered economy. Eleven foreign firms have moved to the area, investing more than $30 million and bringing with them more than 500 new jobs.

gies to more traditional local problems.

Despite these criticisms, municipal officials are likely to continue their foreign economic development programs. By 1981, foreign assets in the United States totaled $400 billion, including $180 billion in property, plants and equipment. New York led the nation in attracting foreign firms last year, followed by North Carolina, California, Texas, Illinois and Georgia. Today, up to 5 per cent of U.S. workers may owe their jobs to foreigners, up from just 2 per cent in 1975. *(See table, next page.)*

The potential for export expansion may be even greater. Only 10 per cent of U.S. firms export products and less than 1 per cent account for more than four-fifths of all exports. Government surveys have identified 20,000-30,000 U.S. firms, mostly small and medium-sized companies, that produce goods that could be exported. Tapping that pool could mean thousands of new jobs because the government estimates that every $1 billion of export volume translates into 25,000-30,000 new U.S. jobs.

WASTEFUL JUNKETS?

One of the most publicized and criticized methods of attracting foreign business are the foreign trade and investment missions. Political opponents and the press frequently write off these trips as expensive wasteful junkets.

Antoinette Vazquez, a consultant with the Illinois Commerce and Community Affairs Department, said the cost of sending one person abroad on a mission ranges from $3,500-$7,500, depending upon the destination. The average mission includes from 5-10 local officials and staff in addi-

tion to local business representatives. Although the costs often are defrayed by private businesses, a city that foots the bill for its officials can end up spending as much as $75,000 for such a trip.

Some local trade missions, however, have been surprisingly successful. Consider Young's 1983 trip to Jamaica. "I thought the country was too poor to have many opportunities for us," he said. "But the chamber of commerce and universities insisted. We took a delegation of 70 business people, 20 from the universities and a soccer team from the local YMCA." The soccer team provided "cover," said Young—plus good press. "In the meantime," he said, "the business people got to see the Jamaican decision makers who previously had been unavailable to them."

As a result of the trip, Atlantans agreed to build a $100 million resort in Jamaica and to import flowers from Jamaica at a cheaper price than from Europe. And an Atlanta firm specializing in low-cost housing forged a deal to exchange its services with Jamaica for rum.

Even so, said Young, "I feel guilty about going out of town so much and I still get criticized. But if I could travel about two weeks out of every two-month period, we could generate much more economic activity for about half the businesses in Atlanta."

But critics charge that Young's preoccupation with international trade has hurt the city by allowing relationships between local Atlanta neighborhoods and downtown business interests to deteriorate. And they blame the mayor for failing to aggressively push for an agreement with Rouse Co. to redevelop Underground Atlanta.

Others suggest that investment missions are not a wise use of city resources, in part because most of the foreign firms that the cities are wooing have already made American investments.

Marsha R. B. Clark, deputy director of the National Association of State Development Agencies, said: "Cities should use [state] resources to maximum advantage." Clark believes that cities should have a greater role in promoting the sale of local goods through trade missions, but that the costs of those missions can be borne by the private sector.

But Vazquez believes trade missions are politically acceptable. "As a tax-supported agency, we are asked to quantify our efforts," she said. "That's a lot easier to do with a trade show or mission because one can attribute direct sales to such efforts and those dollars can then be translated into jobs and tax revenues."

In addition to Young, Miami Mayor Maurice A. Ferre, Mayor Ernest N. (Dutch) Morial of New Orleans and Seattle Mayor Charles Royer, have led successful trade missions. But most cities have not tried this strategy. Less than 20 per cent of the National League of Cities' members with populations above 100,000 have conducted or seriously considered trade missions, the league says.

Foreign trade zones have emerged as another way to attract foreign business. The zones are federally designated areas in the United States where imported goods can be stored, assembled, combined with domestic components and distributed under greatly reduced U.S. tariffs and duties. Cities hope that by having the zones they can attract foreign manufacturers and domestic companies that use imported parts in their products.

The Foreign Look to U.S. Investment

Foreign investment in the United States has produced millions of jobs. The table shows the value of manufacturing and land investments in 1981, in billions of dollars, and the number of direct jobs all foreign investments had created by 1981.

	Value of foreign-owned property, plants and equipment	Direct jobs resulting from foreign investment
Texas	22.4	172,564
California	19.6	240,774
Alaska	9.6	8,578
Louisiana	8.2	45,718
New York	7.1	204,393
New Jersey	6.4	131,764
North Carolina	5.5	86,349
Illinois	5.4	111,850
Florida	5.4	69,983
Pennsylvania	5.4	129,110
South Carolina	5.2	64,898
Ohio	5.0	97,018
Michigan	4.1	65,070
Georgia	4.0	73,742
West Virginia	3.9	34,835
Tennessee	3.7	55,285
Arizona	2.9	29,396
Virginia	2.9	49,115
Minnesota	2.8	32,536
Alabama	2.8	26,501
Oklahoma	2.6	24,459
Washington	2.3	25,329
Wisconsin	2.2	59,666
Colorado	2.2	23,961
Wyoming	2.0	4,070
Maryland	2.0	43,900
Missouri	1.9	31,123
Delaware	1.8	35,340
Indiana	1.8	44,881
Utah	1.8	17,188
Kentucky	1.8	25,366
Maine	1.6	17,692
Massachusetts	1.6	52,578
Mississippi	1.4	10,905
Connecticut	1.2	40,128
Montana	1.2	2,830
Hawaii	1.1	16,143
Iowa	1.1	21,741
North Dakota	1.0	3,255
New Mexico	1.0	8,005
Kansas	0.9	14,206
Oregon	0.8	12,281
Arkansas	0.6	17,397
Nevada	0.5	5,854
New Hampshire	0.4	13,355
Nebraska	0.4	5,225
Rhode Island	0.4	9,423
Vermont	0.3	5,889
Idaho	0.3	3,795
South Dakota	0.3	1,324
U.S. total	**$180.0**	**2,343,115**

SOURCE: Commerce Department

The zones are particularly popular with auto companies, and several have had their factories and warehouses designated as special subzones. Parts can be imported into the zones, duty free, and there is no duty on the finished cars if they are exported. If the cars enter domestic markets, they are considered to have been imported whole and the duty is far less than if each imported component were taxed separately.

The zones range from a 640-acre site in Oklahoma City to a 48-acre zone on two sites in Grand Forks, N.D. There are seaport trade zones, such as the New Orleans Wharf, and zones adjacent to international airports and on land near the Canadian and Mexican borders. Inland cities have zones, too; one of the nation's most active is in Kansas City. The largest zone in dollar volume of imports was in the Mexican border town of McAllen, Texas, which processed more than $1 billion worth of goods in 1983.

The 60 active foreign trade zones in 1983 processed $11 billion worth of goods, up from $7 billion in 1982. The 1,400 firms using the zones last year employed 40,000 U.S. workers and were responsible for an additional 72,000 spin-off jobs, according to the National Association of Foreign Trade Zones.

Some import-sensitive domestic firms do not like trade zones. They contend that the duty and tariff concessions chiefly benefit foreign industries and economies without creating many U.S. jobs. And they argue that the original purpose of the zones—to encourage exports—is being undermined because most of the zones' finished products are sold domestically.

INCREASING EXPORTS

Most cities also hope their international efforts will increase exports of local goods. For more than 100 firms in northeastern Alabama, for example, exports have become big business because of the export promotion program sponsored by the Top of Alabama Regional Council of Governments, which has generated more than $48 million in overseas sales and nearly 900 jobs in the past five years. English and Asian companies are buying 10 per cent of the wire connector cables produced by Beowulf Corp., which is in Huntsville. Kappler Disposables Inc. in tiny Guntersville sells its throwaway protective uniforms, worn in cleaning up toxic wastes, to Europe, the Orient, the Middle East and Canada. Nigerians eat popcorn produced by a firm in rural Jackson County, and China may join a group of nations that buys $7 million worth of air-ventilation grills each year from the Barber-Coleman Co. in Huntsville.

Increasing exports is not easy for many cities. "Too many small and medium-sized companies have strong export potential but don't export because of a lack of expertise about selling overseas," said Vincent C. Burke III, assistant director of the Commerce Department's Office of Export Trading Company Affairs. "There are inadequate financing opportunities, and some fear the risk of antitrust liability if they join together with their competitors for purposes of exporting."

The 1982 Export Trading Company Act may provide relief. It permits cities, states and the private sector to establish special one-stop export companies that would buy goods from private firms and assume all the risks and complications of selling them overseas. (See NJ, 5/14/83, p. 992.)

At least two cities, Philadelphia and Newport News, Va., are working to set up municipal export trading companies. Two port authorities are among the 15 export trading companies that have been certified by the Commerce Department, and many cities are hoping to spur private firms to set up trading companies in which the cities might become partners.

Increasingly, cities also see economic opportunities in tourism. In 1982, an estimated 24.3 million foreign visitors came to America and spent almost $17 billion, a 16 per cent increase from 1981. The federal government estimates one new job is created by every 54 foreigners who visit the United States.

Seattle sponsors seminars for local businesses to help them understand and prepare for the influx of Japanese tourists. Seattle restaurants and hotels print menus and instructions for using the telephone in Japanese and other languages, and a special international tourist welcoming booth has been set up at the airport. In Phoenix, the city brings foreign tour operators to town for "familiarization" tours. Knoxville, hoping that the 1982 World's Fair opened the way for a continuing stream of foreign visitors, has developed a language bank and currency exchange. And Kansas City, St. Louis and Tulsa are jointly arranging tours for foreign travel writers.

The city programs are partially a response to complaints that the federal government does not do enough to help promote international tourism. The U.S. share of international tourists has dropped from 13 per cent to 10.6 per cent in recent years. The United States ranks 56th worldwide in funding for tourist promotion programs.

But city officials do not believe that local or federal government funds are the key to promoting foreign trade and tourism. In fact, a reason local trade programs are attractive is that they do not need to be financed by local tax revenues. Atlanta, for example, spends no city

funds for Mayor Young's trade missions, which are privately financed. Nor do cities need to pass tax incentives to attract foreign investment. "Incentives are not an important factor in attracting foreign trade to the U.S.," said David Bauer, an economist with the Conference Board. "What is more important for the foreign firm is some indication that the community itself welcomes the investment."

Many cities look to the private sector to help finance trade promotion. In Los Angeles, the International Trade Development Corp. is housed free of charge in the Bank of America tower. Copy machines and word processors have been donated by Xerox Corp. and the development corporation's general manager is an executive on loan from Security Pacific Bank. In Columbus, Ind., a town of 35,000, private firms contribute $150,000 annually to help support the city's international promotion efforts.

The cities also look to more than 150 local world trade clubs for help. Typically, the clubs have from 50-500 members drawn from private manufacturing and service firms, universities and government. Most sponsor meetings and seminars on trade issues, and a few offer technical assistance to local firms. The Export Club of Baltimore is applying to become an export trading company, and Florida's 14 world trade clubs send missions to Latin America.

The academic community supports the municipal efforts by supplying translators when foreign industrialists visit their communities and providing city officials with information on a country's history. San Diego colleges sponsor a Japanese language program to help support the Japanese business community there, which has created 13,000 local jobs in the past five years. Atlanta has designated a triad of local universities to work with Caribbean students who have been sent to learn about business by working in Atlanta firms.

The University of Pennsylvania's Wharton School houses, staffs and helps finance the Philadelphia Export Network, a consortium formed in 1981 to promote exports by small and medium-sized companies in the Delaware Valley.

OPPORTUNITIES FOR ALL

The opportunities for greater international ties are not limited to large coastal cities. "The potential is so enormous," Young said, "that almost any city with a local corporate base can do something."

The Conference Board's Bauer agrees. "Trade patterns in the U.S. are changing quite rapidly," he said. "No longer do the Japanese trade only on the West Coast and Europe on the East." As foreign investors have become more sophisticated, they are branching out beyond large cities and into smaller communities,

he said. "Ten years ago it was unlikely that a smaller midwestern city, for example, had a crack at attracting foreign investors, but that is no longer true."

A midwestern city, Battle Creek, Mich., is relying heavily on foreign trade and investment to rebuild a recession-shattered economy. Battle Creek Unlimited Inc., a nonprofit organization funded by the city, has turned to Germany and Japan for new employment opportunities. Since the late 1970s, the organization has conducted 20 investment missions. Eleven firms, six German and five Japanese, have moved to Battle Creek, investing more than $30 million and bringing with them more than 500 new jobs. The latest arrival is Musashi USA Inc., a Japanese auto parts firm, which broke ground in March for a 30,000-square-foot plant that will initially employ 50 workers. And with the aid of state and foundation money, Battle Creek is working to establish itself as an international agricultural marketplace where companies from around the world can come to purchase farm equipment and products.

Foreign trade may also bring new opportunities for minority entrepreneurs. "Over all, the development of Atlanta has been mostly to the north because that's where whites live," Young said. "But the airport is to the south. Foreigners see that and, without such cultural prejudice, are looking to that predominantly black area for investment." German investors, Young said, have already entered into a joint venture with black entrepreneurs.

The National Conference of Black Mayors has made international trade a top priority and has sponsored several trade missions. "Trade opportunities are going to escalate, and we want to begin to try to [channel] the billions of dollars that are going, particularly from African countries, into cities headed by black mayors," said former conference chairman Johnny L. Ford, mayor of Tuskegee, Ala.

In New York City, the Harlem Third World Trade Institute is aggressively seeking African trade opportunities for minority-owned firms. The nonprofit institute, founded in 1980 with a Commerce Department grant, has hosted delegations from nine African nations. By last fall, the institute had garnered more than $14 million in international trade for minority firms, including a $10 million construction deal with Guinea, a $500,000 contract with Zaire for American hair care products and the sale of $10,000 worth of air conditioners to Trinidad and Tobago and $1.8 million worth of boats to Nigeria.

BARRIERS

Despite the apparent promise of increased foreign trade, most cities are still not heavily involved in international efforts. "The biggest problem we face as Americans in dealing with world trade is that we are frankly afraid of the world," said Young, who with San Antonio Mayor Henry G. Cisneros co-chairs the National League of Cities' two-year old international economic development task force.

That task force last year identified lack of knowledge about foreign trade opportunities and resources as another serious barrier to increasing cities' international efforts. This year, the league is organizing trade missions and providing technical assistance to cities wishing to expand trade development programs.

Some cities have also been stymied by complaints from citizens who do not want certain foreigners in their communities, particularly Arabs. Opposition has also emerged to specific types of foreign investments such as acquisitions, mergers and real estate deals.

"In general, opponents of foreign acquisitions fear that these takeovers entail a loss of U.S. sovereignty without the compensating benefits, such as new jobs and tax revenues, generated by new enterprises," said Jane Sneddon Little, an economist with the Federal Reserve Bank of Boston.

Foreign investment in farmland has been particularly controversial. Amid reports that the Arabs were buying up acres of agricultural land, Congress voted in 1978 to require foreign individuals and corporations to report their holdings of agricultural and forest lands. A few states enacted statutory limits on foreign investment in agriculture. Annual surveys by the Agriculture Department, however, show that only about 1 per cent of U.S. farms and forests are foreign held.

Although in many cities the private sector has spearheaded efforts to attract foreign business, local firms sometimes have opposed foreign investments. Some businesses in Denver, for example, contended in the late 1970s and early 1980s that Canadian investors were unfairly driving up real estate prices.

Some critics also fear that cities seeking international investments may be raising public expectations too high. Foreign trade zones and export trading companies generally take years before they generate any jobs or tax revenues. Few of the foreign trade zones are highly profitable. McAllen's spectacularly successful zone in Texas lost money for a decade.

"A lot of cities are looking for a magic formula for restoring their economic vitality, and that just isn't going to work," said James Petkovits of the Philadelphia Industrial Development Corp.

Cities may become too dependent on foreign trade. Miami is still reeling from the loss of a sizable portion of its Latin American export market because of the Latin American recession. Its exports declined 28 per cent last year, and local leaders and businesses are trying hard to cultivate new export markets in Europe, Asia and Africa, to develop Miami as an international medical center and to expand the city's role as a receiving point for overseas cargo destined for other parts of the United States.

Occasionally, cities find their international efforts undermined by state government. City officials in California, for example, fear foreign investors will make good on threats to bypass that state if it retains its unitary taxation system, which taxes the worldwide earnings of multinational corporations, not just the income earned within the state. *(See NJ, 2/25/84, p. 373.)*

Some city officials and many in the private sector believe that the lack of a coherent federal trade policy and coordinated trade programs are the most serious barriers to expanded trade. Eight federal departments and numerous agencies within them offer hundreds of trade-related programs and information services.

Despite their complaints, most city officials agree with the Reagan Administration that states and cities, not the federal government, should be the focal point for trade promotion. A 1980 General Accounting Office report concluded that "the most effective federal role is to facilitate the states' efforts."

Young agrees. "Business-government relationships are easier at the local level," he said. "A mayor can go in and represent the business of his city. That can't be done at the federal level."

And so, in June, Young will be off again, this time seeking investments from Sweden and Finland. The same month, Cisneros will be flying in the opposite direction but on the same course, seeking to entice Japanese high-technology firms to locate in San Antonio.

ACHIEVING ENERGY INDEPENDENCE BY REVIVING AMERICA'S CITIES

"It would appear to be in our nation's energy interest that cities and city living prosper and that the movement of people out of cities and into non-urban areas be reversed."

Neil Goldstein and Amey Winterer

Mr. Goldstein is the Sierra Club's National Conservation Representative in New York City. Ms. Winterer was formerly a Mead Government Scholar on the Center's staff.

"A whole new value of the city has emerged, one which may well be decisive. Not a new value, really: It was always there, but we couldn't see it because we had always acted as though land, energy, and resources were inexhaustible. They have suddenly turned out to be seriously depleted and are becoming even more scarce and costly. Thus the city has a new and vital function as the Great Conservator of land, energy and resources." These are the words and the vision for the future of cities of Congressman Henry Reuss (D.-Wis.), chairman of the House Subcommittee on the City. It is a vision shared by many other urban environmentalists. According to Reuss, cities in the past grew and prospered as a focal point for communication and trade and a birthplace for the arts and learning. Technological changes and population shifts subsequently altered American lifestyles and permitted decentralized trade, communications, and cultural options. Many of our nation's cities, therefore, fell into decay, decline, or distress. Still, as Reuss points out, cities today can play a vital new role in America's fight to achieve energy independence.

Statistics bear out Reuss' argument. *The Costs Sprawl,* a detailed study funded by the Council on Environmental Quality, the Department of Housing and Urban Development (HUD), and the Environmental Protection Agency (EPA), found that " 'planning' to some extent, but higher densities to a much greater extent, result in lower economic costs, environmental costs, natural resource consumption, and some personal costs for a given number of dwellings." This reduced energy consumption in higher-density areas is achieved by substituting walking or mass transit for driving over long distances, by containing within adjacent units heat that would otherwise escape from dwellings, and by reducing the energy needed to build and maintain the infrastructure of sewers, electric lines, telephones, and roads, since less area must be served. In a comparison of three community types, *The Costs of Sprawl* study found that "Low Density Sprawl" development consumed energy at almost twice the annual rate of a "High Density Planned" community of the same population.

In practice, these savings may not fully be achieved. Due to population-density-reducing abandonment of inner-city housing and commercial structures, and because of a lack of appropriate mass transit and of adequate insulation in buildings, most cities do not approach the theoretically possible energy savings of the study's hypothetical communities. For example, the per capita consumption for even the nation's densest city, New York, is only half the national average. Much more effort within each city would be required to achieve these savings in other, less-dense cities. Yet, even though energy savings in cities are less than theoretically possible, actual savings are nonetheless significant; the average city dweller expends a great deal less energy than residents of non-urban areas. For San Francisco, Minneapolis, and Atlanta, single-family detached houses use, respectively, 46, 26, and 33% more energy than do row houses with insulation of comparable quality. Other savings also are achieved by city dwellers, whose commuting distances are generally shorter than their suburban and rural counterparts, who require less infrastructure per person than in non-urban areas.

Promoting compact city living

With facts and potential such as these, it would appear to be in our nation's energy interest that cities and city living prosper and that the movement of people out of cities and into non-urban areas be reversed. Some people argue that the energy-conserving advantages of cities are so great that this return-to-the-cities movement will occur automatically as people search for ways to reduce their energy costs, and that there need be no special effort or change in national policies to encourage a return to the cities. Is this view correct? Are the energy cost savings associated with city living significant enough to encourage people to move back into cities despite such obvious disadvantages as crowding, financial decay, poverty, and crime? A 1979 HUD publication concluded:

with the exception of Los Angeles, the net migration flow of whites continues to be from the central city to the suburbs. At the same time, the number of blacks migrating to central cities has been declining. . . . *These analyses suggest that the spontaneous revitalization of central cities is not yet imminent.* (Emphasis added.)

Since this study, energy prices have escalated at an ever-increasing rate. Yet, even this phenomenon could be offset by new countervailing pressures. Between 1950 and 1975, the suburban home-buying age group (30-49 year olds) increased 17%; between 1975 and 2000, there will be a 60% increase in this age group, over three times the former rate as a result of the post-World War II baby boom (despite a reduction in the *current* birth rate). Even if the rising price of transportation fuels and single-family heating or cooling costs force a significantly higher fraction of this group to live in cities than has historically been the case, the pressure for single-family suburban homes will still far exceed current demand. In short, despite rising fuel prices, slowed population growth, and rising mortgage rates, both the demand for suburban housing and the impact of sprawl are going to increase by the turn of the century. The chances of the energy crisis overcoming these trends without the aid of a conscious Federal urban policy seem slight.

Federal policy today often works toward just the opposite end, encouraging energy-wasteful sprawl and urban decline. Although over 60% of our national population lives in cities, Federal legislation appears to have had a consistent bias toward suburban and rural area development at the expense of cities. The Federal investment tax credit for new construction is but one example. According to George Peterson of the Urban Institute, "By providing benefits for new structures that did not apply to the maintenance and rehabilitation of existing buildings, Federal tax policy exercised a bias in favor of suburban and fringe development and a bias against preservation of the older parts of American metropolitan areas." Added to this tax credit, FHA mortgages promote the construction of rural and suburban single-family homes, while Industrial Revenue Bonds make it possible for rural communities to offer tax-free assistance to

factories locating in their area, thereby draining cities of both industry and people.

Nor does national policy stop short of providing the infrastructure required by new sprawl construction. Until recently, national land and transportation policy primarily promoted highway construction. This highway construction has enabled people to commute long distances from suburban homes to their metropolitan workplaces, promoted strip development along highway routes, and, within cities, degraded or demolished the neighborhoods through which highways were built. To cite another example, until recently, national water resource policy has offered Federal funding assistance for building new infrastructure for flood control, irrigation, navigation, and regional water-supply, but it has neither earmarked funds for municipal water supplies nor for rehabilitation and maintenance of existing conveyance systems. As a consequence, funds for water resource infrastructure, essential for growth, flow to underdeveloped, rather than already-developed, areas. As John Altschuler, president of the Hartford (Conn.) Policy Center indicated at a New York City Urban Coalition energy conference, even energy policy adds to this financial drain on cities as money is transferred to synthetic fuel-, oil-, and coal-producing states.

To be sure, some Federal programs include measures to counteract the policies listed above. Many attempt to achieve this goal by applying to cities policies which were not initially designed to help cities and which created suburban growth and sprawl. For example, Federal subsidies are now available for the construction of multi-family housing, as well as single-family homes, and an Investment Tax Credit is now also allowed for rehabilitation. This approach of generalizing and extending to cities laws initially designed for other purposes does not always work, however. As the Northeast-Midwest Congressional Coalition pointed out in 1980, for example, despite the extension of the Investment Tax Credit to rehabilitation, "The current tax system favors investment in new structures . . . recent data suggests that the offsetting value of the rehabilitation tax credit has been marginal."

There are some notable recent attempts to get to the root causes of city decline and suburban sprawl, rather than merely extending existing (and perhaps inapplicable) programs to cities. The Community Conservation Guidance of November, 1979 (sometimes referred to as the "shopping sprawl policy"), ordered Federal agencies to desist from assisting the creation of shopping centers which would impose "significant negative consequences" upon

a neighboring city. The Office of Management and Budget has ordered all Federal agencies to use consistent population projections in order to ensure that no sprawl-inducing development of infrastructure occurs beyond what is necessary to meet the actual population growth expected in a given community. The EPA has especially taken care to incorporate this policy in its sewer and sewage treatment plant capital grants program.

Energy policy and city viability

Attempts such as these to counterbalance the harmful effects of previous national programs on cities and to preserve cities as the "conservator" of our natural resources and energy can not work as long as national energy policy itself favors suburban sprawl-type development and works against city revival. Energy policy is especially important because it affects the relative energy-efficiency and, therefore, cost-efficiency of cities, since it is this relative efficiency that serves as the basis for much of the hope for urban revitalization. Even pro-environment programs which promote conservation and reliance upon renewable resources in rural and suburban areas can reduce the *relative* energy advantage of cities unless carefully planned to avoid this pitfall. Without such care, the consequent sprawl will prevent theoretically achievable energy savings.

For example, until 1980, Federal energy policy to promote installation of solar energy equipment and insulation relied exclusively upon tax credits provided to people who installed these energy-saving devices in their homes (so-called "owner-occupied units"). What seems at first glance to be a foolproof program to promote conservation and solarization fails to consider the needs of the inner-city poor, who can not possibly benefit from a tax credit since many pay no taxes. Direct grants, loans, or weatherization job training could possibly serve the poor, 39% of whom live in central cities, but tax credits can not. According to the House Subcommittee on the City's analysis of the tax credit program, "the housing of income groups most in need of financial help is locked out of the program. Only five per cent of solar energy systems will be installed by families whose incomes are below the national average, according to an estimate made for the Department of Housing and Urban Development." In 1978, an aide to Congressman Charles Rangel (D.-N.Y.) put it even more strongly: "The tax credit system is a subsidy of what's in people's economic self-interest. Rather than waste a lot of money that way, we'd like to see the money routed to those who can't afford weatherization. . . ."

187

Rangel has worked with government officials to design just such a program to provide direct assistance (on a pilot basis) in his district and to train and employ currently unemployed inner-city residents. The Rangel program and other similar efforts such as the Community Services Administration's weatherization program provide evidence that solarization and conservation *can* work in cities *if properly planned.* Programs *must* be carefully planned in this way if we are to avoid the anti-urban, energy-wasteful consequences and fulfill the promise that solar energy and conservation offer.

Solar and insulation programs must also be designed to consider the large number of people in cities who *rent,* rather than own their own homes. According to the Subcommittee on the City, "Less than one-third of suburban and less than one-fourth of rural families rent their homes. By comparison, the majority of city families are renters. In New York, Chicago, and San Francisco, the proportions of renters are 74, 62, and 64%, respectively."

Weatherization and solar energy programs must cover rental units as well as owner-occupied units to meet the needs of cities, but even the extension of these programs to rental units does not in itself solve the special problem of renters. Legislated limits upon the total funding available for any one building may discourage landlords of large buildings from participating in the program. The staff of the Anacostia Alliance, a Washington, D.C.-based group providing assistance for converting to energy alternatives, has pointed out that many landlords are less inclined to begin with to participate than homeowners because fuel costs are a deductible business expense for tax purposes. In some cases, they can even pass along part or all of their fuel costs to their tenants; in most cases throughout the U.S., tenants pay utility bills. The divergence between the tenants' and landlords' interests in these cases is complete—the landlord has *no* reason to install energy conserving equipment. Tenants are discouraged from taking direct action to lower utility bills in these cases by legal limitations upon the modifications they may make in the landlord's property. Even where such limitations can be overcome, tenants are unlikely to invest in energy-saving improvements which have a moderately long pay-back period since the annual turnover rate in rental housing averages 30%; benefits in such cases would accrue to subsequent tenants and not to the tenant paying for the improvement.

Federal legislation passed in 1980 has to some extent corrected problems in prior solar and conservation programs which interfered with use of solar energy and weatherization in cities. The National Energy Security Act established a Solar Energy and Conservation Bank. The program, according to the Subcommittee on the City,

authorizes several programs which provided funds for renewable energy and energy conservation improvements in existing rental housing on an equal basis with existing owner occupied units. Tenants, homeowners, and landlords whose income is less than 80% of the area median may apply to local financial institutions for grants that cover up to 50% of the cost of allowable energy conservation improvements such as caulking, insulation, and more efficient burners. Local banks or other participating financial institutions will then be reimbursed for their services by a solar bank. The Act also establishes a program of loan subsidies for energy investments in existing residential, agricultural, and commercial buildings. . . . The subsidy rate ceiling for conservation loans ranges from 20 to 50%, dependent on the recipient's income and the type of building being improved. . . .

Clearly, the development of the solar bank is an improvement on Federal energy policy, since the bank expressly provides assistance for lower-income households, renters, and multi-family residential buildings. The exact impact of the bank is impossible to predict and it will take time to measure the effect of its operation, but, even with these improvements, as the Subcommittee on the City points out, "The programs of the solar bank will not end the conservation dilemma faced by rental properties; the divergence of interests of landlords and tenants remains." Nor does the Act sufficiently meet the needs of low-income households. Furthermore, in the effort to trim the budget, Pres. Reagan has proposed eliminating funding for the solar bank in fiscal year 1983 and rescinding the $22,000,000 appropriated for it in fiscal year 1982.

Urban complexity

Perhaps the most important question in assessing energy policy is whether current policies recognize the special energy problems posed by the very same feature of cities that provides the vast potential for energy savings that Rep. Reuss and others hope to rely upon. The cities' inherent energy asset of having higher densities than rural and suburban areas poses unique energy problems. Essentially, the problems are of three types: those which stem from the scarcity of space, those which arise because of the interdependence of people who live in dense urban settings, and those which derive from air pollution and the population at risk due to inevitable concentration of pollution in urban areas. Specific problems range from

such issues as space limits for scrubbers necessary for electric power plants to convert from oil and coal, to the difficulty of ensuring access to the sun ("solar rights") in cities where one building may cast its shadow on another. Even electric vehicles may prove difficult to use in cities; many city dwellers have no garage where they can store their car overnight linked to an electric outlet to recharge their battery. Alternatives such as parking meters with electric outlets would appear to be a simple solution, but answers such as this require government initiative and do not lend themselves to individual action. Similarly, guaranteeing solar access will require legislated guarantees or specific zoning solutions, and preserving air quality during coal conversion will require strict government pollution control, enforcement, and careful monitoring. In short, urban social systems will necessitate coordinated government energy policy-making to address complexities which do not arise in a simpler, rural setting.

Cities offer some special solutions to the nation's energy needs, but these also require complex organization and concerted action. Mass transit, district heating systems, and the use of waste as a fuel resource have special potential in cities. However, district heating, a process in wide use in Europe, requires investment in a distribution system to deliver steam or hot water to homes, apartments, shops, offices, and factories. In already-built neighborhoods, this investment may be quite expensive. Installation of a distribution system in abandoned urban areas is a less expensive, but highly speculative, enterprise. Moreover, some method must be devised to shut down local boilers and guarantee customers for the new system to ensure both the economic viability of the system and attainment of air quality standards which might be violated if a new power-generating source were introduced into a community without shutting down the boilers already in operation. Problems such as these blocked proposals by local environmental officials for district heating in New York's South Bronx.

Heat from burning waste similarly can create pollution problems unless carefully controlled through government regulation and monitoring or unless refuse-derived fuels are shipped out of the city and sold for use in less dense, non-urban areas. Resource recovery therefore requires careful planning.

Decentralization to reduce complexity

Solutions which attempt to reduce complexity and interdependence and provide individual freedom and the opportunity for private energy decision-making would provide evident advantages, but even programs such as these can create problems of their own in cities. Proliferation of neighborhood or single-dwelling-unit power systems using cogeneration devices to generate heat and electricity may add to air pollution since many low-level sources will be administratively more difficult to control than a few central generating stations. Also, while cogeneration appears to have promise, diesel cogeneration potentially can raise nitrogen oxide levels and emit suspected carcinogens directly into the air of densely populated inner-city neighborhoods. Requirements that only methane be used for cogeneration (one alternative to diesels) to avoid pollution problems such as these would require governmental regulation both to delimit the permitted classes of cogeneration equipment and to assure that the methane would be available in cities for this purpose.

While decentralizing power production has some evident advantages, the pollution problem is not the only possible problem. While solar energy and cogeneration systems appear to make economic sense, city residents who convert to these systems more slowly than their neighbors may suffer disproportionately until they convert. According to Steven Ferrey in a 1978 article in *Planning* magazine that dealt with some of the complexities of this conversion process:

Use of solar equipment for heating will not reduce the amount of expensive generating capacity needed to satisfy *summer peak demands* for electricity. Further, to the degree that solar heating displaces electric heating, solar heating will diminish the volume of electricity sold during the winter. When overall volume drops, utilities could experience decreased revenues despite the high construction costs involved in building for peak demands. Each kilowatt of electricity consumed would bear a greater share of the billions of dollars of fixed construction costs. *The consumer's electricity bill would soar.* (Emphasis added.)

In other words, while solarization and cogeneration seem to make a good deal of sense both environmentally and economically, if the inner-city poor can not afford the capital investment to take advantage of these technologies, they may instead face *increased* costs. Steps must therefore be taken to ensure that *all* people are given the opportunity to use renewable resource technologies. The problem that Ferrey pointed out, and other problems like it, can not be solved by market forces alone; it will take conscious planning at the Federal, state, and local levels. The evidence shows that it *can* happen. In specific cases, groups and individuals are working to conserve energy, install solar equipment, and find innovative solutions to the special energy problems of cities. They are overcoming obstacles and proving that city energy problems can, with thought and hard work, be solved. What is needed now is a national urban energy policy and specific program to make the task less difficult.

WHEN PUBLIC SERVICES GO PRIVATE

Taxpayers save 20% or more by using contractors to provide government services—sweeping streets, manning air control towers, running golf courses. Risks crop up among the opportunities, but canny officials are learning what to watch out for.

Jeremy Main

OLD BUT STILL hotly controversial, the idea of letting private industry do more of government's work has caught fire in the 1980s. Pressed by tax revolts and spending limits, federal and local officials are buying more and more services from corporations. They have accumulated enough evidence lately to evaluate the risks and rewards. What they find is impressive. Turning government work over to business can cut costs 20% or more—often much more—without loss of quality. Although there's no way of accurately measuring the growth of these contracts, county and city governments, especially those in the West and Southwest, seem to have moved faster than the federal government.

Private industry has always provided services such as garbage collection and road mending in many places. Not only are governments now contracting for more of these traditional services, such as public transportation, but they are also finding new functions to put out to bid. At some small airports—such as Enid, Oklahoma, and North

RESEARCH ASSOCIATE *Robert Steyer*

Myrtle Beach, South Carolina—the Federal Aviation Administration no longer staffs control towers. The FAA provides funds and local authorities hire entrepreneurs to control air traffic. Los Angeles County and New York City have turned public golf courses over to private operators.

Government is starting to reach far beyond contracting for services by looking to private industry to finance, design, build, and run public facilities from waste-water treatment plants to prisons. The U.S. Army has invited the biggest engineering companies in the U.S. to consider creating and operating an entire base for the new Tenth Mountain Division at Fort Drum in New York State. The contractor would have to find the financing, which could run to $1 billion. (The Army would furnish the soldiers.)

All this activity quickens the entrepreneurial juices. Companies have sprung up to operate jails and airport towers. Two big accounting firms, Arthur Young and Touche Ross, help cities and states figure out what to turn over to the private sector. Writers and lecturers churn out books and schedule seminars on what's awkwardly known as privatization.

Big players in the game expect to grow bigger. Browning-Ferris Indus-

tries of Houston is second among industrial waste-removal companies only to Waste Management Inc. of Oak Brook, Illinois. Browning-Ferris's contracts to collect city garbage have increased from 220 in 1981 to 340 today. Parsons Corp. of Pasadena, California, a big international engineering company, sees a lot of business coming from government. Parsons is financing and building the $20-million first phase of a waste-water treatment plant it will operate for Chandler, Arizona. Chandler plans to double, and then redouble, the plant's capacity. Parsons is also bidding on a $100-million treatment plant for Jefferson Parish, Louisiana, and is interested in the Fort Drum scheme.

The long and redolent history of government contracting, from Revolutionary War scandals right up to some of today's bloated defense contracts, gives ample warning that a private contract is no guarantee that the work will be done honestly or efficiently. The idea of contracting raises troublesome questions. Will a contractor motivated by profit faithfully perform a public service? Or will he make a low-ball bid just to get a contract and then goose up his price—or worse, walk away from a vital function if it becomes unprofitable?

Experienced public officials have

From *Current*, October 1982, pp. 50-56. First appeared in *Vital Issues*, Vol. 31, No. 3, 1982. Reprinted by permission.

come up with good answers to these questions. They are leery of the bargain-basement offers competitive bidding may produce. In certain cases, if the law allows, they may rely on other approaches, such as "requests for proposals." A request for proposal lets officials choose the most promising all-around contractor. When they have to use competitive bidding, tough standards can weed out unqualified bidders. Canny officials write careful standards into contracts, monitor performance closely, and invoke cancellation and penalty clauses. Big cities seldom turn all of any function over to private enterprise. By keeping active in, say, garbage collection, the municipality can maintain competitive pressure on contractors and step in to replace one who fails.

New York City ignored these rules in dealing with Broadway Maintenance Corp., which monopolized streetlight maintenance in three boroughs from 1953 to 1978. Broadway Maintenance always made the lowest bid, and the city didn't fuss much if it didn't do all the work agreed on. When officials audited performance in 1978, City Controller Harrison J. Goldin said the deal with Broadway Maintenance "smelled to high heaven." But New York's plight worsened that year, when Welsbach Electric Corp., which already had a monopoly in the city's two other boroughs, underbid Broadway Maintenance and won the contract for the whole city. After receiving a record 180,000 complaints in one year about lights that didn't work, New York got smart. In 1981, it divided the city into eight service areas, allowing no company to contract for streetlight maintenance in more than two areas. Complaints are down 57%.

"There is absolutely no advantage in replacing a public monopoly with a private monopoly," says Professor Dick Netzer, director of the Urban Research Center at New York University. "What you really are after is competition." Phoenix, a well-run city of 866,000, encourages municipal departments to join the competition with private contractors. Beginning in 1977, Phoenix opened areas of the city to bids for garbage collection. Browning-Ferris won the first area with a bid of $2.47 per household per month, against the city's bid of $2.64. SCA Services of Boston won another section in 1980, and National Serv-All

Inc., a small Indiana company, took on a third area in 1983. Along the way an interesting thing happened. The more the city's public works department competed, the sharper it got. In 1984 the department won back the sector awarded to SCA, which has since been split up and absorbed by Waste Management and a Canadian company.

AS IT TURNS OUT, the city made a mistake in signing up National Serv-All, which had bid only 1 cent per household per month less than the city. Serv-All couldn't work that cheaply. Within months, the company was raising cash by selling equipment given it by the city. Service fell apart last Thanksgiving and Christmas, when garbage piled up faster than Serv-All could collect it. Waste Management took over the contract in January. Says Phoenix Mayor Terry Goddard, 38, "The Serv-All case makes me a lot more cautious. It was a false economy to take a bid that was low by 1 cent." But Phoenix still wants to open more services to private contractors.

Los Angeles County and four counties around it have created the largest and most varied showcase of government contracting—and furnished the most convincing evidence of success. Barbara J. Stevens, a former Columbia University professor who runs a New York research company, Ecodata Inc., studied the area and wrote a 573-page report on the counties' performance, published recently by the Department of Housing and Urban Development. Stevens analyzed eight types of service in ten cities that contracted for each service and ten that didn't. The contractors won by a wide margin.

The municipal departments held their own only in preparing payrolls. In the other seven services, they were markedly more expensive, averaging from 37% more for maintaining trees to 96% more for laying asphalt on city streets. Stevens also made careful comparisons of quality: Were garbage-can lids replaced? Was grass cut to uniform heights and properly edged? She found no significant qualitative difference between municipal and contracted services.

Stevens's research showed that government tends to pay more than necessary for low-skilled jobs. For example, the cities paid janitors $1,234 a month on average; contractors paid

them $881. Contractors get more work out of employees because government gives more vacations, holidays, and sick leaves, and tolerates more absenteeism. Contractors use more part-timers and give foremen greater freedom to hire and fire, while making them responsible for equipment. Contractors paid bottom dollar on labor-intensive jobs, but on the capital-intensive jobs they used better equipment than the cities and paid to get the most skilled workers. Asphalt-paving crewmen earned $29,049 a year on the average from contractors, compared with $18,384 from cities.

The 84 cities of Los Angeles County have the choice of furnishing their own services, buying them from the county government, or contracting for them privately. Many are choosing contractors. Pasadena discovered that it could save $250,000 a year, or 25%, by hiring janitorial services. About 21% of the city's $130-million operating budget goes to contractors. City Manager Donald F. McIntyre says the list of contractors will keep growing.

At the southern end of Los Angeles County, Rolling Hills Estates broke off a contract it had with the county prosecutor to handle all its cases, mostly involving violations of building and other town codes. City Manager Harry R. Peacock says the service "was totally inadequate." Rolling Hills Estates now pays a private law firm to act as town prosecutor. Rancho Palos Verdes, next door, closed its public works department and turned the care of parks, buildings, and roads over to an engineering company.

After much political controversy, culminating in the election of a new Board of Supervisors in 1980, Los Angeles County plunged into contracting. By the end of 1984 the county had signed 434 contracts worth $108 million to do work that civil servants had done before. The county estimates current savings at $21 million a year in a budget of $6 billion. After Touche Ross had helped the county department of health services identify where it could save by contracting, the county turned feeding, housekeeping, laundry, and other nonmedical services in several hospitals over to private companies. The county has put contractors in charge of half its 20 golf courses. Parks Director Ralph S. Cryder says the privately run courses are more attractive and popular and make more money than those the county runs. But Cryder plans to keep some courses under the county wing in case a contractor defaults. He is also putting some parks under private management.

CONTRACTING in Los Angeles has survived a lot of opposition. Civil service unions represent 63,556 out of 74,852 Los Angeles County employees and don't like the spread of contracting. Paul D. Nawrocki, research director of Local 660 of the Service Employees International Union, put together a 2½-inch-thick volume of complaints about the performance of contractors in Los Angeles County. "Contracting," Nawrocki says, "is an ideological program—a philosophical attack on government—that overrides any consideration of cost." He complains that government workers displaced by contracts are mostly blacks and Mexicans in low-skilled jobs who get replaced by lower-paid workers. County officials reply that only 34 workers have actually lost jobs. Most workers in the 2,200 positions eliminated by contracts have found other jobs with the county or work for contractors.

Nationally the fiercest opposition to contracting comes from the American Federation of State, County, and Municipal Employees. In *Passing the Bucks*, a book the union published in 1984, it cites a string of horror stories about contracting, apparently in the belief that readers live in some Utopia where corruption or incompetence among civil servants would be unimaginable. Because of political and labor opposition, contracting hasn't spread as much in the rest of the country as it has in the less-unionized Southwest and West. Nevertheless, city governments in the Midwest and East have made some interesting deals.

Three years ago Louisville faced the awful prospect that it wouldn't be able to open a new $73-million, 404-bed downtown hospital, built to replace the old General Hospital. The owner, the University of Louisville, decided it couldn't afford projected deficits even greater than the old hospital's $5 million a year. No government body was willing to pick up more than part of the deficit. Then Humana Inc., a Louis-

ville-based chain of for-profit hospitals, agreed to lease the hospital for 40 years, starting at $6.5 million a year for the first four years; it also promised to subsidize the medical school, treat all the county's indigent patients for a fixed government payment, and turn over 20% of the pretax profits to the university. Last October, Humana gave the university $205,000 as its share of profits over 16 months, plus a voluntary $327,000 bonus. Humana earned $1 million even though it says it absorbed $21 million in unreimbursed costs for indigent and other patients. This year Humana Hospital-University, as it is known, expects to make more, according to executive director Gary V. Sherlock—but he acknowledges that as an inner-city hospital, it will probably never match the profits of other Humana hospitals.

Humana claims tough management and the economies of mass purchasing for its 85 U.S. hospitals enable it to operate 17% more efficiently than competing hospitals. In Louisville, Sherlock has cut the hospital payroll by 18% relative to the number of patients and fired managers who failed to meet newly written objectives. Private admissions are up from an average of 34 to 58 a day. Sherlock attributes this success with paying patients in part to 28 new programs and services the old hospital didn't have, including burn and acute dialysis units.

IN NEWARK, New Jersey, a basket-case Eastern city with a tradition of machine politics and an entrenched bureaucracy, Mayor Kenneth Gibson has pushed contracting with surprising success. In 1977 Newark gave out a tree-trimming contract that got the job done for $19 per tree, compared with $50 per tree when city workers did it. In 1978 the city hired private snowplowers, and in 1979 contracted for garbage collection in one-third of the city. Other services, such as catch-basin cleaning, the demolition of abandoned buildings, and some street sweeping, are also being contracted out.

The New Jersey attorney general recently filed a civil complaint against 40 companies, alleging that they rigged garbage collection bids. Included in the complaint were Pet-Am Co., which had the Newark garbage contract for the first three years, and

James Petrozello Co., which now has it. The case has yet to be tried, but Newark officials say they are satisfied with privatization.

Private collectors use bigger and better vehicles than the city and have a work force with an average age of 25. The average age of the city's sanitation men is 55, according to Alvin L. Zach, the director of engineering, and many are slowing down. An independent survey in 1982 showed Pet-Am collecting 5.4 tons of garbage per man per day compared with 3.4 tons for the city, though the private workers were more likely to spill garbage and leave it. The study estimated the city was saving $2.5 million to $5 million over the three-year life of the contract. Newark is about to privatize garbage collection in another third of the city.

Government bafflegab makes it hard to determine just how well the federal government is doing with privatization. The Eisenhower Administration began the program to push contracting, which is now governed by the Office of Management and Budget's Circular A-76. That document requires federal agencies—except where restricted by Congress—to buy commercially available services and products unless the savings wouldn't exceed 10%. But civil service unions and bureaucrats who would rather build than dismantle empires continue to resist. Joseph R. Wright Jr., deputy director of OMB, admitted to Congress last fall that A-76 "has not been effectively implemented."

In most cases the federal experience seems to be about the same as the municipal experience. For instance, a 1984 Department of Defense survey of 235 contracts found that private bids on average were 24% below government estimates, which had already been cut 7% when competition loomed. A 1981 General Accounting Office report said it cost 50% more to use federal employees to clean government buildings than to use contractors. Congress has since limited the General Services Administration's contracting for custodians; existing civil service jobs for custodians can be contracted only to workshops for the handicapped.

The OMB estimates that federal officials have identified $15 billion in annual operating expenditures that could be privatized under Circular A-76, saving $3 billion a year. The President's Private Sector Survey on Cost Control, more commonly known as the Grace Commission after its chairman, J. Peter Grace, makes even grander forecasts. It says the government could save $11.2 billion over three years by privatizing Washington's Dulles and National airports, the government's fleets of vehicles, all military commissary stores, and much of the Coast Guard's work.

The Grace Commission may have gone overboard, but who would have expected airport control towers to go private? The impetus to contract at airports came out of the controllers' strike of 1981, which forced the FAA to shut down 80 towers at small airports. After finding that contractors could run these towers at less than half its own cost of $240,000 a year, the FAA decided to let local authorities contract with private operators for the service, with the FAA putting up the money. The scheme is in effect for about a dozen towers, and the FAA would like to farm out 120 more. Mark A. Jones, director of operations for a Kansas company called Midwest Air Traffic Control Service, says he can run a tower with fewer people than the FAA and pay controllers $16,000 to $18,000 a year compared with the typical FAA pay of $24,000 to $31,000. The FAA says the contract towers have an excellent safety record.

The idea of privately financing public works may seem bizarre, but look how it worked for Chandler, Arizona. Chandler lies in what is becoming known as Silicon Desert, and its population grew from 30,000 in 1980 to 60,000 today. Back in 1982, Chandler realized it would need another wastewater treatment plant by 1985. Without the new plant, Motorola, Intel, and other prime industrial catches with facilities in Chandler would have had to go elsewhere to expand. But Chandler learned that it wouldn't become eligible for a federal grant before the late 1980s. In 1983 Parsons Corp. was willing to take the risk of borrowing with a variable-rate tax-exempt industrial bond, which turned out to be cheaper than any financing Chandler could arrange. Parsons figured it could finish by the end of 1985 and is meeting the deadline. Chandler's sewage fees will go up less than half as much as they would have with a city-built plant.

THE SQUEEZE of having to uncrowd jails quickly while cutting budgets has forced federal and state officials to look with favor on companies that will finance, design, build, and run jails. The Nashville-based Corrections Corp. of America operates five facilities, including detention centers built for the Immigration and Naturalization Service in Houston and Laredo, Texas. At Houston in 1984, the company charged the INS $23.84 a day per detainee, compared with the U.S. average of $26.45 a day it costs the INS to run its own facilities—and Correction Corp.'s figure includes capital costs, while the INS's covers only operating costs. The company completed the Houston center more than a year ago; had the INS built it, cumbersome review and approval procedures would have delayed completion until 1986.

Turning prisoners over to profit-seeking companies bothers many officials. Another new company in this field, Buckingham Security Ltd. of Lewisburg, Pennsylvania, has bought the land to build a $25-million maximum-security prison in North Sewickley Township, Pennsylvania. But the state will make no commitment to turn prisoners over to Buckingham until a lot of questions are answered. Who chases escapees? Who is liable for the prisoners when they are in jail or being transported? A recent conference of governors in Washington suggested that "states may wish to explore the option" of contracting prisons but should do so "with great care and forethought."

The limits of how much of its functions government can pass to profit-seeking companies aren't visible yet. Most authorities would balk at turning police and fire departments over to the private sector, yet Scottsdale, Arizona, has an excellent for-profit fire department. It grew out of a private fire-protection service that existed before the town was incorporated. Rural/Metro Corp.'s $2.3-million contract with Scottsdale averages out to $20 per capita per year, compared with an average of $50 for public fire departments in similar cities. Scottsdale's fire insurance rates, the best measure of the firemen's effectiveness, are average.

Even where no policy to contract services exists, a kind of privatization may occur. In a sense the country's police are being privatized. Because Americans feel the need for greater protection, the number of private guards has grown much faster since 1970 than the number of publicly sworn law enforcement officers. The U.S. has about 1.1 million guards, compared with 580,000 police officers. The mail is also being privatized as users grow fed up with the plodding U.S. Postal Service and turn to more efficient and reliable commercial couriers, such as Federal Express and Airborne Freight.

In theory, since the public sector doesn't have to make a profit or pay taxes and can generally borrow money more cheaply than the rest of us, government should be able to underbid the private sector. But it doesn't work that way. The bracing winds of competition more than make up for the built-in advantages of government.

City-States: *Laboratories of the 1980s*

David Morris

DAVID MORRIS, director of the Institute for Local Self-Reliance, is an expert on urban development. He is the author of *Neighborhood Power: The New Localism* (Beacon Press) and *Self-Reliant Cities: Energy and the Transformation of Urban America* (Sierra Club Books).

The signs are there, harbingers of a new way of thinking. From the hills of Seattle to the arid flatlands of Davis, from the industrial city of Hartford to the university town of Madison, cities are beginning to redefine their role in our society. Long viewed as little more than real estate developers and social welfare dispensers, the municipal corporation is asserting the more important function of overall planning and development. Buffeted by natural resource crises beyond their control, cities are encouraging local sources of energy, food, and raw materials. Burdened by deteriorating physical plants, cities are designing new, less expensive, and more efficient life-support systems. Vulnerable to branch plant closings, cities are beginning to favor development that comes from within, that relies on hundreds of small businesses rather than one or two large factories.

The city is becoming an ecological nation. As such, the city maximizes the long-term value of its finite piece of land by creating elegant, biologically based systems. Local self-reliance is the goal. The term "local self-reliance" is defined in various ways by different disciplines. To the ecologist, local self-reliance means "closed loop systems" where the wastes of one process become the raw materials of another. To the economist, local self-reliance means capturing for the benefit of the local community the greatest amount of "value added" to the original raw material through processing and marketing. Local self-reliance, to biologist Russell Anderson, is "a type of development which stimulates the ability to satisfy needs locally." It is "the capacity for self-sufficiency, but not self-sufficiency itself. Self-reliance represents a new balance, not a new absolute."

Consider the garbage we dispose of each day. Garbage is nothing more than mixed raw materials. Once separated from the rest of the waste stream, the individual materials have a value. The self-reliant city captures as much of this additional value as possible for the local economy.

The self-reliant city views itself as a nation. It analyzes the flow of capital within its borders and evaluates its "balance of payments." It recycles money much as it recycles goods. Businesses are evaluated not only for the services or products they offer but for the way they affect the local economy. "Stop the Leakages" has become a rallying cry for those demanding local self-reliance. Whether the leakages are raw materials dumped into landfills, or branch stores that take the majority of their earnings out of the community, or retired people who can't find places to offer their time and skills, the result is the same—the loss of valuable resources.

This new way of thinking about cities defies traditional political classifications. It is ideologically neither right nor left. To John McKnight of Northwestern University, the liberal sees everyone as a potential client; the conservative sees everyone as a potential consumer. The liberal thinks people want services; the conservative believes we want commodities. Each agrees that the individual citizen is not the actor but the acted upon. Those encouraging local self-reliance see the individual as a producer of wealth and an active participant in the political process of resource management. Production rather than consumption is the explicit priority for self-reliant cities.

Self-reliant cities minimize government but not necessarily governance. Practically, as communities take an active role in promoting local self-reliance, the traditional distinction between public and private sectors begins to blur. A good example is

From *Environment*, July/August 1983, pp. 12-20, 36-42, a publication of the Helen Dwight Reid Educational Foundation.

is assuming an aggressive and innovative role.

The New Localism

Local self-reliance is an inward-looking process. But its dynamic may have a major effect on our national economy. By viewing themselves as nations, cities emphasize spatial considerations that undermine one of the principal tenets of our Constitution—the continental free-trade zone. The unencumbered mobility of goods, capital, and people across state and city boundaries was for many of the founding fathers the chief purpose of the Constitution. By the late nineteenth century, the Supreme Court was striking down almost any local restriction on commerce as unconstitutional.

Yet, a century later, localities are being given considerable authority to influence the ease with which we transport people, goods, and capital across political jurisdictions.[1] Cities have been granted the right to limit population growth, in effect limiting people's right to move. Cities enact returnable bottle bills, in effect prohibiting corporations from selling products in certain kinds of containers within the city's political jurisdiction. Cities require public employees to live within city limits. Cities favor local businesses over those outside the city.

In an age of scarce resources the issue of spatial bias will not disappear. As we become more aware of resource flows, the justification of "place" as the basis for decision making increases. For example, most states require municipal corporations to purchase products at the lowest possible price. Cities may not pay more for a product simply because it is produced locally. These laws were enacted to simplify contracting procedures and to reduce the possibility of corruption. But what happens when the advantages of local production become significant?

Take the case of Carbondale, Illinois: It owns 110 vehicles and now imports 100 percent of its fuel. The

To the ecologist, local self-reliance means "closed loop systems," where the wastes of one process become the raw materials of another.

Oceanside, a rapidly growing, conservative Republican city in southern California with a significant number of retired people. Its citizens believe the community should take an active role in promoting the general welfare. With rising energy prices cutting into fixed incomes, the city council investigated the potential for using solar energy to lower hot water bills.

Because traditional financial institutions would not provide adequate financing for people to pursue this option, the city council unanimously approved a program whereby homeowners lease solar hot water systems directly from private firms. The city helps to market the systems, guarantees them, collects lease payments, and reduces red tape associated with permits, building code applications, and the like. To participate in the program, the private firm must post performance bonds, agree to a consumer complaint process, and charge less than a maximum monthly amount. Within 60 days of the commencement of the program, more than $15 million had been committed by private firms for investment in this city of 80,000 people. Thus, the city is not only capturing the value of an indigenous resource—the sun—but it

4. URBAN SOCIAL POLICIES

Table 1.

CITIES, BY POPULATION SIZE: 1960 TO 1977 (covers incorporated places of 10,000 population or more)

POPULATION SIZE*	NUMBER OF CITIES			POPULATION (mil.)			PERCENT OF TOTAL		
	1960	1970	1977	1960	1970	1977	1960	1970	1977
Total.................	1,654	2,031	2,177	91.0	107.7	100.0	100.0	100.0	
1,000,000 or more.........	5	6	6	17.5	18.9	17.7	19.2	17.5	15.8
500,000–1,000,000.......	16	20	17	11.1	13.1	11.2	12.2	12.2	10.0
250,000–500,000........	30	31	33	10.8	10.7	11.5	11.8	9.9	10.3
100,000–250,000........	79	99	104	11.4	14.1	16.1	12.5	13.1	14.4
50,000–100,000.........	180	234	249	12.5	16.3	17.4	13.7	15.0	15.6
25,000–50,000..........	366	474	536	12.7	16.4	18.6	14.0	15.2	16.6
10,000–25,000..........	978	1,167	1,232	15.1	18.2	19.3	16.5	16.9	17.3

* America is a nation of cities, but not large cities. Less than 10 percent of the total population lives in the handful of cities with more than one million people. More than 30 percent live in the 800 municipalities that are home to between 25,000 and 100,000 people.

SOURCE: U.S. Bureau of the Census, *Census of Population: 1970*, vol. I, part A, and *Current Population Reports*, series P-25, Nos. 814-863.

vehicles could, at minimal expense, be converted to operate totally on alcohol. The alcohol could be produced locally from local waste products. Even if the price of the local alcohol were slightly higher than that of imported gasoline, the benefits to the local economy and, as a result, to the city through higher tax revenues would offset the price difference.

The new localism involves social as well as economic issues. To protect its citizens from possible runaway mutations, Cambridge, Massachusetts, imposed a 6-month moratorium on research into recombinant DNA within its jurisdiction, affecting research at MIT and Harvard. The city of Morton Grove, Illinois, banned handguns. New York City banned the transportation of nuclear waste across its boundaries; hundreds of cities have voted in favor of a nuclear weapons freeze.

A New Context

The new activism stems in part from a new generation, but mainly from a new context. In the 1970s, American cities had to deal with an unusually varied series of hard knocks. A prolonged coal strike

forced many West Virginia, Pennsylvania, and Ohio cities to deal with social tensions and even violence. Oil disruptions forced farm communities to seek alternative sources for diesel fuel, and New England and midwestern towns to develop programs to keep their elderly from freezing. The oil and coal developments in the western states spawned boom towns, sorely burdening the planning capabilities of localities. The collapse of the domestic automobile industry brought unemployment rates above 35 percent in some car-based cities. Floods, tornadoes, hazardous waste dumps, carcinogenic water supplies, the worst recession in 40 years, the harshest winter in modern times are only some of the problems cities have had to deal with in recent years.

Another factor prompting a more entrepreneurial attitude on the part of cities is the increasing cost of maintaining municipal life-support systems. Simply stated, these systems were built for a different era. They are based on nineteenth-century technologies. The systems that provide us pure drinking water, safe and fast transportation, waste disposal, energy, heat, and power have become prohibitively expensive. The subway

system currently under construction in the Washington, D.C. area will cost $2,500 for each man, woman, and child in the metropolitan area. The five nuclear power plants owned by more than 40 municipalities in the state of Washington will cost more than $6,000 per household when, if ever, they are completed. A proposed tunnel under Chicago to reduce the backup of sewage into neighborhood basements will cost $1,000 for every resident.

Built a century ago, our industrial cities are wearing out. Two out of every five bridges are in need of major rehabilitation or replacement. Street potholes have become a major financial drain on public as well as private pocketbooks. The problem promises to get worse. The 756 urban areas with populations over 50,000 will have to spend up to $100 billion over the next two decades just to maintain their water systems.

Newer cities are not immune to these problems. Dallas must raise some $700 million for water and sewage treatment facilities over the next decade and more than $109 million to repair deteriorating streets. Booming Denver has begun informally delaying its repair and maintenance schedules.

More Problems, Less Money

All these factors combine to plague cities just as another combination of factors reduces their financial ability to respond. Congress has limited the ability of cities to issue tax-exempt bonds to finance certain types of development. Cities are borrowing money at such a rate that tax-exempt interest rates have risen almost even with taxable interest rates. Local and state tax revolts have limited property tax revenues, a major source of revenue to localities. At the same time, the "new federalism" of the Republican administration has sharply reduced federal grants to localities. As proposed, federal expenditures for non-welfare programs will be cut by more than 50 percent by 1985 and welfare programs will be cut 25 percent. The cost is to effective local government.

Even as the physical underpinnings of our cities deteriorate, the federal government is cutting public works money. This policy is particularly painful because the portion of federal aid for state and local public works had increased from 10 percent to 40 percent between 1957 and 1980. After having become accustomed (some would say addicted) to federal leadership, many cities are being asked to go cold turkey.

Yet, this reduced ability to raise local revenues is occurring as ever more responsibility is delegated to local governments. For example, the federal government eliminated direct financial assistance to low-income families to allow them to install energy conservation measures in their homes and apartments. The federal government delegates that responsibility to the local community, but no money accompanies the delegation of responsibility. Federal aid reductions to individuals also add to the burden on city budgets.

In such an era, innovation and ingenuity are the best allies of cities committed to meeting the short- and long-term needs of their constituents. James Madison argued in favor of powerful small towns to encourage experimentation and diversity. If an innovation fails, the damage is minimal and all the other towns can learn from the failure. If an experiment is successful, the lessons of that success can be quickly learned by hundreds of communities.

The very number of America's cities virtually guarantees widespread experimentation. America is a nation of cities, but not large cities (see Table 1). Only eight percent of our population lives in seven cities of 1,000,000 or more. Thirty percent live in the 800 cities that have populations between 25,000 and 100,000. Shunned by the mass media that are headquartered in a handful of cities, these small- and medium-sized cities will be the laboratories of the 1980s.

Energy, Integration, Recycling

The 2,000 percent increase in world crude oil prices between 1970 and 1980 adds to the burden of sore-pressed local economies. It also provides the motivation for a new conceptual model of the city. As gasoline, heating oil, natural gas, and electricity prices soar, transportation becomes an important design consideration. The price of energy makes local self-reliance not only philosophically palatable but also economically viable.

Even as our school textbooks continue to extol the efficiencies of an integrated world economy, the rising cost of long distribution systems encourages us to think again. No longer is it economical to build a house with glue imported from one continent, wood from another, nails from another and fixtures from still another, to heat it with fuel that comes from still another part of the world, and to bring in water and electricity from several hundred miles away.

To illustrate the rising importance of distribution, today it costs twice as much to get food to our tables as it does to grow the food. Integration

rather than separation will become the design criteria of the '80s. Rather than raise a tomato in California and eat it in Boston, we will raise vegetables in Boston in greenhouses warmed by waste heat from nearby factories or buildings. Small-scale steel mills (the industry calls them mini-mills, or even neighborhood mills) already compete with conventional mills 10 times their size because they use locally available scrap metal. Once again, by integrating business and residence we can avoid the need to require a resident who wants a pack of cigarettes, a loaf of bread, or a gallon of milk to drive a two-ton automobile to a regional shopping center.

Energy efficiency also encourages recycling. As the shortages become more pronounced, the marketplace finds recycled materials more attractive. A city of the size of San Francisco, for example, generates about 1,500 tons of solid waste per day. Broken down into component materials, San Francisco disposes of as much aluminum each year as is extracted from a medium-sized bauxite mine, as much copper as a small-sized copper mine and as much paper as is made from a good-sized timber stand. The city itself is a mine. Its waste stream becomes the basis for new industries. If our cities become mines for recycled material, we can expect industries to locate nearby.

Rising energy prices also encourage decentralized energy generation. In an age of political uncertainty, long distribution lines have made our communities vulnerable. Social upheaval in Iran brings gas lines to Toledo. Grand Forks, North Dakota, waits to see whether Canada will cut off its natural gas supply.

Cities have begun to react to this dependence by moving toward energy self-reliance. Oceanside and Davis, California, mandate solar hot water systems for new homes. Springfield, Vermont, expects to complete the construction of a hydroelectric facility that will allow it to export power to the same central utility from which it had been purchasing power for almost 30 years. Burlington, Vermont, gets about 15 percent of its electricity from wood.

Integration again becomes the key design element. Modesto, California, uses the methane generated during the digestion of its sewage to fuel its entire municipal vehicle fleet. Hagerstown, Maryland, uses its sludge to fertilize 500,000 hybrid poplar trees, which, in turn, are converted into fuel and industrial chemicals.

Cities whose bureaucracies have been fragmented now realize that there is a synergy to municipal development. The way it uses the land area, the kinds of economic activities it encourages, and the way it uses natural resources combine to foster the general health of the city. Municipal planning for self-reliance must take into account many factors previously considered outside the province of the municipal corporation.

This new understanding comes as we enter the electronic age. New analytical technologies and low-cost computers give communities a much better understanding of their environment. The new resource maps are dynamic. They track the movement of capital—money—across city borders; analyze the composition of the solid waste stream; check the quality of the air, water, and soil; estimate the costs of new development; identify where buildings are losing heat; and evaluate the skill levels of the unemployed. The inward orientation of local self-reliance is complemented by the outward orientation of new communications systems. New technologies allow communities to horizontally communicate with others, to share information outside the mass media networks.

Thus, the global village becomes a complementary metaphor to the globe of villages. Cities become enmeshed in a global network of information while they use modern science to convert sunlight, plant matter, and abundant locally available materials into useful products. Long-distance trade in materials declines, while trade in information, culture, and knowledge rises. Elec-

Most jobs in cities come from the start-up of new firms and the expansion of existing small businesses, not by plant relocations by big corporations.

tronic trade replaces molecular trade.

Prevention Minimizes Treatment

The new city-states must rebuild an infrastructure that is more compatible with resource limitations. Future city builders will have many fewer natural and financial resources to build the systems that deliver pure water, remove sewage and garbage, bring in fuels and electricity, and allow for the transport of goods and people. Today's city designers must develop more elegant systems (see box on page 18) that are durable, yet flexible, in the light of changing resources.

While Chicago attempts to attract billions of dollars in federal aid to build gigantic tunnels under the city to divert rainfall that·clogs up sewer systems, a neighborhood-based organization proposes a simpler, prevention-based solution. The Center

for Neighborhood Technology (CNT) concludes that the central problem is that, as a result of paving over most of the urban land, almost all rainfall enters the sewer system at the same time. The solution is to slow down the raindrop before it aggregates. CNT recommends detaching rooftop drainpipes and putting splash blocks on the ground. It argues that delaying a raindrop is cheaper and easier than harnessing a flood.

The principle of prevention works as well in the energy sector. In 1977, the Seattle City Council voted to buy a 10 percent share in two nuclear reactors to meet future electrical demand. A citizens' organization sued the city, claiming it had not looked at alternatives to new generating capacity. The city council agreed to re-examine its initial decision. A consultant was hired. Six months later, with the Seattle 1990 report before them, the city council reversed its vote and decided instead to aggressively encourage energy conservation. They found that saving a kilowatt was less than half as expensive as generating an additional kilowatt. Increasing efficiency prevents the need for expenditures for new capacity.

A Model Development

One model of the future city might be Village Homes, a 70-acre, 200-unit development in Davis, California. The developer, Michael Corbett, stressed prevention. To reduce automobile traffic, each street ends in a cul-de-sac. The streets are narrow, half the conventional 45-foot width. Eight homes form a cluster. Homeowners are encouraged to fence their property facing the street, leaving the yards open to a narrow common strip between the two rows of lots.

A natural drainage system allows the soil to retain water after a storm and reduces the cost of sewers. Because the water does not drop below ground level, pumping stations are not required. Blocks in surface drainage systems merely raise the water level instead of stopping the flow. They are easily spotted and removed. "Each winter I get a pleasant feeling of warmth and righteousness around the Christmas season," Corbett notes contentedly. "As storm drains back up and pumps fail in other parts of Davis, Village Homes is beautiful with its multitude of little streams and waterfalls."

Village Homes made believers out of private developers because its design saves money. Natural drainage systems save $800 per building site. Narrow streets reduce construction costs and open up more land for development.

It was more difficult to convince city departments. The city engineer disapproved natural drainage systems, the fire department disapproved narrow streets, the policy department disapproved cul-de-sacs. Over departmental objections, the city planning commission and city council approved the project, responding to pressures from a political constituency mobilized in large part by graduate students of ecology at the University of California. On a citywide scale, prevention can secure huge savings.

The dynamics of prevention are quite different from those of treatment systems. The more we prevent, the smaller the system, the less the capital expense, the greater the role for para-professionals, and the greater the citizen's involvement. Prevention systems, whether they be in health or other social service areas, could preclude the kind of soaring costs seen in hospital treatment. Indeed, neighborhood and family cohesion might dramatically reduce one of our growing problems—mental illness. Eric Fromm once expressed confidence that an investigation would uncover a direct correlation between the disappearance of the neighborhood bar and the rise of psychiatrists.

The criminal justice system also illustrates the validity of these principles. The concept of neighborhood team police has proven successful. The officers are assigned exclusively to a specific neighborhood in which they also may live. They patrol by foot and get to know the community and its residents. In Dayton, Ohio, the neighborhood itself has become the police force. Working with the regular police, they intervene in family quarrels and handle 80 percent of the complaints. Halfway houses have proven their worth compared to prisons. The cost of keeping one teenager in prison is now around $15,000 a year, and the incidence of recidivism is high. Halfway houses cost less than half as much, and the recidivism rate is much lower.

Neighborhood Power

The principles of prevention rather than treatment, and of integration rather than separation, lead to a third basic principle of self-reliance—subsidiarity. As Daniel Patrick Moynihan describes it, "Th(e) principle is that you should never assign to a large entity what can be done by a smaller one. What the family can do, the community shouldn't do. What the community can do, the states shouldn't do—and what the states can do, the federal government shouldn't do."

The principle of subsidiarity reinforces the principle of integration. Both reduce the most costly characteristic of urban life, its tendency toward separation. Both emphasize a sense of place. Both tend to move us toward a city comprised of neighborhoods where people can fulfill most of their basic social and economic needs. By doing so, they lessen our dependence on travel, especially travel by automobile.

Neighborhood authority stems from pedestrian power. Its advantages to the city as a whole, when weighed against the automobile, are varied and significant. Currently at least one-third of the typical city's land area is devoted to the automobile. In Los Angeles more than half the city's entire surface is devoted to vehicles. That land area cannot be developed, and it is often tax-exempt. The cost of building and maintaining roads has become a major part of local capital budgets. By paving over large sections of the city, rainfall quickly overloads sewage systems. Vehicle exhausts and rubber from tires represent some of traffic's residues. They pollute the air and run off the streets to complicate the processing of sewage.

Neighborhoods constitute a source of strength only if they are cohesive. Cohesion comes in part from stability. Some cities have used their political power to stabilize neighborhoods by protecting their citizens from the upheaval caused by absentee ownership of housing and real estate. Once again, a sense of place is given precedence over the mobility of capital. Since the majority of most city residents are tenants, this attitude leads the municipal corporation to protect the stability of neighborhoods by imposing restrictions on rent increases or evictions.

The self-confidence and aggressiveness of the municipal corporation on behalf of its citizens have set a precedent for the exciting period of experimentation that will follow in the 1980s. A new relationship between levels of government is evolving. In addition, the issue of "development for whom" and the relationship between the public and private sectors are now being examined.

The Cost of Growth

During the post-World War II era cities were addicted to growth. Yet they found that growth brings costs as well as benefits. Environmental legislation forced cities to estimate the impact of growth. Increasingly sophisticated computer models permitted cities to monitor the flow of resources through their borders. What they found was profoundly disquieting.

For example, one suburb of San Francisco, Fairfield, found to its surprise and dismay that total tax revenues from a proposed new subdivision would pay only half of the required new police services and nothing for other services. A 1974 study of Madison, Wisconsin, estimated the cost of a new acre of development was $16,500 for installing sanitary sewers, storm drainage, water mains, and local streets. The figure did not include the acre's prorated share of the cost of new schools, fire stations, arterial streets, wells, landfills, etc.[2]

As cities gained sophistication in the planning process they began to reevaluate the favored practice of courting big corporations to locate branch plants in their community. The mating dance between cities and giant corporations, they discovered, had become too one-sided. One business magazine described the situation as a "rising spiral of government subsidies as companies play off city against city and state against state for the most advantageous terms."[3] Atlanta advertises its wares on Cleveland television programs and has opened an industry-recruitment office in New York. In tiny Bossier City, Louisiana, the chamber of commerce encourages school children to write more than 900 letters to corporate executives telling them of the city's need for jobs, and its abun-

Only eight percent of our population lives in seven cities of one million or more. Thirty percent live in the 800 cities that have populations between 25,000 and 100,000.

dance of assets, such as clean air.[4]

Such self-promotional activities constitute the benign side of the competition between cities for corporate investment. Cities have often used their right to seize land to put together a site large enough to lure a corporation and then, at its own expense, to install the physical infrastructure necessary to service the industry, and finally, borrow money, while writing off local taxes for 10 or 20 years as a further enticement. When the stakes were high, a growing number of local officals were willing to exercise the full authority of the municipal corporation to attract large plants, even at the cost of destroying existing communities.

One of the best examples occurred when General Motors announced it would build plants in cities in Kansas, Oklahoma, and Michigan only if the local governments met its demands. Cities that failed to accommodate GM, the third largest private corporation in the world, were informed they would not be considered. Several

cities, including Detroit, agreed to all conditions. According to GM, its plant there would generate 6,000 jobs; in return, GM wanted the city to clear a 465-acre site.

Unfortunately, the 465-acre site was home to many people—Poletown, as it was called, was predominantly Polish and had strong social cohesion. When 90 percent of the neighborhood owners refused to sell, Detroit used a recently enacted Michigan statute called the "quick take" law that allowed a city to condemn private property for public purposes and take title within 90 days, whether or not the value of the property for compensation purposes had been agreed on. In March 1981, the Michigan Supreme Court ruled in favor of the city and its Economic Development Corporation. The court ruled that the city was exercising its powers of eminent domain for a public purpose, the creation of "programs to alleviate and prevent conditions of unemployment." However, in this instance, in order to create a maximum of 6,000 jobs, the city of Detroit razed 1,300 homes, 16 churches, and 143 businesses, destroying an entire cohesive community.

Ironically, attracting outside investment may well increase economic instability. Absentee-owned businesses tend not to be good neighbors. They cut back employment during down cycles and recessions more than locally based companies, and they are less likely to purchase local services and products, such as legal assistance, financial consulting, capital borrowing, and factor inputs.

Cities are losing control over their capital as they lose control over their jobs and factories. In the late 1970s, an older ethnic neighborhood in Chicago discovered that its residents had deposited $33 million in a local savings and loan association but had received back only $120,000 in loans. That discovery led to the enactment of a federal law requiring financial institutions to invest a significant amount of their locally generated deposits in a local area. But no legislation could stop the hemorrhage of capital that accompanies the advent of electronic banking and money market funds. Not only neighborhoods within larger cities, but entire small- and medium-sized cities are now witnessing the largest outflow of local dollars in history. To individual residents and local financial institutions, the money market fund offered security and a higher interest rate. But the price was a lack of funds lendable to local residents and businesses.

The Municipal Corporation

Caught in a vicious cycle, cities end up competing for fewer and fewer companies. In 1971, there were 12.4 million business enterprises of all sizes and kinds in America, including 3.3 million farms. Of that 12.4 million, over half (6.4 million) had gross sales of less than $10,000. Another 3.4 million failed to reach $50,000 in sales, and still another one

million had $100,000 in yearly sales. Thus, nearly 11 million of the nation's 12.4 million firms, or 87.2 percent, had sales of less than $100,000 in that year.[5]

On the other hand, less than one percent of the service firms had multistore operations. Of the 275,000 manufacturing companies in the United States, about 10 percent had more than 99 employees.[6] Three companies sold 80 percent of the cold breakfast cereal in 1975. Three companies sold 80 percent of the home insulation in that year. Four sold 70 percent of the dairy products. One sold 90 percent of the canned soups.[7] Fewer than 30 giants owned over 20 percent of the cropland. Eight oil companies controlled 64 percent of proven oil reserves, 44 percent of uranium reserves, 40 percent of coal under private lease, and 40 percent of copper deposits.[8]

Yet it turns out that small businesses, not the giant corporations, are the backbone of local economies. A massive study of 5.6 million firms (representing 82 percent of the nation's private jobs) was conducted by David Birch. He tracked these firms over a seven-year period, from 1971 to 1978, and concluded that the country's biggest job producer was small firms. Two-thirds of all new jobs were created in companies employing fewer than 20 people. The top 1,000 firms on the *Fortune* list generated only 75,000 jobs, or just a little more than 1 percent of all new jobs created between 1970 and 1976.[9] Birch found that most jobs came from the start-up of new firms and the expansion of existing small businesses, destroying the myth that economic development is created by plant relocations and expansion by big corporations.

These figures gave an ironic twist to the frenzied competition among cities for giant plant locations. Cities, built on a foundation of thousands of small businesses, often found themselves in the position of forcing out small firms in order to make room for a branch of a larger corporation.

By the end of the 1970s, cities were

beginning to understand the nature of their dilemma. They began to directly involve themselves in economic developments. In 1974 the Housing and Community Development Act provided Community Development Block Grants (CDBG), lump sum payments to cities that enabled them to coordinate community development and economic development planning. The 1977 amendments to this act expanded the economic development activities permitted under the CDBG program.

Increased funds and authority gave rise to dozens of local economic development corporations, with the power to acquire land, lease land, construct buildings, and provide short- and long-term financing to businesses. Cities directly control vast human, physical, and financial resources. There are at least seven counties or cities in California that have over $100 million in public pension funds. The city of Washington, D.C., owns over 4,000 buildings and hundreds of acres of land.

Cities have an important lever in encouraging local small business development: government purchasing. The dollar volume of state and local government purchasing has grown dramatically in the past decade, and it now exceeds that of the federal government.

This abundance of resources is now combined with expanded municipal authority. The judicial system has accepted the right of cities to favor local commerce. Detroit and Livermore, California, have purchasing provisions awarding contracts to local suppliers even if they bid up to 5 percent higher. The state legislature in Maine mandates that state institutions such as penal institutions, vocational and technical schools, and state hospitals purchase food produced locally, even if it is 5 percent higher in price. In Washington, D.C., the city government is required to purchase 25 percent of all its goods and services from local minority-owned firms.

Cities are also wanting to leverage their own government bank accounts to benefit the local economy. Until the 1970s, even large cities that deposited hundreds of millions of dollars in local banks imposed no conditions on these deposits. In many cases, the cities earned little interest and the vast majority of the money was loaned outside of the community. By 1982, a number of cities, such as the District of Columbia and Santa Monica, required financial institutions in which they deposited their money to re-invest this money in local mortgages or consumer loans.

The municipal budget is only a small part of the powers the municipal corporation can exercise on behalf of its citizens. The bonding capacity of cities is often much larger than their budgets, giving them the ability to develop long-term construction projects and provide low-interest loans for economic development purposes. In fact, between 1970 and 1978 the dollar volume of new debt for municipalities was about double the total issuance of all corporate debt.

Sometimes the city itself operates a business. Since the turn of the century, cities have owned and operated energy, water, sewage, and transportation utilities. Cities have been involved in other business enterprises, but the courts have not always upheld the city's determination of what constituted a "public purpose."[10] However, the new generation of city leaders tends to believe less in direct municipal ownership than they do in the city as an overall economic planner, the mechanism that establishes the rules for private investment and channels resources into those areas of the local economy that would most effectively benefit large segments of the local population.

Expanding Authority

Formerly little more than a handmaiden to private real estate developers, the municipal corporation began to exercise its authority to encourage the best social use of its land, not just the use that would generate the greatest private profit. This interplay of the private and public sector is nowhere more evident than in the land-use restrictions that state and local governments have imposed on private development.

A most revealing set of restrictions is the Vermont Land Use and Development Law enacted in 1970. Nine district environmental councils oversee a population about the size of a small city. The Chittenden Environmental Council denied a permit to a regional shopping mall containing 80 stores and 44,000 square feet of commercial space, in the town of Williston. The reason was that the stores would reduce tax revenues of the city of Burlington, causing the state to compensate it for some of the lost tax revenues that would have supported the educational system. This development was denied because it would draw away commerce from neighboring towns, reducing the tax base for the local government.

In short, the municipal corporation is an evolving creature. Once viewed as nothing more than a "mere tenant," cities now possess immense economic and political authority. They are still subordinate to the state legislatures. But in an increasing number of states, the burden of proof that they can exercise power is no longer on the cities, but on the states to prove they can't.[11]

Because of complex legal rulings, municipal authority has not been expanding linearly. Recent judicial decisions indicate a reluctance to give the municipal corporation unlimited powers. In January 1982, the U.S. Supreme Court overruled a lower court, deciding that the city of Boulder, Colorado, had violated anti-trust statutes in a case involving a privately owned cable T.V. company.

Boulder argued that cities with home-rule governments sanctioned by state legislatures automatically shared that immunity. The Supreme Court said no. Justice Brennan, writing the 5–3 majority opinion, said that the state anti-trust exemption embodies

the federalism principle that the states possess a significant measure of sover-

eignty under our Constitution. But this principle contains its own limitation. Ours is a 'dual system of government' which has no place for sovereign cities. . . .

A state could delegate its anti-trust exemption to localities but it could not be assumed through a generalized grant of home-rule authority.

The thrust of the new federalism as conceived by the Republican administration will still further complicate the issue of local authority. Conservatives appear ambivalent as to whether they prefer to delegate authority to lower levels of government or wield the federal authority to curb the exercise of power at any level.

The Department of Transportation attempted to preempt the authority of New York City to regulate the transport of radioactive waste through its jurisdiction. The courts ruled in favor of New York. The White House Commission on Housing proposed federal regulations cutting off federal housing assistance to cities that institute rent controls. The Senate almost enacted a law prohibiting cities from regulating cable television systems. At the last moment, the law was sent back to committee for further deliberations.

Where the administration genuinely wants to delegate authority, the power is to be given to the states, not the cities. That attitude is consistent with the Constitution, which does not mention cities at all. But it is inconsistent with the current demographic realities.

The administration argues, and the governors agree, that state governments in the last 20 years have become modern and sophisticated. No longer the rotten borough of the American political system, they now have the capability to meet the needs of the time. Moreover, the one-man/one-vote judicial decision of the 1960s eliminated the lopsided, rural state-legislative majorities in urbanized states.

Still, urban dwellers are worried that such a transfer of power back to the states would be harmful to their interests. The fear is especially strong in smaller cities, where there has never been the political clout or lobbying strength of the larger municipalities. Rather than receiving direct federal aid, as has been the case since the mid-1970s, under the new federalism, these cities could compete with one another and with more rural communities for aid from state governments.

Overlapping the issue of the prerogatives of each level of government is the issue of the relationship between the private corporation and the public corporation. In ancient Greece a citizen was considered a shareholder rather than a taxpayer. At the beginnings of this nation no distinction at all was made between a business and a city. But by the end of the nineteenth century, the pendulum had swung to the other extreme: cities had almost no right to regulate or operate private businesses. Today the courts and the country are trying to find a reasonable path between these two poles.

This philosophical issue becomes all the more difficult to resolve because since World War II another form of corporation—the public authority—has grown to prominence. Begun by Franklin Roosevelt as a principal tool for implementing his massive public-works programs, public authorities are not tiny parts of the political system; they are central to it. They are the largest category of borrowers in the tax-exempt bond market, raising more money for capital investment than all state or municipal governments. Thus, the power of the municipal corporation is not absolute. But the analytical tools and technologies at its disposal are greater than ever before in history.

As we enter the 1980s, one central issue remains. How far can our cities go toward achieving self-reliance? Can we realistically conceive of the city as a nation, producing a significant amount of its goods and services?

The City as Nation

The city has never been viewed as a producer of basic wealth. Mining and extraction are considered outside the capacity of urban areas. Even manufacturing is considered to need so much land area and to serve such large markets that it must locate outside cities. The urban community generally is seen as the site of finance, commerce, and service industries. The self-reliant city changes this definition. The city becomes a *producer* of basic wealth and a *processor* of raw materials as well as a *site* of commerce and trade.

One of the most important problems will be to identify new sources of energy to heat our buildings, power our machines, and fuel our vehicles. In moving toward an energy-efficient community, cities can also rely on new technologies. Infrared cameras can locate building heat losses. Lights are now available that turn themselves off automatically when people leave the room and adjust their intensity levels to the amount of sunlight coming in the windows.

Existing buildings can save up to 80 percent of their energy with investments that repay themselves in fewer than ten years. Today's automobiles use 250 gallons of gasoline a year compared to the 1,000 gallons a year used by those purchased a decade before. Thus, the city seeking self-reliance can reduce its imported energy simply by making its physical stock more efficient.

Moreover, new technologies now make it feasible for the city to become an energy producer. For example, buildings can now tap into the warmth of the soil, ground water, air, or sun around them, and a municipality can tap into small deposits of natural gas around them.

Some startling breakthroughs have also taken place in electrical generation. Next to the car, the power plant has been the symbol of modern America. For a century, the average power plant grew in size. The largest central electric station served 3,000 households in 1900. By 1980, the largest facility under construction would serve 3,000,000 households. As power plants grew larger, they also became more remote. In 1982, the average kilowatt hour travelled 220 miles.

Currently, it takes more than a decade to plan, construct, and begin to operate an electric power plant. Between 1880 and 1970, demand for electricity increased predictably by seven percent a year, doubling every 10 years. But after the price hikes of the 1970s, industry began to develop more efficient electric conversion devices and households began to use electricity more wisely. Demand for electricity is now doubling nationally every 40 years. In some parts of the nation, demand is actually declining. Thus, power plants now coming online that were planned in 1973 are no longer needed. Even as the ability to predict far into the future diminishes, rising interest rates and construction cost overruns increase the financial penalty associated with wrong guesses.

Another implication of rising energy prices is more efficient power plants. Traditionally, more than 70 percent of the fuel burned in central stations is lost as waste heat. Less than a third is delivered as electricity. Today, more and more companies are building power plants that not only generate electricity but also can capture the waste heat for useful purposes. But since the cost of transporting heat long distances is very high, the best location for these cogeneration facilities is near the customer. Thus, the combination of smaller power plants and cogeneration moves generation of electricity back into our communities, reversing a century-long trend.

Rising energy prices also encourage the use of decentralized fuels. Unlike coal, uranium, petroleum and natural gas, renewable fuels such as sunlight, water, plant matter, and wind are located more or less equally around the globe. As conventional fuel prices increase, the economic potential for renewables expands exponentially. For example, only gigantic hydroelectric dams were competitive with diesel generators in the 1950s. But in the 1970s, rising electric prices made smaller rivers economically exploitable. Tens of thousands of backyard streams suddenly took on renewed economic importance and cities that had been founded 200 years before on the shores of fast-flowing rivers for a source of mechanical power began refurbishing their abandoned damsites.

Recognizing the need to encourage decentralized and efficient power plants, the federal government in 1978 enacted the Public Utility Regulatory Policy Act, abolishing the century-old monopoly utilities held over power production. From March 1981 onwards, utilities have had to purchase independently produced power at premium prices. They must allow independent producers to interconnect with the grid system and must not place any undue burden on these producers. Although utilities have often only reluctantly agreed to the tenets of this new law, and law suits blossomed immediately against the authority of the federal government to enact such legislation, there is no mistaking the tenor of these times. The grid system has become a giant, guaranteed market.

In 1920, 4,000 power plants served the nation. In 1980, the same number did so. By 1990, as many as one million power plants will be in operation and by the year 2000 more than four million. These will be tiny plants, but they will represent a considerable political constituency. One of the major tasks of cities will be to develop institutional mechanisms to integrate these new technologies into existing structures.

Solar storage units, rooftop collectors, and another form of solar energy—food production—will require considerable space—a need that appears to be incompatible with the prevailing image of the congested American city. However, the fact is that the average city of more than 100,000 people has a density of fewer than seven people per acre, closer to that of Staten Island than Manhattan—the classic example of an urban area with a density of 140 people per acre. John Jeavons and Michael

Shepard determined, on the basis of three years' growing experience, that a full, balanced diet may eventually be grown on as little as 2,500 square feet per person in a six-month growing season.[12]

To grow food, we need adequate water and fertilizers. The city is a giant nutrient machine, spewing out organic and human wastes that can be used as fertilizers. In fact, municipal composting operations are increasingly commonplace around the country.[13] It is quite possible that cities would want to use the land surrounding the city as a giant greenbelt, much as Davis, California, and a number of other cities are planning. Given cooperation among metropolitan authorities, or annexation power by the municipality, the land area involved and, therefore, production potential could be greatly extended.

What other resources are available to the city? Our schools should be able to contribute greatly to our community. A student can learn trigonometry while sizing a solar collector as well as by doing abstract exercises in the back of a textbook. A student can learn chemistry by analyzing soil to be used to raise vegetables, or by analyzing the nutritional content of those vegetables, as well as he or she can by doing lab exercises.

As cities look to retain as much economic value within their borders as possible, they will inevitably turn their attention toward manufacturing and processing. Just as we have had to reconceptualize our cities to see them as mines or power plants, so we too must change our thinking about the scale required for efficient manufacturing. The self-reliant city can increasingly make it at home.

The City as Factory

Researchers have recently come to the conclusion that most of the things we need can be manufactured within our larger urban areas. One study found that, if automobiles and petroleum products were excluded from the total, 58 percent of final goods consumption, by value, of a

population of one million could be produced locally in small plants. Sixteen percent of the consumption needs could be produced by plants for a market population of 200,000.[14] Even the use of very small factories raised production costs only slightly.[15] Since production costs represent only a small fraction of the selling price, such increases could be offset by eliminating middleman profits or reducing transportation expenses. Cities could, through a variety of capital and labor tradeoffs, such as through their taxing or procurement policies, value locally produced items higher than those that are imported.

The idea of effective tradeoffs in manufacturing was proven most dramatically by Ernst Schumacher and his London-based organization, the Intermediate Technology Development Group. In 1972, while visiting Zambia, he discovered a serious economic crisis: the farmers could not get their eggs to market because of a labor strike at the egg carton factory—in the Netherlands. Schumacher subsequently asked the president of the company whether it might be feasible to design a factory to meet only the needs of the small market of Zambia, which required but one million egg cartons a year. The president, speaking from 30 years' experience, answered that his factory was designed to be more efficient, and that if any factory were to produce egg cartons at less than the rate of one million a month, it would have to produce them at a higher cost.

Undaunted, Schumacher set his team to work. Eighteen months later an egg carton manufacturing plant was operational in Zambia. It produced not one million egg cartons a year, but only a third of a million, for there were three distinct egg market areas in the country, and three factories were needed. The plants produced egg cartons at the same unit costs, were more labor intensive than the Netherlands factory, and used local materials. When industrial engineers were asked why they never designed a factory like that before, their answer was "Because no one asked us to."

Localism and Globalism

Local self-reliance is a positive concept. It implies strengthening the local economy, and building self-confidence and skills at the local level. But it can also imply parochialism and rivalry.

Parochialism can be combatted only by a massive dose of information. Currently the mass media tell us what the corporate and national leadership are doing, thinking, and wearing. But cities striving for local self-reliance can provide a basis for a dramatic increase in city-to-city and neighborhood-to-neighborhood information transfer of innovations in this country. Exchanges on an international level might be another result.

Aiding this horizontal flow of information are the extraordinary developments in communications and electronics. We can have a global electronic village as we develop a globe of materially self-reliant villages. The growth of the electronics, computer, and communications industries is based on the ability to get more productivity out of fewer raw materials. The objective is to store more information on a given area. Every two years the semiconductor industry quadruples the amount of memory that can be stored for the same price.

We can ship vastly greater quantities of electrons from one part of the globe to another—along the "magnetic spectrum"[16]—using much less energy. That we could exhaust the potential of the electromagnetic spectrum appears unlikely—it is a constantly renewable highway for transporting information. This aspect of the nature of the resource is crucial, because an energy-efficient society is a knowledge-intensive society.

The discovery that the electromagnetic spectrum is a major source of wealth comes at a propitious time for municipalities; they have the authority to issue franchises for cable televi-sion. A century ago, cities learned of the value of the electricity franchise and slowly gained an ability to design franchises that enhanced the public welfare. The communication franchise is more complex but amenable to the same process.

Already about three dozen municipalities have decided to own their own electronic highways. Conway, Arkansas, a town of 20,000, will not only provide entertainment over its channels but fire and burglar alarms, load management for the municipally owned electric system, banking, and meter reading. It estimates that, over a 15-year period, the municipally owned system will generate almost $10,000 a year more in city revenues than if it were privately owned.

The controversy over cable T.V. and the role of the city in its regulation and ownership is only another of the many resource issues that characterize our era. There will be many hard choices involved in deciding what we will do with our resources. Questions of equity, scale, and environment will arise; yet to decide these issues is, above all, the role of the political process.

Only recently has politics been a process by which we vote for people. Originally, it was a process by which we actively participated in allocating resources. Hundreds of cities still allow their citizens to make decisions directly. As Alexis de Tocqueville wrote, "Town meetings are to liberty what primary schools are to science. They bring it within the people's reach. A nation may establish a free government, but without municipal institutions it cannot have the spirit of liberty."[17]

And, of course, there is the problem of confronting those centralizing forces that are so powerful today. The 1980s will be a period of social turmoil. Those who want to use local self-reliance as an excuse to drop out of society will find it impossible. Although local self-reliance, recycling, small-scale production, solar energy, and preventive rather than treatment systems may make more sense, we have to confront and transform institutions built in another era, when resources were plentiful, growth was the objective, and affluence was a never-ending spiral.

We are cursed with giant central power plants, interlocking directorates between big corporations, big factories, big government, production systems far removed from their markets, bloated bureaucracies that are on the whole unproductive, if not downright destructive, and hierarchical organizational structures that remove the top policy makers from the impact of their decisions. We are cursed but not condemned.

We are at a turning point in history. The opportunity exists to marry local political authority to the advantages of modern technology to make more independent, self-reliant communities. Only at the local level can we design humanly scaled production systems that meet our unique local requirements. We can seize the opportunity and potential that comes from a period of rapid social change, and design a society in which we, and our children, would want to live. So far, to be sure, the positive signs are few. Yet they point the way to a new vision, a new context, and a new way of thinking.

NOTES

1. The courts have been ambivalent about spatially oriented policies. Some municipal bottle bills have been overturned as unfair burdens on interstate commerce. Zoning ordinances that favor small businesses have been overturned as unfair discrimination to large firms. Growth limitation ordinances have in some cases been overturned when the courts concluded that the severity of the action had not been justified by the local conditions.

2. Elizabeth Carswell. **Less Is More** (Madison, Wisc., 1974).

3. **Business Week**, June 21, 1976.

4. **Wall Street Journal**, March 22, 1978.

5. Charles Mueller, testifying in hearings on "The Future of Small Businesses in America," **Report to the Committee on Antitrust, Consumers and Employment of the Committee on Small Business**, U.S. House of Representatives, 95th Congress, 1978.

6. Barry Stein and Mark Hodax, **Competitive Scale in Manufacturing: The Case of Consumer Goods** (Cambridge, Mass.: Center for Community Economic Development, 1977).

7.   Representative Morris Udall, **National Journal**, July 30, 1977.

8.   Jeremy Rifkin and Ted Howard, **Who Shall Play God?** (New York: Dell Publishing Co., 1977), p.105.

9.   David Birch, **The Job Generation Process** (Cambridge, Mass.: MIT Press, 1979).

10.   The Arizona and Oklahoma constitutions specifically grant municipal corporations the right to engage in business. Relatively new undertakings, such as low-rent housing, airports, off-street parking facilities, have gained acceptance as public purposes by the courts. Less often, approval has been given to such commercial undertakings as hotels, restaurants, and liquor stores. Cities in Ohio have been permitted to own a railroad that operates outside municipal limits. Thirty cities own their own cable television systems.

11.   Forty-one states had home rule provisions by 1975, either as part of their constitutions, or by statute. Some, such as Maryland, Alaska, and New York, used language such as is in the Tenth Amendment to the U.S. Constitution. Before home rule, cities could exercise no powers that were not explicitly given them by the state legislatures. Under many home rule provisions, cities can exercise any powers which are not explicitly denied them.

12.   John Jeavons, **1972–1975 Research Report Summary on the Biodynamic French Intensive Method** (Palo Alto: Ecology Action, 1976).

13.   One study of the Omaha-Council Bluffs area in Nebraska found that from sludge alone "more nutrients are available . . . than the average supplied by Nebraska farmers." It concludes, "By the year 2000, with increasing waste volume and rising fertilizer prices, benefits to the region's farmers in terms of supplying crop nutrients could exceed $1 million annually. Roger Blobaum, **The Use of Sewage and Solid Waste in Metropolitan Omaha** (Washington, D.C.: Roger Blobaum and Associates, 1979). Another report concluded that the combined nitrogen disposed of by municipalities in America is greater than the total amount used in nitrogen fertilizers in the early 1970s.

14.   Stein and Hodax, note 6 above.

15.   See, for example, F.M. Scherer, "Economics of Scale and Industrial Concentration, in Harvey J. Goldschmid et al. (eds.), **Industrial Concentration: The New Learning** (Boston: Little, Brown & Co., 1974).

16.   David Morris, **Self-Reliant Cities: Energy and the Transformation of Urban America** (San Francisco: Sierra Club Press, 1982) p. 214.

17.   Alexis De Tocqueville, **Democracy in America** (New York: Washington Square Press, 1968).

Suburban Population Ages, Causing Conflict And Radical Changes

Joann S. Lublin

Staff Reporter of The Wall Street Journal

FALLS CHURCH, Va.—Late on a fall afternoon, a strolling, gray-haired man pauses to gaze at a barking dog on Rosemary Lane, an almost deserted residential street in this prosperous Washington suburb. A nearby sign, bent askew, reads, "Watch for children."

But there are no children to be seen. Thirty of them lived and played on this street in the early 1950s when the neighborhood was fairly new. No more than 10 do today. Instead of one elderly couple with adult children, there now are a dozen.

"Many of us grew older. Our children went on to someplace else. We stayed. We like it here," explains 71-year-old Jessie Thackery. She and her husband raised a family of five in a squat green bungalow that bulges with a lifetime of memories—old photos of youngsters, glass knickknacks, overflowing bookcases and a thrice re-covered couch.

SHARP 10-YEAR INCREASE

Rosemary Lanes exist all over the land. America's suburbs are graying, as many original home-owners reach retirement age and stay put. Their mortgages typically paid off, older suburbanites see few housing alternatives as cheap and attractive, even though they may find their big homes hard to keep up. The 1980 census found that 7.9 million Americans 65 and over lived in suburbia, a one-third increase from 1970. It was the first time they outnumbered their central-city cousins.

The aging of suburbia is causing radical changes in the character and politics of countless bedroom communities. It is leading to school closings, property-tax revolts, and demands for new or expanded housing, transportation and recreation services for the elderly. Few suburbs are prepared to meet the needs of an older population. Subdivisions of single-family homes sprang up like crab grass outside major cities after World War II, and their towns' zoning laws and institutions catered to households with young children.

The demographic shift "will become a state and national issue as communities find they don't have the resources to deal with the problems," predicts John Logan, an associate sociology professor at the State University of New York at Albany. The older suburbs generally have the weakest property-tax bases and the highest tax rates, the oldest housing stock, and the heaviest dependence on recently trimmed federal and state aid for social services.

YOUNG OLD AND OLD OLD

Prof. Logan expects that more suburbs soon will fall into similar straits as their senior citizens' ranks swell and more advance from active "young old" to over 75 years old, the nation's fastest-growing age group. The "old old" homeowners, often limited by frail health and lack of cash, tend to be the least able to fix the roof, mow the grass, and drive or take a bus to the grocery store.

Edmund Becker, 75, still trims his bushes and removes dead ones from the quarter-acre yard around his Falls Church home. His doctor wishes he wouldn't, because of his heart condition. There are few teen-agers in the neighborhood, Mr. Becker complains, "and the ones there are don't want to work."

The elderly also become more susceptible to crime in suburban neighborhoods, where adults with-out children mingle less and may not realize who is a stranger. Yet the "frozen occupancy" or "aging in place" of older suburbanites locks out families with young children by keeping houses off the market and house prices high. Upwardly mobile young couples instead buy newer, less costly homes in the outlying exurbia, tempting inner-city em-ployers to relocate. Some demog-raphers fear that close-in suburbs could turn into unintended retire-ment communities, dominated by limited-income householders living in increasingly run-down homes and sapped of their economic and social vitality.

FALLS CHURCH TAKES ACTION

Any community "has the power to become a Miami Beach with 100% elderly," observes Claudia Passen, the director of housing and human services here. The proportion of Falls Church residents aged 65 and older increased from 5.7% in 1960 to 13.8% in 1980, and two of its three elementary schools have closed fully or partly.

So Falls Church created an Ad Hoc Committee to Attract Families with Young Children. The group has distributed 20,000 leaflets to real-estate agents and local em-ployers that emphasize its "family values" and its school system.

Some suburbs are devising other ways to prevent the decay of older residents' homes and attract younger persons. Hundreds of other communities have changed their zoning so as to permit separate rental units, called "accessory apart-ments," in single-family homes, thus providing the elderly owners with a new source of income. And many communities now arrange home-sharing by unrelated individuals; older homeowners trade unneeded empty rooms for needed mainte-nance and security from young tenants.

The space available is plentiful; 12.2 million owner-occupied homes in the U.S. have one or two persons over 55 occupying five rooms or more, according to Patrick Hare, a community planner for suburban Montgomery County, Md.

Despite crippling emphysema and his wife's death in May 1983, 72-year-old Robert Moore con-tinues to live in his three-bedroom Falls Church rambler. A Washing-ton-metropolitan-area home sharing program that began in Montgomery County, just across the Potomac River, matched the retired English professor with a 23-year-old aspiring writer last June. In exchange for free room rent, the young man cleans house, washes dishes, cuts the grass, empties gutters and takes Mr. Moore to the hospital when he suffers bad emphysema attacks. "It would crowd me (financially) to have to pay somebody to be here" to help, says a grateful Mr. Moore. "I've lived here 30 years and I don't want to move."

Babylon, N.Y., adopted an ac-cessory-apartment ordinance in 1980 after a spurt in foreclosures of homes owned by elderly persons; they were pinched by soaring up-keep and energy costs. The Long Island suburb overcame residents' resistance to the zoning change by arguing, "Would you rather live next door to an abandoned house that would be an eyesore to the com-munity or a two-family house that would be regulated and an asset to the community?" recalls Richard Spirio, Babylon's planning and development commissioner.

Accessory apartments can serve different generations' needs, too. Marjorie Schneider of Weston, Conn., a widow who now is 73 years old, originally put a two-room addi-tion on her home to help care for her aged parents. They are dead now, and last June Mrs. Schneider rented the addition to her 36-year-old son and his bride because they lacked the money to buy a house in that expensive suburb. "I felt guilty about being the only person in all these rooms," she says, "when I knew there were young people who can't afford halfway-decent housing these days."

Some aging suburbanites move to nearby luxury town houses, re-tirement complexes or subsidized apartments. Others move to "con-gregate living" apartment buildings that provide common dining space. Winston Place, a 299-unit congre-gate in a Knoxville, Tenn., suburb, is being marketed primarily to resi-dents of the surrounding neighbor-hoods. "They're going to feel very comfortable living within 10 to 15 minutes of where they've lived for 20 years," says Bernard Schreft, executive vice president of Green-man Group Inc., a real-estate mar-keter in Hollywood, Fla. When completed, Winston Place will fea-ture amenities offered by singles complexes, including tennis, bil-liards, a pool and a greenhouse.

But apartment rents there will range from $750 to $1,500 a month —too much for many older people. Advocates for the elderly contend that suburbs don't provide nearly enough housing alternatives for their less affluent older residents. Waiting lists for subsidized units are five years long in some suburban areas.

Many communities simply lack vacant land to build housing for the elderly. So suburbs of Chicago, Buf-falo and Washington, D.C., are turn-ing closed schools into subsidized senior-citizen housing. The venture can be costly, however. Fairfax County, Va., is spending $475,000 to convert the second floor of a former McLean elementary school into 21 congregate-living apart-ments for low-income and moder-ate-income elderly and handicapped individuals.

One reason for the cost is that laborers must work around child-resistant walls that are very solid and very thick, says Leo Berger, the head of a nonprofit church group managing the project. He steps around ladders and over nails litter-ing a dim hall to point out the exten-sive renovation. Amid the new ceilings, light fixtures, carpets and door, a water fountain remains about the last artifact of an era when school-children roamed the build-ing. Mr. Berger admits, "In many instances, it would have been cheaper to do new construction."

TRANSPORT VOUCHERS

Neighboring Falls Church today is starting a transportation program that could help somewhat. "Fare

Wheels" will provide vouchers worth up to $20 a month for each low-income elderly and handicapped resident. The chits will subsidize trips anywhere any time, using taxis and a variety of specially equipped vehicles. The voucher idea, tried in some cities, has rarely been applied in suburbs, county planners say.

Other suburbs are expanding or reorienting their recreation services to meet older residents' needs. Park planners in Nassau County, N.Y., soon may replace part of a rarely used playground with a miniature golf course for adults. A softball league begun three years ago for those over 65 has eight teams now. "The largest number of our users in our parks are seniors and adults, not children," says Francis Cosgrove, a deputy commissioner of recreation and parks.

Urban planners believe that close-in suburbs increasingly will feel the political muscle of "gray power." They expect older citizens to press for funds for police, fire, ambulance and home-health services—rather than certain long-term investments such as roads.

Intergenerational clashes already occur. In Niskayuna, N.Y., a Schenectady suburb, a retiree-dominated taxpayers' group has led the fight to defeat the school system's budget three times in the last four years. Charles Mongin, the president of the taxpayers' association, explains that a typical pensioner may fear that "my house is paid for but if taxes keep going up, I can't afford to still live in it." To win allies, the school board soon may offer older persons classes, day or night, in crafts, exercise and vocational skills.

Day-care homes have turned into young-old battlegrounds in two Connecticut towns—Hamden, a New Haven suburb, and West Hartford.

MORE CONFLICTS FORESEEN

Experts believe that the pressures and the conflicts posed by a growing phalanx of older suburbanites will persist for a decade or more—because of the elderly's increased longevity and their general reluctance to move.

"We do nothing about the shrubbery, plantings or the gardening; we just don't have the strength anymore," says Eleanor Silverman, a 75-year-old retired economic analyst. She and her husband gaze out a picture window at the expansive, woodsy back lawn of their Bethesda, Md., home, where a fence rots and lawn furniture sits rusting on the patio, unused. The couple paid $22,500 for the three-bedroom house, their first, in 1954. They currently spend less than $350 monthly on housing—for taxes and utilities.

"Where could we go as cheap as this?" asks Mrs. Silverman. "We really plan to stay here until we die."

Urban Futures

The future of urban communities will have a serious impact on the population of the entire world and therefore is a continuing concern of social scientists. The unplanned growth of the urban community so characteristic of the past will most certainly promote ecological disaster. Therefore, it is essential that serious planning for the future take place. Good plans are developed out of clearly stated goals and objectives. In recent years, however, a debate over these goals and objectives has begun.

Ironically, the study of the future has a long history. Philosophers and writers, for example, have already designed utopian communities or described the new world that they envision. In the past twenty years, they have been joined by social scientists, engineers, architects, and others from the physical sciences in an attempt to visualize new ways of intervention to better control the quality of life in urban areas.

The scientific study of human behavior is based upon the assumption that most behavior is both patterned and structured. This allows the social scientist to predict, after thorough study, behaviors that are likely to occur. Among social scientists, there is little or no argument that urbanization will continue to be an important aspect of societies around the world and that the demand for change and adaptation will increase. There is also agreement that problems will emerge out of the urbanization process and an effort should be made to develop policies to solve these problems.

The last section begins with Oscar Niemeyer's essay on the city of the future. This is followed by a series of articles by Lucia Mouat on the future of urban America. She explores such topics as the need for new civic leadership, downtown revitalization, and the future of the urban "rust belt." The promise and problems of suburbia are reviewed by Marilyn Gardner. Neal Pierce, Robert Guskind, and John Gardner examine the economic and political future of urban America. S. Kenneth Howard calls for intergovernmental cooperation, an end to conflictual politics, and the need for fiscal restraint. In conclusion, Laurence Rutter urges state and local governments to adopt a philosophy of "skeptical federalism," and to develop strategies that will promote increased autonomy and institutional flexibility.

Looking Ahead: Challenge Questions

How likely is it that the world in the year 2000 will resemble today's world? Why, or why not?

What can people learn from today's world that will prove helpful in designing the world of the future? Is it inevitable that humankind will make the same mistakes?

What dangers does America face in determining its urban future? Are there signs that these dangers can be avoided?

What steps should local governments take to meet the challenges of the future? Do the cities possess the resources and the will to meet this task?

How has technology altered the character of urban life? What impact will high-tech have on tomorrow's cities?

What factors have contributed to the lack of intimacy and community in urban America? Can this trend be reversed?

Is it possible to build a more just and decent society? If so, how?

Is it inevitable that the cities will be forced to make do with less in the future? If so, what are the short- and long-term consequences?

How must tomorrow's leaders differ, if at all, from today's

leaders? Is there evidence of such new leadership?

Is the future of America's industrial cities salvageable? Have these cities outlived their usefulness?

What can be done, if anything, to revitalize America's downtown areas? Is it possible to attract new business and industry to the central cities?

Is urban America addressing the racial crisis which divides many communities? If not, what should be done?

Will black empowerment enhance the quality of big-city life in the future? Why, or why not?

What stake do the suburbs have in the cities?

Are there signs of a new Renaissance in America's cities? If so, what?

To what extent will the states shape the local future? What role will the federal government play?

What can private citizens do to shape the future of urban society? Is there clear evidence of such interest and resolve?

A city for the year 2000

Photo Paolo Gasparini, Unesco

Unlike Brasilia, created to be an urban area in harmony and contact with nature. São Paulo has experienced rampant growth and virtually all its green spaces have disappeared. Photo shows São Paulo's Coán building, designed by Oscar Niemeyer.

Oscar Niemeyer

OSCAR NIEMEYER, of Brazil, is one of the leading exponents of modern architecture in Latin America, and won a worldwide reputation for his work on Brasilia, the new capital of Brazil. In 1956, the recently elected Brazilian President, Juscelino Kubitschek, asked him to design the government buildings for Brasilia. At Niemeyer's suggestion a nationwide competition was held for the master plan of the city. The competition was won by Niemeyer's former teacher, Lucio Costa.

CITIES have always changed under the impact of progress, technological change, new forms of communication, and human indifference.

In the past, city life was easy; it was more natural, and there was a greater sense of community. Then the little squares where people got together, the markets which brought animation to the narrow streets, and the quiet tree-lined residential districts all disappeared, with the spread of shops and businesses created to satisfy everyday needs.

The development of new means of production and transport, new urban activities, and, above all, the industrial revolution, transformed cities into dynamic metropolises bustling with life but lacking the intimacy which is so indispensable and which was theirs in the past.

Cities have existed for thousands of years... and perhaps the people of Nineveh and Babylon—certainly those of Rome and Alexandria—faced some of the problems which confront the modern city-dweller. But metropolitan centres were then very rare, and they may be considered a

"... it will be a vertical city, one where distances will be reduced, thus fulfilling its principal purpose". Drawing by Oscar Niemeyer.

twentieth-century phenomenon. In his essay *On the Populousness of the Ancient Nations,* the eighteenth-century philosopher David Hume (1711-1776) maintained that no city would ever have more than 700,000 inhabitants. William Pelter was convinced that the maximum population of London would be five million. More realistically, Jules Verne (1828-1905) envisaged cities with a population of up to ten million. But the demographic growth of cities in the modern world was to exceed all these expectations.

Houses for five persons were replaced by apartment blocks for two hundred; cars and pedestrians packed the streets; the population density of urban areas skyrocketed; traffic, noise and even security problems began to preoccupy the city-dweller.

"Urban surgery" drove thoroughfares, viaducts and level crossings through the city fabric, and inevitably left scars, while man, a forgotten and frustrated figure in the anonymous crowds, was stifled by his own lack of foresight.

Old tightly packed city districts were an inviting target for demolition as magnates constructed vast unsightly building complexes which disfigured the landscape with their total indifference towards man and nature.

As the implacably monotonous glass cubes of rationalist architecture rose above the streets, the old cities lost their former unity.

Such is the explanation usually given for the phenomenon of urban growth by those who almost invariably forget the odious social discrimination which it involves. New possibilities have emerged only in those countries where the institution of landed property has been abolished. On the other hand, the same errors continue to be made in all Western cities: the rich have taken them over, while the poor are relegated to wretched quarters on the periphery.

From the "industrial city" project drawn up in 1907 by the French architect and city planner Tony Garnier to the Charter of Athens of 1933, countless urban planning projects have been proposed but all, including the Charter itself, are today strongly contested. Solutions must be more coherent and more human; the streets must be restored to pedestrians; the urban fabric must again possess the organic unity it has lost; and the creation of large areas which are deserted outside working hours must be avoided. Specialists talk passionately about the problems of big cities and issue a barrage of criticism: of pollution, of the power of vested interests, of intolerable crowding, of ex-

cessive distances between work-place and home, etc. But when it actually comes down to the *favelas* (shanty-towns), and children wandering through the streets, and the workman who leaves home at dawn and only gets back at night without ever seeing his children, the discussion conveniently evaporates, as if these were natural and acceptable phenomena.

In such an appalling social context, the city of the year 2000 cannot be built. As envisaged today, this city would merely reproduce, perhaps more aesthetically, the discriminations and injustices of the capitalist world.

So what is to be done? How can we Latin Americans, still oppressed by the old privileges created by the bourgeoisie, conceive of a city which calls first and foremost for a classless, just and interdependent society?

How can we imagine this ideal city if we live beneath the yoke of dictatorships and the chains of servitude, and when privileges, landed property and authoritarianism frustrate all our efforts. How can we define the nature of the city of the future if poverty besets us and injustice forces us away from the drawing board to respond to the promptings of our con-

"It will be a multipliable city. A series of cities will be stretched along an axis... Parallel to them areas will be allocated to agriculture, scientific research and the major industries." Drawing by Oscar Niemeyer.

Agriculture

Scientific research

Industries

Cities

science and sense of solidarity, take part in politics and cry out our indignation and revolt?

But we can always dream a little and present our modest proposal for the city of the future. At the outset let us say that it should not, in our opinion, be backward-looking; it should not turn towards those medieval cities which attract us so much today, but at the same time it should preserve something of their tranquillity and their human dimensions, two essential qualities which have fallen victim to human progress and incomprehension. The city of the future will not be conceived for the machine; it will be built for man, who will be able to walk through it from end to end, as he did in olden times.

Thus it will be a vertical city, one where the distances will be reduced, thus fulfilling its principal purpose. The population density will be fixed in advance, in order to avoid the rampant growth which has disfigured the world's great cities. To enable pedestrians to move around freely, all vehicles will be left in outlying car-parks with direct access to the different sectors of the city, including the centre, with its administrative buildings, offices and shops. Sectors for health, culture, education and housing will stretch, according to the logic of urban organization, from the centre to the limits.

It will be a multipliable city. A series of cities designed on this model will be stretched along an axis, divided by immense green spaces for recreation and leisure. Parallel to these, areas will be allocated to agriculture, scientific research and the major industries.

This is the formula we propose. Many others are bound to be put forward, but we believe that it is in this smaller, more intimate, more human city, that man will one day rediscover the lost sense of community and the charm of city life, for which he has always felt nostalgia.

Need for new vision stirs city leaders

Willingness to change course — to broaden a city's economic base, bring minorities into government, rethink social policies — is the way to break the self-fulfilling prophesy of urban decline, experts say.

Lucia Mouat

Staff writer of The Christian Science Monitor

Chicago

THE future of America's large older cities depends partly on how willing they are to give up the past and take up a new role.

Urban experts say that most major Midwestern and Northeastern cities will never again be the centers of population, wealth, and semiskilled jobs that they were after World War II. Their economic vitality will depend — at least for a while — on much more outside help than in years past.

But that doesn't mean they are destined to become the hole in the metropolitan doughnut.

Many urban experts are convinced that these smokestack cities do have a future. But their shape, makeup, responsibilities, and strengths are undergoing some radical changes.

As urban sprawl continues, most such cities are becoming smaller. It is a fact no mayor likes to face. Becoming a medium-size city means having a smaller tax base and less clout in winning state and federal funds.

"Most mayors want desperately to believe that it's all a mistake and that they have the power to change what's happening," says Charles Leven, professor of urban affairs at Washington University, over a lunch of sole at the Faculty Club.

"Their only mistake is a slavish devotion to trying to recapture a halcyon past which is just not recoverable."

"One has to have deep sympathy for these guys," says Cleveland State University urbanologist David Garrison of such mayors. He likens them to managers of large corporations whose assets are deteriorating but cannot be moved for a fresh start. He counts it a significant sign of progress that managing urban decline is now an acceptable discussion topic in public forums.

The populations of these more compact residential, financial, office, and government centers in the frost belt are increasingly lower income, less skilled, and more minority. Some neighborhoods are becoming more racially mixed in response to determined citizen efforts. But residential segregation in many industrial cities remains noticeably strong. Cleveland's East Side, St. Louis's North Side, and Chicago's South and West sides, for instance, are predominantly black.

If middle-income whites are to be encouraged to stay in the city or move back from the suburbs, a more energetic effort must be made to break the "self-fulfilling prophecy of ghettoization," insists University of Chicago political scientist Gary Orfield.

"It's a problem we're capable of solving collectively, but not by talking around the edges of it."

'I'm not talking about a Renaissance, but relative stability,' says Donald Haider, a professor at Northwestern University's Kellogg School of Management. 'I don't think you're going to see a Gary, Ind., for instance, rising Phoenix-like from the ashes. But you might be able to do some things at the margin that will help it stabilize and have economic activity without total dependency on manufacturing.'

A few large industrial cities now have black mayors. Longtime Detroit Mayor Coleman Young, who won a voter-approved payroll-tax hike and city worker wage concessions during a financial crisis a few years back, has successfully integrated much of the city's work force and linked local development with stepped-up minority hiring.

But National Urban Coalition president Carl Holman says blacks tend to get the top job only when cities are almost past saving. More blacks, he says, should also run for state and suburban offices that still control much of what happens to cities.

Most industrial cities have been working hard to diversify their job bases. In Pittsburgh, for instance, where the steel industry has been cutting jobs for the last 20 years, the University of Pittsburgh is now the No. 1 employer.

"This is no longer a steel town," insists United Steelworkers of America spokesman Gary Hubbard at union headquarters. One of the hottest local disputes, he adds, is whether to turn an old Jones & Laughlin mill into a jail annex or a museum.

And Baltimore, trying to build on its strength as a hospital center, now claims an even mix of government, service-sector, and manufacturing employees. "Employment levels have stayed the same, but the composition has changed," says Bernard Berkowitz of the Baltimore Economic Development Corporation.

That kind of success in stemming losses prompts Donald Haider, a professor with Northwestern University's Kellogg School of Management, to rate Baltimore as the most successful in economic development of any of the major industrial cities.

"My guess is that Baltimore would have lost a lot more jobs, had far less economic activity, and less sense of its future and identity if it hadn't done what it did," he says.

"I'm not talking about a Renaissance but relative stability. . . . I don't think you're going to see a Gary, Ind., for instance, rising Phoenix-like from the ashes," Professor Haider explains. "But you might be able to do some things at the margin that will help it stabilize and have economic activity without total dependency on manufacturing."

Haider also credits the leaders of many industrial cities with a new "sobriety" in assessing their cities' strong and weak points and in no longer assuming that the downtown shopping center, the domed stadium, or the high-tech park will save the day. "There is no single panacea," he says.

Federal policies often make a large difference. It is widely agreed, for instance, that the building of Interstate highways through cities and the availability of tax credits to homeowners encouraged the suburban exodus. But now that large industrial cities are at a strong disadvantage in the competition for new jobs, urban experts say the city impact of development policies must be more carefully thought through.

"Should federal and state tax funds subsidize removal of low-income jobs from central cities already collapsing to places where it's impossible for the poor to live or have access?" asks Chicago's Dr. Orfield.

Some contend that welfare, job training, and housing policies must also be rethought with an eye to the social effects they help produce. The National Urban League's 1984 report notes that 83 percent of all black children are born to unwed teen-age mothers. Other studies indicate that few of the young mothers get back into high school or have any contact with those who have jobs, go to college, or get married.

"If nothing is done, we're just creating a whole separate culture," Orfield insists.

Robert C. Embry Jr., former assistant secretary of Housing and Urban Development (HUD), suggests that the US may be the only developed country in the world which in effect "blesses" an event that used to be censured by giving unwed mothers a welfare check.

"I'm not saying they have children to get the money, . . . but the whole structure of our society is set up in a way which encourages what is happening."

Roosevelt University urbanologist Pierre deVise suggests that the US could take some cues from the European practice of group day care, in which some mothers tend the children while others take paying jobs.

"In Chicago we'd have the setting for something like this with public housing, where 90 percent of the families are headed by women. But it would be so contrary to middle-class values that it probably wouldn't have a chance," he says.

The Reagan administration's largely hands-off policy on cities calls for $9.2 billion more in domestic spending cuts in next year's budget. But in response to strong mayoral insistence, it does continue urban- and community-development grants.

It is generally agreed that the administration's proposed enterprise-zone legislation, aimed at helping distressed urban areas draw new business and jobs by tax incentives, is worth a try. But many urban experts say they doubt it will work without the additional stimulus of seed money.

"The administration offers no carrot," says Roger S. Ahlbrandt Jr., a former HUD deputy assistant secretary in the Reagan administration's early days.

There is widespread skepticism that the new Job Training Partnership Act will make much of a dent on the double-digit employment that prevails in many large industrial cities.

"It's cleverly written," but the way it's structured will cause only the most able job candidates to be trained, says Lois Work of the urban coalition New Detroit.

But most distressing of all to those who care about cities is the apparent general lack of interest in the subject in 1984. They argue that presidential candidates in both parties, for instance, perhaps echoing a lack of concern among voters at large, have had little to say on urban issues. "There's very little discussion of what our policy ought to be," says Embry.

"When you say cities," adds the Urban Coalition's Mr. Holman, "people think of blacks, Hispanics, and poor, but it's a vital part of leadership to make it clear why it's important to focus on this. . . . I can't believe we're going to permit the continued deterioration of our cities."

THE SUBURBS' STAKE IN CITIES

'Within our federal system there is tremendous diversity and a capacity for regeneration. There are self-correcting forces at work.'

Chicago

"YOU can't build a wall around a city — we all are one."

As Pittsburgh Mayor Richard Caliguiri sees it, major cities and their suburbs stand or fall together. He says he's convinced that more suburbanites will move back to the city as they realize they did not leave urban problems behind and that areawide, metropolitan government is on the way. "There's no doubt in my mind that economic necessity will dictate it before the turn of the century."

In the meantime, he says, suburbanites must do more to support the city services and facilities they use than the maximum $10 per-capita annual charge now allowed under Pennsylvania law. Mayor Caliguiri insists he has just as much garbage to collect, fire and police services to provide, and bridges and roads to maintain as when his city had 200,000 more residents.

That kind of steady demand for services in the face of rising costs and shrinking revenues poses a growing dilemma for all of the large older cities of the Midwest and the Northeast.

Most urban experts say metropolitan government could help but won't come. Suburbs strongly oppose the added tax burden. And some city halls would rather go broke than yield authority. "It will happen only if the suburbs become convinced that if the city goes down, they will be losers, too," says Roosevelt University urbanologist Pierre deVise.

Much more likely is the continued spinoff of city functions — from wastewater treatment to museum management — to the county or state. Most states now pick up the nonfederal share of welfare. The state of New York has taken over many of New York City's court, hospital, and university expenses.

"The states are getting stronger and stronger vis-à-vis the cities, and they will increasingly play an equalizing role," says John Shannon, assistant director of the Washington-based Advisory Commission on Intergovernmental Relations.

In some cases where there is a common area interest, special districts may be formed. The St. Louis region, which resoundingly defeated a metropolitan government proposal in 1961, recently set up a new zoo-museum district, and is talking about setting up another for economic development.

More than half the states now limit city authority to raise taxes. Many cities, claiming they have the responsibilities of New Federalism without the dollars to go with them, are pushing hard to remove those limits.

But many urban experts argue that only more federal help can really make a difference to the adjusting economies of the most troubled industrial cities.

Cleveland State University's Paul R. Porter, co-editor of "Rebuilding America's Cities: Roads to Recovery," argues that some kind of government-supported jobs program and temporary aid along the lines of a "Marshall Plan" is vital. "Without such help these cities won't even make it through the transition," says this former assistant administrator of the Marshall Plan.

Urban sociologist Philip Morris Hauser, professor emeritus of the University of Chicago, argues that the federal war on poverty did not try to do enough in a comprehensive way and that only massive federal help now, including a full-employment policy, can successfully rescue the large older industrial cities. "And there's no doubt in my mind," Dr. Hauser says, "that the additional revenues would represent the most enlightened kind of investment — that in the human being — with the greatest possible return."

"The key to saving our cities is getting the people in them to be employable and employed — everybody benefits with everybody working," agrees John E. Jacob, president of the National Urban League. "People say that government spending isn't the desirable way, but the job is too big for the private sec-

tor alone. And whether we like it or not, our cities have to be repaired and rebuilt. It's not make-work."

The case may be strong for more federal help — particularly for federalizing the urban welfare burden — but many proponents admit that the prospects are limited regardless of who moves into the Oval Office. "Anyone who thinks there is going to be fiscal salvation for the cities from Washington over the next 10 years is dreaming," says Donald Haider, a former Chicago budget director. The 1983 federal deficit alone was $24 billion more than all taxes collected by state governments that year, Mr. Shannon notes.

But many say Washington must at least think through its responsibility to cities and set some priorities. "We definitely need a national policy for dealing with displaced employees — we haven't really explored what we should be doing," says Alan Beals, executive director of the National League of Cities.

One reassuring note for those concerned about the financial health of the industrial big cities: A strong mix of fiscal and accounting safeguards have been added since New York's troubles in the mid-1970s. The more professional approach may not preclude other close calls. But Mr. Haider, now a professor at Northwestern, insists it removes most of the "mystery" and ensures advance warning. "A revolution has been going on beneath the surface in cities in the adoption of technology, management by objective, and strategic planning that's every bit as good as what's going on in the private sector," says Mr. Beals.

Although recovery of the large industrial cities depends in part on how well the economy of the region rallies, urban enthusiasts insist that with enough vision, effort, and time the cities of the Midwest and Northeast will make it.

"I'm constantly reminded that within our federal system there is tremendous diversity and a capacity for regeneration," Shannon notes. "There are self-correcting forces at work."

Progress Begins Downtown

Abandoned warehouses and rundown waterfronts have become the raw material for successful marketplaces in many cities. These spur the return of businesses, which in turn find they need to help nearby neighborhoods.

Lucia Mouat

Staff writer of the Christian Science Monitor

Baltimore

Stroll past the jugglers and the sea gulls as you visit the boutiques and restaurants of Baltimore's trendy Harborplace—a one-time slum site—and you feel you're somehow part of an artist's drawing of what a thriving piece of downtown really should look like. Nearby, watching a group of seals cavort in an outside pool, is a long line of people waiting patiently to get into the recently built National Aquarium.

Stand with Robert Pease high up in Pittsburgh's US Steel Building and scan the array of new and rehabilitated landmarks below—from the sun-reflecting Pittsburgh Plate Glass headquarters and greenly lush Point State Park (once a rundown warehouse district) to new office towers such as Oxford Centre and remodeled Heinz Hall, center of a proposed new arts complex.

Long gone, although the reputation lingers on, is the soft, smoky coal haze that used to hang so thick over the city that street lights had to be left on all day.

"The only way we seem able to convince people this is a decent place to live is to get them to come here," observes Mr. Pease, executive director of the Allegheny Conference on Community Development. That group of top local business leaders dates back to the 1940s, and played a key role in the crackdown on air pollution, the revamping of Point Park, and other civic rescue missions.

Drive along the once-rundown Mississippi riverfront in St. Louis and notice the restored shops and streets of Laclede's Landing and, nearby, the park with the majestic arch. Wend your way through many blocks of new downtown housing, offices, and hotels under construction and look in on such mammoth recycling ventures as the red-brick Wainwright Building, Louis Sullivan's 1891 masterpiece, which now serves as a state office building, and Union Station, which, in the hands of Maryland's Rouse Company, is fast becoming St. Louis's answer to Harborplace.

The efforts are varied, but they all add up to economic development. A lot of it is going on in city cores across the Midwest and Northeast. It is by far the most visible and dramatic sign of progress in the region's battle against urban decay. Often it is the result of years of careful planning and close collaboration between local government and business leaders.

James O'Flynn, president of the St. Louis Regional Commerce and Growth Association, remembers that when he graduated from college in the mid-'50s, the Famous-Barr department store and the financial district were "the only things good about downtown." Improvements since then, he says, stem largely from a plan evolved by city and business leaders. He attributes the "saving" of downtown St. Louis to several factors: the decision to complete the arch and to build a new stadium downtown rather than to the North, as some proposed; and a longtime Missouri law prohibiting branch banking, which anchored business activity downtown.

James Rouse, chairman of the Rouse Company, which launched many of the nation's most successful downtown shopping malls, has long stressed the importance of vision. In his view, those who care about cities must leap over a preoccupation with urban problems to visualize what cities really could be like if they worked and charted a course of action.

Most urban experts say the involvement of top local leadership in clearing the way and getting needed government dollars has often been vital to downtown development successes. Recently, Baltimore Mayor William D. Schaefer, now in his fourth term and widely considered a master in snaring every available federal and state dollar, set up a number of quasi-public commissions (with fewer public-participation and disclosure requirements than most public bodies) to speed up development action.

Federal aid through Urban Development Action Grants (UDAGs) and Community Development Block Grants (CDBGs) is widely regarded as crucial. In some cases it has helped cities reach a certain economic threshold where the private sector picks up the momentum.

Baltimore developer Robert C. Embry Jr. notes, for instance, that a few years back, no developer wanted to build a hotel in the city's harbor area without a $10 million UDAG. But when a harbor lot recently became available, "there were at least 15 developers falling all over themselves to get it without any sort of public assistance."

Generally the downtown development boom is credited with giving a needed boost to local morale, increasing entry-level jobs, and, eventually, improving the city's tax base.

Baltimore's Harborplace, which drew more visitors in its first year than Disneyworld and brought in more than $1 million in local taxes, has given the city "sparkle," says the Melvin Levin of the University of Maryland's School of Social Work.

But some neighborhood leaders argue that the benefits of downtown development do not trickle down to the neediest and alone are not enough. Some political leaders accordingly insist on spending as much in government subsidies in neighborhoods as in a city's core. San Francisco requires downtown developers to build low- and moderate-income neighborhood housing in exchange for the privilege of downtown action.

Chicago Mayor Harold Washington's proposed new economic master plan would award extra help to the poorest neighborhoods and require downtown developers using city subsidies to buy 25 percent of their supplies from local companies owned by women or minorities.

A growing number of sophisticated neighborhood groups are quashing some of the criticism, too, by helping finance widely scattered commercial development.

Walk around Pittsburgh's East End, for instance, with David Feehan, director of East Liberty Development Inc., and he'll show you just which businesses are coming back and where the new jobs are in this rundown, racially mixed, blue-collar neighborhood once known as the city's second downtown.

The revitalization project aims at recruiting minority-owned businesses in particular. And Mr. Feehan clearly sees no reason for tolerating deterioration in any part of East Liberty. Passing a tavern which is a reported hangout for drug dealers, he insists: "There's plenty you can do about something like this. You can keep after the police to crack down on it, or buy it and put the place out of business.

"If all I do is build confidence in this area, it will eventually work," he adds.

Several hundred miles to the east in Indianapolis, Joseph Perilli, executive director of the Metropolitan Area Citizens Organization (MACO), is trying to work similar wonders in a 20-acre neighborhood on the city's north side. He describes his organization as a broker between neighborhood groups that set policies and private developers that carry them out.

Although MACO is involved in both housing and commercial development, its first priority is with the latter. "That's where most of the visible blight is, and if you can make money off that, you can use it for other things," Mr. Perilli explains.

MACO's major accomplishment to date: the rehabbing of Devington Plaza, a shopping center where the vacancy rate was high and remaining owners refused to make repairs. MACO, funded in part by the foundation and business-supported Local Initiatives Support Corporation (LISC), which is helping 240 community groups around the country, will get half the profits as half-owner. "If this country were as committed to restoring neighborhoods over the next 50 years as it is to defense spending, we wouldn't have a problem," says Perilli.

Many of the funding is increasingly coming from American business. Recently the First National Bank of Chicago set up a $100 million loan program to help revitalize both businesses and housing in distressed neighborhoods in that city. Others, such as Bank of America, have contributed through LISC to help in various urban efforts.

In some cases a corporation has taken the lead in revitalizing its own neighborhood. When the owners of the Ralston-Purina Company decided some years ago to stay and expand their headquarters in St. Louis rather than head for the suburbs, they soon realized they could not ignore the increasingly shabby south-central neighborhood around them. "It was very much a slum," recalls Fred Perabo, a Ralston lawyer. So for a mix of reasons, including protection of its own investment, Ralston embarked on a 140-acre housing project, with the help of substantial urban-renewal funding.

Mr. Perabo, now president of the LaSalle Park Redevelopment Corporation, which did the job, drives

Chat with a Mayor

Industry and government give and take to aid Indianapolis

Many here thought that building the $80 million downtown Hoosier Dome without a firm contract for a team to play in it was a rash gamble.

But Indianapolis Mayor William H. Hudnut III had long insisted publicly that the dome's main purpose was to strengthen the city's standing as a convention center. Any sports use beyond that would be a bonus.

The city's coup this spring in capturing that bonus with the sign-up of the National Football League's Baltimore Colts quieted much of the earlier criticism and reinforced the point that vision and hard work often precede victory.

Civic leaders here have long been clear on what they want their city to become. They want it to grow into a major medical, convention, and sports (both amateur and professional) capital. To back up their goals, they cleared the way and garnered funds to build such facilities as the dome, a downtown basketball arena, and a large track-and-field stadium, Olympic-size swimming pool, and bike-racing arena at the combined Indiana-Purdue University campus.

The mayor of this city of the Indianapolis-500 motor speedway says, "We set ourselves some sights, and we're trying to go for them." He sees the hosting of a Super Bowl and a bid for the Olympic Games as distinct possibilities.

Indianapolis has had it easier than many cities in the industrial belt. It has relied less heavily on manufacturing than many, and its loss of population and jobs have cut less deeply. The city's partial merger with many surrounding suburbs in a "uni-gov" arrangement in 1970, which strengthened its tax base, and the steady generosity of local benefactors such as the Eli Lilly Foundation, which contributed $25 million to the dome project, also set it apart.

Nationally, Indianapolis is considered one of the prime examples of a city making progress through close public-private partnerships.

"It's the new civics, and it's really the key to the salvation of the city," said Mayor Hudnut, a former National League of Cities president, interviewed in his office. "Government can't do it all—and neither can the private sector."

As examples of how that partnership has worked here, the mayor cites the American United Life Insurance Company's decision to build a 38-story office building—now the state's tallest—downtown rather than in the suburbs. As its part of the bargain, the city relocated several sewers and steam pipes, closed off some streets, and offered a tax abatement. "I call it 'creative leveraging'—it goes both ways."

It was a financial package of dollars and tax credits from various government sources that he says managed to keep the local International Harvester plant going when it was weighing a shutdown. And when one local developer wanted a traffic light that the city felt it could not afford, "we went halves with him," Hudnut says.

Mayor Hudnut admits that federal cuts have hurt his city, but says cities have become too prone to hold out the "tin cup" to Washington for every need.

"We're learning that there's a lot [of economic progress] that can be generated by cooperation with the private sector," he says. "I personally don't feel we have to weep and wail and gnash our teeth every time some program is cut in Washington. We've got to rein in deficit spending everywhere."

Taxpayers, too, he says, must lower their expectations or pay the freight.

"We can't just give everybody everything they want, and people can't expect government to do that," says this former Republican congressman and Presbyterian minister. "People are going to have to realize that the cost of delivering services goes up like everything else."

a visitor around what he calls "the campus"—a mix of new public-housing apartments and restored century-old brick homes. It is home now to 1,400 city dwellers. Ralston's effort was recently singled out from 60 contenders for the George S. Dively Award for corporate leadership in urban development.

Business' rapidly expanding view of what action is in its own self-interest is helping considerably in the citywide fight against urban blight. Some local groups, such as Pittsburgh's Allegheny Conference, now involved in everything from improving local schools to infrastructure, took that broad view early on, when city air pollution hampered company recruitment efforts.

"It's terribly important that it be a mandate on the part of business leadership to make sure that our major urban centers don't go bankrupt," says St. Louis's Mr. O'Flynn.

R. Scott Fosler, co-editor of a Committee for Economic Development book on case studies of public-private partnerships, insists that the once-clear distinction between business operations and philanthropy is no more. "Business is beginning to see giving programs as investments rather than throwaway money," agrees Pittsburgh's David Feehan.

Most urban experts agree that recent economic development efforts have left cities of the "rust belt" better off than a decade ago. Pablo Eisenberg of the Washington-based Center for Community Change, says: "It's not necessarily going to bring in the millenium, but it is certainly a chipping away."

America's Urban 'Rust Belt' Cinches Up For the Future

The nation's aging Midwest and Northeast industrial centers can't afford to wait for things to get better. So they're using the strengths they have to reverse the forces of urban decline. Report from seven cities.

Lucia Mouat

Staff writer of The Christian Science Monitor

Chicago

What's ahead for the proud cities that were once the backbone of industrial America?

In recent years these large older cities of the Midwest and Northeast have been pushed and pulled by strong economic and population forces that have left parts of them looking like bombed-out war zones. Anyone driving through Chicago's West Side, New York's South Bronx, or down Detroit's once riot-torn Rosa Parks Boulevard sees ample evidence.

In part, it's a reflection of the big-city exodus to the suburbs and Sunbelt that's been going on for years. Those with more job skills and the means to leave have been the movers. Increasingly, the jobs have moved with them. Over the last two decades, for instance, Chicago lost almost 100,000 jobs, while its surrounding suburbs gained six times as many.

The central cities of what is now often called the "rust belt"—as the United States shifts from a strong manufacturing emphasis to a more service-based economy—are increasingly poorer, blacker, and smaller.

Of the seven cities visited by this reporter in the course of writing this series—Baltimore, Pittsburgh, Cleveland, Detroit, Indianapolis, Chicago, and St. Louis—all but Indianapolis hit their population peaks in 1950. St. Louis, for instance, once the nation's fourth-largest city and now 25th, has lost close to half its residents over the last three and a half decades. In

Detroit, now 63 percent black, 30 percent of all city dwellers live below the poverty line—a 7 percent hike just since 1980, according to the latest Census Bureau data.

Since Southern blacks began flocking to Northern cities during World War II, when manufacturing jobs were plentiful, the nation's black population has become increasingly urbanized. Seventy-five percent of all blacks now live in cities. Currently close to half of all black households are headed by women. A high percentage of working-age black men are unemployed.

"Over the last two decades, distressed cities have even become more distressed," says Robert C. Embry Jr., a former assistant secretary of the US Department of Housing and Urban Development under President Carter and now a private developer in Baltimore. "The poor population has increased, and the situation of the poor has grown worse."

Mr. Embry says he is particularly concerned about the departure from cities of large numbers of middle-class blacks, who are often churchgoers and put a high premium on education, hard work, upholding the law, and having children only after marriage.

Their presence in cities and strong endorsement of that value system, he argues, have long served as important models for other city dwellers farther down on the poverty scale.

Roosevelt University urbanologist Pierre deVise estimates that as many as one-fourth of those living in major cities really shouldn't live there and often don't want to. "They're people who are dependent and unable to work. But the institutions to help them—from public housing to welfare—are there, and it is hard to leave."

For many of these older industrial cities, crime, poor schools, and decaying infrastructure are increasingly serious problems. Yet federal cutbacks and a shrinking local tax base make it harder than ever to finance improvements.

Some economists and demographers argue that the forces of urban decline now at work in these cities are self-reinforcing and virtually irreversible. They note that the exodus of jobs and middle-class residents continues—though at a somewhat lesser rate—despite all-out local efforts to encourage businesses to start or expand within city limits and to lure suburbanites to buy city homes.

"Right at the moment the immigration back in is only a trickle," observes George D. Wendel, director of the Center for Urban Programs at St. Louis University. "The developer tends to see that as the forerunner of a flood. The social scientist is inclined to say, 'Show me the flood when it gets here.' "

In recent years two major studies on urban decline—one by the Brookings Institution and one directed by Richard Nathan, head of Princeton University's Urban Research Center—concluded that positive efforts to rebuild the nation's older cities have not kept pace with the decay and that the situation is unlikely to be reversed anytime soon.

Still, there are many urban dwellers in these United States who are fiercely pro-city—relishing the camaraderie and adventure as well as the many cultural and recreational assets—who are unwilling to accept such a verdict. They say the adverse trends are not set in concrete and that a Renaissance of sorts is under way.

With enough support and imagination, they say, it can make a significant difference.

"It's going to take unremitting guerilla warfare—you just have to keep plugging away," cautions Melvin Levin of the University of Maryland's School of Social Work.

There are some encouraging economic and demographic signs.

The general aging of the population, for instance, means fewer urban residents in the high-crime teen years and should mean less competition for jobs among those of working age. Recent studies also suggest that many who grow up in poverty are not necessarily locked into it as adults.

Although three of the rust-belt cities—New York, Cleveland, and Detroit—have faced serious financial trouble in the last 10 years, all have escaped bankruptcy. New York, in dire straits in 1975 and a city that has now largely shifted its job base away from manufacturing, expects to end the year with a $200 million surplus.

There are visible signs in some cities of the recovery now under way. In Detroit, the parking lots of auto assembly plants are filling up again, and the auto production count on signs over city freeways increases every few seconds.

The downtown core of almost every major industrial city is undergoing a significant construction boom. Sometimes, as with Cleveland's renovated Arcade Building—an indoor shopping mall with live music that has become a popular luncheon spot—a fresh start with an old building makes the difference.

Most cities are also working hard to improve local housing options and recruit every possible tourist and convention.

Helping in all this is an almost tangible new spirit of cooperation and determination to meet the urban challenge.

"We've raised more money and provided more services to the community since Reagan became President than at any time in the 14½ years I've been here," insists the Rev. James Hannah, pastor of Cleveland's Central Christian Church and head of the Inner-City Renewal Society there.

"When black people are laid off and jobs are few, they have a tendency to come back to the church."

"Most of the successful efforts in community renewal are led by people who are going to continue living in these cities—they're essentially survivors, and they are making progress," says Ken Allen of Volunteer: The National Center for Citizen Involvement.

Still, there is a growing consensus among urban analysts these days that the older industrial cities are changing in major ways that will force them to play a new role on the national scene.

Just between 1980 and 1982, for instance, Chicago slipped from the nation's second-largest to third-largest city, while Detroit led the nation with a record 5.3 percent population loss, according to new census data.

"The demographic forces that have begun to empty these cities out are huge and can't be changed in fundamental ways," says David F. Garrison of Cleveland State University's Urban Center. "The challenge for the leadership in these cities is to recognize these forces for what they are and try to bend them a little but not to spend a lot of time wringing their hands."

While industrial production and employment are unlikely to reach peak 1979 levels again, manufacturing will remain the region's economic mainstay.

"We need to think about rebuilding the industry we have left to make it more competitive—high-tech is not going to be the salvation of this region," says Vijay Singh, director of the University of Pittsburgh's Center for Urban and Social Research.

But forecasters say the growth in service jobs in the rust belt over the next decade will not match the decline in manufacturing jobs. Numerous studies, including one by the Federal Reserve Bank of Chicago, say years of difficult regional adjustment lie ahead.

Chat with a Mayor

A city's age can be its advantage, says Cleveland's Voinovich

"I'm confident that we're going to come out of this transition period a star."

Cleveland Mayor George Voinovich sinks into one of the upholstered, high-backed chairs in his spacious office to explain how he thinks his city of "urban pioneers" can adjust to a more service-based national economy and trounce the local forces of urban decay.

Long an iron-and-steel town, Cleveland now produces a broad mix of industrial products, from electrical equipment to fabricated metals. Noting that a certain level of manufacturing strength is vital for national defense, Mayor Voinovich credits Cleveland manufacturers with working particularly hard to modernize and diversify. "Many are doing a darn good job."

A city's age and the assets it acquires over time can be an advantage, in his view. Yes, repairs and upkeep are often vital. The entertainment area of the Cleveland Playhouse, the nation's oldest resident theater, for instance, is in the midst of a $25 million renovation. But the mayor argues that repairs are often cheaper than starting fresh, as many Sunbelt cities must do.

Much of Voinovich's confidence that Cleveland will not only survive but thrive in the decades ahead is based on his conviction that most local business, labor, and civic leaders here now share an unwavering commitment to that goal.

"This community has decided it's going to solve its problems locally and do what has to be done," says the Republican mayor. "We know, frankly, we're not going to get a lot of help from Washington."

Several shiny new shovels resting near the door of the mayor's outer office serve as a reminder that he is a very frequent participant these days in ground-breakings for businesses and new housing, both downtown and in the neighborhoods. One major recent boost for the downtown core: Standard Oil of Ohio's decision to build a 45-story, $200 million corporate headquarters there.

Cleveland's business community and city government were openly at odds as recently as 1978, when the city defaulted on a short-term bond payment. But most urban analysts agree that the relationship changed dramatically when Mayor Voinovich was elected in November 1979. He promptly persuaded local banks to refinance the city's debt, asked a task force of accountants and auditors to assess the city's financial position, and tapped a group of top business executives to suggest ways to streamline city government.

That kind of cooperation has since blossomed into more joint ventures, such as Cleveland Tomorrow, a group of 40 top business leaders ("all heavy hitters," says the mayor) offering seed money and professional services to new development ventures. Another coalition—the Cleveland Roundtable—has an active labor-management committee aimed at keeping friction levels low.

"This city's situation has been about as difficult as any, but we now have a very good community response," says urban expert Paul R. Porter of Cleveland State University. "The mayor has done a great deal to help build the kind of confidence that's paying off."

Although Cleveland has been widely hailed in recent years as a "comeback" city, it still faces tough problems. On May 8 voters for the second time this year turned down the mayor's request for a payroll-tax hike to head off an expected deficit.

Voinovich, who is currently first vice-president of the National League of Cities, says local officials have often been "cowards" in asking for money needed and that states have often been reluctant to give cities the authority they need. But most of all, in these days of sharp federal tax and program cuts, he blames Washington for failing to warn taxpayers that there is no free lunch.

"The President is carrying out a policy of getting the federal government out of our lives, but he hasn't tied the circle together by saying, 'Look, we're cutting your taxes on the federal level, but your state and local taxes are going to have to go up . . . to fund essential programs.' Doggone it. He hasn't done that. And that's good old conservative Republicanism."

Voinovich is also critical of Washington for not recognizing sooner what was happening to America's competitive position in manufacturing and more carefully weighing the impact on it of foreign policy decisions.

"There's been a kind of oblivious attitude," Voinovich says. "I happen to believe that there needs to be closer cooperation among government, labor, and business, and that we should have some type of national industrial policy. If we don't . . . we're not going to compete in the new world."

Anthony Downs, a senior fellow at the Brookings Institution and one of the authors of its study entitled "Urban Decline and the Future of American Cities," says the real-wage advantage Midwestern auto and steel workers have had over most of the nation's other industrial workers is going to have to come down if the region is to regain its economic viability. "It's hard to get people to give up what they've got, but it seems to me the Midwest in particular is in for an adjustment period."

Chase Econometrics vice-president Lawrence M. Horwitz suggests that such evening out of regional differences is already under way. He points to the recent shutdowns of General Motors and Ford plants in California (presumably because of the high cost of shipping parts from the Midwest) and the willingness of foreign-car manufacturers to locate in more traditional high-wage areas—such as Honda in Ohio and Nissan in Tennessee—as signs.

SUBURBS
Revising the American Dream
Main Street Runs into the Future

Marilyn Gardner

Living page editor of The Christian Science Monitor

Cupertino, Calif.

Ten years after the gold rush of 1849, when strains of "California or Bust" still echoed across the country, a hunter and trapper named Captain Elisha Stephens became the first settler of Cupertino. Born in South Carolina, Stephens is credited with leading the first wagon train across the Sierra Nevadas. He was already in his mid-50s when he built a home and established a vineyard along the banks of the river now named after him by a careless speller—Stevens Creek.

Within a few years Stephens found his little corner of Santa Clara Valley becoming "too durn civilized" for his tastes. In 1864 he moved on, a true American and a true son of Cupertino—a community originally known only as the Crossroads.

Today the civilization Stephens was fleeing covers nearly every square acre of the valley. The rich soil has been plowed under, paved over, built upon to make room for shopping centers, industrial parks, and the subdivisions that house the 38,000 residents of Cupertino. Only a token orchard still stands here and there, like a museum piece. The new crossroads has become the intersection of two thoroughfares: Stevens Creek Boulevard and Highway 9.

Cupertino is a state of traffic. "So what we have here," explains Linda Lauzze, a Cupertino planner, "is this: In the morning everybody goes south to north"—to Santa Clara, to Sunnyvale, to all the centers of Silicon Valley where the high-tech industries—Apple, Hewlett-Packard, Tandem—hum. "Then in the evening, when work lets out, everybody goes north to south."

It is as if all the westward-ho pioneers, like Elisha Stephens, who have invaded California over the years could not stop—condemned to become a community in perpetual motion.

The lots in Cupertino average around 6,000 square feet—small by the standards of the American suburb. But almost every lot is outlined by a fence—not a symbolic rail fence, as in the East, or a chain-link fence, as in the Midwest, but a cedar fence, surrounding and towering above its tiny plot, as if to keep it, too, from being carried away in the traffic.

How does a community achieve a measure of stability in a sea of change? The traffic and the fence—perpetual flux and fragile fortress—these opposing presences in a California suburb seem to symbolize the challenge of the suburb everywhere in 1983.

Everybody sees the traffic—everybody understands the state as the state-of-mind Scott Kaufer wrote about in a recent issue of California magazine:

"Something about California has always attracted dreamers and sages who would fashion a perfect society for the rest of us to emulate. Utopians need to believe that the impossible is plausible—and California has traditionally radiated that impression."

But don't forget those fences.

"California, like any other state, is not a homogeneous unit," says Barbara Rogers, a member of the Cupertino City Council. "We have out here all the funny cults. But lots of people in California think they're very peculiar, too."

Something called "Sound-Offs" allows the residents to voice often conservative gripes to the Cupertino council in a monthly newsletter, the "Cupertino Scene." Cries like "Don't destroy Cupertino! We'll have another San Jose" are typical (San Jose grew from 17 square miles and 95,000 people to 135 square miles and a half a million people between 1950 and 1975.)

There are un-Californian recommendations to "restrain small motorbikes-cycles," especially on weekends.

This town, once a center of orchards, now has planted new cherry trees in Memorial Park, producing a nostalgic yearning for more trees—particularly around the post office ("It's like a desert in the summer," one resident writes.)

The sleek-looking, low-profile architecture that makes even the town hall resemble a particularly attractive fast-food chain, the traffic crawling north and south—all that is most modern about Cupertino—lies between green foothills of the Santa Clara mountains, declaring a kind of permanence and continuity.

Councilwoman Rogers, born and brought up in New Jersey, lived in Florida and Indiana on her way to

Cupertino. Rather than finding her Californians self-absorbed in experimental life styles, she keeps encountering "people who care about the community and get involved in it."

Cupertino seems to long to stop the traffic, find a new crossroads, and gather itself together.

Shopping centers like the award-winning Vallco Fashion Park, a million-square-foot monument to consumption, have become social and cultural gathering places. Residents come in from the California sun to skate in a lower-level ice rink. Musical groups perform in the center of the mall. And department store seminars often replace club meetings, luring patrons with talks on financial planning.

There is both a charm and a certain pathos to the custom that summons guests in Cupertino's chic restaurants to their tables by calling out their first names.

But it's hard to be open, relaxed, and informal when you're running out of space. A visitor keeps coming back to those fences that enclose and protect Cupertino's most precious asset. "There's just no land," says Glenn Rupp, a real estate broker who has lived in the area since 1955, the year Cupertino was incorporated. Where his office now stands, a cherry orchard flowered. Indeed, for years Cupertino was one big 11-square-mile orchard, producing prunes as well as cherries. Lockheed was the big industry. The price of an average house was around $10,000—$99 down. Now, Mr. Rupp estimates, the average price is around $130,000.

The frontier is squeezing, in every sense.

"When we moved into our house 13 years ago, it was a nice average tract house," Nancy Madson says. "We thought: 'This is a nice start. We'll be here for five years, then we'll build our own home.' That was the American dream as I knew it from my own experience—that's what I had grown up with.

"Now we have come to the decision that what we need is to simplify our lives and relieve ourselves of some of the burdens of responsibility that include our house and its maintenance and care. We've turned away from that original goal of having the big beautiful house, realizing we're not there enough to enjoy it. If we were to put money into something, it would probably be something recreational that we could enjoy together in our spare time, rather than something that would require constant care."

Mrs. Madson, the mother of an 8-year-old son, is a cheerful woman of considerable energies. Like 51 percent of the women in the country, she works. She is assistant principal at Cupertino's Homestead High School.

For the Madsons, as for many working couples everywhere, home ownership has shifted to what Mrs. Madson calls "managing, rather than doing ourselves." If the old orthodoxy was do-it-yourself—a blend of the Protestant work ethic and Jeffersonian self-sufficiency—the new, often desperate credo is: Hire it done. To meet that need, suburban services in Cupertino, as elsewhere,

have sprung up like dandelions. From cleaning services to day-care centers, caterers to house sitters, the suburbs increasingly are running on remote control.

City manager Robert Quinlan, still enthusiastic and confident after 12 years on the job, acknowledges the unpredictable condition of a California suburb.

"For one thing, the whole strategy of development has changed," he says. "Prior to Proposition 13, office buildings would have been a real plus, because they would have provided a better property tax than housing. Now property tax is not so important a thing to us nor to our schools. But sales tax has become extremely important—the revenue generated by shopping centers and high-quality restaurants.

"A lot of the problems have no respect for town lines. Many of the communities are working together to come up with joint solutions—on solid waste disposal, for instance, and delivery of power and other services." Suburbs no longer dependent on a central city now find themselves dependent on each other.

"Environmental concern has become extremely important," Mr. Quinlan continues. "The rule seems to be: The lower the income, the more people are interested in services rendered by government—social services, police services, fire service, whatever. The higher the income, the more people are concerned about land-use planning, zoning issues, quality-of-life issues.

"All these things kind of play against one another. When we try to predict five years down the road, we're really just guessing. People around here don't think in terms of permanence much.

"On the other hand, maybe that's the wave of the future. Maybe we don't think in terms of permanence. Maybe we're going to have Kleenex houses in the future. We're going to have blocks of land owned by corporations and they'll be maybe leasing the land like they do in Hawaii, and a person will buy a home but won't own the land. They'll just lease the land. And they'll only build homes to last 15 years, because things are changing so rapidly that particular configurations may not make any sense later on."

What will the suburb of the future look like?

When the Monitor asked this question, other experts were equally cautious.

Constance Perin, a cultural anthropologist teaching a course at Harvard in "The Social and Cultural Geography of Suburbs," told the Monitor: "I predict that renters' social status is going to improve. The definition of the American middle class is tied up with home ownership. The important status distinction that supersedes a lot of class distinction is between owning and renting. Renting is going to come out from under the cloud. If the polarization between owners and renters can diminish, that's all to the good."

David Riesman, whose classic "The Lonely Crowd" seemed at the time to be a label for the suburbs, sees them becoming more urban. He notes "a good deal more isolation among people."

He also speaks of the "hedonism of families," which "makes life more costly and sacrifice often less common. Children don't mow the lawn or run paper routes. Families live in a cocoon of television. They eat out a lot. This has made the suburbs more urban, as though these were singles living in the suburbs.

"Peer culture is in charge," he continues. "One has a feeling of parents running a motel for their kids rather than a home."

He wonders "whether the children will survive the working mother. We have gotten a little too cavalier about this question," Professor Riesman told the Monitor. "Children from birth to the age of six who have not had a mother at home are showing up having stress in college."

But on the plus side, he concludes: "There are no boondocks left in America. There's no Siberia. There's hardly any place you can find that doesn't have a little theater, doesn't have some kind of chamber music group, doesn't have a literary circle. So we have to balance the people who eat out at restaurants with the people who go to museums. There's been a general upgrading of American taste, American culture—this has changed the suburbs."

Herbert J. Gans, author of "The Levittowners" and now on the faculty of Columbia University, has become more and more cautious about generalizing as the years go by. "All the suburbs have in common," he told the Monitor, "is that they're outside the city limits."

"What's happening now is more a function of necessity," he says. But he finds that whatever romance of the American heart the suburb represents, the attraction is still there. "The dream has gotten more expensive," he concludes. "The dream has been cut down a bit. But the dream goes on."

Robert C. Wood, who wrote "Suburbia: Its People and Their Politics" almost a quarter of a century ago, sums up suburbs as "republics-in-miniature that have survived." After the '50s, he remarks, not too much attention was paid to the suburbs. In the '60s, the subject was the cities. In the '70s, it was the environment. Now, he suggests, fiscal and social problems are bringing attention back to the suburbs. Civil rights, feminism, "swinging" life styles, drugs, industrial pollution—every-thing affecting the rest of society—has invaded the suburbs, whether the suburbs are ready or not.

Professor Wood told the Monitor that the revisionism—the "recycling"—of the suburbs will go on. He sees the apartments "catering to the new life style with tennis courts and swimming pools" filling in those swimming pools for day-care centers when the "mini-baby-boom" comes along.

He sees the suburbs growing older, in every sense, as the number of people over 65 increases, threatening to produce a "defensive, aging suburban population" protecting a status quo—the kind of zoning that becomes a form of discrimination.

He concludes:

"If you were going to do straight projections, which economists and analysts like to do, you would have a set of quite different forces than those that began the suburbs and the American dream of housing and roots. You could say sort of more of the same—the reinforcement of the fortress mentality—and sort of decline into shabby gentility of what they thought they were getting, with the physical structure of the houses built, the shopping centers, with these being sort of inappropriate forms for the world we're talking about.

"But that's projections. There's another possibility on this—a sea change. It may very well be that we're at a point of history in this country when we're going to have a sea change and just throw the projections out the window.

"But if that sea change comes, it's going to require some kind of political coalition of parties that have been adversaries—the conservationists sitting down with housing developers; some reconciliation between the races; some major renewal of institutions, of which central-city public schools constitute, in my judgment, the most urgent task. We would have a fundamental shift of values that would begin to address suburbs and their cheapening qualities—and center cities and their unrealized potential."

Professor Wood's description of the mood that would bring about such a renaissance—such a "sea change"—is curiously like the mood that first gave birth to the suburbs: a "disposition to fraternity."

Politics Is Not the Only Thing That Is Changing America's Big Cities

NEAL R. PEIRCE, ROBERT GUSKIND AND JOHN GARDNER

Times are changing in America's big cities, as this year's mayoral elections amply showed. Of eight mayoralties in a *National Journal* survey of cities that elected mayors in 1983, all were held a decade ago by white males. Today, only three are: Boston, Baltimore and San Diego. Chicago and Philadelphia have elected black mayors, Denver elected a Hispanic and Houston and San Francisco chose women to run their cities.

Politics is by no means the only arena of change. In key civic and economic developments accompanying the changing of the political guard, the survey found that improving race relations and meeting the needs of their neighborhoods ranked highest. Other issues of concern were schools, housing, transit and pollution.

In virtually all the cities, conflicting demographic forces were a hallmark. Strong downtown growth was accompanied by large dependent populations; "gentrification" of decaying neighborhoods was found cheek-by-jowl with pockets of deep poverty.

Not surprisingly, serious problems were found in some cities. The deep political divisions of Chicago—long proud of its moniker, the "city that works"—presented the most troubling picture in the survey. A bitter standoff prevails there between Mayor Harold Washington and his city council opponents. And in Houston, newborn economic pains and continuing traffic and transit quandries have burst the bubble of "boomtown U.S.A." Yet, in contrast, Boston, San Diego and San Francisco appear to be in such good shape that the task of controlling—not stimulating—additional growth seems to have become their principal concern.

BOSTON: MODEL FOR CHANGE?

Kevin H. White this year concludes 16 years as mayor of a city at once richer and poorer, more hopeful and more perplexed, than when he took office as one of the "hero mayors" of the 1960s. Downtown Boston's multi-billion-dollar building boom is expanding into Back Bay and other areas. Middle-class gentrification is reported to be under way in almost every neighborhood. A high-technology marketing center, called Boscom, is planned for the waterfront. And in a dramatic shift for a school system wracked by mismanagement and a furious busing fight in the 1970s, the city has formed an innovative partnership with business in the Boston Compact, to guarantee high school graduates jobs if the schools improve their performance.

The recent mayoral contest between Raymond L. Flynn, from the white ethnic bastion of South Boston, and Melvin King, a symbol of black power from the racially mixed South End, was notable for a remarkable degree of racial amity. Under Flynn, the city's attention seems sure to shift from downtown development to the neighborhoods.

Still of concern, however, are long-standing racial and ethnic tensions and the city's shaky fiscal condition. Inner-city poverty persists at high levels, and a chunk of the middle class has been lost to the rise of both poor and rich populations. "In many ways, the economic structure is worse now; poverty in the city is extraordinarily severe," said Paul Harrington, an economist at Northeastern University. A sixth of Boston's families in 1979 were poor. Its black and Hispanic population grew by a third over the decade, to 28.8 per cent in 1980, while over-all population declined by 12 per cent.

Boston is a center of the much-heralded high-tech boom under way in selected areas of the nation. Digital Equipment Corp., Teradyne Inc. and Wang Laboratories Inc. have assembly plants in the city. Still, high technology accounts for only 10 per cent of the metropolitan area's employment.

Two state-run facilities may attract more high-tech employment. Boscom, a high-tech "merchandise mart" under construction near the South Boston waterfront, is designed as a trading center that officials project will create 2,000 jobs. City leaders also hope the Massachusetts Technology Center, located near Logan Airport, will attract more manufacturing and research facilities.

Another area of continuing economic growth is the field of health services, which Harrington predicted will account for about 20 per cent of all new jobs in the state by 1990. The key to capturing a large share of the growth, however, said Lynn Browne, an economist at the Federal Reserve Bank of Boston, will be to capitalize on the research strengths of the city's universities.

The city is extending the compact model it used for the schools to form a housing partnership to combat the serious shortage of low and moderate-income housing. As in many other big cities, gentrification and real estate speculation have engulfed many poor and ethnic neighborhoods and are rapidly encroaching on others.

In the meantime, downtown development continues at a pace of more than a billion dollars a year and is spreading outward from the city, according to the mayor's office. Now opening in stages is Copley Place, a $550 million mixed-use hotel-office-premium retailing project built over air rights beside historic Copley Square. Neiman-Marcus will open its first New England store there, but the project's low-income neighbors should also benefit from guaranteed shares of the construction jobs and 6,000 permanent jobs the project will create.

On the drawing boards are more than $1 billion in new structures for the derelict South Boston waterfront, where local developers expect to renovate the entire unused port area within the decade.

Boston's fiscal condition deteriorated substantially under White. In addition to the normal pressures faced by other cities, it was hit by the passage of Massachusetts's Proposition 2½, which slashed taxes and revenues. In 1981, Moody's Investors Service suspended the city's bond rating for a time, and then revised it to a low Ba1 rating.

BALTIMORE: CINDERELLA CITY

Baltimore has emerged as the Cinderella city of this decade by virtue of a combination of factors—a white mayor's phenomenal success in a mostly black city, strategic federal grants during the 1970s and a long-term civic and business commitment, culminating in the 1980 opening of Harborplace, the Rouse Co.'s "festival marketplace" on the city's inner harbor.

Old-fashioned American boosterism now thrives in this lunch-pail city of row houses with white marble steps. Mayor William Donald Schaefer, perhaps its biggest fan, easily defeated a black challenger in this year's mayoral primary and then won the general election with 94 per cent of the vote.

The thought of a revived Baltimore might have sounded preposterous a few years ago, when a visitor standing on the site of Harborplace would have looked out on a vista of rotting and rat-infested piers, abandoned buildings, parking lots and a polluted harbor. But today, the waterfront redevelopment, so successful in attracting visitors, is being complemented by an expanded Lexington Market and a subway system that opened its first eight-mile stretch this month.

Sales are booming at Harborplace, and the city's hotel occupancy rates (ranging from 80-90 per cent), boosted by a new convention center, underscore the need for a projected 2,000 new first-class hotel rooms. (The Hyatt near Harborplace posted a 92.3 per cent occupancy rate recently, only second in its chain to the Hawaiian island of Maui.) And the city's image has been reinforced by the revival of its multiracial and ethnic neighborhoods (237 by one count), where self-help housing measures, some private, some government-assisted, have thrived.

While Baltimore remains a manufacturing and port city, its jobless rate remained below the national average throughout the recession. Unemployment stood at 8.9 per cent in May, despite major layoffs at the plants of General Motors Corp., U.S. Steel Corp. and Armco Inc., evidence that the downtown business boom had cushioned the reces-

sion's impact. What is more, the largest manufacturing employers have made big new investments in their old facilities. While employment levels at the plants may never reach previous peaks, the modernization efforts represent a significant investment in the city's future. U.S. Steel is spending $1 billion to upgrade its production facilities, and GM is embarking on a $270 million modernization program, according to Bernard Berkowitz, president of the Baltimore Economic Development Corp. (BEDCO).

Shipping remains a Baltimore mainstay. "Baltimore's container facilities are second only to New York and New Jersey's on the east coast," said David Carroll of the city planning department. Its port, one of the city's biggest employers, is the second-largest coal handler in the nation and handles 30 per cent of all auto imports on the East Coast.

Even a revitalized Baltimore, however, faces serious problems. Fully 19 percent of the city's residents receive some form of public assistance. Almost one in three of the city's blacks—who made up 55 per cent of the population in 1980—live below the poverty line.

But Baltimore has emerged relatively unscathed from the fiscal problems that have strained other cities in the East. Its bonds, rated A1 by Moody's, remain the highest-rated of any major city in the region. The new city budget in June raised property taxes and further curbed city spending. In the past two years, Baltimore has cut more than 10 per cent of its municipal work force.

PHILADELPHIA: UP AND DOWN

Through most of the 1970s, Philadelphia seemed more deeply mired in divisive racial politics than any other major U.S. city—a phenomenon symbolized by ex-police commissioner Frank L. Rizzo, who capitalized on white fears of crime and black neighborhood incursion to win two terms as mayor. Tensions abated under his successor, Bill J. Green. Last winter, when Rizzo emerged from political exile to seek the Democratic mayoral nomination against black ex-city managing director W. Wilson Goode, many Philadelphians feared a return to the bad old days. But it was not to be so: Rizzo put aside his polarizing law-and-order rhetoric, emerged as a changed and mellowed politician and seemed to symbolize Philadelphia's move to moderation. The calmness with which Goode subsequently won the general election in November appeared to confirm the trend.

One of the big issues in the campaign turned out to be the direction of economic and downtown development in the city, along with such neighborhood-oriented issues as health care and housing. Phila-

delphia is having a difficult time making the transition from a manufacturing to a service economy. "Philadelphia has very rapidly divested itself of its manufacturing labor force," said Theodore Hershberg, director of the Center for Philadelphia Studies at the University of Pennsylvania. Only 17 per cent of Philadelphians now have factory jobs, compared with 26 per cent just 10 years ago. In the same period, total jobs declined by about 140,000.

Another problem has been the business establishment's traditional, low-risk approach to city investments and its lack of involvement in city affairs. While Baltimore's business community has had a concerted program and a vision of urban revival since the 1950s, Philadelphia's private-sector response has been sporadic and unfocused.

Philadelphia, at one time, was on the ground floor in America's technological explosion. The world's first computer, Eniac, was built there in 1945 at the University of Pennsylvania. But the city never capitalized on the opportunity to become a center of that industry, in part because of the lack of investment capital. Seeking to avoid that error, today's economic development plans focus on building on the area's already large base of rapidly expanding, high-tech medical and health services firms.

In the area of downtown development, Philadelphia's $860 million Market Street East project, on a street that a few years ago was in rapid decline, is continuing to expand. New retail stores and restaurants—most recently this autumn's opening of the Rouse Co's "Gallery II"—have begun to draw a wide economic and racial cross-section of Philadelphians. In addition, young professionals now populate the chic 18th-and 19th-century townhouses in the Society Hill area near Independence Hall. But the newly elegant neighborhood scarcely masks the urban scars just a few miles to the north and west, which harbor some of America's most squalid slum neighborhoods.

Candidate Goode estimated that more than 22,000 buildings in the city are vacant or abandoned. And while the city has cleaned and sealed many of the buildings to prepare them for rehabilitation, progress has been slow in comparison to the speed of downtown redevelopment. Philadelphia's public housing agencies, plagued by patronage and inefficiency, remain bogged down in controversy. The Office of Housing and Community Development still maintains a backlog of over $100 million of unspent funds.

CHICAGO STALEMATE

Chicago's transition to its first black mayor remains far from complete in the throes of a power struggle between the reform-minded mayor, elected in April, and the city council majority led by Alderman Edward Vrdolyak. Many believe the stalemate is bad for business, especially downtown development; others suggest Chicago's political debate has opened up for the first time in living memory and that the raucousness of the discussion simply underscores how long open politics was repressed under the machine of Mayor Richard J. Daley.

"The differences between the mayor and the council are really irreconcilable," said Louis Masotti of the Northwestern University School of Urban Affairs. "Race is a factor, but they are fighting over something very basic: power."

Other city business has been stalled by the political turmoil and lengthy budget fight. Issues that are on hold include land acquisition for the North Loop business district, the fate of funds for the city's $750 million 1992 world's fair and negotiations for a $285 million retail project to be built by Rouse in the lakeside Navy Pier area.

Despite the political turbulence, basic city services have been uninterrupted. A compromise was reached to eliminate a projected 1983 deficit of $59 million, but not before Standard & Poor's Corp. lowered Chicago's bond rating from an A-minus to a triple B-plus, citing the city's history of "chronic fiscal stress." A real test will come early next year when the next city budget is drawn up.

Washington's fiscal reforms have made some headway. In September, Illinois courts upheld his firing of 734 city employees (the municipal work force totals 41,000). By executive order, he decentralized decision-making power in several departments and recently broke a long-standing city tradition by limiting the campaign contributions that the mayor can receive from those doing business with the city.

The mayor and council also reached agreement in time to submit an application for $147 million in federal community development block grant funds, and the city also received two state-designated enterprise zones under a new Illinois law.

If Washington has his way, more public spending for public facilities and economic development will flow into the neighborhoods rather than downtown. But this orientation and his combative political relations have produced lukewarm support for Washington among some downtown business leaders.

Chicago will hold an election for some aldermen in 1984, and Masotti suggested that some of Vrdolyak's organization types "may be put out of office by the same coalition [of blacks and white liberals] that elected Washington." If not,

Chicagoans may look forward to another three years of stalemated government.

PLANNING ON DENVER

The June election of Denver Mayor Federico Peña, 36, who defeated 72-year-old Mayor William McNichols, the incumbent since 1969, was a milestone. While Peña's ancestry is important in a city that is 19 per cent Hispanic, the new mayor is "not seen so much as an Hispanic but as an embodiment of the New West," said Marshall Kaplan, dean of the University of Colorado's Graduate School of Public Affairs. "Denver was a city in search of a leader," he added.

The city's explosive growth during the mid-1970s was largely fueled by the mountain region's energy and mining industries. In 1979, it had eight million square feet of office space; four years later, it had more than 35 million square feet. The energy industry was responsible for leasing almost half of that, according to United Bank of Denver's chairman, Richard Kirk. But when energy growth slowed, the office vacancy rate jumped from 0.7 per cent in February 1982 to 13.4 per cent in February 1983. Economists at United Banks of Colorado estimated that 26 per cent of the job growth in the Denver area during the 1970s was directly related to the energy industry.

Denver needs "long-term comprehensive planning," said Peña. "It doesn't make any sense to sit back and watch buildings literally spring up all over the city without some sense of over-all direction. We don't want Denver to become another Houston or Los Angeles."

Working with private developers, Peña has pledged to involve citizen and neighborhood groups more closely in the planning process. In a soon-to-be-developed 600-acre tract adjacent to downtown, the mayor is opposing the idea of office towers exclusively and is instead proposing significant open space, recreational and mixed-use development and housing for various income groups. Peña's election establishes a "different set of criteria and priorities with regard to city allocations" away from large-scale development and toward neighborhoods, Kaplan said.

A new downtown attraction is the year-old 16th Street Mall, a pedestrian-transit project of the city and the Denver Partnership, a business group formed three years ago that has led efforts to make the downtown a magnet for pedestrian traffic, enhance historic preservation and create ties between the downtown establishment and surrounding neighborhoods.

Denver's sprawling development has created serious pollution and transportation problems. In addition to the light rail system long under debate, Peña is consid-

ering a voluntary system under which people would leave their autos home one day a week.

Although Denver finished its last fiscal year with an $8 million surplus, it will have to enact some wide-ranging spending cuts and tax hikes to meet a projected $20 million deficit next year. It currently has an Aa bond rating from Moody's.

RETOOLING HOUSTON'S BOOM

Like a Texas sheriff looking for an outlaw, the recession finally found Houston. By early summer, it had an unemployment rate as high as the nation at large. The unfamiliar bout with economic reversal has caused some to rethink the city's traditional dependence on the energy industry, Houston's great economic engine but also the cause of skyrocketing joblessness in 1983. The city's legendary policies of free growth and rapid development have come under fire too, and the city council, while rejecting comprehensive zoning, has approved a mild ordinance controlling building setbacks.

"Houston's economy is still pretty closely tied to petrochemicals," said Jim Edmonds, chairman of the mayoral campaign of oilman Bill Wright, who lost to incumbent Mayor Kathryn J. Whitmire earlier this month. Economists estimate that 35-40 per cent of the city's economy depends on the energy industry.

The oil and gas recession has dramatically affected Houston. The city lost 50,000 jobs in 1982 as a result of shutdowns, bankruptcies and cutbacks in the energy business and related firms. From 1981-82, office leasing dropped 50 per cent, leading to a vacancy rate of 16 per cent early this year. That translates into 20 million square feet unoccupied and many new buildings nearly vacant. Even the residential market is in a deep slump. Just a year ago only 2 per cent of the apartments in the metropolitan area were vacant, but in the past several months more than 20 per cent of the units, many new and expensive, have been empty. Many city hotels are struggling to maintain a 50 per cent occupancy rate.

Diversification has become a buzzword on the political agenda. Ben Reyes, a city councilman, faults Whitmire for "inaction on her part to go out to try to solicit more business." Echoing the growth management debate heard in Denver, Reyes emphasized the need for "vision and leadership in the mayor's office."

Compounding the mounting economic problems had been the steady stream of unemployed workers from the industrially troubled Midwest. That migration has slowed, however, as Houston's unemployment rate has risen. "If they came down as blue-collar workers," said city councilman George Greanias, "my guess is a fair number of them have left."

Some have cited Houston's defeat last June of a referendum for a $2.4 heavy rail transit system as confirmation that Houstonians have yet to address the sometimes horrendous traffic problems occasioned by rapid growth and overdependence on private autos. The city's traffic congestion has reached such epic proportions that today's rush hours are twice as long as they were just 10 years ago. Planners estimate that 55 new expressway lanes would be needed to handle the existing traffic crunch. Houston voters opposed the high cost and limited size of the heavy rail system, said Neil Tannahill, a political science professor at Houston Community College. In September, Harris County residents did approve a $900 million toll road proposal.

SAN DIEGO ON THE MOVE

Three times in the past century, San Diego has lost major transportation facilities to Los Angeles. Railroad, port and interstate highway systems all chose to locate up the coast. Yet while Los Angeles may be the country's third-largest city, few would now say that San Diego has suffered greatly in its shadow.

Roger Hedgecock, the Republican who was elected in May to fill the vacancy created by Mayor Pete Wilson's successful Senate bid, inherited a prosperous city that has applied at least mild controls to the physical growth threatening to engulf it. Hedgecock also strongly supports the major downtown development project, Horton Plaza, now under construction after years of delay.

Part of the motivation for San Diego's model growth efforts—which Hedgecock has promised to maintain and even strengthen—has come from the city to the north. "Los Angeles has not grown in a particularly attractive fashion," said Lee Grissom, president of the San Diego Chamber of Commerce. "L.A. has done a lot of bad things for us in terms of attracting business away, but it has also done one good thing: given us an example of what we don't want to become."

Still, the city has problems. One is air pollution, though not on a Los Angeles scale. Another is untreated sewage from Mexico that has been washing up on city beaches. Still another is the office vacancy rate, nearly the nation's highest.

San Diego has to an extent shaken the image of company town for the Navy, but defense contractors and military personnel still account for about a fifth of its economy. About a fourth of the Navy's personnel and a fifth of the Marine Corps's are located in the city. Military spending, says the Chamber of Commerce, has declined in relative importance but still poured $4.75 billion into the local economy last year. Increases in Pentagon spending have also meant new business for the area's defense contractors.

But while San Diego's defense-related industries are prospering, the part of its economy that depends on Mexico is not. The devaluation of the peso has hurt area producers that supply goods to Mexico and has slowed the stream of Mexicans who come north to shop. Mexican spending accounted for $461 million, or 7 per cent of local retail sales in 1981, but last year plummeted to $50 million.

Pacific Basin trade is playing a growing role in the city's economy. *San Diego Union* editor Gerald Warren speculated that San Diego could become the center of U.S. Pacific trade. The city is home to a large number of Japanese firms, including the Matsushita Electric Industry Co. Ltd. and Sanyo Mfg. Corp. About 1,050 companies in San Diego County are now involved in exports, according to the Chamber of Commerce.

Fiscally, San Diego enjoys the same relative health and high bond ratings as other Sunbelt cities. While its ability to levy taxes is limited under Proposition 13, forcing it to cut back on capital spending to maintain services, a rapidly expanding tax base has kept revenues up.

Federal budget cuts have not severely hurt San Diego because it was less dependent on federal money than many other cities of comparable size. But with the shrinkage of state aid, it has increasingly sought federal money for some projects. The first line of its trolley system from downtown to the Mexican border at Tijuana was completed without federal money, on time and under budget. To complete the second line, however, the city is turning to the federal government for partial help.

SAN FRANCISCO DOWNSHIFT

Mayor Dianne Feinstein had little difficulty repulsing a recall effort sparked by a radical political group last spring or winning reelection earlier this month. Fiscally, San Francisco appears to be one of the nation's soundest cities, despite the perils of Proposition 13. The city expects to spend $6.5 million as host to the Democratic national convention next summer, but thousands of delegates, press and visitors should substantially enrich its already thriving economy.

There are prices to be paid for prosperity, however. San Francisco's small size, high real estate costs and limited access have compounded the problem of being a major corporate headquarters.

Housing costs have escalated so rapidly that many low and middle-income residents have been driven from the city. A 1982 law required developers to contribute to housing construction as a trade-off for office construction, and developers have contributed $18.8 million to build 2,303 new housing units. "Housing is the critical catalyst of urban life in the 1980s," Feinstein said. "It's up to us to find solutions, and waiting may be hazardous to our civic health."

As San Francisco struggles with prosperity, the most vital question may be whether it will be able to exert planning controls to minimize further Manhattanization resulting from unchecked high-rise development. Sharp limits would be placed on building downtown development by a new city plan announced in August. Endorsed by Feinstein, it would set height limits for buildings, regulate their design, require that development permit more sunshine to penetrate streets and sidewalks and protect more than 200 historic buildings from demolition or alteration.

The new plan is not without its critics, however. The emphasis on downtown means the city has "just physically moved the development to the other side of Market Street," charged preservationist Sue Hestor. Some developers, planners and businessmen have reacted cooly to the proposal on the ground that it may drive business out of the city.

On Nov. 8, San Francisco voters narrowly rejected a referendum that would have restricted development even more than the proposed city plan. Most city officials fought against the measure, and developers poured more than $650,000 into the campaign to defeat it.

The current moratorium on new projects pending approval of the plan could encourage builders to look to eastern suburbs in Contra Costa County and Walnut Creek, where housing and land costs are lower. Also waiting with open arms is Oakland, across San Francisco Bay and connected to the city by a subway system. Downtown Oakland has the West Coast's heaviest concentration of Art Deco buildings and now offers many restored offices spaces that are awaiting tenants.

Dimensions of the Civic Future: Fiscal Restraint and Intergovernmental Impacts

S. Kenneth Howard

S. Kenneth Howard is former executive director of the U.S. Advisory Commission on Intergovernmental Relations. This is based on his address at the 90th National Conference on Government, November 18, 1984, in San Antonio.

Will there be a civic future? Although the subject is broad and elusive, the answer is yes. And that civic future will be heavily intergovernmental in nature, recognizing, of course, that "civic" connotes a whole lot more than local governments and their activities.

One of John Naisbitt's megatrends notes a shift from centralization to decentralization. In govermental terms, that means that the tide is turning toward the local level. In fact, in the last annual public opinion poll conducted by the Advisory Commission on Intergovernmental Relations, local governments, by a substantial plurality, were selected most often by citizens as the level of government from which they feel they get the most for their money. Of the eight polls taken in the 1970's, local governments were rated first only once, in 1979. Of the five polls taken thus far in the 1980's, local units have been first or tied for first three times.

A FUTURE OF FISCAL RESTRAINT

Despite the widespread rejection in November of referenda that would have imposed some rather Draconian tax and expenditure limitations (see the REVIEW, January 1985, page 26), the fiscal future at the local level remains one of very real constraints. We often ignore the fact that for just about a decade now there has been a steady decline in per capita spending at the local level when measured in constant (non-inflated) dollars. Indeed, for domestic spending, that same trend has applied for some years to all levels of government, but for shorter periods than at the local level. The public expectation of fiscal restraint actually began at the local level and spread to the other tiers of government. Thus, fiscal constraint is a grass roots movement of long standing, and it is not about to go away just because of a strengthened economy.

Local fiscal restraint will also be induced by efforts to reduce the national deficit, which increased by approximately $190 billion in the last fiscal year. Through expenditure reductions and tax system changes, the national government can find additional money for its purposes in ways that will significantly affect local governments. The restraining effects of reductions in appropriations for the many grant programs localities now implement are fairly obvious. Only slightly less obvious in their implications are tax code changes which would eliminate or reduce the ability to deduct state and local tax payments when calculating federal tax liability under the personal income tax, or would eliminate or reduce the tax exemption which is extended to interest earned on state and local bonds. Because we have never experienced anything similar to this combination of tax changes, we cannot fully assess their implications, but their restraining effects are apparent.

In short, the local fiscal future, at least for the rest of this decade, will probably be marked by restraint and the increasing use of fees for services.

STATES WILL SHAPE THE LOCAL FUTURE

It is scarcely news that local governments are creatures of the states. The roles and leadership of the states, however, are becoming more and more important as they set the framework within which local futures will unfold. In September 1983, ACIR

"Dimensions of the Civic Future: Fiscal Restraint and Intergovernmental Impacts," S. Kenneth Howard, *National Civic Review*, April 1985. Reprinted by permission.

233

concluded "that the states are pivotal actors in our federal system. . . .[T]he kinds of responses that the states—both individually and sometimes collectively—provide to the challenges facing them will determine the future resilience, effectiveness and political balance of our federal system." The commission concluded further that the best way to measure just how well states are doing in responding to the challenges facing them and their "creatures" is to assess the leadership states show in establishing better state-local-private partnerships. How the states deal with the current and future problems confronting their localities will have a great deal to say about the nature and strength of our federal system for the next several years.

Because the fiscal situation of the states appears to be easing somewhat, some might conclude that the fiscal restraints facing local governments will be eased by state actions. Indeed, some such easing is likely, but probably not as much as some recent projections of state "surpluses" would suggest. For the first time in this decade, states are not confronted by a combination of high unemployment, double-digit inflation, and binding tax and expenditure lids. Compared to the recent past, the fiscal future does indeed look better. But part of this relative well-being is also a direct result of states' own actions as they cut spending and increased taxes to keep their budgets balanced, as all but one are required by law to do. They now face deferred expenditure expectations and expiring temporary taxes that were adopted to stay out of recession-induced deficits. They do so, however, with a heightened appreciation for the wisdom of making themselves less cyclically sensitive economically through such devices as rainy day funds. The setting is rife with demands on resources. Like their localities, the states also face federal grant reductions and tax changes. In short, a recovering economy does not assure the wherewithal to make policy choices easier for state policymakers; nor does it diminish the challenge states face in providing the framework within which the civic future will unfold.

SPECIFIC LOCAL IMPACTS

Three specific aspects of the civic future have important intergovernmental implications. First, efforts to find new alternative ways to deliver public services are having and will continue to have their greatest impact in localities. Because most public services are "delivered" in one local setting or another, it seems natural that there would be more interest and exploration of alternative delivery mechanisms here. It is local governments more than any others that will help us discern the effects of providing a service with public funds while not necessarily having that service

delivered by a public agency and public employees. It is localities that will help us learn just what voluntarism and co-production mean in an era of more single-parent households and two-wage-earner families.

Second, public policymaking is not fun at any level of government when there are heavy fiscal constraints, as the President and Congress are showing the entire nation. Our future is going to be one of conflictual politics as all participants realize that the current system of achieving compromises by giving everybody a little something is less and less feasible. How do we make sustainable and tolerable public policy decisions in such an environment? All governments face this problem, but localities will most likely be the pacesetters in finding new devices and approaches. Local experimentation and hardearned experience will lead us all in this era of political conflict.

Finally, because our society has steadily lost confidence in its authoritative institutions of all sorts (family, church, government and others), it is localities that will have to lead in regaining the needed appreciation for public service as a valued career. Indeed, even the term "public service" seems quaintly out of step with the times. Berating bureaucrats has long been an American practice, and it is properly protected by the freedom of speech. What is missing now is adequate underlying appreciation for government careerists as dedicated persons who are highly competent in their chosen specialties. At one time, teaching, the ministry and "public service" were about equally revered careers. All have lost their luster, but particularly the last. Fortunately, "bureaucrat busting" is practiced less in local politics than at other levels. If we are to attract into public service and retain there the talented people a complex and free society requires, localities must initiate a grassroots rebalancing movement so that the political advantages of degrading government careerists begin to decrease.

CONCLUSION

Although localities can and will shape their own futures in important ways, they cannot escape the economic, fiscal and political environment created by forces well beyond their purview. The character of their future is very much an intergovernmental issue, and it will be affected by actions at all levels of government. But localities can also lead the nation in trying to find new and better ways to deliver public services, to mitigate the debilitating effects of conflictual politics, and to regain appreciation for government careerists as a necessary and positive part of our system of governance.

Strategies for the Essential Community:

Local Government in the Year 2000

Laurence Rutter

Laurence Rutter is associate director of the International City Management Association, 1140 Connecticut Avenue, N.W., Washington, D.C. 20036. He is a political scientist, teacher, and author of numerous publications and articles on topics such as public policy, urban problems, and government. He was principal staff on ICMA's Committee on Future Horizons of the Profession and authored *The Essential Community*, which presents the findings of that committee.

How will cities, counties, and regional councils of governments meet the challenges posed by economic changes, demographic shifts, new urban patterns, and technological and political changes in the next two decades? The International City Management Association's Committee on Future Horizons of the Profession, in a recent study, concluded that the best approach is what they called nurturing the essential community through four strategies: getting by modestly, regulating demand, skeptical federalism, and finding the proper scale and mix for government services.

Getting By Modestly

The prevailing view of local government—what can be called its current paradigm—assumes future growth. This expectation pervades our thinking about cities, counties, and councils of government (COGs). The paradigm calls for budgets to grow, federal grants to increase, incrementalism to reign, wealth to rise, roles to expand, and benefits to improve. Nearly every decision made in city halls or county courthouses has been based on the assumption that growth is inevitable.

The paradigm has been relatively valid for the last 30 years or so. Cities and counties have grown steadily and, it seems, inexorably. Local governments were inadequately prepared for a great deal of the growth; "better" governments were those that prepared for growth better.

Reality may be outstripping the paradigm, however. Straws in the wind indicate that growth—both economic and demographic—is not inevitable. Holding the line indefinitely may become the order of the decade for public sector organizations. For successful negotiation of the 1980s and 1990s, policy strategies will be based on the assumption that the scope of local government can just as easily contract or remain constant as grow.

Budgets. Getting by modestly will translate into budgeting strategies that are not based on the assumption of incremental growth. These strategies do not yet have names, but they will be in great demand and will be difficult to implement. The difficulty arises because without incrementalism it will be hard, if not impossible, to cover up who wins and who loses—the politics of the shrinking pie. If the pie grows, losses can be masked because everyone's slice increases at least a little even though proportions change. No growth means it is harder to buy off the losers.

Emerging budgeting strategies must be based on the recognition that it will be much harder to reallocate resources in both the short and the long run. Surprising though it may seem, when inflation is brought under control the problems for municipal budgets will be exacerbated. Inflation at least gives the appearance—a false and pernicious one, admittedly—of growth.

Public/private cooperation. Getting by modestly also will require increased involvement of the private sector in traditionally public sector concerns—meaning greater pressures to transfer services from one sector to the other. Contracting out will be much more popular, but writing these contracts with the good of the public in mind will test local government ingenuity. Private sector support will become much more important in local government decision-making. And cities and counties will have an interest in improving the climate for the private sector, especially in the area of unnecessary regulation and red tape.

Volunteers. The trend toward professionalization of the municipal work force will be halted. Volunteerism will become necessary if not fashionable.

The key to use of volunteers is to distinguish between truly professional and quasi-professional services and between essential and nonessential activities. Volunteers can perform quasi-professional and nonessential services in the interest of getting by with less.

Quasi-professionalism is not the

same as unskilled activity. Volunteers can be trained, as thousands of volunteer firefighters can testify. They can perform medical, patrol, maintenance, and other functions on a par with paid employees.

Self-help. Another way in which local governments can get by with less is to help people do for themselves what they have come to expect local government to do for them.

This is not volunteerism, where people contribute to the common good, but rather individual self-help, where people take control of their own lives—a control that could be even more tenuous in the future. Local government can help people recognize their own skills, resources, and abilities to deal with the problems that beset them.

Citizens are losing the opportunity to help themselves, to learn about their own capacities to cope and grow. Machines and government have taken over, and both are likely to take over more unless checked in the future.

The programs and the machines have laudable objectives and frequently are necessary. But they have contributed to people's loss of control. People remain passive toward the machine, which cannot provide sympathy, cannot be reasoned with, and cannot handle capricious or out-of-the-ordinary activities.

People increasingly assume that their personal problems can, or at least should, be handled by government. But consumer protection is no substitute for caveat emptor. Safety helmets are not tantamount to defensive driving. Safety regulations are not a substitute for prudence.

There is every indication that people's sense of powerlessness will increase in the future. The demographic projections for the next 20 years suggest a real possibility of great atomization—smaller families, fewer marriages, and more divorces. And the growth of telecommunications as a substitute for personal contact will increase the tendency toward anomie among individuals.

At the same time, local govern-

ments and the public sector at large will no longer be able to assume a great many social burdens. Surely one solution will be for cities and counties to help citizens themselves shoulder some of the responsibilities for their lives.

With some initial assistance, citizens and commercial establishments can undertake a great many activities for which they may not be willing to pay taxes. They can sweep the streets in front of their homes or buildings, especially if receptacles for the sweepings are readily available. If proper tools are provided, they can trim and spray trees in front of homes or businesses and even maintain neighborhood parks and clean up after their animals. In a few cases, local governments have succeeded in changing from back door to curbside refuse pickup, but with considerable protest.

Political and civic leadership is the key to changing the psychology from "this is someone else's responsibility" to "this is my responsibility." And leadership should primarily be by example.

Risk. Getting by modestly also may require coming to grips with what might be called the zero-risk ideal, the tendency to overprotect at the expense of taxpayers. The question to examine is how many public policies and standards for municipal services are based on the belief that the risk of failure or of an undesirable event should be zero. The question is, Can the public sector afford to pay for reducing the risk to zero?

In fire safety, for instance, should we work toward zero risk of property loss? Or is some degree of risk acceptable—providing we continue to reduce loss of life? Is having a community volunteer fire company more important than a certain small loss of property? How much do we pay for a decrease of 1% in the risk of property loss? In police protection, how much patrolling would be necessary to reduce the incidence of mugging? Can we afford the cost? Or is there an acceptable level of risk given the cost?

The answers to such questions do not preclude a city or county

from working toward zero risk. But it may cause them to assess the cost more accurately and appreciate the cost of government generally. It also may make people recognize that they are willing to run certain risks, that such risks are implicit in almost all public policies, and that exposing the public to some risk is not inhumane.

Labor. Getting by modestly involves some important challenges for the public employer and employee. One of the straws in the wind is a reduction of upward mobility in the work force. Too many people will be competing for too few jobs at the top.

The new paradigm will require facing up to the fact that within each jurisdiction the possibilities for advancement will decrease. The problem can be ameliorated only through finding ways to improve working conditions, involve employees in management-level decisions, and encourage interjurisdictional mobility.

Rigid job classifications must be relaxed so that employees can change the nature of the tasks they perform, learn new skills, and have an opportunity for variety if not upward mobility in their work.

Advancement in the future also will require the ability to move between jurisdictions. Patrol personnel wanting to become sergeants should be able to change jurisdictions to advance when opportunities arise. To permit such mobility, a great many local personnel policies and traditions will have to be changed. Pension requirements will need to be altered. Future entrance and examination requirements should not penalize outside applicants. Department managers will need to appreciate the importance of at least not discouraging mobility among personnel.

Few of these policies are going to be easy to implement. Yet the lack of growth in the public sector and the economic adjustments and demographic changes in the future make them necessary.

Regulating Demand

Some of the same forces—economic and demographic—that will require local governments to get by modestly will also require them to find ways to influence the demand for both public and private goods and services.

Price. One important and under-utilized way to reduce demand for government services is the use of a pricing system. A price on a service increases the threshold of use. People learn to think twice about taking advantage of a city or county service if there is a personal, out-of-pocket cost. The cost need not reflect the full cost of the service, but it should be high enough to discourage unnecessary or spurious use. It also causes users to take more personal interest in the delivery of the service.

Prices or fees can be associated with services in numerous ways. Weekly trash pickup may be viewed as a necessity in some communities, twice weekly pickup a useful service, and three times weekly a luxury. It may be possible by imposing fees on a block-by-block basis to allow people to choose the level of service they prefer. Wealthier neighborhoods may want pickups three times a week. Others may be satisfied with a weekly pickup at no charge—the cost being borne by taxes.

The same may apply to police patrol. In Maryland, for instance, the state police literally lease their officers on a county-by-county basis in a "resident trooper program." Some counties are willing to pay for resident troopers; some are not. There is no reason to preclude the same kind of program with municipal or county police on a neighborhood-by-neighborhood basis for patrol purposes.

The price creates a threshold to dampen demand; yet it allows all citizens to receive at least a minimum level of service. Taxes can be minimized and government held to a market-determined size.

Prices also can be used to reduce aggregate demand for consumer and industrial goods and to reduce the side effects of this demand. For example, pricing systems can be built into land subdivision policies to reduce urban sprawl (and the high governmental costs associated with sprawl) and to better control both initial and long-range

costs for transportation, water and sewer services, and other services that will be provided in the new area. Much of this pricing is not new: most cities for many years have required land developers to install streets, sewer and water lines, sidewalks, street lights, and other facilities at their own expense for the land within the subdivision boundaries.

Pricing also can be used by local governments to reduce waste and pollution, the costs of which are eventually passed on to citizens through the tax system. Instead of building waste treatment plants, local governments could concentrate on placing a price on collection of effluent and solid waste from both residential and commercial establishments, a price large enough to discourage the waste itself. The price could be based on a unit of waste collected.

Two caveats must be offered here.

One is to recognize the complexity of the market system itself, a system in which prices are a prime ingredient. Price levels can affect all facets of the economic system and cause ripples throughout the community. Prices should not be imposed without analysis of the possible consequences far beyond the immediate goods or services involved.

The second caveat relates to equity. Prices can deprive people of services they badly need. Local governments must be careful to use highly targeted subsidies to prevent the very poor from choosing to forgo vital services.

Energy. Energy is the most important area in which demand needs to be reduced throughout society. Local government has a role to play, a role that is part regulation, part pricing, and part leadership.

Building codes need to be updated to reflect community concerns for energy conservation, and they need to be flexible enough to accommodate unanticipated future technological developments. New buildings especially are susceptible to codes that set standards for insulation, site, and types of heating units. Codes can specify that build-

ings should be capable of being retrofitted for solar energy when it becomes more competitive with oil and electricity. A number of communities, such as Davis, California, have already updated their codes.

It may be that the process of enforcing energy-related building codes needs to be updated along with the codes themselves. Some communities are using "energy audits," whereby inspectors use visual inspection and/or computers to identify opportunities to save energy costs in heating and cooling. One community in Minnesota uses federally supported employees to help citizens identify ways to make their homes and business establishments more energy-efficient.

Many local governments are directly involved in supplying energy to citizen-customers through their own public utilities. These governments can increase energy efficiency over the next two decades by establishing pricing systems that reduce peak load demand for electricity or penalize users for excessive energy consumption.

Many other local governments have taken the view that leadership by the city, county, or COG is an important element in encouraging individual conservation. The new city hall in Vineland, New Jersey, is an example of what has been called a "smart building," with a computer-based system that constantly monitors and adjusts temperatures to conserve energy. Sherman, Texas, has developed a comprehensive plan of energy use designed to help identify short- and long-term conservation opportunities for the city. Springfield, Missouri, has converted a bus into a mobile educational lab, teaching citizens how to conserve energy.

These activities are the wave of the future for local governments as they mobilize to limit demand.

Skeptical Federalism

Still other strategies for nurturing the essential community should be considered by local citizens, elected officials, and their management staffs.

One is a skeptical federalism, one that contemplates buying back local independence from the national government. It will be no easier than getting by modestly. And it could be very costly.

The committee believes that cities, counties, and COGs run considerable risk of being swallowed up by the central government. They run the risk of losing the ability to determine their own priorities, run their own programs, hire their own personnel, and fashion their communities in the way their citizens desire.

It is conceivable that by the year 2000 most local governments will get substantially more than one-half their revenue from the central and state governments and raise few of their resources locally. Moreover, it is conceivable that if local governments raised no resources independently, the vast majority of their essential activities would be circumscribed by the central government.

There is only one way to prevent this from happening with any certainty, and that is for local governments to buy back their independence from the central government while they have the resources to do the job.

In simple terms, it is a matter of money. Given the interpretation of the Constitution by the courts, when local governments accept federal money, they are subject to any conditions that might legally be placed on that money. The trend in recent years has been for Congress to impose more and more conditions, and as yet no court has declared a condition unconstitutional. The more dependent local governments become, the bolder will be the Congress and the president in imposing conditions on them.

A reversal is vastly easier said than done. Short-term political considerations make it extremely difficult to turn down grants from the central government. Yet some way needs to be found at least to make programs, from revenue sharing to historical preservation, less attractive.

Taxes. First, locally raised taxes should be made more palatable. The property tax as it is currently structured in most places is a very unpopular tax—and with good reason.

Many local governments make annual reassessments of real property, a policy intended to keep the property tax equitable. But experience in California and other states has shown that annual reassessments force assessed property values to keep in step with market prices and, therefore, with the relentless forces of inflation.

Another frequently cited problem with the property tax is that it measures only the present market value of the property and not the owner's current ability to pay tax on it. Thus, the tax falls most heavily on the poor and those living on fixed incomes, except in places that have some sort of circuit breaker for these groups.

Many people have called for the abolition of the property tax because it is widely perceived to be one of the most unfair taxes currently levied. Yet without it, many local governments would be at a loss to replace that local revenue base and would further lose their independence. And a persuasive argument can be made that land and buildings are an appropriate base for many local taxes and the services these taxes pay for. Many essential local government functions exist for the maintenance and protection of property. Water and sewer services, zoning, and waste collection maintain or enhance the value of property. Police and fire services protect property. Zoning and land use controls and building and occupancy codes regulate the use of property.

The nature, value, and dispersion of property are important determinants of the nature, cost, and intensity of a great many municipal services. A community with all frame homes has different fire suppression and code enforcement problems and services from one in which homes are brick or masonry. Apartments have a police protection problem different from that of single-family dwellings.

So it may not be entirely wise or equitable for local governments to abandon this tax. But changes are needed to make any tax in which property is a factor more equitable and politically palatable.

Cities and counties may want to consider:

• A property tax that is scaled to income as determined by a state or federal income tax.

• A property tax that delays the effects of rapid inflation—and perhaps rapid deflation as well—in land values (income averaging on the federal income tax may be a model for consideration).

• A tax that is levied on the sale of property.

• A tax that distinguishes more between land itself and the improvements on the land.

The fee-for-service concept also needs full exploration by local governments; it uses price to affect demand and is compatible with the notion of public/private cooperation.

Grants. Maintaining a local tax base is only one part of the price of skeptical federalism. The other price is taking a particularly cold look at grants from the central government.

The governing body may want to set an annual ceiling on the level of federal and/or state money in the community. And it may want to consider reducing the level of this ceiling annually until it reaches a satisfactory minimum. Every community would have a different ceiling.

Skeptical federalism, in short, means knowing how and when to look a gift horse in the mouth, even when the family thinks the nag is charming—and then finding the money to get your own mount when the "free" horse looks suspicious.

Scale and Mix of Government

The fourth facet of the strategy for local governments over the next 20 years is finding the proper scale and mix for government services.

Scale. The scale of services has been debated for years. The issue is whether local citizens, elected officials, and professional staff people should work to regionalize and/or decentralize the level at which local government programs and services are delivered.

The answer is that it all depends.

The future, we believe, requires both regionalization and decentralization. But if there should be a pattern, it will be in the direction of decentralization of local services and programs.

Regionalism reexamined. Regionalism is undergoing reexamination. For decades, the doctrine among urbanists was that local government should be regionalized. That consensus has broken down. Now some argue with equal conviction that small is always better, that smaller government is closer to the citizen and can operate municipal services more effectively.

The committee was impressed, but not completely convinced, that small is always better. It did come to realize, however, that many virtues of small-scale policymaking and service delivery have been overlooked. At the same time, however, large metropolitan areas have a compelling need for some regional units and decision-making bodies.

Decentralization. The most important trend in terms of the scale of local government services will be in the other direction—decentralization.

Today a great many cities and counties are experimenting with decentralization. Administratively, the neighborhood "city hall" has been tried in Dayton, Ohio; Boston, Massachusetts; and other cities. The neighborhood planning commission is being tried in Washington, D.C. Politically, some communities are experimenting with having neighborhoods construct their own annual budgets, allocating funds among various services according to their preferences. Citizen groups naturally will focus on the neighborhood, following the decentralization of administrative and political activities.

The objective of decentralization should be to facilitate access of citizens to local government.

As with regionalism, however, decentralization eventually has limits. Some decisions must be made uniformly for the entire jurisdiction. Major zoning decisions cannot, and should not, be dealt with in isolation; but many variances are only neighborhood matters. The basic requirements for hiring police patrol personnel should be standard; but some neighborhoods may need specialized skills. Solid waste requires centralized collection control, but collection schedules can vary by neighborhood. Overall budget decisions must be made at the city or county council level, but neighborhoods can have many options within the framework of these decisions.

There are, in short, no easy rules. As a general proposition, localities should concentrate on the question of decentralization over the next decade or so. Yet a time will come when they will reach the limits of this important action. At the same time, they cannot ignore the regional picture and the need to strengthen their COGs. But the rules will invariably apply differently in every region and for every jurisdiction within the region.

Citizen involvement. One of the important keys to adjusting the scale of government to provide more direct access by citizens is the mechanisms to be used. Traditional methods will still be needed—public hearings, citizen representatives, complaint offices, neighborhood meetings, advisory committees, boards, commissions. But the telecommunications revolution offers added possibilities for reducing both the physical and the psychological distance between citizen and government.

Cable TV is a natural for increasing access. Experiments in Columbus, Ohio, with the QUBE system, which offers two-way communication between subscriber and studio, open entirely new horizons. Cable systems can bring into everyone's home a forum for two-way discussions of vital community issues—zoning, land use, budgets, important ordinances, or whatever.

Cable TV also can allow more direct access by citizens to information from local governments. Video display terminals could be used by citizens in their own homes, or in nearby neighborhood offices, to renew drivers' licenses, check tax records, record complaints, change addresses, request special services, and perhaps even engage in some forms of personal counseling.

There are some obvious, and perhaps unobvious, problems inherent in this adaptation of telecommunications to citizen involvement. People have learned to trust television (through Walter Cronkite, for instance) and to take numbers (such as opinion polls) at face value. But there is nothing inherently authoritative about a TV screen. Misinformation can be communicated as easily as correct information. Viewers may or may not be a representative sample—and they may or may not be recording their true reactions. Moreover, there may be a great temptation with these systems to encourage direct as opposed to representative democracy. They could serve to bypass elected officials rather than assist them in reflecting the views of the public.

Another problem is confidentiality. Local governments should be particularly sensitive to this problem because much of the data held locally is of the most personal nature: personal property tax declarations, medical records, and so on.

Mix. The mix of services provided by cities, counties, and COGs in the next 20 years will be determined in large part by the mix of people they serve. Demography is destiny. As the populations served by local governments change, so, too, will the priorities of the governing bodies.

We only can speculate about the effect population changes might have on local government priorities. But the speculation is important because some of these changes in priorities should be anticipated before they overtake our cities, counties, and COGs.

The elderly. The specter of "gray power" has been sighted on the horizon as associations of retired people begin to gain local clout. The form such clout will take in the future depends on what makes this population group unique. Will it have a separate and distinct set of needs that local governments can serve? Will it cause distinct problems? Here the committee finds itself of two minds. On one hand, it can identify a number of unique needs of the elderly, needs that will have to be given more attention in the next two decades. On the other hand, it questions whether the definition of "elderly" that we use today will apply in 2000.

Today we think of the elderly as those over 65 years of age, because they are very likely to be retired, to live on fixed incomes, to have high mortality rates from disease, and to be approaching the limits of their life expectancy.

It is not at all clear that those over 65 in the year 2000 will be so easily categorized. Given the continuing trend toward elimination of mandatory retirement, the fact that life expectancy is probably increasing, and the inability of the working part of the population to pay for early retirement and a sustained income throughout life, it is possible that what we once defined as elderly—65 and older—may no longer fit. It may be 70 and older. Or 75.

If "elderly" is redefined, the population with similar needs will become smaller. Nonetheless, local governments will need to begin now anticipating some changes in the mix of services based on the aging of the population.

Transportation is one area of major concern. The jitney bus, the short-run shopping bus, and the subsidized cab may all be in considerable demand. The elderly probably will require this service, because most will be highly mobile, probably gainfully employed part-time, but unable to afford the very expensive automobile fuels of the future.

In housing, there will be an even greater demand for multihousehold dwellings, conveniently located close to shopping and entertainment facilities. The dwellings need not be publicly subsidized, but they will present some challenges, especially in land use planning. It is conceivable that single complexes will be devoted exclusively to the elderly who are dependent on public transportation and who need to be within walking distance of major commercial areas and medical care facilities. This de-

mand may require specialized police patrol and assistance programs and specially equipped fire service personnel.

The elderly, no matter what their age, will have special recreation needs that have been largely overlooked by most local governments. Swings, jogging tracks, and, in some cases, swimming pools may not fill the bill.

Another problem is clearly pensions. The growth in the percentage of the work force that will be retired in the next 20 years is alarming. Politically and economically, it will be very difficult for pension programs to require, as many do today, that current workers pay for the currently retired.

This will hit local governments' own pension programs hard. Those not fully funded now will find it increasingly difficult to shoulder the burden.

The result almost certainly will be that current workers will contribute some more, but retirees will be getting relatively less in the way of retirement benefits. This alone will present local councils with some nasty political decisions. Another result will be that people who once planned to stop working at retirement age will have to return to the work force at least part-time.

Employment opportunities will be one order of the problem, largely for the public sector. But the support services to sustain part-time employment will be a local problem. Transportation has been mentioned. Now we support those who work on a full-time basis by rush-hour bus service and automobile traffic control measures. With more part-time elderly, the non-peak hours of the present will become peak hours of the future. Recreation facilities, too, may need more flexible hours.

As the elderly increase in number, political influence, and personal freedom, we may see some changes in local politics. Many more of the elderly may be interested in seeking public office, serving on boards and commissions, and presenting their cases to councils. Some observers allege

that today's officeholders are younger than they once were. Tomorrow the reverse may be true, thus bringing different orientations, values, expectations, time horizons, and energy to public life.

The young. There will be proportionately fewer young people in the year 2000 than today. We can see this happening already, with the closing of schools throughout the country for lack of sufficient enrollment. This was a trend that took most of us by surprise, and we are determined that similar trends should not do so in the future. To that end, the committee urges communities not to dispose of their school buildings and youth recreation centers too quickly. Between 1982 and 1992—depending on what assumptions are made—the Bureau of the Census, in *Social Indicators, 1976,* sees an upswing in the number of people under 24 years of age. These people will be needing the schools that are being closed today.

Women. Women will continue to be a larger proportion of the population than men and to enter the work force in increasing numbers. Their effect on the mix of services provided by local governments will change accordingly.

The day of the woman volunteer subsidizing vital local services is about to end. Local leaders should recognize the growing unpopularity of volunteering among many women, who now are demanding full pay for such activity. This may serve as a counterforce to the desire of local governments to change many services from a professional to a volunteer basis. But as women become more independent and need independent income, they will find volunteering less attractive.

Day care is no passing need. In the future, day care is likely to play an even greater role in the lives of children than it did in the past. It will extend beyond preschool to school-age children who require care in the early mornings or late afternoons—and to children of mothers who travel on the job or on weekends. Recreational facilities may assume the job of providing day care-type services seven days a week, eight to twelve hours a day, to accommodate the needs of these mothers.

Male underemployment may be another consequence of women's growth spiritually, politically, and economically in society, especially if the economy does not produce sufficient jobs for both sexes. The result, once the considerable problems of personal adjustment are mastered, may be that men will become the volunteers of the future—and campaigns to recruit, train, and deploy volunteers to help the community should begin planning for such an adjustment.

Minorities. Over the next 20 years, as today, minorities will be concentrated in certain areas. A great proportion of blacks will be in the Northeast, the Midwest, and the South. Hispanics will be found in large numbers in the Southwest; Native Americans in the Midwest and West.

Affirmative action among all these groups will still be needed, but its implementation in 2000 may be unrecognizable by today's standards. Although we must not slack off our current local governments' commitment to bring minorities into the work force of our cities, counties, and COGs, the new affirmative action will be focused more on preventing slippage and dealing with the problems of people at midcareer, who will then be part of the baby-boom cohort competing for limited jobs.

Beyond affirmative action, local governments will need to be aware of the needs of Hispanics in particular. Language will be the most important problem, as many Hispanics will not speak English adequately to compete in the labor market.

Special efforts will be needed on two fronts. The first will be to make every effort to help Hispanics compensate for language barriers by installing bilingual signs; hiring bilingual local government employees, especially in reception areas; and producing special printed and broadcast material for Hispanic communities. The second should be a strong effort to provide English-language training for non-native speakers. This will mean incorporating language instruction into adult education and recreation programs and building it into special regular school curricula.

Smaller households. The declining size of the household will bring about some changes similar to those required for the elderly—the need for multifamily dwellings, for example. Indeed, the change in household size may revamp many traditional images of the ideal home setting for a large number of Americans.

We can see the image changing from the half-acre lot with the four-bedroom house and two-car garage in the planned unit development. In its place will be much smaller homes, many garden apartments, and town houses. People will make much more use of recreation and social settings outside the home (since no one will be home in many more cases).

Smaller homes and lots will have several implications for local governments. The number of water and sewer hookups will continue to grow, but the use of these facilities per thousand population may decline. At any given time, fewer homes will be physically occupied by the tenant, making neighborhood security and patrolling by police more important. In some suburbs with very large houses, there may be more demand to use the houses for "group homes" or even to subdivide them into apartments.

As local governments enter the 1980s and the 1990s, these are just a few of the changes in the mix of services provided, changes brought about by the fluctuating demographics of urban living.

So the mix of local services as well as the scale of their delivery will need adjustment over the next 10 to 20 years. This will be another strategy for nurturing the essential community, along with learning how to get by modestly, beginning to regulate demand for services, and buying back independence from the national government.

All this is a very complex, difficult, and challenging agenda for the future horizon of citizens, elected leaders, and their top professional managers.

Index

abandoned houses, homesteading in, of Philadelphia, 125-126, 128-130
ACORN: 117; success of, 131-133; and urban homesteading, 125-133
Advisory Commission on Intergovernmental Relations, 155
affirmative action, 241
agriculture, man's transition from nomadism to, 8
architecture, and New York City, 42-45
Atlanta: Andrew Young as mayor of, 94-95; and foreign trade, 181
autonomy: federal government efforts at encouraging local, 101-106; and local government in future, 236; of suburbs and Reagan's New Federalism, 49; see also self-help movement

back-to-the-city movement, see gentrification
Baltimore, 67-69, 216, 218, 219, 222, 230
Barry, Marion, Jr., 93
BART, 98,99
Berkeley, California, Citizen's Action group of, to help poor, 137, 138, 141-144
Birmingham, 34
black mayors: 216, 229; evaluation of efforts of several, 90-96
Bombay, 107, 108
Bonus Expeditionary Force, as example of squatting in U.S. history, 126
Boston, high-tech boom in, 229
Britain, and enterprise zone legislation, 192
Bushmen of Kalahari in Africa, 7
businesses: self-reliance of small city, 201, 202; see also, small businesses
"bus therapy," 71

California: homeless in, 71; suburbs, 46
capital city, 39
Carter, Jimmy, 102
Center for Neighborhood Technology (CNT), 198
centers of prehistory, 6-9
Central Park, creation of, 15-16
CETA, 153, 158, 159, 160, 161, 193
Chicago: 219, 222, 230, 231; substandard housing in, 67-68; traffic congestion in, 78; Harold Washington as mayor of, 93-94, 111-115
China, prehistoric cities in, 9
cities/city: crowding in, 78-79; as key to economic health of America, 145-151, 153; fear of, 12-17; in future, 212-214; historical origin of, 6-11; historical perspective of, 33-41; industrial, 36-41; international trade and investment by, 181-185; and need for national urban policy, 27, 146-156; impact of New Federalism on, 101, 103-106, 113-114, 157-161, 197, 202; state of American, 18-28
Citizens Budget Review Committee, and Berkeley plan for city development, 141-143
City and Town Development Act, 139, 140
city planning: and Hartford, 136-144; and self-reliance, 194-205; and triage, 176-180
city revitalization, see urban revitalization
Civic Center Authority, Hartford, 139
civilizations, origin of, and decline of nomadism, 6-11
civil rights, 155

closed loop systems, cities as, to be self-reliant, 194
Colorado, suburbs of Denver, 47
Columbus, urban homesteading in, 130
Community Development Block Grants (CDBG's), 219
Committee of 100, 137
co-ops: 142; in New York City's West Side, 56-60
Coordinated Energy Response Center, 141
councils of government (COG's), 235, 238
crime: neighborhood organizations to prevent, 158-160, 199; personal account of, by packs of young men, 80-89; in suburbs, 48-49; and urban congestion, 79
crowding, urban, 78-79

Dallas, and urban homesteading in, 130
day care, 240
decentralization, 239
deinstitutionalization, as contributor to homeless, 70, 71, 74, 75
demographic trends: and aging population of suburbs, 207-209; impact of, on growth of suburbs vs. cities, 54
Denver, 231
Detroit: Coleman Young as mayor of, 90-93; substandard housing in, 67
developing countries: population growth in, 29-32; see also, Third World
displacement of poor, due to gentrification, 23, 52-55, 61-66
District of Columbia, black mayors of, 93
downtown development: 218-221; in Boston, 229

economic development, and battle against urban decay, 218-221
economy: national, and health of cities, 145-149; role of United States in world, 27
elderly: displacement of, in New York City's West Side, 61-66; and local government in future, 239, 240; effects of, on suburbia, 207-209
Emerson, Ralph Waldo, opinion of, on cities, 13
Empire State Building, 43
employment: and city plans to increase, 137; and national urban policy, 152; and self-help groups in neighborhoods, 158-161
energy: and city self-reliance, 186-189, 197, 198, 203, 204; conservation and town planning, 32; role of, in future local government, 237; effect of, on urban revitalization, 55
energy programs: in Berkeley, 143; cost reduction in Hartford, 140, 141; self-help movement in neighborhoods, 158, 159
engineering challenges, of New York City, 42-45
enterprise zones, 190-193, 216
evictions: 23; and tenant harassment, 61-66
exports, city and foreign trade, 183, 184

family planning, in Third World, 109
farmland, urban development as threat to American, 25
fear of the city, 38-39
federal government: impact of policies of, on cities, 20-23, 26-27; relationship of,

to cities, 101-106, 113-114; role of, in housing for homeless, 75; and national urban policy, 146-148, 150-156; response of, to squatting in abandoned homes, 126-127
federal urban policy: 216; see also, national urban policy
fiscal restraint, future of local, 233
Florence, 34
food, cost reduction programs in Hartford, 140, 141
foreign trade, city involvement in, 181-185
France, center of prehistory in, 7
frostbelt vs. sunbelt, 22-23
future: city of, 212-214; of local government, 235-241; model city of, 199; suburbs in, 227, 228

general revenue sharing, 102
gentrification: 229; displacement of poor due to, 23, 52-55, 61-66; and energy independence, 186, 187; and New York City's West Side, 56-66; reason for, 53-54
Gift Property, and urban homesteading, 127, 128
government services, need to reduce, in future, 235-241
group behavior, and conflict in early cities, 10

harassment, tenant, 61-66
Hartford, 136-141, 194
Hartford Plan, and city planning for poor people, 136-141
homeless people: due to deinstitutionalization, 70, 71, 74, 75; and gentrification, 61-66, 72; private and voluntary organizations for, 73-74
Home Mortgage Disclosure Act, 158
home rule, 26-27
Homestead Act, 126, 127
homesteading, 126-131
Hong Kong, 40
Hoosier Dome, 220
House of Umoja, 159, 160, 161
Houston, 231, 232
housing: lack of low-income, in New York City's West Side, 61-62; and self-help movement, 157-161; shortages in city, 79; waiting list for federally subsidized, 68; substandard, 65-69; cost of, in suburbs, 48
H.U.D., 125-133, 137, 157, 186-189, 216
hunter-gatherers, origin of cities from, 6-8
hunting parties, of young robbers, 80-89

"imagineers," 45
income maintenance programs, 150
independence, city striving for energy, 186-189
Indianapolis: and downtown development, 220; urban decline and aging industry in, 222
industrial cities, 36-41
industry, aging of, in Northeast and urban decline, 222-225
inflation, effect of, on city economic health, 146
infrastructure: and city planning for future, 198; city problems of, 196, 197; and need for national urban policy, 147, 148; of New York City, 42-45
insulation, 187, 188

integration, and local self-reliance of cities, 197, 198
interest rates, 146
international trade, city involvement in, 181-185
Iran, archeological study of prehistoric, 8

Jackson, Jesse, 95, 96
Japan, 147
Jefferson, Thomas, opinion of, on cities, 12-13, 35
jobs, mismatch between, and skill levels, 19
Johnson, Lyndon, 101

Kalahari Bushmen of Africa, 7

labor, future problems of, 236
landlords, vs. tenants' rights, 61-69
legislation, enterprise zone, 216
Les Eyzies region of France, 7
literature, mention of the city in, 33-41
literary artists, views of, on city life, 12-17
litter, and urban congestion, 79
local government, see state and local government
London, 34, 35
Los Angeles, substandard housing in, 67, 68
low-density development, see urban sprawl
Lower East Side, and VISTA, 118, 119, 120, 121
low-income housing: Hartford and Berkeley Plans for, 137-143; and self-help movement, 157-161; and urban homesteading, 125-133

major capital improvements (MCI's), 62
man, as nomad vs. city-dweller, 6-8
Manchester, 37
mass transit: alternatives to, 100; arguments against, 97-100
mayors, black, 216, 229
megastructures, 171, 173-175
Melville, Herman, opinion of, on cities, 14
mentally ill: homeless, 70, 71, 74, 75; in England, 72; in Soviet Union, 72; in Sweden, 72
Mesopotamia, 8-9
metropolitan areas, see city
Mexico, prehistoric cities in, 9
Mexico City, 107
Ministry of International Trade and Industry, as example of cooperation between city and government, 147
minorities: 241; need for, in city government, 215, 216
Mobilization for Youth (MFY), 118, 119, 120, 121, 122, 123
muggings, personal accounts of, by packs of young men, 80-89
municipal corporation, 201, 202

national development policy, see national urban policy
national economy, relationship of, to cities, 145-149, 195, 196
National Energy Security Act, 188
national industrial policy, and urban decline, 224
national urban policy: 27, 146-156; criticism of, 151-156
Near East, center of prehistory in, 7-9
negative income tax, 152

neighborhoods: and Hartford revitalization, 137-141; revitalization of, and triage, 176-180; and self-help movement, 157-161, 199-200
New Deal, 150
New Federalism: 148, 150; and autonomy for suburbs, 49; impact of, on Chicago and Boston, 113-114; impact of, on cities, 101, 103-106, 197, 202; and home rule, 26-27; effect of, on self-help movement in communities, 157-161
new localism, 195, 196
New York City: a century ago, 15-16; engineering feats in building of, 42-45; suburbs of, 47; traffic congestion in, 78; new class in West Side of, 56-66
Nixon, Richard M., 101, 102
nomadism, decline of, and origin of cities, 6-8

Olmsted, Frederick Law, 15
One Liberty Plaza, 43

parking, problems of, in cities, 78
parochialism, 205
peer culture, 228
Philadelphia: 230; and export trading companies, 184; homesteading in, 125, 126, 127, 128-130; traffic congestion in, 78
Phoenix, homeless in, 72, 74
Pittsburgh, 222
"planned shrinkage," 21, 22, 177
plazas, and study on use of space by people, 162-172
police: in early cities, 10; decoy squad description of robberies by packs of youths, 80-89
polycentrism, 32
Poe, Edgar Allan, opinion of, on cities, 13-14
poor/poverty, see poverty/poor
population growth: in cities of world, 29-32; of cities vs. suburbs, 46-47; among nomad vs. city-dwellers, 11; in Third World cities, 107-110
poverty/poor: displacement of, due to gentrification, 23, 52-55, 61-66; impact of federal policies on, 21; in Hartford, 136-141; homesteading of abandoned houses by, 125-127; and triage urban policy, 176-180; and VISTA program, 116-124
power plants, need for efficient, 203, 204
privatization, 103, 190-193
Proposition 13, 141, 143, 227, 232
property tax, 238
public transportation, as distinguished from mass transit, 97, 100; need for, 78

racial tension, in suburbs, 49
rail rapid transit, arguments against, 98-100
Reagan administration: impact of policies of, on cities, 21, 101, 103, 106, 113-114; criticism of, 23, 26; impact of policies of, on poor, 21; impact of policies of, on self-help movement in neighbors, 161; impact of policies of, on suburbs, 49; and VISTA program, 117
recycling, and energy efficiency in self reliant cities, 197
redevelopment: 143; see also, urban revitalization

redistributive policy, and Hartford's program for poor, 136-141
redlining, 158
regionalism, 239
rehabilitation, and urban homesteading, 129
religion, role of, in early cities, 10, 11
rental housing: and Berkeley Citizen's Action group, 142; and loss of single room occupancies, 61-66
rent control, 23
return-to-the-cities movement, see gentrification
revitalization, see urban revitalization
Riis, Jacob, 15, 16, 17
Rio de Janeiro, 40, 107
robbers, packs of young, 80-89

St. Louis, 218, 222
San Diego, 232
San Francisco, 78, 232
Sao Paulo, 107
Seagram Building, and study of use of space by people, 162-172
self-help movement: development of neighborhood, 157-159; effect of Reagan administration on, 161; and urban homesteading, 125-133; see also, autonomy
Settlers Association, 125, 126
7A, 121, 122
sharecropping, 126
shoe industry, national urban policy to help U.S., 148
single room occupancy (SRO), disappearance of, due to gentrification, 61-66
sitting patterns, 165, 166
skid row, impact of deinstitutionalization on, 70, 71
skyscrapers: New York as city of, 42; and steel skeleton construction, 42-43
slums, nineteenth-century, 17, 37
small businesses, impact of gentrification on, of New York City's West Side, 63-64
social classes: of cities vs. suburbs, 49; in early cities, 9; disparity of, in New York City's West Side, 56-66
social mobility, 20
solar bank, 188
solar energy, 187, 188, 204
soup kitchens, opposition to, for homeless, 73-74
Southern Tenant Farmers Union, 126
special revenue sharing, 102
sprawl, see urban sprawl
squatting: government response to, 126, 127; history of practice of, 125, 126; and low income housing, 125-133; and Philadelphia, 125, 126, 128-130; success of, 131, 132
standing patterns, 164
state and local government: and city planning, 194-205; future needs of, 233-241; reaction of, to Reagan's New Federalism, 103-106; role of, in urban problems, 26-27
steel skeletons, and structures in New York City, 42-43
street, as important to plaza success, 169, 170
Street Life Project, 162-172
street people, see, homeless people

structural unemployment, 147
subsidiarity, 199
substandard housing, 65-69
suburbs: effects of aging residents on, 207-209; impact of, on cities, 46, 217; of future, 227, 228; growth of American, 46-49; problems in, 48-49
sunbelt vs. frostbelt, 22-23
suntraps, 168
supercities, in Third World, 107-110

tenants' rights: vs. landlords, 61-66, 67-69; suggestions for, 23
Tent City, 130
Teotihuacán, 9
Third World, population growth in cities of, 29, 31; urban growth in, 107-110
tourism, economic importance of, to cities, 184
town planning, need for, 32
trade: and evolution of cities, 10; international, and cities, 181-185
traffic congestion: in city, 78-79; in suburbs, 48; in Third World cities, 29, 31
trains, see rail rapid transit
traveling conversations, 164
triage, and urban policy, 176-180
triangulation, 172

unemployment, and mismatch between skills and jobs, 19
Upper West Side, 56-66
urban centers, see city
urban congestion, 78-79
urban decay, 218
urban decline, and aging industry of Northeast, 222-225
Urban Development Action Grants (UDAG's), 219
urban homesteading, 125-133
urbanization: in nineteenth century, 36-39; in twentieth century, 39-41
urban policy: federal, 187, 216; need for, 146-156; as poor answer to city problems, 151-156
urban renewal, see urban revitalization
urban revitalization: 44-45; and displacement of poor, 23, 52-55, 61-66; federal role in, 22-23, 224; as cause of homeless, 72; and New York City's West Side, 56-66
urban sprawl, pros and cons of, 24-25

Venice, 34
veterans, 126
Village Homes, as future city, 199
VISTA, 116-124, 158, 161

volunteerism, trend toward, in future local government, 235

waffle slab construction, in concrete skyscrapers, 44
War on Poverty, 116-124, 150
Warsaw, 34
Washington, D.C., suburbs of, 47
Washington, Harold, 93-94, 111-115
Washington, Walter, 93
weatherization, 187, 188
welfare, 150, 152
West Side of New York City: new class in, 56-60; displacement of poor in, 61-66
Whitman, Walt, opinion of, on cities, 14-15
World Trade Center towers, 43, 44
Wyatt v. Stickney, 70

Young, Andrew, 94-95
Young, Coleman A., 90-93
youth, personal accounts of robberies committed by packs of, 80-89
Yuppies, of New York City's West Side, 56-60

zero-risk ideal, and municipal services, 236

Credits/ Acknowledgments

Cover design by Charles Vitelli

1. Urbanization
Facing overview—Department of Public Works, State of California. 14—Maryland Historical Society. 16—Museum of the City of New York.
2. Varieties of Urban Experiences
Facing overview—Dover *Pictorial Archives* Series.
53—Greater Boston Convention & Tourist Bureau.
3. Urban Problems
Facing overview—UN Photo. 112—Marc Pokempner.
4. Urban Social Policies
Facing overview—United Nations.
5. Urban Futures
Facing overview—WHO photos.

We Want Your Advice

ANNUAL EDITIONS:
URBAN SOCIETY, Third Edition
Article Rating Form

Here is an opportunity for you to have direct input into the next revision of this volume. We would like you to rate each of the 41 articles listed below, using the following scale:

1. **Excellent: should definitely be retained**
2. **Above average: should probably be retained**
3. **Below average: should probably be deleted**
4. **Poor: should definitely be deleted**

Your ratings will play a vital part in the next revision. So please mail this prepaid form to us just as soon as you complete it.
Thanks for your help!

Annual Editions revisions depend on two major opinion sources: one is our Advisory Board, listed in the front of this volume, which works with us in scanning the thousands of articles published in the public press each year; the other is you—the person actually using the book. Please help us and the users of the next edition by completing the prepaid article rating form on this page and returning it to us. Thank you.

Rating	Article	Rating	Article
	1. How Man Invented Cities		23. Assuring the Economic Health of America's Cities
	2. Fear of the City, 1783 to 1983		24. Urban Strengths/Urban Weaknesses
	3. Symposium: The State of the Nation's Cities		25. Reagan vs. the Neighborhoods
	4. The World's Urban Explosion		26. Small Space Is Beautiful: Design as if People Mattered
	5. The Industrial City: The Environment of the City		27. The Case Against Urban Dinosaurs
	6. Building the Empire City		28. Triage as Urban Policy
	7. America's Suburbs Still Alive and Doing Fine		29. Cities Are Setting Their Sights on International Trade and Investment
	8. People of the City		30. Achieving Energy Independence by Reviving America's Cities
	9. The New Class		31. When Public Services Go Private
	10. The Dispossessed		32. City-States: Laboratories of the 1980s
	11. For Rent, Cheap, No Heat		33. Suburban Population Ages
	12. Home on the Street		34. A City for the Year 2000
	13. Crowds and More Crowds—No End to Urban Hassles		35. Need for New Vision Stirs City Leaders
	14. Hunting the Wolf Packs		36. Progress Begins Downtown
	15. Black Mayors: Can They Make Their Cities Work?		37. America's Urban "Rust Belt" Cinches Up for the Future
	16. The Myths of Mass Transit		38. Suburbs: Revising the American Dream
	17. American Cities and the Future		39. Politics Is Not the Only Thing That Is Changing America's Big Cities
	18. Supercities: The Growing Crisis		40. Dimensions of the Civic Future: Fiscal Restraint and Intergovernmental Impacts
	19. A Mayor's Dilemma		41. Strategies for the Essential Community: Local Government in the Year 2000
	20. I Was a Spear Carrier in the War on Poverty		
	21. The ACORN Squatters' Campaign		
	22. Running the City for the People		

(cont. on next page)

ABOUT YOU

Name _____ Date _____

Are you a teacher? ☐   Or student? ☐

Your School Name _____

Department _____

Address _____

City _____ State _____ Zip _____

School Telephone # _____

YOUR COMMENTS ARE IMPORTANT TO US!

Please fill in the following information:

For which course did you use this book? _____

Did you use a text with this Annual Edition?   ☐ yes   ☐ no

The title of the text: _____

What are your general reactions to the Annual Editions concept?

Have you read any particular articles recently that you think should be included in the next edition?

Are there any articles you feel should be replaced in the next edition? Why?

Are there other areas that you feel would utilize an Annual Edition?

May we contact you for editorial input?

May we quote you from above?

URBAN SOCIETY, Third Edition